Human Relations

Third Edition

Marie Dalton, Ed.D.
San Jacinto College, Pasadena, TX

Dawn G. Hoyle
Aerospace Academy, Houston, TX
Hoyle and Associates, Seabrook, TX

Marie W. Watts, SPHR
Marie W. Watts and Associates, Muldoon, TX

SOUTH-WESTERN
CENGAGE Learning

Australia • Brazil • Japan • Korea • Mexico • Singapore • Spain • United Kingdom • United States

SOUTH-WESTERN
CENGAGE Learning™

Human Relations, 3rd Edition

Marie Dalton, Dawn Hoyle, and Marie Watts

VP/Editorial Director:
Jack W. Calhoun

VP/Editor-in-Chief:
Karen Schmohe

Acquisitions Editor:
Jane Phelan

Project Manager:
Penny Shank

Consulting Editor:
Laurie Wendell

VP/Director of Marketing:
Carol Volz

Marketing Manager:
Valerie Lauer

Marketing Coordinator:
Georgianna Wright

Production Editor:
Diane Bowdler

Production Manager:
Patricia Matthews Boies

Manufacturing Coordinator:
Kevin Kluck

Art Director:
Tippy McIntosh

Copyeditor:
Margaret E. Sears

Media Production Editor
Ed Stubenrauch

Production House:
Electro Publishing

Cover and Internal Designer:
Tippy McIntosh

Cover Image:
© GettyImages/PhotoDisc, Inc.

Photo Researcher:
Darren Wright

Printer:
Phoenix Color Corp
Hagerstown, MD

ASIA (including India)
Cengage Learning
www.cengageasia.com
tel: (65) 6410 1200

AUSTRALIA/NEW ZEALAND
Cengage Learning
www.cengage.com.au
tel: (61) 3 9685 4111

LATIN AMERICA
Cengage Learning
www.cengage.com.mx
tel: +52 (55) 1500 6000

Represented in Canada by
Nelson Education, Ltd.
www.nelson.com
tel: (416) 752 9100/(800) 668 0671

UK/EUROPE/MIDDLE
EAST/AFRICA
Cengage Learning
www.cengage.co.uk
tel: (44) 207 067 2500

SPAIN (includes Portugal)
Cengage Learning
http://www.paraninfo.es/

Continue Your Personal Development with other titles from South-Western Cengage Learning

Human Relations for Career Success 6E *by Eggland/Williams* is designed to help students increase their self-awareness and self-esteem and learn how to get along better with others in the workplace environment. Development of three foundational skill areas are highlighted: (a) basic communication skills, (b) thinking skills, and (c) personal qualities such as responsibility, self-esteem, self-management, and integrity.

Text 0-538-43876-2   *Instructor's Manual* 0-538-43877-0

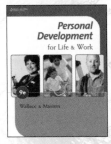

Personal Development for Life & Work 9E *by Wallace/Masters* is designed to help students recognize the important role personal qualities play in the workplace. Successful attitudes, interpersonal skills, critical thinking skills, and strong work ethics are qualities today's employers seek and demand. This book focuses on preparing entry-level workers for success in the workplace with an interactive format that provides students with the framework for successful skill development.

Text/CD 0-538-44148-8   *Instructor's Resource CD* 0-538-44149-6

Professional Development Series consists of short learner guides designed to teach cross-functional skills that involve leadership, teamwork, problem solving, and analytical thinking. These short, comprehensive learner guides provide the reader with immediate "know how" to feel comfortable in any type of work situation.

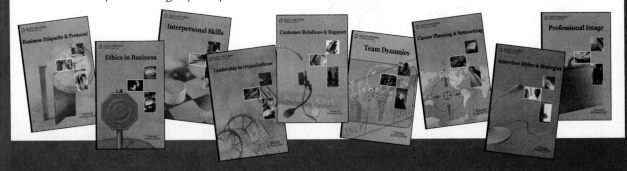

SOUTH-WESTERN CENGAGE Learning   *Join us on the Internet at school.cengage.com*

Brief Table of Contents

Table of Contents

Preface

The world has changed, and a major theme today is connection—electronic, social, personal, intellectual, global—and that is the way learning should occur. Increasingly, learners want more than just an understanding of the concepts of human relations. They want to be able to apply the concepts through connections that are important in their daily lives. This edition of *Human Relations* connects you to the issues, challenges, and applications you will encounter in the 21ST century.

The original intent of the book remains:

1. to provide some of the most intriguing and important aspects of human relations as seen in action in organizations and in personal lives;

2. to serve as basic study in business or social sciences; and

3. to form a solid foundation for further study, practice, and training in a variety of disciplines and industries.

This third edition contains over 30 percent new material representing new trends, additional concepts, and up-to-date connections communicated through the combined experience of three human relations professionals. The content has been reorganized and a new chapter on diversity added in order to reflect current trends in human resources.

FEATURES OF HUMAN RELATIONS 3RD EDITION

The following features have been updated in the third edition of *Human Relations*:

• New high impact *Connections* features on technology, global and diversity issues, and ethics

• *Case Studies in the News* with readings and discussion topics pulled from today's business headlines

• *Fast Chat* questions for review, discussion, and personal reflection throughout each chapter

• *Chapter Projects* with workplace communication applications

• *QuickTips* success strategies from human relations and business professionals and others from a variety of fields

• *Application* scenarios for small group discussion and role-play

• New chapter organization that reflects current human resource trends

REAL-WORLD PERSPECTIVE

Offering a dynamic real-world perspective to human relations, this book highlights more of the contemporary issues faced by employees today:

 • Diversity and global issues

 • The impact of technology and the Internet

 • Ethics and social responsibility

 • Case studies from real workplaces and contemporary events

Additionally, this text maintains an emphasis on the personal and professional concerns in business today, including:

- Communication in the workplace
- Creative problem solving
- Customer service
- Group dynamics and teamwork
- Change dynamics
- Job search and career planning strategies

The book also has more applications for learners to build skills and solve problems through hands-on activities, chapter projects, and extensive questions for review and self-assessment. Graphic icons identify activities that focus on:

 • Role-playing and teambuilding activities

 • Workplace writing and communication

 • Internet and technology applications

TEXT ORGANIZATION

Chapter 1 is an introduction that motivates students by making clear why studying human relations is important. This chapter also provides an organizational and historical framework for the study of human relations.

Chapter 2 explains how our perceptions of people, events, and things can determine the nature of our relationships, while **Chapter 3** is a summary of current and past thinking about what motivates people to act as they do.

Chapter 4 is a comprehensive study of communications. It covers various types of communication—verbal, nonverbal, written, listening, and electronic—and explores barriers that impede communication between people. **Chapter 5** suggests effective ways to solve problems and improve the quality of decisions. It also includes a lively discussion of creativity, its importance to organizational survival, and ways to foster it in others and ourselves.

Chapter 6 identifies organizational structures and discusses the strengths and weaknesses of the most common types of organizations. **Chapter 7**, Group Dynamics, stresses the evolving importance of groups at work and explores aspects of group interaction. **Chapter 8** discusses the need for team concepts in the work environment and how teams can increase productivity. Several types of teams are presented as well as techniques for building an effective team.

Chapter 9 introduces the importance of diversity in business today and makes recommendations on how to thrive in a diverse environment. **Chapter 10** presents a helpful, "how-to" oriented approach to setting and achieving objectives. Its discussion of performance appraisal is unique in that it suggests ways that employees can make this a more pleasant, useful experience with growth opportunities for themselves and their supervisors.

Chapter 11 covers function and styles of leadership, while **Chapter 12** discusses sources and uses of power. It challenges readers to develop their own bases of power and shows them how to do it. **Chapter 13** discusses change dynamics and includes a helpful section on coaching and counseling.

Chapter 14 presents a subject gaining renewed respect in today's depersonalized world, business etiquette. It emphasizes the important role that etiquette plays in our success and presents guidelines regarding the current topics of office politics, networking, and mentoring.

Two chapters in particular challenge students to think for themselves by addressing contemporary topics. **Chapter 15** discusses ethics at work, and **Chapter 16** is a comprehensive look at today's employee rights and unions.

The last two chapters are additional strengths of the book. **Chapter 17** presents information on maintaining work-life balance, and **Chapter 18** discusses career management with a focus on the future of work and how to find a job.

CHAPTER ORGANIZATION

This textbook was written to develop critical thinking skills and to encourage learners to make connections with critical issues. To this end, each chapter is introduced with objectives that the reader should meet after studying the chapter.

Throughout the chapters are activities, experiential exercises, and "Fast Chats" calling for personal involvement. Since human relations means interaction among people, the more participative the class can become, the more students can learn from each activity.

SUPPLEMENTARY MATERIALS

Human Relations, 3rd Edition is supported by a comprehensive *Instructor's Resource CD* with extensive tools that make teaching and training easier:

- Instructor support files offer an explanation of the focus of each chapter, a chapter preview, presentation outline including suggested placement of exercises and applications, teaching-learning suggestions, key terms definitions, suggested responses to review and discussion questions, and opportunities for readers to analyze real human relations issues.

- PowerPoint Presentations and Teaching Masters provide lecture support for chapters and supplementary activities.

- ExamView test generator software and chapter test banks contain hundreds of questions for review and assessment.

- Seminar outlines allow instructors to design customized courses with emphasis on specific human relations topics.

Additionally, a support web site for this text (**school.cengage.com/career/dalton**) contains online resources, links to key government and business web sites, online chapter activities, and vocabulary games.

ACKNOWLEDGMENTS

Many people have contributed to the development of this text. The authors and publisher are grateful for the suggestions and feedback of the following reviewers for this edition of *Human Relations*:

- Karen Boyle, Okefenokee Technical College, Waycross, GA

- Michael Cicero, Highline Community College, Des Moines, WA

- Mike Courteau, The Art Institutes International Minnesota, Minneapolis, MN

- Susan Eckert, Consultant/Coach, Brightwaters, NY

- Helen Hebert, Remington College West Campus, Cleveland, OH

- Helene Hedlund, Minnesota State Community and Technical College, Detroit Lakes, MN

- Jeannie Hobson, San Joaquin Valley College, Fresno, CA

- Nancy Porretto, Katharine Gibbs School, Melville, NY

- Jo-Anne Sheehan, Briarcliffe College, Patchogue, NY

- Daphne Zito, Katharine Gibbs School, Melville, NY

Again, we offer our gratitude to our past and present students who helped clarify our thinking of what a human relations book should be and to future students and instructors who use this book as a reference and learning aid.

If this book makes your teaching-learning journey more pleasant, we would like to hear from you. Please contact us through South-Western, Cengage Learning (**school.cengage.com**) if you have suggestions for how we might incorporate additional connections in future editions. Have a pleasant journey in getting to know yourselves and others!

Marie Dalton
Dawn Hoyle
Marie Watts

ABOUT THE AUTHORS

Marie Dalton, Ed.D.

Dr. Marie Dalton is Executive Vice President, San Jacinto College District in Houston, Texas. In this role, she heads up the Aerospace Academy for Engineering and Teacher Education, a unique K-18 multi-partner education/industry/government collaboration created to address workforce shortages. Her extensive professional experience includes positions as manager of business process reengineering, dean of continuing education, community college instructor, university professor, corporate trainer in the retail, petrochemical, and aerospace industries, and consultant to business and education in the areas of human relations, management, and communications. A successful author and popular speaker, Dr. Dalton has published four texts and numerous articles and has made dozens of presentations to international, national, state, and community groups.

Dawn G. Hoyle

Dawn G. Hoyle is a Human Relations Specialist and President of Hoyle and Associates. She has developed and conducted training seminars for major private industry and public sector organizations in the areas of communication, leadership, change dynamics, strategic planning, and time and stress management. Ms. Hoyle has also worked with NASA-Johnson Space Center for 37 years in various human resources, contract administration, and office of the comptroller positions. She has also been an instructor at San Jacinto College, teaching courses on Human Behavior and Effective Supervision. In her current work with the Aerospace Academy, she helps bring business, technology, medical, and academic representatives together with school teachers and students to encourage education in science and engineering.

Marie W. Watts,
SPHR

Marie Watts is the owner of her own human relations consulting firm, Marie W. Watts and Associates, that specializes in training in human relations skills, mediation, and discrimination investigations. Prior to starting her own business, she worked as a human resource director and manager and was with the Equal Employment Opportunity Commission (EEOC). At the EEOC, Ms. Watts investigated and supervised investigations of charges of discrimination in the workplace. From these activities, she developed a heightened awareness of how crucial human relations skills are to success in the workplace. Additionally, she is the coauthor of a novel about diversity and starting over called *An American Salad*.

Human Relations:
The Key to Personal and Career Success

focus

Why are certain people successful? A December 2003 article in *Fast Company* featuring an interview with Jack Mitchell, Chairman and CEO of Mitchells/Richards Clothing Stores, helped answer this question. Mitchell believes that most stores say they give customer service, but they're really just thinking about product and price.[1]

They don't really think about the customer, so the experience is not personal and exciting. The shopping experience should put customers at the center of the universe. He calls every personal act a "hug," like remembering someone's first name, what soft drink he/she prefers, or what his or her kids' names are. He recommends four simple hiring criteria: people must be honest, be self-confident, have a positive attitude (be up and come to work with a smile), and, most importantly, have a real passion to listen, learn, and grow to be the best. He says, "You have to hug employees and they will hug others. It starts at the top for real success."

Based on the above news story, how do you think human relations skills can help business owners? How will human relations help you? What might you expect to learn in a study of human relations?

After studying this chapter, you should be able to:

1.1 *Explain the meaning of human relations.*

1.2 *Discuss the importance of human relations skills.*

1.3 *Trace the development of human relations in business.*

1.4 *Explain what factors influence human relations in organizations.*

1.5 *Identify how you can contribute to the objectives of an organization and how the study of human relations will help you succeed in your career.*

1.6 *Discuss some ways that technology is changing the world of work and affecting human relations.*

in this chapter

You will find the study of human relations to be helpful and interesting because it is about you and your interactions with others. Also, you will be able to use the material immediately. **Human relations** is the study of relationships among people. Your relationships can develop in organizational or personal settings and can be formal or informal, close or distant, conflicting or cooperating, one-on-one or within groups. Through this study, you will learn skills that will help you achieve your personal and professional goals and help you contribute to organizational goals. Away from work, your relations may include parents, siblings, children, spouses, and friends. On the job, your relationships may be with subordinates, coworkers, supervisors or other superiors, or clients.

Poor human relations skills can cost us.

"The next time something's about to go wrong, I want one of you losers to speak up."

© 1999 Ted Goff www.tedgoff.com

Human relations, the study of relationships among people, will help you interact effectively with others.

Strengthening your human relations skills involves an understanding of your own psychology and that of others, the use of effective communication skills, and an appreciation for groups and their dynamics. The more you know about what motivates people and affects their morale, about setting goals and monitoring performance, and about how change can be managed, the stronger your human relations skills will be.

Other key elements of good human relations skills are being aware of the sources and uses of power, gaining problem-solving and decision-making skills, and understanding creativity, team building, and legal and ethical considerations.

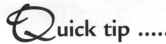

Quick tip ··

Dale Carnegie, in the classic 1936 book, *How to Win Friends and Influence People,* provided these guidelines, which are as valid today as they were then:[2]

1. Show interest in others.
2. Smile.
3. Use people's names.
4. Listen carefully.
5. Talk about topics of interest to the other person.
6. Make the other person feel important.

···

CASE STUDIES IN THE NEWS

Robert Derocher reported in *Insight Magazine* that the management style of the CEO might predict a company's success. Citing a study done by a leading executive search firm, Korn/Ferry International, the *Insight* article said that today's CEO needs to be a team builder, a communicator, open to new ideas, and a good listener to be effective in the 21st century.[3]

Why do you think that listening and communicating are so important in today's work environment? What kinds of problems do you think poor skills in these areas are likely to create?

*Fast*Chat

1. What is human relations? How can human relations skills help you?

2. Give examples from your own experiences, movies, or TV shows of successful human relations and of human relations gone wrong.

Organizations are concerned about the relationships among people because people are their most important resources. Increasingly, companies are adopting the **total person approach**, which takes into account employee needs and goals. Realizing that when they hire you, they are employing a whole person, not just your skills, they strive for win-win situations that allow the company and you to get what you each want. Organizations know that they can be more productive and their employees more satisfied when effective human relations skills are used. Those companies that try to provide fair and just treatment for all employees and to fulfill both personal and organizational goals will normally be more successful than organizations that do not. They usually have less conflict, fewer errors in their products, less illness and absenteeism, lower employee turnover, and higher morale.

> The total person approach acknowledges that an organization employs the whole person, not just his or her job skills.

Effective human relations skills may be the greatest contributor to the success or failure of your career. According to the Dale Carnegie Foundation (as cited in Wray, 1996), 85 percent of the factors contributing to our job success are personal qualities, while technical knowledge contributes only 15 percent.[4]

TECHNOLOGY CONNECTION

Few would argue with the idea that engineers today need to possess technical skill and a basic understanding and competence in such business areas as oral and written communication skills, marketing, and finance. In addition, today's companies place a premium on developing and improving certain extras or "soft skills."[5] When decisions have to be made during right-sizing in today's global market, those with extra skills will be the ones remaining. According to Ted Hissey in *Today's Engineer*, in today's work environment, those "extra skills" include having a global perspective, being a team player, and having sufficient professional depth and versatility to provide a multifunctional capability. Multinational companies are forming product and system teams that are truly global. A global perspective and sensitivity are needed to deal within these widely varying international cultures and conditions.[6]

Think of other jobs usually associated with technology. What are some of the human relations skills people in these jobs must use? What steps would you take in your job to increase your "soft skills"?

Human relations skills may be the greatest contributor to your career success.

The Harvard Bureau of Vocational Guidance has reported that 66 percent of people fired from their jobs were fired because they did not get along with others, while only 34 percent were fired because of lack of technical knowledge.[7] Additionally, *The Wall Street Journal* has reported that managers spend hundreds of hours each year dealing with employee personality clashes.

The average worker will make three major career changes during his or her life. When someone changes careers, he or she may need different technical skills. However, because few people today work in isolation, all positions require similar human relations skills. People with these skills and the necessary technical skills will be in great demand.

Human relations skills are becoming increasingly important as our economy evolves. We are moving from an economy that produces goods to one that provides services, is information and technology based, and expects speed. This economy requires that you and other employees communicate and interact effectively in complex situations.

*Fast*Chat

1. Explain the statement, "Human relations skills may be the greatest contributor to your career success."

2. Will human relations skills or technical skills be more important as you progress in your career? Explain your choice.

3. Think about the career you envision for yourself over the next 5—10 years and, in your own words, discuss how human relations skills will be important to you and to your employer.

To understand how organizations discovered the importance of human relations, we must look at the history of the U.S. economy and management practices. If you had lived here in the 1700s, you would have probably been a farmer or craftsperson living in a rural area. Likely, you would have grown your own food and made your own supplies. This era, known as the Agricultural Era, came to an end in 1782 with the invention of the steam engine. This machine revolutionized work by providing a cheap source of power to run factories.

During the 1800s, the United States shifted into the Industrial Era, during which factories sprang up and towns grew. Had you lived during this period, your work might have shifted from the farm to a factory.

The Information Age is characterized by rapidly expanding technology, increasingly large and complex organizations, and better-informed employees.

Factory managers realized that they needed to manage the behavior of their employees to increase productivity, and studies of management and worker relationships began. By the beginning of the 1900s, the United States had entered the most dynamic period ever in the history of work.

Studies of management-worker relationships began during the Industrial Era.

The invention of the computer in the 1950s ushered in another new period, called the **Information Age**. As you may have observed, this current age is characterized by rapidly expanding technology, increasingly large and complex organizations, and better-informed employees. The complexity of organizations and heightened expectations of employees have made human relations skills more important than ever. This importance will increase as world economies become more global and work forces more interactive. The Information Age will be discussed further in later chapters.

The search for new management techniques began with a base in the social sciences—psychology, sociology, and anthropology. These studies deal with the institutions and functioning of society and how individuals interact as members of society. In studying human relations, we are concerned with why individuals and groups behave the way they do and how their interactions might be improved. These foundational disciplines are described in the figure below.

Social Sciences Basic to Study of Human Relations		
Psychology	Of primary importance because it focuses on the behavior of individuals and why they act the way they do.	Industrial psychology looks specifically at motivation, leadership, decision making, and use of power within the organization.
Sociology	Important because we must all function in a variety of groups, and organizations consist of small groups.	Centers on the interaction of two or more individuals and their relationships in group settings.
Anthropology	Focuses on the origins and development of various cultures.	Increasingly important as society and work force become more multicultural and economy more global.

Armed with knowledge from these three disciplines, people began to study how to increase productivity at work. Their studies identified three different and distinct ways of treating employees, called classical, behavioral, and management science, each developing at a different time in American history.

THE CLASSICAL SCHOOL OF MANAGEMENT—
1900 TO 1920s

The **classical school of management** focused on efficiency. Two branches of this school developed: **scientific management theory**, promoted by Frederick W. Taylor and Frank and Lillian Gilbreth, and **classical organization theory**, based on the work of Henri Fayol.

Frederick W. Taylor was an engineer and inventor who became known as the "Father of Scientific Management." He had an inside understanding of industry, having begun his career as a laborer at the Midvale Steel Company, later becoming its chief engineer. He believed that management could be improved by thinking of it as a science-based art and that tasks could be scientifically analyzed to make them more efficient.

His work during the late 1800s and early 1900s led to the idea of mass production, and his system influenced the development of every modern, industrialized nation. Although Taylor believed that maximum productivity could be achieved through cooperation of management and labor, some managers carried his system to extremes, causing resentment and the feeling that workers were being dehumanized.[8]

Frank and Lillian Gilbreth, a husband-and-wife team, tried to measure and improve the motion of work. The Gilbreths used still and motion photography to identify the distinct steps required to do a task and then deleted the nonessential ones. The combination of the ideas of Taylor and the Gilbreths resulted in the famous "time and motion" studies that became a popular means of improving productivity.

As more studies were done, emphasis shifted from viewing the work itself to viewing the management of the organization as a whole. In 1916, Henri Fayol, a French industrialist, published his 14 principles of management, which included division of work, authority, discipline, chain of command, and other concepts still used in management today. His belief was that management could be viewed holistically, with human relations, productivity, and the general administration of the organization being improved by applying basic principles.[9]

THE BEHAVIORAL SCHOOL OF MANAGEMENT—
1940s TO 1950s

Managers continued to look for ways to improve productivity. Many were disenchanted with the authoritarian, task-oriented approach of the classical school, and by the late 1920s, the **behavioral school of management** had begun. Employees had started to unionize to protect their rights and

---

Frederick W. Taylor is the "Father of Scientific Management."

Taylor focused on efficient use of time; the Gilbreths aimed for efficient use of motion.

Fayol developed 14 basic principles of management.

to demand a more humane environment. The Depression, World War II, and post-war boom contributed to growing concern.

The behavioral school also had two branches, the first of which was the **human relations approach**. From the mid-1920s to the early 1930s, Elton Mayo and his associates from Harvard Business School conducted research at Western Electric's Hawthorne plant near Chicago. These studies, which came to be known as the Hawthorne studies, considered how physical working conditions affect worker output.

The researchers found that regardless of changes—such as heating, humidity, lighting, work hours, rest periods, and supervisory styles—productivity levels increased significantly during the study. Finally, the researchers realized that productivity increased because the workers were receiving attention and felt that someone cared about them. This became known as the **Hawthorne effect**, the idea that the human element is more important to productivity than technical or physical aspects of the job. Mayo's work earned him recognition as the "Father of Human Relations" and provided discoveries that contributed to an understanding of human relations in organizations.[10]

Mayo's Discoveries about Human Relations in Organizations

1. Attention given to people can change their productivity—the Hawthorne effect.

2. Employees have many needs beyond those satisfied by money.

3. Informal work groups can be very powerful within an organization, particularly through their ability to influence productivity levels.

4. The relationship between supervisors and employees is very important, affecting both quantity and quality of employee output. Good human relations is the key, not popularity.

5. Employees have many needs that are met away from the job. Therefore, managers cannot always control motivation.

6. Relations between coworkers affect their performance. These interactions allow employees to meet their social needs.

The second branch of the behavioral school was known as the **behavioral science approach**. In the mid to late 1950s, researchers began to use scientific methods to explore efficient management techniques. The studies included both workers and managers to get a total view of human behavior in the workplace. During this period, psychology, sociology, and anthropology first came into use as tools for understanding the organizational environment.

THE MANAGEMENT SCIENCE SCHOOL OF MANAGEMENT—1960s TO PRESENT

During World War II, both the British and the U.S. military needed to solve complex problems, such as coordinating massive troop movements and seeing that supplies arrived at appropriate places and in correct quantities. The military enlisted the help of mathematicians, physicists, and other scientists, leading to the **management science school**. The results were so successful that companies later used the techniques developed to solve complex business problems.

The computer made **statistical models** easier to use. Models are analytical tools that help managers to plan and control organizational activities. Examples of models developed during this period are the **Program Evaluation and Review Technique (PERT)** and the **Critical Path Method (CPM)**.

PERT is frequently used when a major project to be finished by a deadline is made up of many separate activities or steps, each of which requires a certain amount of time to complete. Usually, one activity must be completed before another can be started. A PERT chart helps coordinate these activities. You can use PERT charts for projects ranging from planning a sales conference to building new corporate headquarters and moving employees to it.

The critical path is the sequence of activities in a PERT chart requiring the longest time for completion. It will show the minimum time needed to complete a project.

> Two statistical models to help planning and control are PERT and CPM.

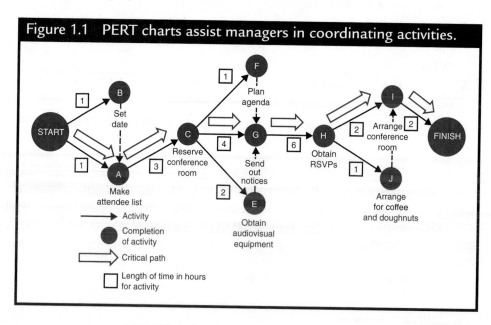

Figure 1.1 PERT charts assist managers in coordinating activities.

Today, computer models help managers make decisions. For instance, a model can predict how many units your company is likely to sell at a certain price. However, the computer is simply a tool; it is not infallible and cannot make decisions, and it does not reduce the need for effective human relations in the success of a project.

Quick tip

Typifying the human relations approach to high productivity, Gene Kranz, head of Missions Operations Directorate during some of NASA's most exciting space explorations, suggests that managers should use one or more of the following, every day and in every conversation, to get the most from their workers:[11]

1. You did a good job.
2. What is your opinion?
3. I made a mistake.
4. Will you please...
5. Thank you.
6. We...

PRACTICES OF THE 2000s

Research continues for ways to improve productivity. Current theory revolves around worker involvement and information technology and emphasizes redefining the work and identifying new approaches. **Reengineering processes** involve eliminating unnecessary work, reducing cycle time, improving quality, and improving customer relations. **Process innovation** blends information technology and human resources management. Consider these examples. Thomas H. Davenport, author of *Process Innovation*, relates that, by changing processes to integrate technology, IBM reduced preparation time for quotes to buy or lease computers from 7 days to 1 day, while preparing 10 times as many quotes. The Internal Revenue Service collected 33 percent more from delinquent taxpayers with only half the staff and one-third the branch offices.[12]

Reengineering can be considered only one part of the change process, a design of what to do with a process. The Process Innovation model involves 1) envisioning radically new work strategies, 2) creating and documenting the process design, and 3) implementing the change. It is usually based on the need to improve financial performance. Process innovation is an approach to business performance improvement that

> Today, computer models assist managers in making decisions.

> Practices of the 2000s: worker involvement and information technology.

uses information technologies and highly motivated workers to realize significant improvements in cost, time, and quality and to carefully track efficiencies. Its lofty goals are to formulate a strategy, design the process, and implement the strategy with full support from senior management across multiple business functions.

 **uick tip** ···

When you're an unhappy customer, using effective human relations in your communication can win you a fast and happy resolution. These words can serve you well in any negotiation situation:

"I'm not upset or angry at you—but I am very upset."	Acknowledge your anger while remaining detached, professional and non-accusatory.
"What I want from you is..."	Remembering that this business transaction is a negotiation, think of a remedy that makes sense and say what you want.
"What would you do if you were in my shoes?"	Your goal is to break through the other person's shell and help him or her see your point of view.

···

*Fast*Chat

1. Discuss examples from your own life of when you experienced the Hawthorne effect. This might have resulted from the attention of a coach, teacher, boss, parent, or other person.

2. Describe a project you have faced and how PERT or CPM or a computer model could have helped you. Sketch a simple PERT or CPM for your project.

3. Review Gene Kranz's advice on the previous page. Then review the "focus" section at the beginning of this chapter. What do they have in common? How might you apply Gene Kranz's advice to your personal life?

4. Think of a significant process you might want to change to which you could apply the Process Innovation model. Discuss how effective it might be. What barriers exist?

Organizations will continue to change dramatically during the 21st century if they want to remain successful. James Martin identified the following characteristics of 21st-century organizations in his book, *Cybercorp*.

Characteristics of 21st Century Organizations

1. **Speed**—Things happen fast, calling for quick decisions.

2. **Turn-around time**—Actions and results must occur quickly.

3. **Uncertainty**—Change and uncertainty create problems and opportunity.

4. **Virtual corporation**—Staff and employees are not in one location.

5. **Unique capabilities**—An organization's unique abilities provide its competitive edge.

6. **Agility**—Flexibility is key.

7. **Knowledge infrastructure**—A base of knowledge is needed to capture, create, store, improve, clarify, disseminate and use information.

8. **Geographical Diversity**—Organizations are product specific and geographically diversified instead of geographically specific and product diversified.

9. **Learning**—The emphasis is on growing human potential as fast as technological potential.[13]

An important part of using effective human relations in these cybercorps, or in any other organization, is knowing how you fit into the overall organization. The quality and type of interaction among individuals and how it changes in organizations is influenced by many factors, including goals, cultures, conflicts between groups, and outside influences.

GOALS OF ORGANIZATIONS

Being aware of the goals of organizations to which you belong (work, social, or civic) can help you understand why management makes the decisions or takes the actions that it does.

Strong human relations skills can help you function and contribute more effectively while your organization is trying to meet its goals and can help you adapt to and cope with changes.

Every organization has goals. A primary goal of any business is to make a profit. If a profit is not made, the business will fail.

Goals, cultures, conflicts, and outside forces can influence relationships in organizations.

Government and nonprofit organizations, while not seeking to make a profit, still have the goal of providing services. They must provide services that the public needs or wants at a price the public can afford. Since these organizations, like businesses, must remain within their budgets, government and other nonprofit organizations often practice the same management and cost-saving concepts that private enterprise uses.

ORGANIZATIONAL CULTURE

Organizational culture: a mix of the beliefs and values of society, workers, and the organization's leaders and founders.

Every organization has its own distinct culture. **Organizational culture** is a mix of the beliefs and values of society at large, the individuals who participate in the organization, and the organization's leaders and founders.

CASE STUDIES IN THE NEWS

A January 2002 Webdesk.com news release profiled Continental Airlines. The airline was implementing new airport procedures and offering passengers step-by-step tips for stress-free check-in. These steps were part of Continental's renewed efforts to improve customer relations. After the once-struggling company survived bankruptcy court and, under the astute leadership of Gordon Bethune, rose to the number one position among airlines, Continental focused on meeting strict federal requirements and providing helpful service to its passengers. "Check flight status before leaving home; allow additional check-in time; bring something to read and toys for the children while waiting after security check-ins; and please be patient" are just some of the tips made available on Continental's web site. They alert travelers to the hazards of security procedures post-9/11 and prepare passengers for what lies ahead by easing tensions and readying them for possible delays.[14]

What human relations skills could have been used to change the overall corporate culture at the airline? What effect do you think the change had on the employees? How is Continental using human relations skills on passengers? Do you think these techniques are working? Why, or why not?

The culture determines what goals the organization wants to accomplish and how it will go about accomplishing them. Some organizations have strong values that are expressed. Here are some examples of expressed values with which you may be familiar.

Examples of Expressed Values

The Girl Scouts—"Do a good turn daily"

DuPont—"Better things for better living through chemistry"

Caterpillar—"Twenty-four hour parts and service anywhere in the world"

Sears, Roebuck—"Quality at a good price"

The Boy Scouts—"Be prepared"

Other cultural norms may not be as openly communicated but must be learned. Organizations, for instance, may have heroes—people with the beliefs, attitudes, and behavior that the organization wishes to reinforce. These people with the "right stuff" are identified as individuals after whom members or employees should model themselves. Disney Productions, for example, reflects Walt Disney's values.

Most organizations develop some standards of behavior. These standards may include unwritten rules concerning appropriate clothing, formats for meetings, language standards for interpersonal communication, decision-making styles, and activities in which employees or members participate outside the organization. Some organizations have rituals and rites, such as awards programs, sales seminars, banquets, or the like.

Good human relations skills can help you learn the cultural norms of companies in which you work. Armed with this knowledge, you will cope more effectively with the expectations of the organization.

QUICK WIT
"Ride the horse in the direction that it's going."
Werner Erhard,
Controversial
philosopher and
seminar developer

SPECIAL FUNCTIONS WITHIN THE BUSINESS ORGANIZATION

Organizations have formal structures that help them carry out their goals and objectives. Because one person cannot perform all functions of a large organization, duties are delegated to individuals or groups of individuals. You should understand that groups or departments must work together to avoid or reduce conflicting objectives.

The basic functions of most business organizations are shown in the following table along with some human relations skills needed in those jobs.

Special Functions Within the Business Organization	
Function	**Human Relations Skills Needed**
Marketing & Sales	Understand the goals of the organization.
	Communicate with clients and customers.
	Coordinate work with others in the organization.
Production	Use teamwork effectively to meet production and delivery deadlines and maintain quality. Use other skills such as motivations, goal setting, job performance problem solving, and decision making.
Finance	Make decisions, listen, and communicate effectively.
Human Resources	Handle confidential information and legal and ethical matters.
Accounting	Use effective oral and written communication.

Often, each part of an organization has its own goals. For instance, the accounting department may be concerned with seeing that an accurate account of inventory is kept, while the production department is concerned with completing its work on time and may not see the importance of filling out routine forms accurately. If you are to function effectively at work, you must recognize the needs of others in the organization and respect what they are trying to accomplish as a part of overall organizational goals. The development of sound human relations skills will help you.

OUTSIDE FORCES AT WORK

All organizations, profit and nonprofit, are vulnerable to their environments. If they do not adjust to a changing environment, they will lose jobs or go out of business. Human relations skills can help you adapt to and understand these changes. The following table shows 10 environments that may affect a business organization.

Ten Environments that May Affect a Business Organization

Function	Cause	Possible Effect
Macro	Increased use of personal computers	Greater speed and communication
	Shifts in interest rates	More expensive business expansion
	Changing attitudes about work	Different work habits
	Concerns about the natural environment	How/where work is conducted
Economic	Large strike or natural disaster	Prices rise
	General recession	Postponement of luxury spending
Competitive	New business down the street	Lower prices
Legal-Political	An increase in taxes	Limited funds for salaries and expansion
	Road construction in front of a business	Fewer customers and less sales
	Change in export regulations	Less foreign sales
	Political unrest in foreign countries	Less oil exploration and drilling
Socio-Cultural	Demographic shifts, aging baby boomers, changing ethnicity, patterns of literacy and shrinking middle class	Change in lifestyle and buying habits
Changing Technology	Widespread use of computers and the Internet	How business is done, how work and personal lives are organized, how people communicate and learn, patterns of residence, relationships, work, and leisure
Unexpected Disasters	Fire, tornado, earthquake	Expense and anguish
	Plane crashes, product tampering	Deaths, injuries, litigation
Corporate Mergers	Newly merged organization	Laid off employees
Management Changes	Retirements and new managers	Change in philosophy and work methods
Global Economy	No economy stands alone	What happens in one economy affects the economy of other countries. Increased need to interact with people of many different nations with sensitivity to their customs, values, and attitudes.
	Goods produced less expensively in some countries	Businesses move factories outside U.S. or have part of the work done overseas.
	Young, well-educated workers from undeveloped countries relocate to cities in developed nations ("brain drain").	Human relations challenges arise Clashes may occur over relative importance of work and leisure, ethics, social responsibility, and copyrights.

GLOBAL CONNECTION

Globalization offers unprecedented opportunities for people and nations to improve the quality of their lives. But the rapid changes are causing widespread concern. In the United States, many people argue that globalization poses great risk to the environment and lower-skilled workers who could lose jobs to intense global competition. In other parts of the world, the impact of globalization on local culture is the source of great concern. Some fear that excessive exposure to foreign cultures will undermine valuable elements of their own cultural traditions. Others argue that globalization offers people of all cultures opportunities to enhance their lives. By promoting increased interaction of people and ideas, globalization brings increased respect for and understanding of foreign cultures. By increasing international commerce and expanding the range of consumer choice, globalization promotes economic well-being that can help preserve local cultures.[15]

What impact is globalization having on lower-skilled workers? How are cultures affected?

The global economy may have a significant impact on organizations. Today's businessperson must be aware of what is happening globally and flexible enough to adapt to changes as they occur.

To continue to compete globally, many organizations are merging. Such actions have the potential to affect thousands of people in many different ways. For example, a study done on the many mergers occurring in the global banking industry indicated that employees not only suffered increased job insecurity but also had heightened workplace stress levels. Often, employees first learned about their company's merger or acquisition over coffee and a bagel while reading the morning newspaper before leaving for work. The study by the International Labor Organization (ILO) revealed that one of the main causes leading to failure of mergers was the neglect of "key human element issues." Open communication between staff and management was vitally important to assure a smooth transition and lessen the development of insecurities and dispel uncertainties. Although supporters of mergers tout increased efficiencies and an improved competitive edge, others would say that mergers often fail in achieving those objectives through the difficulty of adequately blending cultural and other human factors. Merging offers a challenge for both employees and the organization.[16]

Human Relations

Global sales of pirated music compact discs rose almost 50 percent to an all-time high of 950 million units in 2001. Global sales of legitimate music compact discs dropped in 2001 with many industry analysts pointing the finger at the increased production of illegal copies. Jay Berman, IFPI Chairman, said, "Piracy is sometimes and mistakenly called a 'victimless crime'. It is not. The economic losses are enormous and they are felt throughout the music value chain. Piracy nurtures organized crime across the world and it stunts growth and jobs." The chairman called on governments across the world to crack down on copyright theft with tougher laws. Rick Dobbis, president of Sony Music International, said piracy was a global issue that affected both artists and record companies. The hardest-hit victims of this growing problem are the local economies.[17]

Discuss examples of music piracy and the impact of these actions. How serious do you consider it to be? What do you think the impact is on a country's economy if music is bootlegged and sold illegally there? How would you feel if a friend borrowed your new CD, made 12 copies, and distributed them to 12 friends for money? Discuss other examples you may know of piracy and its effects.

*Fast*Chat

1. Why should you understand the goal of organizations of which you are a part? Identify the goal of several organizations with which you are familiar.

2. What is organizational culture? Why do organizations differ in their norms or rituals? Describe the organizational culture of some organizations with which you are familiar.

3. Describe the various kinds of human relations skills that were needed in jobs you may have held.

4. Think of an organization that has undergone significant recent change. What created that change? How did the organization respond?

Employees should have the right attitude, be flexible, retrain, and use human relation skills.

If you join an organization with the attitude that your responsibility is to help the organization accomplish its goals, you are off to the right start. Having the necessary skills, understanding your objectives, accomplishing them as well as possible with the least expense and fuss, and making others' jobs easier by carrying your own weight are how you demonstrate that you have the right attitude. Human relations skills are essential. An employee or member who does not help the organization grow and prosper will not be a valued member of the team.

CONTRIBUTING TO THE ORGANIZATION

Your contribution: a job you do well.

You can contribute to your organization by having a positive attitude and by performing your job or role well. Knowing your tasks, using effective human relations, and being polite and helpful to others are important. Ignoring or being rude to a customer may cause the shopper to go down the street to another business to trade. In their book, *In Search of Excellence*, Peters and Waterman point out that one key to business success is superior customer service. A study for the White House Office of Consumer Affairs found that 96 percent of unhappy customers never complain about discourtesy, but up to 91 percent never return. In addition, the average unhappy customer will tell at least 9 other people about the discourtesy, and 13 percent will tell more than 20 people.[18]

Another contribution to your organization: your effective communication.

Another way in which you can contribute to your organization is through effective communication. If you do not understand an assignment, you should ask for clarification. If you know that you will not meet a required deadline, let the person in charge know as soon as possible. At work, doing your tasks the way your supervisor wants, not the way you think they should be done, is vital. If your supervisor gives you instructions to do the assignment in the manner that you think best, which will probably happen once you have acquired experience and have demonstrated your responsibility, then you may do it your own way. Most organizations have room for honest discussion on the best way to approach a task. However, when your supervisor has made a decision following discussion, you should comply with these guidelines.

BEING FLEXIBLE

The growth of employment in small businesses and the restructuring of large organizations make flexibility more important than ever. Your positive attitude coupled with a willingness to follow orders, help other workers, help with tasks not specifically assigned to you, or take on new tasks, will make you a valued employee. And when decisions regarding layoffs or promotions are being made, employees with cooperative, helpful attitudes definitely have an edge over those who are inflexible and always complaining.

The willingness to retrain is another aspect of flexibility. As technology changes, work changes, and employees are regularly expected to handle new and different jobs. Chip Bell, author of *Managers as Mentors,* said that in his work with corporations he found one interesting common thread among the "winningest" corporations: "Incessant learning. Nonstop learning. Daily learning. In fact, the ability to learn faster than the competition may be the only sustainable competitive advantage of the 21st century."[19]

CASE STUDIES IN THE NEWS

 A recent issue of *Today's Engineer* highlighted the importance of human relations skills in discussions with a high-level management team from a Midwestern U.S. utility company that was in the middle of merger negotiations. When the company reviewed a list of desirable extra skills and characteristics derived from a prior consensus of managers and executives, the human resources director said that those were the very skills criteria the company was using to determine which employees they would keep as part of the post-merger organization.[20]

What conclusions can you draw from this case study about the importance of continuing to develop your human relations skills to both individuals and organizations?

According to *Worklife Visions,* by Jeffrey Hallett, 50 percent of the actual jobs performed in 1987 did not exist in 1967. The rate of change will increase, and by 2007 almost all work will be new. This means you will need to learn new skills at an increasing rate. Knowing how to learn will be as important as knowing what to learn.[21] Determining your learning style and taking steps to understand how you learn best can help you become a life-long learner.

PERSONAL NEEDS VERSUS ORGANIZATIONAL NEEDS

People work or belong to organizations for different reasons. Money, social relationships, power, prestige, status, and growth are only a few of the motives. Sometimes the needs and styles of the individual and the organization clash.

As an employee or member of an organization, you must understand yourself and your own wants and needs and be aware of the written and unwritten rules of the organization. Often you must play a role. For instance, you may prefer to wear jeans, but if an employer's unwritten code calls for dressier clothing, then you should adapt to this standard. If you are unable or unwilling to meet organizational expectations, you may not thrive professionally in that particular environment and should probably consider finding a position or joining an organization that is more in line with your values.

Most jobs today do not last forever. Technology comes and goes and businesses open and close. However, the skills of human relations can be used in any setting and can prove indispensable in helping you adapt to the changing world.

*Fast*Chat

1. Think of people you consider to be contributors to their organizations—work, church, civic, community, or other. What contributions do you see them making? Describe their attitudes and behaviors.

2. Think about technological changes of the last 10 years and people you know who utilize technology in some way. In what topics or skills did they have to retrain—on their own, through on-the-job training, or in formal classes? What skills do you think you will need to learn or update in the near future?

3. How can you demonstrate your flexibility at school and/or work?

4. What do you hope to get out of working? Why should you be willing to continue learning and to retrain?

Throughout this text, you will learn about the ways that technology is changing the world and how it is affecting people both at work and away from the job. The invention of the computer in the 1950s ushered in the Information Age, and technological changes since then have advanced into many other fields while changing how people live and do business. For example, OnStar in our automobiles can guide us to a location or unlock a car door. Retinal scanners improve security identification options in high-risk areas. Cell phones can save us time and money, text-message, and even take pictures. Cyberspace consists of millions of web pages of information and is growing with incredible speed.

Hand-held computers perform a full range of functions and allow greater mobility than ever before. Soon, nanotechnology will bring unheard-of capabilities, as our understanding of molecules and atomic particles increases. Whole new industries support our daily need for the continued use of technology. If you are not already involved with technology, you no doubt soon will be among the growing numbers who work directly or indirectly with computers or some form of the many technological advances used today.[22]

Computer and information networks have made possible the **virtual office**, allowing people in different ("remote") locations to communicate with each other through telecommunications, or machines linked by telephone lines.

> The virtual office allows people in different locations to communicate with each other through telecommunications.

TECHNOLOGY CONNECTION

According to a 2000 Gallup Poll, 62 percent of Internet users thought the Internet was a better use of time than TV, compared with 25 percent that valued TV more. Those percentages flip-flopped, however, when users were asked which was more enjoyable: 59 percent said watching TV, while 33 percent thought surfing the Internet was more enjoyable. The study found that overall, 72 percent of current Internet users believe the Net has made their lives better.[23]

If you are a Web user, for what specific purposes do you use it? If you do not currently use the Web, think of ways it might help you.

Various technologies have been developed to support telecommunications. These include fax machines, centralized voice mail, teleconferencing, and e-mail, which is certainly the most popular means of communication used today. Everybody wants your e-mail address—some for legitimate reasons and some to send you unwanted "spam" mail. Companies and individuals have to worry about installing and maintaining anti-virus capabilities to ward off attacks that can destroy important and costly data. Protecting our privacy and our security is another important part of why new technologies continue to be developed.[24]

Telecommuters are people who use technology networks to send and receive work and information to and from different locations.

The term **telecommuters** was coined to describe people, frequently based at home, who use technology networks to send and receive work and information to and from different locations. Many companies offer the option of working at home to help employees with family responsibilities, to save office space, or for other reasons. In the workplaces of the 21st century, many people are telecommuters because modern offices are more mobile and geographically scattered. Businesses are experimenting with alternative workstyles, such as telecommuting, hoteling (sharing an office space through reservations), and shorter workweeks. Yet many executives at companies that offer workstyle options think that telecommuters do not advance as quickly on the career track as office-based executives. One consequence of telecommuting and virtual teams may be increased worker isolation. Without in-person interaction, workers' social skills can deteriorate.

TECHNOLOGY CONNECTION

Search engines are catalogs for finding information on the World Wide Web. To use them, you start by typing in keywords that describe what you are looking for. This will get you a list of related sites, which you can then visit by clicking on their names. You probably will find that many are irrelevant. To avoid this, narrow your request to a more focused topic. Some of the Web's current search engines include, among others, Yahoo, Google, Lycos, HotBot, AltaVista, WebCrawler, Metacrawler, and Ask Jeeves.

1. *Go online and briefly explore each of the above search engines. What is the focus of each?*

2. *Search the Web to find a book that you would like to buy. Determine how much it will cost. Check out any reviews provided by others who may have already read the book.*

Additionally, some companies worry about employees spending too much time on the Internet. While the benefits for everything from market research to business communication still outweigh the negatives for a company, it can be a distraction for some employees.

TECHNOLOGY CONNECTION

In 1975 Bill Gates and Paul Allen had a simple vision for a powerful new company: Microsoft. They wanted to put a PC on every desk in every home. Then, in 1999, the vision statement changed to emphasize empowering people through great software. Today, in the 21st century, Gates has a new mission to "enable people and businesses throughout the world to maximize their full potential." These statements bring about changes for the entire industry. Advanced software and technologies along with the Internet have made people demand 24/7 access to the bounty of available Web-based services. Ever smaller and faster microprocessors will continue to increase access to services.

While the PC will maintain its lead as the most important home, work, and school computing tool, other intelligent devices and appliances, like hand-held computers, Web-TVs, in-car computers, and advanced cell phones, will share the limelight. Advanced services and software will allow information access any time, anywhere. Microsoft is willing to help households and businesses remotely manage their tasks and easily access information with universal connectivity.[25]

Think of ways technology could make you more productive. What forms of microprocessors are you currently using? How do they affect your work life?

*Fast*Chat

1. What is the virtual office?

2. How might telecommuting affect human relations?

3. Do you know anyone who is telecommuting? What have been their reactions to it? What do they like or dislike about it?

Key Terms

human relations

total person approach

Information Age

classical school of management

scientific management theory

classical organization theory

behavioral school of management

human relations approach

Hawthorne effect

behavioral science approach

management science school

statistical models

Program Evaluation and Review
  Technique (PERT)

Critical Path Method (CPM)

reengineering processes

process innovation

organizational culture

virtual office

telecommuters

CHAPTER SUMMARY

Human relations is the study of relationships among people. The major reason for studying human relations is to learn to interact more effectively with others, thereby becoming a more valued member within organizations and of society as a whole. All jobs and roles require some human relations skills.

The need for improved human relations in the workplace became obvious once workers moved from the farm to the factory. Knowledge of psychology, sociology, and anthropology was used to study human relations, especially as it related to the desire for increased productivity. Three schools of management came out of these studies: classical, behavioral, and management science. Today in the Information Age, with its large, complex organizations, better-informed employees, global economies, and emphasis on speed, the need for human relations skills is even greater.

Human relations in organizations can be influenced by such factors as goals, organizational culture, job function, and outside forces. Outside forces can include the economy, legal-political environment, socio-cultural environment, changing technology, unexpected disasters, corporate mergers and sales, management changes, and the global economy. Strong human relations skills can help you cope with these forces.

You have a responsibility to help employers or organizations accomplish their goals. You can contribute by having the necessary technical and human relations skills, communicating effectively, being flexible, retraining, and meeting organizational expectations. Solid human relations skills will also help you adapt to rapidly changing technology.

REVIEW QUESTIONS

1. Explain the meaning of human relations.

2. Why is human relations important in our personal and work lives? What do you think would happen to a business that did not use effective human relations skills?

3. List the three schools of management and tell what they contributed to the study of organizations.

4. What is the purpose of an organization? What can cause changes in an organization? Explain how you can contribute to an organization.

5. How is technology changing the world of work and affecting human relations?

DISCUSSION QUESTIONS

1. Identify some situations from home and work in which poor human relations skills were used. What happened? How could the situation have been improved?

2. Compare the three behavioral sciences (psychology, sociology, and anthropology). How do they differ? What does each contribute to the study of organizations?

3. Name the three schools of management theory and explain why they evolved.

4. Discuss the job skills needed in the Agricultural Era, the Industrial Era, and the Information Age. How are they different? How are they the same?

5. What changes are taking place in your community that affect local businesses? Identify the environment that causes the change.

CHAPTER PROJECT

Work in small groups to research the most current technologies being used by companies and individuals to maintain state-of-the-art efficiencies—in the field, hoteling, telecommuting, or at on-site job appointments. Use library or Internet resources for your research. In light of what you have learned in this chapter, these examples will be varied and may range from simple to very complex means of data usage. Together write a one-page summary and analysis that can be shared with the class.

Format the report in an attractive, efficient, and effective informal memorandum style. It should include To, From, Date, and Subject at the top of the page and topic headings to break up the paragraphs in the body.

Give your recommendations and conclusions first, followed by the supporting evidence on the technologies you have decided are most beneficial. Be sure to explain your decisions. You may use informal language such as first- and second-person pronouns (we, you).

APPLICATIONS

In small groups, analyze the following situations.

Chaos Is Cooking

Samantha is the production supervisor of a small company that manufactures specialty kitchen items. She has four employees. Juan is just out of high school. Ling Sao, in her early 40s and with the company 2 1/2 years, is absent frequently because she is taking care of her elderly mother. Mike, a 15-year employee, takes a lot of breaks. Kesia, the oldest employee, is the most productive.

Samantha is experiencing all sorts of problems: one of the machines is turning out bent pots, the workers frequently drop some of the lids when carrying them across the room to the packing machines, costly rush orders have to be placed for needed supplies, and production is not what it should be.

The company owner has told Samantha that she has six months to improve production or the company will be forced to close. The owner calls Samantha into the office and shuts the door.

1. What do you think the boss will tell Samantha?

2. Identify the problems that the owner needs to correct. Which management schools may provide ideas to assist the owner?

3. Identify the problems Samantha needs to correct. Which management schools may provide ideas to help her solve these problems?

Computer Crunch

Sam Keystone, the owner of a mid-sized computer manufacturing company, knows that proposed legislation to restrict exports to foreign countries will seriously affect his company. He is also concerned about the less expensive computer models some of his competitors are developing. And, of course, he lies awake at night wondering if he will read in tomorrow's paper that someone has developed a computer that totally revolutionizes the industry, making his models obsolete.

Human Relations

1. What environments are affecting Sam's company?

2. What changes might Sam have to make to stay in business?

3. What human relations skills will Sam's managers need to adapt to these changes? His employees?

ADDITIONAL READINGS AND RESOURCES

Ford, Loren. *Human Relations: A Game Plan for Improving Personal Adjustment.* New Jersey: Prentice Hall, 2000.

Forsythe, David P. *Human Rights in International Relations.* New York: Cambridge University Press, 2000.

Mitchell, Jack. *Hug Your Customer: The Proven Way to Personalize Sales and Achieve Astounding Results.* New York: Hyperion, 2003.

Murtha, Thomas P. *Managing New Industry Creations: Global Knowledge Formation & Entrepreneurship.* New York: Stanford University Press, 2001.

For additional resources, refer to the web site for this text: school.cengage.com/career/dalton

CHAPTER 2
OBJECTIVES

Perception:
Different Views of the World

After studying this chapter, you should be able to:

2.1 *Define perception.*

2.2 *Explain why people may have different perceptions of the same events, objects, persons, or situations.*

2.3 *Use your understanding of perception to improve communication.*

2.4 *Use the Johari Window to analyze your relationships with others.*

2.5 *Explain the importance of a good self-image.*

2.6 *Recognize and understand your different life and work roles.*

2.7 *Recognize perceptual defense mechanisms, what can trigger them, and how they hinder relationships.*

2.8 *Explain how perceptions can affect employee/supervisor relationships.*

focus

Headlines in two recent studies done in U.S. technology companies reveal that women are paid less than men with similar experience and qualifications. A survey conducted by CareerBuilder.com stated that men and women differ markedly when it comes to their assessments of working conditions and career advancement opportunities. Nearly a third of women said they were paid less than men with similar experience and qualifications.[1]

The other study, reported in the *Houston Chronicle*, found that while the United States leads the world in technological advances, women are still denied many of the high-tech industry leadership roles. Women and men both perceived a lack of acceptance of women. One common theme was an assumption that women are less equipped to take on leadership roles than men. For example, some people may assume that women are too emotional to be effective leaders or that a woman who has a family won't be willing to travel, which can automatically exclude her from a more high-profile job.[2]

Discuss reasons you think may contribute to these perceptions. Name some examples in which women are paid less than men in the same job. What can be done to lessen the gaps?

in this chapter

Perception is an important element in human relations. It is the process by which you acquire mental images of your environment. Through it you organize, interpret, and give meaning to sensations or messages that you receive with your senses of sight, smell, touch, taste, and hearing. Many factors influence perception—culture, heredity, needs, peer pressures, interests, values, snap judgments, and expectations are only a few examples. These factors contribute, in varying degrees, to the way you think and feel about people, situations, events, and objects.[3] The following figure illustrates how perceptions can differ.

> Awareness of factors in perception is vital to good human relations.

> Is it a rabbit or a duck?

The Rabbit/Duck illustration originated early in the 20th century. The original artist is unknown. This version was created by Gabor Kiss for Scientific American magazine. Used by permission.

*Fast*Chat

1. How do our perceptions influence the meaning of messages?

2. What is your perception of the difference between work and play?

3. How does, or will, this perception affect your perception of a job?

People develop certain attitudes and tend to make decisions based on these attitudes. Some of the things that influence perceptions and contribute to attitudes are so much a part of us (culture, heredity, interests) that they are difficult to recognize. Others, such as peer pressure, needs, or conditions, might be easier to identify. We should, however, try to view each new problem or situation separately and objectively and base decisions on the facts.

Among the many factors that can influence perception are the **halo effect** and **reverse** or **tarnished halo effect**. With the halo effect, we assume that if a person has one trait we view positively, all other traits must be positive. For instance, imagine that you are the owner of an office supplies store. Jane has been a bookkeeper for you for several years, doing an excellent job in the back office, so you promote her to manager. You soon realize to your dismay, however, that she is not an effective manager because she lacks the necessary people skills to meet the public and supervise other employees. You were probably influenced by the halo effect here.

Under the influence of the reverse halo effect, we allow one negative characteristic of a person to influence our whole impression negatively. That is, we consider one behavior or characteristic of a person to be "bad" and, therefore, view all other characteristics or behaviors of that person as bad. For example, you are operating under the reverse halo effect if you believe that people with poor handwriting are not intelligent or will not perform well.

Conditions and Characteristics Influence Perception

Time and place	Employees sometimes erroneously assume that an order from a supervisor is not as important when it takes place in the hall as when it occurs in the boss's office.
Emotional state	We are more receptive to ideas when we are relaxed than when we are feeling nervous or tired.
Age	A building or room that you thought was large when you were a child may seem small once you are an adult.
Frequency	If your supervisor starts including you in weekly planning sessions, you may feel uneasy at first but become comfortable after a while.[4]

Human Relations

Postpone judgment until you see how people function in a variety of situations.

Stress is another condition that distorts perception. When we are under stress, we are frequently unable to evaluate situations objectively. By learning to recognize situations that are stressful to you, you can make allowances for distortions that may cloud your perceptions.

"Of course we can do the impossible, in less time, and at a lower cost than our competition."

© 1997 Ted Goff www.tedgoff.com

Perceptions play an important role in the relationships we have with coworkers and supervisors.

*Fast*Chat

Many times when we lack information we fill in the void with negative thoughts.

1. Cite instances from your own experience when you or someone you know jumped to the wrong conclusion and expected the worst, but once all the information was in, discovered that the worries were unfounded.

2. How can you avoid situations where not having enough information draws you into negative thinking?

3. How can you tell when you are experiencing negative thinking? What steps can you take to overcome this experience?

Perceptual awareness allows more self-control.

Being aware of your own perceptions and what influences them, as well as others' perceptions, is extremely important in today's workplace. With such awareness, you can withhold judgments until you have analyzed situations. Ask yourself why you are feeling the way you are, whether your feelings are justified, and whether you should act on those feelings. Perceiving situations accurately can prevent or resolve human relations problems in your personal life and at work. You may refrain from doing or saying things that could create difficulties.

Being aware of what may have influenced the perceptions of others can help you understand people and will help you be tolerant, even sympathetic. When you accept the fact that others have equal rights to their feelings or points of view, even if you do not agree with them, you can deal with situations better.

Open communication concerning feelings can be helpful in personal and work relationships. If people disclose their feelings to each other, they can develop better mutual understanding. Stronger relationships, built on honesty and openness, can help coworkers develop respect for each other's beliefs and opinions. Respect, in turn, can lead to fewer conflicts, greater job satisfaction, and growth, resulting in higher morale. In addition, productivity may increase because ideas flow more easily.

GLOBAL CONNECTION

Tensions continue worldwide between different ethnic, racial, and religious groups—Protestants and Catholics, Jews and Palestinians, whites and blacks, and ethnic Albanians and Serbs. Age-old conflicts rage on with little sign of demise. Recent horrific bombings in Spain, Indonesia, Russia, and in New York, Washington, and Pennsylvania on 9-11 give vivid evidence of terrorism and heightened tensions among societies. Other random acts of violence and harassment toward racial, religious, and ethnic groups provide proof of the ongoing presence of hate crimes in our society.

1. *What role do perceptions play in the continuation of violence?*
2. *What changes might contribute to the elimination of these problems?*
3. *Do these types of problems spill over into work?*

Other people can learn about your perceptions when you practice **self-disclosure**, which means sharing honestly, but appropriately, your thoughts, feelings, opinions, and desires. Self-disclosure can increase the accuracy of your communication and may reduce stress because you no longer have to hide your feelings. Additionally, you can increase your self-awareness by being open to both positive and negative feedback. **Feedback** is information given back to a person that evaluates his or her actions or states what the receiver understood. For instance, someone may tell you, "I missed your point. You are speaking too softly for me." After evaluating their feedback, you may want to make changes within yourself. A theory that may help you understand the importance of open communication and feedback is the Johari Window.[5]

Self-disclosure and feedback increase the accuracy of communications.

© 1999 Ted Goff www.tedgoff.com

Perceptions can affect the accuracy of information.

*Fast*Chat

1. What types of disclosures would facilitate a working relationship?
2. Who is responsible for verifying the accuracy of communication?

The **Johari Window** is a model that helps us understand relationships and interactions among people. It is named for **Jo**seph Luft and **Har**ry **In**gham who developed it.

Each of us has information within us of which we are aware and habits, attitudes, or talents of which we are not aware. Similarly, information about us or our habits, attitudes, or talents may or may not be known by others. Luft and Ingham combined these concepts to create four window-panes, depicted in the figure below. These panes are called the arena or area of free activity, hidden or avoided area, blind area, and unknown area. The meanings of these terms are defined below.[6]

The ideal Johari Window is one with a large arena and a small unknown area. To achieve this pattern, practice self-disclosure and be willing to accept and learn from feedback (negative or positive). At work, obvious ways in which you can do this include making suggestions and expressing opinions as appropriate and by being receptive to appraisals and suggestions made by your supervisor.

Your relationships away from work can also be improved by changing your arena. Ways to do that include accepting feedback from your family and friends about your actions and sharing your feelings and opinions in appropriate ways.

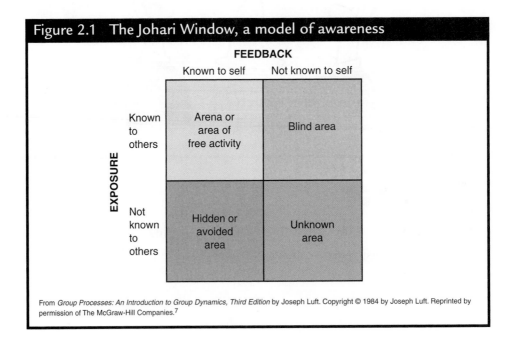

Figure 2.1 The Johari Window, a model of awareness

From *Group Processes: An Introduction to Group Dynamics, Third Edition* by Joseph Luft. Copyright © 1984 by Joseph Luft. Reprinted by permission of The McGraw-Hill Companies.[7]

Human Relations

Explanation of the Areas of the Johari Window

Arena

The arena contains information that you know about yourself and that others know about you. This pane will be bigger if you have effectively communicated your thoughts and ideas. It can include information about your job, preferred movies, disliked foods, and many other facts or feelings.

Hidden Area

The hidden area contains information that you know about yourself but do not divulge to others. The size of your hidden area suggests how trusting you are of those with whom you associate. Experiences, hopes, and dreams can be included in this window if you have not shared them with others.

Blind Area

The blind area is the section that represents what you do not know about yourself but what others do know about you. Blind areas can get in the way of interactions with others and can make people appear to have poor human relations skills. The size of this pane is an indication of how willing you are to listen to feedback about your behavior. Included in the blind area can be habits, attitudes, prejudices, weaknesses, and strengths.

Unknown Area

The unknown area is the undiscovered or subconscious part of you. It contains information about you that neither you nor others know. This information can include unremembered experiences or undiscovered talents.[8]

Disclosures, as described in the Johari Window, should be done carefully, particularly in the workplace. Telling too much about intimate matters or revealing personal information too soon can be harmful to careers. We all know people who blurt out their personal problems to almost everyone they meet. Such behavior is considered inappropriate in almost any setting, but especially so at work. Being critical under the guise of sharing your feelings can also hamper human relations. People who make rude or hurtful or inappropriate comments and excuse their behavior with "I'm just being honest about my feelings" have large blind areas.

> Self-disclosure must be done carefully and appropriately.

Use great caution in sharing intimate information with people at work. Such information may detract from the professional image that you wish to create. Although all of us need people with whom we can share our confidences and problems, people away from work may be more appropriate choices for discussing intimate matters.

Subjects that should be shared only with caution include marital problems, financial difficulties, problems with children, many health-related

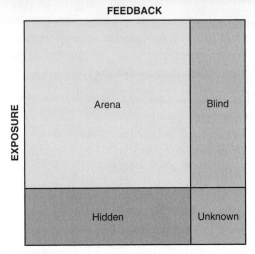

Figure 2.2 The ideal Johari Window for effective relationships has a large arena and small unknown area.

FEEDBACK

EXPOSURE

| Arena | Blind |
| Hidden | Unknown |

From *Group Processes: An Introduction to Group Dynamics, Third Edition* by Joseph Luft. Copyright © 1984 by Joseph Luft. Reprinted by permission of The McGraw-Hill Companies.[9]

matters, and opinions of coworkers. When deciding to disclose information, consider carefully the individuals with whom you will share information. What will their reaction be? Will they understand and be considerate of your feelings? Will they perceive what you have to tell them as a professional weakness that will inhibit your performance, or will they work with you to enhance your abilities? Is this the right point in your relationship to reveal such information?

If you determine that information can be shared, select an appropriate time and place for disclosures. Look for a time when the other person is most able to pay attention and distractions are least likely to occur. For instance, taking your supervisor's time to discuss a personal problem when the supervisor is working on a deadline project or has others waiting to be seen may create additional stress for the supervisor and hinder your communication.

*Fast*Chat

1. What topics are not appropriate for disclosure at work?

2. What should you do when someone discloses inappropriate information about himself or herself? Coworkers? Your boss?

Another aspect of perception important in human relations is how people feel about themselves, their **self-esteem**. Feeling good about ourselves is *the* key to success. All people, even those most confident and secure in their personal and professional lives, must work on their self-perceptions continually. We are never finished with this task. Psychologist D'Arcy Lyness offers the following tips for improving self-esteem.[10]

> Self-esteem takes time and practice.

Suggestions for Raising Self-Esteem	
Love yourself	We can love and respect others only if we love and respect ourselves.
Believe in yourself	Realize that almost everyone is afraid to try new and different experiences. However, we must be willing to take reasonable risks to pursue our goals.
Analyze yourself	Know your strengths and weaknesses and set goals to overcome your weaknesses and enhance your strengths.
Forgive yourself and accept the fact that you are not perfect	Although we cannot change events of the past, we can learn from them and not make the same mistakes again.
Practice positive thinking	You will feel better about yourself and the world.

POSITIVE THINKING AND ITS IMPORTANCE

Positive thinking is looking on the bright side. People who think this way are called **optimists**, whereas people who frequently have a negative outlook are called **pessimists**. Research has shown that optimists are more successful than pessimists, and it is easy to see why. After all, few of us enjoy being around people who are pessimistic. Then, too, people who are pessimistic probably give up in their endeavors too soon, not believing that positive results can occur.[11] The difference between optimists and pessimists is demonstrated in the figure on the next page.

Three steps can be taken to develop positive thinking: (1) change your thought processes, (2) engage in positive self-talk, and (3) use visualization. Each step is discussed in the following sections.

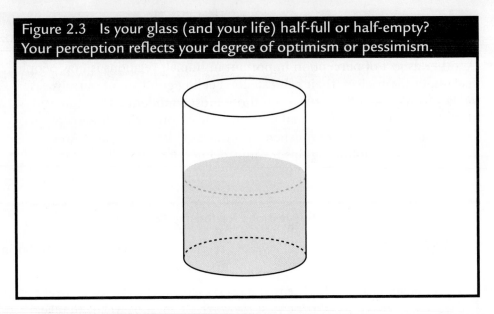

Figure 2.3   Is your glass (and your life) half-full or half-empty? Your perception reflects your degree of optimism or pessimism.

Change Your Thought Processes. Dr. David D. Burns, in his book *Feeling Good*, describes thought processes that prevent us from thinking positively. One is seeing things in black-and-white categories, so you consider your performance a total failure if it is not perfect. Another is exaggerating or minimizing the importance of your mistakes or someone else's achievements. Some other thought processes that interfere with positive thinking are over-generalizing so you see negative events as part of a failure pattern, disqualifying positive experiences as "not counting," and jumping to conclusions. Being aware of these processes and realizing when you are using them will help you begin to develop positive thinking patterns.[12]

Reach positive thinking by changing thought processes and using positive self-talk and visualization.

Engage in Positive Self-Talk. Positive **self-talk** involves making favorable statements to yourself. Making statements such as "I can do that job," or "I performed well," can help strengthen your positive self-image. Stephen Strasser, in *Working It Out—Sanity & Success in the Workplace*, points out that self-confidence, self-worth, self-direction, self-respect, self-dignity, and self-esteem are necessary before we can solve problems of job and career.[13]

Use Visualization. Taking time to practice **visualization**, or seeing yourself as a good, productive person, can also help you develop a positive attitude. Make time each day to picture yourself doing well. For example, if you have a test coming up, imagine yourself sitting at the desk, reading the questions, and writing the correct answers. If you are to make a workplace presentation, visualize yourself successfully making the presentation and seeing your supervisor pleased.

Remember, however, that visualization does not take the place of hard work. If you have studied hard or prepared thoroughly and are rested and healthy, visualization can enhance your performance.

Quick tip

Elwood N. Chapman, in his book *Attitude—Your Most Priceless Possession*, says you can use the "flipside technique" to adjust your attitude. When a negative enters your life, immediately flip the problem over and look for whatever humor may exist on the other side.[14]

Signals Give Clues to Your Attitude

Several attitudes and the signals they give off are described below. Some represent positive attitudes and others represent negative attitudes. Do these describe anyone you know? Can you add others to the list?[15]

Attitude	Signals Given Off
Complaining	Nothing you do will make me happy.
Determined	Nothing can stop me.
Fearful	I worry about everything.
Rejecting	People don't like me.
Superior	I'm great at everything.
Inferior	I'm not good at anything.
Insecure	I'm not sure what I should say or do.
Arrogant	I'm pretty important.
Humble	We are all equally important.
Intimidating	I'll bully you.
Belligerent	Oh, yeah? Just try it.
Persevering	I'll keep trying until I make it.
Victimized	Poor me.
Optimistic	Things are going to be okay.
Pessimistic	Nothing works out right.
Enthusiastic	Okay, let's try it.
Caring	You are important to me.
Resilient	Nothing keeps me down for long.
Uncooperative	No, I'm not going to try anything new.
Confrontational	Make me.
Defensive	It's not my fault.

from the School-to-Work Series: *Attitude*, by Career Solutions Training Group, © 1996 South-Western/Thomson.

Take time each day to visualize yourself succeeding.

©Getty Images/PhotoDisc

ALWAYS BEING POSITIVE IS DIFFICULT

All individuals face difficult periods in their lives. The "down" periods can be caused by stress from fatigue, tension, or illness. Other experiences, such as the death of a loved one, loss of a pet, loss of personal belongings through fire or natural disaster, divorce, robbery, moving, job loss, and retirement, also trigger stress. Even good things cause stress if they involve major changes, deadlines, or lots of details (such as a wedding). When these events occur, we may have difficulty remaining positive. Stress can distort perception and our ability to identify truth or view matters realistically.

The grieving process affects our outlook.

Difficult events (even some that are positive, like leaving home and moving to a new state to start a new job) can trigger a natural grieving process that was first identified by the Swiss psychiatrist Elisabeth Kubler Ross. She discovered five stages of grieving: denial, anger, bargaining, grieving, and acceptance. By understanding this process, we can work through our grief and return to our positive perspective of life.

GLOBAL CONNECTION

Because of jet travel and modern communication and information technology, we now operate within a global, rather than regional, economy.

1. *How can differing perceptions cause problems when working in a global economy?*

2. *Do you think that the world could eventually meld into one culture because of modern communication techniques? Why, or why not?*

Individuals enter the stages of grieving at different times. Those persons who do not move through the stages or who stay at one stage too long may need professional help.[16]

Check Out My Attitude

Evaluate your attitude by responding Yes or No to each statement.

1. I complain immediately when I don't like something.	Yes	No
2. I can't stand do-gooders.	Yes	No
3. You had better not try to pull a fast one on me, or I'll get you back.	Yes	No
4. If you don't succeed the first time, give up because you'll embarrass yourself.	Yes	No
5. I think it's good to complain; then people know exactly how I feel.	Yes	No
6. Being positive most of the time is just too unrealistic.	Yes	No
7. If anything goes wrong, it ruins the rest of my day.	Yes	No
8. If I do a good job, nobody cares about the way I act.	Yes	No
9. Backing down makes you look weak.	Yes	No
10. Few people understand what I go through.	Yes	No

If you responded Yes to one or two statements, you think negatively sometimes.

If you responded Yes to three to five statements, you see the bad side too often.

If you responded Yes to more than five statements, life must be tough for you. You need to learn coping behaviors.[17]

from The School-to-Work Series: *Attitude*, by Career Solutions Training Group, © 1996 South-Western/Thomson.

---

*Fast*Chat

1. What events can cause people to grieve?
2. Have you ever seen someone stuck in a phase of grieving?
3. When you have a loss, should you allow yourself to grieve? Why, or why not?
4. What difficulties can occur at work when someone is going through the grieving process?

Conforming to expected roles can help us succeed.	Everyone has different **roles** to fill. Employee, parent, church member, student, volunteer, teacher, and friend are examples. Each role has its own acceptable behavior and dress. Realizing which role you are playing and behaving appropriately for that role is important. People feel more comfortable dealing with individuals who fit roles as the roles are perceived. For instance, we expect our auto mechanic to wear work clothes made to withstand oil and grease. A mechanic who is not dressed "appropriately" may be perceived as being unable to perform the tasks necessary to service cars. Parents expect teachers not to swear and frequently complain if swear words occur in classroom lectures, even though their children may hear these same words numerous times in a single evening of watching television.

Because of this phenomenon, be sensitive to the roles that you play and the perceptions and expectations that others have of you in those roles. Learn what the expected behaviors are and then conform to them when appropriate. Conforming to expectations of dress and behavior at work will help you do your job effectively, will enhance your image, and will help you move ahead professionally.

Some people feel more comfortable in one role than in another. For instance, a mother who is returning to school after 20 years will feel more comfortable in her role of mother than in her role of student.

GLOBAL CONNECTION

Cultures perceive things differently. For instance, Americans see time as linear, with a beginning and end. Americans have sayings such as "a stitch in time saves nine." Many other cultures see time as circular; the seasons come and go, and punctuality is not as important.

1. *What problems might this cause for individuals from other cultures who come to work in America? For Americans working abroad?*

2. *Should American companies operating overseas follow the customs of U.S. companies or of the country in which they are located?*

The employee promoted to supervisor may feel ill at ease initially. Realize that being uncomfortable in a new role is natural. If you are aware of the behavior that the role requires and keep in mind that changing your behavior to conform to that role is expected and acceptable, you will handle transitions into new roles better.

Sometimes roles are ambiguous. Most people feel awkward the first day on a new job or as a new member of a group because they are not sure what is expected of them. Again, this unease is natural. Learning a new role and developing confidence in it takes time.

Sometimes, too, roles can conflict. A father may need to be at work at the same time that his child's Scout meeting is being held. A mother may feel guilty about being at work and not at home with her children. Such conflict can cause anxiety. Recognizing the source of anxiety will help us cope with it.

©Getty Images/PhotoDisc

©Getty Images/PhotoDisc

©Getty Images/PhotoDisc

We all play many roles in life.

*Fast*Chat

List your roles.

1. How do you behave differently in each of these roles?

2. How does your role at work differ from your role at home?

3. What might happen if you behaved at work as you do with friends?

Everyone faces anxiety. Anxiety can be caused by a number of factors such as role conflict, ambiguity, or low self-esteem. To function satisfactorily, we need to feel adequate in our activities and acceptable to others. High feelings of acceptability can compensate for low feelings of adequacy. The weak student who is well liked because of a kind personality is an example. The reverse is also true: high feelings of adequacy can compensate for low feelings of acceptability. An example is the student who makes good grades but has no friends or social life. However, when both adequacy and acceptability are low, a person's overall feelings of worth suffer.

Perceptual defense mechanisms are used to cope with anxiety.

Individuals frequently cope with anxiety through the use of **perceptual defense mechanisms**. These unconscious strategies serve to protect our feelings of worth and to avoid or reduce threatening feelings. Note that both positive and negative outcomes can result from the use of defense mechanisms. The trouble is that defense mechanisms may keep us from confronting the real problem. Some common defense mechanisms are explained on the following page.[18]

While at work, be aware of the behavior of others. *Stop to think* before you *react*. Perhaps your supervisor has had a fight at home and now seems angry with everyone in the department. If you are aware that displacement is occurring, you will be less likely to take the gruffness personally. Taking a minute to think through interactions before responding can greatly improve your human relations skills.

*Fast*Chat

1. Examine your own thoughts and behaviors. Are you using defense mechanisms regularly? Which ones?

2. Does use of defense mechanisms cause you to avoid dealing with your problems?

3. Are there times when using these mechanisms is healthy?

4. Can you be more tolerant of others' behavior if you realize they are using defense mechanisms? Why, or why not?

Perceptual Defense Mechanisms

Denial   Denying that anxiety exists
<u>Work example</u>: "I'm not worried about my upcoming performance appraisal." "I never become nervous before a presentation."
<u>Home example</u>: "Death doesn't frighten me." "I don't become nervous about tests."

Repression   Pushing stressful thoughts, worries, or emotions "out of mind"
<u>Work example</u>: The cashier who was robbed cannot remember the incident.
<u>Home example</u>: The child cannot remember being abused by a parent.

Rationalization   Explaining away unacceptable feelings, thoughts, or motives
<u>Work example</u>: "It's just as well that I did not get that promotion. I would not have been able to spend as much time as I want with my family."
<u>Home example</u>: "I know Joe didn't call me, but I am sure he likes me. He just had important things to do."

Regression   Returning to previous, less mature types of behavior
<u>Work example</u>: Ann's supervisor is reprimanding her for sloppy work. Ann starts to cry.
<u>Home example</u>: Mike wants to be waited on when he is sick, as he was as a child.

Scapegoating   Blaming another person or group for a problem
<u>Work example</u>: "It's the Human Resource Department's fault. If they would hire better people, we wouldn't be in this mess."
<u>Home example</u>: "It's Billy's fault that I didn't get any of my chores done. He kept talking to me."

Projection   Attributing an unacceptable thought or feeling about yourself to others
<u>Work example</u>: The supervisor routinely comes in late and accuses employees who are on time of being late.
<u>Home example</u>: The husband accuses the wife of wanting a divorce when he is actually the one considering a separation.

Displacement   Finding safe, less-threatening people or objects and venting frustration on them
<u>Work example that goes home</u>: An angry manager yells at a supervisor (who cannot yell back), the frustrated supervisor yells at an employee (who cannot yell back), the irritated employee yells at the spouse (who cannot or will not yell back), the furious spouse yells at their child (who cannot yell back), and the upset child kicks the dog.

Sublimation   Directing unacceptable impulses into socially acceptable channels
<u>Work example</u>: A person who is aggressive may make a career in the military or sports.
<u>Home example</u>: A suicidal person may take up a risky sport, such as skydiving.

Compensation   An attempt to relieve feelings of inadequacy or frustration by excelling in other areas
<u>Work example</u>: The employee who feels unappreciated by an immediate supervisor may take on tasks in other areas, such as committee or community projects, to experience success or receive positive feedback.
<u>Home example</u>: A physically handicapped person may become a computer expert to show that his or her mind is not impaired.[19]

Perceptions play an important role in the relationship we have with supervisors and others above us. How you perceive superiors will determine how you act around them.

Feeling intimidated by authority figures with whom you have not had an opportunity to interact is quite natural. If you become so frightened by authority figures that you cannot communicate comfortably, look for opportunities to interact in casual ways. For instance, you might speak briefly in the hall or, if appropriate, stick your head in their doors for a quick "hello." This type of assertive behavior will help you see authority figures in a new light.

FEELING UNSURE OF AUTHORITY FIGURES

Perception of superiors influences work behavior.

You may feel unsure of authority figures when a coworker is promoted over you or uncomfortable when you are promoted over coworkers. This type of change creates what psychologists call a loss of perceptual anchorages. An adjustment period is normal while everyone involved learns new roles and what each expects of the others in these roles.

Another event that can produce anxiety is getting a new boss. You may miss the old boss and resent having to start from scratch in showing the new supervisor what you are capable of doing. You must remember that some time will be necessary for both of you to become comfortable with each other. Being ready with suggestions if asked and offering to help the new supervisor will encourage a good relationship. Keep an open mind and avoid prejudging the new boss.

VIEWING THE BOSS

The most effective way to view bosses is as humans with their own feelings and own jobs to do. They have their strengths and weaknesses, good days and bad days. Recognize this fact, and learn when to approach them. For instance, if you approach your supervisor about a trivial matter when she is in a hurry or has just arrived late to work because of a flat tire, you can probably expect a less-than-enthusiastic reception.

Also, be sensitive to bosses' moods and viewpoints and do not challenge them in front of others or when they are not feeling well. Remember that bosses will appreciate tact and kindness just as much as you do.

Quick tip

Try this tactic when bringing a problem to your supervisor:

1. Define the current problem/situation as you see it.

2. State how you feel the situation should be and why.

3. Suggest a solution.

4. State specifically what you would like the supervisor to do.

5. Affirm your support and offer your assistance.

MANAGING THE BOSS

Just as supervisors manage their staffs to meet goals and deadlines, you can manage your bosses to meet your own objectives. This behavior is called **upward management**. Upward management can result in better relationships, increased flexibility in assignments, and a greater understanding of how your work fits in with the overall organizational picture. As a result, you may be more committed to the job, have higher morale, and increase your productivity.

Walter St. John, in an article in *Personnel Journal,* pointed out that supervisors have the same concerns, fears, and anxieties as others. We can help ourselves by understanding and learning to cope with their fears:[20]

1. Looking bad to their bosses or others and/or being criticized.

2. Not being respected or appreciated.

3. Appearing inadequate, perhaps because of outdated skills or sharp, aggressive subordinates.

4. Being rejected as a leader.

> Managing your supervisor increases job satisfaction.

ETHICS CONNECTION

We are all confronted with situations requiring us to use ethical judgment every day. What is your obligation concerning the confidentiality of information revealed to you by others while at work? What if the individual reveals stealing money from the company? Taking company equipment or supplies? Falsifying a time sheet?

Tips for Managing Your Supervisor

1. Present your supervisor with suggestions for solving problems rather than just problems.

2. Keep your supervisor informed of the progress of your work so those managers higher than your supervisor can be informed. No one likes surprises. (This will help lay the groundwork if you must ask for extra time or help later.)

3. Be honest about problems. Most supervisors will tolerate some mistakes as part of the learning process.

4. Be sensitive to the effect that you have on others and take responsibility for your own behavior.

5. Do not try to change your supervisors. Study their preferences and try to conform to them.

6. Try to make your supervisors look good. Build on their strengths and compensate for their weaknesses.

7. Be sure that your priorities are in agreement with your supervisor's and be aware of changing priorities.

8. Know your supervisor's goals and understand how you can help meet them.

9. Recognize that you can learn from criticism. Learn how to ask for specific information and feedback.

10. Try to see things from your supervisor's perspective. Supervisors may not always have the right perceptions, but they do have the power and do determine goals.[21]

*Fast*Chat

1. Did you ever have difficulty viewing your boss as "human"? Why?

2. What is your current perception of authority? Where did it come from?

3. What can you do to see your boss as more human?

CHAPTER SUMMARY

Perceptions differ greatly depending on a number of factors, including your upbringing, values, and culture. Recognizing and appreciating differences in perception is vital to your ability to function in the workplace. Others learn about our perceptions when we practice self-disclosure. We learn theirs by accepting feedback.

The Johari Window suggests that ideally we should have a large arena, the result of self-disclosure and openness to feedback. Positive self-esteem, an optimistic outlook on life, and an understanding of the roles people play in life are other important ingredients in a successful career. Positive thinking can be enhanced through changing our thought processes, engaging in positive self-talk, and using visualization.

Learning about the defense mechanisms that individuals use to cope with anxiety can help you deal more successfully with yourself and those around you. Defense mechanisms sometimes have positive outcomes, but they may prevent us from confronting the real problem.

Remember that the most effective way to view bosses is as humans and deal with them accordingly. Learn to manage them by using the concepts of upward management.

Key Terms

perception

halo effect

reverse halo effect

self-disclosure

feedback

Johari Window

self-esteem

optimists

pessimists

self-talk

visualization

roles

perceptual defense mechanisms

denial

repression

rationalization

regression

scapegoating

projection

displacement

sublimation

compensation

upward management

REVIEW QUESTIONS

1. Explain why people have different perceptions of the same events, objects, persons, or situations.

2. Name the panes of the Johari Window and explain what they mean.

3. What is self-perception? Why is it important?

4. Name and explain the common perceptual defense mechanisms.

5. How can your perceptions of your supervisor affect the relationship you have?

DISCUSSION QUESTIONS

1. Name three reasons why different people might view the same situation differently. Are these differences acceptable? Why, or why not?

2. Draw the Johari Window of three people with whom you interact frequently at work or at school. Explain why you have drawn each pane a particular size, and describe examples of the person's behavior. How might they enlarge their arenas? What effect would enlarging their arenas have on them? On you?

3. What is your self-image at work? At home? Around friends? What can you do to improve it?

4. Describe an incident from home or work showing each of the defense mechanisms in operation.

5. Why is recognizing that supervisors are human important? How can you allow your supervisor to be "real"?

6. How would you describe an ideal worker? An ideal boss?

CHAPTER PROJECT

WRITING Invite a psychologist, social worker, or therapist to your class to discuss self-esteem. Write a plan on how you will raise your self-esteem. The plan should include action items (steps you will take), target dates, a list of resources and people who could help you, barriers you will need to overcome, and a maintenance plan for how you will keep your self-esteem high.

APPLICATIONS

In small groups, analyze the following situations.

The Screaming Supervisor

"You really messed this up!" Isaac yelled at Bobby and Maria. "I want it done right by noon or both of you are fired!" Isaac turned and stomped away.

"Oh, he makes me so angry!" Maria exclaimed under her breath. "What's been eating him? Nothing I've done has made him happy!"

"I heard he's split up with his wife," Bobby said. "They separated last weekend."

"That's true," said Ted, "but you two have really been doing a poor job lately. I don't blame Isaac for being upset."

1. Why do you think Isaac is behaving this way?

2. Is Isaac using a defense mechanism? If you think so, which one? Are Bobby and Maria using a defense mechanism? If so, which one?

3. What would be a more appropriate way for Isaac to deal with Bobby's and Maria's performances?

4. What would be an appropriate action for Bobby and Maria to take if they think that they are being unjustly criticized?

Viewpoint

"Don't ever take my tools again without asking," Ann growled at Dan as she stormed out of the room.

"I don't understand it," Dan said, turning to Sally. "I had ten brothers and sisters and I had nothing that was my own. We shared everything."

"Well, I understand," replied Sally. "My mother always taught me to ask permission before I borrowed anything."

1. Which viewpoint is right?

2. Should Dan respect Ann's feelings?

3. Does Dan have to agree with Ann's feelings to respect them?

ADDITIONAL READINGS AND RESOURCES

Beaumont, Peter, and Nick Wood. "Fragile Peace Shatters as Balkan Hatred Overflows." *The Observer,* March 11, 2001, pp. 24-25.

Carroll, Rory. "West Struggles to Contain Monster of Its Own Making." *The Guardian,* March 2004.

Harris, Thomas A. *I'm OK, You're OK.* New York: Avon Books, 1996.

Hoover, John. *How to Work for an Idiot: Survive and Thrive without Killing Your Boss.* N.J.: Career Press, 2004.

Kubler Ross, Elisabeth. *On Death and Dying.* New York: Touchstone Books, 1997.

Kushell, Jennifer, and Scott M. Kaufman. *Secrets of the Young & Successful: How to Get Everything You Want Without Waiting a Lifetime.* New York: Simon and Schuster, 2003.

Lee, John, and Bill Stott (Contributor). *Facing the Fire: Experiencing and Expressing Anger Appropriately.* New York: Bantam Doubleday Dell, 1995.

Lyles, Dick. *Winning Habits: 4 Secrets that Will Change the Rest of Your Life.* New Jersey: Prentice Hall, 2004.

McGraw, Phillip C., Ph.D. *Self Matters: Creating Your Life from the Inside Out.* New York: Simon and Schuster, 2001.

Peck, M. Scott. *The Road Less Traveled.* New York: Simon and Schuster, 1998.

Richardson, Cheryl. *Life Makeovers: 52 Practical and Inspiring Ways to Improve Your Life.* New York: Broadway Books, 2000.

Rubin, Theodore Isaac. *Compassion and Self-Hate: An Alternative to Despair.* New York: Touchstone Books, 1998.

Rubin, Theodore Isaac. *The Angry Book.* New York: Touchstone Books, 1998.

For additional resources, refer to the web site for this text: school.cengage.com/career/dalton

Motivation:
Maximizing Productivity

focus

A Great Place to Work! The lead story in the October 2003 issue of *Fast Company* magazine illustrates how the Principal Financial Group, a diversified insurance company, motivates employees in today's work environment.

More than 3,500 employees in their Des Moines home office location can use a new state-of-the-art athletic facility to try tae kwon do classes, tai chi, Pilates, spinning, or body sculpting or perhaps to join a volleyball, basketball, or softball league to stay fit. Additional benefits include free or subsidized parking, free financial counseling, and a subsidized Weight Watchers Program (one of the largest in the United States.) The Wellness Center also provides these parenting perks: an annual "Stork Fair" for expectant parents, lactation centers for new mothers, childbirth classes for expectant mothers, and a Daddy Boot Camp for soon-to-be fathers to learn diaper-changing skills and other required abilities.

A sign of their global nature includes the Muslim prayer room provided at the wellness facility. Principal believes that these means of motivating employees have been beneficial in competing for and retaining quality workers in today's tight labor market.[1]

How would you like to work for this company? What would be motivators to you? What are some of the motivating factors offered in places where you have worked?

After studying this chapter, you should be able to:

3.1 *Explain why motivation is important to organizations and individuals and understand the basic motivational behavior model.*

3.2 *Identify two basic categories of individual needs and explain the differences between needs and wants.*

3.3 *Identify the major theorists and describe their contributions to the study of human motivation.*

3.4 *Discuss positive versus negative behaviors to fulfill needs and identify the motivational source fields in individuals.*

3.5 *Discuss motivational techniques that are increasingly important in motivating employees.*

in this chapter

3.1   What Is Motivation?

Motivation is the emotional stimulus that causes us to act. The stimulus may be a need or a drive that energizes certain behaviors. At work, motivation is a combination of all factors in our working environment that lead to positive or negative efforts. If we understand what motivates us, we are more likely to achieve our personal and professional goals. Likewise, if organizations know how to motivate employees, they can increase productivity. This ability to boost production is increasingly important as U.S. organizations compete in the global market. While all companies make some effort to motivate employees, a growing number of organizations are introducing new strategies, including different compensation packages, as a means of motivating today's workers.

CASE STUDIES IN THE NEWS

In a recent interview with *InfoWorld*, Allan McLaughlin, Sr. Vice President and CTO of LexisNexis, a global information publisher, explained his belief that the key to motivation is communication. In today's fast-paced, changing work environment, employees can often feel disconnected without clear communication from their management. McLaughlin feels that when employees feel disconnected they will not be fully motivated. To improve communication and boost motivation, he began holding informal "skip-level" meetings every other week with 10 to 15 employees randomly chosen from his 830 staff members. The meetings are totally open, no-rules, any-way communication to allow employees to have access to management and to know what is going on within the company. He also tries to "know" his employees' interests, provide interesting work, and develop new skills training as other means of motivating his employees.[2]

How would you feel about working for this company? Why would training be a motivator? What would be the advantage to knowing your employees' interests?

Understanding motivation helps individuals and organizations.

Predicting motivation is difficult. To understand what motivates someone, we must guess what physiological and psychological processes underlie behavior. For example, if Allen works much harder than Sid,

Human Relations

we assume that Allen is more highly motivated than Sid to achieve some goal—perhaps a bonus, a promotion, or the prestige associated with being the top producer in the organization. Allen seemingly has a stronger need to work hard. However, unless Allen tells us why, we can only presume what his motivation or need may be.

Through studies of motivation and behavior, psychologists have generally concluded that all human behavior is goal-directed toward satisfying a felt need. The figure below illustrates a basic behavioral model with an unsatisfied need as the starting point in the process of motivation. According to the model below, an unsatisfied need causes inner tension (physical or psychological). The individual engages in some action to reduce or relieve the tension. The individual wants to do something that will satisfy the perceived need. For example, a thirsty man needs water, is driven by his thirst, and is motivated to drink.

Human behavior is goal-directed toward need satisfaction.

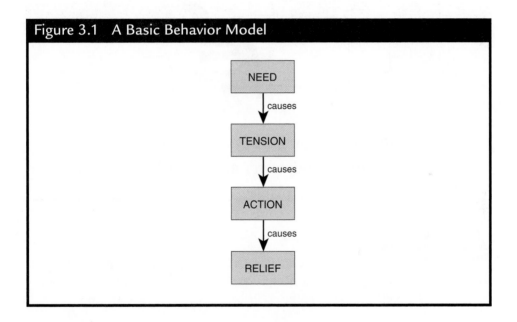

Figure 3.1   A Basic Behavior Model

All humans have needs. They need to breathe, eat, drink, and rest. But these needs are only part of a much larger picture. People also need to be accepted, fulfilled, recognized, and appreciated. They need to dream, aspire, desire, acquire! Many are the motives of individuals and groups. Understanding the complexity of these motives or needs—our own as well as those of others—is essential in establishing and maintaining good human relations.

QUICK WIT

"A mighty flame
followeth a tiny
spark."

Dante, Italian poet

Our behavior is clearly motivated by needs, and yet we often do not understand the complexities and the subtleties of our motives and needs. How often have you done something and then asked yourself, "Why did I just do that?" or "What caused that?" Try a simple exercise to experience the full range of activities involved in the motivation. Think of something you "need" and your motive for that need. What will you do to satisfy that need? Could the action you take actually cause you to be dissatisfied? An awareness of these actions will help you understand your behavior.

Until basic needs are satisfied, other needs are of no importance.

"What's this on your resume about requiring food, water and sleep?"

*Fast*Chat

1. What is motivating you most today?

2. What actions might you take to satisfy the needs behind that motivation?

People's wants may be very different from their needs, as in the following scenario.

Wimberley's New Car
••••••••••••••••••••••••••

Wimberley just graduated from college in June and is about to start her first big job. The new job is located almost 20 miles from her modest apartment, so she will need reliable transportation. As Wimberley shops for a car to satisfy this need, she finds one that greatly exceeds her budget allowance but is what she calls her "dream machine."

Wimberley reasons, "I *want* one of these convertibles with the deluxe option package, but all I *need* is this economical gas-saver. I need safe transportation from point A to point B and that doesn't require deluxe extras. Besides, the economy car fits my budget and will be easy on gas, and I can afford the insurance, too."

Often we are conditioned to think that our "wants" are "needs," when, in fact, a need can be satisfied much more simply. We all have needs, which differ greatly in origin and occur in varying degrees of intensity. Needs fall into two categories: primary (physiological) or secondary (psychological).

Primary needs are the basic needs required to sustain life, such as food, water, air, sleep, and shelter (for individual survival) and sex/reproduction (for survival of societal group). Because these needs are so basic to survival, we can easily understand why and how they affect a person's behavior.

> Primary needs are physiological and secondary needs are psychological.

Secondary needs are psychological and are far more complex. They include the need for security, affiliation or love, respect, and autonomy. Secondary needs are a result of our values and beliefs. These needs are not identical in everyone, nor are the same value or priority placed on satisfying them.

Gary Applegate, in his book *Happiness, It's Your Choice*, states that we have eight secondary needs: security, faith, worth, freedom, belonging, fun, knowledge, and health. Everything else, according to Applegate, is a want. He suggests that wants can be seen as pathways to meeting our needs.[3]

*Fast*Chat

1. What primary needs do you satisfy each day?

2. How are you satisfying your secondary needs?

Many theories have been developed about motivation. Four of these theories apply to individual behaviors in the work setting. Abraham Maslow, Frederick Herzberg, David McClelland, and Victor Vroom have contributed the most to understanding motivation in the workplace.

MASLOW'S HIERARCHY OF NEEDS

Maslow, Herzberg, McClelland, and Vroom explained motivation in the workplace.

Like many other psychologists, Maslow agreed that only a felt need motivates and that once a need is satisfied it ceases to motivate. However, he went on to identify a **hierarchy of needs**. The figure on the next page illustrates Maslow's five need levels and briefly describes the needs associated with each level. The five levels are physiological needs, safety and security, social needs, esteem, and self-actualization. Maslow's Hierarchy of Needs Theory was presented in 1954 in *Motivation and Personality*. This theory became an important building block in the understanding of human behavior, laying a foundation for the work of other theorists.[4]

Maslow identified five levels of needs.

Physiological Needs: **Physiological needs** include our desire for food, sleep, water, shelter, and other satisfiers of physiological drives. These are our most basic needs and, until they are satisfied, other needs are of little or no importance. In the workplace, adequate air conditioning and heating, water fountains, cafeteria or snack machines, and other satisfactory working conditions are designed to meet some of these needs.

Safety and Security Needs: Today, **safety and security needs** are more often reflected in our need for economic and emotional security than for physical safety. Examples of how the safety need can be met in the workplace are safe working conditions, job security, periodic salary increases, adequate fringe benefits, or a union contract.

Social Needs: **Social needs** center around our desires for love, affection, acceptance in society, and meaningful affiliation with others. These needs are often satisfied in the workplace by compatible friendships in the work group, quality supervision, and membership in professional associations or organizations.

For most people, the need for satisfactory relations with others and a place in society is so important that its lack is often a cause of emotional problems and general maladjustment.

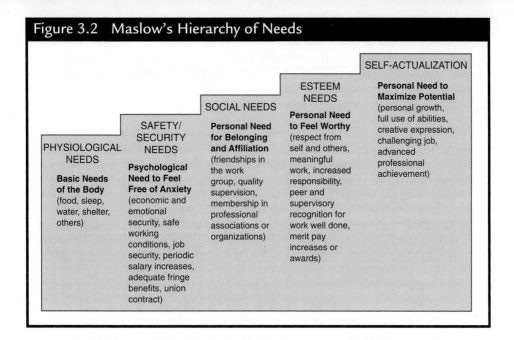

Figure 3.2   Maslow's Hierarchy of Needs

PHYSIOLOGICAL NEEDS

Basic Needs of the Body (food, sleep, water, shelter, others)

SAFETY/ SECURITY NEEDS

Psychological Need to Feel Free of Anxiety (economic and emotional security, safe working conditions, job security, periodic salary increases, adequate fringe benefits, union contract)

SOCIAL NEEDS

Personal Need for Belonging and Affiliation (friendships in the work group, quality supervision, membership in professional associations or organizations)

ESTEEM NEEDS

Personal Need to Feel Worthy (respect from self and others, meaningful work, increased responsibility, peer and supervisory recognition for work well done, merit pay increases or awards)

SELF-ACTUALIZATION

Personal Need to Maximize Potential (personal growth, full use of abilities, creative expression, challenging job, advanced professional achievement)

Esteem Needs: Often called the ego needs, **esteem needs** include our need for respect from self and others. Fulfilling these needs gives us a feeling of competence, control, and usefulness. In the workplace, these needs are generally met through meaningful work, increased responsibility, peer and supervisory recognition for work well done, and merit pay increases or awards. People whose esteem needs are not met often feel inferior and hopeless.

Self-Actualization Needs: **Self-actualization needs** refer to our desire to become everything of which we are capable, to reach our full potential. These needs include the desire to grow personally, to use our abilities to the greatest extent, and to engage in creative expression. In the workplace, these needs are most often met through a challenging job, the opportunity to be creative, and advanced professional achievement.

People actualize at different levels.

A common question asked about self-actualization is whether we ever fully actualize. The answer lies in the individual. People actualize at different levels.

Some people, for example, are satisfied with a bachelor's degree from a local college, whereas others feel a need for a master's or doctoral degree from a prominent university. Some individuals reach their full potential at a simple job; others have a capacity far beyond that level.

Some self-actualized individuals tend to be creative and will thrive on feedback. Satisfying this need level is, therefore, highly individualized.

Maslow believed that we generally satisfy these needs in a hierarchical order, fulfilling the lower-order needs first before moving on to the higher-order needs. However, he added that we can move up and down the hierarchy depending on the situation at hand.

For example, in recent years many companies have merged, downsized, and streamlined to become more competitive in the global marketplace. With the mergers and downsizing, jobs are often eliminated or greatly reduced in level of importance. Successful, often long-term employees

Individuals can move up and down the hierarchy of need levels.

TECHNOLOGY CONNECTION

An item reported by CNetAsia tells of high burnout at Indian call centers operating as hotlines for Western banks, credit card, and tech companies. Over half of the employees quit due to tough working conditions and high levels of stress. To answer calls during the Western daylight hours, Indian call centers need to maintain around-the-clock hours. Most of the calls come from the United States and Europe. Staff members assume more Western-sounding names and, through voice coaching, change their speech patterns to accommodate the target customer. Some of the U.S. companies using the services of these call centers include GE Capital, Citibank, and Dell Computers. Other companies are outsourcing operations to India and other nations with low labor costs. Business Process Outsourcing (BPO) has become one of India's growing job markets with revenues of slightly under US$1 billion in 2002 and growing steadily in 2003.

A recent study revealed human resource professionals were looking for ways to motivate and retain call center employees given the increased stress and workload. Erratic working hours, assuming false identities, copying foreign accents, and changes in social and family life topped the list of problem spots. While new workers came in highly motivated and excited with the attractive salary levels, the glow soon faded when the job stressors kicked in.[5]

How do you feel about this report? Which of Maslow's need levels are being satisfied at the call centers? How might the supervisors motivate the workers beyond burnout?

Human Relations

who may have been operating at the esteem and self-actualization levels may suddenly be without a job. These people are compelled to return to the more basic levels of safety and security needs—they need work and an income. Most likely, these people will resume their natural progression through the need levels once the security of a paying job satisfies their lower-order needs.

HERZBERG'S TWO-FACTOR THEORY OF MOTIVATION

In 1959, Frederick Herzberg presented his **two-factor theory of motivation**. After questioning over 200 accountants and engineers about what in their work led to extreme satisfaction or extreme dissatisfaction, Herzberg concluded that two sets of factors or conditions influence the behavior of individuals at work. He called the first set hygiene factors and the second set motivational factors.[6]

Hygiene Factors: **Hygiene factors**, also known as maintenance factors, are necessary to maintain a reasonable level of satisfaction among employees. Included in the category of hygiene factors are company policies and procedures, working conditions and job security, salary and employee benefits, the quality of supervision, and relationships with supervisors, peers, and subordinates. Although the absence of these factors may cause considerable dissatisfaction among workers, their presence will not necessarily lead to motivation. Generally, these factors prevent employees from being unhappy in their jobs. However, happy employees are not necessarily motivated workers.

Motivational Factors: According to Herzberg, **motivational factors** build high levels of motivation and job satisfaction. These factors include achievement, advancement, recognition, responsibility, and the work itself. Another important finding in Herzberg's research was that highly motivated employees have a high tolerance for dissatisfaction arising from the absence of adequate maintenance factors. This fact probably has to do with employees' perceptions of motivational factors. A factor that motivates one individual may be perceived as a mere maintenance factor by another. The two-factor theory (see diagram, next page) compares sets of satisfiers and dissatisfiers and their effects on job attitudes.

Herzberg's theory extended Maslow's ideas and made them more specifically applicable to the workplace.

> Herzberg defines two sets of factors in worker behavior.

> Hygiene factors maintain satisfaction.

> Motivational factors build motivation and job satisfaction.

Figure 3.3 Herzberg's Two-Factor Theory of Motivation

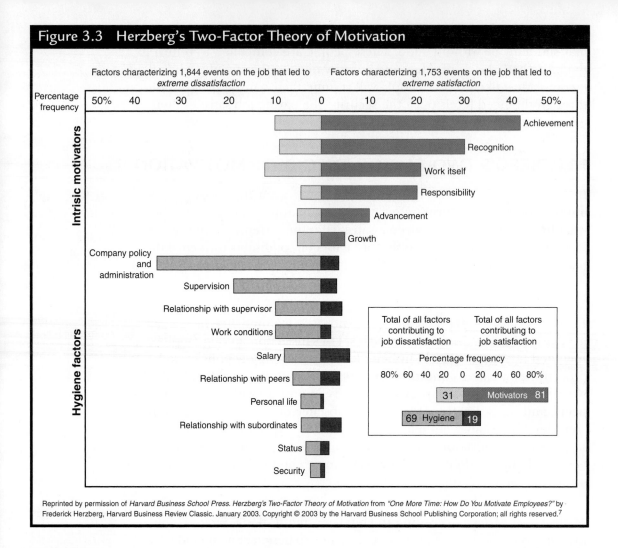

QUICK WIT

"If you want the rainbow, you gotta put up with the rain."

Dolly Parton, American singer, songwriter

Additionally, it reinforced the concept that while some factors tend to motivate employees, others have little to no effect on worker productivity. We tend to be motivated by what we are seeking rather than by what we already have. Maslow's hierarchy of needs theory is compared to Herzberg's two-factor theory in the following illustration.

Before we can successfully apply any motivational technique, we must assess the need level of the person concerned. Some people are both satisfied and motivated by hygiene factors, such as an adequate salary and comfortable working conditions. Others are only motivated by opportunities for additional responsibility or advancement to a higher-level position. This variation in need levels has been explored by other theorists with interesting results.

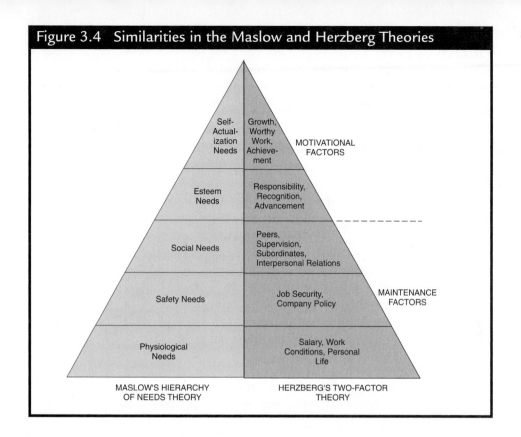

Figure 3.4   Similarities in the Maslow and Herzberg Theories

Self-Actualization Needs / Growth, Worthy Work, Achievement — MOTIVATIONAL FACTORS

Esteem Needs / Responsibility, Recognition, Advancement

Social Needs / Peers, Supervision, Subordinates, Interpersonal Relations

Safety Needs / Job Security, Company Policy — MAINTENANCE FACTORS

Physiological Needs / Salary, Work Conditions, Personal Life

MASLOW'S HIERARCHY OF NEEDS THEORY | HERZBERG'S TWO-FACTOR THEORY

MCCLELLAND'S ACQUIRED NEEDS THEORY

In 1955, David McClelland developed a theory of motivation that says our needs are the result of our early personality development. Calling it the **acquired needs theory**, he wrote that through cultural exposure, people acquire a framework of three basic needs: achievement, power, and affiliation. McClelland's premise was that these three needs are the primary motives for behavior. His theory is outlined on the next page.[8]

Following McClelland's theory, if we recognize which of the needs is most important to others, we can create the right environment for them. For example, people with a high need for achievement have a natural tendency to become leaders or managers. Planning, setting objectives and goals, and controlling the methods of reaching those goals are a basic part of their workstyle.

People with a strong need for affiliation are less concerned with getting ahead than they are with developing close relationships and friendships with others at work. They tend to enjoy jobs that require a variety of interpersonal contacts. People with a strong need for power naturally seek positions with a great deal of authority and influence. McClelland found

McClelland says most people are motivated by achievement, affiliation, or power.

QUICK WIT
"Just what you want to be, you will be in the end."
Justin Hayward, British songwriter, musician

that people who are considered highly successful tend to be motivated by the need for power.[9]

McClelland's Acquired Needs Theory

Individuals with a high need for:	Personality Trait Tendencies:
Achievement	• Seek and assume responsibility • Take calculated risks • Set challenging but realistic goals • Develop plans to achieve goals • Seek and use feedback in their actions
Affiliation	• Seek and find friendly relationships • Are not overly concerned with "getting ahead" • Seek jobs that are "people intensive" • Require high degrees of interpersonal action
Power	• Seek positions of influence • Enjoy jobs with high degrees of authority and power • Are concerned with reaching top-level, decision-making positions • Need autonomy

---

McClelland's acquired needs theory provides additional insight into the kinds of needs and motives that drive individual behavior and strengthens our knowledge of how to influence the behavior of others. The theory also helps us determine our own motives and understand our behavior.

VROOM'S EXPECTANCY THEORY

Victor Vroom, another motivational theorist, took the basic ideas of Maslow, Herzberg, and McClelland one step further. His **expectancy theory** views motivation as a process of choices. According to this theory, you behave in certain ways because you expect certain results from that behavior. For example, you may perceive that if you study long and hard for an upcoming examination, you stand a strong chance of making an "A" in the course. If you have a need for the prestige or achievement inherent in making an "A," you will more than likely study long and hard, expecting to receive the high grade to fulfill your need.[10]

Vroom was careful to emphasize the importance of the individual's perceptions and assessments of organizational behavior. Not all workers in an organization place the same value on factors associated with job performance. What individual workers perceive as important is far more critical to their choices than what their supervisors view as important. This idea still intrigues researchers, and further work is being done in the area of the expectancy theory of motivation.

Although many other theories on motivation have been developed, these capture the main ideas. The most persistent theme in motivational theories is that all behavior is directed toward some goal to satisfy a need. If the action taken leads to positive outcomes, it will probably be repeated. If the action taken leads to negative results, the behavior will usually not be repeated. Understanding these basic concepts enables us to lead ourselves and others toward desired results.

NEW METHODS OF MOTIVATION

Managers and supervisors in today's workforce are faced with motivating a diverse group of employees. Making people of all ages and cultural backgrounds feel important, connected, useful, and motivated is a major challenge. In these times of shrinking budgets, some unconventional and cost-effective means are being used to increase staff motivation. Examples include offering inexpensive rewards such as movie tickets and gift certificates, bringing in guest speakers to discuss the latest technology trends, or offering perks such as extended holiday breaks, flexible work schedules, casual dress days, telecommuting options, or a special parking spot. Managers should examine the types of things that might motivate their staff, within reason, and follow through with a plan to make some of those things happen. It may be something as simple as offering training for a new job skill or sponsoring an office ball team. These small investments can bring huge returns in benefit to the organization and the employee.

One of the most frequently overlooked methods of motivating employees is the use of applied attention. Managers can provide motivation simply by talking with employees to ensure life on the job complements their professional and personal interests, acknowledging outstanding employee contributions in front of their peers, regularly complimenting and thanking staff members, occasionally holding lunch meetings with the staff to encourage networking and camaraderie, and always sharing information.

*Fast*Chat

1. What are the five levels of Maslow's Hierarchy of Needs?
2. What similarities exist between Maslow's and Herzberg's theories?
3. What three basic needs make up the framework of McClelland's theory?
4. According to Vroom, what is the motivation for behavior?

Knowledge of motivational theory can help us as individuals in a variety of ways. Understanding the difference between a want and a need, recognizing what motivates us, learning alternative ways to fulfill needs, and learning how to motivate others when we are in leadership situations can help us reach our personal and professional goals. Learning to recognize the difference between wants and needs can help us be satisfied with what we have. This lesson can also assist us in being patient and planning alternative ways to fulfill our needs and wants.

FINDING FULFILLMENT

The illustration below expands the behavior model discussed in the beginning of the chapter to show possible reactions. Here again, an unsatisfied need creates tension and motivates a search for ways to relieve that tension. If the goal is achieved, the individual will usually engage in some form of constructive behavior. If the goal is not achieved, the individual has a choice of behaviors with positive or negative results.

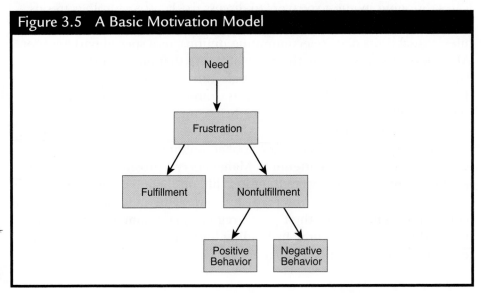

Figure 3.5   A Basic Motivation Model

Recognizing possible outcomes and realizing that we have choices in our behavior can help turn difficult situations into positive ones. By avoiding negative behaviors and by considering which behaviors might benefit us in the long run, we can often find the need fulfillment we desire. Two situations are described below. Determine the types of behaviors that may result from each of these real-world situations. Once you have identified the behaviors, discuss what would motivate you to react in such ways.

Motivation Theory Applications

As a student, you may really want an "A" on a term paper that took a great deal of time and effort to prepare. The high grade is needed to improve your overall semester grade for the class. Unbelievably, you get your paper back with a grade of "C" boldly appearing at the top of the page.

You can choose to react in the following ways:

POSITIVE   **NEGATIVE**

a. _____   _____

b. _____   _____

c. _____   _____

d. _____   _____

As an employee, you really want the supervisory position that is open in your work unit. You are very qualified to do the job and the extra money is needed to help with the expenses of a new baby. You have always been a team player and the boss seems to like you. Unbelievably, you get word on Friday that Jose was chosen for the position.

You can choose to react in the following ways:

POSITIVE   **NEGATIVE**

a. _____   _____

b. _____   _____

c. _____   _____

d. _____   _____

Note: Possible answers to these applications are available at the end of the chapter.

From the exercise above, you can see that you can choose and apply positive behaviors that result in preferred future outcomes. From your discussions, you can also realize the negative effects that poor choices may have. Understanding why we act and react to any given situation may often help us avoid destructive behaviors that may limit future opportunities.

MOTIVATING OTHERS

Leaders must assess the motivation of followers.

Both at work and in our personal lives, we may be placed in positions of leadership and held responsible for accomplishing a goal. For example, you may be elected president of your local civic group or you may be selected for a supervisory job at work. In either of these two leadership roles, understanding motivation is important.

Leaders are frequently judged by the performance of their group. The output of followers usually depends on their motivation to do what they are asked to do. Performance and motivation are closely linked. Obviously, a large part of any leader's job is to assure maximum output of the group. This is not an easy task. Encouraging others to maximize their potential and contribute their enthusiasm and energies at peak levels requires a sound understanding of motivational concepts and techniques. When we are sensitive to what increases motivation and we understand the behavior of others, we are better able to make the group more productive.

Although motivating followers is one function of the leader, the leader cannot do it alone. Because the decision to move comes from within us, we have a shared responsibility whether we are the leader or the follower. A leader, however, can influence a person's level of motivation. Through psychological research, three **motivational source fields** have been identified that are believed to influence individual behavior. The diagram on the next page illustrates the fields and their degrees of influence.[11]

QUICK WIT

"Never confuse movement with action."

Ernest Hemingway,
Author

A leader works to assure maximum output from the group.

©Getty Images/PhotoDisc

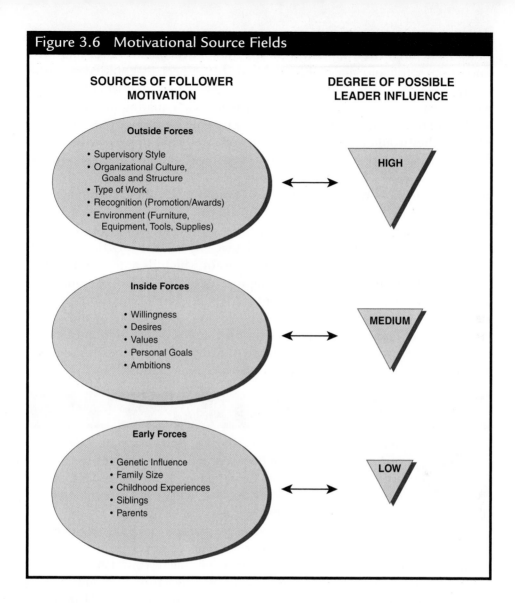

Figure 3.6   Motivational Source Fields

SOURCES OF FOLLOWER MOTIVATION

Outside Forces

- Supervisory Style
- Organizational Culture, Goals and Structure
- Type of Work
- Recognition (Promotion/Awards)
- Environment (Furniture, Equipment, Tools, Supplies)

Inside Forces

- Willingness
- Desires
- Values
- Personal Goals
- Ambitions

Early Forces

- Genetic Influence
- Family Size
- Childhood Experiences
- Siblings
- Parents

DEGREE OF POSSIBLE LEADER INFLUENCE

HIGH

MEDIUM

LOW

Outside forces offer the greatest opportunity for influencing motivation. A few of these tools are praise, variation of the work task, and financial rewards. Praise involves positive reinforcement for tasks that are completed properly. Task variation can occur through enlargement or enrichment of a job, assignment to special task forces, or rotation through different work assignments.

Financial rewards, which include pay raises, bonuses, and stock options, are the most misunderstood of the outside motivators. Our society is increasingly materialistic, and we are constantly bombarded by advertising telling us what we need.

Outside motivators include money, praise, and changing the task.

According to Peter Drucker in *Management: Tasks, Responsibilities, Practices,* we are driven to want so much that our income is never large enough to satisfy our needs. For some people, especially knowledge workers (people who earn their living by what they know rather than from what they produce), money is a form of feedback, equating to their value to the organization. If organizations paid us what we thought we should be paid, they would not be able to function. We begin to see pay raises and bonuses as a "right" rather than a "privilege" and become discontented with our salaries and, ultimately, our jobs. Organizations, then, cannot rely on financial rewards alone to satisfy employees. Other outside motivators must be used.[12]

As testimony to the effectiveness of titles as motivators, Lee Svete, Director of Career Services at Colgate University in New York, has noticed employers dressing up the titles of the jobs for which they are recruiting college students. Instead of advertising for sales representatives, companies will advertise their "management leadership development program." Rather than getting 10 resumes for the sales job, they get 90 for the "management leadership" offer. Apparently, some college graduates will sacrifice money for a title and the hope of future promotion. This seems to support the belief that money is not always a motivator.[13]

CASE STUDIES IN THE NEWS

In an article in *Washington Technology,* Bob Nelson, the author of *1001 Ways to Reward Employees* and a management consultant based in San Diego, California, explained his belief that although money is nice, employees really want recognition for a job well done. One of his favorite examples is BMC Software Inc. of Houston, TX. Identified as one of *Fortune* magazine's top 100 companies to work for, the company provides an array of incentives to attract and retain employees. An on-site barber shop, bank facility, car wash, dry cleaner, health clubs, well-stocked kitchens, incentive trips, and on-the-spot cash awards are but a few of the "perks" offered. However, Nelson will tell you that the employees work hard and put in long hours with this company because the company has created a productive environment for their employees. What the employees value most is the challenging work, well-planned career paths, and a quality management team that appreciates their performance—a job well done.[14]

Why do you think BMC provides the extras for their employees? What need levels are being satisfied with these perks in most cases? Would you feel a sense of loyalty to BMC?

Inside forces are less easily manipulated. Consider, for example, the company that wants its employees to learn a certain computer software program. Offering training on it may increase a worker's motivation. If the new ability promotes some personal goal, the worker will want to excel in its application. Influencing people's motivation through the areas of early forces is virtually impossible. These forces were established early in life and are firmly fixed within value and belief systems.

Methods for Enhancing Motivation

1. *Sell, don't tell.* Selling a course of action by explaining the benefits and the reasons for doing it is more likely to persuade employees to act than simply ordering, "do it."

2. *Let your followers make their own decisions.* Employees must feel some control and authority over their own jobs.

3. *Delegate, don't dump.* Delegating only unpleasant tasks is called dumping and is considered an abuse of power. When delegating, give challenges that will develop a subordinate's abilities—and delegate authority with the responsibility.

4. *Set goals with your followers.* Regular goal setting improves performance. Define subordinates' work in terms of goals and objectives.

5. *Listen to your followers and let them know that you are listening.* Schedule regular meetings to let them express what is on their minds. Followers tend to work harder if they feel that you care.

6. *Follow through.* Effective leaders take action to make their promises happen and keep their followers informed on what is happening.

7. *Don't change course midstream.* Followers need continuity. Be consistent.

8. *Build in a monitoring system.* Check with your group daily. You should be aware of possible problems to prevent disruption to the work environment. Encourage employees to report problems without being asked.

9. *Give criticism gracefully.* Reprimanding or ridiculing followers in public can cause problems. If criticism must be given, it should be done in private and in a constructive manner.

10. *Have a plan for employees' future.* People who cannot envision career growth will probably leave. People are more likely to work hard if they see a possibility of growth in their jobs.

11. *Avoid hasty judgments about workstyle.* Individuals will handle tasks differently than you expect. Allow the freedom of personal choice as long as the task is completed in an acceptable manner.

12. *Use rewards and incentives.* Use praise immediately when a task is well done. Praise is an important method of motivating some individuals.

13. *Encourage camaraderie and friendship.* Allowing employees time to socialize in the workplace can create a team atmosphere. Given a chance to be sociable, employees can form essential networks and expand their means of being creative and productive.[15]

Effective leaders develop an atmosphere conducive to motivation.

Understanding the motivation sources available gives the leader a framework to develop steps that may energize followers. Albert Bernstein and Sydney Rozen conducted research on successful methods that corporate leaders use to create environments that will motivate employees. They concluded that the steps shown on the previous page could enhance motivation. You may recognize some of these methods and choose to apply them in your role as a leader at work and elsewhere.[16]

CASE STUDIES IN THE NEWS

A popular North American clothing manufacturer opened a new factory in Central America. Management quickly implemented a reward and recognition program to motivate garment workers there using the same successful program used in its North American shops. The U.S. program had increased productivity and morale and decreased turnover rates. Employee productivity was measured by numbers of completed garments each day, and the worker with the most completed pieces received a recognition reward. The recognition was to have the employee stand up at the company's weekly meeting to receive applause, a green baseball cap that said "I'm Number 1" and a paid day off.

After only 90 days of this program in the Central American factory, 40 percent of the workers had quit, citing this program as the reason, even though many of them had won the award. Almost 80 percent of the world's cultures are group oriented and support the group's interest before the individual's. Being singled out meant these top workers were no longer able to be an effective part of the team. Good workers actually reduced their productivity to prevent being singled out.[17]

Which of the motivation theories apply to this situation? Why is it important to learn cultural differences when motivating employees? How would you solve this situation?

*Fast*Chat

1. What forces offer the greatest opportunity for influencing motivation? The least?

2. What methods other than payment can be used to reward employees?

Managers and supervisors are recognizing a significant change in what motivates employees in today's workplace. The changes have come about because we now have four generations fully engaged in the workplace: the Traditionalists, born before 1946; the Baby Boomers, born between 1946 and 1964; Generation X, born between 1965 and 1979; and Generation Y (or Millennials), born after 1979. Each brings far different values and expectations into the workplace. While each generation has certain characteristics, not every member of a generation will share the values and characteristics listed below.

GENERATIONAL EXPECTATIONS

Traditionalists were influenced by the Great Depression and war. Deeply patriotic, they are also loyal and have faith in institutions. Fiscal restraint and a strong work ethic characterize this generation.

> Today's employees are motivated by new factors.

Baby boomers, on the other hand, are more motivated by work that provides a sense of identity—interesting and challenging work, recognition and appreciation for a job well done, more participation in decision making, and more leisure time. With their entry into the workplace, demands for a flexible work environment grew more prominent. Employers responded by devoting more time to the development of their employees through training, job enrichment, and job enlargement.

Generations X and Y have "untraditional" mindsets when compared to their "baby boomer" parents. The boomers were at least familiar with a structured work environment and an established reporting process through a chain of command, they demonstrated good interpersonal skills, and they had reasonable written and oral communication skills.

Outspoken Gen Xers tend to have a confident attitude and statistically may be weaker in written and oral skills than the boomer generation. Sometimes described as cynical about the future and unwilling to conform, Gen Xers are known to jump from job to job if the work bores them or is not fun. But, put them behind a computer and hang on to your hat! Generation X workers are quick thinkers and risk takers, want immediate gratification, and often have advanced technical skills. They are completely at ease cruising the Information Highway, using cyber tools for problem solving, and researching issues on the Internet.

Generation X is entrepreneurial. Individuals in this age group create new businesses faster than all other age groups and maintain successful start-up companies at a rate three times higher than any other age group. They want to control their destiny, make all the decisions, and keep all the money. Some Gen Xers enter the general workforce and deliver a challenge to supervisors who must manage to motivate them. These represent the cynical, non-conformist group.[18]

Ralph Schomburg, a training leader and manager in the aerospace industry, has spent many hours learning what it takes to motivate Gen Xers. He believes we must take a look at the factors that influenced their values and belief systems. Unlike the baby boomer generation, many Gen Xers grew up with divorce, as latch-key kids, in struggling single-parent families, and as day-care youths. The threat of AIDS and other medical menaces, crooked politicians, pollution, and other ecological concerns were looming large in their lives. He believes this group of workers places different priorities and values on traditional motivational tools and is more loyal to their personal careers than to "the company." The box below represents Schomburg's experienced view of Gen X motivators.

Motivating Generation X Workers

1. *MONEY:* Money can be a strong motivating force to Gen Xers. The desire for things and gadgets moves this group to work for reward. Money is a scoreboard, a measure, for their sense of accomplishment. Money also provides independence and identity.

2. *TRAINING*: This means of increasing their skills and abilities is important to Gen Xers. It makes them more marketable and mobile—and appeals to their need for self-fulfillment.

3. *FEEDBACK*: The need to know how they're doing is strong. Providing positive (or negative) feedback helps them gauge the next move to make.

4. *REWARDS*: Traditional "Employee of the Month" recognition won't work, but hand them free theater tickets, ball game passes, or dinner tickets immediately following good behavior, and you'll have a winner.

More than 60 million strong, Generation Y (Millenials) is the second largest workforce in America's history, and members are viewed as loyal and hardworking if they see value in what they are doing. "Why should I?", "Why does it matter?", and "Why should I care?" is the mantra to make certain they understand.

Technologies (computers, e-mail, the Web, interactive multimedia, cell phones, instant messaging) are commonplace to Gen Yers and have had considerable influence on their personalities, attitudes, expectations, and learning strategies. They multitask easily, expect constant access to information with zero tolerance for delays, and have a strong need for continual stimulation and challenge. They admire honesty and integrity and place high value on volunteer work within their communities.[19]

Motivating Generation Y Workers

1. *MONEY*: They expect and believe that they will be better off than their parents. They have a very optimistic outlook on life, work, and the future, and that carries into their pay expectations. Lofty financial and personal goals are the norm.

2. *TRAINING*: Gen Yers are the most education-minded generation in history. Influenced by baby boomer parents who value education and a workplace that demands it, Gen Yers realize the key to their success lies in advanced learning and continuing education.

3. *FEEDBACK*: They prefer to work with highly motivated teams of committed people and get immediate feedback on their performance.

4. *REWARDS*: Managers must figure out a way to offer incentives at work that few competitors are willing or able to offer. Money matters, but Gen Yers are willing to meet specific work standards—goals, deadlines, and parameters—in exchange for financial and non-financial rewards.

NEW METHODS FOR MOTIVATING WORKERS

The challenge of managing, motivating, and retaining these varied generations will require a new set of attitudes and skills. The assumptions that money alone will motivate and that the workplace is of prime importance in workers' lives are no longer valid. In order to develop interesting and challenging work, employers will need to devote more time to employee development in the form of education and training, job enrichment, and job enlargement. Employees will need continuous training to acquire new skills and knowledge. This training will include classroom as well as on-the-job training. Rotating jobs will continue to be another way to motivate employees. This additional experience and training will empower individuals with the tools needed for success.

In a survey reported by Bernstein and Rozen, great disparity was found between what people say motivates them and what their companies are actually providing. For example, although 91 percent of the individuals in the survey stated that recognition for good work is important, only 54 percent felt that they were actually receiving appropriate recognition. This finding points out that the old "Way to go!" still works and that today's managers often fall short by using "management by exception."

QUICK WIT
"If you don't think every day is a good day, just try missing one."
Zig Ziglar, Author and motivational speaker

The old "Way to go!" still works in motivating some individuals.

In 1998, a chief engineer with Toyota, Tetsuya Tada, presented his concept car designed specifically to attract the Millennials. If Toyota hoped to win over the 18- to 23-year-olds worldwide who will dominate global car sales by 2020, it needed to revise both its product and its thinking. To surpass GM as the world's biggest automaker, they would have to reach beyond the baby boomers and target the 60 million–strong Generation Y. Tada brought the Toyota Scion into the market configured to fit Gen Y needs: priced affordably and with high-tech stereo equipment that played MP3s and received satellite radio signals. Toyota carefully crafted special sales centers within existing dealerships where Gen Y consumers could comfortably hang out, look up information on the Net, and browse without having to speak to a salesperson. Tada and his team knew it was not the way things had been done, but it would be the way of the future.[20]

What will really motivate the Generation Y consumer to purchase this vehicle? Why?

Under this technique, the boss only says something to you when you do something wrong.[21] One of the key success concepts of the *One Minute Manager* says that the fastest way to motivate individuals is by applying a little praise. In fact, the book's advice is to "catch them doing something right!" It stresses that praise should be specific, appropriate, and immediate.[22]

Smart leaders have discovered that words of encouragement given to a person who has done an outstanding job pay real dividends. By contrast, an old adage states, "Label a man a loser and he'll start acting like one." These practices illustrate the self-fulfilling concept that people tend to act in accordance with their self-image. If they see themselves as successful, respected, and contributing members of the work force, their behavior is likely to reflect this perception.

A strong motivational factor influencing worker behavior today is the desire for more leisure time. Increasingly, employers are finding their work places deserted by 2:00 or 3:00 P.M. on Friday. Employees slip away for an early start on the weekend's activities. This practice obviously affects productivity through lost work time, but it can also have an effect on employee morale. Dedicated employees who stay on the job until closing time resent having to handle the work left by those who skip out.

QUICK WIT
"Man is what he believes."

Anton Chekov,
Russian author

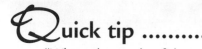
"Where the needs of the world and your talents cross, there lies your vocation."

Aristotle, Ancient Greek philosopher

....

Some methods used by organizations to cope with employees' desire for more leisure time include changing work shifts to four ten-hour work days and instituting more flexible work hours on Fridays to accommodate earlier arrival and departure times. Other employers are allowing individuals the freedom to choose which two days of the week they prefer as their "weekend." For example, employees may choose Sunday and Monday as their days off as opposed to the traditional weekend combination of Saturday and Sunday. For some employees, this choice satisfies a desire for leisure time that is less crowded and ends the "skip out early" syndrome.

One employer's innovative method of using the increased desire for leisure time to solve a motivational problem was reported in *Inc.* magazine. Walter Riley, president and CEO of Guaranteed Overnight Delivery, devised a solution to stop accidents. Tired of the $440,000 a year that accidents were costing his company, he felt that he could reduce costs by instituting a new safety program. First he scrapped the pin, patch, plaque, and $50 driving record award system. He replaced it with a 35-foot-long motor coach for vacation use by drivers who worked one year without an accident. The accident rate dropped by 89 percent the first year the program went into effect. More and more of these innovative approaches to motivating today's workers may be seen as we adjust to the changing needs of the workforce.[23]

QUICK WIT
"In the middle of difficulty lies opportunity."
Albert Einstein, Theoretical physicist

*Fast*Chat

1. What challenges do employers face in motivating a new generation of workers?
2. What methods work well for motivating today's workforce?

Key Terms

motivation

primary needs

secondary needs

Maslow's hierarchy of needs
theory

physiological needs

safety and security needs

social needs

esteem needs

self-actualization needs

Herzberg's two-factor theory

hygiene factors

motivational factors

McClelland's acquired needs
theory

Vroom's expectancy theory

motivational source fields

CHAPTER SUMMARY

The study of motivation is an ongoing attempt to understand a complex side of human behavior. From past studies, we know that a significant relationship exists between needs and motivation. Motivation is defined as the needs or drives within individuals that energize certain behaviors. Only a felt need motivates. Once that need is satisfied, it will no longer be a motivator.

Maslow developed a hierarchy of needs arranged in a specific order. He believed that individuals normally address these needs in a natural order, fulfilling lower-order needs first before moving on to higher-order needs. Herzberg was able to identify two categories of needs. He believed that hygiene factors are necessary to maintain satisfaction among employees, whereas motivational factors build high levels of motivation. McClelland's theory states that individuals acquire needs for achievement, affiliation, or power through cultural exposure during early personality development. Vroom believed that people behave in certain ways based on expected results from that behavior.

The most persistent theme in motivational theories is that all behavior is goal-directed toward satisfying some need. If an action leads to positive outcomes, it will probably be repeated. If it leads to negative results, the behavior will usually not be repeated. Needs vary in importance and intensity with each individual but generally fall into one of two basic categories, primary or secondary. Primary needs are basic to physical survival, and secondary are psychological. By understanding the difference between wants and needs, individuals can learn how to make constructive choices that do not damage careers while fulfilling needs.

Outside, inside, and early motivational source fields influence behavior, and leaders can influence motivation by working with the outside source fields.

Interesting and challenging work, recognition and appreciation for work well done, being included in key decision making, and having more leisure time have replaced some of the traditional motivators such as money and job security.

REVIEW QUESTIONS

1. Why is understanding motivation important to organizations and individuals?

2. What is the basic motivational behavior model from its point of origin through its completion?

3. Who are the major motivational theorists, and what are their contributions to the study of human motivation?

4. What are the two basic categories of individual needs?

5. What are the differences between needs and wants?

6. What are the possible constructive and destructive behaviors that individuals use to fulfill needs?

7. What are the three motivational source fields in individuals?

8. Which motivational techniques are becoming increasingly important to motivate employees today and in the future?

DISCUSSION QUESTIONS

1. Describe a personal situation in which the basic motivational behavior model was evident. What was the need you felt you had to satisfy? What action did you take to relieve the tension?

2. Using the above situation, describe whether the action resulted in constructive or destructive behavior. How might you have handled it differently?

3. Identify several sets of your personal "wants" versus "needs." How do they differ? What other ways can you find to fulfill your needs?

4. Identify a situation in which you were able to apply one or more of the motivational source fields to influence the behavior of a coworker. Which source did you use, and why was it effective?

5. Discuss your personal position on Maslow's hierarchy of needs. Describe what self-actualization will mean to you.

6. What changes in your work environment indicate a shift in motivational techniques being used? Describe some of the methods. Describe how you might choose to motivate the new age worker.

CHAPTER PROJECT

Using any one of the popular Internet Search Engines (Yahoo, Google, Excite, etc.), select a job search location. Browse through job listings to find one that would motivate you to apply for that job. Prepare a written report on how you selected your new job and what motivated you to choose that job field. Format your report in an attractive, interesting, and informative format. You might include a copy of the application, copies of your search pages, or other indicators of why you were motivated to make this choice.

APPLICATIONS

In small groups, analyze the following situations.

The Case of Ron the R.I.P.

Rosa is the supervisor of a small group of resource analysts for a major research and development company. Three of the four analysts have been in her group for less than two years and are highly motivated by opportunities for career growth and promotions to higher salary levels. They have much to learn in their advancement toward a journeyman level position.

Ron, the fourth analyst, has been with the company for 26 years. He is 52 years old, financially comfortable, and happily married with no children living at home. He and his wife travel frequently and enjoy an active social and leisure life.

Ron reached the journeyman level almost 15 years ago. Although his performance is satisfactory, he has become known as an R.I.P. (Retired in Place). He has openly stated to Rosa that he does not want any responsibility added to his current workload. He does not desire a promotion because that would put him into a stress-filled management position, and he has no aspirations to become a star performer. Ron steadily arrives at work on time, works his eight-hour shift with an appropriate lunch break each day, and leaves on time. He strictly avoids overtime hours. When occasional new assignments are added to Rosa's work group, Ron often suggests which of the other analysts is best suited to the task, indicating his obvious lack of interest in accepting the assignment.

Rosa has been unsuccessful in her attempts to force Ron to accept any additional work. Assignments made to Ron most often go unattended or result in incomplete products that require more time to redo.

The other analysts are beginning to resent Ron's passive attitude and feel that they are having to carry him by shouldering tasks that should be more evenly distributed among all office personnel.

1. According to Maslow's theory, at which need level is Ron operating?

2. At what level of Maslow's theory does Rosa wish Ron were operating?

3. How do you think the others in the group will eventually react if Ron's behavior does not change?

4. What do you think will happen to Ron if his behavior does not change?

The Times They Are A-Changing

TEAMWORK

In his six years at Hoffman Manufacturing, David has always been preoccupied with plans for his days off and has been known to call in sick when his shift is due to face heavy periods of production. His supervisor, Carl, expects all employees to carry their load in the shop and to work overtime to meet production output schedules as required.

David's shift was nearly over when a lathe in the shop broke down, requiring a four-hour repair. Carl immediately called in a maintenance crew to make the repair and asked all production shift hands to work whatever hours it took to complete the day's order. David's reply was simply, "I have plans for this Fourth of July weekend, and I'm leaving." Carl was angry and took immediate steps to discipline David. He documented the case against David and found that the company policy requires a three-day suspension without pay as the usual disciplinary action.

When David returned to work and heard the news, his only request was, "Great, can I add the three days to a weekend period so I can plan for the extended time off?" Carl felt defeated but knew David's skilled experience was valuable to the company. He decided instead to try some different method to motivate David. Carl took the challenge of turning this negative situation into a positive one.

1. What motivates David?

2. Why do you think Carl's method of discipline was ineffective in this situation?

3. What will eventually happen to David if he continues to behave in this fashion and Carl continues to motivate him with suspensions?

4. What should Carl try?

ADDITIONAL READINGS AND RESOURCES

Bennis, W. B., and R. J. Thomas. *Geeks and Geezers.* Cambridge, MA: Harvard Business School Press, 2002.

Katzenbach, Jon. *Why Pride Matters More Than Money: The Power of the World's Greatest Motivational Force.* New York: Crown Business, 2003.

Lamb, Mary Beth. "Boosting Productivity through Recognition Requires Cultural Understanding." *link&learn Newsletter,* March 1, 2003.

Lancaster, Lynne C., and David Stillman. *When Generations Collide: Who They Are. Why They Clash. How to Solve the Generational Puzzle at Work.* New York: Harper Collins. 2002.

Martin, Carolyn, and Bruce Tulgan. *Managing Generation Y.* Amherst, MA: HRD Press, 2001.

Overholt, Alison. "Des Moines, the Hippest City in the USA?" *Fast Company Magazine* (October 2003): 96-98.

For additional resources, refer to the web site for this text: school.cengage.com/career/dalton

Possible Responses to "Motivation Theory Applications" (page 69)

As a student:

Positive	Negative
a. Ask the instructor why you received the grade.	Complain bitterly.
b. Study harder for the next test.	Cause a class disruption.
c. Learn the instructor's style of grading.	Drop the class.
d. Reflect on the learning experience.	Ignore the situation.
e. Analyze the failure. (What could you have done better?)	Spread insults about the instructor.
f. Pay more attention in class.	

As an employee:

Positive	Negative
a. Take a class in supervision/management.	File a grievance over the selection.
b. Continue working as a team player.	Cause disharmony among staff.
c. Develop better rapport with supervisor.	Spread insults about Jose.
d. Volunteer to help train Jose.	Withdraw from office involvement.
e. Learn what the supervisor wants.	Do only what you are told
f. Improve your skills.	from that point forward.

Communication:
The Essential Skill

focus

The use of e-mail, voice mail, faxes, text messaging, and instant messaging permits communication to occur more quickly and more frequently. With the advent of wireless technology, access to these communication devices will be simpler than ever. However, that speed and frequency may mean less thought is put into the tone and meaning of messages, leading to potential problems in human relations and communication. Concern over these potential problems, as well as other problems that have already cropped up, has resulted in the creation of numerous instructional materials–in print and on the Internet–designed to assist people in "coping at work." It is essential that both the sender and the receiver understand the positives and negatives of using these methods of communication and take responsibility to head off miscommunication and ill will, both electronically and in person.

What do you think are some of the potential human relations and communications problems that might result from reliance on e-mail, voice mail, faxes, text messaging, and instant messaging? What advantage might face-to-face communication have over electronic communication?

After studying this chapter, you should be able to:

4.1 *Define communication and explain its role in human relations.*

4.2 *Discuss the communication process and the importance of feedback.*

4.3 *Identify barriers to communication and learn how listening skills can be improved.*

4.4 *List ways to improve your spoken communication.*

4.5 *Identify the qualities of strong written communication.*

4.6 *Discuss forms of nonverbal communication and why it is important.*

4.7 *Explain the importance of time, timing, context, and medium of a message.*

4.8 *Discuss common forms of electronic communication.*

in this chapter

Communication is the process by which we exchange information through a common system of symbols, signs, or behavior.

Communication is the process by which we exchange information through a common system of symbols, signs, or behavior. This process sends messages from one person to another. Symbols can be written or spoken words; signs can be shapes and colors; and behavior can be any nonverbal communication, such as body movements or facial expressions.

Listening, speaking, writing, and reading are the four basic skills that we use in communicating. Of these skills, the first two are the most frequently used, but unfortunately, they are the two in which we receive the least training. However, any communication skill can be sharpened, either through experience (which can sometimes be a tough teacher) or through training.

WHY IS COMMUNICATION IMPORTANT?

We have become an information society, and every technological advance seems to bring us into contact with more people. We communicate by phone, letter, e-mail, and in person with people at home, at work, and everywhere in between. We spend the majority of our waking hours communicating in one way or another—10 to 11 hours of each day. Strong communication skills are becoming an asset in all aspects of life.

Because communication is the most important element of human relations, being able to interact effectively with people around you at work will enhance your work experience and theirs. The more sensitive and knowledgeable you are about communication, the stronger your human relations skills will be.

 **uick tip** ....

Phillip J. Harkins has been studying leadership for 30 years. High-impact leaders, he says, have powerful conversations. A powerful conversation is "an interaction between two or more people that progresses from shared feelings, beliefs, and ideas to an exchange of wants and needs to clear action steps and mutual commitments." The outputs of a powerful conversation are advanced agendas, shared learning, and stronger relationships.[1]

....

THE ROLE OF COMMUNICATION IN HUMAN RELATIONS

Examples of the role communication plays in effective human relations are shown below:

Effective Human Relations

Away from Work	At Work
1. The wife who explains to her husband that she is bothered by the clothes he leaves lying on the floor and offers alternatives rather than yelling at him.	1. The employee who asks the boss for clarification of a written work order rather than doing a job incorrectly and causing a problem.
2. The father who asks his child about a broken lamp and gives the child a chance to explain rather than yelling, blaming, and punishing immediately.	2. The boss who calls employees together to discuss a major company change rather than letting them hear it as gossip or sending it in a memo.
3. The neighbor who calls and asks nicely that the stereo be turned down the first time that it is bothersome rather than immediately calling the police.	3. The employee who waits for the "right time" to ask the boss for a change in schedule, not when the boss has just arrived late after being snarled in a traffic jam.

---

*Fast*Chat

1. What is communication? Why is effective communication so important?

2. Which of the four basic communication skills do you use and enjoy the most? Why?

3. What have you seen in the movies or on TV that you consider to be effective communication? What made it effective?

COMMUNICATION FLOW

Looking at the flow of communication can be fascinating. In any organization, communication will flow upward, downward, or horizontally. In each instance, the communication process includes three elements: the **sender**, the person who transmits (sends) the message; the **receiver**, the person to whom the message is sent; and the **message**, the content of the communication. Communication may be verbal (either spoken or written, such as questions and responses), or nonverbal (such as nodding, smiling, or frowning). In addition, communication can be one-way (such as a speech or bulletin) or two-way (such as a conversation or correspondence).

> Feedback should be **T**imely, **O**ften, and **P**recise (TOP).

To be effective, a message must be understood by the receiver. Whether you are the sender or the receiver, you are responsible for determining that the correct message has been received. A process known as feedback will help you. **Feedback** is information given back to a sender that evaluates the message and states what the receiver understood.

Because of the role feedback plays in clarifying communication, verifying understanding, and overcoming communication barriers (distortions and blockages), it is an extremely important part of the communication process. To be most effective, feedback should be timely, often, and precise *(TOP)*.

ETHICS CONNECTION

Some employees pretend to be productive at work. However, with the advent of telecommuting, acting as if you are being productive is easier than ever. By utilizing wi-fi (wireless fidelity) and the cellular telephone, you can check e-mail and voice mail frequently (especially at odd hours) while being absolutely nonproductive.[2]

1. *Is it easier to fake white-collar or blue-collar work?*

2. *What other behaviors do people use to pretend to be working?*

3. *What are the short- and long-term consequences of pretending to be productive?*

4. *What, if anything, do you owe your employer? yourself?*

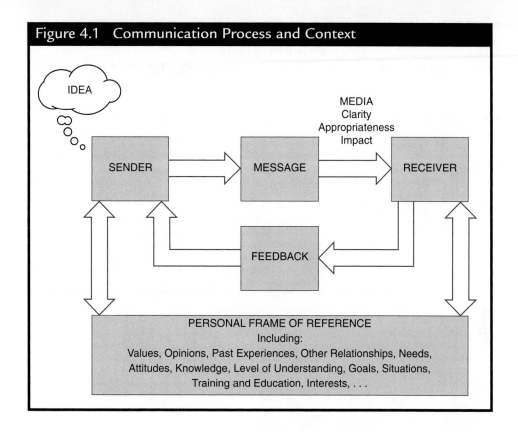

Figure 4.1   Communication Process and Context

IDEA

MEDIA
Clarity
Appropriateness
Impact

SENDER → MESSAGE → RECEIVER

FEEDBACK

PERSONAL FRAME OF REFERENCE
Including:
Values, Opinions, Past Experiences, Other Relationships, Needs,
Attitudes, Knowledge, Level of Understanding, Goals, Situations,
Training and Education, Interests, . . .

THE IMPORTANCE OF FEEDBACK

The figure at the top of this page depicts the communication process and the relationship of feedback to the sender and the receiver. Effective feedback improves communication, saves time, and reduces the possibility of errors and human relations problems. In face-to-face communication, feedback can be fast, with both the listener and speaker continuously giving feedback to each other verbally and nonverbally. Examples of ways in which we do that include frowns, nods, verbal expressions of agreement or disagreement, questions, statements, and silence. Silence can be a surprisingly powerful form of feedback, communicating power, uncertainty, agreement, or disapproval.

As the sender of messages, you will want feedback from the person or persons for whom your messages are intended to help you determine whether your message has been received and interpreted correctly. Some possible ways you can obtain feedback are shown on the next page.

> Sender, receiver, message, and feedback are the elements of the communication process.

Ways of Obtaining Feedback

When Face to Face with the Receiver

1. Ask questions that determine whether the receiver has understood.

2. Ask the receiver to restate what you have said.

3. Watch for signs for understanding (such as nods) or confusion (such as frowns).

When Not Face to Face with the Receiver

1. If you have sent a memo or letter, request either a written answer to the memo or a written estimate of when the answer will be available.

2. If a written or oral answer is not received, follow up and check for compliance. (Repeat your request or see whether the action you requested has been taken.)

Ask questions and watch for signs of understanding to be sure your receiver has understood your message.

©Getty Images/PhotoDisc

*Fast*Chat

1. How can you make sure that feedback occurs?

2. How does your frame of reference differ from that of your parents, peers, neighbors, teachers, or others? Why does it differ?

What Are Barriers to Communication and 4.3 How Can Listening Skills Be Improved?

BARRIERS

Miscommunication can create serious problems in our personal lives and at work. Communications experts have identified a number of factors that can cause distortions and blocks in communication. Some of them lie in our senses, in word meanings, and in the emotions and attitudes of the sender and receiver. Others are role expectations, personality, appearance, prejudice, changes, poor organization of ideas, poor listening, and information overload. The chart on the next two pages describes some of the barriers to communication and how they can be overcome.

LISTENING

One of the most important elements—perhaps the most important—in strong human relations skills is the ability to listen. The International Listening Association says we spend 45 percent of our time listening, but only 2 percent of us have had any formal educational experience in listening. Listening is vital at all levels of activity but becomes more important as we move up in an organization. Communication authorities have identified seven barriers to listening:[3]

Listening Barriers

1. Lack of interest in the subject or the speaker.
2. Outside noises, distractions, or fatigue.
3. Limited vocabulary of the sender or receiver or both.
4. Poor delivery of the message.
5. Thinking ahead to our responses or back to what the speaker said earlier or turning attention to other matters. (We speak at about 125–150 words per minute, but listen at 1000–3000 words per minute.)[4]
6. Lack of knowledge in the speaker or listener.
7. Prejudices, or listening for what we want to hear.

Barriers in Communication

Barrier	Possible Problem	Potential Solution
1. Sensory organs	1. Poor eyesight or hearing can cause us to misunderstand or misinterpret. Or, other noises or sights might distract, so full attention is not given to sending or receiving a message.	1. Periodic checkups can detect vision or hearing problems that hinder communication. If distracted, try to reduce the number of sights and sounds around you.
2. **Semantics** (study of meanings and changing meanings of words)	2. Words may have multiple meanings, which can cause difficulty. The more abstract a term, the less likely people are to agree on meaning. Also, words change meaning, and new words are introduced.	2. Use feedback to ensure correct interpretation. Ask questions, such as "Do you mean ...?"
3. Emotions	3. Our emotions can cause us to overreact to a message or prevent us from hearing all of it. Attitudes can cause us to have preconceived ideas that affect how we interpret what we hear.	3. Calm down before you send or receive messages. Have an open mind and withhold judgment until you have adequate information to evaluate the message.
4. Role expectations (how we expect ourselves and others to act on the basis of the roles played)	4. We may identify others too closely with their roles and discount what they say. Or we may not allow others to change their roles (such as a coworker who becomes a supervisor or a family member who has grown in maturity). People in positions of power may act superior to others or misuse their power.	4. Try to separate people from the roles they are playing, and recognize that roles change. Also, be sensitive to the effect that power may have on perception, especially if you are in a position of power. (For example, ask for compliance rather than making demands.)
5. Personality and appearance	5. Some messages are rejected because the personality or appearance of the sender is inappropriate (such as wearing ragged clothes on a job interview) or the message itself is messy and full of errors.	5. Strive to make your behavior and appearance appropriate to the roles you play. Also, your correspondence should reflect the image you wish to present.

Human Relations

Barriers in Communication (continued)

Barrier	Possible Problem	Potential Solution
6. Prejudice	6. Sometimes our opinions regarding the sender's race, religion, color, sex, national origin, age, or disability can alter our perception of the message. For example, someone might think a person "too old" to be creative.	6. Recognize the contribution different people can make. Try to evaluate communication on the basis of the message itself, not on preconceived ideas about the sender. See Chapter 9 for further information.
7. Changes	7. Failure to recognize changes can cause confusion and make more communication difficult. Sometimes we are so close to objects or people we don't notice changes. Other times changes occur too quickly, causing fear or mistrust.	7. Try to recognize that people, objects, and situations can change and interpret communication in that light.
8. Poor organization of ideas	8. We may present ideas (spoken or written) in such a disorderly fashion that listeners or readers find following difficult and lose interest. Also, credibility is lost when ideas are poorly organized.	8. Organize and revise correspondence and presentations so that they are clear and logical. If organization is a problem for you, consider classes or workshops in written and oral communications.
9. **Information overload** (More messages and stimuli coming at us than we can process successfully.)	9. Because of our busy society, increased communication, and hectic pace of life, too many messages and stimuli come at us at one time. When we become overloaded with information, we lose the ability to continue processing and remembering information, fail to listen carefully, and forget information. The result is a breakdown in communication.	9. Develop coping strategies for dealing with information, such as making notes and grouping activities (telephone calls, e-mail). Recognize overload, then work to relax, reduce noise, and focus. Getting enough rest and eating healthily are important, and delegating, saying no, getting an answering machine, and doing work before it builds up also help.
10. Poor listening	10. Most of us listen effectively to only about 25 percent of what we hear.	10. To listen effectively, determine what the speaker is saying and consider the speaker's emotions about the message.

To prevent the common difficulties and damaged relations caused by poor listening, we must want to improve and must engage in active listening. **Active listening** is a conscious effort to listen to both the verbal and nonverbal components of what someone is saying, without prejudging. Here are some steps to help you improve your listening skills.

How to Improve Listening Skills

1. Don't anticipate or plan rebuttals. Don't jump to conclusions. Keep your thoughts in the present.

2. Avoid prejudging the speaker. Be aware of your biases and prejudices.

3. Eliminate distractions by providing a quiet, private location for communication. Face the person speaking to you so that you can concentrate.

4. Ask for clarifications; restate important points by paraphrasing the speaker. Ask questions that make the other person go deeper, such as who, what, when, and where. (However, you should avoid the use of the word *why*. This word puts some people on the defensive.) Remain neutral and restate the person's viewpoint. Put the person's feelings into words.

5. Be ready to give feedback.

6. "Listen" to the nonverbal communication. It is through nonverbal communication that we can pick up the emotional message.

7. Avoid unnecessary note taking. (Some may be necessary, as we forget one-third to one-half of what we hear within eight hours, but don't focus on your notes and risk missing what is being said.)

8. Listen for major ideas; don't try to remember everything.

9. Don't fake attention; it takes too much work and is distracting. (It's hard to disguise feigned interest.)

FastChat

1. Discuss barriers in communication that you may have observed or experienced. How might these barriers have been minimized?

2. Give examples from your own experience of when listening was blocked. What can be done to avoid the problem in the future?

Human Relations

Verbal communication is any message that we send or receive through the use of words, oral or written. Effective verbal communication requires good listening skills and an ability to use the written and spoken word. To improve your spoken communication, consider the following vital aspects.

Aspects of Spoken Communication	
Voice	Our voices should be pleasant and appropriate for the situation. Be aware of surroundings, and match tone and volume to situation. To learn how you sound to others, you may want to try recording yourself.
Word Choice	Correct grammar is important. We should develop an ability to use descriptive, specific verbs, adverbs, and adjectives. Slang should be used sparingly and carefully, so as not to confuse listeners.
"I" Phrases	Beginning communication with "I think," "I believe," "I feel," or "I don't understand" is much more effective than comments such as "You made me angry," or "You are wrong," or "You are confusing me," which can make people defensive.
Following Up	Follow up verbal directives or complex instructions in writing. The International Listening Association states that we usually only recall 50 percent of what is said immediately after we listen to someone talk. Our ability to recall what we heard drops as time passes. Parts of a message are lost or distorted after passing through two people.[5]
Willingness to Speak Up	Don't worry excessively about what others will think. The insight you offer may help others. Also, your participation may be encouraging to others. Ask precise questions to show that you are paying attention and want to contribute.
Choosing the Right Level	We communicate on many levels and need to pick the right level for the situation or relationship: conventional with strangers or casual acquaintances; exploratory when the communication is about facts or other people; participative when we start talking about ourselves, expressing ideas and feelings; and intimacy, the deepest level of communication, when we expose our intimate thoughts and feelings.
Keeping a Secret	Know when not to speak. Being discreet is extremely important in human relations. The importance of confidentiality in our work and personal relationships cannot be overemphasized.

In addition to working on the mechanics of good spoken communication (from grammar to voice control), we should remember other keys to good communication as shown here.

Suggestions for Improving Spoken Communication

1. Listen to the message in the words and the feelings.

2. Don't let your own ideas get in the way. Listen to what others are saying.

3. Know when to *just* listen. Sometimes one person may withdraw, and you will need to be patient and supportive and just wait.

4. Question assumptions. Appearances can be deceiving. Keep in mind that you are communicating with another distinctly individual human being who feels the need to like and be liked.

5. Tell the truth. You might never consider telling a "serious" or big lie, but even small white lies such as "I like it" (if untrue) or "I'll get back to you soon" (when you won't) can create hurt, confusion, and resentment.

6. Think before speaking. Ask yourself, "What do I want to communicate?" The key to communication is truly understanding what must be communicated.

7. Now is the best time to get it correct. "I should have said..." will never be enough.

ETHICS CONNECTION

You've heard the saying, "It's not what you know, it's who you know." Is it ethical to engage in such communication behaviors as name-dropping in order to get ahead? Under what circumstances would it be appropriate or inappropriate to drop names?

1. *Another common saying is "Sex Sells." Is flirting ethical in order to achieve goals? What about the use of profanity? Slang?*

2. *In what ways can these types of behaviors backfire?*

GLOBAL CONNECTION

The use of the Internet grew worldwide during 2002, although the increase was slower than 2001 according to figures released by the United Nations in 2003. Despite the rapid growth of the number of Internet users in developing countries, the digital divide between the United States, which has the highest rate of Internet users in the world, and developing countries is still quite large. Slightly less than 10 percent of the world's population had access to the Internet by the end of 2002.[6]

United Nations Secretary General Kofi A. Annan said, "Technology can improve the lives of millions of the Earth's poorest people." With this in mind, attendees of the UN-sponsored World Summit on the Information Society held in Switzerland in 2003 set a goal of ensuring that more than half the world had access to some form of electronic media by 2015.[7]

1. *Have computers, the Internet, and mobile telephones improved your life? How, or how not?*

2. *Do we have an obligation to assist developing countries with this technology? Why, or why not?*

*Fast*Chat

1. Review the aspects of spoken communication and determine where your skills are strongest. Explain.

2. Did any of the suggestions for improving communication surprise you? Which ones?

3. Think of a situation where having known this information might have made communication better. What happened, and how might you have improved it?

4.5 How Can You Improve Your Written Communication?

The purpose of writing, like speech, is to communicate, not impress.

Follow the KISS rule in writing: **Keep It Short and Simple.**

Good writing skills are essential to career success. Writing, the most durable form of communication, is used frequently, particularly at higher levels of an organization. The purpose of writing, like speech, is to communicate, not impress. Inexperienced writers sometimes think that they must change their personalities completely and write in a showy, unnatural manner. This is neither necessary nor desirable. Every written communication creates a mental image of the sender. Will your writing style cause you to be viewed as pompous and wordy, as disorganized and possibly unreliable, or as an intelligent, clear thinker with a sense of purpose? Here are some suggestions to help you make your writing a positive reflection of you.

WRITING

Suggestions for Improving Written Communication

What	How
1. Sentence length	1. Educators and publishers suggest keeping your average sentence length between 15 and 20 words, cutting down on long sentences, and varying the length of your sentences.
2. Wordiness	2. Avoid thinking aloud on paper. Follow the KISS rule: "Keep It Short and Simple."
3. Organization	3. Think about what you want to communicate and the logical progression. Outlining and creating a rough draft can help you.
4. Appropriate style or tone for the intended audience	4. Know when writing should be formal and when informal writing would be effective.
5. Clearly stated purpose	5. Ask yourself, "Why am I writing this message" and then tell the reader.[8]

Human Relations

In writing, you should follow the **4 Cs of communication:** Writing should be complete, concise, correct, and conversational or clear. After you have written a memo or letter, check it against the suggestions given below.

WRITING

Checklist for Written Communication

Criteria	Questions to Ask
1. Complete	1. Have I included all necessary facts and answered all questions?
2. Concise	2. Have I deleted unnecessarily long words? Is my message one page or less? Are my paragraphs short and easy? Is important information obvious?
3. Correct	3. Is my message accurate? Does it agree with company policy? Are the grammar, spelling, and punctuation correct? Are corrections neat?
4. Clear	4. Is my writing easy to understand and friendly without being flowery? Have I avoided argumentative words or expressions?

At work, written communication should be complete, concise, correct, and clear.

©Getty Images/PhotoDisc

Quick tip ···

Human Relations Practices in Writing E-mails:

1. Be courteous, brief, and specific, using one subject and one message per e-mail.

2. Don't write something you wouldn't want public. Even if the e-mail is erased, it can be retrieved.

3. Read the message for clarity several times before sending.

4. Don't immediately send or respond to an angry message.

5. Don't clog up others' mailboxes with jokes or chain letters.[9]

*Fast*Chat

1. Have you ever received a written message that was so poorly written that you had difficulty understanding it? How might it have been improved?

2. How would you describe your own writing style? Which of the suggestions in this section do you think will help you improve your ability to communicate effectively in writing?

Nonverbal communication—communication without words—has been mentioned several times in this chapter. **Nonverbal communication** is any meaning conveyed through body language, through the way the voice is used, and through the way people position themselves in relation to others. How you say something is frequently just as important as what you say. Tone of voice, facial expression, gestures, or haste may determine how listeners interpret your words and may even overshadow them.

Recognizing nonverbal communication is an important human relations skill.

People with strong human relations skills are usually good at reading others' body language and in using nonverbal communication. In a well-known study, Dr. Albert Mehrabian, an expert in nonverbal communication, found that nonverbal communication accounts for at least 93 percent of the impact of our communication, and words account for only 7 percent. That 93 percent is made up of pace, pitch, and tone of voice (38 percent) and facial expressions (55 percent).[10]

Common nonverbal transmitters are posture, facial expressions, eye contact, voice, body movements, personal space, and seating.

Understanding others' nonverbal communication is important because people often show their feelings and attitudes by their actions rather than their words. When we appreciate others' thoughts and feelings, we can interact more effectively with them.

Examples of Nonverbal Communication

Behavior at Work	Possible Message
1. The computer operator who averts her head or turns her body away when the supervisor leans over to explain a graph.	1. May mean she is uncomfortable with the closeness.
2. The employee who in a meeting rambles on in long, involved, unfinished sentences.	2. He may feel insecure.
3. The employee who engages in much unnecessary body, hand, or foot movement.	3. Can signal tension.
4. The employee who sits at the head of the conference table and participates.	4. May be signaling confidence and interest. (Environment, location, and seating can influence the kind of interaction that occurs.)

Examples of Nonverbal Communication (Continued)

Behavior at Work	Possible Message
1. The mother who puts her hands on her hips and looks sternly at her young daughter.	1. Wants the child to understand that she had better do as she is told.
2. The father who smiles as he tells his son that he is disappointed the boy left the house last night without permission.	2. A mixed message, with his words saying one thing and his body language saying another. When such a split occurs, we tend to believe the nonverbal communication. The message that the son will perceive is approval.

Some common means of communicating nonverbally are shown here. Be aware of them in yourself to make sure that you are conveying the message you wish to send. Noticing them in others will enhance your communication skills.

Common Means of Communicating Nonverbally

Nonverbal Transmitters	Examples
1. Posture while sitting and standing	1. A woman who sits in a chair with her legs wrapped around the chair legs, holding her head rigidly to one side, clasping her hands tightly or holding a clenched fist, is tense. Another tense person may be the man wandering about the room or continually moving his hands and feet, or twisting his head from side to side. Individuals in high-status positions usually display their status through relaxed positions, such as one arm in their laps and the other across the back of a chair; they keep their heads level and face forward. Those in lower-status positions keep their heads down and hands together or at their sides.
2. Facial expressions (must be considered in the total context of what is being said; some people do not show emotions on their faces)	2. Happiness, anger, surprise, disgust, and fear are displayed most often through facial expressions, particularly through the eyes and lower face. Smiling can detract from a serious message. (Women tend to smile more than men, which can create misunderstandings for them at work and in their personal relationships.)

Common Means of Communicating Nonverbally (continued)

Nonverbal Transmitters	Examples
3. Eye contact (direct and powerful form of nonverbal communication)	3. We generally use eye contact to signal a desire for communication, as when we try to make eye contact with a waiter in a restaurant. When we wish to avoid talking to someone, we look away and avoid eye contact as when our instructor asks a question we cannot answer or when we approach someone in the hall. A failure to make eye contact can indicate embarrassment, fear, or dishonesty.
4. Voice (pitch, clarity, breathiness, articulation, resonance, tempo, rhythm, and speech rate)	4. The voice can often tell us something about a speaker. For example, when people feel comfortable or secure, their voices tend to sound smooth and well modulated and their sentences are normal. A loud voice, fast rate of speech, and high pitch may express active emotions; while sadness, disgust, or boredom may be indicated by a quiet voice, low pitch, and slow rate of speech. A fast but not excessive rate is more persuasive and is viewed as more trustworthy and enthusiastic.
5. Body movements	5. Hand, arm, and body movements can reveal openness, suspicion, honesty, confidence, nervousness, or defensiveness.
6. Personal space (an invisible bubble around us, the size of which varies from culture to culture). Effective human relations skills demand that we respect others' personal space.	6. In general, people in the United States tend to have larger bubbles than people in other cultures. We will permit a smaller personal space when situations are comfortable or non-threatening or we feel close psychologically. When our personal space is violated, we may react with embarrassment or move away to create distance. Common reactions to intrusions include turning our heads, placing an elbow between the intruder and ourselves, ignoring the intruder, or leaving the area.
7. Seating	7. High-status, dominant individuals tend to sit in the head table position and participate more than those who sit along the side. Conflict is more likely between people sitting across from each other than between people sitting next to each other.

The meanings of many movements are detailed on the next page. However, no clue should be considered in isolation. Always look for what other nonverbal transmitters may be saying and consider them in the context of what is happening or being said.

Nonverbal Communication Clues

Clue	Possible Meanings or Interpretations
1. Shaking hands	Limp hand—person may be ill at ease or doesn't like to be touched. Firm handshake—confidence
2. Arms crossed on chest	Defensiveness or disagreement
3. Closed fists	Defensiveness or nervousness
4. Sitting with a leg over the arm of a chair	Defensiveness or indifference
5. Crossed legs	Defensiveness
6. Moving of the crossed leg in a slight kicking motion, drumming on table, tapping with feet, head in hand, or doodling	Boredom or impatience
7. Open hand with palms upward	Openness
8. Men unbuttoning their suit coats and even taking them off	Openness, friendliness, or agreement
9. Hand to cheek gestures	Evaluation
10. Hand over heart, palms uplifted, looking the person in the eye when speaking, or touching gesture	Honesty
11. Short breaths, "tsking" sound, tightly clenched hands, wringing hands, or kicking the ground or an imaginary object	Frustration
12. Steepling (fingertips brought together), hands joined together behind the body, feet up on the desk, elevating oneself, or leaning back in a seated position with both hands supporting the head	Confidence
13. Clearing throat, "whewing" sound, whistling, smoking cigarettes, fidgeting in a chair, tugging at clothes while sitting, jiggling money in pockets, clenched fist, wringing hands, playing with pencils, notebooks, or eyeglasses	Nervousness
14. Avoiding eye contact, touching or rubbing the nose, or rubbing behind or beside the ear with the index finger when weighing an answer	Suspicion, secretiveness, or doubt

The National Institute of Business Management suggests that by using the following suggestions you can make your nonverbal communication work for you.[11]

Making Nonverbal Communication Work for You

Desired Result	How To Accomplish the Desired Result
1. Act confident.	1. Look people in the eye, stand straight, move quickly and with determination, speak loudly (within reason) and distinctly, and avoid nervous gestures.
2. Look efficient.	2. Dress well and keep a neat but not sterile office.
3. Get people to open up to you.	3. Lean forward when listening, look people in the eye, sit with arms and legs uncrossed, and nod occasionally. Smile, have a relaxed posture and movements, and shake hands in a firm but not overpowering way. Mirror the other person's posture or match the voice tempo of the other person to build rapport.
4. Be more effective on the telephone.	4. Explain the purpose of your call and indicate how long it will be. End calls gracefully, summarizing key points and thanking the other person, using a rising, upbeat tone of voice. Vary your tone, loudness, and speed. Using natural gestures, especially smiling, can help make your voice sound more natural and expressive.
5. Improve your speeches and presentations.	5. Be prepared. Practice in front of a mirror. Choose appropriate visuals, examples, anecdotes, and analogies. Keep your message short and simple. Look confident and calm, and your voice will relax. During the first half minute of your presentation, smile, walk confidently to the podium or front, establish eye contact by scanning the group, and say thank you to your introducer and audience. Begin with a humorous or light remark or just a friendly "Hello, how are you today?" to encourage the audience to participate, which takes the pressure off you. Vary your distances from sections of the audience to stop their talking or to get them to participate. Lean forward when asked a question and look at all people in the group. Draw in nonattentive or nonresponsive people by looking at them or asking them a question.
6. Appear more credible.	6. Avoid self-deprecating words or expressions such as "This may be a dumb idea" or tag questions such as "Don't you think?" Do not use expressions that hedge, such as "sort of" or "kind of" or excessive superlatives like "really, really great." Have notes to build confidence and add security in case you lose your train of thought. Be prepared with short answers if asked negative questions.

Nonverbal communication is used differently in different cultures.

©Getty Images/PhotoDisc

𝒬uick Wit ....

"This 'telephone' has too many shortcomings to be seriously considered as a means of communication. The device is inherently of no value to us."

—Western Union internal memo, 1876.

"The wireless music box has no imaginable commercial value. Who would pay for a message sent to nobody in particular?"

—David Sarnoff's associates in response to his urgings for investment in the radio in the 1920s.

Where do you think communication technology is headed in the next 20 years?

....

People from various cultures use nonverbal communication differently. For this reason, Americans who will work abroad are frequently given training in cultural differences. For instance, the handshake is common in this country between men, women, and men and women. In many other countries, customs differ about who shakes hands with whom. In Australia, for example, women do not usually shake hands with other women; in India, men and women do not usually shake hands with one another; and in South Korea, women usually do not shake hands at all.

What differences in nonverbal behaviors have you noticed in your interactions with people from other cultures?

When using nonverbal communication, certain cautions must be kept in mind:

1. Nonverbal communication must be considered in conjunction with the verbal message and the situation. If you try to interpret meaning from an isolated nonverbal cue, you may be wrong.

2. Nonverbal communication such as closeness or touching may be misinterpreted at work and may lead to charges of sexual harassment. Even an innocent pat on the back or hand on the arm can be mistaken for sexual interest. These gestures should be avoided in the workplace.

3. Recognize that nonverbal communication varies from culture to culture and that individuals from other cultures cannot be accurately assessed using the cues presented in this chapter.

*Fast*Chat

1. What are some familiar nonverbal messages that you have seen?
2. Think of instances when you felt your personal space was being invaded. What did you do? Have you ever been made aware of having invaded someone else's bubble? What did the other person do?

Several other factors can make a difference in the success or failure of your communication:

Time: The way you use time is important. Frequent tardiness will make you be viewed as disorganized and disrespectful. Using tardiness as a manipulative ploy to put yourself in a higher-status position will simply cause frustration and anger and will cost you respect. At work, tardiness may result in your being disciplined or even fired. Developing the habit of punctuality can enhance your human relations skills and professional image.

Timing: If you are to be effective in your communication, you must remember that at times everyone needs to be left alone or at least have fewer interruptions. Your supervisors may be tired, preoccupied, rushed, angry, or frustrated. If you force them to talk with you at those times, you should not be surprised or hurt if they seem disinterested.

    Most employees feel that they do not have enough communication with their supervisors. Supervisors will not necessarily ask for communication, so you must use your own judgment in determining what to tell them and when. You should definitely keep your supervisor informed about matters for which your supervisor is held accountable and about upcoming proposals from you.

Context: **Context** refers to the conditions in which something occurs that can throw light on its meaning. Being yelled at to "stop that machine" creates a different response if we are about to be injured than if we are in trouble or our boss is having a bad day. Hence, the context of a message must be considered along with its verbal and nonverbal components for accurate understanding.

Medium: The **medium** is the form in which a message is communicated. If you receive a registered letter from an attorney, it may create more anxiety than one through regular mail.

Humor: A healthy sense of humor can create a favorable long-term impression. People usually like people with whom they can share a laugh. However, most people are offended by distasteful jokes and lose respect for someone who is constantly clowning around.

QUICK WIT

"The art of communication is the language of leadership."

James Humes,
Author and former
White House
speechwriter

A sense of humor can also help you get over some of the rough spots in life. Putting matters into proper perspective and not taking yourself too seriously becomes easier to accomplish. Some health experts have even suggested that humor can make us physically healthier and better problem solvers. Common sense must be your guide. When does humor become silly, sick, inappropriate, or counterproductive? When does it save the day?

"How can I listen to you if you don't say the things I want to hear?"

© 1998 Ted Goff www.tedgoff.com

Many factors can make a difference in the success or failure of your communication.

*Fast*Chat

1. Can you think of a situation in which a message you received had a different emotional impact simply because of one of the factors in this section? Explain.

2. Can you think of a time when humor would have helped a situation? When it hurt a situation?

Electronic communication has evolved rapidly. A decade ago, e-mail was exotic. Today, it is so commonplace that when the Tom Hanks-Meg Ryan movie, *You've Got Mail,* was released, everyone understood the meaning. Experts say that the 21st century is ushering in a second Information Age that will cause us to think of the ability to communicate electronically as a natural part of the environment. Rapidly improving technology, falling prices, and the advent of wireless technology will allow us to send images, text, and sound from virtually anywhere.

Electronic communication allows data to be communicated by computers and other technology from one sender to one or more receivers. If you are not already using electronic communication, it's likely that you will be before too long—in both your personal and professional life—with e-mail and voice mail probably being the two you will use most.

Voice mail is a system that extends the capabilities of your telephone. While voice mail offers more options than the traditional answering machine, it also does the job of an answering machine, receiving and storing incoming messages for you. This is probably the most common application of voice mail that people use. It is also capable of responding to messages, or of transmitting the same messages by telephone to different groups on the voice mail system. Voice mail capabilities differ and depend on the service provider.

TECHNOLOGY CONNECTION

Mannersmith Monthly lists five questions you should ask yourself before answering your cellular telephone:[12]

- Will I disturb those around me?
- Will I be ignoring the people with whom I am currently spending time?
- Will I be discussing something that should not be overheard by others?
- Will I be missing out on something that I may regret later?
- Will I be putting myself or others in danger?

If you take a cellular telephone call in one of these situations, will you be giving 100 percent of your attention to the communication? Why, or why not? What consequences could result?

Electronic mail or **e-mail** uses a computer, keyboard, and an Internet service provider to create messages and send them through electronic networks. The message appears in text rather than in voice. E-mail is an extremely popular form of communication and for good reasons: it is easy to use, allows time to compose, crosses the traditional lines of communication, is very fast, and can be sent to people who are not in their office. This communication tool also allows senders to include pictures, worksheets, charts, or other attachments with the message. However, some experts feel that workplace interpersonal skills are suffering from the overuse of e-mail. In some cases, it is better to make a phone call or meet in person.[13]

Instant messaging is a method of sending and responding to written messages in real time over the Internet. This process is similar to talking over a telephone but the communication is written and not verbal. Both sender and receiver must have Internet access and software that allows instant messaging. These messages are meant to be brief. Longer communications should be sent by email or telephone.[14]

Text messaging allows users of cellular telephones or other integrated voice and data devices to send text messages rather than voice messages. Text messaging can be used when it is inconvenient to talk. Group text messages can also be sent. Senders and receivers must have a cellular telephone with text messaging capabilities. Like instant messaging, this communication method should only be used for brief messages.[15]

Quick tip ....

Frank Thorsberg, author of *Instant Messaging Etiquette,* reminds us to be respectful when sending an instant message. Start out by asking if the other person is free to chat and, if the answer is no, respect the decision. Don't be afraid to say you are too busy to chat. Use the built-in "busy" or "away" features to tell others you will be out of touch.[16]

*Fast*Chat

1. Name four forms of electronic communication. What are the positive and negative aspects of each type of communication?
2. What are some techniques you have used to make your communication more effective?
3. What do you think will be the impact of future communication technology on human relations?

Key Terms

communication

sender

receiver

message

feedback

semantics

information overload

active listening

verbal communication

4 Cs of communication

nonverbal communication

context

medium

voice mail

e-mail

instant messaging

text messaging

CHAPTER SUMMARY

Communication, the process by which we exchange information through a common system of symbols, signs, or behaviors, is very important today because we live in an information society and we must interact with a variety of people. Communication can flow up, down, or horizontally in an organization. It can also be one-way or two-way and includes three elements: the sender, the receiver, and the message. Feedback helps the receiver understand the message as the sender intended it.

Communication can be distorted or blocked because of barriers. Our verbal communication can be made a strong part of our human relations skills if we develop good listening skills and an ability to use the written and spoken word.

Nonverbal communication is any meaning conveyed through body language, the way the voice is used, and the way people position themselves in relation to others. It accounts for at least 93 percent of the impact of our communication. Time, timing, context, medium, and humor contribute additional dimensions of meaning to messages and communicators.

Electronic forms of communication are emerging rapidly and continue to alter some of the ways we interact.

REVIEW QUESTIONS

1. Define communication, its process, and its role in human relations.

2. Describe common communication barriers and strategies for overcoming them.

3. What is information overload? What are some effective ways of avoiding it?

4. How can listening skills be improved?

5. What are some guidelines to make your verbal messages and presentations more effective?

6. Why is an understanding of nonverbal communication important in organizations? What are the different components of nonverbal communication?

7. Name four common forms of electronic communication.

DISCUSSION QUESTIONS

1. Think of five words that have either gone out of style or are no longer used and five words that have developed new meanings. Share them with your classmates.

2. Think of ways in which you have used nonverbal communication today, both as a sender and as a receiver. Share these instances with your classmates.

3. Think of instances in the news, in movies, or on TV in which communication has broken down. With your classmates, analyze what created the breakdown and how it might have been avoided. How might the outcomes have been different if the breakdown had not occurred?

CHAPTER PROJECT

In the library or over the Internet, find several articles regarding e-mail etiquette. In a small group of two or three classmates, write and prepare a 10-minute lesson based on your findings that you will deliver to your other classmates. Follow these steps: (1) relate the article to the Electronic Communication section of this chapter; (2) follow the suggestions for improving spoken communication given in this chapter; (3) determine who will teach what information; and (4) deliver the presentation.

(5) After the presentation, write a brief summary of your observations: (a) verbal and nonverbal communication in your team, (b) feedback you observed or heard during or after the presentation, and (c) problems in listening you may have observed in the team or during the presentation. Format the report in an attractive, efficient, and effective memorandum or e-mail to your instructor.

APPLICATIONS

In small groups, analyze the following situations.

The Medium Is the Message

Today was going to be a big day for Mac DeLorian. He finally had a chance to show management that he had some good ideas about how the company could be improved. Because of a new policy allowing employees to submit written suggestions for changes to top management, he planned to send a memo to the president for consideration. Having worked in the mailroom for three years, he had seen the great amount of time wasted by sorting and putting mail in individuals' boxes and then retrieving it and handing it to them at the front window. He thought that if each department were given a key to open its own box, much mailroom personnel time could be saved, speeding up distribution of mail and reducing the need for overtime.

Knowing that his suggestion had to be received before the 8 AM managers' meeting, he hurriedly prepared an e-mail and sent it without proofing it or asking someone else to read it for clarity or tact. After he sent it, he called the president's secretary to make sure she gave it to the president before the meeting. The e-mail the president received said, *"Want to save a lot of money? Give everyone a key to the mailbox so they can get their own mail and not waste so much of my time."*

Mac eagerly waited for some response to his recommendation. Finally, he received a brief written memo thanking him for his suggestion and stating that, after consideration, management had decided not to make a change. He later learned that management did not consider his proposal because they did not understand it. They thought he was recommending that everyone, including managers, go to the window to retrieve his or her own mail rather than having office staff pick it up twice a day. Amazed, Mac said, "What? I told them what I thought would work. Why didn't they understand?"

1. What did happen? Why didn't the managers understand what Mac was recommending?

2. How could he have handled this situation better? Rewrite Mac's message so that it is complete, concise, correct, and clear.

Breakdown in Communication

TEAMWORK

It was the holiday season at Terry's Terrific Toys. The employees were exhausted and had been putting in twelve-hour days. Sleet was beginning to fall outside, which caused Anna Marie, the manager, to be late arriving. As she entered the store, she noticed that it was extremely crowded. Shoppers nudged each other in the aisles, fighting over the few remaining toys. The telephones were ringing, and cash register three was malfunctioning.

Suddenly Anna Marie heard loud voices arguing. As she moved closer, she saw the stock clerk, Samuel, and a well-dressed, attractive lady in her late 20s or early 30s. Both had raised their voices and were waving their hands excitedly.

"Buzz off!" Samuel yelled. "That Samuel," thought Anna Marie angrily. "He's always causing trouble."

Anna Marie ran up to Samuel and yelled, "You're fired! Out!" Samuel looked up at Anna Marie in surprise and began to protest. "You're fired!" yelled Anna Marie.

"Yeah!" responded Samuel, equally as loud, as he stomped off. "And a Happy Holiday to you, too, Miss Scrooge."

A bit later, Darrell, the assistant manager, came into the manager's booth where Anna Marie was filling out Samuel's termination papers.

"You know, Anna Marie, Samuel didn't start that. The woman yelled at him and demanded that he quit helping an elderly lady with two grandchildren. When he didn't, the younger lady came over and grabbed him by the arm and jerked him away. That's when Samuel told her to buzz off."

1. Identify all the communication barriers in this scenario. How should Anna Marie have handled the situation?

2. What communication skills should have been used by Samuel? By the customer? What do you think the outcome would have been if these skills had been used?

ADDITIONAL READINGS AND RESOURCES

Green, John O. and Brant R. Burleson. *Handbook of Communication and Social Interaction Skills.* New Jersey: Lawrence Erlbaum, 2003.

Knapp, Mark L. *Nonverbal Communication in Human Interaction*, 5th Ed. Wadsworth Publishing, 2001.

Lee, Larry, Ph.D., and Kittie W. Watson, Ph.D. *Listen Up: How to Improve Relationships, Reduce Stress, and Be More Productive through the Power of Listening.* New York: St. Martin's Press, 2000.

Martin, Phyllis. *Word Watcher's Handbook—A Dictionary of the Most Misused and Abused Words:* Backinprint.com, 2001.

Rosenberg, Marshall B., Ph.D., Arun Gandi, and Lucy Leu. *Nonviolent Communication: A Language of Life: Create Your Life, Your Relationships, and Your World In Harmony with Your Values* 2nd Ed. California: Puddledancer Press, 2003.

Wainright, Gordon R. *Teach Yourself Body Language* 2nd Ed. New York: McGraw-Hill/Contemporary Books, 2003.

For additional resources, refer to the web site for this text: school.cengage.com/career/dalton

Creative Problem Solving:
Making Good Decisions

focus

Creativity often takes strange twists. Many products fail their initial trial runs and take off in totally new directions. A 2003 article in *Fast Company* magazine explained how in five short years, W.L. Gore & Associates became a leading manufacturer of guitar strings through a failed experiment. Yes, the Gore-Tex Company that puts floss between your teeth and rubber on your rain slickers also brought you greatly improved guitar strings quite by mistake.
In 1997, at a Disney theme park, a Gore team was testing one of its new materials, expanded polytetraflouroethylene (ePTFE), made for puppet cables. The tests failed—but the strings were given to guitar players to try out, and the rest is history. The strings did not go flat, and they lasted up to five times longer than other available strings on the market. Gore trolled festivals handing out free samples, bought magazine ads, and got guitar makers to install their strings on new models. Today, more than half the music stores in the country sell Elixir Strings.[1]

How important do you think creativity is in successful organizations? What is the relationship between problem solving and decision making?

A popular definition of a problem is a puzzle looking for an answer. Whether the problem is an organizational one or a personal one, it can be defined as a disturbance or unsettled matter that requires a solution if the organization or person is to function effectively. Problems become evident when expected results are compared to actual results. The gap is the problem that needs solving. Determining that solution involves decision making.

Problems may be of three types, as shown here:

Three Types of Problems

Types of Problems	Examples
1. Occurring now and must be addressed now	• The economy is forcing the XYZ Company to lay off several employees. • You have returned to school, requiring you to allocate part of your budget to school expenses.
2. Expected in the future and plans must be made for dealing with them when they do occur	• The ABC Company has a deadline of May 1 to complete a project and is now behind schedule. • You have a major paper due in two weeks and have not started writing it.
3. Foreseen for the future but so serious that actions must be taken immediately to prevent their developing	• Earnings projected for a company reveal that it will be unable to meet its payroll by the middle of the last quarter. • The term paper that you have not yet started and that is due next week is a minimum requirement to pass the course.

Once a problem has been identified, specific steps should be taken to solve it. Decision making is an important part of the problem-solving process. Deciding which solution to choose is always necessary.

HOW ARE PROBLEMS SOLVED?

Regardless of your position in an organization, you are or will be faced with problems and the need to make decisions. Your personal life also requires problem solving and decision making. Human relations, if they are effective, can prevent or help solve problems. If they are not effective, they can create problems of their own. For this reason, problem-solving skills are considered an important part of human relations.

Problem solving and decision making are related. Effective decisions must be made if problems are to be solved satisfactorily. Identifying a problem and its possible solutions is important, but the process is incomplete until we decide which option(s) to implement.

Numerous ways exist for making decisions, some more effective than others. You should understand and be able to use a systematic approach to problem solving so that you do not have to rely on generalizations, snap judgments, or intuition. The following process can help you attain personal and career success.

A helpful maxim says, "A problem well defined is a problem half solved." Instead of saying, "We are behind schedule," say, "We have only two weeks in which to complete this project." Collect and analyze all information pertinent to the problem—people, processes, materials, equipment, or other matters. Although you do not want to overwhelm yourself with information, try to uncover all relevant objective data.

©Digital Vision

Brainstorming is a group problem-solving technique that involves spontaneous contribution of ideas in a nonjudgmental environment. It is freewheeling and fun.

PROBLEM SOLVING EXAMPLE

In looking at information related to a project that is behind schedule, you might find that absenteeism has been high, materials have been late in arriving, and a new computer system used on the project has had start-up difficulties. Consider what factors caused the gap between the expected and actual results. In this example, try to imagine the impact of each change—the absenteeism, late materials, and new computer system.

Steps in Problem Solving

1. Identify the problem, defining it clearly and specifically.

Be objective. See the situation as it actually is, not as you think it is. Don't let emotions color your perception. Quantify the problem if possible. Examine all facets of the issue and identify the source of the problem. Collect relevant data. List possible causes. Select most likely cause(s).

2. Generate ideas; use brainstorming to develop as many alternative solutions as possible for removing the causes of the problem.

Brainstorming is a group problem-solving technique that involves the spontaneous contribution of ideas from all members of the group. The goal is to generate as many ideas as possible—more ideas means better results. Reserve judgment—no ideas should be eliminated initially. An idea that seems ridiculous may trigger a feasible idea in someone else. By throwing ideas back and forth and adding to them, members can form a plan. Brainstorming is a freewheeling, fun activity that encourages creativity.

3. Evaluate alternatives for practicality.

Analyze the implications of each alternative by evaluating the pros and cons. Rather than just saying that one solution is better than another, define "better." Develop criteria such as cost and speed. Consider the information gathered in Step 2 and possibly discuss the criteria with experts. Try to anticipate problems that some alternatives might create.

4. Select a solution.

Select your "best" solution. This step is the decision phase in the problem-solving process. Weigh all the chances of success against the risks of failure. The strengths of your solution should exceed its weaknesses. Develop a plan of action for carrying out your solution. What will be done, how, by whom, where, when, and at what cost?

5. Implement the solution.

Implement the idea by carrying out your "best" solution. Consider that you may have to alter your plans and be ready.

6. Evaluate results; follow up and modify actions when necessary.

Make sure that your actions accomplish your objectives by examining the situation carefully. If your goals are not being met, you may have to study the problem further and apply other alternatives.

Human Relations

Using a process of elimination, imagine what difference returning a changed factor to its original condition would make. If that does not solve the problem, keep checking. Would the project be on time if absenteeism had been at its usual rate, or if materials had arrived on time, or if the computer system had not been changed? After considering these options, you might decide that the most likely cause was the late materials.

© 1998 Ted Goff www.tedgoff.com

When analyzing a problem, be sure to view the situation clearly, collect relevant data, and identify the source.

TECHNOLOGY CONNECTION

An ad for Hewlett Packard introduced its e-services with a scenario of a daughter driving her parents' vintage Jaguar while they were out of town. A security chip in the car recognizes the daughter's key and engages a "soft limit" that won't allow the car to exceed 65 mph. When she immediately does, the car sends a signal to the parent three thousand miles away who speed dials the daughter to slow down, thereby heading off a potential problem. Hewlett Packard points out that businesses are using the Internet in ways that go far beyond today's web sites, and the next chapter of the Internet is about to be written.

Chip technology in this case has been applied in a creative way to prevent a potential problem. What other creative uses of this technology to solve problems can you envision?

In this example, what can you do to assure the timely arrival of materials in the future? You may, for instance, consider ordering earlier, or ordering from a different source, or even changing the design so that other materials can be substituted for the late ones.

Then, anticipate the likely results of each alternative. You may discover that some alternatives create more problems than they solve. If you choose to substitute materials in our example, you may create design problems. Although ordering from another source seems reasonable, you may find that the second source is more expensive. You may decide that ordering earlier seems the best alternative, but you may not always have advance notice of the need.

The basic question is whether your projects are being completed on time using the specific plan for ordering supplies. If you are still running behind, you need to study the situation further and try other solutions.

Pitfalls in Problem Solving

When trying to solve a problem, be alert to pitfalls or problem areas. Common ones are the following:

- Overanalyzing, which can lead to inaction.
- Not taking necessary action or acting too quickly.
- Erring in judgment or execution.
- Not having a backup plan.
- Not involving others in the problem-solving process.
- Perceiving the problem incorrectly.

Following the steps in the problem-solving process on page 120 can help you avoid these pitfalls.

*Fast*Chat

We are frequently called upon to solve problems. Name three problems you have had to solve at home or work.

1. What process did you use to solve them?

2. Was your process similar to the one presented in this chapter?

3. Would the process in this chapter have been more effective? Why, or why not?

TECHNOLOGY CONNECTION

Computers and other technologies are eliminating entire categories of jobs (such as telephone operators), but they are also constantly creating new jobs. They are changing our work as well, particularly problem solving and decision making. An article in *Modern Maturity* pointed out that technology-savvy frontline personnel are now responsible for decisions formerly made by supervisors. Managers also have more control over their own work. Desktop PCs equipped with software that does everything from keeping appointments to formatting business letters and writing contracts have largely replaced personal assistants. When people feel they have more control, they are usually more satisfied with their jobs.[2]

Technology is also speeding up the rate at which decisions can be made. Sophisticated software used by NASA, for example, allows the agency to analyze numerous moving components of the Space Station simultaneously, thereby permitting decisions to be made more quickly and moving the project along faster.

On the other hand, computers permit the creation of so much data that even though most businesspeople seek more information for decision making, they are drowning in a sea of data and detail. Additionally, a recent survey suggested that computers are eliciting rage in the workplace, or at least taking the brunt of it. The study found that 83 percent of corporate network administrators reported "abusive and violent behavior" by employees toward their computers—smashing monitors, throwing mice, kicking hard drives, and shattering screens. A follow-up study concluded that employees might be merely taking out the frustration they feel toward their bosses and work in general on their computers.[3]

Technology is changing the way we make decisions.

1. *Overall, what do you see as the strengths and weaknesses of using technology in decision making?*

2. *Describe experiences you have had when technology enabled you to make better decisions. What technology did you use? How did it facilitate the decision-making process?*

3. *Have you had an experience in which technology actually hampered your problem solving or decision making? Describe the situation and explain what you could have done differently.*

All organizations and people are faced with the need to make decisions. In fact, we make dozens of them daily, from what to wear to which e-mail to answer first.

Decisions are made when we must choose actions, opportunities, or solutions.

Whenever we have more than one way of doing something, we must make a decision. Sometimes the decisions we must make include problem solving, as discussed earlier in this chapter. In such cases, we are trying to overcome the gap between expected and actual results. At other times, we must choose among a number of opportunities facing us. For example, at some point you considered whether to go to college, to go to work, or to combine the two. If you decided to go to college, you then had to consider your major field of study. You may have considered several occupations with different rewards such as travel, money, or flexibility.

Many people overlook opportunities for decisions, both personal and professional ones. Managers and individuals alike become comfortable with the status quo. We should, however, keep in mind the important point that *no decision is a decision*. By not making another choice, we have, in effect, decided to remain with the status quo. People sometimes fail to make conscious decisions because they fear change.

Tools such as decision trees, cost-benefit analyses, ABC analyses, PERT charts, quality circles, Six Thinking Hats, and Six Sigma can help identify when decisions need to be made and what those decisions might be.

The decision tree illustrated in this figure shows various decision points and chance events that may occur in the growth of a company. Should additional employees be hired, should employees be asked to work overtime, or should the owner decide not to increase business?

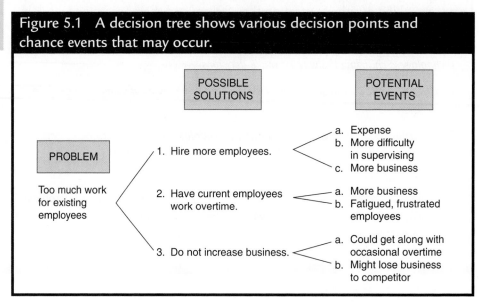

Figure 5.1　A decision tree shows various decision points and chance events that may occur.

TOOLS FOR DECISION MAKING

Several well-known tools and techniques for making personal and work-related decisions are explained in the box below.

Decision-Making Tools

1. **Decision tree**—graphic depiction of how alternative solutions lead to various possibilities.

   Helps people and organizations see the implications that certain choices have for the future. Can be used formally by actually drawing them or informally in our heads.

2. **Cost-benefit analysis**—examination of the pros and cons of each proposed solution.

   Popular in the public sector, frequently used for evaluating proposals to provide a nonprofit service to the community, such as hospitals or child care. Involves comparison of all costs against value of the service to the community.

3. **ABC analysis**—concentration of decisions where the potential for payoff is greatest.

   Involves concentration on the vital few items ("A" items), not the trivial many ("C" items). Example: In choosing a builder for your home or office, the quality of the construction would be considered an "A" item, paint color a "C" item, and brand of appliances probably a "B" item.

4. **PERT chart** (Program Evaluation and Review Technique chart)—a graphic technique for planning projects in which a great number of tasks must be coordinated.

   Shows the relationships between tasks and helps identify critical bottlenecks that may delay progress toward a project's completion. The critical path is the sequence of activities that must be done one after another and that requires the longest time for completion.

5. **Quality circle**—committee of 6 to 15 employees, generally volunteers from the same work area, which meets regularly to examine and suggest solutions to common problems of quality. Committee usually receives training in group processes, problem solving, brainstorming, and statistical quality control.

   A form of participative management that encourages employees to provide input to key decisions. Widely used in Japan beginning in the 1950s and in the United States beginning in the 1970s and 1980s; still used but not as widely.

6. **Six Sigma**—sophisticated method of continuous process improvement that uses a structured statistical approach to improve bottom-line results. Involves statistically measuring baseline performance to improve performance processes, product quality, and process engineering.

   A disciplined, data-driven method on which to base decisions about process defects and errors. Can be used in manufacturing and service industries. When implemented strategically, can help companies improve bottom-line results by minimizing waste and non-value-adding tasks.[4]

7. **Six Thinking Hats**—A form of group decision making designed by Edward de Bono that gives each person a role to play in wearing the six hats of intelligence. Each "hat" represents a different way of viewing the situation or issue. White hat presents the facts; red hat says how one feels about the issue; black hat is the pessimist looking at the negative side; yellow hat is the optimist looking at the positive effects; green hat offers alternatives and what ifs; and blue hat is the coordinator and facilitator.

   Encourages participation and open communication, and gives validation to the many different ways a problem can be solved. Postpones judgment longer so more ideas can emerge. Claims to reduce time spent in meetings by 20 to 90 percent.[5]

THE 80-20 RULE

Because you are faced with a multitude of decisions every day, you simply cannot devote much time, thought, or effort to all of them, nor should you want to do so. Economists point out that only a few problems or opportunities (20 percent) are vital, and many (80 percent) are trivial. They call this fact the "**80-20 Rule**," meaning that 20 percent of your problems will account for 80 percent of your losses or gains. The value of the 80-20 Rule is that it reminds us to focus our time, efforts, and resources on the 20 percent that matters. (In the ABC analysis identified above, this 20 percent would be the "A" items.) This rule is also sometimes referred to as "Pareto's Principle" because it uses the 80-20 ratio that Italian economist Vilfredo Pareto used to explain distribution of wealth in his country.[6]

GROUP DECISION MAKING

Whatever decision-making technique is used, most work-related problems and many personal ones require that decisions be made by groups of people rather than by individuals alone. Such situations require strong human relations skills, skills that can be enhanced by knowledge of group decision making.

In general, groups make better decisions than individuals because of the increased input and suggestions. However, there are pitfalls, such as wasting time and engaging in groupthink (in which the group may be led to a conclusion without fully exploring or even considering creative solutions). The first step, then, is deciding whether a group should be used in making a decision. Factors to be considered are listed in the chart on the next page.

Review the factors carefully. Notice that group decision making assumes that members are knowledgeable, will participate, can be creative in their solutions, and are likely to support what they help create. Human relations skills can help groups arrive at consensus decisions.

Group decision
making seeks
consensus, a
solution that
all members
can support.

The goal of group problem solving is to reach **consensus**—to develop a solution that all members can support, even if it is not each member's first choice. *Webster's* defines consensus as "group solidarity in sentiment and belief" and "the judgment arrived at by most of those concerned." It does not mean that the final solution is the one each member thinks is the best one, but rather that the solution is one that all members can at least support. If group decision making is not approached carefully and the process not monitored for real input, a potential risk is that a consensus decision can be a "watered down" decision that tries too hard to make everyone happy.

Human Relations

Individual Versus Group Decision Making

Situational Factors Supportive of Individual Decision Making[7]	Situational Factors Supportive of Group Decision Making[8]
1. When time is short.	1. When creativity is needed.
2. When the decision is relatively unimportant.	2. When data for the solution rest within the group.
3. When the leader has all the data needed to make the decision.	3. When acceptance of a solution by group members is important.
4. When one or two group members are likely to dominate the discussion.	4. When understanding of a solution by group members is important.
5. When destructive conflict is likely to erupt among group members.	5. When the problem is complex or requires a broad range of knowledge for solution.
6. When people feel they attend too many meetings, don't feel they should be involved, or are pessimistic about the value of group meetings.	6. When the manager wants subordinates to feel part of a democratic process or wants to build their confidence.
7. When the relevant decision-making data are confidential and cannot be shared with all group members.	7. When more risk taking in considering solutions is needed.
8. When group members aren't capable or qualified to decide.	8. When better group member understanding of each other is desirable.
9. When the leader is dominant or intimidates group members.	9. When the group as a whole is ultimately responsible for the decision.
10. When the decision doesn't affect the group directly.	10. When the leader wants to get feedback on the validity of his ideas and opinions.

Adapted from Sussman, Lyle, and Samuel D. Deep. *COMEX: The Communication Experience in Human Relations.* © 1997 South-Western College Publishing.

For a group to have the greatest likelihood of reaching consensus, certain guidelines should be followed. Consider the recommendations shown in the chart on the following page when you are working with a problem-solving group.

A healthy **"win-win" situation** occurs when both sides of an issue feel they have won. If one side runs roughshod over the other, the situation is considered to be a "win-lose" one. Aggressive, bullying people are not effective negotiators in the long run because other people are not likely to feel satisfied at the end of the negotiations. Because negotiation is a

Recommendations for Group Problem Solving

1. State the idea or proposal in the clearest terms possible. Writing it on a chalkboard or flip chart will help.

2. Poll *each* member for opinions by asking, "What do you think of the idea (or proposal)?" Use an open-ended question such as this one rather than "do you agree?"

3. If everyone expresses positive opinions for the idea or proposal, you have total consensus.

4. If someone disagrees, ask why and ask for an alternative idea or proposal.

5. Restate any opposing ideas or proposals to ensure understanding.

6. Use problem-solving techniques to resolve the differences. For example:

   a. Find common ground and work toward another suitable alternative.

   b. Use a best-estimate approach to weigh alternatives, such as a decision tree or ABC analysis.

   c. Strive for a substantial agreement among group members and encourage willingness to try the idea or proposal for a limited time.

   d. Use negotiation that results in a "win-win" situation. **Negotiation** is discussion that leads to a decision acceptable to all.

7. Avoid forcing unanimity, voting, "averaging," "majority rule," or horse trading ("I'll do this if you do that"). Voting divides the group into a win-lose situation.

8. If one group member changes his or her mind, poll opinions from each member again.

9. If someone still disagrees, return to step 4.

10. If only one person, or a small subgroup, continues to disagree, get that person or group to give permission to try the idea or proposal for a limited time period. The permission might include the stipulation to test the counter idea or proposal if the first one fails to accomplish its objective.

11. If all parties now agree to support the decision, consensus has been achieved.

part of our daily lives, learning to negotiate properly will increase your effectiveness on the job and the satisfaction of everyone involved. Establishing a reputation of trust will also help you in negotiating. If you are seen as someone who can come through in a tight spot, keep your word, and never betray confidences, you are ahead in the process. Phrases such as "How do you think this idea would work?," "What are your feelings about…?," and "Have you ever considered…?" convey respect and are helpful during negotiations. Other aspects of communication useful in negotiations are listening carefully, finding out what the other person wants, and watching that person's body language. Various tools can be used to improve the quality of decisions, including the use of group decision making.

While effective organizational decision making is vital in today's global business environment, it can produce stress. Humor is a great way to deal with stress, and humorous buzzwords are constantly created to describe aspects of business. Some terms used today, identified and defined by Bill Schadewald in the *Houston Business Journal*, are:

- *analysis paralysis*—The result of studying a problem in search of a perfect solution until everyone involved becomes stuck and unable to take any action until precisely the right course of action is identified (which may be never).

- *blamestorming*—Group discussion of why a particular project failed. (Often results in outplacement of those who brainstormed the original concept.)

- *mousemilking*—Making a maximum amount of effort for a minimum possible benefit. You can milk a mouse, but is it really worth it?

- *scope creep*—This occurs when a project gets incrementally bigger and more sprawling after being imperceptible at first.

- *stratical*—Describes a project that is perceived as both strategic and tactical.[9]

Think of other buzzwords you are currently hearing that deal with problem solving, decision making, or creativity.

1. *How do you think they originated?*

2. *What do they communicate about their subjects?*

*Fast*Chat

List several major activities you will face in the next three days.

1. Label them as A, B, or C following definitions in this chapter. Explain your rating.

2. Can something rated a "C" become an "A" later? Why, or why not?

As pointed out earlier, an important factor in problem solving is the need to be creative. In fact, creativity is so important in today's economy that many experts are suggesting that it is the only way for businesses to survive.

Creativity is a thinking process that solves a problem or achieves a goal in an original and useful way. Simply stated, it is the ability to come up with new and unique solutions to problems. A creative person has the ability to see practical relationships among things that are not similar and to combine elements into new patterns of association. Imagination, rather than genius, is a necessary ingredient. Creativity has been the subject of intensive research since the 1960s. That research suggests that creative professionals are no different than others in intelligence. However, they are open to new ideas and have learned how to respond to their intuition and to their environment. They also will investigate ideas that arouse their curiosity without immediately judging the ideas too harshly.

We all have the potential for creativity. Some people simply develop their potential more than others. Cultivating the vivid imagination that we have as children allows creativity to occur later in life. If we listen to Maslow's advice that creating a first-rate cake is better than creating a second-rate poem, we may be less judgmental of others and ourselves.

Creative people have been found to have several characteristics and traits in common, as summarized on the next page. Of course, not all creative people will possess all of these traits, and some of the traits or characteristics may be found in other people.[10]

QUICK WIT
"Everything that can be invented has been invented."
Charles H. Duell, Commissioner, U.S. Office of Patents, 1899

Creativity comes in many forms. Devising a more effective office procedure is a worthwhile example.

©Getty Images/PhotoDisc

Innovation, the end product of creative activity, is vital to the success of organizations and individuals today. Businesses must be able to respond quickly to today's changing world in order to stay competitive. Failing to change and develop new products or techniques will eventually lead to the deterioration of a company.

Characteristics and Traits of Creative People

1. Creative people possess a sensitivity to problems and deficiencies, the ability to flesh them out, and the ability to perceive in a way different from the traditional or established method.

2. They possess flexibility rather than rigidity, openness to new ideas and experiences, tolerance of ambiguity, a wide range of interests, curiosity, enthusiasm and energy, vivid imaginations, playfulness, commitment and concentration, comfort with change, capacity for hard work, persistence, and divergent thinking.

3. Because creativity involves new approaches and the production of something new and untried, it also involves the risk of failure. Two characteristics of the creative person are particularly significant: self-confidence, based on a strong self-concept, and independence, the strength to hold fast against disagreement or resistance by others and the courage to persist when others may be threatened by a new idea or discovery.[11]

4. Creative people can make "leaps of reasoning" from one fact to a seemingly unrelated fact and build a bridge of logic across the two.

5. They probably were nurtured to be creative by their social and educational environment rather than being born creative or intelligent.

6. Creative people tend to view nature as fundamentally orderly.

7. Creative people engage in divergent rather than convergent thinking first. They use divergent thinking to search for answers in many directions and convergent thinking to make choices based on analysis, reason, and experience.

8. They may sometimes appear sensitive, self-centered, or unconventional with chaotic lives and unconventional choices. Because they are inner-directed, they tend not to worry about the approval of society.

9. They also tend to be introspective, open to new experiences, and spontaneous, with an inner maturity.

10. On the job, creative people may prefer ideas and things to people, have a high regard for intellectual interests, have a high level of resourcefulness, have a high tolerance for ambiguity, be less concerned about job security, not enjoy detail or routine, and be persistent.[12]

Innovation cannot take place without creativity. Many business experts point out that the ability to come up with new ideas and make them work is, for most companies, the only way to stay alive today. Companies are, therefore, interested in learning more about creativity, how to identify it, and how to foster it. For this reason, employees who develop their own creativity skills and produce more and better ideas for their organizations will become more valuable members of the workforce.

WHAT ARE THE STAGES IN CREATIVITY?

Although the creative process is still somewhat mysterious, experts on creativity generally agree on five stages as the phases a person goes through in the creative process. These stages are not necessarily distinct and usually involve a complex recycling of the process.[13]

1. **Preparation**—acquiring skills, background information, and resources, sensing and defining a problem. This stage requires a creative and different viewpoint. Sometimes it simply involves looking for relationships; at other times it means questioning accepted answers.

2. **Concentration**—focusing intensely on the problem to the exclusion of other demands. This is a trial-and-error phase that includes false starts and frustration.

3. **Incubation**—withdrawing from the problem; sorting, integrating, clarifying at an unconscious level. This stage often includes reverie, relaxation, or solitude. Incubation is the most mysterious part of the creative process. Numerous people have compared this stage to a bird sitting quietly on a nest of eggs waiting for them to hatch. Although not much action can be observed, a person in this stage may be mentally reviewing many ideas and much information, even in dreams. This stage can range in length from a few hours to many years. Several important global concerns are now in the incubation stage, including how to deal with terrorism, cope with trade deficits, prepare for workforce shortages resulting from a high retirement rate, solve food and water shortages, find new sources of fuel, reduce production costs, and develop effective mass transit systems.

4. **Illumination**—the Aha! stage, often sudden, involving the emergence of an image, idea, or perspective that suggests a solution or direction for further work. The illumination stage is the flashing light bulb that cartoonists like to use. This breakthrough to conscious thought lasts for only a few moments, but it is the result of lengthy thought. Its occurrence is unpredictable and can come at totally unexpected times.

5. **Verification** or **Elaboration**—testing out the idea, evaluating, developing, implementing, convincing others of the worth of the idea. The last

stage of the creative process is verification. Thomas Edison once said, "Creation is 1 percent inspiration and 99 percent perspiration." Productivity is the ability to make new and unique solutions effective. This stage often requires working closely with others and, hence, having finely tuned human relations skills.

GLOBAL CONNECTION

Changing world markets and economies are literally forcing companies and individuals to expand beyond the limits of what they previously thought they could accomplish, to constantly learn new ways of working. A lifelong career now means lifelong learning:

1. "The qualities that once nearly guaranteed lifelong employment—hard work, reliability, loyalty, master of a discrete set of skills—are often no longer enough." —Radcliffe Public Policy Institute

2. "The will to succeed is important. But, the will to prepare is even more important." —Bobby Knight, basketball coach

3. "If I had six hours to chop down a tree, I would spend the first four hours sharpening the ax." —Abraham Lincoln

4. "Learning is what most adults will do for a living in the 21st century." — Sydney Joseph Perelman, American writer/humorist

Lifelong learning is crucial to survival in the global workplace.

1. *What do you think is the connection between learning and problem solving? Between learning and creativity?*

2. *What is the most recent thing you have learned? What skills and information are you particularly proud of learning? How will the skills and information you have learned help you in your personal and professional lives?*

3. *What plans do you have for continuing your learning?*

*Fast*Chat

Creativity requires "thinking outside of the box."

1. Is this hard to do? Why, or why not?

2. Is doing things the way they have always been done easier than finding new ways? Why, or why not?

3. Why is getting others to try something different frequently difficult?

Effective organizations will listen to their customers, clients, and employees, who can identify drawbacks to products and point out needs for new products or services. Ideas can then be developed based on these findings. For example, 3M inventor Richard Drew noticed that painters on automobile assembly lines had a hard time keeping the borders straight on two-tone cars, so he invented masking tape. Thomas Edison invented wax paper because he became tired of chocolates sticking to the tissue paper wrapping.[14]

Executives at many organizations today believe that their companies must be more than lean and fast to create a successful future. They must transform their industries by reinventing themselves. Hamel and Prahalad in *Competing for the Future* say that industry transformers:[15]

1. change the rules of engagement in an industry (as Charles Schwab did in the brokerage business),

2. redraw the industry boundaries (as Time Warner did with "edutainment"), and

3. create new industries (as Apple did with personal computers).

To imagine and create the future, managers need to unlearn the past, develop foresight, create a strategic architecture that helps identify core competencies needed for market leadership, create stretch goals that inspire, and preempt competitors.

HOW CAN A WORKER PROMOTE CREATIVE IDEAS?

As a worker in an organization, you may be more familiar with the processes involved in the performance of your job than anyone else. Therefore, you are in a good position to be able to identify creative approaches. What should you do if you think of a better procedure or better product? Knowing how to successfully present ideas and get others to act on them is a crucial skill for creative individuals.

New ideas are not usually immediately embraced in a company. They must be cultivated and supported from conception to implementation. The idea must have a champion, someone who is willing to speak up for it, and to commit to it.

Being a champion of an idea takes enthusiasm and the willingness to take risks. After all, the idea may prove to be fruitless. The champion, who may be you or someone else such as your supervisor, must put together a team to develop the idea. Few ideas and projects are implemented by one person alone. Working as part of a creative team will not only require creativity, but it will also require well-developed skills in human relations, including problem solving, decision making, and communication.

If you are trying to get an idea through an organization, be prepared to persist. Even the most successful projects have their downsides when the going is tough and participants become discouraged. As the champion of an idea or as a member of a team developing an idea, you should be emotionally prepared for these periods. Having supportive family, friends, or coworkers can help tremendously.

Ideas must be sold to others. Effective communication and networking skills will help the champion develop a coalition and gather others who are willing to support the idea. You or the person serving as the champion must then work to maintain their support.

The above discussion points out the importance of effective human relations skills and explodes the myth that creative people work alone and, therefore, do not need people skills. Creative people have a much better chance of bringing their ideas to fruition if they are able to work effectively with others.

A strong trait in people with effective human relations skills is the willingness to share credit. When a creative group project or idea is successful, the person in charge must be sure to share the credit. While patents and copyrights exist to protect individuals' creations, taking individual credit for a group project is an excellent way to ensure that no further successful group projects will be completed. Learning and sharing information can contribute to a creative atmosphere.

QUICK WIT
"History doesn't repeat itself, but sometimes it rhymes."
Mark Twain,
American writer
and humorist

HOW CAN SUPERVISORS STIMULATE CREATIVITY?

Wren and Greenwood in *Management Innovators* suggest that managers can learn a lot by knowing the history of business. Events in today's telecommunication industry are echoes of long-ago events in the telegraph industry. Sam Walton's retailing innovations at Wal-Mart paralleled Richard Sears's earlier innovations at Sears, Roebuck.[16]

If you are a supervisor in an organization, you have a responsibility to stimulate creativity among your employees. Several methods for accomplishing this are

- suspending judgment,
- tolerating a reasonable amount of failure,
- supervising carefully,
- offering constructive criticism, and
- tolerating some different behavior.

The National Institute of Business Management has pointed out that managers skilled in stimulating creativity among workers make it to the top faster than anybody else. They have overcome several common myths about creativity. Being aware of the myths shown here can help you move up in your organization.[17]

Myths about Corporate Creativity

Myths	Facts
1. Creativity is only important in the arts.	Creativity is essential to any organization's success, and managers skilled in tapping their employees' creativity rise faster in the organization.
2. Only a small number of people are creative.	Actually, most people can be creative. Companies should learn to spot creative ideas and use public recognition and money as incentives.
3. Creativity is intangible and uncontrollable.	Although people cannot be made to produce brilliant ideas on demand, an innovative spirit can be nurtured.
4. Creative thinking is needed only in the creative fields of an organization, such as research and product development.	Innovation can occur in policies, processes, and techniques as well as people's activities and behaviors. Additionally, innovation in one area can set off a creative chain reaction throughout the organization.
5. Creative thinking is play, not work.	Intensive thought about innovative problem-solving strategies can be draining. Companies should convey the message that creative work will be rewarded.
6. Creative thinking is risky and leads to unnecessary change.	Creativity is necessary for companies to survive today.[18]

Supervisors interested in stimulating creativity must be sure that they suspend critical judgment during brainstorming sessions. They must make sure that no one insults, demeans, or evaluates another participant or a response. They should also coach participants to be uninhibited in their responses and not to feel liable for any seemingly outrageous or unconventional comments they might make during the session.[19]

Supervisors must also stress that failure will be tolerated. Failure is a natural part of innovation and risk taking. As individuals and as employees, if we never fail, we are probably setting goals that are too "safe" (which will be discussed at greater length later in Chapter 10 on goal setting). Many companies stifle creativity because they do not tolerate a certain amount of failure or reward those persons who develop creative ideas. Employees then become afraid to present an idea for a project or product that might not be successful.

Supervising creative people takes some practice. Some creative individuals find breaking, stretching, or overlooking rules to be natural. For this reason, they must be supervised carefully. Goals and timetables may need to be established for them while they are allowed to work at their own pace. If your supervisor does this for you, view it as an attempt to help you succeed professionally, not hinder you.

Creative people usually work best in an atmosphere of freedom. They may prefer to be autonomous and independent and to work with little or no supervision. They may also need quiet time to allow their unconscious mind to work. Supervisors should help ensure that such times are available.[20]

Feedback in the form of careful constructive criticism, praise, and evaluation must be given even if the project is indefinite or long postponed. As pointed out in the discussion of Maslow's hierarchy of needs, creativity falls under the heading of self-actualization needs and is associated with a desire for personal growth and opportunities to use abilities to the fullest. Feedback is an important part of the process of fulfilling this need.

Finally, creative people can be unconventional in their attitudes and behaviors, and others in the company may become impatient with their progress or be bothered by their behavior. Creativity is not always a visible process. The person who is staring out the window with feet on the desk may indeed be working very hard. At times a supervisor may need to defend creative individuals, protect them from harm, and nurture them in the corporate political environment.

QUICK WIT
"I think there is a world market for maybe five computers."
Thomas Watson, Chairman of IBM, 1943

QUICK WIT
"He who is not courageous enough to take risks will accomplish nothing in life."
Muhammad Ali, American boxer

Nine Supervisory Steps toward a Creative Workplace

1. Help people see the purpose of what they do.
2. Expect a lot.
3. Tell employees what you expect, not how to do it.
4. Realize that people are different.
5. Be really available.
6. Get the word out in 24 hours or less.
7. Provide the proper tools.
8. Say thanks.
9. Have fun.[21]

WEB

TECHNOLOGY CONNECTION

Making a success of small new start-up businesses requires creativity. Today, the Internet is the most powerful tool for experimentation and exploration, transforming how companies and people work and interact. Prime examples are eBay, providing person-to-person commerce via the Net; the Apollo Group, satisfying the demand for lifelong learning with its Web-based University of Phoenix; and Cemex, creating a revolutionary high-speed communication approach for delivering cement to construction sites. Each of these businesses grew from the use of cutting-edge technology to reshape an old-line business.[22]

1. *How do you think the Internet would be beneficial in business planning phases?*
2. *Have you taken any Web-based courses? If so, what was your experience? If not, why not?*

*Fast*Chat

Creativity in the workplace is extremely important today.

1. Where do you think businesses today can gain creative ideas?
2. How might you be a champion for a new idea?
3. If you were a supervisor in an organization, what might you do to encourage your employees to work creatively?

Human Relations

Creativity can be developed and nurtured. It can also be hampered in a variety of ways. Researchers have identified many different blocks to creativity that can be categorized as thought processes, emotional blocks, cultural blocks, and environmental blocks.

*Q*uick tip ....

"Knowing is not enough, we must apply. Willing is not enough, we must do."

Johann Wolfgang von Goethe,
German poet and dramatist

1. *What do you think Goethe meant by this statement?*
2. *How does it apply to your life and work? To problem solving and decision making? To creativity?*

THOUGHT PROCESSES

To stimulate creativity, we must learn to modify our problem-solving habits and develop new ways of thinking that enhance creativity. The first block to overcome is the inability to isolate the real source of a problem. People often stereotype a dilemma and see only what they expect to see. To overcome this limit, develop the habit of taking a "big picture" perspective. Look at every angle and take a wide view of the dilemma.

Sometimes we become overloaded with information and cannot recall familiar information because our minds are cluttered with trivia that we are unable to clear away. This clutter can interfere with our creativity. Changing our activities can frequently help us overcome this block. For example, if you have been working in your office, you might go to the library for a short period; or you might temporarily put the problem out of your mind only to have the solution come to you when you are out walking that evening.

> Thought processes that block creativity can be overcome.

Failing to use all of our senses is an additional way that thought processes block creativity. Using sight, sound, smell, taste, and touch as inputs into the creative process can help. Many people, for example, find that watching playful kittens or happy children stimulates their creativity. The sights, sounds, and smells of nature inspire others.

EMOTIONAL BLOCKS

We must become aware of emotional blocks to creativity.

QUICK WIT

"There is the risk you cannot afford to take, and there is the risk you cannot afford not to take."

Peter Drucker, Management consultant and author

Fear of taking a risk or making a mistake is one of the biggest emotional blocks to creativity. Not all ideas are successful, and the creative individual must be willing to risk negative outcomes. We should, therefore, refrain from letting others (or ourselves) engender such fear in us. If fear is a problem for you, you may benefit from reading the section on attitudes that bring success and confidence in the chapter on goal setting.

Being overly critical will also kill creativity. Most people would rather judge an idea than generate one. Many ideas die because they are judged too early, before they have been fully developed. Review the steps in the creative process and recall that generation of ideas and evaluation of them are two different parts of the process.

The ability to tolerate ambiguity is essential in the creative process. When something is ambiguous, it can be understood in two or more possible ways. That is precisely what you want in creativity. If you are able to look at a problem in a different way, you are closer to coming up with a novel solution. Black and white, either/or thinking is a communication barrier. If such thinking impedes communication, it will certainly inhibit creativity. Most people have an overriding desire for order and predictability, but the creative process is a "messy" one. New ideas or projects are not orderly or predictable, and people working on them can become frustrated if they cannot tolerate ambiguity. Being aware of this emotional block may help you overcome it.

If we are to be creative, we must **unlock our unconscious minds.** When we are tense or preoccupied, we are unable to be creative.

Relaxation and the ability to "sleep on it" are helpful. Many excellent ideas have been conceived on the golf course, in the shower, on the way to work, or during routine chores.

Another emotional block is **fear of change.** Some people find tradition more comfortable. Because creativity by its nature is newness and change, we should develop a positive attitude toward change if we wish to be more creative. Engaging in new activities, sports, or hobbies can help stimulate our creativity.

Egos, too, can be the source of emotional blocks to creativity. People who feel that they can never be wrong and will not back down or who will not support an idea presented by another person even when it is a good one stifle creativity. Be careful of such behaviors in yourself.

Finally, some people are unable to **distinguish fantasy from reality.** The creative individual needs to be able to distinguish what is feasible from what is not. Remember that an important step in the problem-solving process is the evaluation of ideas for practicality.

CULTURAL BLOCKS

Some cultural taboos stand in the way of creativity. As noted above, the creative process is not always visible, and time spent gazing out the window may seem wasteful and might make an individual appear lazy. Playing is seen as an activity for children only, not for adults, and pleasure is considered unproductive and inefficient. To be creative, we must rid ourselves of such notions and allow our minds to float in a random fashion sometimes, to see figures in clouds. Of course, this only works if you have done the real work first of filling your mind with ideas and information with which your mind can build and create when you do let it float.

Cultural blocks to creativity include taboos against daydreaming, intuition, and humor.

Quick tip

"Great works are performed not by strength, but by perseverance."

Dr. Samuel Johnson,
English essayist and poet

1. *What do you think this quote means?*
2. *Describe some examples of "great works" that resulted from perseverance.*
3. *How might these examples apply to your life and work?*

Other cultural biases lock out the use of intuition and qualitative judgment in favor of logic, reason, numbers, and practicality. Reality, however, dictates that a balance be maintained between these two sets of forces.

Another cultural block is the idea that problem solving must always be a serious business. Humor not only relieves stress, it can also unlock creativity. Studies have suggested that laughter enhances creativity because it frees up the childlike part of us. It also can help to strengthen team relationships. And, if used appropriately, humor can deflect anger and reduce tension.[23]

ENVIRONMENTAL BLOCKS

Be aware of supervisors and subordinates who can set up environmental blocks to creativity.

A lack of trust and cooperation among colleagues can short-circuit creativity. Group interactions are particularly vulnerable when members of rival groups are thrown together to resolve a problem. Autocratic bosses and those who provide little or no feedback can also hinder creativity. They may value their own ideas and not support those of subordinates, blocking contribution to the brainstorming process.

In some situations, groups become merely a rubber stamp and approve ideas without exploring them. This block may happen for two reasons. Sometimes, people are afraid to speak up and present opposing views. At other times, they fear jeopardizing harmony, so they make a decision that satisfies both sides but that is not the most practical or realistic.

CASE STUDIES IN THE NEWS

Two Harvard professors, Barry Nalebuff and Ian Ayres, found in their research that sometimes a creative answer comes before we know there is a problem. Then the idea will spring from the solution with multi-level applications. For example, Spin Pop, introduced in 1993, was one of the most successful new interactive candy launches ever with over 85 million of the motorized lollipop holders sold worldwide. Hold your tongue steady and the candy spins against it. Roaming the aisles at Wal-Mart, Spin Pop creators found another "problem" to solve with their innovation, the SpinBrush™. In less than four years, a $1.5 million investment paid off when Procter & Gamble bought them out for $475 million. Another example is Hunt's and Heinz tomato ketchups, which are now putting their labels upside down on the bottles so we don't have to turn the bottle over to get the ketchup out.[24]

What other products are benefiting from innovative packaging and design? What problems do they solve?

A sense of humor in the global environment can place misunderstandings and potentially stressful problems in proper perspective, as shown by these examples from Roger E. Axtell's book, *Do's and Taboos of Humor Around the World*. After all, one form of communication understood wherever we travel is the smile.[25]

- In Belgium, General Motors used a tag line, "Body by Fisher," but when that was translated into Flemish, it became "Corpse by Fisher."

- In China, KFC's (Kentucky Fried Chicken's) famous slogan "finger-lickin' good" came out as "eat your fingers off."

- When Braniff Airlines translated a slogan about its luxurious upholstery ("Fly in leather") into Spanish, it came out as "Fly naked."

- An American traveler in England asked an Englishman how Thanksgiving is celebrated in Britain. The Englishman with a smile dryly responded, "I suppose you could say in Britain we celebrate Thanksgiving on the Fourth of July."

- A traveler called the front desk at an Indonesian hotel to request a wakeup call and was told to use the alarm clock. Upon asking what happens if it didn't work, the traveler was told by the desk clerk, "Just call me."

- A detour sign in Japan: "Stop: Drive sideways."

1. *What is the relationship of humor to creativity?*
2. *Think of instances when the right humor could have enabled a group you know to move forward and develop a creative response to a problem.*
3. *Have you personally witnessed a problem that was alleviated with humor? What was the situation and its outcome?*

*Fast*Chat

Review the blocks to creativity.

1. Does your work environment block or encourage creativity?

2. What are specific elements in your work environment that influence creativity positively or negatively?

3. How do you overcome the elements of your work environment that block your creativity?

Because of the important role of creativity in innovation and problem solving, you might want to consider ways to improve your own creativity—something we can all do. Ways to improve your creative ability, suggested by Jimmy Calano and Jeff Salzman in *Working Woman* and Eugene Raudsepp in *Nation's Business*, include the following:[26, 27]

Ways to Improve Your Creativity

1. Believe that you have the ability to be creative.

2. Listen to your hunches, particularly while relaxed.

3. Keep track of your ideas by writing down your insights and thoughts. Keep a pad near your bed, in your car, and in your pocket or purse on which to record your ideas as they occur.

4. Learn about things outside of your specialty to keep your thinking fresh.

5. Avoid rigid patterns of doing things. Change your rhythms. Draw your problems instead of writing them down. Change your scene or environment by taking a trip or walking. Try a different route to work occasionally.

6. Observe similarities, differences, and unique features in things, whether they are situations, processes, or ideas.

7. Engage in an activity at which you are not an expert and that puts you outside of your comfort zone, such as tennis or playing a musical instrument.

8. Engage in hobbies, especially those involving your hands. Keep your brain trim by playing games and doing puzzles and exercises.

9. Take the other side occasionally in order to challenge and scrutinize your own beliefs.

10. Have a sense of humor and learn to laugh easily. Humor helps put you and your problems into perspective and relieves tension, allowing you to be more creative.

11. Adopt a risk-taking attitude. Nothing is more fatal to creativity than fear of failure or resistance to change.

12. Think positive! Believe that a solution is possible and that you will find it.

13. Turn your ideas into action; follow through. Use positive reinforcement with yourself and reward yourself as a payoff for completing a project.

In a *Business Week* excerpt of their book, *Managing Generation Y,* Bruce Tulgan and Carolyn A. Martin observe that the latest wave of global citizens are coming of age and streaming into the workplace—29 million over the last five years with ten more years to come. Born between 1978 and 1998, Gen Yers are very certain about what they want from their careers and how they want to be managed. They are self-confident, optimistic, independent, goal-oriented, and "masters of the PC." Most Gen Yers were booting up computers before they were hopping on bikes. They are the most education-minded generation in history, and the expectation of lifelong education is a fact of life. They are also the most cross-cultured, cross-creed, and cross-color generation in U.S. history. And they are the most socially conscious generation since the 1960s, embracing our environment, poverty, and community problems. Given all of the above, they are known as "the Self-Esteem Generation" and require special attention in the workplace.[28]

To tap the strengths and creativity of these young workers, managers must respect their unique characteristics. Managers should recognize that Gen Yers want meaningful roles and meaningful work that helps others. They would like to feel their job is truly contributing something to the organization. They also want to work with a highly motivated team of committed people. And managers will need to develop means of helping these employees meet personal and professional goals with flexible schedules, work locations, and job descriptions along with desirable financial incentives. Flexibility is key with Generation Y.

1. *Why are Generation Y workers so well suited for the new high-tech job markets?*
2. *How can managers develop the creativity of these young workers?*

*Fast*Chat

Reread the suggestions for improving your creativity.

1. How many of these ways have you used in your creative processes? Which suggestions do you follow routinely? Which ones are you most comfortable in using?

2. Which suggestions could you start practicing now?

3. How do you think your performance would change if you were to begin practicing these suggestions? (Be specific—don't simply say, "I'd be more creative.")

5

CHAPTER SUMMARY

Problems are disturbances or unsettled matters that require solutions if organizations or individuals are to function effectively. Problems become evident when expected results are compared to actual results. They can best be solved by following specific steps beginning with defining the problem and ending with following up and modifying when necessary.

Decisions are needed when we must make choices among actions, opportunities, or solutions. There are several well-known techniques or tools that can be effective for making personal and work decisions. Decision making may be done by individuals or by groups. The goal of group problem solving is to develop a solution that all members can support. Negotiation, discussion that leads to a decision acceptable to all, is important. To be an effective negotiator, you should try for win-win solutions.

An important factor in problem solving is creativity, the ability to come up with new and unique solutions. We all have the potential for creativity, but it must be nurtured and developed. Innovation, the end product of creative activity, is vital to the success of organizations and individuals today.

Creativity involves several steps, and creative ideas can come from many sources. An employee trying to get a new idea through an organization should be prepared to persist, develop a coalition, sell the idea, work as part of a team, and share credit.

Supervisors wishing to stimulate creativity among their workers must be aware of the myths about corporate creativity. Blocks to creativity include thought processes, emotional blocks, cultural blocks, and environmental blocks. You can take several steps to overcome blocks and develop your own creativity, starting with believing that you can be creative. Thinking positively helps, and following through is essential.

REVIEW QUESTIONS

1. What is a problem, and what are the steps in problem solving?

2. Define decision tree, ABC analysis, cost-benefit analysis, PERT chart, quality circle, Six Sigma, and Six Thinking Hats.

3. What is the role of creativity in problem solving, and what are the basic steps in the creative process?

4. What are the sources of creativity in organizations, and what are ways to encourage creativity and to get new ideas through organizations?

5. What are the blocks to creativity? Give some examples. How can they be overcome?

6. How can you improve your creativity?

DISCUSSION QUESTIONS

1. Think of a problem with which you were recently confronted. Apply the problem-solving process to it. Would you take the same action now that you did at the time? (Remember that no decision is a decision!) Share your answer with the class.

2. Think of two problems that you are currently facing. Apply a decision tree to one and ABC analysis to the other.

3. Think of a time when you came up with what you considered to be a novel solution to a problem. Think back carefully to the process you used. Try to identify the five basic steps in your creative process. Share this experience with the class.

4. If you are currently working or have worked, think about your organization. What is the level of creativity in it? What steps is the organization or your supervisor taking to stimulate creativity? What are you doing to develop your own creative ability?

5. Review the different blocks to creativity. Name examples of each kind and consider them in relation to yourself. Are they blocks to your own creativity? (Try to be objective!) If not, good for you. If so, identify what you can do to overcome each block.

CHAPTER PROJECT

Do an Internet search for "creativity tools" or "creativity techniques." Identify two creativity techniques that will help you examine an issue or product from different angles to see if you can find a way to improve it. Working with a group of classmates, choose a product you know well.

Use the creativity techniques to break down its component parts and then consider how each part could be made better so that the resulting product is a more innovative one. Then think about products or services that you consider truly creative. In your group, discuss how you think the companies that invented these ideas came up with them. Research the companies online to determine the actual history of the products. Share your findings with the class in a short report.

APPLICATIONS

In small groups, analyze the following situations.

The 80-20 Rule

Paige, the head of the continuing education program at the local community college, finds that summer is the best time for her to develop new programs and courses. In looking at her "to do" list for this summer, she sees so many projects that she cannot possibly do all of them. In reviewing the list, she finds the following:

1. *Courses for professional groups.* Some professional groups are required to complete state-mandated continuing education hours each year in order to remain licensed or certified. The state expects community colleges to provide such training, and Paige is interested in offering courses if they will have satisfactory enrollments. These groups include real estate sales people, Certified Public Accountants (CPAs), and insurance agents.

Paige has tried to provide some courses for CPAs in the past; enrollments were low, yet she knows that other community colleges are experiencing high enrollments. One of these colleges said that it set up an advisory committee made up of members of the local CPA society. The advisory committee recommends courses, helps find instructors, and assists in publicizing the courses. Paige thinks that perhaps she should set up an advisory committee before offering additional courses for CPAs.

Paige has not yet offered courses for insurance agents, but she knows of a college nearby that does. That school reports low enrollments. Paige is uncertain whether she should try courses in this area, set up an advisory committee, or even devote effort to it.

2. *Other new courses and programs.* Paige also has several other programs and course possibilities on her list. They include classes for senior citizens and a "fear-of-flying" course for white-knuckle flyers. Other colleges report great success in targeting classes to local citizens over 55 years of age.

Paige does not know of any colleges that offer the flying course or even who would teach it for her (although her college does have a pilot training program). She is considering a dental assistant program and a gerontology program as well. Her community has several medical complexes in it, and students would probably be able to do internships in them.

3. *Business/industry contracts.* Paige would also like to devote some time to developing additional training contracts with businesses and industries in the community. She has been successful in building up good working relationships with a number of companies around her college and would like to do more. Such contracts develop goodwill in the community, bring in additional money to the college, and provide jobs for teachers. Besides, Paige enjoys setting them up.

Although Paige can ask some of the other people at the college for input, she has to do most of the work herself designing and marketing courses and programs. As Paige looks at her list of potential projects, she grows both excited and frustrated. She enjoys creating new programs and courses, but she also knows that she will not be able to do all of this work in two and one-half months.

1. Apply ABC analysis to Paige's dilemma. Categorize each task, label it A, B, or C, and explain your reasoning.

2. Based on your ABC analysis, what recommendation would you make to Paige about her priorities for the summer?

Help! Help!

Two years ago, Daniel started a roofing business. Most of his customers are homeowners and small businesses. His business has been so successful that six months ago he hired an employee to help him. He was lucky enough then to find someone who was experienced and fast.

TEAMWORK

WRITING

Last month, Daniel hired a second person when he found that work was stacking up and deadlines were not being met. The second employee is not experienced but is eager to learn and, in fact, seems to be a quick study. However, because of all the rush projects, Daniel has not had much time to train him and, hence, has to give him the less complex jobs.

Daniel is beginning to feel overwhelmed. One of his saws has been acting up for the last two weeks, resulting in some downtime. He and his employees frequently run out of needed supplies in the middle of a job. Another common problem is realizing that a job calls for a particular roofing material, and the local supplier does not keep it in stock. Daniel is dismayed to find that even though he has an additional person on the payroll, deadlines are still not being met and jobs are backing up.

In fact, some projects have even been put aside and not bid until the customer called once or twice, causing much embarrassment. Daniel feels that he cannot blame anybody in particular, as whoever is free is the one who takes requests from customers, orders supplies, and moves on to the next project.

1. Imagine that you are a consultant hired by Daniel to try to bring order to his business. Using the problem-solving process described in this chapter, summarize your conversation with Daniel. Be specific.

   a. What do you think is the real problem? What information are you using to determine it?

   b. What do you think are the possible causes of the problem? Again, what information are you using?

2. Based on the conversation with Daniel and the application of the problem-solving process, what advice would you give him? Be specific.

   a. How practical are the ideas you have generated?

   b. What alternatives for removing the causes of the problem would you suggest? Identify the implications of each alternative.

   c. What would you recommend as the most likely solution to Daniel's problem? The next most likely?

   d. Write an action plan for solving Daniel's business problem. Be sure to explain how the plan should be implemented and followed up.

ADDITIONAL READINGS AND RESOURCES

Ayres, Ian, and Barry J. Nalebuff. *Why Not? How to Use Everyday Ingenuity to Solve Problems Big and Small.* New York: Harvard Business School Press, 2003.

Breyfogle, Forrest W. *Implementing Six Sigma: Smarter Solutions Using Statistical Methods.* New Jersey: John Wiley & Sons, 2003.

Maxwell, John C. *Thinking for a Change: 11 Ways Highly Successful People Approach Life and Work.* New York: Warner Books, Inc., 2003.

Pande, Peter S., Robert P. Neuman, and Roland R. Cavanaugh. *The Six Sigma Way: How GE, Motorola, and Other Top Companies are Honing Their Performances.* New York: McGraw-Hill, 2000.

Thaler, Linda Kaplan, and Robin Koval. *Bang! Getting Your Message Heard in a Noisy World.* New York: Reed Business, Inc., 2003.

For additional resources, refer to the web site for this text: school.cengage.com/career/dalton

Working within the Organization:
Structure and Climate

CHAPTER 6
OBJECTIVES

focus

In his 2003 book *Re-imagine!*, influential business author Tom Peters sets out to redefine business thinking. He challenges the traditional rules and organizational barriers that can stand in the way of creativity and success and says:

We are in the midst of redefining our basic ideas about what organizations and enterprises are...in a brawl with no rules. What can we do? Relish the Mess! Enjoy the Fray! We must destroy virtually all our business organizations and re-imagine them in order to respond to the new technological and social imperatives of our era. If we don't, we are dead.... It is as simple as that. Big, established companies invariably fail to innovate. Destruction is a harsh word. And yet I firmly believe—I insist—that it is the right word for our time. The call for today must be "Destroy and Rebuild."[1]

What changes in organizational structures have occurred during the new millennium? Why have these changes occurred? What changes do you expect to happen in the future?

After studying this chapter, you should be able to:

6.1 *Explain the purpose and importance of organizational structure.*

6.2 *Discuss the hierarchical pyramid and identify its roots.*

6.3 *Describe the ways power is distributed within the chain of command.*

6.4 *Understand the concept of span of control.*

6.5 *Define formal and informal communication and discuss the dangers of the grapevine.*

6.6 *Recognize the various types of organizational structures used by businesses today.*

6.7 *Identify corporate life cycles, reasons they exist, and how they affect organizational structure.*

in this chapter

Structure is the relationship among parts. In the case of a business or other organization, structure helps the organization divide its work and delegate tasks. Without structure, employees do not know what their jobs and responsibilities are, which results in frustration, low morale, conflict, and other human relations problems. An effective structure also helps people avoid duplication of work and delays that occur when work must be reviewed by numerous layers of management.

Structure divides and delegates responsibility.

There is no single correct way to structure an organization. Organizational structure affects productivity, quality, employee morale, customer satisfaction, and, ultimately, the success of the entire business. For these reasons, many organizations study their structure on an ongoing basis and make changes to boost efficiency. Increasingly, companies are experimenting with radical new ideas concerning structure, attempting to flatten and decentralize control in order to spark innovation and allow a more rapid response to changing market demands.

The chain of command directs the flow of authority and information.

An understanding of organizational structure will help you function more effectively within any type of organization and to understand and adjust to organizational changes. The heart of organizational structure is the chain of command, of which you should be aware and to which you should be sensitive.

*Fast*Chat

Describe the structure of an organization to which you belong, such as your job, your school, or a volunteer organization.

1. According to Tom Peters' prescription, how would you help your organization "Re-imagine!" its structure?

2. What resources would be most helpful in making these changes? Why?

Organizational structure originally developed around the **chain of command**. The chain of command is the direction in which authority is exercised and policies and other information are communicated to lower levels. Authority begins at the top, and each level gives commands, delegates authority, and passes information to lower levels. Information and requests going up the line follow the chain upward. The idea of the chain of command developed in the military and is prevalent in today's organizations. It forms the classic **pyramidal hierarchy**, illustrated below.

Employees and members of an organization must respect the chain of command and exercise great caution in skipping levels. Such respect and caution will reduce the potential for human relations problems. One of the few occasions when you can safely ignore the chain is in emergencies or when time is crucial and your immediate supervisor is not present.

Figure 6.1   The business chain of command can be compared to that of the military.

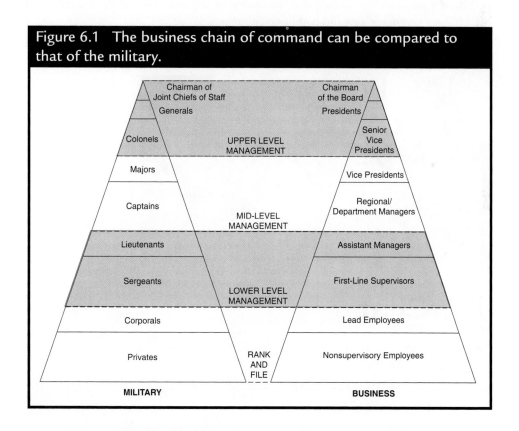

In *The Boundaryless Organization: Breaking the Chains of Organizational Structure*, the authors introduce the idea that today's organizations must learn how to adjust quickly, proactively, and creatively to the changing times by sweeping away the boundaries of hierarchy, turf, and geography that they believe get in the way of outstanding business performance. They advocate a very open flow of knowledge, ideas, resources, and talents up and down, across, and in and out of the organizational structure, a paradigm shift for success in the 21st century.[2]

1. *How is this idea different from the classic pyramidal hierarchy?*
2. *What skills would the workers in a boundaryless structure need that they would not need in a traditional pyramidal hierarchy?*
3. *Are you currently working in a "Boundaryless Organization"? If so, describe your experience with this type of organization.*

Organizational structure allows companies to divide work and delegate tasks.

©Getty Images/PhotoDisc

*Fast*Chat

Think of a company or organization in which you have worked or participated.

1. Describe the chain of command. How would the organization function without the chain of command?
2. Do you think the chain of command will eventually disappear? Why, or why not?

As organizations grow in size and complexity, their leaders find that making all decisions becomes increasingly difficult. Presidents of companies with thousands of employees cannot possibly make every decision and supervise all employees. With so many companies globally scattered and field teams in remote locations, decision-making methods have had to change and authority has had to be delegated to lower levels.

Two forms of authority distribution are common. The organization is said to be **centralized** when those high up in the organization closely hold authority and are responsible for making all major decisions. When important decisions are made at a lower level and authority is delegated, the organization is **decentralized**.

> Authority is distributed because organization heads usually cannot make all decisions.

Centralization and decentralization have their positive and negative sides. A centralized purchasing function, for instance, can ensure that quality of supplies remains consistent among locations. Additionally, buyers of large quantities frequently receive discounts. A drawback to centralization is that decision making can be slow and innovation can be difficult. Reporting through several layers of managers instead of making decisions immediately and acting on them at the lower level can take time.

Decentralization can face problems from weak managers who may not have the maturity or expertise to make effective decisions. To create the type of innovative, creative, fast-paced global company for which the new millennium calls, organizations must work collaboratively and draw on the strengths of the entire employee base. The decision-making capability needs to be delegated up, over, around, and throughout the organization.

In January 2004, the Associated Press (AP) announced an agency-wide move to a "much more horizontal structure." The structural reorganization combined several technology groups from across the company and consolidated them into a services and technology organization. Four Manhattan offices were combined into one smaller building. These changes moved the AP toward a much more horizontal structure with the intent of improving journalism.[3]

> QUICK WIT
>
> "How do you induce innovation? Simple: Decentralize! What's the problem with decentralization? It almost never works."
>
> Tom Peters,
> Author and
> business guru

*Fast*Chat

1. The "outsourcing" of jobs offshore is among the many changes occurring in organizations across America and abroad. What does this mean for the people in middle management positions?
2. How will outsourcing affect entry-level positions for American college graduates seeking jobs?

You can effectively supervise 12 to 21 employees, depending on the industry and type of work.

The number of employees that can be supervised effectively by one person generally ranges from about 12 to 21, but will vary based on the industry and type of work. More people can be successfully supervised at one time if the employees are capable of working independently and their tasks are very similar. However, the higher up in the organization you go, the more complex jobs become, and the fewer people you can supervise.

The number of people that an individual can supervise is called the **span of control**. The span may be either tall or flat, as shown below. Not having the appropriate span of control can sometimes result in behavioral or performance problems. Employees may feel unnoticed—good performance may be unrewarded and poor performance may go uncorrected.

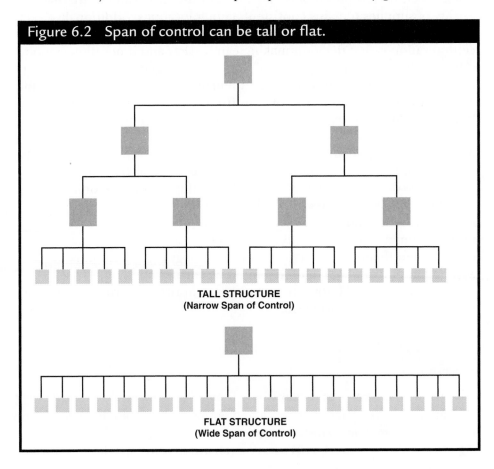

Figure 6.2 Span of control can be tall or flat.

TALL STRUCTURE
(Narrow Span of Control)

FLAT STRUCTURE
(Wide Span of Control)

One way that you can broaden your span is by delegating authority to others within your group. Broadening the span can lessen red tape and increase morale. Individuals allowed to perform higher-level tasks feel heightened job satisfaction. Using "lead" employees to oversee the work of others might expand span of control. These could be senior level individuals who would continue to perform their work but who would also monitor the performance of others. While lead people generally would not have authority to discipline or appraise performance, they would be given authority to direct work and give orders.

For your delegation of authority to be successful, you must communicate fully. The person receiving the authority must understand the new role and be willing to act accordingly. Likewise, the other employees must be informed of what is expected of them and of the person receiving the authority. Without this communication, serious human relations problems can develop. If you are the one being given such authority, ask your supervisor whether coworkers are aware of your new responsibilities. If they are not, suggest that your supervisor inform them. If that does not happen, you should probably communicate this information to your coworkers as early as possible in your new role.

QUICK WIT

"The intermediary is doomed: Technology strips him of effectiveness. The flattening of the vertical order . . . is already clear."

Pat McGovern,
Founder, International
Data Group (IDG)

*Fast*Chat

Some organizations today are attempting to flatten their spans of control in order to bring products to the marketplace more quickly and to improve customer service. This has increased the need for supervisors to delegate, although they often have little experience in delegating and sometimes find it difficult.

1. Why do people have trouble delegating authority?

2. How do you feel when you are not in control of something but responsible for it?

3. What can you do to get your supervisor to trust you with delegated tasks?

Formal communication, communication that flows up or down the formal organizational structure, is controlled by the chain of command. Organizational communication varies in the direction it flows, whether it is one-way or two-way, and in its chance of distortion.

DIRECTION AND DISTORTIONS OF COMMUNICATION FLOW

Communication flows upward, downward, or horizontally.

In any organization, communication will flow downward, upward, or horizontally (sideways). **Downward communication** is communication that begins at higher levels of the organization and flows downward. Typical forms of downward communication are meetings, memoranda, policy statements, newsletters, manuals, handbooks, telephone conversations, and electronic mail.

Downward communication can become distorted for a variety of reasons. Long messages not in writing tend to be forgotten or misinterpreted. Furthermore, sometimes so many messages are received that a communications overload results. For example, the employee receiving 20 e-mails a day may fail to read all of them carefully. (Communication—how to make it effective and avoid problems—is discussed in greater depth in Chapter 4.)

Various tools can be used to communicate formally within an organization.

©Getty Images/PhotoDisc

Upward communication consists of messages that begin in the lower levels of the organization and go to higher levels. Upward communication can be in the form of memos, grievances (presented formally or informally), meetings, attitude surveys, or suggestion systems.

Upward communication can also become distorted. Frequently, subordinates who must deliver unpleasant messages misrepresent situations for fear the receiver may blame the messenger who delivers the bad news.

uick tip ···

When you must talk about a problem that no one wants to talk about, remember the following:

1. Spend time identifying the problem. Explore your motivation for bringing up the issue. Imagine how others will react.
2. Work to overcome your fear of presenting the problem. Use visualization (Chapter 2) to assist.
3. Be direct but tactful. Give the listener time to react.
4. Stay with the message. Continue to seek support for your point of view.[4]

Michael Warshaw, *Fast Company*

···

GLOBAL CONNECTION

Boeing leaders from all over the world attended the annual leadership meeting to hear Boeing President and CEO Harry Stonecipher deliver a speech to the organization about the organization. The purpose of the meeting was to plan, review strategies, and assure that all global business units were working toward consistent goals. Stonecipher's key message was to communicate better throughout the organization. He encouraged managers and leaders around the world to communicate strategies and to have ongoing conversations that help all company people see where they fit in. He suggested practicing and having genuine conversation—the real two-way kind so people can ask questions. He also asked them to have ongoing discussions with the people about their performance and development and to ask employees how they, the leaders, could improve their own performance. "People appreciate good, crisp communication about what's going on," he said.[5]

1. *What kind of communication is Stonecipher suggesting should happen between Boeing employees and management?*
2. *Have you ever been encouraged to tell your managers how they "could improve their own performance"? If so, please share the experience.*

Horizontal communication occurs between individuals at the same level in an organization. These messages can be in the form of telephone conversations, memos, meetings, informal gatherings, or electronic mail. These communications, too, can suffer from distortions whenever messages are not clear, perceptions differ, or attitudes get in the way.

ONE-WAY AND TWO-WAY COMMUNICATION

Communication within organizations is either one-way or two-way. **One-way communication** takes place with no feedback from the receiver. Some examples are memos or videotaped lectures. Although one-way communication can present problems, it is used frequently because it is

ETHICS CONNECTION

A recent article in *Fast Company* reported on the ease with which today's organizations can identify who is buying what kind of groceries, driving through what tollbooth, accessing what kind of e-mail, and even having what kind of medical problems. They can even monitor traffic and public activity using hidden cameras and monitors. Via a grocery scanner, an ATM, a convenience store video camera, your home or office computer: somewhere today you have likely been part of a network that captured information about you and delivered it electronically to an organization.

The interesting thing about this networked world is that many organizations have now become "transparent." That is, networks enable us to see their inner workings.[6] For example, Fed-Ex has embraced the concept of transparency, scanning packages all along each delivery route and allowing customers to track packages online. EBay provides seller history to each online bidder. This transparency helps make a company more competitive, faster, and cheaper, sharpening its competitive edge. This can be profitable and leads to open communication among employees, management, and customers, but what are the ethical implications of this situation?[7]

1. *How many times today (this week) have you been "networked"? Make a list of all the electronic transactions you have made, such as store purchases, ATM withdrawals, online transactions, frequent buyer cards, etc.*

2. *What form of communication/network was used? Was there any human interaction or two-way communication during the process? Or was it just a swipe of the card?*

3. *What type of information did you provide? What will these organizations do with your information? What control do you have over your information?*

quick, easy to generate, and orderly. Can you imagine the president of a corporation of thousands of employees attempting to communicate a new benefits program using two-way communication? In addition, one-way communication is less threatening for the sender because no one is present to give negative feedback.

Two-way communication is communication in which feedback is received. Although two-way communication is slower and less orderly than one-way communication, in general it is more accurate. The receiver of the message is able to provide feedback, and the sender is able to evaluate whether the message has been correctly interpreted.

INFORMAL COMMUNICATION

Informal communication is another type of communication that occurs in organizations. This form of communication, the most common type, can either help or hinder an organization's efforts. If you discuss a new company policy with someone in another department, you are using informal communication. Informal communication does not follow the formal channels of communication but travels through a channel often called the **grapevine**. The grapevine is an informal, person-to-person means of circulating information or gossip. It serves several functions for both employees and management. Many managers have learned to respect and even use the grapevine because of its speed. However, because of its unreliability, it must be used with caution. As an employee or organization member, you can satisfy some of your social needs through the grapevine, clarify formal orders, and use it as a release for your feelings and

Use the informal grapevine with caution.

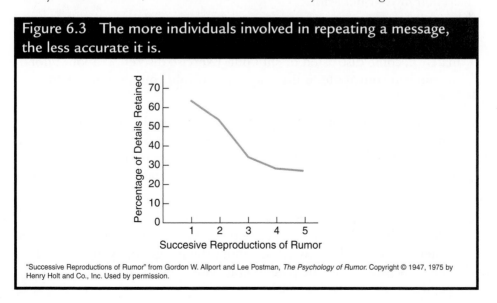

Figure 6.3 The more individuals involved in repeating a message, the less accurate it is.

"Successive Reproductions of Rumor" from Gordon W. Allport and Lee Postman, *The Psychology of Rumor.* Copyright © 1947, 1975 by Henry Holt and Co., Inc. Used by permission.

concerns. When employees feel that upward communication will be threatening, blocked, or ineffective, they frequently turn to the grapevine.

The problem with grapevines is that often messages are distorted, exaggerated, incomplete, or even totally wrong. Grapevines are the primary means for transmitting rumors. The chance of misinterpretation increases with the number of individuals through whom the messages pass, as shown on the previous page. Because downward communication is sometimes ambiguous and upward communication is often nonexistent, rumors too often occur. Such situations are fertile soil for problems in human relations. Grapevines exist in every organization, and you should understand how grapevines work and respect their potential, both good and bad. Be careful that you do not contribute incorrect or inappropriate information to the grapevine. Information can easily be introduced into the grapevine or garbled once it is in, but correcting it is almost impossible. Probably the best rule of thumb for good human relations is to ask yourself the question, "Does this need to be said?" The most valuable asset in human relations is common sense!

Communications authors Barry L. Reece and Rhonda Brandt developed the following guidelines and cautions concerning grapevines. Understanding the grapevine can keep you out of trouble.[8]

1. No one can hide from the grapevine, even though it may know only part of the truth. Our reputations are created by the grapevine and are hard to change. Be careful about what information about you makes its way into the grapevine. Watch what you tell others about yourself, choose carefully those with whom you share information, and use discretion in your behavior.

2. The message (gossip) of the grapevine tends to be negative. People who consistently communicate negative information about others ultimately become distrusted or shut out. Exercise discretion about information you contribute to the grapevine. Would you want others to know what you said?

3. Several grapevine networks operate in every organization. Each one is composed of people who have common experiences and concerns. In a particular network, usually only a few people pass on most of the information, and that is usually downward or horizontally. Do you want to be labeled one of these people?

4. The role you play in the grapevine will reflect your ethics, decision-making skills, and maturity. Mature people anticipate the consequences of their actions and words. Think about the image that you create of yourself before you participate in grapevine communication.

CASE STUDIES IN THE NEWS

 According to the *Houston Chronicle*, you will soon be able to open an office in the mall Shops at Willow Bend in Plano, Texas, just outside Dallas. The mall's coffee court is becoming part of a research project that will offer a free wireless Internet access (WiFi) area, network printers, conference tables, fancy Herman Miller chairs, and live news and stock reports on 52-inch plasma TV screens. There will be loaner laptops for checking e-mail by an increasingly mobile workforce. A consortium of high-tech companies including Best Buy, IBM, Microsoft, Panasonic, Cisco Systems, and Herman Miller are part of this Internet Home Alliance and will run the experiment for one year, providing workstations, cubicles, and meeting tables but not exterior walls. If successful, they hope to sell products and gear to these mobile offices of the future.

Other retailers are already exploring WiFi usage. UPS offers free usage in 66 of their stores. FedEx Kinko's already sells WiFi access in every one of its stores, and based on the popularity of its usage, plans are underway to expand the offerings of perks to their customers. Coffee for conferences, newscasts, and large conference tables with built-in electrical outlets will be added to the list of videoconferencing, computer, and conference room rentals. Tens of thousands of public locations across the nation now offer WiFi access points; McDonald's, Starbucks, Borders bookstores, and most major hotels, airports, and train stations are just a few readily available locations. This is a new twist on telecommuting.[9]

1. *Have you used a WiFi center? What are the benefits of these locations?*

2. *How could a mobile office location be useful to you in your career?*

*Fast*Chat

1. Think of an organization in which you have worked. How was communication handled? How could communication have been improved?

2. What problems can occur if organizations do not formally release information and most of the information comes through the grapevine?

3. Can you name a time when you heard information through the grapevine? How accurate was the information? Were you able to correct inaccurate information?

Various structures have been developed for large, complex organizations.

Warren Bennis, in *Organizing Genius*, reminds us to be aware of the organization's culture as it relates to its structure. Unlike a mission statement, a culture is never written down, but it is the "soul" of an organization and determines much of how things get done and by whom. It is a collection of unspoken rules and traditions that determine which offices are most important, who speaks to whom and in what tone of voice, and whether men wear ties or tennis shoes on Friday. He says although these rules are not visible, they are there 24/7 and drive the quality of life within that organization's structure.[10]

A variety of new structures have developed as organizations have become larger and more complex. The basic pyramidal hierarchy no longer meets all organizational needs. However, no one specific type of organizational structure is best. The most efficient structure depends on the size of the organization, whether it provides a service or produces a product, and the number of different products or services involved.

The formal structure can be organized by function (what each department does), by geographic area, by customer, or by product. Large, complex organizations may use a variety of these structures, depending on their needs. The figures on the next page represent the various ways of organizing. Developing an organizational structure is a complicated process and is a whole study in itself.

Complex organizations have developed other structures to enhance organizational effectiveness. Some use a line and staff structure, others use a matrix structure, and still others mix the two.

LINE AND STAFF STRUCTURE

Line employees are directly involved in production activities. The **staff** employees support line employees through advice and counsel on a variety of subjects in their areas of expertise. This support may be in the form of legal, safety, personnel, or computer assistance, or may involve maintenance of equipment or facilities.

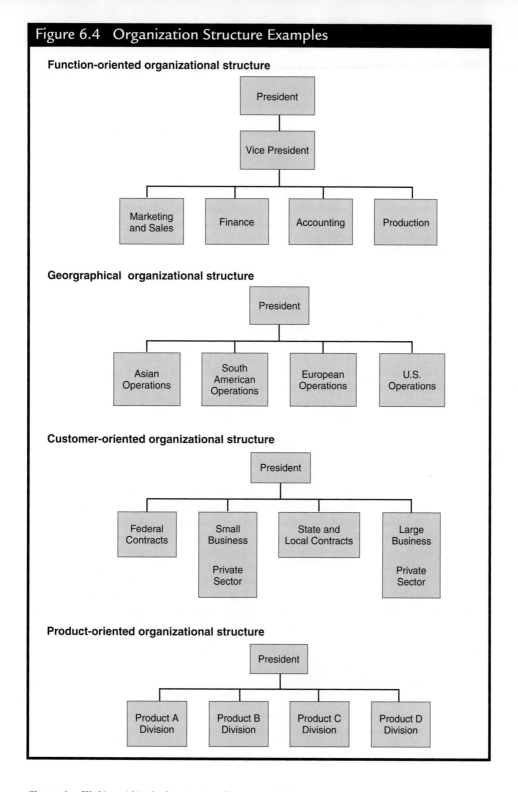

Figure 6.4   Organization Structure Examples

Function-oriented organizational structure

President

Vice President

| Marketing and Sales | Finance | Accounting | Production |

Georgraphical organizational structure

President

| Asian Operations | South American Operations | European Operations | U.S. Operations |

Customer-oriented organizational structure

President

| Federal Contracts | Small Business Private Sector | State and Local Contracts | Large Business Private Sector |

Product-oriented organizational structure

President

| Product A Division | Product B Division | Product C Division | Product D Division |

Figure 6.4 (continued)   Organization Structure Examples

A company using a variety of organizational structures

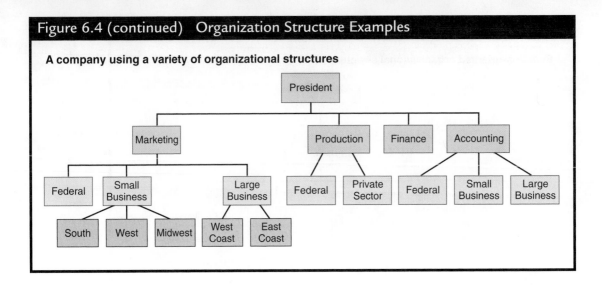

Many problems can arise from line and staff relationships. One common problem is that staff members usually have no authority to force line employees to cooperate. Staff people must frequently rely on their skills of persuasion to convince line workers that staff instructions should be followed. For this reason, some staff members are given **functional authority**—the authority to make decisions in their area of expertise and to overrule line decisions.

MATRIX STRUCTURE

Matrix structures are frequently used by organizations that manage many projects. Therefore, the matrix structure is sometimes called project structure. A **matrix structure** uses groups of people with expertise in their individual areas that are temporarily assigned full or part time to a project from other parts of the organization. The project has its own supervisor and can last a few weeks or a few years. For instance, an engineering firm may pull together a group of engineers to oversee the design and construction of a new plant and dissolve the group as soon as the plant is finished. The employees then return to their original supervisors, and the plant continues operation under its own management.

Some companies utilize the matrix structure to develop products or operate in markets where decisions need to be made quickly. These

GLOBAL/TECHNOLOGY CONNECTION

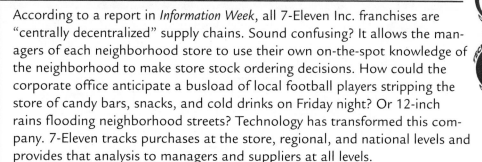

According to a report in *Information Week*, all 7-Eleven Inc. franchises are "centrally decentralized" supply chains. Sound confusing? It allows the managers of each neighborhood store to use their own on-the-spot knowledge of the neighborhood to make store stock ordering decisions. How could the corporate office anticipate a busload of local football players stripping the store of candy bars, snacks, and cold drinks on Friday night? Or 12-inch rains flooding neighborhood streets? Technology has transformed this company. 7-Eleven tracks purchases at the store, regional, and national levels and provides that analysis to managers and suppliers at all levels.

7-Eleven's store managers use its Retail Information System to place orders, do bookkeeping, obtain replacement reports, and even get area weather forecasts for awareness of how storms may affect upcoming sales. The system provides the store managers with daily, weekly, and monthly sales tallies for making the best decisions on re-orders. The company's CEO, Jim Keyes, spends about one-third of his capital budget on IT and lobbies with Oracle CEO Larry Ellison to integrate a system that will make 7-Eleven a "high-end, role model technology corporation."

With $33 billion in worldwide sales, 7-Eleven can benefit from such technology and can negotiate with major manufacturers for good merchandise deals for its nearly 20,000 stores worldwide.[11]

1. *How does 7-Eleven's decentralization improve the store managers' ordering decisions?*
2. *How is technology transforming 7-Eleven?*

groups are given the power to make decisions to speed their work, and they may be assigned experts on a number of fronts. Matrix structures can cause difficulty. The individual assigned to head the temporary team may have no formal authority or control over the rest of the group, and power struggles may erupt as a result.

If you find yourself in this type of situation, the best approach is to discuss it with the person who delegated the project to you and ask for formal authority. Someone higher in the chain of command than the participants should instruct them to cooperate and emphasize that they will be appraised on their participation and performance.

John Katzenbach, a well-known management consultant and author, believes "pride building" is at the core of many high-performing organizations. In his book, *Why Pride Matters More Than Money*, he suggests that organizations return to building pride by nurturing, engaging, and recognizing the actions of their employees. His concern is that in many organizations, the message has changed from "What can we do to keep you happy and keep you here?" to "You're lucky to have a job, sit down or move out." He says that too many leaders have focused their ambitions on them-selves rather than on the organization and have looked for personal gain, and the result has led us straight to the Enrons and Tycos that recently lit up the newscasts.

Katzenbach believes there is a groundswell of "pride builders" who personalize the workplace and create close-knit communities inside large, often impersonal corporations, instilling self-esteem in workers and building strong support for tough assignments. (Sound like infor-mal organizations?) Pride building is becoming an institutionalized process at GM and is widely used by McDonald's, Westinghouse, Aramark, Pfizer, Fannie Mae, Microsoft, and Marriott. This may be a new fix to another old organizational problem. There is certainly noth-ing to lose—it's always important for people to be proud of what they are doing every day.[12]

1. *Do you know any "pride builders"?*
2. *How successful do you perceive "pride builders" to be, and what do you think is their "secret to success"?*

*Fast*Chat

Globalization and modern technology will cause organizations to experiment with structure.

1. To what structures have you been exposed?

2. Have you ever had two supervisors with different priorities? How did you handle the situation?

Organizations change for many reasons. New technology brings fresh products and makes old ones obsolete, new markets open and old markets fade away, and competition or the lack of it increases or decreases demand. All of these changes may call for a modification in organizational structure. Another reason organizations change, according to Joseph L. Massie and John Douglas in *Managing—A Contemporary Introduction*, is that they go through **life cycles**, as shown below. After birth or start-up comes growth. The next stage is stabilization. After that, the organization begins to slow down. Then it either closes or it revitalizes.[13]

This concept can be illustrated by companies that produced only black-and-white TVs when color TVs came onto the market. The demand for black and whites died out. The color TV was very expensive initially, but as the production of those televisions increased, the price dropped. Then sales rose and television manufacturing companies grew to handle the demand. Soon the majority of households in the U.S. had color TVs, and the demand stabilized. Technology has begun to change again with high-definition TV and now disc TV. With technology developing at lightening speed, an organization's life cycle may only last a short while.

> Structures change as companies go through life cycles.

Frequently, businesses and organization's close or die for natural reasons over which you may have no control. For the successful death of a company, some experts suggest that employees plan a formal grieving process and mourn the death—even if it means having a "wake" to celebrate the demise. They suggest maintaining strong ties through networking to see the group through the transition times, and placing no blame. If you experience this last stage in an organization, remind yourself that you made a contribution.[14]

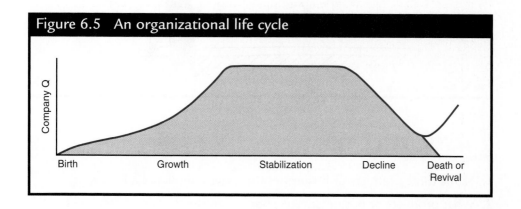

Figure 6.5   An organizational life cycle

Company Q

Birth   Growth   Stabilization   Decline   Death or Revival

GLOBAL CONNECTION

Offshore outsourcing is a defining political influence on organizational change. One recent major impact was the shift affecting well-paid knowledge workers. In 2004, IBM reported they would ship 5,000 white-collar jobs—engineering and managerial jobs paying $75,000 to $100,000 per year—to India where the talent pool could and would do the work for one-fifth the cost. Offshore outsourcing has become so substantial now that Intel is opening a glittering new $41 million campus in Bangalore to house 1,000 of its workers. To stay profitable, many employers are concluding that they have no choice but to go overseas.[15]

Various concerns are being raised about offshore outsourcing, such as, "Is it short-sighted or risky?" What impact do you think offshore outsourcing has on the global economy? On organizational structure and climate?

In many organizations, the customer has the greatest authority.

© 1996 Ted Goff www.tedgoff.com

*Fast*Chat

1. Name three products or businesses that have completed a life cycle.
2. What products or businesses will soon be on the decline of their life cycles?

CHAPTER SUMMARY

Structure is the relationship among parts. Organizations require structure to arrange their workload and allow smooth operations. Organizational structure originally developed around the chain of command, the direction in which authority and communication are utilized within the organization. The classic business structure, the pyramidal hierarchy, developed from the chain of command.

Authority in an organization can be either centralized or decentralized. Each choice has advantages and disadvantages. An organization must also consider the most effective span of control for its particular situation. The span of control indicates how many employees a supervisor manages.

Communication in an organization can be either formal or informal. Formal communication can travel upward, downward, or horizontally and can be either one-way or two-way. Each type of communication and flow has its positive and negative aspects. Informal communication ranges from conversations between employees to rumors that travel through the grapevine.

Organizational structure can take many forms besides the classical pyramidal hierarchy. Work can be organized according to function, geography, customer, product, or a mixture of these. Some structures, such as the matrix structure, while offering advantages, are complex and can cause difficulties for the employees involved. Organizational structures often change as organizations go through life cycles and tailor structures to meet their current needs. Understanding how organizations function and why structural changes are needed can help us in the organization.

Key Terms

chain of command

pyramidal hierarchy

centralized

decentralized

span of control

formal communication

downward communication

upward communication

horizontal communication

one-way communication

two-way communication

informal communication

grapevine

line and staff structure

functional authority

matrix structure

life cycles

REVIEW QUESTIONS

1. What is the purpose of organizational structure, and why is it important?

2. What is the hierarchical pyramid, and where are its roots?

3. How is power assigned in an organization? How many employees can be supervised effectively at one time?

4. What is formal communication, and in which directions can it flow?

5. What factors decrease the effectiveness of formal communication?

6. What is informal communication, and what are the dangers of the grapevine?

7. Describe the types of structures used by businesses today.

8. What complex organizational structures exist? What problems arise from their use?

9. What is the corporate life cycle, and why does it exist?

DISCUSSION QUESTIONS

1. Describe an organization that restructured of which you are or have been a member. What were the results? Is restructuring always the best step?

2. Have you ever received an inaccurate message through the grapevine? What happened as a result of this misinformation?

3. Should all firms attempt to decentralize authority? Why, or why not?

4. Identify a company in your community and describe where you believe it is in its life cycle.

5. Why are we usually more willing to accept authority of those above us than those at our level or below?

6. Think of several organizations with which you are familiar through experience or the news. What organizational structure does each have?

CHAPTER PROJECT

Search the Internet or your public library for the works of Henry Mintzberg, one of the world's most influential teachers of business strategy. Find the definitions of his five types of organizations:

1. Simple Structure (or Entrepreneurial Startup)

2. Machine Bureaucracy

3. Divisionalized Form

4. Professional Bureaucracy

5. Adhocracy (or The Innovative Organization)

Answer the following questions about each type of organization:

1. What are the pros and cons of each of these structures?

2. Can you name organizations today with these types of structures?

3. Define your ideal organizational structure.

APPLICATIONS

In small groups, analyze the following situations.

Nowhere to Run, Nowhere to Hide

Jacob sat at his desk staring out the window. He did not know what to do. Yesterday, his boss, Carla, had told him to fire Lisa immediately for having one too many complaints. A patient complained about how Lisa had treated him. Carla's boss, the director of nursing, was furious and had threatened to demote Carla.

TEAMWORK

However, when Jacob spoke with Janet, the human resources specialist, she voiced concern. Janet did not think that Jacob had followed the company's progressive discipline policy and said that Lisa should be given a final warning before being fired. Janet cautioned Jacob that terminating Lisa without following company policy might result in a grievance from the union and a charge of discrimination filed with the Equal Employment Opportunity Commission.

Jacob reported this concern to Carla, who exclaimed, "I don't care what those human resources people say. We just can't let lazy, incompetent people continue to work here! I want Lisa fired immediately, and I want anyone else who makes another mistake fired, too."

1. What type of organizational structure is being used in this scenario?

2. What problem has the structure caused?

3. Could this problem have been avoided if Janet had been given functional authority? How?

4. Whose orders should Jacob follow? Why?

Order from Chaos

Lester's t-shirt company is growing rapidly, and problems have emerged. The factory makes 20 varieties of shirts with different logos. A special division does custom orders for teams and corporations. The factory employs 61 individuals, and each of his two sales outlets has 20 employees.

However, matters are getting out of hand. Supplies are late, paychecks are not coming out on time, and employees at the second outlet are sneaking off early after Lester leaves the shop. Yesterday, because Lester forgot to pay the bills, the electricity was turned off at the first outlet, and he had to close for the day until power was restored.

Currently, Lester has a plant manager to oversee production and two lead store clerks, one in each store. Lester takes care of ordering supplies, paying bills, writing paychecks, and hiring personnel. He makes all major decisions at the outlets and most of the decisions at the plant.

1. Does Lester need to restructure his organization? If so, how?

2. Should he add more layers of management? Why, or why not?

3. Should management decisions be decentralized? Why, or why not? In which areas should he add management?

4. What would be a better span of control?

ADDITIONAL READINGS AND RESOURCES

Champy, James. *X-Engineering the Corporation: Reinventing Your Business in the Digital Age.* New York: Warner Books, 2002.

Champy, James, and Michael Hammer. *Reengineering the Corporation: A Manifesto for Business Revolution.* New York: Harper Business, 2001.

Foster, Dick, and Sarah Kaplan. *Creative Destruction: Why Companies that are Built to Last Underperform the Market.* New York: Doubleday, 2001.

Hammer, Michael. *The Agenda: What Every Business Must Do to Dominate the Decade.* New York: Crown Business, 2003.

Lawler, Edward. *Treat People Right.* New Jersey: Jossey-Bass, 2003.

Peters, Tom. *Re-Imagine! Business Excellence in a Disruptive Age.* London: Dorling Kindersley, 2003.

For additional resources, refer to the web site for this text: school.cengage.com/career/dalton

Group Dynamics:
The Advantages of Working with Others

focus

Anita's alarm goes off at 6:00 AM. She quickly dresses for work and goes downstairs for breakfast with her family and her dog, Fiesta. A horn blast beckons her to the carpool van already loaded with her fellow workers. Anita is a manager at NASA's Johnson Space Center. She has a full day and evening ahead.

FRIDAY, AUGUST 19

9:00 AM Division Staff Meeting	1:00 PM Windows XP Training class
10:00 AM Contractor Status Meeting	3:00 PM Fact finding for cost proposal
12:00 noon Lunch—Ralph	5:00 PM Journal entries and callbacks
	6:00 PM Aerobics class at gym

After work, another meeting begins at 7:00 PM. Anita is chairperson for the National Management Association Conference scheduled for later in the year. Committee reports of current and planned activities are expected with limited time to cover the topics. After the meeting, Anita plans to join friends for dinner and a birthday celebration. What a day!

How many groups did Anita interact with after the 6:00 AM alarm? What types of human relations skills will be most important for her throughout the day?

After studying this chapter, you should be able to:

7.1 *Understand the characteristics of a group.*

7.2 *Explain the importance of studying groups and why people join groups.*

7.3 *Distinguish among types of groups.*

7.4 *Discuss the different types of leaders.*

7.5 *Recognize factors that influence group effectiveness.*

7.6 *Identify the pitfalls of groups and discuss various group roles.*

7.7 *Discuss the importance of groups in the future.*

in this chapter

From the time we wake up each morning, we are involved in and influenced by group interactions. Individuals may act alone, but their behavior has in some way been influenced by the values, attitudes, and perceptions formed from previous group interactions.

Anita's busy schedule, discussed on the previous page, brought her in touch with many small and large groups throughout the day, ranging from personal to professional. Her experiences represent the wide range of group activities that many people with today's busy lifestyles encounter. Increased encounters with groups make the understanding of group dynamics an important part of effective human relations.

We interact in many groups daily.

A **group** consists of two or more individuals who are aware of one another, interact with one another on a regular basis, and perceive themselves to be a group. Group interaction often occurs face-to-face. Increasingly, however, groups are becoming geographically—even globally—dispersed, relying on a variety of modern communication media to interact. This reliance on technology can create minor barriers to effective interactions but can also be used to greatly facilitate communication and collaboration.

QUICK WIT

"Alone we can do so little; together we can do so much."

Helen Keller,
American author
and lecturer

Groups take many forms and evolve from many sources. However, all groups have a common thread: the purpose of satisfying organizational or individual needs. Members of a group tend to receive some degree of satisfaction from their association or they will drop out of the group. For example, a dissatisfied member of a work group may ask for a transfer to some other department or simply resign to find another job.

Groups satisfy organizational and individual needs.

A group can be as small as Anita's family at breakfast or as large as a U.S. Marine Corps battalion. The ability to function effectively in any group setting is important. The focus of this chapter will be on the expected behaviors and problems you may encounter when dealing with groups.

*Fast*Chat

1. Discuss the variety of group settings Anita encountered throughout the day.

2. What new forms of electronic communication have you used in your group interactions?

The formation of groups in the workplace is natural. Groups tend to form whenever people are located close together and see and talk to one another on a frequent basis. They are then able to share ideas, opinions, and feelings and to pursue similar activities.

Work groups influence the overall behavior and performance of individuals in the workplace. The figure below illustrates the relation of behavior and morale to performance and productivity. As can be seen, the behavior of a work group does influence productivity. A positively motivated group can increase productivity. Unfortunately, a negative group can construct roadblocks to an organization's success.

> Groups influence behavior and performance at work.

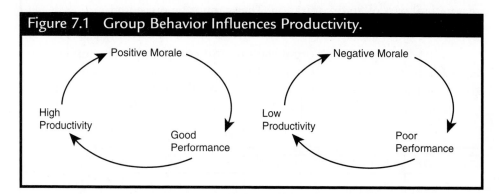

Figure 7.1   Group Behavior Influences Productivity.

This fact was first substantiated during the late 1920s when the Hawthorne experiments studied several work groups to determine the physical effects of lighting on the productivity of workers in the Hawthorne Plant of Western Electric. Two groups were observed. One experienced various changes in lighting. The other, a control group, experienced no lighting changes. The production in *both* groups rose because the attention and concern of the observers increased group morale, and morale, in turn, increased productivity. The experiment further revealed that the plant workers had definite group norms related to work output, preferred channels of communication, acceptable behavior among group members, and roles for each member.[1]

> The Hawthorne Studies provided insight into group behaviors.

Harold Leavitt, an expert on groups, summarized the findings from the Hawthorne experiment and from other studies done from the 1930s to the 1950s. The studies left little doubt about the importance of group dynamics in the workplace. Leavitt's summary (in the following box) showed that groups are important and should be taken seriously in the workplace:[2]

Importance of Work Groups

1. Small groups satisfy needs within individuals and are good for them.

2. Groups can promote creativity and innovation and solve problems.

3. Groups can make better decisions, in many instances, than individuals.

4. Group decisions are more willingly carried out because group members are committed to the decisions.

5. Group members can frequently control and discipline their members more effectively than the formal disciplinary system can.

6. Small groups lessen the impersonality of large organizations, allowing better communication and a sense of belonging.

7. Groups are a natural part of an organization. They cannot be prevented.

For these reasons, many organizations and companies use team concepts (discussed further in Chapter 8), participative management, and group decision making when appropriate. Additionally, today's workforce members expect a greater voice in decisions that affect them.

GLOBAL CONNECTION

The Royal Dutch/Shell Group of Companies is a global group of energy and petrochemical companies that operates in over 145 countries and employs more than 119,000 individuals. The company operates retail gasoline stations, explores for oil and natural gas, provides products for industry uses, generates electricity, produces petrochemicals, develops technology for hydrogen vehicles and markets, and transports and trades oil and gas. The company uses technology to connect its worldwide groups, processing 200,000 Internet-based e-mails every day. Employees who are away from their home locations use hotdesks—designated workstations for visitors. At the hotdesks, they can connect their laptops to the Shell network to check e-mails and access shared networks.

In order to ensure that the company taps the talent of all its employees, a process called GameChanger has been established. This process helps capture, nurture, and mature great ideas from employees worldwide.[3]

1. *What do you believe would happen if groups within Shell operated independently?*
2. *Does technology help lessen the impersonality of the large group? Why, or why not?*

The reasons that we join groups vary depending on our needs and which needs are strongest at any given time. Studies in the area of need satisfaction have identified the four most common reasons for joining groups as social connection, power, self-esteem, and goal accomplishment. Groups are important to both organizations and individuals.[4]

Reasons that Individuals Join Groups

Social Connection (Affiliation)
Groups can provide us with a sense of belonging and reduce our feelings of aloneness. Being a member of a social group gives us an opportunity to share ideas or to exchange information, making us feel needed and increasing our sense of worth. People tend to feel a stronger sense of affiliation when they join a group on a voluntary basis than when they are assigned to a group.

Power (Security)
The fact that there is power in numbers is no secret. Groups may give us the confidence and courage to speak out and make certain requests. This sense of power and security can also provide us with the confidence to tackle difficult tasks by removing the feeling of facing the task alone.

Self-Esteem (Ego)
People frequently join groups for self-esteem or ego satisfaction. Membership in some groups can raise our sense of being "somebody." This is especially true if the group is a prestigious one (known for its power, unique skills, social status, or innovative and profitable ideas). Few people want to be "outsiders."

Goal Accomplishment (Strategy)
Joining a group may enable us to accomplish goals more easily because we can learn skills and acquire knowledge from other members of the group. Individual members may either have their own goals and objectives or simply agree with the goals desired by other members of the group.

---

*Fast*Chat

1. Why did **both** groups in the Hawthorne Plant improve their productivity?

2. How have groups affected your performance at work or school?

3. Make a list of three groups to which you belong (such as a volunteer group, a sports team, a professional organization). Which of the four reasons above prompted you to join each group? How are your needs met by being part of a group?

Two basic types of groups exist. The **primary group** consists of family members and close friends, whereas the **secondary group** is made up of work groups and social groups. This chapter focuses on the secondary groups that are essential to workplace operations and evident in our social surroundings.

` Within the secondary group category are two types of groups, the formal group and the informal group. Both group types are important in the workplace. Although they may support similar organizational goals, they may also satisfy different needs.

FORMAL GROUPS

The **formal group** is generally designated by the organization to fulfill specific tasks or accomplish certain organizational objectives. Group members may have similar or complementary skills, responsibilities, or goals clearly related to the organizational purpose. Positions within the formal group are officially identified, usually "assigned" to individuals, and meant to provide order and predictability in the organization.

Formal groups are assigned in the workplace.

©Getty Images/PhotoDisc

Human Relations

Two kinds of formal groups exist. The first is the **functional group**, which is made up of managers and subordinates assigned to certain positions in the organizational hierarchy performing the same tasks. If you have ever held a job and reported to a supervisor, you have been a member of a functional group. Group positions or assignments in functional groups are usually permanent and serve as the skeleton of the organizational structure.

The formal group is officially set up for a task or objective.

The second kind of formal group is the **task group**, which is formed for a specific reason with members drawn from various parts of the organization to accomplish a specific purpose. Also known as a cross-functional group, this group consists of individuals who may represent two or more different functional specialty areas. For example, in a hospital, a cross-functional group is most commonly used in a trauma center's emergency room when specialties from various medical disciplines are required.

Another common example of a task group is the **committee**. Committees may be formed to develop procedures, solve problems, form recommendations for decision making, or exchange ideas and information. Committees may be considered ongoing or ad hoc.

TECHNOLOGY CONNECTION

In January 2004, *Information Week* explained how a group of architects, engineers, and builders came together to create new and innovative database applications for the building industry. This technology includes three-dimensional drawings and related project data and can help a company perform certain tasks with half the staff normally required and can greatly streamline building processes. This information-modeling software can bring design and construction projects into the 21ST century and will improve building and construction group performances in its wake. From schedulers to concrete pourers, carpenters to electricians, painters to carpet layers—each group will have a new sense of speed and efficiency as the software allows improved specifications, drawings, and models. Only cost, training, and deeply entrenched labor habits stand in the new growth path. As groups slowly succumb, there will be no turning back, and they will wonder what took them so long to convert to using software for design collaboration.[5]

1. *What other work groups could make good use of design collaboration software to improve operations or productivity? How would you suggest putting it to work?*
2. *Why do you think some groups are reluctant to convert to a collaborative effort?*
3. *What are the real benefits you see that can come from this to the builder? To the client/owner?*

Ongoing committees are relatively permanent groups that address organizational issues on a standing or continuous basis. Examples might include plant safety committees, employee promotion boards, or the local rodeo and livestock show committees.

Ad hoc committees, on the other hand, have a limited life, serving only a one-time purpose, and disband after accomplishing that purpose. Examples of an ad hoc committee might include the Warren Commission formed to investigate the assassination of President Kennedy, a committee formed to create a new corporate logo, or a committee gathered to plan a celebration for the birth of the supervisor's first child.

INFORMAL GROUPS

Informal groups are formed by individuals to satisfy personal needs.

In addition to formal groups, informal groups may exist in the organizational setting. Unless you are a loner, you no doubt are a member of one or more informal groups at work. The group members themselves create **informal groups** because the formal group seldom satisfies all of their individual needs. They form spontaneously when members with similar interests get together voluntarily. Although the informal group does not appear on the formal organization chart, it does have a powerful influence on members' behavior. Informal groups exist in all organizations and do not necessarily indicate that the formal group is inadequate or ineffective.

Informal groups may be peer groups that form because members have common interests, such as politics, recreational preferences, or religion.

Informal groups may form to share a common interest.

©CORBIS

Types of Groups

Formal	Informal
Has recognized authority.	Has little or no authority.
Has a mission or direction.	May have a mission.
Has organized structure.	Has no organizational legitimacy.
Has organizational legitimacy.	Is considered a shadow organization.

Peer groups also form to satisfy members' needs for informal job training, to provide them opportunity for status, or to help them gain information concerning the organization.

Group Identity Quiz

Identify each group as a:

A. Primary Group
B. Secondary Group
C. Formal Group
D. Functional Group
E. Task Group
F. Informal Group
G. Ongoing Committee
H. Ad hoc Committee

_____ Independent council members
_____ Company softball team
_____ UN members meeting on current issues
_____ High school friends planning a reunion
_____ Workers setting new safety policies
_____ Firefighters on a ladder truck
_____ Office workers planning a conference
_____ Doctors and nurses in a trauma center

The various types of groups are not mutually exclusive and do overlap at times. While working in an organization, you can have relationships on both personal and professional levels that fulfill your needs within the organization. Furthermore, the wider your circle of acquaintances is, the easier time you will have fulfilling your needs.

FastChat

1. Discuss the purpose of an informal group in which you have participated.

2. Identify a committee on which you have served and determine if it was ongoing or ad hoc.

Within any group there may be two leaders: a formal leader and an informal leader. The **formal leader** is the one who is officially given authority over other group members, such as a supervisor or a team captain.

Dr. Warren Bennis writes in his book, *The Secrets of Great Groups*, "…the problems we face are too complex to be solved by any one person or any one discipline. Our only chance is to bring people together from a variety of backgrounds and disciplines…in common purpose. The genius of Great Groups is that they get remarkable people—strong individual achievers—to work together to get results." Dr. Bennis believes that group leaders of these Great Groups vary widely in style and personality. Some are facilitators and some are doers, but all take on any role necessary for the group to achieve its overall goal. Effective group leaders will understand the chemistry of the group and the dynamics of the work and help provide direction and meaning.[6]

Recognizing the formal and informal leaders of a group is important.

The **informal leader** is the person within the group who is able to influence other group members because of age, knowledge, technical skills, social skills, personality, or physical strength. This leader is also known as the **emergent leader** because he or she will emerge without formal appointment but can exert more influence than the formal leader. The formal leader must be able to recognize the informal leader, determine that person's purposes and goals, and deal with them. If the formal and informal leaders have different objectives, conflict will arise.

Types of Group Leaders

Formal	Informal
Is the boss.	Is a recognizable force.
Is appointed to the position.	Is unofficially designated.
Has legitimate power.	Emerges because of being
Is officially designated.	—respected, likable, knowledgeable,
Has authority with responsibility.	technically competent, a senior team
Has a mission.	member, strong physically, or older.

---

*Fast*Chat

1. Think of a good leader and discuss why this person is so effective.

2. Have you been aware of an informal leader within a formal group? How did this situation develop, and how did it affect the group?

Groups are in a constant state of change. Some of the changing factors in group effectiveness are behavior of members, synergy (combined action or operation) of the group, its degree of cohesiveness, group norms that evolve, size of the group, status of group members, and nature of the task to be accomplished by the group.

Group effectiveness depends on behavior of individuals.

BEHAVIOR OF INDIVIDUALS

The behavior of individuals is in a constant state of fluctuation. As people begin to perceive things differently, they may alter their behavior within the group. Changes in behavior may occur for a number of reasons, such as the influence of family, peers, continued education, or acquisition of new skills. These behavior changes may have a positive or negative effect on the group. For example, you may once have been a member of a group of friends that socialized together every weekend. As individual members became involved in personal relationships, other friendships, or work or school responsibilities, the group grew smaller or broke up. The group can also cause individuals to behave differently while they are within the group setting. Some people, for instance, behave one way in a one-on-one situation and completely differently in a group atmosphere.

SYNERGY

Synergy is the cooperative interaction of two or more independent elements or individuals to create a different effect from that which they would attain separately. More simply stated, it means that, with synergy, the whole is greater than the sum of its parts.

Groups can take advantage of synergy to develop better ideas and make superior decisions through the process of brainstorming. As discussed in Chapter 5, **brainstorming** involves generating ideas freely in a group without judging the ideas at first. The group then selects the best ideas and forms a plan of action. These decisions are generally more effective because group members have a greater pool of ideas from which to draw. Studies have shown that decisions made by effective groups generally produce better results. The collective creativity of the group increases the number of alternative solutions generated, and group consensus assures commitment from individual group members. The effort is more likely to become a self-fulfilling prophecy.

Additionally, our involvement as group members in the decision-making process enhances our feelings of worth (as contributors) and of belonging to the group (as members). These are but a few of the benefits of using groups when making decisions.

COHESIVENESS

Another of the factors influencing a group's behavior is cohesiveness. **Cohesiveness** is the degree to which group members are of one mind and act as one body. In general, the more cohesive a group is, the more effective it is, and, as the group becomes more successful, it becomes even more inseparable. This effect occurs because cohesive group members stick together, supporting and encouraging one another. Also, this support helps reduce stress for group members, leading to greater job satisfaction.

Group cohesiveness develops through a number of factors, one of which is group size. Smaller groups tend to be more cohesive because they can readily communicate and exchange ideas, goals, and purposes.

Similarity of the individuals in a group is also a factor in cohesiveness. The more that individuals share similar values, backgrounds, and ages, the more cohesive they tend to be. Sometimes groups become more cohesive because of outside pressures. The "It's you and me against the world!" attitude draws members together to support and assist each other.

The more individuals are similar, the greater the cohesiveness.

Human Relations

Synergy and cohesiveness can help groups develop better ideas and make superior decisions.

©Digital Vision

GROUP NORMS

Another factor that influences group effectiveness, **group norms**, are shared values about the kinds of behaviors that are acceptable to the group. These norms are standards of behavior that each member is expected to follow—similar to rules that apply to team members. They develop slowly over time and usually relate to those matters of most importance to the group as a whole. Expected conformity to these norms applies only to behavior and does not affect private thoughts and feelings.

Nonconformity, or **deviance**, from group norms may provoke obvious displays of displeasure, ranging from rejection to physical violence or vicious harassment. Of course, if the group in question is a business and the deviance involves breaking company rules, the signs of displeasure may be formal and might include poor reviews, docked pay, reprimands, and even termination. However, in smaller groups, displeasure is more likely to take the form of more informal sanctions.[8]

> Norms determine group behavior.

CASE STUDIES IN THE NEWS

University of North Carolina Coach Roy Williams was named one of the 2004 Tar Heels of the Year and is one of the top winning coaches in the school's coaching history. He believes many young ball players want to win but have to learn to fight off selfish, individual desires. For example, he says, "Michael Jordan may have wanted to win, to take the big shot and make the big play. But he was totally able to pass the ball to Paxson or Kerr and let them make those winning shots that won the championships." Although some say Jordan should have taken those shots for himself, Jordan was part of the group—the team—who wanted to win. Williams says, "Michael Jordan was selfish, there's no doubt in my mind, but great players fight that off."[9]

1. *Why is it important for a standout member of a group to fight off selfish, individual desires?*
2. *When would it be acceptable for a group member to demonstrate his or her special skills?*

The following list represents a few of the more common types of informal **sanctions**, actions taken to force compliance with established norms.[10] Each is considered in the context of a work group of four administrative assistants, of whom only one, James, smokes. James has disregarded the suggestions from the other three assistants that he not smoke during work hours.

Common Sanctions Provoked by Deviance

1. *Ostracism* (cold-shoulder treatment). The nonsmokers have quit inviting James to lunch with them and do not include him in their coffee breaks and informal discussions.

2. *Verbal criticisms.* The nonsmokers frequently make critical comments to James about his clothes smelling like cigarettes and about the time he wastes on smoke breaks.

3. *Open ridicule.* The nonsmokers have started imitating James, both in front of him and behind his back, blowing exaggerated smoke rings in the air.

4. *Malicious gossip.* The nonsmokers begin gossiping about James's actions both on and off the job.

5. *Harassment.* The nonsmokers begin to save the pleasant tasks for themselves, giving James the most undesirable jobs to do.

6. *Intimidation.* The nonsmokers exaggerate James's mistakes or inaccurate work and threaten to report any problems to superiors.

The type of sanction taken may depend on how important group members perceive the violated norm to be. Some norms are considered more important than others. **Critical norms** are considered essential to the survival and effectiveness of the group as a whole. The sanctions for violating critical norms can be severe, with physical violence sometimes used in extreme cases. Personal safety and career success may depend on an individual's ability to operate within the established acceptable group norms.[11]

Other norms are considered **peripheral norms** because they are not perceived as damaging to the group and its members. The sanctions for violating these norms are less severe than those for critical norms but can be just as meaningful.[12]

We learn about group norms in various ways. In formal groups, we learn norms through formal orientation programs, classroom training, and on-the-job training. In informal groups, we grasp group norms through conversations with other group members and observation of their behavior.

Often group norms enhance group effectiveness. For instance, the group may ostracize or criticize members who fail to do their fair share of the work or fail to behave in a way that is constructive on the job. These individuals are considered "social loafers" and will be punished if they do not pull their weight within the group. The individuals may react to this unpleasant treatment by increasing their productivity or in some way changing their behavior.

Nonconformists at work can expect sanctions.

Unfortunately, group norms sometimes prevent members from working toward the goals of the organization. For instance, an assembly line worker may not work as fast as possible because coworkers would reject him. In this case, the sanctions and rewards of the informal group are stronger than those of the formal organization.

Group norms can become counter-productive.

If you become the target of group sanctions, evaluate your situation carefully. Are the sanctions being applied because you have not followed group norms meant to increase organizational effectiveness? If so, determine why you are behaving the way you are and how you can change your behavior so that you contribute to the effectiveness of the group.

You may choose how to handle sanctions.

If you determine that the sanctions being applied are counterproductive to the organization and your career, you have several choices. You can conform to the group norms (which may jeopardize your career), attempt through persuasion and the use of effective communication skills to persuade group members to change the norms, tolerate the sanctions, or ask for a transfer to another area that would limit your interaction with the group. After all, norms are simply meant to keep a group functioning as a system instead of as a collection of individuals.

GROUP SIZE

The size of a group will also influence its effectiveness. Studies have shown that the preferred group size for maximum effectiveness in problem solving and decision making is five or seven members. Groups of any larger size begin to experience problems with communication and coordination. Groups with even numbers of members may have greater difficulty in obtaining a majority opinion if members are equally divided in their opinions. Not having a person to act as a tiebreaker can cause increased tensions. The uneven-numbered group size offers an easy solution to this problem. The chart on page 190 identifies the characteristics of group interaction in certain group sizes.[13]

QUICK WIT
"It's a sad commentary on one's competitive nature if you're happy to be the top man on a sinking ship."
Jim Cleamons,
Assistant Coach,
Los Angeles Lakers

Characteristics of Group Sizes

Fewer than five	More than seven
• Fewer people to share task responsibilities.	• Fewer opportunities to participate.
• More personal discussion.	• Members feel inhibited.
• More participation.	• Domination by aggressive members.
• More convenient for frequent interaction.	• Tendency for "cliques" to form.
• Increased tension among group members.	• More diverse opinions shared.
• Greater sense of satisfaction.	• Greater likelihood of absenteeism and turnover.
• Greater cohesion.	• Coordination of activities more difficult.
	• Less cohesion.
	• Team effect lost.
	• Individual identities tend to be retained.

STATUS OF GROUP MEMBERS

Success, education, possessions, and physical appearance are factors that can contribute to a person's status within a group.

The status of group members can also influence group effectiveness. What gives a person status may vary from group to group. In some groups, higher social class and economic success may confer higher status. In these groups, members who are financially successful, come from "good" families, or have college degrees may have more status. They may be given more respect, and other group members may pay more attention to them. People in white-collar jobs are often viewed as having higher status than those in blue-collar positions. Similarly, salaried workers may be seen as having higher status than those paid by the hour.

Clothing and cars can also make a difference in how much status people are perceived to have. In some groups, individuals who dress fashionably in expensive clothes and drive costly cars are perceived as having higher status. In other groups, the reverse may be true; expensive clothing and cars would be considered showy.

Physical appearance is another factor that can influence perception of status. Some studies have suggested that people who are overweight may be viewed negatively. Individuals who are tall are sometimes seen as being more competent and powerful.

Status at work is conveyed in a variety of ways. For instance, those in higher-status positions may have an office with a window, a larger or corner office, reserved parking, and nicer office furniture and decorations. Executives may even have special dining rooms separate from other employees or have memberships in private clubs. Groups whose members have high status are more effective because they are able to get things done.

NATURE OF THE TASK

The last of the factors influencing group effectiveness is the nature of the task itself. When a decision is required on a subject that is simple and uncomplicated, a highly homogeneous group whose members have similar backgrounds and compatible beliefs may be best.

When the task is complex and difficult, group members should be of dissimilar backgrounds and drawn from a variety of sources. This makeup will ensure diversity of ideas, foster creativity among the members, and result in a wider selection of alternatives from which to choose a solution.

To foster creativity for complex tasks, group members should be diverse.

©Getty Images/PhotoDisc

*Fast*Chat

1. What types of sanctions have you seen administered in group situations?

2. When you have been in a large group, did people act differently when asked questions? Did anyone raise a hand and offer answers or opinions right away? Did you feel differently? If so, explain the feelings you had and how they influenced your behavior.

Wasting time, groupthink, and role ambiguity worsen group decisions.

Chapter 5 discussed group decision-making techniques and benefits. In general, groups make better decisions than individuals because of the increased input and suggestions. However, three factors may negatively influence group decision making and must be managed carefully in a work group. These factors are wasting time, groupthink, and role ambiguity.

WASTING TIME

The group decision-making process is time consuming. If it is not handled correctly, it can waste time and cause costly delays, indecisiveness, and diluted answers. For this reason, groups must be handled with skill.

Because the group decision-making process is time consuming, groups should not make emergency or small decisions.

Not all situations lend themselves to group decision making. For example, an emergency situation such as an office fire is hardly the time to call the office staff together for ideas on how the fire should be extinguished or who will call 911. The fire chief, barking out orders, gets the job done more effectively. Or perhaps the decision is such an easy one that it needs only a quick fix. For situations like this, making the decision yourself is certainly acceptable.

If it is not handled correctly, the group decision-making process can waste time and cause costly delays.

"Wow! This meeting lasted longer than I thought. It appears the year is now 2053."

©2002 Ted Goff www.tedgoff.com

However, if the situation lends itself to group decision making, using a group process is the preferred method. For example, if office policy is to be revised and enough time remains to seek office staff opinions, you would do well to apply the group problem-solving recommendations outlined in Chapter 5.

GROUPTHINK

Irving Janis identified the phenomenon of **groupthink** and defined it as "the process of deriving negative results from group decision-making efforts as a result of in-group pressures." Through groupthink, a group may be led to a conclusion without fully exploring or even considering creative alternatives.[14]

For example, a supervisor may call a meeting of subordinates to determine how a new office procedure is to be implemented and start the meeting with the statement, "I believe the best way for us to do this is to…; don't you agree?" The pressure to accept the leader's approach and to retain group cohesion results in a "rubber stamp" of what may appear as a predetermined conclusion. The supervisor may even interpret the group's silence as a resounding and unanimous acceptance of the "proposed" approach rather than an attempt at retaining group cohesion.

Our peers, especially those with more status or greater expertise, influence us all. We should, however, try to avoid falling victim to groupthink.

ROLE AMBIGUITY

Roles of individual members are readily apparent when the group is a formal one with certain positions identified. This formal identification helps to define the role an individual is expected to play. However, in informal groups, these roles may not be as clearly designated. Expected behavior may never be stated or in any way formalized. **Role ambiguity** occurs when individuals are uncertain about what role they are to fill or what is expected of them. All of us experience some initial feelings of role ambiguity when we join new groups. The following chart on group member roles defines several of the roles most frequently expected in group situations.

Group Member Roles

Information Seeker: Asks for facts, feelings, suggestions, and ideas about the group's concern.

Information Giver: Gives information about the group's concerns, stating facts and feelings; gives ideas and makes suggestions.

Coordinator: Pulls all the group ideas and suggestions together and recommends a decision or conclusion for the group to consider.

Gatekeeper: Keeps communication channels open; facilitates participation.

Harmonizer: Reduces tension and reconciles differences.

Observer: Provides feedback on the group's progress; remains neutral and uninvolved in the process.

Follower: Goes along with the group; offers no resistance to suggestions or ideas.

Blocker: Resists any suggestions or ideas of the group; acts negatively toward group purpose and members.

Avoider: Resists interacting with group members; keeps apart from interaction.

Dominator: Forces opinions, ideas, and desires on the other group members; manipulates group behavior by asserting status or authority, using flattery, interrupting others, or other aggressive and obnoxious measures.

You may recognize some of these roles from groups in which you have been involved. You may recognize roles that you have played in group interactions. Many of the roles are important in making the group highly effective and productive. Some, however, can be destructive and should be managed by the group leader, a facilitator, or the other members themselves. These roles are also common in workplace teams, as will be discussed further in Chapter 8.

*Fast*Chat

1. Have you experienced "groupthink"? Give an example and discuss how it may have been prevented.

2. What other pitfalls in group interactions have you experienced?

3. Which of the group member roles have you played in group interactions? Which are you most comfortable performing?

In a world that is faster, harder, leaner, more downsized, merged, and streamlined than ever before, you might expect the demands of the work environment to curb the appetite for group interactions. In reality, the opposite is true. People will naturally band together to increase their effectiveness. Group interaction will become more important, and the ability to work well in groups will be a vital part of your career success. Indeed, competing in the "knowledge era" environment will require continual shifts from traditional thinking about the way we work.

One of the expected trends will be an increased shift in the types of groups toward an approach called **Communities of Practice** (COPS). Considered critical for a knowledge-based company, COPS are small groups of peers who have worked together over a period of time, have a common sense of purpose, and a strong need to know what each other group member knows. They are not a team, not a task force, and probably not identified as an official or authorized group. Their benefit to the organization derives from their potential to overcome the inherent problems of a slow-moving traditional hierarchy in a fast-moving virtual environment, their potential to share information outside the traditional structural boundaries, and their ability to develop and maintain long-term organizational memory. All of these benefits are increasingly important in today's changing economy.

Knowledge workers will continue to be influential and highly respected work groups in the near future. Highly creative and talented employees are already sought by companies to share their innovative new ideas with others in the company—often even to change a corporate culture that may need a makeover. Some examples of companies with a strong base of knowledge workers would include Dell Computers, Microsoft, General Electric, Hewlett-Packard, and Sun Microsystems. Businesses are learning to provide knowledge-sharing, interactive-learning environments for workers as a means of retaining these employees.

Knowledge workers are valuable assets and make their livings in the creation and exploitation of information for profit. Intellectual properties will become closely guarded as work groups and companies vie for their winning edge. Applying sound human relations skills when managing groups of knowledge workers will be important in retaining their desired advantage.[15] Although the systems, methods, and tools used in group interactions may evolve, groups will remain a vital part of our environment.

Further proof of the growing importance of groups is the computer software that has been developed to facilitate the use of groups. Sometimes called "**groupware**," this class of technology relies on modern computer networks, such as e-mail, newsgroups, videophones, or chat to improve group interactions. Specifically, these computer aids are designed to improve meeting capabilities, global group interactions, knowledge worker exchanges, and other group interactions. The software simplifies problems encountered by groups trying to work in long-distance, multicultural settings. It allows groups of colleagues attached to a local area network to organize their activities and is sometimes called work group productivity software.

Some examples include chat groups that allow group members to meet online with controlled access and have direct transcripts of the conversations provided in multilingual translations. Screen sharing is another example, which allows a single user's application to be viewed or shared by multiple users. It can combine the input from users or limit input to only one user at a time. Collaborative writing allows multiple people composing text together to access a database or document.[16]

Describe experiences you have had with any type of groupware and how it improved the capabilities of your group.

*Fast*Chat

1. Why does closely guarded information present challenges for today's groups of knowledge workers?

2. How can you prepare to meet these challenges in our competitive and ever-changing work environments?

3. How can groupware facilitate the interaction of a group?

CHAPTER SUMMARY

We all interact with a variety of groups on a day-to-day basis. Organizations encourage groups because they increase productivity and effective decision making. Individuals join groups because they fulfill needs such as power, affiliation, self-esteem, and goal accomplishment.

Secondary groups can be formal groups, which the organization creates for certain purposes, or informal ones, which spontaneously develop because individuals work close to one another. Each group may have two leaders, a formal and an informal (emergent) one.

Groups are influenced by many factors that can affect their productivity, such as behavior of individuals, synergy, group cohesiveness, group norms, group size, status of members, and nature of the group task. Although groups do, in general, make better decisions than individuals, pitfalls occur. Groups can be time wasters, give in to groupthink, and produce role ambiguity. Small decisions and emergency decisions are best left to individuals. In the future, groups will continue to evolve and to be a vital part of our collective work environments.

Key Terms

group
primary group
secondary group
formal group
functional group
task group
committee
ongoing committee
ad hoc committee
informal group
formal leader
informal leader
emergent leader
synergy
brainstorming
cohesiveness
group norms
deviance
sanctions
critical norms
peripheral norms
groupthink
role ambiguity
communities of practice (COPS)
groupware

REVIEW QUESTIONS

1. What is a group?

2. What is the importance of studying group dynamics?

3. Why do people join groups?

4. What are the two types of formal groups?

5. Why is it important to recognize the informal or emergent leader in a group?

6. What are the factors that influence group effectiveness?

7. What are the pitfalls of group decision making? Explain.

8. What roles are open in a group setting?

9. Why is it important today at work to use groups in the decision-making process?

DISCUSSION QUESTIONS

1. Examine the opening Focus scenario and identify the various types of groups Anita encounters.

2. Think of a group to which you belong, such as a social club, church group, civic group, or work group.

    a. What type of group is it?

    b. Who is the formal leader?

    c. Is there an informal or emergent leader? Who is it?

    d. Why is this individual recognized as the emergent leader?

    e. What was the reason that you became a member of this group?

3. Give some examples of group norms and describe the groups to which they belong. How might these norms be violated? What would happen if the norms were violated?

4. Discuss the benefits to the formal group leader of identifying the informal leader. Explore the possible negative effects of not identifying this individual.

5. Identify the important roles in group dynamics. Which of these roles do you play most often?

CHAPTER PROJECT

Choose a movie that you feel demonstrates aspects of large and small group interactions discussed in this chapter. Choose the movie carefully. Be certain that it illustrates a variety of group characteristics. Examples are war films with groups ranging from squadrons to close personal friendships, films about sports teams or musical groups, crime capers, or films about explorers or survivors of a disaster. While you watch the film, take notes about the different types of groups, types of interactions, leadership styles, types of role-playing, and any other factors you may recognize as relevant to this chapter material. Prepare a written description of these findings. This is not an invitation to play movie critic. *Do not critique the movie.* Whether or not you liked it is not important. Instead, describe the groups and their characteristics. Be prepared to discuss your findings in a small group of your classmates.

APPLICATIONS

In small groups, analyze the following situations.

Who's the Boss?

Robert had just been promoted into his first supervisory position. Initially, a high degree of camaraderie existed among the eight workers in his office. The lead analyst, Sandy, had a long-standing record of good performance, knowledge of the program requirements, and loyalty to the organization. Sandy had become a guiding force to the junior analysts, offering advice on certain topics and showing them the established office procedures of the job.

Robert seemed somewhat uneasy with the guidance being given by Sandy. He frequently challenged her decisions and questioned the approaches that she recommended to the junior analysts. Obviously, he did not trust Sandy. Rather than relying on her knowledge and experience, Robert set out to gain absolute control and change the general office operations.

It didn't take long for the junior analysts to get the picture. After all, they did not want to do a job twice—the way Sandy suggested and then again the way Robert would require it. Eventually, Sandy was left alone and was seldom made to feel a part of the group. The other analysts still went to lunch but seldom invited her. The feeling of being an "outcast" was a painful one to her.

After several months of seeing the situation deteriorate further, more distance coming between her and the other office members, and feeling out of place, Sandy asked to be moved to some other position within the company. After all, her own work reputation and career safety were being threatened.

1. Into what type of group was Robert promoted—formal or informal? What type of leader was he—formal or informal?

2. Was there an informal or emergent leader in the group? What made this person a leader?

3. What factors influenced this group's effectiveness?

4. What could Robert have done differently to minimize the group's disharmony? What could Sandy have done to assure continued group cohesiveness?

The Explosive Commission

TEAMWORK

The recent explosion at the chemical plant was the worst disaster in the company's 20-year history, killing five workers. A committee of seven people was immediately formed to study the causes of the accident and prescribe protective measures to eliminate any future occurrence. The committee members were carefully selected from a wide cross section of appropriate representatives.

Ralph Windham was brought in from the company's corporate head-quarters to head the committee. He had 47 years of chemical plant experience and had often been used as a troubleshooter in hazardous cases. Derek Soong, the plant manager, had been personally involved in a similar accident with a different company. He was considered the expert in chemical plant accident investigation and would bring a great deal of experience to the committee's activities. Derek was to be the local company representative. The plant's local legal representative, Carol Harnett, would be a member, and, of course, the president of the local union, Tom Filbert, would be representing the employees.

Great consideration was given to including other members of the community. The chief surgeon of the local hospital, Dr. Shardar Kahn, was appointed because of the enormous involvement of rescue teams and medical attendants. The mayor, Sharon Wilson, and Larry Brown from the Chamber of Commerce would represent the community and its members.

After an extensive investigation, the committee's final report was issued almost nine months after the date of the accident. The report cleared the company of any wrongdoing. From the beginning, Ralph Windham's influence on the results was obvious. After all, he was the senior member, the chair, and a highly respected person throughout the chemical industry for his expertise and knowledge.

Other members appeared to have voiced little or no opinion, and the recommendation showed obvious bias toward corporate reasoning. The industry and community members winced with anger and astonishment that the final outcome was not more representative of all members' interests and fairer in its summation and recommendation.

1. What three factors most heavily influenced the formation and selection of the committee?

2. Which factor undermined the committee, and why did it happen? How might this outcome have been prevented?

ADDITIONAL READINGS AND RESOURCES

Bennis, Warren. "The Secrets of Great Groups." *Leader to Leader*, 3 (Winter 1997): 29–33.

Corey, Marianne Schneider and Gerald Corey. *Groups: Process and Practice.* Belmont, CA: Wadsworth Publishing, 2001.

Lawler, Edward E. *Treat People Right*, San Francisco: Jossey-Bass Publishers, September 2003.

O'Leary, Richard. *Leading Innovation and Change: Corning Incorporated Best Practice Case Study*, Boston: Best Practice Publications, Summer 2003.

Stonecipher, Harry. "What Goes Into Flawless Execution?" *Boeing Frontiers*, March 2004.

Surowiecki, James. *The Wisdom of Crowds.* New York: Doubleday, 2004.

For additional resources, refer to the web site for this text: school.cengage.com/career/dalton

CHAPTER 8
OBJECTIVES

Teamwork:
Becoming a Team Player

After studying this chapter, you should be able to:

8.1 *Define a team.*

8.2 *Understand the concept of teambuilding.*

8.3 *Identify the types of teams in use today and the stages of team development.*

8.4 *Name the elements necessary to build an effective team.*

8.5 *Discuss the benefits and drawbacks of teamwork and how to be an effective team member.*

8.6 *Know when the team approach is appropriate.*

8.7 *Explain team conflict and how it can be resolved.*

focus

What's the secret to a great team? *Fast Company* asked several high-profile leaders, and their answers addressed a range of teamwork issues. Tony DiCicco, head coach of the U.S. Women's World Cup Champion Soccer Team, says that a successful team requires a shared culture of preparedness, focus, and respect. Millard Fuller of Habitat for Humanity feels that the most essential ingredients are a cause that everyone agrees on and preparation. Ray Oglethorpe of AOL Technologies says a team should have no more than seven to nine people to form strong connections between team members. Janine Bay of the Ford Motor Co. finds that diversity and a great facilitator are the keys to a successful team. Martha Rogers of the Peppers and Rogers Group says that good teams require a supportive corporate culture. Thomas Leppert of the Turner Corporation says his teams require mutual respect among team members and a common vision about where the team is going. According to Michael Leinbach of the Kennedy Space Center, the most critical element is an open channel of communication between team members.[1]

Think about a team of which you have been a part. What factors made your team successful? What factors made them struggle?

in this chapter

Throughout your life, you will be a member of many different teams, some limited to a business environment, some related to other areas of your life. We commonly think of a team as a group of individuals doing the same activity or task, such as playing a sport. In today's work environment, however, teams may include representatives from a variety of disciplines, departments, or even different lines of business who come together to achieve common goals and objectives that will enhance all their varied areas. When an identifiable group of people are working together toward a common goal and are dependent upon each other to realize that goal, they may be referred to as a **team**. If any of these factors are missing, they may simply be a *group* of individuals that come together with their own agenda and no common purpose.

Teamwork is the work performed by the combined effort of several disciplines for maximum effectiveness in achieving common goals.[2] An example of a team performing teamwork is the group of 16 anesthesiologists, residents, fellows, and nurses at Johns Hopkins Children's Center who successfully separated conjoined twins.[3]

CASE STUDIES IN THE NEWS

Recently profiled in *HR Magazine*, consultant Mark Samuel trains employers to create a work climate that fosters *experiential teambuilding*. Workers take the time to know their team players, developing a personal level of trust through physical and mental activities that build rapport, increase morale, and enhance productivity. An objective facilitator helps team members learn from each other, reveal hidden team talents, and seek hidden conflicts that can sabotage success. Experiential teambuilding assists in managing conflict, overcoming power struggles, clarifying roles, breaking down territorialism, developing effective communication strategies, improving performance execution, and increasing team morale. Developing this type of "team spirit" allows people to support each other because they care about each person on the team and their success.[4]

1. *Describe a work environment with which you are familiar. Was it conducive to teamwork? Why, or why not?*
2. *What experiential teambuilding exercises have you used in a team? Were they helpful?*

©Getty Images/PhotoDisc

Teamwork is a key to improved quality, productivity, and efficiency.

Companies are increasingly using teams to speed up the cycle time in product development and get a better product out to customers faster. To accomplish this, companies assemble a team of marketing, design engineering, quality, and manufacturing people to attack the problem from the beginning. The old process involved having one group do the design, hand it off to the manufacturing team, and then forward the work to the quality crew. The last step was to have marketing people decide how to sell or market the final product. This process is slow and costly. With the team concept, product designs and quality are greatly improved, and total product cycle time is reduced.

*Fast*Chat

Read the Quick Wit by Eileen Hudson.

1. What can you do to ensure that you continue to learn throughout your career?

2. Often people refuse to do tasks saying, "It's not my job." Is this attitude acceptable in a workplace team? Why, or why not?

3. Discuss ways you have benefited from being involved in teams and what you learned through the experience.

Human Relations

Effective teamwork doesn't just happen. It evolves through the deliberate efforts of team members working to strengthen the group's purpose. For this reason many organizations have begun a conscientious effort to develop competent teams through teambuilding. **Teambuilding** is a series of activities designed to help work groups solve problems, accomplish work goals, and function more effectively through teamwork. Constructive teambuilding requires that each team participant accept the team goals and objectives and take ownership of the results. In this way, a high degree of cohesion develops within the group, and the open environment improves the quality of problem solving and decision making. **Synergy** (as you will remember from Chapter 7) involves cooperative action to achieve an effect that is greater than the sum of the individual effects.

QUICK WIT

"You can get anything you want out of life if you just help enough other people get what they want."

Zig Ziglar,
Author and
motivational speaker

CASE STUDIES IN THE NEWS

The De La Salle Spartans lost a football game on December 7, 1991, but not again for the next 11 straight seasons: 138 victories, 0 defeats. Coach Ladouceur leads his small high school team as if it is a business team. He believes that size and talent gaps can be offset by intelligence and quickness, of which he has plenty on his team. He delegates to his line "managers," trusting the players to do what is required. He builds a team with soul, feeling that a team's culture should be one of commitment and responsibility. During the off-season, players go camping and river rafting and do community service volunteering. During game season, the team attends chapel for readings and songs and declarations of specific game expectations. After practice, there is dinner at a player's home, chapel, and team time. Coach Ladouceur says, "If a team has no soul, you're just wasting your time."[5]

1. *What do you think has led to the success of this team?*
2. *What business concepts are being taught to the team members? How will these lessons benefit them in later life?*
3. *Discuss your team experiences that may have involved leaders who showed trust of the team members. How was that trust shown and how did the leader's actions make you feel and perform?*

The team concept, which involves the application of teambuilding and teams bonding together for effective teamwork, is a generic term used to describe the workings of teams in achieving common goals and objectives, with all their human relations complexities. The concept is not new to the work environment.

Quick tip

Try this activity to build trust among team members:

1. One team member puts on a blindfold.
2. Another team member and a spotter lead the team member through an obstacle maze, taking care not to allow the blindfolded member to hit one of the barriers.
3. Each member takes a turn wearing the blindfold and leading the individual.

After the exercise, discuss what happened by answering the following questions:

1. How did you feel when you were blindfolded and had to depend on others to take care of you?
2. Are you able to accept losing control and trusting others on the job?
3. What, as team members, can you do to develop trust?

FastChat

1. Which concepts of group dynamics from Chapter 7 are elements of successful teambuilding? Unsuccessful?
2. Is it your responsibility in teamwork to achieve synergy? What could you do to make this happen?
3. Think of times when you functioned as a leader of a team. Could you tell when the team bonded? How?

Human Relations

Teams have been used since people began to perform complex tasks. The early Egyptians, for instance, used large teams to construct the pyramids. Major corporations in the United States began experimenting with team concepts on a small scale as early as the 1920s and 1930s with the introduction of problem-solving teams.

TYPES OF TEAMS

Many types of teams exist today, and an organization may have several types operating at the same time. A few of the more common types of teams are described below.

Project teams are groups that come together to accomplish a specific project. When the project is over, the team disbands. Project teams are frequently used in the engineering and construction industries to design and construct buildings or plants. Upon completion, the team disbands and team members are generally assigned to other teams.[6]

Self-directed work teams are teams that, to a certain extent, manage themselves. They may or may not have a leader. Often, these teams are responsible for selecting and hiring their members, reviewing member performance, and making decisions regarding corrective action. A common example is a faculty team from several departments that develops a new cross-disciplinary academic program.[7]

Continuous improvement teams focus on continuous process improvement. They are also known as quality circles or kaizen teams. For instance, employees in a manufacturing facility may meet together regularly to discuss how to improve product quality and speed production.[8]

Functional work teams involve employees from one particular function, such as accounting or human resources, who work together to serve various groups. For example, a team consisting of computer programmers, network specialists, and hardware installation experts may work together to install a computer system for a client or for a new location of their own organization.[9] A **cross-functional team** is composed of individuals from two or more different functional areas. They are commonly used to design and bring a new product to market and ensure its long-run success.[10]

The number, types, and function of teams has steadily grown. Teams have become an integral part of the operation of any large organization that hopes to remain competitive in today's marketplace. While there is still room for innovation and individual genius, processes and businesses alike have become increasingly complex, so input from individuals with a

QUICK WIT
"You cannot build character and courage by taking away a man's initiative and independence. You cannot help men permanently by doing for them what they should be doing for themselves."
Abraham Lincoln, American President

Figure 8.1 The world abounds with teams.

quality teams, *functional teams*, cross-functional teams, DESIGN TEAMS, customer support teams, **work teams**, rank-and-file teams, *project teams*, planning teams, COMMITTEES, task forces, advisory teams, steering groups, action teams, **flat teams**, **hierarchical teams**, *leader-led teams*, leader-less teams, TEAMS AS SMALL *as two people* and as large **as 20,000 people**

wide range of expertise is vital for organizations. Companies are revamping their ways of doing business to include more diverse employee resources and team efforts to cope with the rapidly changing global economic environment.

RESULTS OF TEAMWORK

The team concept is ever more important in an increasingly competitive global market.

Studies indicate that work-team systems that allow workers real participation in decision making produce better quality products, improve efficiency, increase productivity, and yield more satisfied employees. Workers who are a part of a team find their jobs more rewarding and stimulating than the usual fragmented or production-line job. Additionally, today's workers are demanding a say in decisions that affect their work environment and want greater responsibility. Building productive teams is, therefore, increasingly important in today's organizations.

TECHNOLOGY CONNECTION

Cornelius Grove, of Grovewell Global Leadership Solutions, raises the following e-mail questions for teams whose members may not work in the same location.[11]
Topics: Which topics are appropriate for e-mail? Which need to be handled in person or over the telephone? What about jokes? Off-color language?
Urgency: What do the terms "ASAP" or "urgent" mean?
Frequency: How frequently should members use e-mail?
Participation: Does every team member need to see every e-mail?
Respect: How can team members demonstrate respect?
Time of day: Should there be a blackout period when e-mails are not sent or received?

1. *How can these considerations be used to improve e-mail communication?*
2. *What rules do your teams follow when sending e-mail communications?*

Teamwork Lessons from Geese

Fact	**Lesson**
1. As each goose flaps its wings, it creates an "uplift" for the birds that follow. By flying in a "V" formation, the whole flock adds 71 percent greater flying range than if each bird flew alone.	1. People who share a common direction and sense of company can get where they are going quicker and easier because they are traveling on the thrust of one another.
2. When a goose falls out of formation, it suddenly feels the drag and resistance of flying alone. It quickly moves back into formation to take advantage of the lifting power of the bird immediately in front of it.	2. If we have as much sense as a goose, we stay in formation with those headed where we want to go. We are willing to accept their help and give our help to others.
3. When the lead goose tires, it rotates back into the formation and another goose flies to the point position.	3. It pays to take turns, doing the hard tasks and sharing leadership. As with geese, people are dependent on each other's skills, capabilities, and unique arrangements of gifts, talents or resources.
4. The geese flying in formation honk to encourage those up front to keep up their speed.	4. We need to make sure our honking is encouraging. In teams where there is encouragement, the production is much greater. The power of encouragement (to stand by one's heart or core values and encourage the heart and core of others) is the quality of honking we seek.
5. When a goose gets sick, wounded, or shot down, two geese drop out of formation and follow it down to help and protect it. They stay with it until it dies or is able to fly again. Then, they launch out with another formation or catch up with the flock.	5. If we have as much sense as geese, we will stand by each other in difficult times as well as when we are strong.

Source: These popular lessons are thought to be based on the work of Pastor Milton Olson and developed for a sermon by Baltimore school Superintendent Dr. Robert McNeish.[12]

Those who work as a team with a common direction and a support system can make great strides.

©Getty Images/PhotoDisc

STAGES OF TEAM DEVELOPMENT

Teams mature through several growth stages. The four stages of team development are forming, storming, norming, and performing.

A team is considered mature when its members help each other and address problems that impede its work. Initially, team members go through a "feeling out" stage, learning what each has to contribute and how to interact with one another. As they continue to work together, they become more comfortable with the team effort, their performance improves, and eventually the team becomes highly effective and focused on the common purpose of achieving team goals. Typically, a team will pass through four stages of development: forming, storming, norming, and performing.[13]

Stages of Team Development

1. **Forming:** Individuals begin to identify what the team goals are and how their own goals may fit with the team. They decide how much time, energy, and effort they wish to commit to the team and become acquainted with other team members. Everyone behaves politely and seldom takes strong stands at this stage.

2. **Storming:** Members may engage in constructive conflicts and disagreements. Individuals may question the team's direction and progress. Some will resist task assignments or attempt power plays to gain control. Some may display frustration with the team's activities. Others become stronger through listening and handling challenges and complaints. Members learn how to deal effectively with disagreements and establish a better balance and clear direction. Real progress occurs.

3. **Norming:** Team members pursue responsibilities and work toward team goals. The team works as a whole to resolve problems, establish action plans, and focus on getting things done. Individuals develop negotiation skills, deal with ambiguity, cooperate, and communicate effectively.

4. **Performing:** Individuals actively help each other complete assignments and tasks in order to achieve team goals. Team members develop a sense of trust and commitment at both individual and team levels. Members acknowledge cooperation and performance, value learning, and imagine future objectives. The team is willing to accept creativity that may lead toward greater productivity. Not all teams reach this stage.

---

*Fast*Chat

1. In what types of teams have you been a member? What has been the impact of teamwork on the members? On the organization?

2. In what stage of development are the teams of which you are a part? How can you tell?

When people cooperate in a true team effort, powerful results are achieved. Several key ingredients are necessary to ensure the kind of synergy that a competent team can produce. The box on the next page labeled "Elements Needed to Build an Effective Team" lists those ingredients.

Studies have shown that employees like participating in group or team activities and appreciate opportunities to contribute their ideas and knowledge toward improving operations. Increasing an employee's sense of responsibility translates directly into greater job satisfaction and loyalty.

Working as a team requires new management methods. It does not mean that the formal leader never leads. Today's formal leader must learn to allow others to assume a guiding role when appropriate. Team leader responsibilities are listed below:

QUICK WIT

"Never doubt that a small group of thoughtful, committed citizens can change the world."

Margaret Mead,
Anthropologist and
social scientist

Formal team leaders must be willing to share control.

Responsibilities of a Team Leader

1. Assign the right people to the right task.

2. Make expectations clear.

3. Encourage participation by nudging, assisting, helping, and answering questions.

4. See the big picture.

5. Plan.

6. Involve "rookie" employees in the team to bring a fresh outlook or approach.

7. Provide encouragement, motivation, and spirit.

8. Administer rewards for performance, including positive reinforcement and acknowledgement of contributions.

9. Remove roadblocks and obstacles that keep the team from performing.

10. Teach, assist, and answer questions.

11. Keep things on track and moving forward.

The choice of leaders in a truly effective team is made by consensus, and the team will usually select the leader based on strengths. Decisions are based on logic and agreed to by team members rather than dictated by authority or position power. The ability to acknowledge others' leadership ability and let go is a sign of an effective formal leader. Leadership will be discussed in greater detail in Chapter 11.

Elements Needed To Build an Effective Team

Vision

To build an effective team, whether at work or elsewhere, you must have a clear idea of the team's purpose, where you want to go, and what you must do. Allowing the team to contribute to the planning and setting of specific goals promotes teamwork. Goals should be specific and result in a mission statement through which team members can clearly understand their purpose. For example, President John F. Kennedy provided NASA's team with a clear and compelling vision that demonstrated the power of purpose. By committing to "place a man on the moon by the end of the 1960s," President Kennedy inspired team members of the Apollo Program to achieve their mission. The clarity and conviction generated strategies and an execution that in fact achieved the goal in the prescribed time frame.

Interdependence

Clearly identifying each person's role is essential in reducing conflict and negative competitiveness. Once individuals are comfortable with their role and mission, true team identity can arise. Members will feel like teammates. Teammates will feel comfortable sharing and will come to rely on one another rather than operate as independent entities. The use of "we/us/our" terms becomes noticeable, replacing the typical "I/me/mine" individualistic view. This togetherness reflects a sense of ownership in what the team is doing and builds team spirit.

Leadership

The leadership role in a team is a critical and often difficult one. Certainly, a leader is needed, but it need not always be the formal, legitimate leader. Sharing the leadership role with other team members when appropriate serves to strengthen the team feeling. Today's formal leader must learn when to let go and allow others to lead. Of course, the formal leader has very real responsibilities to the group, as noted below.

Coordination

Given the dynamic conditions of the team approach, coordination of information is critical. All members need to keep up with new facts or changes in direction. Establishing effective communication lines is essential. Something as simple as notification of meeting times and places can play a key part in the process.

Sharing information is also vital. All team members should be informed of important events, from policy changes to new technologies to priority modifications. Team members should be encouraged to establish networks with other team members and external sources. Maximum cooperation occurs when people know they will have to deal with each other again.

Adaptability

Keeping pace in the rapidly changing workplace requires adaptability and flexibility. People working shoulder-to-shoulder in teams can get things done much faster than individuals out to protect their own turf or those who may be required to obtain dozens of approvals of higher-ups before they can proceed. Meeting the challenge of change can serve to inspire team responsiveness and heighten synergy.

IDENTIFYING EFFECTIVE TEAM MEMBERS

Selecting the best team members possible is crucial to building an effective team. If you are selecting team members, a cross-section of talents with each member representing expertise in a separate discipline is desirable. However, when drawing a team from an existing group, rely on the strengths of certain individuals and develop abilities in others. Cross-train or rotate employees to enhance their knowledge of operations. You should recognize valuable traits in individuals and encourage them to flourish. The freedom to make mistakes allows growth through trial and error.

> *Encourage team members to contribute their strengths and expertise.*

Characteristics of a Good Team Player

A good team member generally:

- Thinks in "we/us/our" terms versus "I/me/mine."
- Is flexible.
- Is willing to share information, ideas, and recognition.
- Gets along well with others.
- Exhibits interest and enthusiasm.
- Remains loyal to team purpose and team members.

IMPORTANCE OF COMMUNICATION, NETWORKING, AND HUMAN RELATIONS SKILLS

Once team members understand their roles and mission, communication, networking, and other human relation skills become important. One of the key ingredients for any team effort is open communication. It enhances creativity, camaraderie, and productivity.

In a study done by Arthur D. Little, Inc., a research and consulting firm, researchers found a common positive attribute in 10 of the United States' most innovative companies. The key was an organizational style stressing easy communication and networking. Innovation increased when collaboration disrupted the hierarchical power flows. Successful corporations such as 3M, IBM, AT&T, and General Foods emphasize internal communications and networking and believe that the enormous information base created fosters new ideas and stimulates creativity.

> *Open communication and networking enhance the team's creativity.*

Because an effective team is able to communicate openly and is highly cohesive, good human relations skills are in constant use. Ask the following questions about your team and its members. Are we supportive of one another? Do we share appropriately how we feel about important things? Do we share information and ideas? Are we effective listeners? Do we handle confrontation or problems within the team fairly, resolving issues well?

Developing these basic human relations skills can go a long way toward improving your team's overall output.

VIRTUAL TEAMS

Thanks to advances in communication technology, a growing number of organizations are relying on the use of **virtual teams**. A virtual team is usually a task- or project-focused team that meets without all members being present in the same location or at the same time. They meet using videoconferences, conference calls, and **groupware**—special software that improves group interactions through computer networks, e-mail, newsgroups, videophones, or chat. Groupware allows the team members in a global organization to communicate without worrying about location or time zone differences.[14] Team experts Jon Katzenbach and Douglas Smith offer the following pointers for working with a virtual team:[15]

Tips for Working with a Virtual Team

1. Hold a *face-to-face* meeting early on to confirm your goals, agree on a working approach, and establish rules for using groupware and e-mail.
2. Save time by determining which tasks should be handled by the team and which can best be done by individual members.
3. Assign tasks and roles to take advantage of different members' skills and experiences.
4. Hold face-to-face meetings as often as needed.
5. Divide up and assign different leadership roles. Virtual work requires more leadership attention than co-located work.
6. Select groupware features as a team so all members are familiar with the technology.
7. To avoid confusion and improve your interactions, agree on your team netiquette and work approaches; for example, return e-mail within 24 hours, record vacation days on the team calendar, let team members know when you will be on-site, etc.

---

*Fast*Chat

1. If you were a team leader, would you try to take shortcuts to hasten the teambuilding process? Why, or why not?
2. Why do you think virtual work requires more leadership than face-to-face work? Why would it be necessary for a virtual team to hold occasional face-to-face meetings?

How Does a Team Affect Its Members?   8.5

Being on a team has advantages. Teamwork creates a cycle of positive dynamics, with each part reinforcing the others. This enables individual team members to reach high levels of performance. Teams are an effective way to stimulate participation and involvement. Most people have difficulty feeling a strong sense of identity with or loyalty to an organization when they think that their impact is minimal.

BENEFITS AND DRAWBACKS OF TEAMWORK

The following box identifies the benefits and drawbacks that exist in the teamwork process. As you review them, think of examples from your own experience with teams.

Benefits and Drawbacks of Teamwork

Benefits

- Increased commitment and ownership of goals
- Higher sustained effort toward goal accomplishment
- Improved self-confidence and sense of well-being for team members
- Increased levels of team member motivation, enthusiasm, and job satisfaction
- Improved decision-making and problem-solving results
- Greater emotional support within team structure
- Greater endurance and energy levels from team members
- Greater reservoir of ideas and information
- Increased sharing of individual skills
- Increased productivity
- Improved quality and quantity output
- Improved loyalty to goals and objectives

Drawbacks

- Fear of individual anonymity
- Restricted opportunity for personal career advancement
- Loss of power and authority
- Need to be generalists versus specialists in career field
- Team commitments overshadow personal desires
- Current leadership not geared to team concepts
- Duplication of effort
- Time wasted in team interaction
- Conflict and infighting
- Diminished opportunity to stand out/obtain rewards

As team members, individuals have a sense of making real, direct, and appreciated contributions. This increased feeling of worth improves their commitment to the goals and objectives of the team and the organization. However, drawbacks do exist in the teamwork process. Because of these personal drawbacks, the team approach is not always welcome. Some individuals may refuse to participate or may even sabotage the team's effectiveness.

ETHICS CONNECTION

You are a team leader and have just been called to the president's office and informed that your team has won an achievement award for the past year. A banquet will be held next month and the award will be presented. You are instructed to be at the banquet to accept the award.

1. *As the leader, should you accept the award and take credit for the accomplishments? Why, or why not?*

2. *Do you think giving credit to other team members would detract from a leader's ability to advance in a company? Why, or why not?*

Lack of participation by some team members can get in the way of successful teamwork.

"Isn't this what teamwork is all about? You doing all my work for me?"

©2003 Ted Goff www.tedgoff.com

BEING AN EFFECTIVE TEAM MEMBER

When you are a member of a team, you can help make the team effective and the experience pleasant if you remember certain suggestions:

1. Know your role and the team's goals. Be aware of your strengths and weaknesses and what you can contribute to the team.

2. Be a willing team player. At times you may be asked to perform tasks that you dislike or with which you disagree. Realize how performing these assignments will contribute to the group productivity and perform them willingly (unless you disagree on ethical or moral grounds).

3. Cooperate with other team members. Using open communication and solid human relations skills enhances harmony.

4. Support other team members by giving them encouragement and assisting them when necessary with their tasks.

5. Share praise. Do not claim credit for yourself if a team effort was involved.

6. When conflict occurs, attempt to turn it into a positive experience.

> An effective team member needs extensive human relations skills.

Give other team members encouragement and assist them with their tasks if necessary.

©Comstock Images

*Fast*Chat

The United States was founded and built both by rugged individualists and solid communities. Americans have sayings such as "if you want something done, do it yourself," and yet "united we stand" is also a vital concept in U.S. history.

1. How might the two different sides of the American mindset contribute to effective teamwork?

2. How might these attitudes make forming teams in America more difficult?

Not every organization is suited to teamwork. Current structures and operating styles may not lend themselves readily to the universal use of teamwork. For the team concept to be successful, management must be fully supportive and have a clear mission and values that sustain this approach.

The other issue is the work itself. There are times when individual effort might be more effective to resolve a particular issue. For instance, a group with a leader who makes the decisions and directs the work may be appropriate, particularly when the activities to be performed are routine and do not require creativity or innovation.

The team approach is not always the best strategy.

Lastly, participants must buy into the premise that, in order to succeed, they must commit to helping those around them succeed and that all the team members will be held personally responsible for the outcome. This adjustment is difficult for most individuals, particularly if they are accustomed to succeeding on their own. Many people concluded this was why America's men's basketball team did not fare better in the 2004 Olympics.

GLOBAL CONNECTION

Global teams bring special challenges. Members first need to understand each other's differences before they can effectively come together as a group. Then, too, they must recognize the role of language difficulties and manners of speaking. Additional time will be needed for team members to become comfortable with each other.

1. *What can you do to be better understood when speaking with others for whom English is a second language?*

2. *What types of difficulties can occur when speaking with others who are native English speakers but have different regional accents and terminology? How can you minimize these problems?*

3. *Do you think individuals should try to remove their regional accents? Why or why not? If your answer is, "It depends," give examples to explain the circumstances.*

However, in situations where team concepts can be used, the benefits are well worth the effort of implementation and adaptation. Successful teams, whose attributes are described below, inspire peak performance and provide a critical, competitive edge.[16]

As you read these characteristics, relate them to teams of which you have been a part or with which you are familiar. Try to think of an example of how each characteristic was displayed by your team.

Characteristics of a High Performing Team

A high performing team...

- Is made up of highly talented people with the right skills and temperament
- Has strong leadership that protects and sponsors its members
- Has members who are able to work together
- Believes its mission is vital and has real meaning
- Views itself as a winning underdog
- Has or creates an enemy
- Concentrates on its mission to the distraction of everything else
- Is optimistic
- Believes no one is too important to do any particular task
- Obtains the resources it needs and is free from unnecessary detail
- Feels the work itself is the reward
- Sees itself as an island with a bridge to the mainland, often creating customs or jokes that make membership exclusive
- Is productive
- Works in a comfortable atmosphere that is supportive of team tasks

---

*Fast*Chat

Atmosphere is important in effective teams.

1. Describe your ideal team environment.

2. What can you do to help ensure a good work atmosphere?

Introducing change sets the stage for conflict. Although conflict is often regarded as a barrier to teamwork, it is actually an essential part of the process. **Conflict** is defined as disagreement between individuals or groups about goals. It is inevitable, and its occurrence should be analyzed as a part of the whole group process. If no conflict occurs in a group, the group may actually be ineffective because members do not care about outcomes or make suggestions. Conflict does become a problem, however, when it is excessive, becomes disruptive, or causes a team to become dysfunctional.

Competition is a healthy struggle toward goal accomplishment without interference, even when the goals are incompatible. Competition can stimulate beneficial and creative ideas and methods by team members, whereas excessive competition typically limits creativity. This occurs because members frequently become reluctant to share ideas.

Conflict can be healthy and positive if handled properly. Team members may be inspired or stimulated to resolve issues and reach new heights of creativity. Although too much conflict may be disruptive or destructive, too little conflict generally results in apathy or stagnation. A moderate amount of conflict controlled through resolution techniques can be of benefit to both the organization and the team members and can assure peak performance.

QUICK WIT
"Every difference of opinion is not a difference of principle."
Thomas Jefferson,
American President

Conflict can be healthy and productive if handled properly.

©Getty Images/PhotoDisc

WHAT CAUSES CONFLICT?

Conflict can be experienced by any team member or by the team as a whole. The causes may be incompatibility, organizational reliance, goal ambiguity, labor-management disputes, and unclear roles. These causes are described below.

Causes of Conflict

Incompatibility	Personality conflicts may arise within the team or even between two teams. Within the team, a conflict may occur between a supervisor and a subordinate or between any two or more team members.
	Between teams, ill feelings may exist for a variety of reasons. For example, plant operators may resent corporate engineers who design and implement changes that do not work well. The engineers may look down on the plant operators. Such conflict may create considerable trouble.
Organizational Reliance	In most organizations, teams rely on one another. For example, machine operators depend upon the maintenance crews to perform periodic maintenance on equipment. A production team may rely on the sales team to provide orders from customers to keep the production line in full operation. Conflict may arise between the teams if maintenance is slipshod or if sales orders force production into overtime to meet unrealistic schedules.
Goal Ambiguity	Team goals may differ from the goals of the organization. For example, the organization may want to hurry processes and jeopardize quality of product in order to get the job out and turn a profit. The work teams may want to take time to assure quality. The goals of the two groups clearly conflict.
Labor-Management Disputes	Labor and management have long had disagreements over work conditions, hours, and wages. However, the trouble often goes deeper. Conflicts may be based on roles that each feels necessary to portray. Management representatives may believe that "squaring off" with union representatives just prior to contract negotiations is necessary to set the stage. These situations are normal when union and management have opposing views.
Unclear Roles	The uncertainty brought on by constant changes in roles and missions breeds conflict. These environmental changes cause instability among team members, and conflict will occur. Good communication among team members helps control this type of conflict.

HOW IS CONFLICT RESOLVED?

Conflict resolution is the active management of conflict through defining and solving issues between individuals, groups, or organizations. Given the fact that conflict is part of any team environment, understanding how to manage it is important. In a study conducted by Ronald J. Burke on methods of resolving conflict, five techniques proved to be the most common and effective ways of handling conflict:[17]

Techniques for Handling Conflict

Avoidance: This technique involves totally refraining from confronting the conflict. Avoiding the situation can buy some time to learn additional facts surrounding the conflict or provide a "cooling off" period. It does not resolve the conflict but is often of immediate help.

Smoothing: Accommodating the differences between the two parties, smoothing plays down strong issues and concentrates on mutual interests. Negative issues are seldom even discussed.

Compromising: This technique does address the issue but seldom resolves it to the complete satisfaction of both parties. There is no clear winner or loser.

Forcing: Forcing results when two groups reach an impasse and allow an authoritative figure to choose one preference rather than work toward a mutually agreeable solution. This is considered a win-lose situation.

Confrontation: Although it sounds like a negative approach, confrontation is actually the most positive. It can create a win-win situation. Openly exchanging information and actively working through the differences assures that some agreeable resolution is reached.

These techniques give you some choices for dealing with conflict. The critical message when confronted with confusion or disagreements among team members is to be alert and aware that the conflict exists, look for the causes, understand the reasons as much as possible, and then meet the conflict head on to bring it to resolution.

*Fast*Chat

1. Describe a time when you were in a group where conflict existed. How was it handled? Was it disruptive? What could have been done differently?

2. How can conflict be turned into a positive experience?

3. Recall a recent conflict that you experienced. Which of these methods did you use to resolve the conflict? How effective was it?

CHAPTER SUMMARY

Organizations use teamwork because it increases productivity. This concept was used in corporations as early as the 1920s, but it has become increasingly important in recent years as employees demand more direct involvement and companies strive to gain a competitive edge in the ever-changing marketplace. Today, many different types of teams exist within organizations.

Five basic ingredients must be present for a team to be effective. The team must have a vision, feel interdependence, have good leadership, use effective means of coordination, and have a high degree of adaptability. Teams go through various stages on their way to maturity, and some teams never reach the fully mature stage.

Although a formal leader will be present in most teams, leadership is commonly shared without fear of loss of power. Good team members can be selected or developed and can be coached to share responsibility in achieving the team's goals and mission.

Effective networking systems and open communication are both required for maximum team effectiveness, and, in virtual team situations, groupware and common protocols for using the technology are essential. The benefits derived from the use of teams outweigh the drawbacks and point to the usefulness of teamwork when increased productivity and improved quality are desirable. In some situations, the team approach is not the best method to use, but these occasions are dwindling as companies seek new ways to meet the challenge of the future.

Competition among teams and team members can stimulate creative ideas and methods for accomplishing goals. Conflict, an active ingredient in the team process, can be healthy and positive. Conflict may also be disruptive or destructive. Excessive conflict typically limits creativity and should be properly managed. Major sources of conflict include incompatibility, organizational reliance, goal ambiguity, labor-management disputes, and unclear roles. However, the five common techniques of conflict resolution (avoidance, smoothing, compromising, forcing, and confrontation) can bring positive results.

Key Terms

team

teamwork

teambuilding

synergy

project teams

self-directed work teams

continuous improvement teams

functional work teams

cross-functional teams

virtual teams

groupware

conflict

competition

conflict resolution

avoidance

smoothing

compromising

forcing

confrontation

REVIEW QUESTIONS

1. Why are team concepts necessary in today's work environment, and why are they successful?

2. How do effective teams increase productivity?

3. What are the elements needed in building an effective team?

4. Why are communication and networking important ingredients in teambuilding?

5. Why are groupware technology protocols necessary for virtual teams?

6. What are some of the benefits and drawbacks of team membership?

7. What can you do to become an effective team member?

8. What is the difference between conflict and competition? Why can they both be healthy for an organization?

9. What are the most common techniques in conflict resolution?

DISCUSSION QUESTIONS

1. You are responsible for building a team to improve quality and productivity in your work unit. Outline your approach and describe your reasoning.

2. Describe a conflict that you have experienced within a team setting. Identify the causes and discuss what conflict resolution techniques might have been used.

3. Identify a problem within your community. If you were the formal leader assigned to correct the problem, what types of individuals would you choose for your team? How would you approach the task of team formation?

4. Think of a team with which you have been involved recently. Identify the disciplines or areas of expertise that were represented in the team. How did they serve the team's purpose?

5. Identify tasks in your work or volunteer organization setting that are more efficiently performed by teams than by individuals.

CHAPTER PROJECT

TEAMWORK

In groups of five, discuss the teams in which you have participated (workplace, academic, activities, committees, etc.). First, identify teams you considered to be effective and then those you viewed as ineffective.

Describe each in detail. In your group, identify the three most important elements of the effective teams and the three worst elements of the ineffective teams.

1. What elements did you develop for the effective teams? For the ineffective teams?

2. How did you feel being a part of the team decision-making exercise in your group?

3. Were there moments during this team exercise when you referred back to the chapter? What examples specifically related to the book content?

APPLICATIONS

In small groups, analyze the following scenarios.

The Magic at Magill Manufacturing

Anna Magill took over as chief executive officer at Magill Manufacturing after her father retired from running the business for 32 years. Magill Manufacturing was a keystone company in Lisbon, Ohio, and provided jobs to a large number of the citizens in the community. She took great pride in continuing the family business but knew that she would run the operation differently than her father had.

After only a short period of time in her new position, Anna realized the company was suffering from symptoms of high absenteeism, chronic tardiness, and low morale. Frequent complaints had been filed, employee attitudes were poor, and a general discontent existed among workers. Management was viewed as coercive, with "little dictators" running isolated kingdoms throughout the company. Employees felt that managers gave little support to their ideas or suggestions. Working at Magill Manufacturing had become a way to draw a paycheck and little more. These conditions were reflected in slumping productivity and declining quality of the products.

Anna knew that she needed to act quickly if she were going to turn this situation around. She felt a strong commitment to improving the quality of product, increasing productivity, and creating company loyalty. Her course was clearly charted.

1. How can Anna use team concepts to improve conditions at Magill Manufacturing?

2. What positive changes might be expected from the use of teams in the problem-solving process?

3. How do you think the employees will respond to the new methods? Support your answer with examples from the chapter.

The Left-Handed Pressure Valve

TEAMWORK

The engineering office issued design drawings for the installation of a pressure valve in the plant. The corporate engineers developed the design without consulting the users of the valve. Reviewing the design drawings, the operations people noticed problems with the design. They said nothing, however, because the engineers had not asked for their input.

The operators waited until the valve had been fabricated and installed before they told the engineers why the valve would not work. Indignantly, they demonstrated that the valve could only be accessed from the left side and could not even be seen if approached from the right side. The entire operation had to be returned to the drawing board and redesigned, refabricated, and reinstalled incorporating the suggestions made by the operators.

1. What was the relationship between the two team groups? How effective was the approach taken by the engineers?

2. What did this conflict cost the company?

3. What techniques might have been employed to prevent the conflict in the first place? How might future conflicts be prevented?

ADDITIONAL READINGS AND RESOURCES

Blanchard, Ken, Donald Carew, and Eunice Parisi. *One Minute Manager Builds High Performing Teams*. New York: William Morrow, 2000.

Conners, Roger, and Tom Smith. *Journey to the Emerald City: Implement the Oz Principle to Achieve a Competitive Edge through a Culture of Accountability*. New Jersey: Prentice-Hall Press, 2002.

Hackman, J. Richard. *Leading Teams: Setting the Stage for Great Performances*. Boston: Harvard Business School Press, 2002.

Maxwell, John C. *The 17 Essential Qualities of a Team Player: Becoming the Kind of Person Every Team Wants*. Nashville: Thomas Nelson Publisher, 2002.

Miller, John G. *QBQ! The Question Behind the Question*. Colorado: Denver Press, 2001.

Patrick Lencioni. *The 5 Dysfunctions of a Team: A Leadership Fable*. San Francisco: Jossey-Bass, 2002.

Samuel, Mark. *The Accountability Revolution: Achieve Breakthrough Results in Half the Time*. Tempe, AZ: Facts on Demand Press, 2001.

Wallace, Donald. *One Great Game: Two Teams, Two Dreams, in the First-Ever National Championship High School Football Game*. New York: Atria Books, 2003.

WEB

For additional resources, refer to the web site for this text: school.cengage.com/career/dalton

Human Relations

Diversity:
A Business Imperative

focus

US Airways is committed to developing a diverse workforce that reflects the talents and perspectives of the customers and communities it serves. To further this commitment, the organization established three affinity groups: the Professional Women's Group, the Minority Professional Association, and Spectrum, which focuses on gays and lesbians in the workforce. Additionally, a religious accommodation policy helps ensure that all employees work in an environment where they can feel comfortable about their religious beliefs.

As a result of its commitment to develop a culture of inclusion, US Airways has been recognized by the Hispanic Association of Corporate Responsibility. They have also been awarded the NAACP Annual Corporate award and a Blue Ribbon certificate for supporting women in the workplace. The Gay Financial Network named the airline one of the Top 50 gay- and lesbian-friendly U.S. corporations for employment in 2000 and 2001. In 2003, the Minority Corporate Counsel Association awarded the airline the Employer of Choice award for the Mid-Atlantic region.[1]

Why do you think US Airways is so committed to developing an inclusive work culture? Would you want to work at a company that is committed to including employees who are different? Why, or why not?

After studying this chapter, you should be able to:

9.1 *Define diversity and explain its importance in the emerging economy.*

9.2 *Understand what internal factors contribute to conflict in diverse environments.*

9.3 *Recognize linguistic styles and how they affect interactions in a diverse workplace.*

9.4 *Know how to thrive in a diverse environment.*

in this chapter

Diversity refers to differences. In people, these differences can be thought of in four layers as indicated in the diagram on the next page. The sum of our individual differences affects how we view others and how others view us.

Businesses have increasingly begun to pay attention to the issue of diversity. The global economy and the rapidly changing composition of our population have opened many markets to American businesses; in order to capitalize on these opportunities, organizations must understand the consumer and the consumer's needs. A diverse workforce is now a competitive necessity—it can help a business create new and more innovative products as well as better meet the needs of customers and clients.

Without input from a diverse staff that understands the consumer and the consumer's needs, some American companies have made major mistakes. American Motors, for instance, tried to sell an automobile named "Matador" in Puerto Rico. However, it did not sell well because "matador" carries the connotation of "killer." Pepsodent's efforts to sell teeth-whitening toothpaste in Southeast Asia was disappointing because many cultures in that area value the habit of chewing betel nuts, which darken the teeth. Some believe this habit strengthens teeth, sweetens breath, aids digestion, and even cures tapeworms. Historically, stained teeth were desirable as a sign of marriageability or "coming of age."[2]

Additionally, the pool from which organizations draw employees has become ever more diverse. The U.S. Bureau of Labor Statistics says that between 1998 and 2008, 4 of every 10 people entering the workforce will be members of minority groups.[3] By 2012, white non-Hispanics are expected to make up only 66 percent of the labor force. Women, people with disabilities, older workers, and people of color will continue to be an increasingly important part of the workforce.[4a]

Lastly, as discussed in Chapter 18, the nature of work is changing. An impending labor shortage and the need for a highly skilled workforce will make diverse groups an increasingly important source of labor. Organizations that fail to utilize the best and brightest from the talent available run the risk of falling behind their competitors. Michael Lewis, the author of *Moneyball: The Art of Winning an Unfair Game* says that the inability to envision a certain kind of person doing a certain kind of thing because you've never seen someone who looks like him do it before is not just a vice—it's a luxury. What begins as a failure of imagination ends as a market inefficiency. When you rule out an entire class of people from doing a job simply by their appearance, you are less likely to find the best person for the job.[4b]

Figure 9.1 Dimensions of Diversity[5]

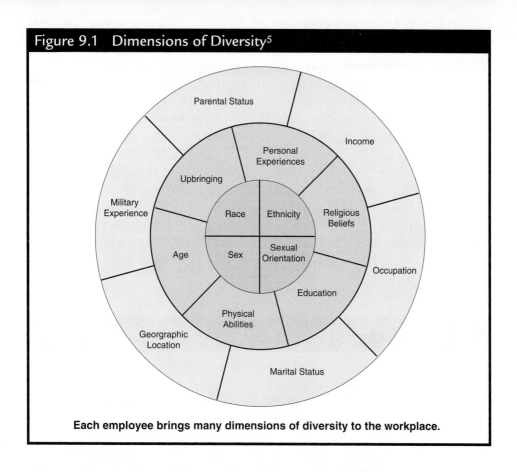

Each employee brings many dimensions of diversity to the workplace.

©Getty Images/PhotoDisc

Diversity is a competitive advantage for any company operating in the global work world.

CHANGING MAKEUP OF THE WORKFORCE

Employers are increasingly expected to accommodate the needs of a complex and diverse workforce that is changing. More minorities, women, and people with disabilities are entering the workforce while older workers are staying longer or returning in increasing numbers. Also, more employees are revealing their sexual orientation.

Women When the United States was a nation of men doing heavy-duty farm and factory jobs, women's jobs were typically those of homemakers, nurses, and teachers. The shift from manufacturing to service industries has provided many jobs that are not gender specific, and the playing field has been further leveled by the Information Age. In today's knowledge-based fields, people earn their livings by what they know rather than through physical labor.

CASE STUDIES IN THE NEWS

The Families and Work Institute reported that in spite of changing attitudes toward women at work, a "social glass ceiling" still exists. Barriers to women's advancement are not merely those erected by employers but the result of social and cultural barriers that are pervasive in society. Society's attitudes and values exert strong influences on educational and career choices of women.

For instance, women are much more likely to work part-time than men and work fewer hours a week than men. Seventy-five percent of the men in the survey reported taking overnight business trips (an indicator of business and financial success) in the past three months, while 13 percent of women reported overnight trips in the same time period. The survey revealed that the more responsibility an employee (male or female) had for routine child care, the lower their earnings.[6]

1. *What barriers in the past discouraged women in the workforce?*

2. *What societal pressures do women face today?*

3. *What do you think were some of the original reasons that women generally earned less than men? How have women's roles changed? How has this contributed to closing the gap between men's and women's wages?*

Women now make up approximately half of the workforce and more than half of college enrollments. More women than men (38 percent versus 28 percent) hold professional and managerial positions. While women's salaries still lag behind those of men, the gap is closing.[7] As demographic changes reduce the pool of educated men, talented and well-prepared women are in stronger bargaining positions.

More working mothers are in the workforce than ever before. Approximately 60 percent of all married women with children under six years of age are working, which is having an impact on the types of benefits and working conditions desired by this segment of the workforce.[8] For example, while practices and benefits vary among organizations, many employers provide excellent family leave policies, flexible work hours, and telecommuting as means of accommodating families with small children. Work life benefits and issues are more fully explored in Chapter 17.

Older Workers **Baby boomers** are those Americans born between 1946 and 1964, during the "baby boom" that followed World War II. For decades, whatever boomers were doing became the most significant factor in demographic studies of U.S. trends. Today, what the boomers are doing is getting older. The Bureau of Labor Statistics states that by 2010, 17 percent of the nation's workforce will be comprised of adults ages 55 and older. By 2050, older adults are expected to account for 19 percent of the workforce while younger workers between the ages of 25 and 54 are expected to decline to 66 percent of the workforce.[9]

A 2003 survey by the American Association of Retired People polled working Americans between 50 and 70 and found that, of those interviewed, 85 percent have never retired while 15 percent had retired but remained in or returned to the workforce. Although age 65 has customarily been considered retirement age, the majority surveyed envisioned themselves working into their 70s and beyond. Not only did those surveyed need extra money, but they also wanted to work for enjoyment, to have something interesting and challenging to do, and to stay physically active.[10]

uick tip ....

"Given the current life expectancies, the proper retirement age will be 79 by 2010."

Peter Drucker

Many retirement age workers will choose to remain in the workforce longer.

©Getty Images/PhotoDisc

CASE STUDIES IN THE NEWS

Dr. Russell B. Clark was named 2003's Oldest Worker in the United States by Experience Works, an organization that helps older workers. Twenty years ago he retired from his practice of medicine.

At 103, however, Dr. Clark has no intention of slowing down. This father of five, grandfather of 23, great-grandfather of 42, and great-great-grandfather of 6 walks three to four miles every day, reads, and cares for his real estate holdings. Once a week he speaks to community groups about the secrets of successful aging. He still drives to St. George, Utah, five hours from his home, where he hops a bus to Las Vegas to visit the industrial complexes he oversees.[11]

1. *In what ways does experience make older employees valuable?*

2. *What do you feel will be lost as they leave the corporate world?*

3. *What barriers exist that limit older workers from continuing to contribute to society?*

4. *How long do you intend to work?*

Race and Ethnicity The Bureau of Labor Statistics states that the workforce will become increasingly diverse racially and ethnically as the chart below indicates. As of July 1, 2002, U.S. residents who were African American or African American in combination with one or more races, made up 13.3 percent of the population, and Hispanics became the largest minority population. By 2012, Hispanics are expected to number 23.8 million in the labor force, and Asians will continue to be the fastest growing of the four labor force groups.[12]

Already, foreign-born people constitute the majority in six U.S. cities of over 100,000 or more (Hialeah and Miami in Florida, and Glendale, Santa Ana, Daly City, and Elmonte in California), according to the U.S. Census Bureau.[13] The Milken Institute says that we can expect one million immigrants annually in the next decade. Most of them will come from Asia and Latin America. These immigrant groups are filling jobs in almost every industry, especially those requiring unskilled labor, such as landscaping and restaurant work.[14] They bring cultural values, ways of communication, and behavior patterns that affect communication in the workplace.

Figure 9.2 Projected Composition of the American Workforce by Ethnic Group[15]

Civilian labor force by sex, age, race, and Hispanic orgin, 1982, 1992, 2002, and projects 2012 (numbers in thousands).

Group	Level 1982	Level 1992	Level 2002 (1990 census weights)	Level 2002 (2000 census weights)	Level 2012	Change 1982–92	Change 1992–2002	Change 2002–12	Percent Change 1982–92	Percent Change 1992–2002	Percent Change 2002–12	Percent Distribution 1982	Percent Distribution 1992	Percent Distribution 2002 (1990 census weights)	Percent Distribution 2002 (2000 census weights)	Percent Distribution 2012	Annual growth rate 1982–92	Annual growth rate 1992–2002	Annual growth rate 2002–12
Total, 16 years and older	110,204	128,105	142,534	144,863	162,269	17,901	14,428	17,406	16.2	11.3	12.0	100.0	100.0	100.0	100.0	100.0	1.5	1.1	1.1
16 to 24	24,606	21,616	22,425	22,366	24,377	-2,990	809	2,011	-12.2	3.7	9.0	22.3	16.9	15.7	15.4	15.0	-1.3	0.4	0.9
25 to 54	70,506	91,429	99,865	101,720	106,866	20,923	8,436	5,146	29.7	9.2	5.1	64.0	71.4	70.1	70.2	65.9	2.6	0.9	0.5
55 and older	15,092	15,060	20,244	20,777	31,026	-32	5,184	10,249	-0.2	34.4	49.3	13.7	11.8	14.2	14.3	19.1	-0.0	3.0	4.1
Men	62,450	69,964	76,052	77,500	85,252	7,514	6,088	7,751	12.0	8.7	10.0	56.7	54.6	53.4	53.5	52.5	1.1	0.8	1.0
Women	47,754	58,141	66,481	67,363	77,017	10,387	8,340	9,654	21.8	14.3	14.3	43.3	45.4	46.6	46.5	47.5	2.0	1.3	1.3
One race																			
White	96,143	108,837	118,569	120,150	130,358	12,694	9,732	10,208	13.2	8.9	8.5	87.2	85.0	83.2	82.9	80.3	1.2	0.9	0.8
Black or African American	11,331	14,162	16,834	16,564	19,765	2,831	2,672	3,201	25.0	18.9	19.3	10.3	11.1	11.8	11.4	12.2	2.3	1.7	1.8
Asian	2,730	5,106	7,130	5,949	8,971	2,376	2,024	3,022	87.0	39.6	50.8	2.5	4.0	5.0	4.1	5.5	6.5	3.4	4.2
All other groups[1]	n/a	n/a	n/a	2,200	3,175	n/a	n/a	975	n/a	n/a	44.3	n/a	n/a	n/a	1.5	2.0	n/a	n/a	3.7
Hispanic or Latino	6,734	11,338	16,200	17,942	23,785	4,604	4,862	5,843	68.4	42.9	32.6	6.1	8.9	11.4	12.4	14.7	5.3	3.6	2.9
Other than Hispanic origin	103,470	116,767	126,334	126,921	138,484	13,297	9,567	11,562	12.9	8.2	9.1	93.9	91.1	88.6	87.6	85.3	1.2	0.8	0.9
White (only) non-Hispanic	89,630	98,724	103,360	103,348	106,237	9,094	4,636	2,889	10.1	4.7	2.8	81.3	77.1	72.5	71.3	65.5	1.0	0.5	0.3

Footnotes: (1) The "All other" group includes those reporting the race categories of (1a) American Indian and Alaska Native or (1b) Native Hawiian and Other Pacific Islanders, and (2) those reporting two or more races.

Source: Bureau of Labor Statistics Monthly Labor Review, May 2002.

QUICK WIT

"Ultimately,
America's answer
to the intolerant
man is diversity,
the very diversity
which our heritage
of religious freedom
has inspired."

Robert F. Kennedy,
U.S. Senator and
Civil Rights advocate

Workers with Disabilities People with disabilities are the nation's largest minority, and cross all racial, gender, educational, socioeconomic, and generational lines. There are approximately 16 million Americans of working age who have disabilities, and 60 to 70 percent of them are unemployed or underemployed. The Bureau of Labor Statistics predicts we will have a 10 million-worker shortage by 2010. Experts believe that the current generation of Americans with disabilites is well prepared to be tapped for the job market and able to provide an added solution for the labor shortages facing American business.[16]

Gays and Lesbians Estimates of the gay and lesbian population in the United States vary but are projected to be anywhere from 1 to 10 percent of the total population.[17] While federal law does not protect gays and lesbians from being terminated from their jobs because of their sexual preference, many state and local governments are moving to give this population civil rights, and many companies are including them in their diversity initiatives. Currently, 92 of the Fortune 100 companies ban discrimination based on sexual orientation, and nearly two-thirds of them offer health benefits to same-sex partners.[18]

UNDERSTANDING DIVERSE NEEDS

While the diverse groups discussed in this section offer many advantages for organizations, they can also be a source of conflict and loss of productivity. Disagreement can evolve from internal factors such as biases and prejudices as well as differences in values. Linguistic styles also contribute to misunderstandings. In order to thrive in a diverse environment, workers must understand these issues.

*Fast*Chat

1. How will older workers be beneficial in our future workforce?

2. Why do you believe so many individuals with disabilities are unemployed or underemployed?

3. How do cultural values, behavior, and communication styles affect communication in the workplace?

4. How do you think the issues discussed in this section will change the workforce of the future?

Biases, prejudices, and value systems are ingrained in all of us, and we base our daily actions on them, often unconsciously. The more diverse a group, the more diverse the internal factors are, thus increasing the likelihood for conflict. By understanding these factors, we can improve our understanding of others and ourselves and work to reduce conflict.

A **bias** is an inclination or preference either for or against an individual or group that interferes with impartial judgment. We begin developing biases early in life and are influenced by our family, personal and educational experiences, the media, and peers. Often, preferences are not spoken but rather are learned by watching and viewing what happens in the world around us. By the age of five, many children have definite and entrenched stereotypes about people of other races, women, and other social groups. They have acquired these beliefs from various sources well before they have the ability or experiences to form their own beliefs.[19]

Prejudice is prejudging or making a decision about a person or group of people without sufficient knowledge. Prejudicial thinking is frequently based on **stereotypes**. A stereotype is a fixed or distorted generalization made about members of a particular group. When stereotyping is used, individual differences are not taken into account. Because people tend to grow up with people like themselves, they may develop prejudices about people they do not know—views that are full of inaccuracies and distortions. The goal of diversity is to increase trust among groups who do not know enough about each other. It is important to learn how to control biases and prejudices and not to let them interfere with the ability to interact with others. Use the quiz on the next page to explore your biases.

> Biases, prejudices, and values are learned at an early age.

> *QUICK WIT*
> *Integrity is doing the right thing, even if nobody is watching.*
> Jim Stovall,
> Motivational speaker and author

Quick tip

In *Workforce America!*, Marilyn Loden and Judy B. Rosener say the key to thriving in a diverse workforce is exploring your own biases and prejudices and dealing with them. They offer these tips:[20]

- Acknowledge the existence of bias and prejudice and accept responsibility for it.
- Identify problem behaviors and assess the impact of behaviors on others.
- Modify your behavior.
- Obtain feedback on changes.
- Repeat steps when necessary.

Rating Your Behavior[21]

Directions

Answer the following questions by rating your behavior on a scale of 1 (Never) to 5 (Always). Circle the appropriate answer.

How often do you:	never				always
Interrupt someone who is telling a racial or ethnic joke?	1	2	3	4	5
Read about the achievements of people with physical or mental disabilities?	1	2	3	4	5
Challenge friends expressing a gender stereotype?	1	2	3	4	5
Send e-mails to TV or radio stations that broadcast news stories with cultural or racial biases?	1	2	3	4	5
Examine your own language for unconscious bias or stereotypes?	1	2	3	4	5
Ask exchange students questions about their countries of origin?	1	2	3	4	5
Recognize compulsory heterosexuality in the media?	1	2	3	4	5
Volunteer your time for a cause you support?	1	2	3	4	5
Donate goods or money to shelters for battered women or homeless people?	1	2	3	4	5
Intervene when a person or group is sexually harassing someone?	1	2	3	4	5
Think about the definition of rape?	1	2	3	4	5
Truly appreciate a friend's differences from you?	1	2	3	4	5
Take the lead in welcoming people of color to your class, club, job site, or living situation?	1	2	3	4	5
Challenge the cultural expectation of slimness in women?	1	2	3	4	5
Protest unfair or exclusionary practices in an organization?	1	2	3	4	5
Ask a member of an ethnic group different from yours how that person prefers to be referred to?	1	2	3	4	5
Think about ways you belong to oppressor and oppressed groups?	1	2	3	4	5
Identify and challenge "tokenism"?	1	2	3	4	5
Examine your own level of comfort around issues of sexual orientation and sexual practices?	1	2	3	4	5
Celebrate your uniqueness?	1	2	3	4	5

Variation

After you have rated your behaviors, examine your responses for patterns. Did you surprise yourself in any regard?

Are there any behaviors you would like to engage in less frequently? More frequently? How will you implement those changes?

Source: Janet Lockhart, M.A.I.S. and Susan M. Shaw, Ph.D. Used with permission.

Values, according to Webster's Dictionary, are those things (as a principle or quality) intrinsically valuable or desirable. We all develop a set of values, or **value systems**, which provide a road map for our behavior in a variety of situations. Our values evolve from the influences of family, society, religious training, and personal experiences. Not only do we have our own value systems as individuals, but organizations do as well. Underlying every decision made at work is a corresponding value. Because these values are so ingrained in us, we are usually not aware of them as we make decisions. In diverse groups, many more value systems are at work, which can cause conflict in decision making.

As a society, for example, Americans tend to expect individuals to speak up for themselves. We value those who speak their minds and do not let themselves be taken advantage of. How many times have you heard the expression, "the squeaky wheel gets the grease"? On the other hand, the Japanese, who tend to value harmony over individuality, have a saying that "the nail that sticks up will get hammered down."

It is important to note that, while certain groups may tend to value certain behaviors, not all members of that group necessarily hold those values. Also, there are no right or wrong value systems. Diverse value systems cause us to define problems and develop solutions to those problems differently. For example, generational values and national values can affect the way people work together in an organization.

While certain groups may tend to value certain behaviors, not *all* members of that group necessarily hold those values.

GLOBAL CONNECTION

Social scientist Geert Hofstede identified five dimensions of cultural values that influence values in global organizations:[22]

Power Distance: Extent to which the inequality between bosses and subordinates is accepted

Uncertainty Avoidance: Degree to which uncertainty is tolerated

Individualism versus Collectivism: Extent to which one views things in terms of 'I' versus 'We'; ties to one another are either loose or cohesive through life

Achievement versus Relationship: Extent to which achievement and success are rated more highly than the quality of life and caring for others

Confucian Dynamism: Extent to which cultural orientation is long term or short term

How could these differences affect an employee's ability to function in a different country's work environment?

Differing Generational Values[23]

Silent Generation "Traditionalists" (born 1933–1945)   **10 percent of workforce**
Tend to value sacrifice, discipline, teamwork, and working within the system

Baby Boomers (born 1946–1964)   **46 percent of workforce**
Tend to value challenging work, personal accomplishment, and competition

Generation X (born 1965–1979)   **29 percent of workforce**
Tend to value feedback, enjoyable work, independence, adaptability, risks, and technology

Generation Y (born 1980–1998)   **15 percent of workforce**
Tend to value integrity, challenges, teamwork, education, and relationships

ETHICS CONNECTION

John is the vice president of sales for Makeamillion Corporation. Mary, his sales manager, is attempting to close a multimillion dollar sale with the Rainbow Corporation to run their computer help desk and maintain all computer operations in their corporate center. Rainbow executives have made it clear that they value a diverse workforce, and Mary is worried her team will not be able to close the deal because her sales force has no minority members. She is pressuring John to assign Efrain Fuentes, a technician, to work on this case, even though Efrain has other assignments that could not be completed if he were to join the sales team.

1. What should John do? Explain your reasoning.
2. How would you feel if you were Efrain?

*Fast*Chat

1. Name three celebrities. Do they fit the stereotypes you grew up with regarding persons of color, older people, females, or persons from certain areas of the country? Why, or why not?
2. Identify some decisions you have made in the past week, such as whether to study, whether to go out to eat, or what television show to watch. What were the values behind those decisions?

Linguistic styles refer to characteristic speaking patterns. Directness or indirectness, pacing and pausing, word choice, and the use of elements such as jokes, figures of speech, stories, questions, and apologies are also included.[24]

Understanding your linguistic style and that of others is extremely important when dealing with a diverse group of individuals. By understanding style differences, you can focus on the message rather than letting the way the message is delivered influence the way you interpret it.

Important factors to consider when dealing with linguistic styles are that they are norms, variations exist, and individuals do not always follow the linguistic norm of their group. Individual personality, culture, class, and sexual orientation can cause these variations. No style is right or wrong—they are just different ways of delivering communication. The more you understand your own style and the styles of others, the more comfortable you will be communicating in diverse groups.

> Understanding linguistic styles is extremely important when interacting with diverse individuals.

CASE STUDIES IN THE NEWS

Four book-manufacturing companies in Ann Arbor, Michigan, joined forces to teach their employees English, as some had so little understanding of the language that they were unable to understand the books they were binding, to read safety signs, or to communicate fully with coworkers. One firm had Albanian speakers from Kosovo as well as West Africans who spoke tribal dialects and French. Another bookmaker had a few employees who spoke only Vietnamese or Chinese. Because of their efforts, the firms, along with Washtenaw Literacy and the Washtenaw Development Council, were the 2004 Optimas Award winners for Partnership by *Workforce Management Magazine.*[25]

1. *What problems can arise when employees are not able to communicate fully with one another?*

2. *What can you do to communicate better with someone whose native language is not English?*

DIRECT AND INDIRECT COMMUNICATION STYLES

Direct and indirect communication styles can be a source of conflict in communication. A **direct communication style** reflects a goal orientation and a desire to get down to business and get to the point, while an **indirect style** reflects a focus on the relationship and is used to develop a rapport before getting down to business.

A supervisor who is an indirect communicator may say something such as, "You might consider adding another paragraph to your report explaining the history behind the project." To the supervisor, this is a nice way to say, "do it" when he or she does not want to appear rude or abrupt. When two communicators have an indirect style, there is usually not a problem. However, if the recipient operates in a direct manner, he or she may ignore an indirect message, much to the frustration of the supervisor. The supervisor will think the employee does not follow directions, and the employee will see the supervisor as "wishy-washy," indecisive, or unclear.

On the other hand, a direct supervisor who hands a subordinate an assignment and simply says, "Get this back to me by 4:00 this afternoon," without engaging in any additional conversation may be seen as cold, uncaring, and callous.

Listen to yourself and to those around you to identify styles. If you have a direct communication style and someone speaks indirectly, you may need to ask questions to ensure you understand exactly what he/she wants you to do. If you have an indirect style, you may need to speak more directly to ensure that your wishes are followed.

At times, you may need to adapt your communication style to match those with whom you interact.

The important point to remember is that there is no correct style. Concentrate on the message and clarifying your understanding of the message rather than on the way it is delivered. At times, you may need to adapt your style to match those with whom you are interacting.

HIGH AND LOW CONTEXT MODES

Cultures and groups can operate in a low context or a high context mode. **Low context groups** value the written or spoken word. They are task oriented and results driven and generally adopt a direct linguistic style. In low context situations, knowledge is more transferable and available to the public. Examples of low context situations are sports and activities where rules are clearly laid out, restaurants, grocery stores, hotels, and airports.[26]

High context groups, however, are more difficult to penetrate. Long-term relationships are important, and communication is less verbally explicit. There are strong boundaries defining who is accepted and who is considered an outsider. Many times, decisions and activities focus on face-to-face relationships and often around one person who has authority. Some examples are small religious congregations, family events, small businesses, regular "pick-up" games, and groups of friends.[27]

Entering low context groups is easier than entering high context groups. And remember, many situations have both high and low context aspects. For example, membership in a nonprofit organization may be open to anyone, but the group may have a high context core group in charge of the organization.

Assess your circumstances and, if you find yourself in a high context situation, be patient. It may be necessary to seek input from an established member of the group in order to learn the unwritten rules and the way the group functions. Lastly, make it a point to assist newcomers in assimilating into high context cultures in which you operate.

Quick tip ....

In *Workforce America!,* Marilyn Loden and Judy B. Rosener offer these tips for improving communication:[28]

1. Identify your own personal communication style.

2. Recognize your own personal filters, and test assumptions you have with other, neutral parties.

3. Acknowledge your own personal style of communication and how it might be perceived as threatening or confusing to others. Disclose personal styles to ease communication.

4. Become aware of whether you are in a low context or high context culture to reduce your frustration.

CONVERSATIONAL RITUALS

Conversational rituals are things we say without considering the literal meaning of our words. The purpose is to make interactions as pleasant as possible.[29] For instance, many of us say, "How are you?" and do not expect or want the other person to tell us about his or her aches and pains. This is just a way to be nice.

However, if others do not understand conversational rituals and take them literally, problems can occur. For instance, some people may say, "I'm sorry," but do not mean this literally. While it may be seen as an apology or taking blame, many times it is intended as an expression of understanding and caring about the other person's situation. Other conversational rituals include saying thanks as a conversational closer when there is nothing to say "thank you" for, "troubles talk" as a form of rapport rather than asking for solutions, asking for input from many different individuals before making decisions, and giving praise.

Some individuals, on the other hand, use conversational rituals, such as fighting. They may argue heatedly to explore ideas and not take the exchange personally. This group may also tend to engage in razzing, teasing, and mock-hostile attacks.

Contrasting Linguistics Styles[30]

STYLE A	STYLE B
Direct	Indirect
Talk about things	Talk about relationships
Convey facts	Convey feelings and details
Compete; one-up	Gain rapport; speak to save face; buffer comments to avoid insults
Solve problems	Look for discussion
Goal oriented	Relationship oriented
Hierarchy, competition	Level playing field
Conversation to give information	Conversation to give information, connect, and compete
Minimize doubts	Downplay certainty
Razz, tease, mock-hostile attacks	Self-mocking

Style A elements are often used by males while Style B elements are often used by females. It is important to note, however, that linguistic styles are affected by a number of cultural and societal factors and many individuals of either gender may use a mix of these elements.

FastChat

1. Do you currently work with anyone who has a different linguistic style than you? What can you do to make your communication more effective?

2. Have you ever tried to enter high and low context situations? How did the experiences differ?

In order to thrive in a diverse workforce, we must not only explore and deal with our own biases and prejudices and understand our own value systems, but also we must develop empathy, engage in positive self-talk, treat others with dignity and respect, be flexible and learn to deal with ambiguity, use inclusive language, and respect work style differences.

DEVELOPING EMPATHY

Webster's Dictionary defines **empathy** as the action of understanding, being aware of, being sensitive to, and vicariously experiencing the feelings, thoughts, and experience of another. To use empathy, use your listening skills to understand other points of view and needs. Ask questions to clarify why others see things differently. Try to see the world through other viewpoints and determine what values influence how others interact with you.

POSITIVE SELF-TALK

The **Pygmalion effect** is a psychological phenomenon whose premise is "you get what you expect." It is important to expect that you will get along with and understand others so this will become a self-fulfilling prophecy.[31] If you train your "inner voice" to expect the best and avoid negativity, you will build self-esteem and be more likely to respect yourself and others.

Positive self-talk can lead to respecting yourself and others.

$\mathcal{Q}$uick tip ....

Cultural Coach Linda Wallace suggests the following ways to increase your cultural IQ:[32]

1. Take advantage of cultural offerings at colleges.
2. Shop in a new part of town.
3. Volunteer for a community-based initiative that works with people who make you feel the most uncomfortable.
4. Seek others to act as advisors on cultural issues.
5. Develop a learning plan using books and films.
6. Talk to a child who has not yet learned to be judgmental.
7. Learn a foreign language and experience the culture.
8. Listen to a radio talk show of a host who angers you and try to understand his/her viewpoint.

DIGNITY AND RESPECT

Find out what dignity and respect mean to an individual and act accordingly.

Most individuals want to have more authentic, honest, and respectful relationships with others. Remembering that others may see dignity and respect differently, try to find out what that means for each individual and act accordingly. This may involve being sensitive to physical needs, work/family needs, language barriers, and cultural taboos and customs. Remember, respecting others' values and viewpoints does not mean you must accept or adopt their way of thinking. It may be necessary to respectfully agree to disagree.

You can communicate dignity and respect by encouraging open communication—share a part of yourself and be open to the differences in others. Be sure to listen actively and be other-oriented, showing interest in what other people have to say. Additionally, speak to others as you would speak to your peers to help create a sense of equality. Body language and tone can help create a genuine, sincere style.

FLEXIBILITY AND AMBIGUITY

Expect ambiguity and learn to deal with it. What you think you see may not be reality to others if they have different viewpoints and perspectives. Observe and analyze situations carefully before taking action. For example, your boss's behavior may create ambiguity because it can be interpreted in two or more ways. Use the Rolling the D.I.E. Quick Tip below to help you evaluate your perceptions of a situation. You may need to think on your feet, be flexible, and adapt to the communication style of the individual with whom you are speaking in order to operate effectively.

Quick tip

William Sonnenschein, author of *The Diversity Toolkit*, suggests using the *Rolling the D.I.E.* self-awareness tool to check our perceptions of a situation.

1. **D**escribe the experience. (*My supervisor snapped at me.*)

2. **I**nterpret it in as many different ways as you can. (*She doesn't like me; she is having a bad day because her mother is in the hospital; she is frustrated because her boss has given her a difficult deadline.*)

3. **E**valuate the interpretations to determine which one is the most accurate.[33]

INCLUSIVITY

Make a conscientious effort to use language and actions that include others. For example, when sending an invitation to a function, you might say that employees may bring significant others rather than husbands and wives. Because many religions and cultures have prohibitions on consuming certain food products, be sure to offer food that is acceptable for everyone. Additionally, make certain that entrances and facilities are accessible and comfortable to everyone. Deliver information in alternate formats if needed, such as Braille or captioning.

Quick tip ....

If someone has said something to offend you, try the following techniques to resolve the issue:

- Be clear about your goals for challenging the individual. (A mentor can be useful for discussing sensitive issues.)

- Try to assume goodwill—that the other person did not realize what he or she said was offensive.

- Talk to the person privately.

- Be honest and direct when explaining how the comments made you feel.

- Use "I" phrases (See Chapter 4).

- Give examples of the comments and behaviors that offended you.

If you are unable to resolve the issue yourself, seek assistance from your supervisor or the human resource department.[34]

WORK STYLE DIFFERENCES

Individual work styles vary greatly along with perceptions of time and priorities. Some people work in a **monochronic** fashion. They do one thing at a time and follow plans closely. **Polychronic** workers may do many things at once, change plans easily, and tolerate interruptions.[35] Respect work style differences and concentrate on meeting goals. Focus on completing tasks in a timely fashion rather than dwelling on *how* tasks are completed.

According to Cybercast News Service, in January 2004 a federal jury found Southwest Airlines not guilty of discrimination in a case brought by two black passengers. The flight attendant used an old rhyme over the address system to attempt to get passengers seated more quickly. "Eenie, meenie, minie, moe; pick a seat we've got to go," she said. The plaintiff said that the rhyme reminded her of a racist version of the rhyme that was used as far back as the mid-19TH century. That obsolete version of the rhyme included a derogatory term for African-Americans. The plaintiff said she was so upset by the rhyme that it caused her to suffer two seizures. The young flight attendant testified that she had never heard the racist version of the rhyme and did not know that the rhyme would be offensive to passengers.[36]

1. *Do you believe the flight attendant was attempting to demean African-American passengers? Why, or why not?*
2. *Have you experienced these types of situations at work where one person unknowingly offends another? How was it handled?*
3. *How should these types of situations be handled?*

*Fast*Chat

1. Is your work style monochronic or polychronic? How might a polychronic boss view a monochronic employee? A monochronic boss a polychronic employee?

2. Have you ever been in an environment where you felt excluded? What could others have done to make you feel included?

3. Make a list of five things you can do in your daily life and work to show empathy and be more respectful of the needs of others.

4. Why is it important to recognize and analyze ambiguity? How should you deal with it?

CHAPTER SUMMARY

As our economy becomes global and our work-place shifts to include more women, people of color, older workers, people with disabilities, and gays and lesbians, companies are paying increasing attention to the issues of diversity. While a diverse workforce allows organizations to be competitive and to attract the best and brightest employees, it can also be a significant source of conflict.

Understanding how biases and prejudices affect our ability to deal with those who are different from us is imperative. Other sources of conflict include value systems, communication styles, and linguistic styles. Skills to thrive in a diverse environment include developing empathy, treating others with dignity and respect, being flexible and learning to deal with ambiguity, acting in an inclusive fashion, and respecting differences in work styles.

KEY TERMS

diversity
baby boomers
bias
prejudice
stereotypes
values
value system
linguistic styles
direct communication style
indirect communication style
low context group
high context group
conversational rituals
empathy
Pygmalion effect
monochronic work style
polychronic work style

"You're not so bad for someone who's different."

©1996 Ted Goff www.tedgoff.com

Chapter 9   Diversity: A Business Imperative

247

REVIEW QUESTIONS

1. What is diversity, and why is it important that businesses pay attention to diversity?

2. What are biases and prejudices? How do they interfere with our interactions with others who are different from us?

3. What are linguistic styles, and how can different linguistic styles cause conflict?

4. What actions can improve your ability to thrive in a diverse environment?

DISCUSSION QUESTIONS

1. Has the racial and ethnic composition of your community changed in the last decade? If so, how?

2. Do you believe you have a responsibility to share information about yourself in order to facilitate better understanding? Give an example of a situation in which sharing information about yourself was helpful.

3. Recall a conflict you have either seen or been a part of at work that you feel may have been caused by different linguistic styles. How could the conflict have been resolved?

4. How can you learn about other cultures? Identify at least five things you could do or resources or people you could consult for more information.

5. Consider this advice: "We should treat others as they like to be treated." How do you like to be treated? Do different members of your group have different ideas about how they would like to be treated? What lessons can you learn from this?

CHAPTER PROJECT

The Internet contains a wealth of information on diversity issues. Locate at least three relevant web sites, and identify five new tips for dealing with diversity in the workplace. Be sure to carefully analyze the web sites to make sure they are reputable, up-to-date, and unbiased.

Write an action plan to improve your own ability to interact in a diverse environment.

An action plan:

- States an explanation of a goal or problem and gives a rationale for your decision or recommendation.

- Indicates what resources, tools, or people you will need to use to implement your plan.

- Identifies any issues or barriers that need to be considered and explains how you can overcome them.

- Gives a schedule or timeline for completing the steps in your plan with deadlines for each step.

- Identifies what alternative steps (contingency plans) will be taken if your plan does not work.

- Is no more than one page in length.

APPLICATIONS

In small groups, analyze the following situations.

Hey, Didn't I Say That?

TEAMWORK

Two hours into an emergency problem-solving meeting of Advent Corporation's production team, Janice raised her hand. Jason, the team leader, opened the floor for her to speak.

"Uh, I don't know if this would work or not, but…" Janice proceeded in a low, tentative voice to suggest a resolution to their current problem. She was ignored and the discussion moved to other areas. Fifteen minutes later, Devan spoke up in a clear, confident voice.

"This is what we should do…" He proceeded to expound on Janice's idea. The team became animated and started a lively discussion. Within 30 minutes, the team had developed an action plan for solving their production problem.

As the team members left the conference room, other team members congratulated Devan on his contributions to the group.

1. Why do you think the team members did not acknowledge Janice for her idea?

2. Why did the team members acknowledge Devan's contributions?

3. What could Janice have done differently to get the members of the group to listen to her? What do you think she learned from this experience?

4. How do you think Janice would have been perceived if she had been more assertive?

5. Does the team leader have an obligation to ensure that team members get credit for their contributions and that the group is aware of these contributions? Why, or why not?

6. How should Jason, the team leader, handle these types of situations in the future?

In the Eye of the Beholder

TEAMWORK

Joyce stormed into her supervisor's office and confronted him in a loud, aggressive, demanding voice. "Why did you hire Tony and Alex anyway? They just make me so mad!"

John looked up, startled. Before he could say a word, Joyce continued. "They don't do what I tell them. I give them an order and they nod and smile and then later, when I get back, they haven't done a thing I asked. When I tell them to come to my office, they just sit in the lobby and never tell me they're here. I tell you, there should be a law not letting people who can't speak English into the United States. I think they just don't want to work for a woman."

"I don't blame them for not doing anything you say. You're loud and rude. You're the one who's wrong. Besides, they do a good job."

"What do you mean it's all my fault? I'm only trying to accomplish what you asked me to do. You know I'm the hardest-working person on this team. You're always picking on me. I'm going to report this to the human resource office."

1. Why do you believe Tony and Alex do not ask Joyce for clarification on assignments or tell her when they arrive at her office?

2. What could Joyce do to improve communication with Tony and Alex? With John?

3. Do you believe Joyce's body language and voice tone caused John to devalue her performance and message? Why, or why not?

4. What could John have done differently to handle this problem?

5. If you were the human resource manager, what would you do to repair this situation?

ADDITIONAL READINGS AND RESOURCES

Bucher, Richard D., and Patricia L. Bucher. *Diversity Consciousness: Opening Our Minds to People, Cultures, and Opportunities.* New York: Prentice Hall, 2003.

Miller, Frederick A., and Judith H. Katz. *Inclusion Breakthrough: Unleashing the Real Power of Diversity.* San Francisco: Berrett-Koehler Publishers, Inc., 2002.

Stern-LaRosa, Carolyn, and Ellen Hofmeier Bettmann. *The Anti-Defamation League's Hate Hurts.* New York: Scholastic, Inc., 2000.

Tannen, Deborah, Ph.D. *Talking From 9 to 5: How Women's and Men's Conversational Styles Affect Who Gets Heard, Who Gets Credit, and What Gets Done At Work.* New York: William Morrow and Company, 1994.

Williams, Mark A. *The 10 Lenses: Your Guide to Living & Working in a Multicultural World.* Virginia: Capital Books Inc., 2001.

Zemke, Ron, Clair Raines, and Bob Filipczak. *Generations at Work: Managing the Clash of Veterans, Boomers, Xers, and Nexters in Your Workplace.* New Jersey: Pearson Custom Publishing, 2000.

For additional resources, refer to the web site for this text: <u>school.cengage.com/career/dalton</u>

CHAPTER 10

OBJECTIVES

Goal Setting:
Steps to the Future

After studying this chapter, you should be able to:

10.1 *Explain the importance of planning to people and to organizations.*

10.2 *Name and define three categories of organizational goals.*

10.3 *Discuss the characteristics and timing of goals.*

10.4 *Understand how goals are set and prioritized.*

10.5 *Describe Management by Objectives and name its benefits.*

10.6 *Grasp the importance of the performance appraisal and how it works.*

focus

In *Life 101*, Peter McWilliams says:

"In order to get what you want, it's very helpful to know what you want. If you don't know where you want to go, you probably won't get there."[1]

In *The Psychology of Winning*, Denis Waitley says:

"The reason most people never reach their goals is that they don't define them, learn about them, or even seriously consider them as believable or achievable. Winners can tell you where they are going, what they plan to do along the way, and who will be sharing the adventure with them."[2]

Why do you think motivational authors and speakers so often talk about goals? Do you know what you want to do next week? Next year? In 5 years? In 20 years? What do you think are advantages of goal setting? Why do many people and businesses fail to set goals?

in this chapter

The cartoon below typifies the way we all too often approach our desires or goals. We might want to accomplish certain things, but we do not think about the steps we must take. Being successful is almost never a matter of luck or fate; we must plan to increase our chances of being successful. Failure to plan is frequently described as taking an automobile trip to a strange place without a road map. You may reach your destination, but getting there will probably take longer and cost more. And you may never arrive.

Planning increases our chances of success.

"Magnificent invention! Now, let's get the people in Marketing to figure out what it can do!"

©1998 Ted Goff www.tedgoff.com

Planning is an attempt to prepare for and predict the future. It involves goals, programs, policies, rules, procedures, and decisions about what resources to commit to future action. These resources can include time, money, supplies, material, and labor. Planning should be ongoing and flexible because goals will change as we grow or face new situations.

Planning is important for organizations *and* individuals (in both our personal and professional lives). Having specific goals gives us a better chance of making things happen and achieving success.

As a recent Smith-Barney ad says, "There's blind luck, dumb luck, and then there's 'get-up-every-morning-at-5:30-and-sweat-the-details-luck.'"

Planning is important for organizations *and* individuals.

Without goals, we just wait, watch things happen, wonder what happened, or criticize what happened. Goals provide direction and assist us in selecting strategies, communicating intentions, and evaluating effectiveness.

Examples of Things That Require Planning In Our Personal Lives

Weddings and events

Daily schedules

Vacations and trips

Classes to be taken next semester

Saving to buy a car

Saving for retirement

Saving for a wedding or other major event is an example of planning in personal life.

©Brand X Pictures

Examples of Things That Require Planning In Organizations

Appropriate use of facilities and equipment

Care of materials and supplies

Conservation of energy and power

Cash and credit management

Workforce management

Information collection and processing

Time conservation

Schedules

Quality management

Cost reduction and control

Productivity

Self-improvement planning

Psychologists suggest that lack of planning is a subconscious desire to create crises or even to fail. In our personal lives, lack of planning may make us feel more spontaneous and alive because of the temporary heightened emotion that results from scrambling to deal with unplanned events.

People fail to plan for a variety of reasons.

In an organization, managers may feel more important because they have immediate decisions to make. This kind of busyness is called "putting out brushfires." These are short-term "benefits" and ultimately are harmful.

WHY MUST ORGANIZATIONS PLAN?

Without planning, organizations have no sense of direction and ultimately are not able to manage resources effectively. No planning or poor planning can result in crisis management (constantly putting out brushfires) and employee frustration. Managers spend their time on emergencies while employees are forced to move from one task to another as emergencies arise. Then, too, coping with change is more difficult without planning.

Planning is the difference between reactive management and proactive management. **Reactive management** is characterized by supervisors being caught off guard when problems arise and spending their time moving from one crisis to the next. (It is often called crisis management.) **Proactive management** involves looking ahead, anticipating problems, and determining solutions to potential problems before they develop. It may require goal setting by individuals.

Proactive management puts you on guard for potential problems.

TECHNOLOGY CONNECTION

Computers and cheap power have made it possible for companies to do extensive planning in the areas of just-in-time inventories, cost benefit analyses, and project planning. Companies can do "what if" scenarios and extensive advanced project planning to envision what might occur in the future.

1. *Why would a company not use these tools to plan into the future?*

2. *Change is increasing at an ever-rapid pace. Is planning worth it?*

3. *Is it possible to plan too much?*

4. *How important is it to be flexible with your plans?*

HOW DO PEOPLE DIFFER IN PLANNING?

People generally fall into three broad categories when planning. Imagine three people playing a game of horseshoes. Here is how each would act if each were in a different category.

The underachiever will stand close to the target. **Underachievers** tend to set goals that are lower than their abilities. This is their way of protecting themselves from risk and anxiety. Because they seldom, if ever, push themselves, they do not achieve much.

The overachiever will stand so far back from the target that hitting it is unlikely. **Overachievers** take on goals beyond their abilities. Their intent is usually to perform better or achieve more success than expected, but this can be very risky. Overachievers may be uncertain of what they can expect of themselves but unable to admit inadequacy. They may also lack self-confidence and try to reduce their anxiety by aiming beyond what they can achieve. Because they may aim for unrealistic goals, they may find it difficult to achieve them or feel satisfied.

The realistic achiever will stand just far enough back to be challenged. **Realistic achievers** tend to have a positive self-image. They are usually successful in their endeavors because they set challenging but attainable goals. They, therefore, become *high achievers*.

Ten Characteristics of High Achievers

1. They like to control situations, and they take responsibility for their behavior.

2. They take reasonable risks.

3. They visualize their accomplishments in advance and allow their behavior to be determined by their goals for the future.

4. They tend to be driven and very focused on the job to be done.

5. They manage their time wisely and prioritize their work effectively.

6. They use effective communication techniques.

7. They value diversity and increase productivity through teamwork.

8. In negotiations, they are fair and seek solutions that are mutually beneficial.

9. They take time to renew themselves physically, spiritually, emotionally, mentally, and socially.

10. They like immediate feedback about their performance.

Perseverance is important in reaching goals.

Consider the traits of high achievers in relation to your own goals. Do you set moderate, attainable goals? Do you become involved in situations so that you may influence what is happening rather than just "going with the flow"? Are you receptive to feedback about your behavior and performance? Do you arrange your tasks to be free from interruptions? Do you allow yourself enough time? Do you persevere? If the answers to these questions are yes, you are probably already a realistic high achiever or well on your way to becoming one. If the answers are no, analyze what you might do to increase your chances for success. If you think back on times when you did practice these behaviors, you will probably find that you were more productive.

If procrastination is a problem for you, think about the pride you feel on accomplishing a task satisfactorily. Giving yourself credit for your accomplishments can provide "energy" for attempting other goals.

People procrastinate for a number of reasons. Some people procrastinate because they have an unrealistic view of successful people. They do not recognize the great amount of planning, organizing, and hard work required to make success seem "easy."

Other people procrastinate because they have poor coping skills or a low tolerance for disappointment. Instead of analyzing situations to determine alternative actions when complications occur or steps are blocked, they give up and do nothing.

If you procrastinate, examine your perceptions, coping skills, tolerance for disappointment, assertiveness, and task organization.

Still others procrastinate as a way of rebelling against expectations, not recognizing the immaturity of such a response. A more effective approach to handling expectations that we consider unfair or inappropriate for us would be to discuss the situation with the person who holds those expectations. Then, we can decide for ourselves what is best and proceed accordingly. However, because many procrastinators lack assertiveness skills, they are uncomfortable addressing a difficult situation, hoping perhaps that the problem will go away. Lack of assertiveness can create additional delays or procrastination if people are reluctant to ask others for resources or help necessary to perform a task.

When you find yourself putting off work on a task or goal, a healthy approach will be for you to examine yourself closely to see why. Then, decide what you want to do about the situation. If you feel overwhelmed, dividing a large task into several smaller ones may be the answer. Do not try to do everything at once. The best way to attack giant projects is to start with small steps and remember that the key to achievement is to think big but act *now*. A small success can motivate you to move on to the next step. Small, steady steps are the key.

Another factor that may help you overcome procrastination is the support of someone who believes in you, such as a friend, relative, or coworker. Developing supportive relationships takes effective human relations skills. (Procrastination will be discussed more thoroughly in Chapter 17.)

Jim Loehr, a performance specialist, has studied the habits and performance of many professional athletes. One of his conclusions suggests a shift in beliefs from the old idea that we should manage our time, avoid stress, and seek rewards to fuel performance. Instead, he now believes we should manage our energy through effective exercise and strength conditioning and seek out stress to heighten our senses. The important part is how we manage our downtime. The effective management and usefulness of the downtime is actually what refuels us. We should realize that life is a series of sprints rather than a constant marathon.[3]

*Fast*Chat

Think back to something that you planned recently.

1. Did the plans go as expected? Why, or why not?

2. Did anything unforeseen happen?

3. Would your planning have been more effective if several people had been involved? Why, or why not?

A **goal** is the objective, target, or end result expected from the completion of tasks, activities, or programs. In your personal life, your goals may include becoming a college graduate, a successful businessperson, or a respected community leader.

Much of what is written about goal setting in organizations can be applied to your personal goal setting. Two management authors, Ramon Aldag and Timothy Stearns, have identified three broad categories of goals in organizations: official goals, operative goals, and operational goals.[4]

Official goals are developed by upper management, are formally stated, and may be published in annual reports or newsletters. They are usually the most abstract category of goals. They tend to be open-ended; that is, the goal itself may not include information about quantity, quality, or deadline. Official goals pertain to the overall mission of the organization. A common example in business today is "to provide excellent service."

Operative goals are those goals for which middle management is responsible. They concern the operating policies of the organization. These goals tend to be more specific than the abstract official goals.

Operative goals usually include a mix of open-ended and close-ended goals. They are usually redefined on a yearly basis. Common examples of operative goals in business today are "to increase the company's share of the market" and "to hire more minorities."

> Organizational goals can be official, operative, or operational.

> *QUICK WIT*
> "There is nothing you cannot have — once you have mentally accepted the fact that you can have it."
>
> Robert Collier,
> Self-help author

CASE STUDIES IN THE NEWS

Despite the fact that companies continue to downsize, unemployment remains relatively low because companies often need to fill empty positions in their new, restructured, and short-handed organizations. Many companies are obsessed with sustaining short-term profitability at the expense of long-term growth. Experts expect downsizing to continue at record levels.

1. *Why would companies lay off workers, then hire for new positions?*

2. *Is this wise planning? What pushes this trend?*

3. *What is the downside of downsizing?*

Peter Drucker, a management expert, has identified eight types of operative goals. They are marketing, innovation, profitability, physical resources, financial resources, human resources, productivity, and social responsibility.[5]

Operational goals are the responsibility of first-line supervisors and employees. They are statements of the expected results of the efforts of the various components of the organization. They include built-in standards of behavior, performance criteria, and completion time. They are concrete and close-ended.

An example of an operational goal is "to increase sales of XYZ chemical by 2006 by 20 percent over the current year by hiring and placing a marketing representative in Southeast Asia." Another example is "to increase the proportion of Hispanic employees in the total workforce of the company to one-fourth within three years by active recruiting and training." Notice that these two goals include specific dates for completion and specify how much.

Following the examples of goals in organizations, we can create specific goals in our personal lives. Here are two examples: "to complete an associate degree within two years by registering for and passing 15 credit hours each semester" and "to save $1,000 for a trip next summer by forgoing movies and eating out only once a month."

Categories of Organizational Goals

Type of Goal	Responsibility of:	Pertains to:	Example:	
Official	Upper management	Overall mission of the organization	Become the global leader in fruit juice brands	Broad
Operational	Middle management	Operating policies and plans of the organization	Increase the company's share of the fruit juice market by 10%	
Operative	Supervisors and employees	Expected results of the efforts of the components of the organization	Increase global sales of fruit juice by 20% by hiring 10 new sales reps in Latin America	Specific

*Fast*Chat

1. What sorts of goals have you established for work, either regarding your own career or as part of your job? Into which category did these goals fall?

2. What are some other areas of life to which you might apply these concepts?

To be most helpful, goals, whether personal or organizational, should have the following characteristics:

Characteristics of Goals
....

1. Goals should be written. Writing increases understanding and commitment.

2. Goals should be measurable. For example, "I want to be more successful in school" is a vague goal because what constitutes success is not specified. Grade point average can be measured; therefore, a better way of expressing this goal would be "I will earn a GPA of 3.0 out of a possible 4.0." If goals are vague and uncertain, they will provide little guidance.

3. Goals should be specific as to time. Otherwise, they are not challenging. At the time specified, they can then be reviewed for correction or revision. Considering the goal above, we can make it time specific by adding a deadline: "I will earn a GPA of 3.0 out of a possible 4.0 during the next academic year."

4. Goals should be challenging but attainable to provide satisfaction and reduce frustration. Goals should be realistic, not wish lists, and should be reasonable expectations of what can be achieved over a given period of time.

5. In an organization, goals should involve participation. Participation increases commitment and communication and, hence, understanding and motivation. The most frequent participation is between the employee and supervisor.

Goals are not just a writing exercise to be put aside until the time comes to write goals for another period. They should be used personally and organizationally to monitor progress throughout the period. In organizations, this monitoring may be as simple as observation by the employee and the supervisor or as formal as written progress reports. Such progress checks help identify changes needed while time still remains. Progress checks must be planned for, and someone must be responsible for them. We should make frequent progress checks of goals in our personal lives as well, recognizing that we are responsible for our own checks and our own progress.

Brian Tracy, in his book *Goals! How to Get Everything You Want*, suggests reviewing your goals every day and every week of every month. He believes it is important to review and reevaluate your goals and objectives frequently to make certain you are still on track toward obtaining your ultimate desire. If not, be flexible and willing to adjust your approach. In the final analysis, persistence will guarantee your success in life.[6]

> Goals should be written, measurable, time specific, challenging, and participatory.

QUICK WIT
"Whatever you can do, or dream you can, begin it. Boldness has genius, power, and magic in it."
Johann Wolfgang von Goethe (1749-1832) German writer and dramatist

HOW FAR AHEAD ARE PLANS MADE?

As noted above, time is a key characteristic of planning. Plans can be long-range, mid-range, and short-range. The time involved will vary from level to level in an organization. For top management, long-range plans may extend over several years, whereas for supervisors, long-range plans may cover only several months. Short-range plans for supervisors may include today or this week, whereas for top management they may cover the current year. In the same way, mid-range plans, which fall between long-range and short-range plans, vary from level to level.

Individuals, too, have long-range, mid-range, and short-range plans. Sometimes we have difficulty completing our long-range plans because we grow tired, forget them, or allow short- or mid-range plans to interfere. Because long-range plans cover a greater period of time, situations and circumstances may change for us, making the long-range plans impractical. In this case, we may need to change them. Psychologists point out that change can be an indication of growth; therefore, a healthy approach for us is to review our plans from time to time to check our progress, modify our strategies if necessary, or perhaps discard the plan as no longer important or possible—and then set new goals.

Developing readily attainable short- or mid-range goals can actually help us accomplish long-range goals because they provide us with periodic feelings of accomplishment. For example, if your plans include a bachelor's or master's degree, setting a short-range goal of satisfactorily completing each course in which you enroll or a mid-range goal of getting a two-year associate degree can help.

Completion of each course and the two-year degree can provide satisfaction and motivation to continue. Patting ourselves on the back can be

GLOBAL CONNECTION

In general, the Japanese spend much more time planning projects than Americans. They get opinions and feedback as well as buy-in from all individuals concerned. The result is that they have fewer adjustments to make after plans are implemented. Americans spend much less time planning and much more time making adjustments after plans are implemented.

1. *Is the American way better? Why, or why not?*
2. *Should Americans spend more time planning?*
3. *Why is it important to gain consensus from the people involved?*

Human Relations

Attaining goals is a thrilling accomplishment. It makes you feel good inside.

1. *Should you attain your goals at the expense of others? Why, or why not?*
2. *Should you embellish your accomplishments to obtain your dream job?*
3. *Should you "advertise" your accomplishments at work to supervisors and other superiors? Why, or why not? In what appropriate ways can you make known accomplishments that might affect your career?*

psychologically healthy, and completion of short- or mid-range goals provides opportunities to do so.

Another of Brian Tracy's recommendations for goal-setting success is to measure your progress. Setting clear benchmarks helps you assess how well you are doing and what corrective actions are necessary. Advance planning and organizing enables most people to accomplish even the most complex goals.[7]

Goals can become obsolete if we have achieved them. They can also become less important as we grow. Think of how your own goals have changed over the years. We can probably all recall various ways in which we answered the traditional question, "What do you want to be when you grow up?" At four years of age, we may have wanted to be a prince or princess, at six a dancer, at ten an astronaut, and in our teens a professional athlete. Somewhere along the line, we lost interest in some of these, decided we lacked the natural ability necessary for others, or found something else of appeal to us. Today we may have a different career goal in mind, one that probably combines dreams and practicality. Then, after we have been working a while, we may decide to set other career goals. Mid-career switches, for instance, are fairly common.

*Fast*Chat

1. Do you ever write your goals down? Why, or why not?

2. Have any plans you've made possessed some or all of the characteristics listed above? Which ones?

3. Have you successfully reached a goal you set for yourself? What steps did you take to reach the goal? Were there intermediate steps (short-range or mid-range goals)?

Both organizations and individuals have multiple goals and priorities. We seldom have the luxury of pursuing one goal at a time.

WHICH GOALS COME FIRST?

Aldag and Stearns have identified four techniques that managers can use to decide which goals to emphasize during periods of conflict. We can apply them to our personal goals and plans also. They include satisficing, sequential attention, preference ordering, and goal changes.[8]

> Prioritize goals by satisficing, sequential attention, preference ordering, and goal changes.

Satisficing Satisficing is a term created to define situations where one perfect and unique solution may not be possible. Satisficing refers to any group of solutions that offers good results under the circumstances. When we are faced with numerous goals, we can reduce our stress by identifying a satisfactory rather than optimum level of performance for some of them. Some tasks just need to be done, and often there are several perfectly acceptable ways in which they might be performed. For example, in our lives, satisficing might consist of light housecleaning when we're pressed for time, rather than sacrificing other goals (such as time with family) or doing nothing and letting it get steadily worse.

In many situations, perfection, or even excellence, may not be that important, and, as a matter of fact, can be costly or stressful. The desire for perfection can create havoc with goal accomplishment and people's lives if carried too far. Save your energy for the things that really do need to be as close to perfect as possible.

Sequential Attention When we have multiple priorities, we may need to shift our attention from one goal to the next over periods of time. Successful working parents frequently adopt this tactic. Work priorities sometimes take precedence over family activities, and at other times the reverse is true. The main point is to keep the overall quality of performance in each area acceptable.

Preference Ordering If we have several goals toward which we wish to work, we may need to rank them according to preference. For example, a company may decide to maximize profit over expansion. Individuals may decide to save for a new car rather than take a vacation.

Goal Changes As pointed out earlier, we may change goals because they become outdated or inappropriate, such as when we complete a degree or buy the car for which we have been saving. A well-known example of goal changing is the Foundation for Infantile Paralysis. Its original goal was to develop a vaccine for polio. Once the vaccine was developed, it changed its goal to conquering birth defects and became the March of Dimes.

HOW DO YOU SET PERSONAL GOALS?

In the book *The Power of Focus: How to Hit Your Business, Personal and Financial Targets*, the authors suggest that your habits determine your future. They help identify bad habits and how to overcome them and illustrate the power of "NO!" Often, we overload ourselves with too many tasks because we cannot say no to friends and family members when asked to take on additional chores or responsibilities that ultimately overload our schedules and bog us down on our path toward success. The authors advise individuals to stay focused, see the big picture, have a "Top 10 Goals Check List," say no to toxic people, find a great mentor, and ask for what you want. These considerations are the basis of the process for setting successful personal goals.[9]

The process for deciding where you want to go next with your life requires that you make a frequent, close examination of your preferences. Asking yourself specific questions can help you determine your priorities in life. Consider, for example, how important the Personal Preferences listed on the next page are to you.

Considering these questions objectively can help you in setting your personal goals. Notice that all of the measures of success require high levels of human relations skills. Once you have examined yourself closely, you are ready to set your goals. Below are some guidelines to help you.

1. Remember to be realistic. If your goals are too high, you may lose confidence. In determining how high to set your goals, consider your own past performance and that of others. If your goals are too low, you will have no incentive or challenge to better yourself. Be careful that you do not underrate yourself. Finally, make your goals worthwhile.

2. Once you have determined your goals, openly commit yourself. Letting others know about them can help. Be sure to say specifically what it is you plan to accomplish, when, where, and how.

3. Your goals may have to be coordinated with other people. An examination of your professional and personal relationships is necessary.

4. Visualize success. Get a mental image of your goal and think when, not if. Carefully applying the above guidelines can help you establish goals that are both meaningful and achievable. Such application must be an ongoing process to be effective.

QUICK WIT

"Our greatest need and most difficult achievement is to find meaning in our lives."

Bruno Bettelheim
(1903-1990)
Austrian-born
American psychologist

Personal Preferences

1. **Affection.** If you are to have your need for affection met, you must obtain and share companionship and affection. Your goals must include other people. Are your goals practical enough to accommodate others?

2. **Expertness.** If this is important to you, you must become an authority in some area and possess the human relations skills to communicate your expertise to others and have it received. Which area? Do your human relations skills need developing?

3. **Independence.** Being independent may require time and at least some money. When will you have that time, and how will you obtain the necessary finances to be independent? Even more basic, what does being independent mean to you? Will it mean the same to others in your life?

4. **Leadership.** To be a leader, you must gain influence. Where? At work? In the community? How?

5. **Parenthood.** Parenthood requires a tremendous investment of time, finances, and physical and emotional energy. Can you afford that investment now? Later? How?

6. **Happiness, contentment.** What is your definition of these concepts? What will it take for you to achieve them? How? Without human relations skills, our lives can be in constant turmoil, which can prevent personal happiness and contentment.

7. **Prestige.** Prestige differs for different people. How will you measure it—by the house in which you live, the organization for which you work, or where you vacation? How will you acquire that house, gain employment at that company, or acquire the money and knowledge for that vacation?

8. **Security.** Security is important for many people but not for others. What kind of security do you need—financial or emotional? If financial security is part of your need, how much will it take, and how will you acquire it? If emotional security is important to you, what does that mean—a supportive supervisor? A caring spouse? Concerned friends? What will you have to do to have that kind of relationship with your boss, spouse, or friends?

9. **Personal development.** Personal development can take the form of growth, hobbies, talents, or knowledge. It implies continuing to learn throughout your life. How will you feed this desire in yourself? Where can you find the necessary direction, guidance, and instruction?

10. **Wealth.** If money is important to you, how will you acquire it? How much will it take to satisfy you? How will you take care of it if you gain it? Human relations skills will be necessary to help you earn more and to keep others from begrudging you money for which you have worked hard.

11. **Service to others.** A sense of duty is important to many people and can make the difference in the quality of life in organizations, communities, and countries. If you desire to make such contributions to others, where and how would you like to use your energy and abilities?

WHAT ATTITUDES BRING SUCCESS?

Personalities have been characterized as Type A and Type B based on a person's degree of aggressiveness and passiveness. Type A personalities are usually driven and aggressive, whereas Type B are patient and passive. Both have problems associated with them. Type A people may create stress-related health problems for themselves while Type B people may not be assertive enough.

Two psychologists, Robert Kriegel and Marilyn Harris Kriegel, suggest that all of us have the potential to perform as a Type C person. Type C behavior is versatile and adaptive. It enables us to perform at our peak and feel vital and full of energy. A Type C attitude combines commitment, confidence, and control.[10]

Commitment Identifying what you want, knowing your innermost desires, and translating them into action will result in harmony between what you do and what you want to do. The more committed you are to something, the less difficult it seems. Low commitment can make a task overwhelming. When Type C people look at a task, they see opportunities. Others see obstacles.

uick tip ....

You can do a reality check to determine how serious a problem is.

> To do a reality check, measure and rate the difficulty, bring the past into the present, and imagine the worst.

1. Measure the difficulty. Rate it on a scale of 1 to 10. Measuring the difficulty may be as simple as writing it down.

2. Bring the past into the present. Think of similar situations and remember your successes. Analyze them. What were your actions, feelings, and thoughts that led you to success?

3. Imagine the worst. Ask yourself, "What is the worst that can happen if I fail in this endeavor? Will I die, lose my job, or lose my spouse?" Because the consequences are not usually that dire, such a reality check will immediately boost your confidence.

4. Visualize yourself accomplishing your present goal.

In doing your reality check, be careful of false confidence, which can lead to being unprepared. If the reality check shows the problem is indeed major, you can at least now concentrate on dealing with it rather than on your anxieties.

....

Confidence Confidence in your own worth does not depend on others' moods, your looks, or other external factors. You may hate to fail, but you do not fear it, because you know that with risks come mistakes and failures, but also the possibility of learning and greater gain. Be alert to your own inner signals of fear. When you notice them, stop, take a few deep, slow breaths, hold each to the count of three, and exhale slowly. This practice can help put matters back into perspective. Doing a reality check can also help you manage your anxieties.

Control Control is the third component of a Type C attitude. After doing a reality check, concentrate on what you can control to improve your performance and effectiveness. You can include your own thoughts, feelings, attitudes, and actions.

Robert Land, executive vice president of a large national human resources management-consulting firm, pointed out that successful people are generally those who work to maintain control over their work environment and a myriad of unanticipated events. In other words, these people are proactive rather than reactive. He advises that we must be responsible for our careers and ourselves. We cannot expect our bosses to take charge of our careers because bosses seldom have the time or interest to help us plan where we should be and how to get there.[11]

One thing you can usually control is how you approach work. Employees must work to keep themselves employable. They need to accept change, learn to adapt, accept responsibility, and continue to develop. Also, bosses look favorably on employees who ease their burden and harshly on those who add to it. Ultimately, the most valuable subordinates are those who make their bosses look good. If you are now working, you can check your "progress pulse" to measure your career success by answering the questions below.[12]

Check Your "Progress Pulse" to Measure Career Success

To assess objectively whether your progress pulse is healthy, ask yourself these questions.

1. Have you had a formal or informal performance review within the last three months?

2. Have you asked your boss lately what you can do to help?

3. Do you know what your boss's goals and missions are?

4. Have you taken the initiative to do things your boss hasn't asked you to do?

5. Have you taken on any special projects within the last three months?

---

6. Have you been sought out recently for information or special advice?

7. Have you created some positive visibility for yourself?

8. Are you keeping notes on your recent accomplishments so you can give them to your boss before your next performance review?

9. Are you a team player and do you help your coworkers meet their goals?

10. Do people, especially your boss, like to work with you?

11. Do people ask you to meetings and copy you on memos?

12. Have you aligned yourself with a confidential peer to get candid feedback on your performance and to determine how others perceive you?

13. Have you set down where you'd like to be in two to five years?

14. Do you know how your progress compares with others in your field at your age?

15. Are you aware of training or experience you'll need to advance to the next position?

16. Are you keeping a list of contacts in your field?

17. Have you been attending professional meetings?

19. Can you name an alternative field where you could transfer your skills if necessary?

20. Have you identified a mentor—someone to help you and to serve as a good role model?

Reprinted with permission from the International Association of Administrative Professionals (IAAP).

*Fast*Chat

Many times in this fast-paced society, we cannot do everything well.

1. Can you name a time you had to attempt satisfaction rather than perfection?

2. In what situations might it be acceptable to do a satisfactory job rather than an excellent one? When might excellence be important?

3. Which personality type do you think you possess: A, B, or C? What would you need to do to become more like a Type C?

A variety of approaches and different degrees of formality are used in setting goals in organizations. One popular technique is **Management by Objectives**, originated by George Odiorne. This technique, sometimes abbreviated to MBO, is a method and philosophy of management that emphasizes self-determination. Its chief purpose is to improve employee motivation by having employees at all levels participate in setting their own goals.[13]

FEATURES OF MBO

MBO emphasizes self-determination for employees.

Proponents of MBO say that it helps increase motivation because of the involvement and commitment of the people participating in the process. Three features characterize it.

1. Employees participate in establishing the objectives and the criteria by which they will be judged. This step usually involves discussions between the supervisor and the employee. Employees should be aware of overall organizational and departmental goals. Then they can set individual goals that are valued by the organization.

2. Both the supervisor and the employee know what the employee is to accomplish. The employee knows what the supervisor expects and can work toward the correct goal. The supervisor, in turn, can guide the employee correctly if deviation should start occurring.

3. If the goal has been written correctly, it will contain specific descriptions of the end result desired (how much and by when). This feature will make evaluation of the employee's performance easier. Additionally, the employee will be more likely to agree with the appraisal because the criteria were selected and agreed upon in advance.

BENEFITS OF MBO

Feedback reinforces desired behavior, discourages unwanted behavior, and helps us plan improvement.

The *George Odiorne Letter* summarizes several benefits to be gained from organizations using MBO:[14]

1. Communicating job objectives helps people understand the purpose of their job, which increases the likelihood of success.

2. People today want to participate in decisions affecting them. Because MBO involves superior and subordinate in discussions about responsibilities and expected results, employees develop greater commitment.

3. MBO makes sense psychologically and may help motivation. Various studies have shown that high achievers are those who set goals, that goals have a powerful effect on behavior, that employees with clear goals achieve more than those without them, and that highly motivated people are those who achieve, especially goals to which they are committed. Odiorne points out that goal-centered people are more likely to be mentally healthy than are people driven by fear, intimidation, punishment, or hostility.

4. MBO can save time and money because people know for what tasks they are responsible and accountable.

5. Because individuals are exercising self-control under MBO, they can measure their own progress against the goals they helped create and adapt their behavior appropriately.

6. MBO allows people to present again their past creative ideas not previously accepted when they set their goals for a new period. This opportunity fosters creativity in organizations, considered vital for success today.

7. MBO makes performance appraisal more reasonable and compensation systems more rational. Because people are evaluated against goals and standards that they helped establish, appraisal becomes easier for both the supervisor and the employee.

*Fast*Chat

MBO helps set goals and objectives upon which both supervisor and subordinate agree.

1. What might be the downsides to MBO?

2. If goals are set for the year, can they change after six to eight months? If so, what should be done?

3. Does MBO keep people from setting goals in areas that are hard to measure such as improving communication skills?

The **performance appraisal** is a measurement of how well an employee is doing on the job. Performance appraisals can be performed by supervisors rating their employees, employees rating their superiors, team members who rate each other, outsiders who rate employees, employees who rate themselves, or a combination of all these techniques. Because of the growing use of teams and a concern about customer feedback, the fastest growing types of appraisals are those that involve team members and sources outside the organization. The most common type of appraisals, however, are those done at least annually by an immediate supervisor.

Performance appraisal is a process that frequently both the employee and the supervisor dread. Being human, supervisors may fear that subordinates will not like them, that employees may do less work if the appraisal is a negative one, that employees may yell at them, or that friendships with subordinates may be jeopardized. At the same time, employees may wonder whether supervisors can be fair, doubt whether supervisors understand the subordinates' jobs, fear an average or below-average rating, or feel that a high rating may interfere with friendships with coworkers.

Organizations appraise employee performance for a number of reasons, as shown on the next page:

Feedback is important. It lets us know what we are doing right and what behavior we need to change.

©Digital Vision

Why Organizations Appraise Employee Performance

1. To encourage good job perform-ance, to discourage unacceptable performance, and to correct inappropriate behavior that interferes with good performance.

   If it is conducted correctly, the appraisal session can help communication. It can result in growth and increased motivation or at least a better understanding of what is expected of us.

2. To let us know how we are doing.

   We want to know where we stand in the organiza-tion. Although we may dislike being judged, human beings need feedback, both negative and positive. Negative feedback allows us to make cor-rections in our behavior and performance, whereas positive feedback lets us know what is appreciated so that we will continue. (Psychologists say that we quit engaging in a certain behavior both if the behavior is punished and if it is ignored.) Feedback also assists us in making plans for personal improvement.

3. To give the organization informa-tion about employees that can be used in later career decisions, such as raises, promotions, demotions, transfers, and terminations.

   Appraisals can help move your career forward or help identify areas that need more work. They also help managers identify the need for training in individuals and in groups of employees.

If performance appraisals are to be effective, both the supervisor and the employee must prepare for them.

PREPARING YOURSELF

You can take two important steps ahead of time and during the appraisal session to help make your appraisal the positive process that it is supposed to be. These steps are explained in the box on the next page. Using a proactive, assertive approach is to your advantage.

Additionally, you can take three steps *during* the appraisal session to make the process effective and to help yourself. They are:

1. Go into the session willing to listen and participate. A defensive, closed mind will sabotage the session before it even starts. The appraisal is a good opportunity to share your career goals with your supervisor.

Steps You Can Take *Before* a Performance Session

1. Make sure that you understand what is expected of you.

Effective supervisors will be preparing for the appraisal session throughout the entire appraisal period. They know what is expected of the employee, make sure the subordinate also knows, observe frequently, and tell you how you are performing. You also can prepare throughout the period. If you participated in the establishment of objectives for your job, you understand what is expected of you. If you did not, do not wait until the appraisal session to ask questions. Keep checking that your understanding of what you are to do is the same as your supervisor's understanding. You can also take the initiative and ask for feedback during the period. This way, you will eliminate surprises in the appraisal session. Open communication with your supervisor is extremely important.

2. Become familiar with the evaluation or appraisal instrument to be used.

Ideally, you should do this at the beginning of the appraisal period. Then, before your appraisal session, take the time to conduct a self-appraisal by completing the instrument as objectively as you can. This activity will help you remember accomplishments that you want to bring up if your supervisor overlooks them. It also can increase communication and understanding during the session. Identify areas that need improvement also.

2. If obstacles have been in the way of your performing satisfactorily, you should have made them known to your supervisor before now. However, if you have not, certainly share them at this time. Are you frequently late in completing a weekly report because the Sales Department is late in submitting figures to you? If so, let your supervisor know what you need to perform better.

3. Make sure that you understand what is expected of you at the conclusion of the appraisal session. For instance, should you continue as you have been, assume other responsibilities, or perform current responsibilities better?

Taking these steps will help you feel more in control of your life and can make the session more effective. Extremely important in each step of this process are strong human relations skills. The greater your skills and those of your supervisor, the better will be the outcome of an appraisal. This outcome, in turn, will benefit you, your supervisor, and the organization.

THE SUPERVISOR'S ROLE

Lester Bittel, the author of *What Every Supervisor Should Know,* found that an effective supervisor will follow a number of steps in conducting the appraisal. Awareness and understanding of these steps can enable you to use them to your advantage and to prepare effectively for your appraisal.[15] The steps are:

Understanding the supervisor's role in appraisals can help you prepare.

1. The supervisor will schedule the appraisal in advance and ask the employee to think about achievements and areas for improvement to be discussed during the session. This step will allow the supervisor and employee time to prepare. Your objectivity and preparation can make a big difference in how smoothly the session runs and can enhance your supervisor's perception of you.

2. The supervisor will read the employee's personnel file and any other performance information available. If your file is open to you, you should review it periodically. This review will enable you to respond to negative information. If positive comments have been made or written about you that have not been put into the file, bring them to the evaluation session.

3. The supervisor will be prepared and will plan in advance what to say. Realizing that your supervisor is not treating you or the process lightly should make you feel more respected and, hence, more comfortable and receptive.

4. The supervisor will choose a quiet location for the session, free of interruptions, will allow plenty of time, and will give the employee opportunity to speak. If you know that the session will not be rushed, you can take the time to listen fully, communicate openly, take notes, and ask the appropriate questions.

5. The supervisor will not usually discuss salary and performance in the same meeting. Recognizing that money should be discussed in a separate meeting frees you to concentrate on issues related to your performance and to avoid distractions.

6. During the session, the supervisor will explain the purpose of the meeting, ask the employee's opinion, stay positive, discuss total performance, reach agreement on standards of performance, document the agreement, and get the employee's signature. If you accept these actions as part of the effective appraisal process, each step will seem less threatening to you. This knowledge will allow you to feel more comfortable and confident during the appraisal.

APPRAISAL INSTRUMENTS

No single perfect technique or form has yet been designed for recording performance appraisals. You may be evaluated by a variety of means during your career because numerous kinds of appraisal instruments exist. Some organizations have created their own forms, whereas others use commercially available ones. In general, the most common performance appraisal techniques fall into four broad categories. They are the narrative, category, comparative, and behavioral approaches.

Narrative Approach The performance appraisals in this category include the essay and critical incident technique.

Essay Appraisal. Using the **essay appraisal** technique, the supervisor writes a paragraph or more about the employee's strengths and weaknesses, quantity and quality of work, current skills and knowledge, and potential value to the organization.

The strength of this method lies in the fact that it probably gives a more complete picture of the employee. However, its use has several drawbacks. First, it takes longer to complete, and essay writing is more difficult. Secondly, it is likely to be more subjective than a graph. Finally, it makes comparison of employees almost impossible because it has no scale. For these reasons, it should be used only in appraising middle- and top-management employees.

Critical Incident. Using the **critical incident** technique, supervisors record in writing actual incidents in behavior that they observe in employees. The note or memo is then filed in the employee's personnel folder. Examples of negative incidents include tardiness, careless work, errors in judgment, and insubordination. Positive incidents may be completion of a project ahead of schedule, willingness to assist others, cooperation, or regular attendance at work. An obvious drawback to the critical incident method is that it is time-consuming. Its advantage is that it provides the organization with the necessary documentation for decisions about transfers, promotions, demotions, and terminations.

Category Approach These ratings include the graphic rating scale and the checklist.

Graphic Rating Scale. As you can see on the sample form that appears on pages 278–279, a **graphic rating scale** lists the factors to be considered and terms to be used. Its strengths are that it is easy for the supervisor to complete and it helps make comparisons of employees easier. However, the categories and factors in the scale may overlap, making a thorough appraisal difficult. For example, individuals appraised with the sample form would almost automatically receive a high score in "effort" if they had been rated high in "quantity of work." Additionally, because descriptions are specified, the scale is rigid and might not give a complete picture of the employee. Because of its weaknesses, the graphic rating scale is often used in combination with the essay method.

Analyze the sample form that appears on the next page. As you review it, think about forms you have used in your own performance appraisals and how they were more or less useful than the graphic rating scale form.

Checklist. Supervisors check statements on a **checklist** to identify those that most represent the characteristics and performance of the employees. Different weights can be assigned to the statements, so they can be quantified. The problems with this method are that the words may have different meanings to different supervisors and that the supervisors can have difficulty explaining the appraisal if the weights assigned are not apparent.

Comparative Ranking Approach These appraisal techniques include ranking and forced distribution.

CASE STUDIES IN THE NEWS

 In a recent article in *Fast Company* magazine, management theorist Henry Mintzberg argued that no one can become qualified to be a manager solely from the classes in an MBA program. He suggested that if individuals are interested in management, they should find an industry they like, get a good job, stick with it, prove themselves, and *then* pursue further education.[16]

1. *What do you think experience can teach you that a business course can't?*

2. *Is there anything you have learned firsthand from your experience with performance appraisals that you did not learn in a business class? Give examples.*

A Graphic Rating Scale Lists the Factors To Be Considered and Terms To Be Used in Appraising Employees

EMPLOYEE:		
JOB TITLE: (GRADE)		
DEPARTMENT:		
DATE OF EMPLOYMENT	DATE OF EMPLOYMENT ON PRESENT JOB:	NUMBER OF MONTHS/YEARS ON PRESENT JOB:
		PRESENT SALARY: $

To Raters:

The value of this rating depends upon the impartiality and sound judgment you use when marking this form. Base your judgment of the employee in relation to others doing similar work, keeping in mind the duties and requirements of the job the employee occupies. Consider only one trait at a time. Do not let your rating of the employee on any one trait influence your rating on any other trait.

Place a check mark in the block on the scale below the expression that most nearly describes your opinion of the employee. You are requested to note any comments which you believe would furnish additional information concerning the employee's performance on his/her job or to record any significant observations made during the discussion in the space provided at the end of this form.

EFFORT: How well does he/she make use of his/her time? Consider his/her physical and mental application to his/her work, his/her energy and attentiveness.	☐ Wastes considerable time. Does only enough to get by.	☐ Keeps fairly busy. Allows idle conversation to keep him/her from work.	☐	☐ Rarely unoccupied. Is energetic and attentive.	☐ Constantly applying himself/herself. Never seems to have an idle moment.
JOB KNOWLEDGE: How well has he/she acquired the knowledge of all elements comprising his/her job? Consider not only his/her own job's fundamentals, but also that of related work: his/her understanding of 'how' and 'why' his/her work is done.	☐ Understands only the simpler or more routine phases of job.	☐ Is steadily acquiring the knowledge necessary to perform the more intricate job phases.	☐	☐ Thoroughly knows most all phases of job.	☐ Has complete mastery of job. Remarkable understanding of all phases.
ACCURACY: How accurate is the employee in performing his/her duty? Consider the number of errors made—the orderliness and thoroughness of work produced.	☐ In need of improvement.	☐ Reasonably accurate.	☐	☐ Very seldom makes a mistake.	☐ Exceptionally precise, orderly and thorough.
INITIATIVE: Is he/she eager and able to attack new problems, advance ideas, better improve his/her work? Consider his/her self-reliance. Aggressiveness—constructive thinking.	☐ Mildly progressive, but lacks certain abilities to go ahead on own.	☐ Possesses a normal amount of initiative.	☐	☐ Usually self-sufficient in his/her work enterprise.	☐ A self starter, enjoys solving difficulties and originating better methods.

DEPENDABILITY: What are your feelings toward him/her when you are not at hand to give supervision? Consider his/her reliability in complying with standard procedures on his/her job following instructions and conducting self properly.	☐ Needs occasional follow-up.	☐ Dependable.	☐ Is very dependable, needs little supervision.	☐ Completely trustworthy, can handle job without supervision.
JUDGMENT: How well does he/she display good common sense in his/her work? Consider how readily he/she grasps a situation and draws a correct conclusion, making best use of his/her experience and the facts at hand.	☐ Apt to make hasty conclusions without due regard for consequences.	☐ Usually displays good common sense.	☐ Is levelheaded, able to draw sound conclusions.	☐ Displays superior discrimination in analyzing facts and coming up with the right answer.
QUANTITY OF WORK: How much work is he/she able to produce? Consider not only his/her regular daily output but also how promptly he/she dispatches those extra or rush assignments.	☐ Pushed to maintain schedule. Sometimes needs help from others.	☐ Turns out satisfactory amount of work.	☐ Keeps well ahead in his/her work—on top of his/her job.	☐ Extremely rapid—"never seems to get enough to do."
ATTITUDE TOWARD ASSOCIATES: How well does he/she get along and cooperate with others? Consider his/her relations with fellow workers, his/her supervisors, business contacts.	☐ Frequently uncooperative. Too critical of others.	☐ Average ability to work with others.	☐ A good team worker.	☐ Very well liked and respected. An exceptional force for good morale.
ATTITUDE TOWARD WORK: What interest does he/she take in his/her job or line of work? Consider his/her eagerness to obtain more knowledge about his/her work—his/her enthusiasm in tackling difficulties—his/her pride in a job well done.	☐ Mildly interested in some phases of job.	☐ Shows normal interest.	☐ Eagerness often displayed. Has pride in work.	☐ Extraordinary interest, wants to learn all about job and any related work.

COMMENTS:

RATING REVIEWED WITH EMPLOYEE: _____   SUPERVISOR: _____

EMPLOYEE'S SIGNATURE: _____   DATE: _____

Ranking. In the **ranking** method, all the employees are listed from highest to lowest in performance. This can cause problems in that someone who is last in one group could be the top employee in another group. Also, quantifying the difference in how far apart the employees are from each other is difficult. For instance, there may not be much difference between #4 and #5 rated employees whereas there is a great deal of difference between #11 and #12.

Forced Distribution. Ratings of performance are distributed along a bell-shaped curve in the **forced distribution** technique. The difficulties are that a supervisor using this system may resist placing employees in a very high or very low group. Further, small groups may not have a bell-shaped distribution.

Behavioral Approach Appraisals These appraisals include the behaviorally anchored rating scale (BARS).

The **BARS** rating technique describes possible behaviors that the employee most often exhibits. The behaviors are then measured against a scale. For instance, a customer service representative taking orders may be rated from "used positive phrases to explain product" to "argued with customer about the suitability of the product requested." These scales take extensive time to develop and maintain, and scales must be developed for each different position.

In addition to these types of appraisals, in which supervisors rate subordinates, a recent rise has been seen in the use of 360-degree appraisals. The concept is that you receive feedback from a range of individuals around you—a 360-degree circle—including other employees, managers other than your immediate supervisor, and even customers. The intentions of the 360-degree appraisal are to find out how an employee interacts with others, avoid any chance of one person's bias either holding that employee back or advancing him or her too rapidly, and making sure that good human relations skills are being used with everyone around the employee, not just with a supervisor the employee is trying to impress.

*Fast*Chat

1. Have you ever been appraised at a job? What was it like? Did it worry you? Do you feel that you now would be better able to prepare for such an event?

2. In what ways do job appraisals differ from grades in school? In what ways are they similar?

3. What do you think makes creating an appraisal a difficult task for a supervisor?

CHAPTER SUMMARY

Planning can benefit both people and organizations by improving the chances of success. Having goals gives us targets at which we can aim. Without planning, organizations tend to become reactive rather than proactive, creating frustration for employees.

Three broad categories of organizational goals are official, operative, and operational. They differ in how specific they are, what activities are included, and which level of management has responsibility for them. To be most effective, goals should be written, measurable, specific, and challenging but attainable. In an organization, for the greatest understanding and motivation to occur, an individual's goals should be developed with participation of both the supervisor and the affected individual. Goals differ in the time allowed for their completion. They can be long-range, mid-range, and short-range. When goals conflict, four techniques can be used to prioritize them: satisficing, sequential attention, preference ordering, and goal changes.

In setting personal goals, we should consider our priorities in life. They can include affection, expertness, independence, leadership, parenthood, happiness and contentment, prestige, security, personal development, wealth, and service. We should also apply four guidelines: (1) be realistic, (2) openly commit ourselves, (3) coordinate our goals with people important to us professionally and personally, and (4) visualize success. A Type C attitude that combines commitment, confidence, and control can improve our chances of personal success.

Management by Objectives is a method and philosophy of management used to formalize goal setting in organizations. The employee performance appraisal is a measurement of how well the employee is doing on the job. Although both the supervisor and employee may dread them, appraisals are necessary. Employees can take steps to make appraisal a beneficial experience. Numerous appraisal techniques exist.

Key Terms

planning

reactive management

proactive management

underachiever

overachiever

realistic achiever

goal

official goals

operative goals

operational goals

Management by Objectives (MBO)

performance appraisal

essay appraisal

critical incident

graphic rating scale

checklist

ranking

forced distribution

Behaviorally Anchored Rating Scale (BARS)

REVIEW QUESTIONS

1. Explain how planning can benefit people and organizations.

2. What are the three categories of organizational goals? Whose responsibility is each category? What kinds of activities are included in each category?

3. Describe the characteristics of well-formulated goals.

4. Define long-range, mid-range, and short-range goals.

5. Name and define the four techniques for prioritizing goals.

6. What is Management by Objectives? Name some of the reasons why an organization may use MBO. How would individuals within the organization benefit from its use?

7. What is an employee performance appraisal? If it is so dreaded, why do organizations do it? How can employees help turn this process into a positive one?

8. Describe the common performance appraisal instruments.

DISCUSSION QUESTIONS

1. Identify some situations in your personal life and, if you have held jobs, at work that developed because of a lack of planning. What happened? How could the situation have been improved?

2. When setting goals, do you see yourself as an underachiever, over-achiever, or realistic achiever? On what do you base your perception? Do you want to be in a different category? If so, what steps can you take? What steps are you willing to take?

3. Is procrastination a problem for you? Why, or why not? If so, what has been the usual result of your procrastination? How might you work to eliminate this problem?

4. Write a goal that would be appropriate for a company with which you are familiar. Write a personal goal. Be sure that the goals are complete.

5. Briefly review your goals so far in life. Analyze why the goals have been accomplished or not. How has their status affected where you are today and your current goals?

6. Again considering situations in your personal life and at work, think about periods of conflicting goals. How was the conflict resolved? How might the four techniques for prioritizing goals described in this chapter have helped you?

7. Review the questions in the section of this chapter dealing with setting personal goals. Choose one long-range goal and develop a plan for accomplishing it. Then write three mid-range or short-range goals related to it.

8. After completing question 7, review the guidelines for setting goals. Examine your goals to see whether you have applied the guidelines for goal setting to them.

9. How can you apply the three components of Type C behavior to your accomplishment of the goals you wrote in question 7?

10. Think about a job that you have held. Did you make your boss's job harder or easier? How? Which approach would have been better for you in the long run? What, if anything, would you do differently today?

11. Have you ever worked in an organization that used MBO? If so, what was the process? What was the outcome of that process for the organization and those involved?

12. We have all received evaluations of our performance. We tested for a driver's license, tried out for sports, or completed tests, for example. Think about specific times when you received appraisals, at work or at any other place. How did you react to the feedback? Were some of your reactions negative? Why? How did you use the feedback? Did feedback help you grow in some way? How?

CHAPTER PROJECT

In a one-page essay, describe what goals you want to have achieved by the year 2025 in the following areas of your life: professional life, personal relationships, spiritual life, and social life. Then, draw up a plan to get yourself from your current status to your desired achievements.

WRITING

APPLICATIONS

In small groups, analyze the following:

You Can't Have It All At Once

Sulynn is a part-time student at the local community college. She is afraid that she will once again have to drop her courses even though she wants an associate degree in management very much. Because Sulynn is a

TEAMWORK

divorced mother with two children to support, she must work full time as a sales clerk in the nearby mall. Additionally, she feels she should serve as a room mother in her son's and daughter's schools each year. Having no help around the house, she also does all inside and outside maintenance and yard work. In fact, the appearance of her home is an area of special pride for her. Needless to say, all of this activity leaves little time for friendships.

Sulynn did not go to college immediately after graduating from high school and feels that she is falling even farther behind by going part time. For the last four semesters, she has tried to play "catch-up" by registering for three or four courses even though her counselor advised against such a heavy load. By the middle of each semester, she felt so overwhelmed that she dropped all or most of her courses.

It is now midway through the fall semester, and Sulynn once again recognizes that feeling of hopelessness.

1. What is wrong with Sulynn's plans?

2. What advice would you give her in setting long-range, mid-range, and short-range goals?

3. How might she prioritize her goals?

MBO Gone Awry

TEAMWORK

Mike Aston is an engineer with a large oil and gas company. Four months ago, he was asked to participate in the budgeting process for the next year. The corporate office cited use of MBO as the rationale for getting Mike's input. Willingly, he spent hours in his office alone, carefully calculating costs for maintaining and operating several oil platforms in Indonesia for which his local office is responsible.

After many hours of hard work, he submitted his budget to his supervisor, Emily Rodriguez, who passed it on to the head of the Houston office, Ronald Wang.

One month after the process began, Mr. Wang gathered the budgets from the different departments in the Houston office and carried them to the corporate office in New York.

Six weeks later, the corporate office issued the overall budget guidelines for the corporation. Mike was astonished to see no resemblance between the guidelines and the budget that he had submitted. Emily asked him to redo his budget to fit the parameters issued by the corporate office, which he did.

Exactly four months after beginning the process and after much frustration, Mike received approval of a budget for his next year's operations.

1. Is this application of MBO correct?

2. What happened to create the overly long time involved and the need to prepare a second budget?

3. What could Mike have done to make a more productive process? Emily? Ronald? The corporate office?

ADDITIONAL READINGS AND RESOURCES

Canfield, Jack, Mark Victor Hansen, and Les Hewitt. *The Power of Focus: How to Hit Your Business, Personal and Financial Targets with Absolute Certainty.* Florida: Health Communications, Inc. 2000.

Covey, Stephen R. *The 7 Habits of Highly Effective People.* New York: Fireside, 1989.

McWilliams, Peter. *Life 101.* Los Angeles: Prelude Press, 1994.

Liker, Jeffrey K. *Toyota Way: 14 Management Principles for the World's Greatest Manufacturer.* New York: McGraw-Hill, 2004.

Loehr, Jim, and Tony Schwartz. *Power of Full Engagement: Managing Energy, Not Time, Is the Key to High Performance & Personal Renewal.* New York: Free Press, 2003.

Loehr, Jim, and Tony Schwartz. "The Making of a Corporate Athlete," *Harvard Business Review* (January 2001): 120-128.

Tracy, Brian. *Change Your Thinking Change Your Life: How to Unlock Your Full Potential for Success and Achievement.* New Jersey: John Wiley & Sons, Inc., 2003.

Tracy, Brian. *Goals! How to Get Everything You Want – Faster Than You Ever Thought Possible.* San Francisco: Berrett-Koehler Publishers, Inc., 2003.

For additional resources, refer to the web site for this text: school.cengage.com/career/dalton

Leadership:
Styles and Skills of an Effective Leader

focus

Michael R. Jones, CEO of Phonak, a hearing-aid manufacturer in Warrenville, IL, tries to remember the names of all 300 employees in his rapidly expanding company. When touring people through his plant, he will acknowledge his employees and have them demonstrate their work. Jones is strong on hiring minorities and immigrants and believes they are highly motivated workers. Everyone is treated with respect. Phonak has 28 nationalities represented among its 300 employees. To encourage communications, the company has open floor plans and no individual offices. There are no physical barriers, desks are all out in the open, and no one is stuck in a back room or cubicle. Jones sits with his sales and marketing team to encourage a collaborative atmosphere within the company and de-emphasize hierarchy. There are also no reserved spaces in the parking lot! Leaders he admires are Colin Powell and Lee Iacocca. They set examples, lead, and cut their people loose to do their jobs.[1]

Based on the above biographical information, what types of leadership skills does Michael R. Jones exhibit? How does he apply human relations skills in his leadership style? Why do you think his company has been so successful?

in this chapter

According to Warren Bennis in *On Becoming a Leader*, three basic reasons explain why society and organizations need leaders and cannot function without them. First, leaders are responsible for the effectiveness of organizations. The success or failure of all organizations depends on the quality of their leaders. Second, leaders provide a guiding purpose, something greatly needed in today's world. Third, current concerns about the integrity of our institutions emphasize the need for better leadership in religion, government, Wall Street, and business. The quality of leadership determines the quality of life in society and in organizations.[2]

 **uick tip** ••

"One person can live on a desert island without leadership. Two people, if they are totally compatible, could probably get along and even progress. If there are three or more, someone has to take the lead. Otherwise, chaos erupts."

Warren Bennis
Business Professor, Author,
and Leadership Expert

Often the terms "leadership" and "management" are used interchangeably. However, a distinct difference can be drawn between the two. A person can be a leader without being in a position of management or supervision. Likewise, a person can be a manager without being an effective leader. Several distinctions can be made between leadership and management.

Leadership is the process of influencing the activities of individuals or organized groups so that they follow and willingly do what the leader wants them to do. To be a leader, you must deal directly with people, develop rapport with them, apply appropriate persuasion, inspire them, and thus influence them to cooperate in pursuing your goals and vision. Without followers, leaders do not exist.

Everyone has the capacity to develop and acquire leadership skills—it is a learned ability—and leaders are seen in many different activities, from politics to play. Not only must leaders be vocationally or professionally competent, but they must also establish and maintain positive relationships with their followers. Developing such skills will help you understand how people feel, what motivates them, and the best ways to influence them.

> You do not have to be a manager to be a leader.

> *QUICK WIT*
> "A leader has the vision and conviction that a dream can be achieved."
> Ralph Lauren,
> Fashion designer

If you ask successful leaders how they get people to help them achieve goals and visions, they will talk about human values, such as empathy, trust, mutual respect, and courage.

Management, on the other hand, is the use of resources, including human resources, to accomplish a goal. It can occur in many settings, but it is most frequently associated with a formal position within organizations and businesses. It may be nonbehavioral if it involves only nonhuman resources—but most managers manage people. A person can be a manager without being an effective leader. This person may lack the ability to inspire or influence others. Influence is a key word in the definition of leadership. Managers can be leaders only if employees allow them to influence their attitudes and behaviors.

Influence is our ability to change the attitude or behavior of an individual or group. This ability is the result of our power (discussed in Chapter 12), which can come from any number of sources. Leaders vary in their use of power sources. Even formal leaders on the same level often vary in their ability to influence others. Although they may have the same official title, for example, one may demonstrate greater knowledge or expertise.

Writer Trevor Gray says leadership and management are as different "...as chalk and cheese" and supports Warren Bennis's belief that "Managers do things right...leaders do the right things." Each has a distinct role.[3] John Naisbitt and Patricia Aburdene in *Megatrends 2000* say that any well-trained person can be a manager, but that a leader is "...an

> **Leadership is the process of influencing the activities of others.**

> **Management is the use of resources to accomplish a goal.**

CASE STUDIES IN THE NEWS

In 2003, *Fast Company* magazine profiled Russell Simmons. Simmons is known as the most creative, successful, and respected African-American entrepreneur in America to begin the millennium. He built a career and fostered an array of other businesses supporting the music and culture of today's urban youth hip-hop culture across the United States and the world. His empire, primarily featuring Phat Fashions, hit an estimated $615 million in sales in 2003 and is growing at 30 percent each year. His successful business dealings give him the power to achieve social and political goals. His main mantra seems to be, "Never quit, always give back, and keep it real!"[4]

How do you think Simmons learned his leadership skills? Do you think he is as effective in his political activities as in his business ones? Do you think his success will be long lasting? Why, or why not?

---

individual who builds fellowship by ethical conduct and by creating an environment where the unique potential of one individual can be actualized."[5]

Leadership is a skill that we all need to develop. To attain goals that we support, whether personal or organizational, we must be effective in directing and coordinating the work of others so that they want to work toward these same goals. For example, you may support a departmental goal of increasing sales by 15 percent by influencing your department members to sell more, whether or not you are their supervisor. A solid understanding of and a conscientious effort to acquire these abilities can enhance your career even if management is not your career objective.

Additionally, leadership skills are needed in situations away from work when we want to influence individuals or groups to work toward certain goals. You may, for example, want to start a Neighborhood Watch program to make your street safer. You might attend city board meetings and speak out, or go door to door and talk to your neighbors in order to influence them to get involved.

In understanding what leadership is, you should also understand what it is not. It is *not* a form of manipulation. Rather, it involves understanding your followers' motives and providing conditions so that their work-related needs are met while attaining your work goals.

EVOLVING ROLES FOR MANAGERS AND EXECUTIVES

Today, the many changes in organizations, employees, and the business environment in general have created the need for a different kind of manager—one who is a good leader. New management styles will encourage creativity, risk taking, healthy conflict, and learning from errors. Good human relations skills, coupled with good technology skills, will be the solid foundation for both effective managers and effective leaders.

The diagram on the next page illustrates the levels of management in a typical organizational hierarchy. Although new ideas about management will "flatten" the hierarchies in many organizations, this management hierarchy will likely survive to a certain degree. Leadership can appear at any level, however, despite management being confined to the upper levels.

Further changes may be ahead for business, and the roles of managers are certain to continue to evolve. In the opening chapter of *Effective Executive*, Peter Drucker makes the case that every "knowledge worker" in any organization has become, in effect, an executive. He says of this worker, "By virtue of his position or knowledge, he is responsible for a contribution that affects the capacity of the organization to perform and to obtain results."

QUICK WIT
"A leader's role is to praise people's aspirations for what they can become and to release their energies so they will try to get there."
David Gergen, Author and presidential adviser

QUICK WIT
"Management's role is to create a vision of the whole, and to empower others to reach it."
Joan Goldsmith, Business consultant and author

In defining effective executives as those who know where their time goes, focus on outward contributions, build on their strengths, and make effective decisions, Drucker makes it clear that future managers who succeed will need to know how to manage themselves as well as their employees.[6]

In *Partnering: The New Face of Leadership*, Marshall Goldsmith insists that the leader of the future will be a person skilled at building partnerships both inside (direct reports, coworkers, and managers) and outside (customers, suppliers, and competitors) the organization. Goldsmith argues that learning to be collaborative with colleagues and to partner across the organization will be critical to share people, capital, and ideas.[7]

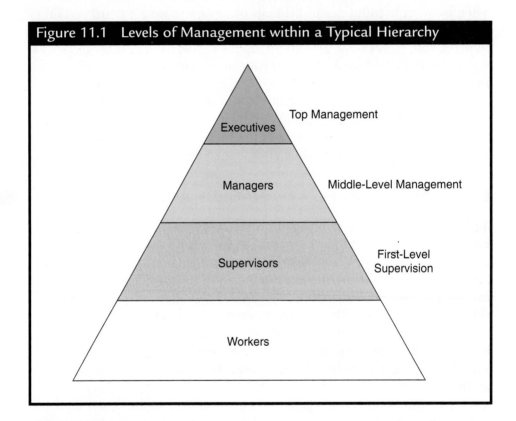

Figure 11.1   Levels of Management within a Typical Hierarchy

*Fast*Chat

1. Thinking of the opening Focus, state whether you think Michael R. Jones is a leader or a manager. On what do you base your opinion?

2. Why do you think people skills are so vital to the success of a leader?

Human Relations

Ideas about leadership have changed significantly over the years and have influenced how organizations and individuals within them operate. The **great man theory**, the first of these ideas to surface, was based on a belief that certain people are born to become leaders and will emerge in that role when their time comes. According to this theory, because of position, education, or mere exposure to other prominent leaders, these individuals develop a certain style or personality. Today, we know that few leaders were born that way. Most people learn to be leaders through study, observation, and hard work. Modern theories of leadership fall into three broad categories—trait theories, behavioral theories, and situational theories. Each of these ideas has evolved with time and research; yet each remains in some way linked to its predecessor.[8]

> Leadership skill is acquired and developed.

TRAIT THEORIES

Wondering whether leaders have certain traits in common, researchers studied the physical, personality, and intelligence traits of prominent leaders in business, military, medical, and other fields. They looked at height, weight, personal appearance, and physique but found no conclusive results. They also looked at intelligence and at personality traits such as confidence, independence, and perception.[9]

Lists of desirable traits were formed, giving weights to some believed to be more important than others. These lists were controversial at best and gave little recognition to the effects of the subordinates or the job itself on the success of the leader. The resulting confusion gave way to a belief that perhaps the success of leaders is based on their behavior rather than their traits. Several theories about leadership behavior then developed.

> Trait theorists sought key physical, personality, and intelligence traits of known leaders.

BEHAVIORAL THEORIES

Theorists in this category believed that successful leaders can be identified by what they *do* rather than what traits they have. In an effort to identify certain behavioral patterns or "styles" of leadership, researchers measured typical leader behaviors such as amounts of control and authority, degrees of flexibility, concerns for goal or task accomplishment, and concerns for subordinates. Several well-known studies developed during this period are still used in identifying the styles of leaders.[10]

In his classic 1960 book, *The Human Side of Enterprise*, Douglas McGregor suggested that leaders treat followers according to the

> Behavior theorists sought patterns or styles of behavior in leaders.

assumptions they hold about what motivates those followers. The traditional view, known as **Theory X**, exhibits a fairly dim view of workers' attitudes and motivation, while the second set of assumptions, **Theory Y**,
takes a much more optimistic view of human nature.[11]

McGregor's Theory X and Y

Theory X contends that people	Theory Y contends that
• have an inherent dislike of work, considering it necessary only for survival	• the expenditure of physical and mental effort in work is as natural as play or rest
• are not ambitious	• people will direct themselves toward objectives if their efforts are rewarded
• will avoid work if they can	• most people are eager to work and have the capacity to accept, or even seek, responsibility as well as to use imagination, ingenuity, and creativity in solving problems
• prefer to be directed, wanting to avoid responsibility	• under the right circumstances, people derive much satisfaction from work and are capable of doing a good job

---

Theory Y con-
tends that peo-
ple are eager to
work and
capable of
doing a good
job.

Leaders who hold Theory X assumptions believe that workers must be
coerced, controlled, directed, and threatened to make them work, resulting in a leadership style that is strict and authoritarian. The Theory Y
leader tends to be less directive and more supportive of subordinates'
needs and uses a democratic or participative approach to leading others.
McGregor thought that the ideal situation is to integrate the needs of
employees with the needs of the organization. He believed that proper
leadership helps employees set personal goals that are consistent with
organizational goals.[12]

The Managerial
Grid® plots
a leader's
concern for
people and for
production.

Another of the well-known theories of this period is the two-dimensional
Managerial Grid® developed by Robert Blake and Jane Mouton. A grid is
used to plot the degree to which leaders show concern for people and
concern for production (or getting the job done), with 1 being the least
concern and 9 the highest concern. The diagram on the next page illustrates the five specific leadership styles identified by Blake and Mouton.[13]

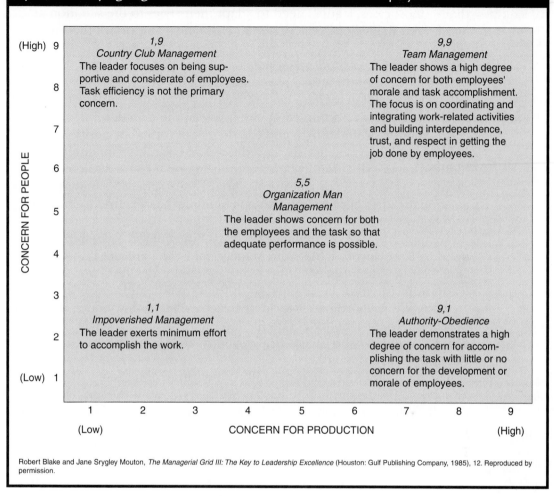

Figure 11.2 Blake and Mouton's Managerial Grid® identified five specific leadership styles with varying degrees of concern for the tasks and the employees.

1,9
Country Club Management
The leader focuses on being supportive and considerate of employees. Task efficiency is not the primary concern.

9,9
Team Management
The leader shows a high degree of concern for both employees' morale and task accomplishment. The focus is on coordinating and integrating work-related activities and building interdependence, trust, and respect in getting the job done by employees.

5,5
Organization Man Management
The leader shows concern for both the employees and the task so that adequate performance is possible.

1,1
Impoverished Management
The leader exerts minimum effort to accomplish the work.

9,1
Authority-Obedience
The leader demonstrates a high degree of concern for accomplishing the task with little or no concern for the development or morale of employees.

CONCERN FOR PEOPLE
(High) 9
(Low) 1

CONCERN FOR PRODUCTION
(Low) 1   (High) 9

Robert Blake and Jane Srygley Mouton, *The Managerial Grid III: The Key to Leadership Excellence* (Houston: Gulf Publishing Company, 1985), 12. Reproduced by permission.

This theory suggests that the 9,9 Team Management approach is the best leadership style because it results in maximum productivity and positive consequences. It is a goal-directed team approach. However, using a 9,9 leadership style in every situation is difficult. For example, in a conflict with an employee or any emergency job, the supervisor may need to use a 9,1 leadership style. The fluctuations in leader-follower situations, thus, gave rise to the next group of theories, which focus on the situation in which a leader is placed.

> Blake and Mouton identified the 9,9 leadership style as the best.

SITUATIONAL OR CONTINGENCY THEORIES

Fiedler said a leader's success is affected by the leader-follower relationship, the task, and the leader's formal power.

As theorists continued their research of leadership styles, they realized that in most cases, leaders need to adapt their styles to the situation at hand. Fred E. Fiedler developed one of the more important theories from this era in his 1967 book, *A Theory of Leadership Effectiveness.* Considerable research evidence supports Fiedler's belief that three important situational factors influence how much power and influence the leader has over the behavior of followers. These factors are the degree of confidence in and loyalty to the leader exhibited by the follower, the degree to which the task is routine or undefined, and the degree of formal or position power held by the leader. Fiedler suggested that some leaders function best in highly directive situations, whereas others are better suited to permissive situations. Therefore, organizations should consider each situation before assigning leaders because the same person may be effective in one situation but not in another.[14]

An application of contingency theory is **Situational Leadership**®, developed by Paul Hersey. Unlike the Managerial Grid® concept that stresses "one best way" to influence others, Situational Leadership® says that leadership style must be adapted to fit the situation and varies with the "readiness" of subordinates. Readiness, according to this model, does not pertain to age or emotional stability but rather to a worker's desire to achieve, willingness to accept responsibility, ability and experience with the task, and confidence.[15]

Situational Leadership® considers follower readiness, task behavior, and relationship behavior.

The diagram on the next page illustrates three dimensions of Situational Leadership®. The bar across the bottom of the model describes the first dimension, **follower readiness**. Followers may be unwilling and unable, not able but willing, able but not willing, or willing and able to complete the task. The second dimension, **task behavior**, has to do with the extent to which a leader may or should be directive or "telling." Does the leader closely supervise followers, telling them exactly what to do and when and how to do it, or does the leader allow a great deal of freedom in how followers accomplish the task? The third dimension of this model, **relationship behavior**, describes leader behavior with people, or the extent to which a leader is supportive of followers and engages in two-way communication with them.[16]

Effective leaders adjust their leadership style to followers' task readiness.

Situational Leadership® suggests that leaders should vary their style as subordinates (either individually or as a group) develop and mature. When a task is new for followers, the leader must engage in many task-related behaviors to instruct them. Once followers begin learning the task, the leader reinforces them with supportive relationship behaviors (such as praise and encouragement) while still offering direction. After followers demonstrate that they are willing and able to perform the task, the leader should stop directing but still offer support and consideration.

Figure 11.3 Situational Leadership® suggests varying the leadership style to match the different situations that leaders face.

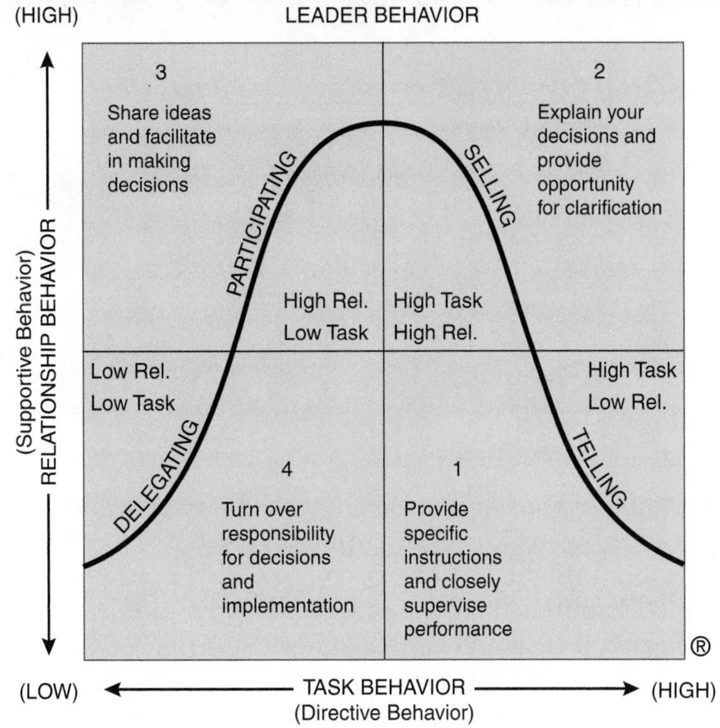

(HIGH)   LEADER BEHAVIOR

3		2
Share ideas and facilitate in making decisions	*PARTICIPATING* / *SELLING*	Explain your decisions and provide opportunity for clarification
	High Rel. | High Task	
	Low Task | High Rel.	
Low Rel. Low Task		High Task Low Rel.
DELEGATING		*TELLING*
4		1
Turn over responsibility for decisions and implementation		Provide specific instructions and closely supervise performance

(Supportive Behavior) RELATIONSHIP BEHAVIOR

®

(LOW) ◄——— TASK BEHAVIOR ———► (HIGH)
(Directive Behavior)

FOLLOWER READINESS

HIGH	MODERATE		LOW
R4	R3	R2	R1
Able and willing or confident	Able but unwilling or insecure	Unable but willing or confident	Unable and unwilling or insecure

Finally, when followers are high in readiness in a particular task, the leader reduces both task-related and relationship behaviors *in regard to that task.*

If followers assume additional new tasks, their readiness level may fall because they lack ability or confidence, and the leader must once again move through the cycle. For instance, if your office assistant is highly skilled in using a certain software package for building presentation charts and is suddenly given a new software version, that person's maturity

QUICK WIT
"Whether you think you can, or that you can't, you are usually right."
Henry Ford
Pioneering automotive engineer and inventor

Your leadership style should allow employees to develop with confidence.

©Digital Vision

level in preparing charts may decline. You will be required to return to the telling leadership style, providing training on the new software with close supervision until the assistant becomes skilled in its use and regains confidence. This approach allows leaders to handle various situations that occur in the workplace in a flexible manner.

Situational Leadership® can be applied to individuals or groups.

Hersey believes that a leader who effectively matches style with followers' readiness motivates the followers and helps them move toward a higher level. You may have to change your leadership style to facilitate growth on the job, whether you are dealing with an individual or a group of employees. Groups and teams may collectively go through the same changes in maturity as they progress through the forming, storming, and norming phases discussed in Chapter 8. Watching for behavior changes is the key to mastering this leadership application.[17]

*Fast*Chat

1. Think of supervisors you have had. Were they more Theory X or more Theory Y in their management style? Why do you categorize them as such?

2. What do you think is the most important feature of the Situational Leadership® method of supervising? Why?

3. Can you think of a situation that would require a change in the leadership style used? How would you react as the supervisor in that situation?

A **leadership style** is a particular pattern of behavior exhibited by the leader. Most leaders have a style with which they are most comfortable and that they prefer to use. Studies of leadership behavior patterns have identified three traditional leadership styles: the autocratic, democratic, and free-rein or laissez-faire styles. The **autocratic leadership** style is also described as authoritarian or directive. Leaders comfortable using this style usually show a high degree of concern for getting the job done. They are task-oriented and tend to provide close supervision, are highly directive, and are not at all comfortable with delegating their authority to others. A close match to this style is the Theory X leader and the 9,1 leader, described earlier in this chapter.

> The autocratic leader is highly directive.

The **democratic leadership** style is often described as participative and is generally the style preferred by modern management and employees. These leaders tend to share authority with their employees, involving them in decision making and organizational planning. Democratic leaders show concern for their employees, especially in matters that directly affect them in the workplace. A close match to this style is the Theory Y leader and the 9,9 leader.

> The democratic leader encourages participation by followers.

Typical of the democratic leader is the department manager who says to her work group, "The corporate office has set an overall goal of increasing production company-wide by 10 percent next year. I would like your thoughts about how much we can reasonably try for and how we might do that."

The **free-rein** or **laissez-faire leadership** style is sometimes called the integrative style. These leaders allow employees more or less to lead themselves, offering advice or information when asked. Little effort is made by these leaders to either increase productivity or nurture employees. They may integrate the activities by handing out tasks and closing out assignments with a signature at job's end, but for the most part they are uninvolved with directing or controlling tasks or employees. This style can be effective if the task is highly routine or clearly defined and the employees are skilled and responsible in the performance of their duties. This leader is most commonly compared to the 1,1 leader of the Managerial Grid® theory.

> The free-rein leader allows followers to lead themselves.

An example of a person using the laissez-faire leadership style is one who hires good people, provides them with an arena to be as good as they can be, and leaves them alone.

> *QUICK WIT*
> "The best of all rulers is but a shadowy presence to his subjects."
> Lao Tzu, Chinese philosopher

Bada-Bing....You're a leader! Yes, someone has correlated Tony Soprano's being "the boss" to being a business leader. Deborrah Himsel, the vice president of Organizational Effectiveness at Avon, has written a book called *Leadership Soprano's Style: How to Become a More Effective Boss*. With a creative approach, she analyzes this perfect specimen of a fully functioning, dysfunctional family and compares it to a working corporation. She explores the leader's techniques, his management style, how his "team" responds, and his unquestionable power skills. Although a slightly flawed, fictional character, he faces many of the same issues leaders in corporate America face each day: motivation, coaching and mentoring, competition, conflict management, and succession planning. He is "the boss"! You may want to use some of these techniques—but only the legal ones, please![18]

1. *What leadership style do you think Tony Soprano uses? How would he lead his team to motivate them?*
2. *How do you think he might handle a conflict management situation on his team? What are the ethical implications of this type of leadership?*
3. *Discuss how you think this family functions like a company and give specific examples.*

   (*Note: if you haven't seen the show, you can find character descriptions and episode plot summaries on the HBO web site.*)

Leaders should vary their style to fit the situation.

Little direction is needed or provided and this leader makes few decisions. In fields that are highly creative or primarily idea- or knowledge-driven, it is counterproductive to hire exceptionally creative or skilled individuals, pay them a huge annual salary, and then tell them what to do at every step. Scientists and doctors working on a research grant may respond quite well to this "uninvolved" type of leadership, as might software developers or creative directors.

Although leaders have a preferred style, they should vary their style to fit the numerous situations that arise in the workplace. Certain factors may influence a leader's preferred style, such as general disposition or personality, skill level or confidence, and perception of others. Failure to adjust to different situations can limit a leader's career.

Gregory Smith, in his *Link&Learn* article, "Using Assessments to Develop Managers and Others for Professional and Personal Growth," states that many organizations today are using behavior assessments and personality trait testing for both hourly workers and managers to help understand these unique differences in people.

A recent American Management Association study reveals that while in the 1990s only 5 percent of large Fortune 500 companies used assessments, in the new millennium that percentage has rapidly risen to 65 percent. Most assessments generate an amazing amount of detail on diverse behaviors, skills, and competencies. By understanding these behavior differences, an organization can maximize the abilities of its workforce in ways to help make all employees star performers.[19]

CASE STUDIES IN THE NEWS

Do the U.S. Army's Elite Rangers' methods of seeking and taking responsibility for one's actions apply to effective leadership? How important is knowing yourself and seeking self-improvement in becoming an effective leader? Brace Barber, author of *No Excuse Leadership,* thinks these are the very core principles that will push you to do more and do it better when your organization needs a good leader. Through his own personal story and those of nine other Rangers, the author relates first-person accounts of the leadership skills and lessons all Ranger School alumni learn. Each chapter provides an insider's glimpse into how Rangers are taught to be persistent, focused, honest, selfless, confident, instinctual, determined, driven, dutiful, and humble. Using these 10 "lessons" taught by the alumni may improve your efficiencies, raise your morale, and truly lead you toward success in your leadership role.[20]

1. *Do you share Brace Barber's opinion that seeking self-improvement and knowing yourself is a core principle in becoming a good leader? Why, or why not?*
2. *Which 2 of the 10 "lessons" do you think are the strongest principles? Discuss your rationale.*

FastChat

1. Have you ever had the opportunity to use one of these leadership styles? Which one(s)? How did it work for work for you?
2. What problems, if any, could you envision with the use of the free-rein leadership style?
3. How do you feel about behavioral assessments being used by employers? Does your workplace use them? How might they benefit the group with which you currently work?

The leader's effectiveness may also depend on demonstrating an adequate level of skills. Fortunately, good leadership skills can be acquired or developed. Substantial research has identified three basic skills most beneficial to competent leaders. If you aspire to be a formal leader in an organization, you will need to pay particular attention to developing your technical, human relations, and conceptual skills, as discussed in Chapter 1. **Technical skills** are those skills required to perform a particular task.

GLOBAL CONNECTION

A recent article in *Training & Development* magazine profiled Ping An Insurance, the second largest insurance company in China with 300 branches and over 250,000 sales agents across the country. Peter Ma, the CEO, understands that the employee of the future must see, think, act, and mobilize with a Chinese mind-set from a global perspective. From 10 employees and $30 million in assets in 1988, the company has grown to more than a $30 billion business today. Peter Ma has learned that in our borderless economy, culture matters more than ever before. Technological advances, the knowledge explosion, globalization, and the rapidity of change are the universal business drivers affecting organizations around the world in the 21ST century.

International competition, the global war for talent, domestic and cross-border mergers and acquisitions, changing employee expectations, management of knowledge workers, and pressures for greater productivity are the demands with which executives around the world are dealing. This company is devoted to lifelong learning for its employees. Peter Ma makes certain his field agents have the latest technologies to manage information required while serving customers. All agents carry the latest in PDAs with state-of-the-art software.[21]

1. *Which leadership style does Peter Ma exhibit?*

2. *What are the disadvantages of having an organization of this size? Can managers ever really know enough about what's going on to manage well?*

3. *What lifelong learning tools would you choose to implement?*

For example, a first-line supervisor may need the knowledge and ability to step into the production line and assemble a part or tear down a mechanism to solve a problem or train employees on the process. Obviously, this skill is more important at levels of leadership closest to the actual work being done.

Conceptual skills are often referred to as administrative skills or "big picture" skills. The ability to think abstractly and to analyze problems becomes increasingly important as a person rises in the hierarchy to levels of top management. Planning and coordinating the overall activities of the organization and its personnel requires an ability to view the operations from a total perspective and anticipate as well as solve problems.

Human relations skills cut evenly across all levels of leadership in organizations. This ability to deal effectively with people includes effective communication, listening, empathy, inspiring and motivating, perceptiveness, and fair judgment when dealing with employees. Too often, the lack of human relations skills is the limiting factor in becoming a good leader.

These skills can be acquired or developed through various means as you progress along your career path. Common ways are exposure and observation, trial-and-error experience, on-the-job training, and some forms of formal education. An important factor in your development as a leader will be your acceptance of the need for lifelong learning or continuing education. John Naisbitt and Patricia Aburdene, authors of *Re-inventing the Corporation*, point out that the constant change created by the new information society requires us to be lifelong learners. We must periodically upgrade our marketable skills and expand our knowledge. We can no longer expect to get an education and be done with it—no education or skill will last a lifetime.[22]

> Competent leaders will develop their technical, human relations, and conceptual skills.

> Lifelong learning will be an important factor in your development as a leader.

©Comstock Images

We must periodically upgrade our marketable skills and expand our knowledge, especially if we aspire to leadership.

Konosuke Matsushita came from humble beginnings as an apprentice for Osaka Electric Light Company, where he learned his wiring skills and won a promotion. In 1917, he started Matsushita Electric and grew that business to $42 billion in revenues—and brought us a brand known to millions around the globe as Panasonic. Along the way, he also became a respected author, educator, statesman, philanthropist, and social philosopher.

Matsushita was an industrialist with a vision. His basic management objective and company creed, established in 1929, read "harmony between corporate profit and social justice." Today, the company's mission statement reads, "Recognizing our responsibilities as industrialists, we will devote ourselves to the progress and development of society and the well-being of people through our business activities, thereby enhancing the quality of life throughout the world." Matsushita's belief was that lifelong learning is the key to peace, happiness, and prosperity. He kept learning and reinventing himself by keeping an "untrapped mind," and that quest for lifelong learning made him the great success he was. According to Matsushita, "The great 'untrapped mind' is open enough to see many possibilities, humble enough to learn from anyone and anything, forbearing enough to forgive all, perceptive enough to see things as they really are, and reasonable enough to judge their true value."[23]

1. *How can you develop an "untrapped mind"? In what areas should learning occur as one grows?*

2. *In what ways, in addition to formal classes, can we pursue the learning and development we need to stay marketable?*

Coaching and mentoring by a senior person will also help you develop leadership skills. The way you function as a follower can also help or hurt your development as a leader. A valuable part of becoming a leader is being an effective follower, a role we all play throughout our lives.

*Fast*Chat

1. Which of the leadership skills do you think are easiest to obtain? Hardest? Why?

2. Why do you think lifelong learning will remain vital to success and achievement?

Lester Bittel and John Newstrom, in their book *What Every Supervisor Should Know*, point out that our personalities can determine under what kind of leader we perform best. You can either try to change your personality or seek out leaders who best complement your style. The suggestions below provide guidance on how you might choose a leader compatible with your personality or personal operating style.[24]

> Our personalities can determine our leadership needs.

Choosing Compatible Leaders

If you are an aggressive, cooperative person, you will probably do your best work under a democratic or free-rein leader. Your self-assertiveness will move you constructively in the right direction.

If you are an aggressive, hostile person, you will probably perform more effectively under an autocratic leader. Such a leader will help channel your feelings toward constructive ends.

If you are insecure, you will probably depend on your leaders for guidance. Such leaders should ideally be autocratic.

If you are an individualist who prefers to work alone and if you know your job well, you will probably perform most effectively under free-rein leadership.

Marshall Goldsmith, author of *Partnering: The New Face of Leadership*, suggests that followers can have a great influence on how successful a project is by taking responsibility, sharing information, and seeing the micro and macro perspectives of the situations. Partnering with management requires followers to learn how to influence "up" as well as "down" and "across."[25] This has great impact on the success of the project and will reflect well on all members of the group, enhancing your image and potential as a leader. Additionally, working on a successful project is an excellent opportunity to observe effective leadership and build your skills for future use.

Learning these effective methods of good "followership" will certainly improve opportunities you may have for demonstrating your capabilities as a leader. Experience is the best teacher and provides excellent hands-on exposure to how projects operate.

> **QUICK WIT**
> "There is the risk you cannot afford to take, and there is the risk you cannot afford not to take."
> Peter Drucker, Business consultant and author

1. Try to understand any problems from top management's point of view. If you need more information to do so, ask for it.

2. Approach the project as an opportunity to learn and grow. After all, you will have a chance to hear various points of view, see different parts of the organization, interact with different people, and observe new skills.

3. Be committed to the project and show that commitment to your fellow team members.

4. If you believe that the project is doomed to failure, do not sit silently. Discuss this belief with your supervisor.

Our personalities can determine under what kind of leader we perform best.

©Digital Vision

*Fast*Chat

1. Which of the types of leaders would you choose to best fit your personality and why?

2. How do you think project experience might be beneficial to you?

Aside from the skills described in the preceding paragraphs, certain other elements have proven critical to effective leadership. These elements include the satisfactory performance of the job functions, common behavioral characteristics, and certain attitudes and behaviors.

FUNCTIONAL ABILITIES

Early in the research on the basic functions of managing and leading, Luther Gulick, cited in Joseph Massie and John Douglas's management book, coined an acronym that has held through time as a quick reference. The letters in **PODSCORB** each represent a function basic to business leadership. They are **p**lanning, **o**rganizing, **d**irecting, **s**taffing, **c**oordinating, **r**eporting, and **b**udgeting. These elements are still needed despite the fact that they were first identified in the 1930s. Leaders and managers must be able to perform these key required tasks before they can motivate others and effectively operate in a business environment.[26]

CHARACTERISTICS

A characteristic is a distinguishing feature or attribute that sets you apart from the norm. Studies that began during the behavioral sciences school of management development identified certain behaviors and abilities that were considered key elements. Successful leaders have consistently been labeled with the five characteristics shown in the box on page 306.

Motivating employees means getting commitment through the gentle art of persuasion and setting examples of excellence. Empathy helps give leaders power. That power comes from the company's success and the leader's staff working well together. A follower's trust of the leader is essential to motivation. Leaders can develop trust by being steadfast in their goals, by "walking their talk" (living what they espouse), by being reliable and supportive, and by honoring their commitments and promises.

Leaders often find delegating the single most difficult thing to do. A mistake often made when delegating is giving the responsibility without the authority to get the job done. As you read through the descriptions on the next page, try to relate them to your characteristics: What kind of feedback have you received from others or how do you see yourself? What skills do you need to work on?

Leadership Characteristics

Communicator   Leaders are able to express themselves well. Certainly this feature includes good oral and written communication skills but goes far beyond that. It means that they know who they are, what their strengths and weaknesses are, and how to use them to their full advantage. They also know what they want, why they want it, and how to get it. They set goals and achieve those goals by communicating to others what they want to gain support and cooperation.

Decision Maker   Leaders are comfortable making decisions. They are able to gather facts, organize information, and apply good judgment in their choice of action. The willingness to make a choice after considering all possible alternatives is essential. Depending upon the complexity of the decision to be made, decision-making models may be used. Most decisions are made independently, with the decision makers held fully responsible. They take risks that the decision is a good one.

Risk Taker   Effective leaders very often operate on instinct, go with their "gut feel," and are willing to try everything that may bring desired results. The willingness to take risks seems to set them apart from the crowd. Risk takers do not fear failure. They view it as a "temporary setback" or perhaps a "mid-course correction" and feel that failure today does not rule out success tomorrow. Some U.S. companies are deliberately making risk-taking part of their corporate culture. Risk takers tend to be achievement-oriented, goal-directed, and self-confident. They are the great experimenters of life. The willingness to try new ideas often reaps great rewards for the individual and the company. Many experts have identified this characteristic as tantamount to being a successful leader.

Motivator   Leaders must be able to influence others to produce good results. In the climate of the 21ST century, motivation of employees will lean away from the autocratic methods of the past toward the new style of inspiring and empowering employees. John P. Kotter, author of *The Leadership Factor,* says that leadership is "the process of moving people in some direction mostly through non-coercive means." A good leader recognizes that people are a key resource to the success of the organization, project, or vision.[27]

Delegator   An effective leader delegates tasks to others to develop their skills and build a stronger team. **Delegation** means assigning tasks to subordinates and following up to ensure that they are completed properly and on time.

QUICK WIT

"*Well done is better than well said.*"

Benjamin Franklin, American statesman and inventor

The steps to successful delegation are to select the person best qualified to perform the task, give good instructions, and ask for feedback to assure understanding of the task directions. Then, leave the person alone to complete the assignment. If you are the leader, follow up to assure completion but do not interfere with that individual's methods of getting the job done.

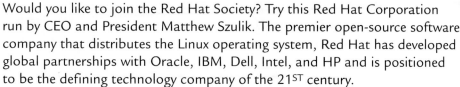
Would you like to join the Red Hat Society? Try this Red Hat Corporation run by CEO and President Matthew Szulik. The premier open-source software company that distributes the Linux operating system, Red Hat has developed global partnerships with Oracle, IBM, Dell, Intel, and HP and is positioned to be the defining technology company of the 21ST century.

Szulik leads by example and works every bit as hard if not harder than other employees and expects them to follow his lead. He maintains an open-door policy and remains approachable to everyone, and that policy has existed since he became the 32ND employee at the Durham, NC, company in 1998. Szulik is passionate about improving educational opportunities for students worldwide. He and a business partner took the company public in 1999 and now have 450 employees. A true success story for a dot.com company: he's still there. Under his watch, this company that began in an apartment in 1994 is a multinational organization that not only distributes operating systems, but also includes the development of future technologies for industry, government, and education.[28]

1. *What is your impression of Szulik's leadership style? Would you want to work for Red Hat? Why, or why not?*

2. *How will his leadership style have to differ from that of Steve Jobs or Bill Gates when they started out in their garage companies, or will it in a newer, more global setting?*

In an amusing analysis of the leadership style of Attila the Hun, author Wess Roberts describes Attila's rules on delegating. Roberts stresses that "delegating demonstrates trust in your subordinates and helps build their skills and improves their loyalty." Specific rules that Attila applied are illustrated below.[29]

Attila the Hun's Rules of Delegation

1. Never delegate responsibilities that require your direct attention.

2. Delegate to those people most able to fulfill the assignment, and grant them authority as well as responsibility.

3. Once you delegate a task, never interfere.

4. Do not give your Huns precise direction on how to accomplish their delegated assignments.

Warren Bennis, in *On Becoming a Leader*, adds that leaders seem to share some, if not all, of the characteristics in the chart that follows. In a related workbook, *Learning to Lead*, Bennis and Joan Goldsmith stress that these characteristics stand out as important for success and are deeply relevant for tomorrow's business environments.[30]

Additional Leadership Characteristics

A guiding vision	Leaders have a clear idea of what they want to do and the strength to persist.
Passion	Leaders love what they do and love doing it. Leaders who communicate passion give hope and inspiration to others.
Integrity	The integrity of leaders has three components: self-knowledge, candor, and maturity. Leaders never lie to themselves, know their flaws and assets and deal with them, are honest in thought and action, and experience and grow through following.
Trust	Trust must be acquired. It is the product of a leader's ability with coworkers and followers.
Curiosity and daring	Leaders wonder about things, are willing to experiment and learn from adversity.

ATTITUDES AND BEHAVIORS

Attitudes and behaviors most commonly displayed by successful leaders are listed on the opposite page. Sometimes described as states of mind or feelings, attitudes play an important role in the workplace. Followers are affected by the example you set and will react to your enthusiasm and dedication. A showing of empathy for them is important and will gain you their respect. Each of these attitudes has a direct bearing on your success as a leader.

Attitudes reflect predispositions, mental states, emotions, expectations, and moods. Keeping attitudes positively focused will assure better leadership and strong followership. Displaying a sense of humor is also a method of maximizing good human relationships. That is not to say you need to be the village (or office) clown, but that you can express feelings and enjoy the workplace.

QUICK WIT
"The mistakes I made were my best teacher by far."
Arnold Hiatt, Chairman, Business for Social Responsibility

Closely related to attitudes are courtesy and enthusiasm. Being courteous toward others and demonstrating civility can create a positive workplace setting. Your enthusiasm and positive attitude go a long way toward inspiring and motivating people. This is an important part of being an effective leader.

Typical Attitudes and Behaviors of Effective Leaders

- Positive thinking
- Dedicated with a sense of mission
- Open-minded
- Enthusiastic
- Spontaneous
- Courageous
- Empathetic
- Flexible
- Responsible
- Ethical with high character
- Self-denying; willing to forgo self-indulgences, such as showing anger
- Competent (both in leadership and technical skills)
- Wise
- Energetic
- Considerate
- Fair

---

*Fast*Chat

1. Which of the characteristics listed above do you feel are most important and why?

2. In which areas do your strengths lie, and in which areas do you think you need to develop?

3. How important do you think attitudes are and what impact do you think they can have on the work environment?

According to Bernard M. Bass, a leadership researcher, leadership can be categorized in two ways: transactional and transformational. **Transactional leadership** encompasses the theories presented in this chapter and requires that leaders determine what followers need to achieve their own and organizational goals, classify those needs, and help followers gain confidence that they can reach their objectives. **Transformational leadership**, on the other hand, motivates followers to do more than they originally expected to do by raising the perceived value of the task, by getting them to transcend self-interest for the sake of the group goal, and by raising their need level to self-actualization.[31]

Other leadership theorists have suggests that today's business environment requires a variation of transformational leadership. Leadership skills should include the following:

1. *Anticipatory skills*—the ability to foresee a constantly changing environment.

2. *Visioning skills*—the ability to induce people to take action that agrees with the leader's purposes or those of the organization.

3. *Value-congruence skills*—the ability to understand followers' economic, safety, psychological, spiritual, aesthetic, and physical needs in order to motivate them on the basis of shared motives, values, and goals.

4. *Empowerment skills*—the ability to share power.

5. *Self-understanding*—the ability to understand one's own needs and goals as well as those of followers.

Recurring themes seem to ripple through all the practices and predictions of the leadership gurus. Indeed, little doubt remains that we all need to prepare in some way or another for the future, the new work environment, the new workers, the new globalization, and the information revolution. There is no question that these clichés have real meaning. But what does all this have to do with leadership development?

The majority of new models still deal heavily with human relation skills. As technology advances, we will necessarily grow and improve those skills to remain a viable part of our environments—at work and at home. Some shifts in paradigms will occur, but on balance people are people and management is management. We are our own raw leadership material and we are our own best teachers. We must "invent" ourselves by discovering our own native energies and desires and then find our own way to act on them.

The challenge of leadership is growing. Numerous experts predict that the days of the "big bad boss" and the hierarchy are gone. We will no longer be "taking or giving orders," but as leaders of knowledge workers, we will learn to influence up, down, and across. Marshall Goldsmith brings us the importance of "partnering" skills and how critical they will be in the future. The next generation of leaders will be more intellectually aware, will be comfortable with and excited by ideas and information, and will anticipate and accept change, seeing it as an opportunity. Many of the important qualities of the past like integrity, vision, and self-confidence will still be required. Warren Bennis suggests new leaders will share the following nine characteristics.[32]

New Leader Characteristics

1. They will have a broad education, maintained through lifelong learning.
2. They will have boundless enthusiasm.
3. They will believe in people and teamwork.
4. They will be willing to take risks.
5. They will be devoted to long-term growth rather than short-term profit.
6. They will be committed to excellence.
7. They will be ready for change.
8. They will demonstrate virtue in their integrity, ethics, and respect for self and others.
9. They will be wise, giving followers a chance to look good.

The effective leader of the future will optimistically embrace change and will continue to do the most important task of helping others to perform to the highest of standards.

*Fast*Chat

1. What do you think is the most difficult task facing leaders in the 21ST century?

2. How would you prepare for meeting the expected challenges facing future leaders?

3. Do you think the challenges will be much different than those faced by Matsushita when he led Matsushita Electric in the 1920s on the trail toward Panasonic in the 2000s?

Key Terms

leadership

management

influence

great man theory

Theory X and Y

Managerial Grid®

Situational Leadership®

follower readiness

task behavior

relationship behavior

leadership style

autocratic leadership

democratic leadership

free-rein (laissez-faire) leadership

technical skills

conceptual skills

human relations skills

PODSCORB

delegation

transactional leadership

transformational leadership

CHAPTER SUMMARY

Leaders, people who influence the behavior of others, may be found at all levels of the organizational hierarchy and in personal life. A person can be a leader and not be a manager and vice versa. Leadership has long been a subject of concern with considerable research to define its origin and identify those traits or behaviors in individuals that single them out to be leaders. From the great man theory, researchers moved into trait and behavioral theories and identified various means of recognizing and even developing leadership abilities. Some of the best-known theories are Theory X and Y, the Managerial Grid®, and Situational Leadership®.

Several distinctive styles of leadership have also been identified. They are autocratic, democratic, and free rein. Most leaders have a preferred style but change their approach to fit the needs of the situation. An effective leader in an organization must be able to apply technical, conceptual, and human relations skills. These skills can be acquired or developed through exposure and observation, trial-and-error experience, on-the-job training, formal education and continuing education, coaching and mentoring, and effective following. Successful leaders will also display certain functional abilities, characteristics, and attitudes and behaviors known to be critical to effective leadership. Future leaders will be transformational, motivating their followers to transcend self-interest for the sake of the group goal by raising their need levels to self-actualization. Leadership experts predict that the next generation of leaders will possess specific characteristics that will allow this transformation to happen.

REVIEW QUESTIONS

1. Define leadership. What is the difference between a leader and a manager?

2. What is the importance of leadership skills to us at work at any level? In our personal lives?

3. Discuss the various leadership theories that have developed throughout history and name and define the three traditional leadership styles.

4. What are the three categories of skills required of leaders? How do they vary with the leader's level?

5. What are the methods of developing leadership skills? Why is lifelong learning now necessary?

6. Identify the basic elements of effective leadership. Name the functions, characteristics, and attitudes and behaviors of effective leaders.

7. How do transactional and transformational leadership differ? Which is expected to be more important in the future? What elements are part of it?

DISCUSSION QUESTIONS

1. Think of a situation in which you have been involved and identify the leader's style. Was that style appropriate for the situation?

2. Describe the leadership style from a situational perspective that should be applied to you in your present job situation or in an organization to which you belong. Is that style being used? Why, or why not?

3. Describe situations that call for each of the three traditional leadership styles. Discuss why that particular leadership style best fits that situation.

4. Cite examples from your experience of leaders you perceive to be transactional and transformational. What skills and special characteristics do they demonstrate?

5. Describe follower roles that you now have. How are your behaviors and attitudes in those roles helping you develop leadership skills?

WRITING

WEB

CHAPTER PROJECT

Develop and design a brochure for a professional training course aimed at preparing employees to be effective leaders in the 21ST century. Create a professional-looking product with serious content. Assume you will be the course leader. Outline and describe the topics you plan to cover, describe why these topics are important, and identify what the proposed benefits of this course will be for the participant. You may want to use the Internet as a source for some materials. Using any of the search engines, you may find that leadership topics render many ideas for your brochure. Embellish this brochure with any other items of interest that add to its professional appeal. Be persuasive; make the reader want to take your course.

APPLICATIONS

In small groups, analyze the following situations.

Do We Want to Follow the Leader?

TEAMWORK

Andy ruled the production crew with an iron fist. He had come up through the rank and file and had many years of experience to his credit. His success was based on technical expertise. He had no formal education but knew more about the manufacturing processes involved than any young college graduate in the company. Although the people in the work unit respected his technical knowledge and abilities, they felt that he was a bit heavy-handed in his method of supervising the day-to-day operations. "He cracks the whip around here and closely supervises every move you make," said Rosa, the lead technician. "He wants to be involved with every detail and won't let go of any responsibility. You would think that he doesn't trust us or that maybe he just doubts we would get the job done."

1. What leadership style is Andy using in this situation?

2. What assumptions has he made about his employees, and what typical behaviors of the leadership style is he demonstrating?

3. How do you think the workers feel about his leadership style? How would you feel?

What Caused the Boat to Sink?

TEAMWORK

The Administrative Office had a staff of seven seasoned employees running daily operations. As a service organization, they helped other company employees with questions about policies and procedures and processed all official paperwork on promotions, reassignments, health and life insurance, and many other administrative matters. Wilma, their supervisor for nine years, respected the knowledge and maturity of her employees and normally left them alone to do the job as they saw fit. When Wilma retired and moved away, Doris was hired from another company to replace her. On her first day as the new supervisor, Doris changed many of the internal office procedures to her way of doing business. She required that all incoming calls from company employees be directed to her. She became the single point of information for the office. She requested a daily prioritized list of activities from each of the staff members for approval by her. She then determined whether the priorities were in order or correct and revised them. Within six months, complaints became common, morale declined, and finally five of the original seven staff members resigned. Doris replaced those employees with members from her previous company's staff, and the operation began to run smoothly again.

1. Using Situational Leadership®, what would you assess the readiness level of the seven office staff members to be?

2. What leadership style had Wilma applied?

3. What leadership style did Doris apply in her new position as head of the Administrative Office?

4. Was Doris's leadership style the correct one to apply in this situation? If not, why not?

5. What might Doris have done to improve human relations in this example?

ADDITIONAL READINGS AND RESOURCES

Barber, Brace E. *No Excuse Leadership: Lessons from the US Army's Elite Rangers.* Hoboken, New Jersey: John Wiley & Sons, 2003.

Himsel, Deborrah. *Leadership Soprano's Style: How to Become a More Effective Boss.* Chicago: Dearborn Trade Publishing, 2003.

Reingold, Jennifer. "One Degree of Russell Simmons." *Fast Company*, November 2003, 71-80.

Rosen, Robert. "Developing Globally Literate Leaders." *Training & Development*, May 2001, 26-28.

Segil, Larraine, James Belasco, and Marshall Goldsmith. *Partnering: The New Face of Leadership.* New York: American Management Association, 2002.

For additional resources, refer to the web site for this text: school.cengage.com/career/dalton

CHAPTER 12

Appreciating Power:
Positioning and Politics

OBJECTIVES

After studying this chapter, you should be able to:

12.1 *Define power and explain why developing power is necessary.*

12.2 *Identify and discuss the basic power sources available to you.*

12.3 *Explain how power sources are linked.*

12.4 *Name and discuss the three basic power personalities.*

12.5 *Identify and discuss techniques used in the planning and implementation of power positioning and applying power politics.*

12.6 *Discuss why empowering others is important.*

12.7 *Discuss the pitfalls of developing power.*

focus

It's oh so Oprah! Oprah Winfrey openly admits she cannot read a balance sheet, has no corporate role models, never met Jack Welch or Michael Dell, and turned down invitations from AT&T, Ralph Lauren, and Intel to sit on their corporate boards. "Being a 'businesswoman' is not a title I like very much," she says. And yet she is at the peak of her power and recognizes the influence she has. She defines power as "the ability to impact with purpose and the privilege to influence." She has made the most of her power applications—22 million U.S. fans watch the Oprah TV show, she's into movie production, has the Oxygen cable TV channel, does an annual self-help speaking tour, and edits her two-year-old magazine, *O, The Oprah Magazine*, the most successful start-up ever in the industry.[1]

How do you think Oprah was able to become such a powerful influence in our modern society? What do you think her sources of power have been? Do you think she will continue to be such an influential force? If Oprah were to leave her talk show after over 20 successful seasons, would the power go with her? Why, or why not?

in this chapter

Power is our ability to influence others to do what we want them to do. It involves changing the attitudes or behaviors of individuals or groups. Power is exercised by nonmanagement as well as management employees and by people in their personal lives.

Power gives us the means to accomplish tasks and can help us reach our goals. Many experts point out that people cannot succeed in organizations today without acquiring some power and learning how to use it. Also, an understanding of power can help you recognize when those around you are attempting to influence you through the exercise of power. The appropriate use of power can be a strong factor in how effective your human relations skills are.

A fine distinction exists between influence and power. **Influence** is the application of power through actions we take or examples we set that cause others to change their attitudes or behaviors. People must possess power from some source before they can influence the behavior of others. Patricia Sellers notes in her article, "The Business of Being Oprah," that only after a four-hour interview filled with hard evidence of her solid business ventures spread throughout multiple interests would Oprah admit the degree of her influence on people, places, and things enough to say, "Yeah, I guess I am a businesswoman."[2]

Too often, the word "power" brings to mind negative images. Terms such as manipulation, control, domination, exploitation, corruption, and coercion are frequently associated with power. Because of the tarnished image of power, many individuals tend to shy away from learning about and practicing positive power.

Pat Russo has confessed that it was her taste of power while at AT&T that made her want to run a big corporation. "It was the first job where I was in charge, and I had control of all the levers and I liked it. I liked choosing, planning, and seeing what worked, what didn't, and why."

> Acquiring power and learning to use it are essential to accomplishing goals.

> Power, sometimes seen as negative, is desirable when used appropriately.

uick tip ·····································

"Professional excellence requires the knack of knowing how to make power dynamics work for us, instead of against us."

John P. Kotter, Business Author

···

Three dozen of America's most powerful businessmen were gathering for a showdown. Members of the *Fortune 500* CEO list, they were participating in the AT&T Pebble Beach National Pro-Am event on the PGA Tour. The heads of Morgan Stanley, Motorola, Sun Microsystems, Comcast, UPS, Wachovia, AT&T, and even "The Donald," Donald Trump, were among those arriving in private jets and limos. Golf remains the true communications hub of America's business elite. Golf is far more than a game. The greatest clubs in the country–Augusta, Oakmont, Pine Valley, and Brookline–were founded by businessmen who wanted to establish an inner circle of corporate chieftains and other power brokers. Golf is about building relationships that move right into the business world: friendship, camaraderie, trust, honesty, and discretion. Golf is a litmus test for a person's character.[3]

1. *What kind of lesson could be learned about a person by playing golf?*

2. *Why do you think the golf club memberships today are still carefully controlled? Is this fair?*

3. *Do you think business is always discussed on the course? Why, or why not?*

After 20 years at AT&T, Russo moved to the number two slot at Kodak, then returned as CEO of Lucent Technologies, an AT&T spin-off. She has used her power positively to advance her career.[4]

Power can be a healthy, desirable attribute when channeled appropriately. It is most effective when its use is not obvious. Positive uses of power include influence, leadership, control, authority, and direction. These strong behaviors are very necessary in both your personal and professional lives.

Acquiring some power and learning how to use it, then, is essential to your achievement of personal and organizational goals. An understanding of the sources of power available to you and techniques for drawing upon them will assist you in strengthening your power base.

*Fast*Chat

1. Why is power a necessary tool?

2. How have you had power exercised over you, and how did you feel about it?

John French and Bertram Raven, two researchers on power, identified five basic power sources: reward, coercive, legitimate, expert, and referent. The first three sources are derived from our position within the organization; the last two are generated from our personal characteristics. Other theorists add derivative and passive power to the list.[5]

REWARD POWER

Reward power is the ability to give something of material or personal value to others. The rewards may be in the form of promotions, bonuses, supplies and equipment, highly desirable job assignments, or reserved parking places. It may also take the form of valued information, praise for a job well done, or a desired position title. At home, reward power may come in the form of an unexpected gift, an allowance, a night to eat out, or a trip to the movies.

Reward power is considered the most important source of power by French and Raven because it places the reward seeker almost totally at the mercy of the reward giver. Only by submitting to the desired behavior can the seeker hope to obtain the reward from the giver. The strength of this power source varies with the amount of rewards controlled by the giver. From the corporate chief executive to the unit secretary who controls the distribution of supplies, a full range of individuals can hold this power source.

> Developing or acquiring power sources is a necessary step in gaining power.

COERCIVE POWER

Coercive power is based on fear and punishment. Demotions, dismissals, reprimands, assignment of unpleasant tasks, and public embarrassment are examples of coercive power. This form of power can be directed toward superiors, coworkers, or subordinates. At home, coercive power comes in the form of spanking, scolding, grounding, or loss of privileges.

Coercive power can be used in a positive manner, such as in an emergency, to let others know that you mean business. When an employee's performance is slipping, being firm and pointing out the consequences of continued nonperformance can have a positive effect.

However, open use of coercive power is generally considered unacceptable in the work environment, and the user may risk retaliation, sabotage, or malicious obedience. Low morale may result, because coercive power is a negative motivator. This counterproductive use of power also places the

> *QUICK WIT*
> "Power doesn't corrupt people, people corrupt power."
> —William Gaddis, American novelist

user at great risk of being removed from any position of power. Because of its potential for harm, coercive power should be used with caution.

LEGITIMATE POWER

Legitimate power is derived from formal rank or position within an organizational hierarchy. A company president holds greater legitimate power than a regional vice president, and a general department manager will hold more legitimate power than a first-line supervisor or a technician on the assembly line. This power source is dependent on the formal, established chain of command within the organization and the perceived authority of the individual in that position of power. Examples away from work include a team captain or a committee chairperson. These individuals are perceived to have an "appointed" power.

However, just because you are ranked higher in an organization does not mean that you hold total power over those under you. An example is the security guard who has the legitimate power to request the president of the company to present identification to enter a secured facility.

EXPERT POWER

While reward, coercive, and legitimate power are linked to position, expert and referent power are derived from personal characteristics.

Expert power develops when an individual possesses specialized skills, knowledge, or expertise. This power source is limited in that it is only useful when the knowledge is of value to the seeker. This power source is not dependent on appointed rank or position. It can be held by individuals ranging from the chief executive officer to the computer technician to the janitor. For instance, when the building heat is malfunctioning, employees will turn to the janitor rather than the company president, who may have no knowledge of machinery or equipment.

Expert power can also be found off the job. You may, for example, defer to a neighbor with extensive mechanical experience when dealing with an automobile that will not start or a dishwasher that does not work.

REFERENT POWER

Referent power is power based on respect or admiration for the individual. This respect or admiration may result from personal charisma and "likable" personal traits. Sports heroes, political leaders, and dynamic religious or business leaders can influence the behavior of others who have a desire to emulate their heroes' perceived success. Bill Clinton may have retained his legitimate power as president but may have lost his referent power with some of the public after the White House scandals erupted.

DERIVATIVE AND PASSIVE POWER

Derivative power comes from close association with a powerful person. We are all familiar with signs and symbols of people using this power technique. Name-dropping and use of the "good old boy" system are examples of using derivative power to gain advantages.

Passive power, the last of the power sources, stems from a display of helplessness. A child often uses this power source effectively on a parent to gain attention or solicit help with some undesirable task. Unfortunately, we sometimes see this same technique carried into adulthood and used in the workplace. For example, an employee will act incapable in order to gain help in accomplishing a task or to escape it altogether. A simple statement that says, "I cannot possibly manage this all by myself and, besides, you are so much better at this sort of thing than I am," will often subtly but powerfully gain the desired results.

Derivative and passive power sources are not dependable in the long haul. They tend to damage the image and credibility of the user. Recognizing that these power sources exist and avoiding their use will aid you in developing more desirable power sources. Being knowledgeable will additionally help you avoid being the pawn that gets duped in the game of passive power.

> Derivative and passive power are not strong or reliable power sources and tend to damage the credibility of those who rely on them.

*Fast*Chat

1. Which of these power sources do you think apply to you?

2. Which of these power sources do you think are more important than others?

3. Who might represent examples of some of these power sources?

The power sources are highly linked. They tend to occur in combinations, as the following example illustrates. As you read the example, note the various sources of power that are used and how they are linked.

Power Source Linking

Thomas, the head of the accounting department, glared down at a young staff accountant sitting in the chair beside him. He was angry at his antics and felt that he had to show him he could not get away with foolishness that reflected negatively on the company. Thomas's brow was furrowed, reflecting a scowl. When he spoke, it was in low-toned, slow phrases that revealed his anger. He was the department chief with full authority to administer the punishment due for the embarrassment caused the company and to delay any promotion until the staff accountant's behavior matured.

Thomas has legitimate power given to him through his position in the organization. Additionally, he is exercising coercive power through his intimidating body language and threats of consequences.

Another example of power source linking would be the prominent sports figure Alex Rodriguez. He has expert power because he possesses special skills and expertise in the sport of baseball, and he has referent power because he is admired and respected for his home-run and fielding talents. He also has legitimate power as a high profile member of his team who has been named the American League Most Valuable Player (MVP) and the Players' Choice Overall Outstanding Player several times.

With some individuals, we don't have to guess or be told which power sources they use or possess. The names or faces of certain individuals are easily recognized because of the impact they have had on us or on our world. We immediately acknowledge and can often easily identify the power sources of people such as those pictured on the next page.

The type of behavior response from individuals will vary in different situations depending upon what the receiver perceives the power source of the sender to be. For example, individuals with a high degree of expert power are usually admired and respected and, therefore, have a high degree of referent power.

Similarly, individuals with a high degree of legitimate power may wield strong reward and coercive power over others.

QUICK WIT
"Life is full of obstacle illusions"
Grant Frazier,
Author

What are the power sources for these individuals?

Tiger Woods   **Bill Gates**   **Oprah Winfrey**   **Donald Trump**

Many combinations of power can be developed. A particularly powerful combination to acquire is expert, legitimate, and reward power sources. Obviously, the more power sources you acquire, the stronger your influence will be in the work environment and on a personal level.

Our ability to use these power sources individually or in combination relies heavily on the perception of those involved. They must believe that our power source is genuine. John P. Kotter, as summarized by James Stoner and R. Edward Freeman in *Management*, suggests that, in order to develop the perception in others that you are truly powerful, you must use your power sources wisely and appropriately. Recognize what sources you do not have and avoid their use. Using undeveloped sources or abusing your power sources weakens your credibility and strips you of what power you do have. Understand the risks and benefits of using each of your power sources and develop your skills accordingly.[6]

> You must use your power sources wisely and appropriately.

*Fast*Chat

1. How were the power sources of the individuals pictured above developed? How are these power sources linked?

2. Which of the power sources do you think link in your personal activities?

3. Have you ever seen or heard about someone who used linked power sources unwisely and inappropriately? What was the outcome?

Some behavioral theorists believe that a person's use of power is based more on individual characteristics, charisma, and acquired personality traits than on other factors. These traits vary in intensity in different people, resulting in three basic power personalities: the power-shy, the power-positive, and the power-compulsive.

Power-shy individuals tend to avoid being placed in positions that require overt use of power. They quickly sidestep or totally shun responsibility and leadership, feeling extremely uncomfortable with decision making and influencing or controlling the behavior of others. Power-shy individuals make excellent followers and will usually excel in positions that require them to operate independently and rely on individual skills and abilities. You may recognize why Oprah Winfrey was once considered a power-shy individual.

On the other hand, **power-positive** people genuinely enjoy accepting responsibility and thrive on the use of power. Highly power-motivated, these individuals enjoy controlling situations and directing and influencing the behavior of others. They express strong views and opinions and are usually risk takers and adventurers. Power-positive individuals can be valuable resources when placed in leadership roles requiring the described qualities. How do you think Ms. Winfrey's success in her field helped her transform from being a power-shy to a power-positive person? Only when the need or desire for power becomes compulsive and is a driving force directing all actions toward selfish goals does it take on negative overtones.

Power-compulsive individuals have a lust for power and are seldom satisfied with the amount of power they have. These individuals constantly seek increased levels of control and influence over others and have a strong need to display power plays for personal gain in all situations. This use of power is destructive and intimidating, seldom benefiting the organization or the individual.

Fortunately, the need and desire for power does vary greatly in individuals. The power-shy and power-positive personalities are both needed in the work environment to create balance. We acquire power in varying amounts, from different sources, and at different times in life. How we choose to use it reflects our positive or negative motives.

The short self-inventory presented on the next page will rate your power personality. Does the need for power control you, or do you constructively use the power that you have for growth and advancement? As in any self-test, you must be honest in your responses to get a true reflection of

---

Some theorists believe that power is based on personal characteristics.

QUICK WIT

"Oh, it is excellent to have a giant's strength, but it is tyrannous to use it like a giant."

William Shakespeare

yourself. You may also want to have your spouse, close friend, or coworker answer the questions about you. Seeing yourself as others see you is an excellent method of gaining insight.

Power Personality Test[7]

INSTRUCTIONS: Answer each question with 2 (often true), 1 (sometimes true), or 0 (seldom or never true). The scoring interpretation appears on the next page.

1. "Get the last word in" is my motto.

2. It is important to me to "wear the pants" in my family.

3. It disturbs me when things are disorganized.

4. It angers me when somebody tries to take advantage of me.

5. When I entertain, it is important that plans go smoothly.

6. For my leisure time, I usually plan things/activities well in advance.

7. People who don't behave the way I expect really irritate me.

8. Nothing angers me more than people trying to dominate me.

9. In my position, I feel it is demeaning to do subordinate tasks.

10. I always conceal my true feelings.

11. I do not tolerate my child publicly displaying poor manners or bad behavior.

12. In a public or business meeting, I make certain my viewpoint is known.

13. I cannot tolerate others humiliating me.

14. I would turn down a tempting job offer with another firm if the position had less prestige and power than my current one.

15. I agree with Michael Korda's quote about the workplace, "Without power we're merely cogs in a meaningless machine."

16. I feel good when I can make others perform menial tasks for me.

17. To show others "who's the boss," I will sometimes humiliate them undeservingly.

18. When people get "out of line" at work, it really irritates me.

19. I never allow other people to push me around.

20. Inconveniencing others, forcing them to adhere to my schedule, or keeping others waiting provides me with a certain degree of enjoyment.

21. It angers or depresses me when a rival at work upstages me.

22. I will feel like a failure if I do not achieve my targeted key executive position in my company.

SCORING INTERPRETATION:

Control Scale: Total the scores for your answers 3, 5, 6, 7, 10, 11, and 18. Your total score reflects the degree to which you seek or need control and order in situations.

Total Score of: 0–3   Little to no need
                    4–6   Moderate need
                    7 or more   High, compulsive need

A high score in the control scale means you seek consistency and prefer predictability. You need or desire the security of certainty. You seldom "go with the flow" or allow yourself the freedom of spontaneity. You prefer rigid control. Learn to be more flexible. Decrease your need for control by enjoying your emotions. Allow your feelings to surface.

Power Scale: Total the scores for your answers to questions 1, 2, 4, 8, 9, 12, 13, 14, 15, 16, 17, 19, 20, 21, and 22. Your total score indicates the degree to which you have a need for or seek power.

Total score of: 0–6   Little to no need
                    7–14   Moderate need
                    15 or more   High, compulsive need

A high score on the power scale means your need for power may be excessive and may require some self-evaluation of your motives. In your interpersonal actions with others, examine your behavior to better understand the origins of your power compulsion. What did you do, and what were the effects of your actions? Why did you feel the need for power in that situation? Did your dominance decrease your overall effectiveness? Compulsive power needs can be destructive to the development or use of good human relations skills. Plan and implement change in your behavior to lessen a strong compulsive drive for power if necessary.

*Fast*Chat

1. If you are power-shy, how might you change that power personality?

2. Was your score on the Power Personality Test what you expected? Are you comfortable with the results? How will you use this information?

Building power is a complex process and seldom comes without planning and careful execution. Some individuals may operate from a totally subconscious level in their quest for power, whereas others consciously and methodically plan their steps to the top. Building and maintaining a strong power base usually requires a thorough understanding of power positioning, power politics, and power symbols.

CASE STUDIES IN THE NEWS

Carly Fiorina was number one on *Fortune* magazine's list of Most Powerful Women in Business for six consecutive years. In 1998, when this list began, a $3 billion business practically guaranteed you a spot on it. Not so today! Fiorina's company revenues hit $72 billion and her competitors are not far behind. The criteria used to judge who makes this list include the size and importance of the woman's business, her clout inside her company, the arc of her career, and her influence on mass culture and society. Fiorina orchestrated the biggest tech merger in history and has done a stellar job improving efficiencies at Hewlett-Packard. She is a world-class risk taker and is currently known to be Microsoft's favorite PC maker. Fiorina is a star in the computer industry.

Carly Fiorina majored in medieval history and philosophy and dropped out of law school in her first year. From job to job–receptionist, teacher– she floated. Finally, she went to AT&T as a sales rep and refused to join the savings plan because she knew she planned not to stay more than two years. Now making in excess of $100 million per year, her savings plan is good, and she is undeniably one of the most powerful women in America.[8]

1. *What power sources do you think Carly Fiorina possesses?*

2. *What do you think Fiorina's power personality is?*

POWER POSITIONING

Power positioning is the conscientious use of techniques designed to position yourself for maximum personal growth or gain. Achieving success is sometimes attributed to luck or being at the right place at the right time. (How often have you heard the cliché, "It's not *what* you know, but *who* you know"?) However, you can apply specific techniques of power positioning that do not rely on luck or influential others.

Some 20 years of research by behavioral scientists have resulted in the identification of major techniques that strongly influence the degree of personal power that we attain. The techniques, shown below and on the next page, should be cultivated in your quest for power, as they will greatly enhance your chances for success.

Seldom are individuals fully proficient in all these techniques. Self-assessment is an important first step in identifying which technique needs attention and which already is fully developed in you. Effective power positioning requires skillful planning and careful implementation.

Techniques to Strengthen Your Personal Power

1. Be goal-oriented.

   Know what power sources you have and how you plan to strengthen them.

2. Learn to take risks.

   Show that you are willing to take action and make decisions.

3. Look for ways to become visible.

   Volunteer for special projects and other activities that expose your strengths and capabilities.

4. Acquire positions of authority and knowledge.

   Controlling resources and information strengthens power.

5. Develop communication skills, including the ability to negotiate.

   These skills are crucial in learning to persuade and influence others.

6. Learn to make decisions.

   Think through issues on which you wish to take a stand. Taking a stand just for the sake of winning and being right can backfire in the long run.

7. Develop commitment.

   Show through your determination and will power that you are committed to your cause. Display that inner drive that shows you are dedicated to excellence.

8. Network.

   Learn to call on individuals inside and outside your organization who can help you accomplish your goals. They can be superiors, subordinates, or colleagues. Discover how to ask for and return favors that will help you build your coalition.

9. Learn how to be a team player.

   Help others reach their goals and objectives. Do not be afraid to delegate authority to others. Display a cooperative attitude.

10. Create a following.

    Be sensitive to the feelings of others and be careful not to abuse your power. Establishing a reputation for being credible, reliable, and ethical will draw others to your side.

11. Select a mentor.	Choose a successful person with whom you can develop rapport to give you advice and guidance. Having a mentor with political savvy is advisable.
12. Develop confidence.	Sharpen public speaking and other communication skills that will enhance your positive self-image. Portray a professional impression through appropriate dress.
13. Develop advanced skills.	Become an authority by developing and maintaining advanced skills in some area that is perceived as important to others.
14. Understand your organization.	Be knowledgeable in the philosophy, politics, communication channels, and structures of your organization. Discover where the power lies and how it is used.
15. Anticipate resistance.	Realize that others may resent your use of power or view you as a threat to their own goals. Develop an information feedback system that lets you know how others perceive you. Then, deal positively with the situation.

POWER POLITICS

In his book *Unlimited Power*, Anthony Robbins says, "The meeting of preparation with opportunity generates the offspring we call luck." Success is not an accident, and **power politics** allows us to develop opportunities for success.[9]

Not all decisions for promotion and rewards are made on the bases of merit, fair play, rationality, or even ethics. The only defense you may have against unfair practices is becoming politically astute. This means developing an awareness of power politics, understanding how it works, and applying those techniques with which you are most comfortable.

A first step in this process is to determine how politically inclined you are. The checklist on the next page is a quick self-test that will give you some insight into your political inclination. It is an abbreviated version of the Organizational Politics Scale developed by business and psychology author Andrew J. DuBrin in *Winning Office Politics*. DuBrin's complete test consists of 100 comprehensive questions that provide an in-depth index of an individual's political tendencies. He places the scores in five categories that illustrate a person's identity as a politician. This shortened test version may help you determine where you would fall in the category scale.[10]

How Political Are You?
....

Directions: Answer each question "mostly agree" or "mostly disagree," even if it is difficult for you to decide which alternative best describes your opinion.

1. Only a fool would correct a boss's mistakes.
2. If you have certain confidential information, release it to your advantage.
3. I would be careful not to hire a subordinate with more formal education than myself.
4. If you do somebody a favor, remember to cash in on it.
5. Given the opportunity, I would cultivate friendships with power people.
6. I like the idea of saying nice things about a rival in order to get that person transferred from my department.
7. Why not take credit for someone else's work? They would do the same to you.
8. Given the chance, I would offer to help my boss build some shelves for his or her den.
9. I laugh heartily at my boss's jokes, even when they are not funny.
10. I would be sure to attend a company picnic even if I had the chance to do something I enjoyed more that day.
11. If I knew an executive in my company was stealing money, I would use that against him or her in asking for favors.
12. I would first find out my boss's political preferences before discussing politics with him or her.
13. I think using memos to zap somebody for his or her mistakes is a good idea (especially when you want to show that person up).
14. If I wanted something done by a coworker, I would be willing to say "If you don't get this done, our boss might be very unhappy."
15. I would invite my boss to a party at my house, even if I didn't like him or her.
16. When I'm in a position to, I would have lunch with the "right people" at least twice a week.
17. Richard M. Nixon's bugging the Democratic Headquarters would have been a clever idea if he hadn't been caught.
18. Power for its own sake is one of life's most precious commodities.
19. Having a high school named after you would be an incredible thrill.
20. Reading about job politics is as much fun as reading an adventure story.

Interpretation of Scores. Each statement you check "mostly agree" is worth one point toward your political orientation score. If you score 16 or over, it suggests that you have a strong inclination toward playing politics. A high score of this nature would also suggest that you have strong needs for power. Scores of 5 or less would suggest that you are not inclined toward political maneuvering and that you are not strongly power-driven.

Source: Andrew J. DuBrin, *Winning Office Politics* (Englewood Cliffs, NJ: Prentice-Hall, 1990)

Human Relations

In *Winning Office Politics,* DuBrin explains the following five categories of power:[11]

- **Machiavellian** The Machiavellian is a power-hungry, power-grabbing individual. Often ruthless, devious, and power-crazed, he or she will try to succeed at any cost to others.

- **Company Politician** This individual is a shrewd maneuverer and politico. Most successful individuals fall into this category. Company politicians desire power, but it is not an all-consuming preoccupation for them. They will do whatever is necessary to address their cause except deliberately defame or injure others.

- **Survivalist** The survivalist practices enough power politics to take advantage of good opportunities. Not concerned about making obvious political blunders, he or she will stay out of trouble with others of a higher rank.

- **Straight Arrow** This person is not particularly perceived as a politician, nor seen as a person intent on committing political suicide. The straight arrow fundamentally believes that most people are honest, hardworking, and trustworthy. The favorite career advancement strategy is to display job competence, but he or she may neglect other important career-advancement strategies.

- **Innocent Lamb** The innocent lamb believes fully that good people are rewarded for their efforts and will rise to the top. This individual remains focused on the tasks at hand, hoping that hard work will be rewarded.

Obviously, some individuals are well suited to applying whatever methods and techniques will advance them toward their goals. The Machiavellian and Innocent Lamb types are extremes to avoid, but falling somewhere in the middle of these categories may prove valuable in power politics.

Organizational politics are unavoidable. The political implications of your actions, and the actions of others, must be taken into consideration whenever operating within an organization, be it large or small. Playing power politics can be negative or positive. Negative methods are manipulative, coercive, exploitative, and destructive. Positive methods are used to achieve common goals, empower others, build cooperation, develop effective personal contacts, and gain credibility and leadership.

The Political Power Checklist itemized in the box below provides a quick reference to methods that you may use to become politically powerful. It can be used to check your progress or map your strategies.

Political Power Checklist

Use this checklist to assess your progress in building a power base.

_____ Do you have a mentor?

_____ Are you sought out for advice or information?

_____ Are your achievements visible?

_____ Do you present your major accomplishments at performance appraisal time?

_____ Have you set your mid- and long-range goals?

_____ Are you tracking (and remaining ahead of) your competition?

_____ Are you paying attention to power dynamics?

_____ Do you attempt to influence others?

_____ Do you get credit and recognition for your ideas?

_____ Are you developing and increasing your power sources?

_____ Do people like to work with you?

POWER SYMBOLS

Power symbols influence perceptions.

Power symbols come in the form of physical traits and personality characteristics as well as external physical factors, such as clothes or cars. Power symbols are everywhere. We turn on the soap operas and watch as the rich, handsome tycoon and his ex-model wife, who is draped in jewels, are driven in their Rolls-Royce to a romantic weekend on their 80-foot yacht. We then pick up the paper only to see that another corporation has built an even larger building designed by a popular architect.

Do individuals acquire these power symbols after they obtain power? Do some persons with little power use them to portray the illusion of power? If you do not have power, will use of power symbols speed your ability to obtain it? The answers are unclear. One thing is certain, however — our perceptions are influenced by these symbols. Understanding power symbols will help us decide how we wish to use them and recognize their use by others.

Traits and Characteristics Do some characteristics identify the potential of an individual to hold power over others? High achievers are generally perceived as powerful, and their traits have been associated with power. These individuals are seen as self-confident, ambitious, dominant, attractive, selfish, ruthless, decisive, strong-willed, determined, accomplished, and goal-directed.

Whether individuals start with these traits or acquire them is undetermined. However, most theorists believe that they are learned abilities nurtured from infancy. Individuals gain these strengths through exposure and experience and cultivate them because of benefits that they derive from their use. The desire for some of these traits is no doubt strengthened through the constant reinforcement by the media that these are the dynamic traits of success and power.

Some studies have supported the idea that certain physical traits make a more powerful impression. For example, people do make a mental connection between height and power, reported Wayne Hensley, a scientist who has done research on whether height provides any real advantage. He found through a survey of some 243 executives that 90 percent of them were taller than the average 5-foot-9-inch male. He also found through a sampling of male university professors that the taller the teacher, the higher the academic ranking. Full professors averaged a two-or-more-inch advantage. The same pattern held true in his research on the last 21 presidential elections. The taller candidate was chosen to be our nation's chief executive in 17 of the 21 elections.[12]

Additionally, some studies have shown that specific nonverbal behavior patterns differ between high- and low-power individuals. These behaviors deal with direct eye contact, facial expression, body gestures, and body positioning. For example, a less powerful person is more likely to *be* touched, whereas the more powerful person is far more likely to *do* the touching.

External Physical Factors Clothing is an external physical factor that may send power signals. The famous adage "Clothes do not the man make" does not hold completely true. Certainly, the idea of "dressing for success" has merit.

Personal appearance does seem to carry importance in most cases. The way we dress, from hairstyle down to shoes, is believed to make a statement about the degree of power we either hold or seek. For some, personal appearance can make desired impressions while others disavow the need for all the fuss. Stylish appearance makes a perceived difference and will let others know you are serious about your career choices.

QUICK WIT
"It isn't a mistake to have strong views. The mistake is to have nothing else."

Anthony Westin,
Ethicist and author

In 1996, Nancy Lublin and three nuns in Spanish Harlem founded Dress for Success with a $5,000 inheritance from Lublin's grandfather. They helped women from low-income referrals get clothing for job interviews so they could enter the workforce. The idea caught on when women from cities across the United States began calling, so she trademarked the name and licensed it to over 20 new affiliates. In 1998, she left law school to become executive director of Dress for Success–Worldwide, which added the Professional Women's Group program to provide career training skills and professional coaching capabilities. Only one year later, Dress for Success had grown to 50 affiliates in four countries and Nancy had been seen on *Oprah*, *60 Minutes*, *The Today Show*, *CNN*, *People* magazine, and *Reader's Digest*. Partnering with representatives from the clothing, cosmetics, travel, shoe, and career counseling industries, Lublin built an impressive array of services needed to prepare women for the workforce. Her distribution system is handled by Vista (Volunteers in Service to America), a service that helps communities and individuals out of poverty.[13]

1. *Why do you think clothing and appearance make a difference in business?*

2. *How many smart business principles do you see applied in Lublin's decisions? Discuss any other growth potential you see.*

Entrepreneurs in fitted suits, board members in the "corporate uniform," and power brokers in the "right kind of suit" all understand the psychological advantages gained from dressing for the part. It is important to make your statement, but know what statement you are making.

We all know many examples of less-rigid appearance requirements. To some, not only the style but also the very nature of executive power has changed. Some attribute the different visions of appropriate dress for success to an "East Coast-West Coast" phenomenon. The West Coast's Silicon Valley originated the "dress-down" or "casual" Friday for winding down a busy business week, and many of today's powerful people have lowered the once-rigid standards for power symbols.

Power is also communicated through use of space. In some cases, powerful people will enjoy large zones of personal space. For example, the corporate CEO may be seated behind a large, executive-style desk issuing orders to a subordinate standing on the opposite side of the desk. A less powerful person will usually make an appointment and wait to be ushered in by invitation to see the power holder, whereas the more powerful person is far more likely to walk right into the smaller office area of a subordinate and be given immediate recognition and respect. Although these cues are subtle, they do leave the impression that an individual is powerful.

CASE STUDIES IN THE NEWS

As part of her "Ask Annie" column in *Fortune*, Anne Fisher asked her readers what was the one piece of advice they wish they had been given when first starting their careers. She received many hundreds of responses on topics including proper ethics, office politics, mentoring, and the importance of making good first impressions. One reader replied, "Dress for the job you want, not the job you have. That way, when your big chance comes, it isn't as difficult for people to see you as someone to be taken seriously. It is interesting that appearances have so much power over perception, but that is reality." First impressions are not easily overcome.[14]

1. *Do you agree with this? Why, or why not?*

2. *Think of an instance when a person's dress influenced your initial impression. Was your impression true or misleading?*

On the other hand, some feel that the "power office" is passé. Robert Tillman, CEO of Lowe's Cos., the giant discount retailer, sets the modern example. He turned down an office on Executive Row at the front of the building. He chose a windowless office smack in the middle of the building instead, saying, "The ideal office layout would be senior executives in the center, with operating areas fanning out from it." It seems to be an idea that has caught on in other arenas. Jim Hackett, CEO at Steelcase, gave up a two-room suite with a marble fountain for a nearly phone-booth-size office. He says, "People don't need to see me in a big fancy office to know that I'm the CEO."[15]

©Brand X Pictures

©CORBIS

Which of these two women is most likely the boss? What external factors are sending power signals?

TECHNOLOGY CONNECTION

It's good to be the president of anything, but especially the United States! Signs of power are ALL around you: a mountain retreat in Maryland where you can pitch horseshoes, hike, bike, and fish; a flying "Oval Office" with a state-of-the-art technology conference room, media room, and dining room for 50; and back at the White House, you have your own tennis court, putting green, jogging track, swimming pool, movie theater, billiard room, and bowling alley. If you want a snack, no need for McDonalds—there are five full-time chefs on duty 24-7. Your hi-tech limo has a master control panel for power accessories and other luxuries. Yes, life at the top is good! Many top executives enjoy similar perks.[16]

1. *Why do you think these "perks" or power symbols are provided to presidents and executives?*

2. *How might it affect the attitudes of their business associates if the hi-tech perks were not there?*

3. *Do you think we overemphasize the importance of "perks" today? Why, or why not?*

Thoughts today about what is appropriate seem to move in extremes from one end of a continuum to the other. This is attributable in part to the rise of the baby boomer, who has moved away from tradition in many areas, and to the dramatic changes in business itself, as technology of the Information Age continues to alter the way we do work. Our work and personal environments will continue to evolve throughout the 21ST century.

Regardless of how the world changes, the power person will always acquire benefits. As an individual rises to a position of power, certain symbols will set that person apart from others. Today, power symbols provided by organizations may include a company car, a personal assistant, a large corner office, and the latest electronic tools/toys. The mailroom clerk who holds a considerably less powerful position seldom enjoys these extras, or perks.

*Fast*Chat

1. How do you feel about power symbols? Are they necessary or useful?

2. Do you agree with the "casual Friday" concept for corporate settings? What effect do you think this idea has had on the work environment?

3. Were you surprised or comfortable with your power category based on DuBrin's political assessment instrument? How will you use this to your advantage?

Empowerment became a trendy management catch phrase in the nineties. This trend has carried right into the 21ST century. A prime example of this is illustrated in the case study below. As organizations continue to flatten, decision making is being pushed to lower levels in organizations. The need for a leaner and meaner operation naturally requires passing the power to those most qualified to make the right decision. **Empowerment** is allowing others to make decisions and have influence in desired outcomes. It involves not only delegation of tasks, but assigning the appropriate authority and supplying the necessary information and training with the task so that the individual has considerable likelihood of being successful. It is the giving of power to others, helping them to develop their own power sources. The ability to empower others is a sign of an accomplished leader.

> Empowerment is allowing others to make decisions and influence others.

Kenneth Blanchard is a world-renowned consultant and author of several books, including *The 3 Keys to Empowerment: Release the Power within People for Astonishing Results.* The title speaks to his strong support of empowering others. Blanchard feels you must start by sharing information

CASE STUDIES IN THE NEWS

Everyone knows the old Bill Gates, the all-powerful computer mogul. He is largely responsible for how our computers behave. He achieved a monopoly in Microsoft's operating systems software and weathered a huge federal antitrust investigation. Still the world's richest man at over $30 billion, he's now out to make a difference in the world by helping others. After an exhaustive study of global health issues, he founded and funded the world's richest charitable foundation aimed at eradicating infectious diseases. He gave up his Microsoft CEO position and now works as their chief software architect—a grand geek helping develop operating systems. He is empowering his management team to run Microsoft and his wife to lead the charity foundation, and he now empowers his team of developers daily to complete the new software code-named "Longhorn."[17]

Have you areas in your life where you feel that, if you were empowered with the authority, you would be able to reach a goal successfully?

with others, allowing others the autonomy to use that information. You must flatten the decision-making process and push the freedom to do that down to the lowest levels at which a competent decision can be made. If these steps are taken, you may expect to get remarkable results from subordinates.[18]

Blanchard points out that many people will be uncomfortable with this newly acquired power, but given the opportunity to use their power and the freedom to make mistakes, they will mature in confidence. This approach is a winning approach for all involved. He states, "The rewards include more tuned-in employees, less turnover, and ultimately, a wealth of brainpower and expertise from which to draw." With the trend toward larger, global businesses, empowerment may become an increasingly important element of successful human relations and effective business.[19]

Knowledge work, with its reliance on project teams and cross-functional collaboration, is naturally resistant to the old forms of authoritarian leadership. Relinquishing power and giving it away will be a method of survival. Companies cannot be fast or global unless people in the field are empowered to make judgment calls and make decisions in a timely manner.

Frances Hesselbein, the woman who modernized the Girl Scouts of America, shares her opinions on empowerment in *WorkingSmart,* a monthly publication of the National Institute of Business Management. "The concept of empowerment requires some adjustments in traditional thinking. Authoritarian managers and leaders who view empowerment as a threat to their personal power are missing the point. In fact, the more power you give away, the more power you have."[20]

One final testament on behalf of empowerment comes from Warren Bennis in his workbook, *Learning to Lead.* He feels that in organizations with effective leaders, empowerment is widely evident. The organizations are successful and its leaders are fulfilled. He states that, "In organizations where leaders lead through empowerment, people feel significant, learning and competence matter, people feel part of a community, and work is exciting." Individuals are motivated through identification with a worthwhile group and feel they make important contributions.[21]

*Fast*Chat

1. How do you think empowerment differs from delegation, or does it?
2. Is empowerment a trendy phase or a real asset in leadership?
3. What other benefits do you think might come from empowering others?

The more power you are able to exert, the more easily you will accomplish your goals. With each goal accomplishment, some degree of additional power is gained that enhances further accomplishments. Each cycle increases the ability to go beyond the previous level.

A number of behaviors, however, can block the development of power. Individuals who are so eager to be liked that they bend over backward to please others will find the development of power difficult. Being eager to please includes being unwilling to face a conflict for fear of offending others or refusing to take some action that will displease others.

On the other side of the coin, being aggressive and coming on too strong at inappropriate times can reduce your power. Refusing to share power by being unwilling to delegate is also viewed negatively.

In an executive coaching session, consultant Bob Cuddy recommends methods of using power more effectively. He advises participants to force themselves to speak for no more than two minutes in any meeting. Other people have many good ideas and thoughts that should be heard.[22]

> Wise use of power allows you to become even more powerful.

Figure 12.1   The Power Spiral

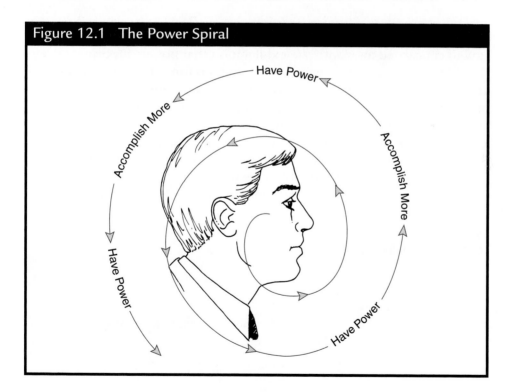

Do women really want power? Maybe yes, maybe no! Some recent studies are revealing that attitudes toward positions of power are changing. Some women are not willing to make the personal sacrifices necessary to hold the corporate CEO and chairperson jobs. They are instead opting for the flexibility that other venues offer. Ann Fudge quit her leading Kraft Food's position to travel with her husband and spearheaded a tutoring program for African-American kids with Harvard Business School. She says, "Women are consciously extending power to broader venues." Strangely, men's attitudes about power are changing, too. They are realizing balance has its rewards.[23]

Why do you think this change is occurring? Do you agree or disagree, and have you seen any evidence of this happening? What effects do you think this will have on women in the workforce? On the work environment?

A major pitfall of power gaming is overconfidence or arrogance. It is easy to get carried away with the exhilaration that power can bring. Care should be taken to guard against becoming too fond of our own abilities and basking too long in the glow of the spotlight. Remembering that others may know how to play the power game would indicate a certain amount of wisdom and maturity. A truly powerful person has the ability to recruit allies and harness resources to accomplish a mission or goal. Power use is most effective when it is an exercise of strength that enables you to achieve your goals and objectives without harm or damage to others and least effective when it is abused for selfish, personal gain.

*Fast*Chat

1. What are some means of reducing your power? How would you safeguard against this happening?

2. In meetings you have attended, who did the most talking? Was the speaker perceived to be more or less powerful?

3. How can you guard against becoming arrogant or self-centered?

CHAPTER SUMMARY

Power is the ability to influence others to do what we want them to do. Despite its sometimes negative image, experts agree that the acquisition and appropriate use of power is necessary for individuals at all levels of an organization if they are to accomplish goals and objectives.

Many sources of power are available and need to be cultivated for maximum effectiveness. These sources include reward, coercive, legitimate, expert, and referent power. Derivative and passive power are sources best left uncultivated. In addition to these power sources, research has defined three basic power personalities: the power-shy, the power-positive, and the power-compulsive.

Developing power is not a matter of luck. It must be planned. Part of this planning and development involves a thorough understanding and respect for power positioning, power politics, and power symbols. Empowering others is also a method of acquiring power and can be beneficial for all parties involved. Crucial to power development is avoiding the power pitfalls and ensuring that you have used power in a positive manner.

Key Terms

power
influence
reward power
coercive power
legitimate power
expert power
referent power
derivative power
passive power
power-shy
power-positive
power-compulsive
power positioning
power politics
power symbols
empowerment

REVIEW QUESTIONS

1. What is power, and why is developing power necessary?

2. Which basic power sources are available to you?

3. What are the three basic power personalities?

4. What techniques can you use in the planning and implementation of power positioning?

5. Why is applying power politics important?

6. How are power symbols used for power positioning?

7. Why is empowering others important?

8. What are the pitfalls in developing power?

DISCUSSION QUESTIONS

1. Think of individuals who are powerful or have power over you. Which power sources do they possess? Which ones are most effective?

2. Review the power sources available to you. Which is your strongest source, and which is your weakest? Do you have linkages?

3. Do you effectively plan the use of your power to gain personal advantages? How, and why?

4. Which of the power personalities best fits you? Are you comfortable with your assessment? Why, or why not?

5. What power symbols do you possess? How do you use these symbols in your power building?

6. How many of the power techniques have you cultivated? How have they benefited your power positioning?

7. Do you agree that playing power politics is an unavoidable means of assuring personal and professional success? Why, or why not?

CHAPTER PROJECT

As a group, collectively pool your resources and decide on a prominent person from somewhere in your community whom you may interview about how they became successful. This person should hold a reasonably powerful position. Based on the chapter topics, prepare a written report on how you believe this individual became and remains powerful. Describe traits, characteristics, power plays, etc.

APPLICATIONS

In small groups, analyze the following situations

Linda Loophole, the Legal Eagle

Linda is the best lawyer the firm has. All the junior associates admire her abilities and pattern their courtroom style after hers. She has been at the business longer than most of them have been living. She is known to be persuasive and shrewd. Just her physical presence in a courtroom demands attention. Her nearly 6-feet-tall, slender frame displays her immaculate and expensive clothing to its maximum flair. She really has it together. Linda knows exactly when to exert her strengths and when to let others have their opinions heard.

Everyone is aware of how she has used every legitimate method available to her to reach the pinnacle of success that seems rightfully hers. She was mentored by the firm's founder, gained visibility by landing two highly controversial cases early in her career, and outpaced most of her peers with little effort.

1. What power sources has Linda developed during her years with the law firm? How are they linked?

2. What power symbols does Linda use to add to her power positioning?

3. What power techniques has she used to aid her in becoming a success?

4. Do you think that Linda used power politics to acquire her status as the best lawyer in the firm? If so, why do you think that?

The Case of the Coercive Commander

Dave Hanks was a retired naval commander who had done a tour in private industry to round out his retirement income. Then came the call to serve his government again. He took the post as a favor to an old Navy buddy who needed help bringing about change at his agency. He was a tall, physically fit individual, a good match for the leadership position. As director of the Technology Commercialization effort, Dave had a small staff of highly skilled, competent individuals, all of whom had many years of experience in the public sector. They were an easy-going, cohesive group with many accomplishments to their credit.

When Dave first arrived, the winds of war began to blow. Wielding his power like a baseball bat, he began systematically "squeezing out" employees he felt had outlived their importance to his organization or just didn't fit the new culture.

He tried to run the office like a private industry business, railing against the bureaucracy of government operations. His demands were often unreasonable. His orders sometimes bordered on unethical practices in government work. He constantly "reminded" people of his connections to his buddy, the agency director, and alluded to his power base being indestructible. Stress levels grew to unmanageable heights among the employees.

Those that could retired. Others sought reassignments to any other part of the agency to escape the constant badgering and belittling. Accusations of fraud and abuse of government funds were leveled at Dave. A few employees filed claims of sexual harassment and mental cruelty. Complaints were made to appropriate sources, but nothing was done to change his behavior. A 150 percent turnover in staff occurred, but no one could please the coercive commander.

1. What power sources did Dave use?

2. Why did the agency employees fear him?

3. What might Dave have done differently?

4. What do you think the agency authorities should have done?

ADDITIONAL READINGS AND RESOURCES

Arndt, Michael. "Living Large in The Corner Office." *Business Week,* February 2004.

Blanchard, Kenneth, John P. Carlos, and Alan Randolph. *The 3 Keys to Empowerment: Release the Power within People for Astonishing Results.* San Francisco: Berrett-Koehler Publishers, Inc., 1999.

DuBrin, Andrew J. *Winning Office Politics.* Englewood Cliffs, NJ: Prentice-Hall, 1990.

Gergen, David. *Eyewitness to Power: The Essence of Leadership Nixon to Clinton.* New York: Simon & Schuster, 2001.

Schlender, Brent. "All You Need is Love, $50 Billion, and Killer Software Code-Named Longhorn." *Fortune,* June 2002.

Sellers, Patricia. "The Business of Being Oprah." *Fortune,* April 2002.

For additional resources, refer to the web site for this text: school.cengage.com/career/dalton

Change:
A Constant in an Inconstant World

focus

On April 15, many Americans will have their income tax preparation done in India. Yes, it's true, and it's legal. Most people will never know that their data have been shipped electronically to Bangalore, checked for accuracy, and put in proper order for submittal to the IRS. In March of 2004, the number of taxes prepared "offshore" jumped to more than 150,000—up from only 1,000 just two years ago. Mark Everson, the IRS commissioner, says, "...it's something we're taking a close look at, but there is no requirement that it be disclosed to taxpayers." Executives using offshore tax preparation companies say the workers are highly competent and the systems are extremely secure with very sophisticated encryption methods used to protect Social Security and other personal information from hackers and identity thieves.

Accounting and tax preparation firms such as SurePrep, Inc. defend the practice as safe and cost efficient. In a *60 Minutes* interview on August 1, 2004, SurePrep's CEO David Wyle revealed to Moreley Safer that they pay $300 to $400 per month for the same specialist support in India that they must pay $3,000 to $4,000 per month to get in the United States. Wyle says, "We are utilizing technologies and a global workforce so that prices come down and service improves." Global offshoring is part of the continual evolution of the U.S. economy.[1]

How would you feel about having your income taxes prepared offshore? Do you agree or disagree with this practice and why? What effects do you see this having long term?

After studying this chapter, you should be able to:

13.1 *Describe significant factors that are changing in today's workplace.*

13.2 *Identify who usually recommends and implements organizational changes.*

13.3 *Explain several effective methods of planning and implementing change.*

13.4 *Understand common reasons for resistance to change and how to overcome that resistance.*

13.5 *Describe the leader's role in facilitating change including coaching and counseling techniques.*

13.6 *Discuss the need for Employee Assistance Programs in change processes.*

in this chapter

13.1   Where Are Changes Occurring?

Companies strive to become globally competitive.

Change is a basic condition of today's work world. In recent decades, the number and speed of changes have escalated. Perhaps the Industrial Revolution is the last time conditions changed as rapidly. Thousands of the world's largest corporations have undergone some form of restructuring. From simple changes such as internal reorganizations to the mega-merger explosions, dramatic changes have been occurring in the corporate world. British Petroleum took over Amoco Oil, Chrysler Corporation merged with Germany's Daimler-Benz, and Exxon merged with Mobil Oil. More recently, Hewlett-Packard and Compaq became one, Chase and Bank One merged, and Cingular acquired AT&T Wireless. The variety of these co-minglings represents the diversity of the multinational business activities prevalent today. Even the government has felt the need for streamlining its ranks.

Millions of jobs have been eliminated throughout the world. The buzzwords "merger," "takeover," "buyout," and "downsizing" are very familiar to a multitude of workers and cause anxiety for many more. Some 2.35 million Americans have lost or left jobs since the beginning

CASE STUDIES IN THE NEWS

The latest mega-merger in the banking industry has raised alarms among smaller community groups voicing concerns about big banks getting bigger. J.P. Morgan Chase & Company announced the absorption of Bank One Corp. to form the second largest bank in the nation effective July 1, 2004. The bank will have assets of more than $1.1 trillion and operations in more than 50 countries. This $58 billion deal will erase about 10,000 jobs by 2006 and the Bank One name even sooner in a series of consolidations in the financial services industry. The concerns are for moderate-income consumers, communities of color, and small businesses nationwide who may be affected. After Bank One, how long before there's only one bank?[2]

1. *What changes might you personally experience from this merger?*

2. *How would you see it affecting smaller community groups? Why?*

of March 2001. Part of the explanation is that the job market has become a global game. Your toys are assembled in Hong Kong, customer service representatives in Manila answer your computer questions, and technicians in Bangalore analyze your X rays.[3]

The watchword for the new millennium is "offshoring," sometimes called outsourcing, or offshore outsourcing. Whatever you choose to call it, it affects the way we live and do business, the way we educate and market ourselves. We trace offshoring to a beginning in manufacturing when automakers set up plants in Mexico followed by garment companies sending their textiles to be sewn by small shops in the Dominican Republic and Sri Lanka. But the big wave, and the noisemaker, has been in the service industry. It is no longer just blue-collar jobs that go abroad. Today, jobs that require even higher skills are quickly being moved offshore. Computer programmers, architects, engineers, accountants, and customer service workers are beginning to see their jobs slip away. Foreste Research predicts 3.3 million technical industry jobs and $136 billion in wages will leave the U.S. economy within 10 years, and this is a conservative estimate. U.S. companies must now send work wherever the work can be done faster, cheaper, and better. Otherwise, they can no longer be competitive, and even more jobs will be lost. Some experts argue that the ultimate response to this outflow of jobs is a combination of new-job creation, a

> No person or company will function long or well without deliberate and intelligent planning for change.

TECHNOLOGY CONNECTION

Challenger Gray and Christmas, Inc., an outplacement firm, reported in June 2001 that the dot.com firms had cut 13,500 jobs that May. The previous month's layoffs had been 17,500. These two months were highest for the years reported since 1999 and perhaps indicated a downturn in layoffs. Job competition is very strong, but Rebecca Dill, executive producer for a New York-based Internet consulting and design firm, says she has openings for a technical project manager and a director of technology. She reveals the key to job selection is bringing the right stuff to the interview. "For some positions, business skills and soft skills may be more important than technical expertise. When several applicants are competing for an IT (information technology) position, the one with good communication skills will most often get the job."[4]

Why do you think soft skills would be more important than technical expertise in an IT position?

return to quality in manufacturing, and corporate policies that encourage critical jobs to remain in the United States.[5]

Although change is necessary to avoid stagnation, it can be difficult. People are often unwilling to step out of their comfort zones or abandon routines to which they have grown accustomed and that they see no reason to change. However, in today's complex environment, the premium is on *adaptability*. No person or company will function long or well without deliberate and intelligent planning for change. A planned change is a method of helping people develop appropriate behaviors for adapting to new methods while remaining effective and creative. The key to an organization making a positive transition is getting people involved in and committed to the change in the beginning. Then, employees are more likely to view change as an opportunity rather than a threat. The application of sound human relations skills will make adapting easier during any transition.

Areas currently experiencing rapid changes include the economy, science and technology, transportation, the general workforce, management styles, and the work itself. Each area has far-reaching effects on the others. We are bombarded daily with these changing elements in our environment.

CASE STUDIES IN THE NEWS

In a 2003 *Fast Company* article, author James Champy wrote that, "America's solution to the outflow of jobs may be found in opportunities presented in research and development, ingenuity and innovation." He explains that the life sciences may hold the secret, and industry, academia, and government should be partnering to bolster business in those fields. "Our hospital systems, pharmaceutical makers, and research facilities make America a premier leader in health care," he says. "Leave the manufacturing and programming to others."[6]

1. *What other areas of the life sciences could be explored to provide jobs here in America?*

2. *How do you feel about Mr. Champy's idea of letting U.S. manufacturing and programming go to other countries? What do you think is the best way for U.S. companies to remain competitive in a global market?*

The illustration below provides a graphic view of the many forces working to change our work world.

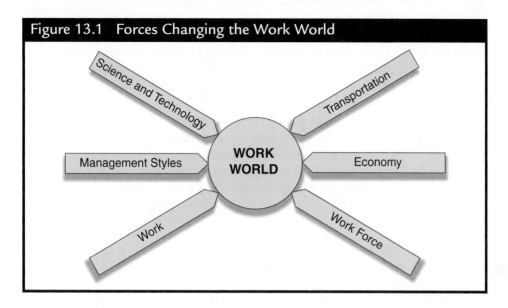

Figure 13.1 Forces Changing the Work World

Science and Technology
Transportation
Management Styles
WORK WORLD
Economy
Work
Work Force

GLOBAL CONNECTION

The use of a single currency, the Euro, by all eleven countries of Europe's Economic and Monetary Union (EMU) has brought a basic and irreversible change to how Europe now deals with foreign friends and competitors. The Euro made its physical appearance on January 1, 2002, to replace all other forms of currency in the EMU countries. This switch to a single currency simplified buying and selling for many businesses, both local and foreign. Small and large companies, manufacturers, and retailers are all finding that the Euro is having a big effect on their trade. The transition was very smooth, often requiring a simple software adjustment to the accounting system. England enjoys the benefits of the conversion as well, but as of February 2003 had not yet joined the EMU.[7]

1. *What impact might this European union have on international trade?*
2. *What impact might it have on U.S. business?*
3. *Why would a European country choose to not join the EMU?*

ECONOMY

As we continue the globalization of business activities, more opportunities for growth are being realized. The opening of the eastern and western European markets in the early 1990s caused an explosion in free trade and created the vast array of entrepreneurial opportunities we enjoy today. Many goods, services, people, and capital move across national borders in Europe as easily as we cross state borders in the United States, creating a major impact on the world market.

The North American Free Trade Agreement (NAFTA) was another international economic decision that opened trade and employment opportunities among countries. Signed into effect on January 1, 1994, NAFTA's main objective was to promote fair competition, increased investments, and enhanced trade cooperation between the United States, Mexico, and Canada. These types of trade agreements continue to shrink the world in which we live.

SCIENCE AND TECHNOLOGY

Advanced space exploration and experimentation are resulting in new scientific discoveries about our universe and the addition of new technologies to our lives. New research in medicine and nutrition science contributes to improving our health and well-being. Technological advancements are increasing as we share our knowledge and experience through joint ventures with other nations.

GLOBAL CONNECTION

American wood furniture manufacturers are losing retail floor space and jobs to Chinese goods that typically sell for 30 percent less. China exported $5.6 billion worth of furniture to the United States in 2003, impacting American manufacturers. The new threat comes from Vietnam's furniture makers who sell their goods 8 to 10 percent cheaper than China. The cost of labor in Vietnam is roughly 20 to 40 percent cheaper than in China. The import of Vietnamese furniture to the United States jumped by 155 percent in 2003. U.S. furniture manufacturers and four unions filed a petition with the government asking for help.[8]

1. *How can the U.S. furniture companies compete?*

2. *How would you suggest this problem be solved? What should the government's role in this be?*

As we continue to move deeper into the Knowledge Era, we have a greater need for computer competencies and other higher-level skills. These requirements are driving the need for a more capable, adaptable, and educated workforce. The need for life-long learning in areas of science and technology affects everyone from the farmer to Wall Street stockbroker.

TRANSPORTATION

While nothing as dramatic as going from horse-drawn carriages to cars has happened until now, the transition from combustion engine automobiles to hydrogen fuel cell forms of transportation will be a major new change in our lives. High fuel prices and hot political issues have pushed the auto and energy industries to work toward developing the new fuel cell cars expected on the highways by 2015. The crush of commuter traffic and pollution has become so bad in urban areas that other alternatives are also being pursued, including forms of mass transit and telecommuting. The need for efficiencies and speed in business has put great pressure on transportation companies to move more products swiftly and economically.[9]

WORKFORCE

Numerous changes are occurring in the workforce. The baby boomers, the Gen Xers, and the Gen Yers/Millennials have all brought their sets of values and beliefs into the workplace, requiring different methods of leadership, motivation, and other human relations skills.

CASE STUDIES IN THE NEWS

The 2004 Congressional Fuel Cell Expo was held with approximately 35 fuel cell industry leaders exhibiting on Capitol Hill in Washington, DC. GM offered fuel cell vehicles to ride and drive along with demonstrations. An impressive list of Members of Congress sponsored this function, which was put on by the U.S. Department of Energy and the U.S. Fuel Cell Council, and also served as speakers to promote the efforts. Meetings and workshops were held among the industry giants to advance the hydrogen fuel cell development.[10]

1. *Why do you think experts say it will take until 2015 for fuel cell technology to become widely available?*

2. *In what other ways do you think we might solve our energy crisis?*

Workers in the twenty-first century feel less strongly about long-term employment security than did previous generations, realizing that these tumultuous times create uncertainties. The hopes are for career development opportunities, training and retraining, and opportunities for job and knowledge improvements. The general workforce is aging, but retirements are fewer. Overall, there are fewer qualified workers to replace those who do leave the workforce. Continued immigration to the United States is affecting the ethnic diversities of the workforce. Considering the variety of changes foreseen in the workplace, the workers who are most likely to succeed are flexible, well honed in human relations skills, and adaptable to changing conditions.

MANAGEMENT STYLES

Peter Drucker, author of *The New Realities*, predicted, "in so-called knowledge-based companies, hierarchies will give way to something resembling a symphony orchestra with dozens or even hundreds of specialists reporting directly to the conductor/CEO." He was right. The age of the standard pyramidal hierarchy is passing. Organizational structures are more open and fluid, able to adapt quickly. Much of this transition has been driven by the continued corporate globalization and multinational company growth. Power is becoming increasingly decentralized, and the use of matrix-style structures is allowing organizations to adjust more readily.[11]

Leadership is more team-oriented and participatory. Managers are delegating more tasks to the lowest levels possible and empowering others with greater responsibility. With the growth of home-based, virtual offices, many companies rely on employees to set their own pace but get the job done. Because of this, managers increasingly appreciate characteristics such as speed, flexibility, risk-taking, and decisiveness in employees.

WORK ITSELF

The evolution from Industrial Era to Information Age has moved us from an emphasis on manual to mental labor. Work is shifting from industrial manufacturing and production to information and knowledge-based goods and services. Increased global competitiveness is forcing U.S. employers to achieve productivity with fewer and better-educated workers with different skills. Characteristic of the required new skills is the ability to interpret information using more abstract and creative methods. Within the general labor force, critical skills are becoming scarcer. Companies are already realizing a gap between basic skills and the highly technical skills required to operate their rapidly advancing equipment.

CASE STUDIES IN THE NEWS

In the spring of 2004, *U.S. News & World Report* indicated that age and wisdom might truly be replacing youth and beauty in the workplace. Americans 55 and over have become the target for corporate recruiters. Employment is on the rise rather than the decline for retirees. A first-ever event is an alliance between AARP's 35 million members to apply for Home Depot's 140,000 expected openings. It is a strange supply-and-demand work equation. Older workers often only want to earn small supplemental income, assure minimal medical coverage, or retain social contact. Businesses are finding cheaper, more reliable, and more flexible labor sources. As the huge numbers of baby boomers enter that labor pool, many companies are bringing them back as part-time employees or working flex-hour jobs from home. AARP is currently negotiating with carmakers, government agencies, and retailers to expand the opportunity to tap their labor pool for employees.[12]

1. *How do you feel about this shift in the labor pool? Explain.*

2. *What benefits would mature workers provide to a company?*

The need for improved quality of product or service continues to be a force shaping the way work is performed. In the new global economy, employees compete in a much broader field.

Work performance in many organizations is taking on a new shape, with decisions being pushed to the lowest level possible in increasingly horizontal organizational structures.

An equal number of more personal changes will influence the immediate work setting. Organizations are examining work patterns and looking for alternatives to the traditional workplace. In 2001, Cornell University's International Workplace Studies Program (IWSP) focused its research on "Offices that Work." The IWSP teams took the business challenge of finding ways to "do more, faster, better, with less." They found the optimum "office setting" for the 21ST century will be more open and conducive to the free exchange of information necessary for high-performing team organization environments. Open offices contribute to the team's productivity in both quality and speed.[13]

Advances in communications systems will continue to provide innovative access to offices, information, and individuals globally. E-mail allows access to hundreds of coworkers worldwide in minutes rather than days. Teleconferencing, web conferencing, and videoconferencing have allowed us to span the continent and have caused a revolution in how information flows and how people are managed. Rapid advancements in technology in all areas of communication will continue to change the workplace.

> QUICK WIT
> "Everybody thinks of changing humanity and nobody thinks of changing himself."
>
> Leo Tolstoy,
> Russian novelist

Research led by Frank Becker at Cornell's International Workplace Studies Program (IWSP) indicates the most productive work setting is one in which employees can openly exchange information and interact socially. The research team determined that communication is a key element of work effectiveness and is best shared in an open office plan. While most employees preferred a closed, private office setting, they often missed communications and weakened the team's performance. The research indicated that in organizations where teamwork was critical and collaboration was important, socializing was the glue that held the team together and built a solid trust foundation. The overall recommendation was for "team-oriented workstation pods" and "shared-closed offices."[14]

1. *Why do you think the team recommended the open office concept as the best environment?*

2. *What do you think the real advantage to the company would be?*

Tomorrow's offices cannot be created without designing physical, social, technical, and organizational systems that are in harmony.

©Getty Images/PhotoDisc

While CEO at Intel Corp., Andrew Grove warned company employees, "The new environments dictate two rules: First, everything is happening faster—second, anything that can be done will be done, if not by you, then by someone else, somewhere in the world. These changes lead to a less gentle and far less predictable workplace." Clearly, one message for survival in the future is to focus on continual self-improvement and to expect the unexpected.

The emerging organizational environment is characterized by three principal trends: intense global competition, rapid technological advancements, and continuing turbulence and uncertainty. The reality of the changing world around us highlights the need for understanding change dynamics.

TECHNOLOGY CONNECTION

While Americans worry about offshoring, their counterparts in India and the Philippines face similar worries. They soon may be replaced by increasingly sophisticated voice-automation technology. In the competitive wireless phone market, this technology will save even more money by providing automated answers to questions about account balances, payment locations, and rate plans. Complicated calls will continue to go through an operator, but it is estimated that over 50 percent of the calls will be answered through automation. Cingular Wireless is expected to be one of the first wireless technology providers to launch a voice-automation pilot program.[15]

1. *How could current technologies contribute to overcoming a communication problem for you?*

2. *Discuss the effects of the information above. If voice-automation is successful, who or what could be replaced next?*

*Fast*Chat

1. In what ways do you think you will be affected by any of the future changes described above?

2. How have changes in science and technology already touched your life? Give examples.

13.2   Who Changes Organizations?

Recommendations for change in organizations originate from a variety of sources. These sources include professional planners and outside consultants who may be hired and brought into an organization to define methods and techniques for increasing effectiveness. Additionally, special task forces or teams may be formed of representatives from within the organization to participate in streamlining operations. CEOs and other top-level managers are also the initiators of change within an organization. Mid-level and first-line managers usually carry out change using unilateral, participative, and delegated methods.

With the **unilateral method**, employees have little or no input in the process. Supervisors dictate the change—what it is, when and how it will be accomplished, and who will be involved. Employees merely follow the directives. In the **participative method**, employee groups are used in the problem-solving and decision-making processes that precede change implementation. Both the supervisors and the employees share in bringing about the change.

In the **delegated method**, employees are given the responsibility and authority to effect the change. They diagnose, analyze, and select the best method for implementation. This method is used most when employees are closest to the situation that needs changing. It is being used more frequently as organizations push decision making further down into the ranks, so knowing how to plan change is an increasingly valuable skill, even at lower levels. You may find the steps below useful in implementing changes. To better understand how organizations bring about change, study companies with successful track records using the following methods.

Personal Guide for Effective Change Planning

- Establish consistent goals—consider present and future conditions.
- Have vision—foresee the future and raise expectations of those involved.
- Have a "big picture" outlook—take a broad view of change effects.
- Make your intentions known—communicate openly for change acceptance.
- Know your options—develop alternative plans.
- Time your change—introduce processes carefully for least resistance.
- Be flexible—adapt or modify process if necessary.

CASE STUDIES IN THE NEWS

In an interview, Tom Peters, author of *Re-imagine!,* says, "I consider this to be a time of chaos." He feels very strongly that technology changes are in their infancies and that each person is totally responsible for his/her own career in this new economy. Peters advocates destroying virtually all business organizations as we know them today and suggests that we "reimagine" them in order to properly respond to this new social and technological era. One of his more important themes is that women should be recognized as a more significant group in our society. They are the larger population, they make the key financial decisions, and they are smart, yet they are fundamentally ignored and not considered or consulted much in the new economy. Women tend to operate more closely on principles of collaboration than on command and control and are frequently better communicators, all of which make them good candidates to be strong leaders in business and communities.

Another of Peters' ideas is "It's a cross-functional world." He believes that open and honest communication between decision makers is absolutely vital to the success of an organization. Without giving this consideration to the human element, you won't be able to change your organization at all.[16]

1. *Why do you think Peters feels we are in a state of chaos? Do you agree or disagree?*

2. *How do you feel about Tom Peters' promoting the welfare of women in the workforce?*

3. *What have you done to take control of your own career?*

*Fast*Chat

1. Think about ways in which you may have participated in change activities in a work or personal group situation. What method do you think was used in that process?

2. How do you think different workers deal with the varied changes occurring in the workplace?

The goals in managing change are to anticipate the need for change and to bring the change about effectively. The most common methods for achieving these results include strategic planning, organizational development, job redesign, and force field analysis.

STRATEGIC PLANNING

The essence of planning is designing a desired future and identifying ways to bring it about. Plans must be designed to fit the unique characteristics of each organization. **Strategic planning** is the systematic setting of organizational goals, defining strategies and policies to achieve them, and developing detailed plans to ensure that the strategies are implemented—always taking into account the unique character of the organization. The process helps determine what is to be done, when and how it is to be accomplished, who is going to do it, and what is to be done with the results. Because changes in any organization's environment are continual, strategic planning must be ongoing and flexible.

Strategic planning is not simply forecasting based on trends, nor is it a set of plans that can be carved in stone to be used day after day. This type of planning for change is more a thought process than a prescribed set of procedures and techniques. A formal strategic planning system links three major types of plans: (1) strategic plans, (2) medium-range programs, and (3) short-range budgets and operating plans. The diagram on page 359 illustrates the information flow and steps in a typical strategic planning process.

In the initial steps, consideration is given to the concerns of outside and inside interests and how they may be affected by the planned goal. For example, as a manager you may ask how the local community will react to the proposed building site for a new factory near the downtown area. Will this expansion please the stockholders by increasing profits and better serving our customers? Will it generate revenue to pay our creditors and increase orders to our suppliers? Will Joe Chang agree to leave his current foreman job to manage and operate the new facility? What has our past performance capability been in the area of pipe manufacturing, and how will the new factory change that performance? Can we forecast with reasonable accuracy the outcome of making this major investment?

What effects overall will this plan for expansion have on the environment and the company? Careful thinking is needed to initiate strategic planning.

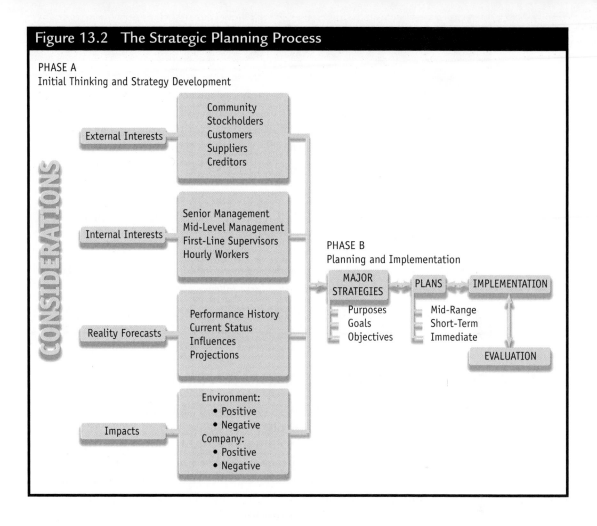

Figure 13.2 The Strategic Planning Process

PHASE A
Initial Thinking and Strategy Development

CONSIDERATIONS

External Interests
- Community
- Stockholders
- Customers
- Suppliers
- Creditors

Internal Interests
- Senior Management
- Mid-Level Management
- First-Line Supervisors
- Hourly Workers

PHASE B
Planning and Implementation

Reality Forecasts
- Performance History
- Current Status
- Influences
- Projections

MAJOR STRATEGIES
- Purposes
- Goals
- Objectives

PLANS
- Mid-Range
- Short-Term
- Immediate

IMPLEMENTATION

EVALUATION

Impacts
- Environment:
  - Positive
  - Negative
- Company:
  - Positive
  - Negative

Once all the questions are favorably answered, the next step is to design a master strategy for implementation. The purposes and objectives are clearly defined and policies are established. Then medium- and short-range steps are developed and the plan begins to take shape. With a step-by-step program plan in place, implementation can begin. The land may be purchased and cleared, building specifications drawn to scale, and contractors hired to build the facility. As construction begins, each phase is carefully reviewed and evaluated to assure maximum efficiency upon completion.

The thought process continues throughout the year that building the facility takes. If new facts arise, changes may be made to accommodate them. No plan is absolute. It may best be described as a fluid or dynamic process that allows change to occur as warranted.

According to *TQM Magazine*, the international magazine for users of total quality management concepts, the United Kingdom is the leading subscriber to TQM methods today, followed by the United States, Europe, and the Far East, based on 2003 statistical data. The European Centre for TQM continues to pioneer ideas and develop solutions to problems that will help businesses deal with contemporary issues. A new report published in 2004 entitled "Critical Factors of TQM Implementation: Theory, Concepts, and Applications through Best Practice Examples" provides excellent guidance to its subscribers.[17]

1. *Read the following information about organizational development and TQM. Why do you think TQM has such a large following in the U.K.?*

2. *Why do you think TQM continues to be such a valuable tool in the workplace?*

ORGANIZATIONAL DEVELOPMENT (OD)

Organizational development (OD) is a planned change process for meeting organizational needs through employee participation and management involvement on a continuing basis. It is similar to strategic planning in concept but not in practice. OD is a holistic approach, involving the entire organization —its people, structures, culture, policies and procedures, and purpose. Undergirding OD is the belief that any planned change process must continuously adapt to the ever-changing environment.[18]

> OD methods involve a high degree of participation by employees and management to improve organizational effectiveness.

Because OD is strongly rooted in human relations management theories, it involves a number of methods to identify degrees of concern for people as well as tasks. Methods might include sensitivity training, team-building exercises, and goal-setting activities to bring about the desired changes in both the employee and the organization. Other methods used in the OD change process include survey and feedback techniques and confrontation meetings. These methods involve a high degree of participation by employees and management to improve organizational effectiveness.[19]

When speaking of OD, buzzwords such as **total quality management (TQM)** and **benchmarking** come to mind. Each of these methods is a new means of accomplishing an old goal—effectively implementing change in organizations. Each has roots in OD, and many high-powered companies are still using these techniques to deal with changing business environments.

TQM focuses on involving employees in continuous process improvements to keep the organization on the cutting edge. TQM has its roots in the theories of the American statistician and educator, Dr. W. Edwards Deming, who became interested in methods of achieving better quality control in the 1930s. Deming's ideas were put to the test in the 1950s, when Japanese business leaders invited him to teach quality control as they tried to rebuild after WWII. In addition to statistical analysis of production as it related to quality, Deming advocated involving employees at all levels in the pursuit of quality. In the 1980s, American companies began to adopt Deming's ideas to compete more effectively against foreign manufacturers. Today, employee involvement in improving quality has become the vanguard of progressive companies.[20]

Benchmarking is a method that involves comparing the company's practices—among internal divisions, against those of outside competitors, or both—to determine which are the best. For example, Johnson & Johnson compared financial report filing in its internal branches and discovered ways to streamline the processes. Xerox matched prices and procedures with a Japanese competitor and improved its bottom line. This method involves employees in the analysis of information, taking action, and reviewing the results for effectiveness.

Instrumental in bringing about any of these change processes is the **change agent**. Also known as an OD practitioner, the change agent's powerful role is to diagnose problems, provide feedback, help develop strategies, or recommend interventions to benefit the organization as a whole. The challenge is to develop a creative, innovative organization that easily adapts in an ever-changing world, yet remains competitive. To foster such flexibility, employees must be made to feel part of a team. Change should be perceived as an opportunity for growth among team members as they accept new challenges and learn new skills.[21]

Actions of a Change Agent

- Be open and honest about why the change is happening.
- Encourage participation and solicit feelings.
- Allow negative comments but not negative actions.
- Explain benefits of change.
- Involve others in initiation/implementation phases.
- Acknowledge loss of the old method.

An organization's culture is often shaped by its customs and personalities and by the community in which it exists. Many companies operate with a culture that has become stale or stagnant and needs revitalizing. To remain creative with dynamic performance and realize sound profitability, an organization may have to enlist the aid of change agents. These teams assist in the training required for a successful transition. Walt Disney, Saturn, and GTE Corp. are fine success stories of how change agents used these methods to facilitate critical internal changes. There are many other good industry guides to illustrate a step-by-step method for making the critical change a reality. Change agents are the key element for the smooth transition.[22]

How can change agents make for a smoother transition during changes in organizational culture?

uick tip ....

"You can't expect people to change if you don't give them the tools. We can create opportunities for people to change, but we cannot change them. People have a personal responsibility to get involved and change themselves." [24]

Thomas M. Kasten,
VP of Information Technology, Levi Strauss

JOB REDESIGN

Job redesign changes the makeup of an employee's tasks.

Job redesign is a method of bringing about gradual, low-risk changes in an organization by changing tasks performed by individuals. Job redesign means changing the makeup of tasks to make them more interesting and challenging for the employee. The goal is to relieve boredom, create interest, and obtain a more satisfied and productive worker. The most common methods used in job redesign are job enrichment, job enlargement, and job rotation.

Common Redesign Methods

Job enrichment Builds greater responsibility and interest into task assignments. Means adding tasks that encourage and motivate employees. Also known as vertical loading or adding tasks of increased responsibility. Excellent means of bringing about positive change within an organization.

Job enlargement Known as horizontal loading, increases the complexity of a job by adding similar tasks to those already being performed. May not motivate employees, but may appeal to their higher-order needs for creative and challenging work.

Job rotation The shifting of employees from one job to another in hopes of reducing boredom and stimulating renewed interest in job performance. The content of a particular job is not affected. May also be used to prepare an individual for permanent assignment to a higher-level position.

REENGINEERING

Reengineering takes redesign to the next level; instead of simply redefining jobs, the organization retools whole divisions or corporations. James Champy defines **reengineering** as the fundamental rethinking and redesign of business processes to achieve dramatic improvements in critical, contemporary measures of performance, such as cost, quality, service, and speed. And in his most recent book ushering in the 21ST century, *X-Engineering the Corporation,* he says modern companies must "e-engineer" or they will be lost to history. Champy believes it essential that companies large and small reengineer their processes, build their business on a platform of IT, and keep pace with technological advances in all phases of their management practices and strategies. Reengineering is the tool of the century.[23] Organizations around the world have been implementing this form of change with dramatic results. Microsoft, UPS, General Electric, General Motors, IBM, Intel, Levi Strauss, Germany's Siemens, Brazil's Semco, and the U.S. Government are only a few of those organizations who have undertaken some form of reengineering.

FORCE FIELD ANALYSIS

Force field analysis is a technique used to analyze the complexities of the change and identify the forces that must be altered. This useful tool, developed by Kurt Lewin, views any situation in which change is to be made as a dynamic balance of forces working in opposite directions.

The forces that move the situation in the direction of the anticipated change are called driving forces. The opposite forces, those which tend to keep the situation from moving in the direction of the anticipated change, are called restraining forces. These two sets of forces working against each other create a dynamic equilibrium or a balance that can be disturbed at any moment by altering either the driving or restraining forces.

A change agent who uses force field analysis to determine how those opposing forces operate in an organization can predict the consequences of altering either set of forces or can alter the forces to create the desired change. The forces may include people, tasks, technology, equipment, or the organization's basic structure. Planning for change is important to ensure a smooth transition with the least resistance possible. Each situation should be analyzed to anticipate the consequences of the change process.

Quick tip ···

"There is at least one point in the history of any company when you have to change dramatically to rise to the next performance level. Miss that moment and you start to decline." [25]

Andy Grove,
Chairman of the Board, Intel Corporation

Change is an unavoidable part of the world of work.

© 1998 Ted Goff www.tedgoff.com

Human Relations

Levi Strauss & Co. is reengineering to remain competitive in the global market. Since the California gold rush in the 1870s, the San Francisco-based jeans company has been a globally recognized symbol of America. But, in 2004, the company announced the closing of the last two U.S. sewing plants and the shifting of production to overseas contractors in China and other cheaper labor markets. The company's global workforce shrunk from 37,000 in 1996 to 12,000 in 2004. The design and sales staff will remain in the San Francisco-based headquarters along with some distribution and operations centers.

Jeff Beckmann, a Levi Strauss spokesman, says, "We still are an American brand, but we're also abroad and a company whose products have been adopted by consumers around the world. We have to operate as a global company."

Even with the move to overseas labor, management faces a big challenge marketing the Levi image. The brand has lost a little luster in the fashion trend scene and there are now many other competitors in the field, too. All these factors played into the reengineering decisions for this global, ultra-competitive apparel company.[26]

1. *How do you feel about America losing the manufacturing of Levi Strauss jeans?*

2. *What do you think would be the most difficult part of a change this great?*

3. *Could Levi Strauss have reengineered its operations in other ways to prevent this loss? If so, how?*

*Fast*Chat

1. Describe a situation in which you may have been a change agent helping to bring about change.

2. What changes have you seen occur in the government that may have been a result of reengineering efforts.

3. During times of significant change, some organizations require employees to reapply for jobs. How would you feel about having to reapply for a job at a company in which you already had a job?

People are naturally resistant to change, both in their personal and their work lives. Their feelings create barriers to effective change. Understanding how people feel about change can help us remove the barriers and ensure an easier change process. Four common reasons for resistance to change are explained below.

Four Common Reasons for Resistance to Change

Fear of the unknown — When situations remain constant, we know what to expect, how to respond, and how things fit together. We have stability, security, and predictability. Change presents us with an unknown and uncertain situation. This disorganization of the familiar often arouses anxiety, fear, and stress.

Fear of power loss — Often our power and status are so tied to the existing situation that any change means a potential personal loss. The change may "cost" us too much.

Fear of economic loss — We may feel threatened by loss of income due to reductions in salary or cuts in benefits or possibly the ultimate loss of our jobs.

Conflict of interest — Traditions, standards, values, or norms of a person or a group may be threatened by the change. Social affiliations may also be jeopardized.

Resistance often provides clues for the prevention of failure.

Resistance to change can result in some benefits. For example, initiators of change may put more thought into clarifying the purpose of the recommended change and identifying the desired results. The fear of the unknown may lead people to examine possible consequences, both immediate and long-range, with more care. When we find a poor flow of information, we can improve communication systems, a vital link to effective change implementation. Resistance often provides clues for the prevention of failure. The following suggestions might help you when facing change. Open communication about any change process is critical in making smooth transitions. Keeping people informed about each step and telling them how it will affect them helps to garner commitment and assure that change is embraced.

Suggestions for Dealing with Change

1. Remember that change is inevitable and that fear of change is normal.

2. Analyze the reasons that you want to resist the change. What fears do you have? What behaviors will you have to adjust in order to effect the change?

3. Search for the positives. How will the changes constructively affect your work?

4. Seek assistance if you are having difficulty adjusting to the changes. A supervisor or a more experienced employee can help.

5. Learn how to learn. The most important skill to acquire for the future is learning to keep abilities fresh and desirable in the job market.

CASE STUDIES IN THE NEWS

During the 1980s, Vince Kosmac of Orlando, Florida, had planned to follow his dad's example as a blue-collar trucker and live a comfortable life delivering steel to plants in Johnstown, Pennsylvania. Then, the steel industry disappeared to low-cost competitors in Brazil and China. Since that plan didn't work out, Vince used the G.I. Bill to go back to school and get a degree in computer science. For 20 years now, he has been a successful computer programmer with a comfortable job, a wife, children, a mortgage, and two cars. But at age 47, his programming job went to India.[27]

Unfortunately, Vince's story is a common one. What would you recommend someone in Vince's situation do to deal with this type of change?

*Fast*Chat

1. What are some of the most common fears individuals may experience? Have you ever been in one of these situations? How did you deal with it?

2. What positive things would you find in a major change situation?

Leaders have an opportunity to facilitate change processes.

Creating a climate conducive to change is an important step in change management. When change is needed, leaders are called upon to act as change agents to facilitate the process. (Conversely, those who are able to act as change agents are more likely to attain positions of leadership.) If you are in a position of leadership at work or in other situations, organizational or personal, and are asked to implement change, the following seven-step process may help you.

Steps in the Change Process

1. Conduct present state assessment (PSA).
Diagnose the present situation. "Where am I now, and what are the current conditions?" Examine why you need to change.

2. Conduct future state assessment (FSA).
Determine the desired results. "Where do I want to be, and how will the conditions change?" Visualize the desired results.

3. Generate alternatives.
Identify the possible approaches through use of "What if . . ." questions. Consider the probable outcomes and reactions. Who will be involved and how will they be affected?

4. Select one alternative.
Make a selection from the alternative solutions. Decide which method will best achieve the desired results.

5. Implement the change.
Put a plan in motion to assure that the change occurs. Alter whatever conditions are necessary or introduce the change method.

6. Evaluate the change.
Allow time for implementation and acceptance; carefully evaluate the results to see whether you have achieved the desired outcome.

7. Modify the change.
Modify as required. You may make only a minor revision or repeat the entire process with a different alternative.

Modifying or changing an alternative is appropriate if the expected results are not achieved or if they prove undesirable. However, making changes too frequently may make us appear indecisive. Use of these steps in your change process may reduce the negative effects on people involved.

As mentioned earlier, communication is an important factor in facilitating change. It helps get more people involved in the process. The more individuals feel involved, the more likely you will be able to keep change moving in the right direction. Communication can also contribute to the ongoing evaluation of both the process and the results. The following suggestions can help individuals adjust to change.

Facilitating Changes

Discuss the change. Communicate early in the process with those who will be affected. Educate them in how, why, and when the change will occur.

Invite participation. Ask people who will be affected by the change to take part in the formulation of the change. Involvement will create "ownership" and commitment to the success of the change.

Be open and honest. Share facts and information with those who will be affected. Stick to the facts and avoid what you "hope" or "think."

Accent the positives. Stress the benefits. In the work environment, increased pay, fringe benefits, lighter workload, elimination of hectic deadlines, or more flexible work hours may be some of the positive outcomes expected of the change. Although individuals are interested in how the change will affect them, they are even more interested in what benefits it will bring them.

Do not downgrade past methods. A mistake often made when introducing change is to tear down old or existing methods. If you imply that the old or existing method is inadequate, individuals may resent the implication that they have not been doing an adequate job using that method.

Follow up on the process. Frequently, resistance to change is shadowed or hidden, only to surface later. Follow up to see whether individuals are having problems accepting it or implementing it, and provide help.

Allow time for adjustments. Changing long-standing habits can take time. Give individuals a chance to adjust to the change. Be prepared to make adjustments if you hit a snag in the process.

Applying these methods will help those involved accept change. The box on page 370 illustrates the stages of acceptance individuals must go through. You may want to try additional human relations approaches when introducing change. For example, you may try the change first on a small scale. Begin the process with some small segment of the whole group to be affected. Other individuals will see the advantages and importance of the change. Their uncertainties will be reduced. A similar approach calls for special timing. Before you begin, find allies who will be supportive of your ideas. This way you may ease the general resistance.

> ## Stages in Acceptance of Change
>
> **Recognition:** Individual must recognize the need for change.
>
> **Choice:** Individual must decide the change is beneficial and act to make it happen.
>
> **Plan:** Individual must think through the change process to develop a specific approach.
>
> **Support:** Individual must seek understanding and assistance of others to help implement the plan.

Finally, you can use special human relations skills to facilitate change. Unwelcome change often results in low morale or motivation, apathy, uncertainty, instability, frustration, and symptoms of stress. Even change that is welcomed can cause some of these symptoms. These behavior changes are hardly the ones hoped for in reaching your change objectives. Additionally, changes that tend toward restructuring, compressing, or reducing the workforce may result in a mismatch of skills and jobs. In this case, you may notice performance problems and a decrease in productivity while change is being implemented.

Coaching and counseling employees are the most effective means of dealing with behavioral problems, performance and productivity problems, and employee training and development concerns brought on by change. Open communication, which is stressed in these methods, is always a good way to cope with problems.

Coaching and counseling skills often help you implement change.

COACHING

Coaching is a method of employee development that closely resembles on-the-job training. Typically, a skilled and experienced employee, usually of high-ranking status within the organization, is assigned to develop or train a junior employee with lesser skills and abilities. A coach may help identify career paths, help define career goals and objectives, explain the organization's culture and established norms, or simply share expertise for skills development. Immediate and ongoing feedback is provided. A popular form of coaching is known as **mentoring**.

A **mentor** is usually a manager with political savvy and an interest in helping employees achieve both career goals and the objectives of the organization. Many corporations are recognizing the benefits of establishing formal mentoring programs. Some companies are providing mentors to help new employees rapidly enter the corporate culture. A mentor and protégé are often matched on the basis of backgrounds, interests, and work style.

If you are not assigned a mentor, you should attempt to find one either within your organization or within your profession. A mentor is often selected on the basis of being a kindred soul. You can best achieve the close rapport necessary in this relationship when the ethics, values, and operating styles of both participants mesh. A foundation of mutual respect must exist. A mentor will listen to you empathetically, suspend judgment, invite you to discuss your concerns, assist with problem-solving and decision-making challenges, and offer specific suggestions regarding training and development opportunities. The selection of a mentor can be a wise investment in career planning and development. While having a mentor is not a requisite to getting ahead, it can make adjustment to the company swifter and the learning curve easier—and it makes it more likely that your skills and accomplishments will be noticed. Many companies have begun to realize the benefits to both the company and the employee by providing this "nurturing" relationship.

GLOBAL CONNECTION

Intel started a new and different method of mentoring that defies the traditional method. They reinvented the idea to fit today's typical competitive environment where it is more important to know how and where to do the right thing right away. They match employees by skill in demand, not by title or years of service. This means that an older manager may be mentored by a younger administrative assistant if she knows the inner workings of the travel management system he now needs to understand. The matching may cross state and national lines, using an intranet and e-mail matching system. This allows Intel to spread best practices quickly throughout its global organization.[28]

1. *How do you think this type of program works? Do you think it would work in your company?*

2. *In what situations could you imagine it working well, and how do you think the junior mentor would react toward the senior mentee? Would you be comfortable in this situation?*

Although the need for mentoring programs over the last 10 years has quadrupled, all situations do not work well. An aging baby boomer and 47-year-old computer engineer had a bad experience with three different Gen X protégés in the company mentoring program. One of them even tried to take his job! A 24-year-old Gen X employee doesn't trust mentors much. After losing his family at an early age, he poured his soul out to a "Big Brother" who vanished after only three weeks—apparently, being a Big Brother looked good on his resume and he was job hunting.[29]

1. *Do you think you would like to have a mentor if you were new to a company? In what ways do you think you could benefit from working with a mentor?*

2. *How do you think a formal mentor program might compare to the informal approach?*

COUNSELING

In most organizations, **counseling** is a technique used to assist employees with problems affecting performance on the job. These problems may be personal or work-related. Employee problems may result in unacceptable quality and quantity of work, absenteeism, and low morale, which cost companies millions of dollars.

Counseling is generally used to assist employees with performance problems.

An article published by the National Mental Health Association pointed out that during any given year 11.6 million adults in the United States suffer from at least one mental health disorder (which can include anything from anxiety to depression to more disabling problems).[30] Not only can problems of this nature affect an individual's performance, but also the behavior of these individuals affects employees who are in contact with them. Of course, the problem may not be related to any "disorder" but rather to such situations as personality conflicts, being overwhelmed by the job, or uncertainty engendered by company changes.

Counseling can be directive, nondirective, or cooperative.

If the problems are not easily resolved, the intervention of a **counselor** may be needed. A counselor may be a supervisor or a trained professional capable of dealing with a wide variety of employee problems. Once a counselor identifies the problem and documents the specifics to be addressed, a counseling session may be scheduled. During the counseling interview with the employee, any of the three basic types of counseling methods may be used: directive, nondirective, or cooperative.

CASE STUDIES IN THE NEWS

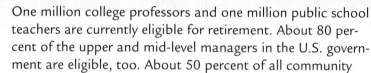

One million college professors and one million public school teachers are currently eligible for retirement. About 80 percent of the upper and mid-level managers in the U.S. government are eligible, too. About 50 percent of all community college presidents, and 1 in 5 of the senior executives of the Fortune 500 companies are poised to go. Many more are ready if only the stock market recovers. When this happens, "succession management" will be a term on everyone's lips, for those going and those staying. Some companies already have plans in place to retain retired knowledge workers in "coaching" positions using phones and at-home computers, as needed.[31]

1. *How do you think retirees will feel about being "coaches" to others?*
2. *What do you think will happen when all this "knowledge" walks out the doors of our businesses and institutions?*

*Fast*Chat

1. How would you tell valued workers they are losing their jobs because of "reengineering" the organization?
2. What situations lend themselves to using coaching and counseling methods?

Some supervisors find counseling a difficult part of the human relations skills required in leadership positions. They prefer to have a professional staff counselor take the responsibility. An alternative solution would be to make a referral of the employee to an employee assistance program.

Employee assistance programs (EAPs) are formal programs designed to aid employees with personal problems such as substance abuse, serious depression, overwhelming stress, family tensions, or psychological problems that affect their job performance and/or disrupt their lives. These personal problems often result in undesirable behaviors at work, such as absences, errors, tardiness, decreased productivity, accidents, or an inability to operate equipment safely. The immediate supervisor generally identifies problems. In some companies, the supervisor is expected to take immediate action. In many companies, employees have the option of seeking confidential help before a problem affects their jobs or is even noticed by coworkers. Sometimes the rate or type of change in a company creates the problems, and stress is a growing issue.

Most companies have specific guidelines for handling situations where employees' personal problems have started to affect their work. The supervisor is usually required to document incidences of unsatisfactory behavior or performance, counsel the employee on performance expectations, and reach an agreement with the employee on a specific time for improvement of performance. If appreciable improvement is not shown within the time limit, a supervisor is expected to refer the employee to the EAP for assignment to a qualified professional counselor.

Whether an employee seeks help or is referred by an employer, the counselor to whom he or she is assigned will recommend whatever treatment is required to aid the employee in coping with personal problems. The problem may be marital strife, financial troubles, substance abuse, parenting problems, care for aging parents, difficulty balancing life and work, or adjusting to foreign surroundings.

Employees are guaranteed confidentiality when entering an employee assistance program. In most cases, the employee begins to handle the problem and job performance improves. In fact, these programs have been so successful that EAPs have virtually exploded, with almost every major U.S. corporation now offering assistance to its employees.

Any planned change must give as much attention to the emotional or psychological dimensions as to the practical and informational aspects of the change process. The most important condition for effective change management is the certainty that the climate is conducive to the change being introduced, implemented, and accepted.

QUICK WIT

"The difference between a mountain and a molehill is your perspective."

Al Neuharth, Founder of *USA Today*

The Federal Occupational Health (FOH) organization assists federal agencies throughout the United States and overseas in improving the health, safety, and productivity of their workers through Employee Assistance Programs (EAPs). Workers and their families are provided an array of services designed to provide prevention and early intervention of problems. The expected return on the investment is the improvement of the worker's health and overall quality of life. It is believed that by reducing behavioral health issues, an organization will realize benefits in productivity, reduced absenteeism and medical benefit usage, and improved workplace environment.

With the global nature of work assignments and events happening around the world that can affect foreign-based employees, the FOH may be called upon to provide its services to families assisting the military deployments and those stationed abroad affected by Severe Acute Respiratory Syndrome (SARS) in China and other situations as they arise.[32]

1. *What kind of support do you imagine families might need in these situations? How might an EAP help them adjust to their surroundings?*

2. *Do you think people actually use EAPs? Discuss.*

 **uick tip** ••

"Creating change, managing it, mastering it, and surviving it is the agenda for anyone in business who aims to make a difference."

Mark Maletz,
Author and Business Professor

•••

*Fast*Chat

1. What types of employee assistance programs do you think are most used in today's "techno-stress" work environment?

2. Do you think that people are more comfortable seeking help these days? Explain.

Key Terms

unilateral method

participative method

delegated method

strategic planning

organizational development

total quality management

change agent

benchmarking

job redesign

reengineering

job enrichment

job enlargement

job rotation

force field analysis

coaching

mentoring

mentor

counseling

counselor

directive counseling

nondirective counseling

cooperative counseling

employee assistance
  program (EAP)

CHAPTER SUMMARY

Change is a basic condition of today's work world. Changes will continue to be a way of life as we move into the 21ST century. Areas experiencing rapid change include the economy, science and technology, the general workforce, management styles, and work itself. The organizational environment of the future can be described as intensely competitive, technologically advanced, and filled with turbulence and uncertainty. Because change can be difficult for employees, organizations must use sound human relations skills to facilitate necessary changes.

Recommendations for change originate from professional planners, special task forces, CEOs, and other top-level executives. However, mid-level and first-line managers usually carry out the change. Unilateral, participative, and delegated methods are used in effecting change. The most common methods of planning for change include strategic planning, force field analysis, and various organizational development strategies such as benchmarking, redesign, and reengineering.

Reasons for resistance to change include a fear of the unknown, a fear of power loss, a fear of economic loss, and a conflict of interest. The steps involved in the change process include a present state assessment, a future state assessment, generation of alternatives, selection of one alternative, implementation, evaluation, and modification, if required. Several methods of overcoming resistance to change may be applied. Coaching and counseling skills are used to help individuals cope with uncertainties of change. Coaching and mentoring are methods of developing employees to their maximum potential. Counseling is a method of assisting employees with personal problems affecting their performance. The most common methods of counseling are directive, nondirective, and cooperative. Employee assistance programs are formal programs provided to help employees with personal problems that may affect their work performance.

REVIEW QUESTIONS

1. Discuss the significant factors that are changing in today's workplace.

2. Who usually recommends and implements organizational changes?

3. Discuss several methods used in bringing about change.

4. What are the most common reasons for resisting change and how might you overcome them?

5. Explain why coaching and counseling are needed in the change process.

DISCUSSION QUESTIONS

1. Which of the major factors changing in today's workplace are affecting you personally? How?

2. What changes in your immediate work environment have you resisted over the past year? Discuss why, and explain what action you took to adjust.

3. Think of the last major change that was introduced in your organization. Was the method used to effect that change unilateral, participative, or delegated? Describe how you were involved.

4. Think about several mergers, takeovers, or outsourcing situations that were mentioned in this chapter or ones with which you may be familiar. How do you think these changes may be affecting you personally?

CHAPTER PROJECTS

WEB

WRITING

TEAMWORK

1. Do you have a mentor? If so, prepare a brief, one-page written description of why you selected that individual as a mentor for your career. If not, think of someone in your organization whom you might select and describe why you would choose that person. Be specific about the advantages you feel might result from this alliance. What skills and information might you exchange? Using the Internet, investigate a few large companies in your career area to see whether they have programs that assist new employees to more easily enter that organization. You may find one that interests you and you may want to apply.

2. As we become more globally involved, understanding the extent to which we will be affected by change becomes more important to our success and well-being. Search the Internet to find an article on the Europe's Economic and Monetary Union (EMU). Write a summary of your findings and explain how the information could affect you in your current environment. Be prepared to discuss the ramifications of Europe's changing economy in small groups in class.

APPLICATIONS

In small groups, analyze the following situations.

Would Somebody Help Me, Please?

TEAMWORK

Marc Tross had been a faithful worker for the Whitaker Transportation Corporation for nearly 20 years. His work record was outstanding with few absences to mar his attendance record and no lateness. He was considered a pillar of dependability and highly respected for the expertise he had developed over the years about the transportation industry.

"I don't understand what's going on with Marc's performance lately," remarked Chauncey, his first-line supervisor. "He has begun to come in late and take excessively long lunch breaks, and he slips out before quitting time. I've spoken with him about the changes in his behavior, but he seems unwilling to admit that he has changed or to commit to correcting the problem."

"Have you documented the circumstances and followed the usual procedures?" asked Patrice, the trained counselor from Human Resources.

"Yes, but I don't know what my next step should be," replied Chauncey. "I am not comfortable with this situation."

1. From the behaviors described, what do you think could be the problem?

2. Do you think Chauncey has taken the appropriate steps to help his employee in this situation?

3. What do you think Chauncey should do next? Why?

Where Will All the People Go?

TEAMWORK

"This new office system will revolutionize your department's operations, increase productivity, and reduce your overhead costs. You can't beat it, and if you plan to stay competitive in this market, you must adopt this system."

Darla knew that she needed to make the decision soon on converting her department to this new system, but it would mean a reduction in her office staff of nearly 60 percent. Then the department would have a period of lost productivity while employees were trained to use the new equipment and adjusted to the changes. Many factors needed to be considered.

1. What methods should Darla consider using to implement the new system in her department?

2. Is there any evidence that Darla's management had planned for this change in technology and prepared for implementation?

3. What will be some of the typical responses to the implementation of the new system, and how will Darla react to the concerns of her employees?

ADDITIONAL READINGS AND RESOURCES

Becker, Franklin, and William Sims. *Offices that Work: Balancing Communication, Flexibility and Cost.* Ithaca, NY: Cornell University International Workplace Studies Program, 2001.

Champy, James. *X-Engineering the Corporation: Reinventing Your Business in the Digital Age.* New York: Warner Business Books, 2002.

Champy, James. "Create Jobs, Don't Protect Them." *Fast Company,* October 2003.

Costlow, Terry. "Fuel Cell Research Moving at Light Speed." *IEEE USA: Today's Engineer,* April 2003.

Dash, Julekha. "Employees Say Hunters Need Soft Skills." *ComputerWorld,* June 2001.

Rothwell, William J. "Beyond Succession Management: New Directions and Fresh Approaches." *Link&Learn Newsletter,* September 2003.

Warner, Fara. "Inside Intel's Mentoring Movement." *Fast Company,* April 2002.

Zaslow, Jeffrey. "Baby Boomer Managers Struggle with Mentoring." *Career Journal,* August 2004.

For additional resources, refer to the web site for this text: school.cengage.com/career/dalton

Workplace Expectations:
Business Etiquette

After studying this chapter, you should be able to:

14.1 *Understand etiquette and protocol.*

14.2 *List five reasons knowledge of etiquette is important today.*

14.3 *Make a good impression through your appearance, table manners, and confident introductions.*

14.4 *Understand cross-cultural etiquette.*

14.5 *Develop effective customer relations and use correspondence and communication technology in appropriate ways.*

14.6 *Understand how to handle new cyber technologies.*

14.7 *Use networking, mentoring, and office politics sensibly.*

14.8 *Differentiate among behavior types.*

focus

There's a gadget war going on around the world! A priest presses a button to keep his sermon serene—free from beeps, chirps, and bell tones. A teenager takes a sneaky snapshot in the gym with his camera phone but gets a blank screen display. A restaurant patron sits blissfully enjoying a meal as other diners puzzle over dead cell phone tones. Jamming—blocking cell phone signals—is illegal in the United States, but pocket-sized "jammers" have brisk sales from foreign sources and even eBay. The Federal Communications Commission prohibits their use, punishable by a year in prison and fines of $11,000. One can argue that doctors may miss important calls from hospitals and parents may miss emergency calls from babysitters. Jammers are more commonly used in the Middle East, Africa, Asia, and Europe.[1]

How do you feel about this approach to controlling cell phone abuse? Have you been in a situation—perhaps at a movie or café—where someone's cell phone ring and/or conversation was a serious annoyance? What would you suggest as a possible solution to the problem?

in this chapter

With the popularity of wireless Internet, hand-held computers, camera phones, cell phones, video phones, home computers, e-mail, text messaging, web conferencing, and other communication conveniences, the electronic age has indeed arrived—and along with it a whole new set of etiquette problems. The following incidents portray only a few of the blunders we are encountering.

Examples of Etiquette Errors

- A world-renowned actor in a Broadway play stopped the production to address a member of the audience misusing a cell phone; he received a standing ovation from the crowd.

- When a pager went off in a business conference, the executive did not excuse himself to a more private place to return the call. He carried on a lengthy cell phone conversation disrupting the other conference participants.

- The head of an executive recruiting firm accidentally faxed a resume of a promising executive to the firm where she was currently working instead of to the one trying to hire her.

- A manager rolls her eyes with a "here we go again" look before suddenly, and painfully, realizing she is in a videoconference and in full view of the monitor.

- A prominent law partner places a client conference call on mute to have a side discussion with a coworker.

- Instead of listening attentively to a human resources presentation, an employee keys e-mail messages on a PDA.

Practically every week, another article appears in the newspaper or in a popular journal about the growing importance of business etiquette. **Etiquette** is defined as "the forms required by good breeding or prescribed by authority to be observed in social or official life." In simple words, when we use correct etiquette, we act appropriately in social and business situations. Etiquette is the oil that prevents friction in business and social settings.

> Etiquette is acting appropriately in social and business situations.

Business publications report that people are signing up for etiquette classes in record numbers, that businesses are sending their employees to etiquette classes, and that business schools are incorporating etiquette lectures and classes into their programs. This renewed interest in manners has been too long in coming. We can trace the breakdown of polite society back to the 1960s and 1970s when dress codes faded, permissiveness was the norm, Vietnam protesters carried the banner of rebellion, and "flower children" were followed by latchkey kids. The traditional household mealtime relaxed—or disappeared. Good manners were mocked, and etiquette was viewed as being old-fashioned and outdated.

Companies now view business etiquette, often called corporate etiquette, as a way of giving them a competitive edge in winning and retaining a solid market share. Knowledge of the finer points of good manners can help build long-term relationships among employees and with customers and clients. Maureen Rauscher, in an article on global etiquette, reports that there is a growing interest in etiquette as young people in senior positions are representing companies at international events.[2] Therefore, social skills are increasingly important. Often, the ability to engage in small talk over dinner or in small groups, listen effectively, and make introductions—all in a natural and sincere way—is a part of corporate protocol and a part of many companies' marketing strategies.

Etiquette provides us with a code of behavior in different settings, much as rulebooks provide us with a set of directions for playing golf, tennis, bridge, and other games. If we know the rules, we can play the game better and enjoy it more. When we walk into a situation and are sure that we know how to handle ourselves, our self-confidence will be obvious to others.

CASE STUDIES IN THE NEWS

According to a *New York Times* article about Jacqueline Whitmore, founder and executive director of the Protocol School of Palm Beach, there is a renewed interest in etiquette as companies lose customers who felt they weren't being treated well. Young business executives are technically brilliant but lack basic table manners and fail miserably at many social graces. She and other experts in the field say that business etiquette programs have grown by 50 percent in the last few years with the increased demand for "manners mania." Classes range from proper table manners, to appropriate netiquette, to acceptable global cultural protocols.[3]

1. *Why do you think so few people know etiquette today?*

2. *What topics besides those listed do you think might be included in one of these courses?*

At a formal dinner party a few years ago, Dr. David C. Jones, president and chief executive of a credit counseling company, was appalled at the table manners of several of his senior managers and made etiquette classes mandatory for all executives. Wendy Lang, a corporate events manager, made the switch between nonprofit sector planning to corporate America activities and realized the need for an etiquette adjustment. She took an etiquette class and now subscribes to *Executive Advantage*, a newsletter by Letitia Baldrige, formerly Jacqueline Kennedy's chief of staff in the White House and author of a renowned guide to executive manners.[4]

Protocol is that part of etiquette dealing with behavior in business, diplomatic, or military situations. It is used in determining matters such as displaying the flag of this country, seating people at formal dinners, determining the sequence for introducing people, and using formal titles correctly. Protocol is designed to simplify meetings. It answers questions and everybody accepts it. At affairs of state, protocol rules unambiguously answer questions about the order in which dignitaries will arrive, how and what flags will be flown, and if or how world leaders will be saluted.

Protocol involves rules for business, diplomatic, or military etiquette.

As our world becomes increasingly global, understanding the effects of good manners and protocol in all cultures becomes more and more important. Dorothea Johnson, founder of a protocol school in the Washington, D.C. area stresses, "I am hearing more and more from top executives that people skills are very important, in many cases more important than the technical skills." A well known reminder is that we never get a second chance to make a first impression. Proper dressing establishes our credibility in today's business arena and is only one of the many lasting impressions that can be made. Much of Ms. Johnson's business today is focused on training corporate "in-house protocol officers." Many global, cross-cultural companies are recognizing the important need for this service.[5]

QUICK WIT
"We cannot always oblige; but we can always speak obligingly."
Voltaire, French philosopher

"Courtesy, up 25%. Effort, up 25%. Quality, up 25%. Customer retention, up 250%."

© 1999 Ted Goff www.tedgoff.com

Courtesy and etiquette are important qualities in business professionals.

Rules, then, are an important component of etiquette, but they are not the only one. Knowledge of etiquette rules alone will not strengthen your human relations skills. You must use two other components: courtesy and good taste. When you act with courtesy, you are combining kindness and politeness. An unkind act is never a courteous one, no matter how correct it may be, and impolite acts are neither courteous nor correct. Several experts point out that being courteous involves the following behaviors.

Behaving Courteously Means

- Considering others, even in little ways.
- Respecting and encouraging accomplishments in others.
- Being thoughtful of others.
- Being democratic in our relations with others.
- Saying "thank you" with sincerity.
- Using a friendly voice.

Good taste is concerned with the suitability or fitness of actions, objects, and other things. An important part of good taste is the ability to recognize good proportions, orderliness, symmetry, quality, and beauty.

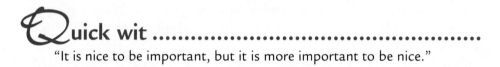

Quick wit

"It is nice to be important, but it is more important to be nice."

John Cassis, Motivational speaker

*Fast*Chat

1. Have you ever had a "good manners" class or discussed etiquette in school? How was it helpful to you?

2. Have you ever been in a situation where you felt uncertain about what to do or how to act? How did you feel? How did you overcome the feelings of uncertainty?

Elena Brouwer, founder of the International Etiquette Centre, points out that mastering business etiquette is important to any person who wants to attain and maintain success in today's rapidly changing, fast-paced business world. Lack of knowledge of protocol can cause embarrassment and misunderstanding. Brouwer and other writers on etiquette emphasize that etiquette is more important than ever and give several reasons.[6]

> Mastering business etiquette is important to any person who wants to be successful.

Why Etiquette Skills Are Important

1 High-tech tools and toys are being used by more people in more places today. The development of high technology all too often results in our being treated impersonally and our treating others that way. This situation leaves us desiring human sensitivity, a need that can be at least partially met through socially correct interpersonal behaviors.

2. The growth of the global economy and our own diverse population requires that we interact with people of all cultures. If we are to be successful in our dealings, we must be careful not to offend people of other cultures by violating their communication or behavioral norms.

3. Because of the influx of women, minorities, and people with disabilities into the workplace, old behavioral rules are being reexamined and new ones created. Some of these behaviors are being determined legally; others fall outside of the legal domain and are less specific.

4. In the 1960s and early 1970s, "doing your own thing" became the norm and children were not taught etiquette, resulting in a generation of business people who may feel awkward and ill at ease in social and official situations. Use of teams and group decision making is more common.

5. Because work has increasingly become technologically advanced, cyber skills change as rapidly as do the technologies. Workers must maintain good working skills in these areas and many times apply cross-cultural etiquette abilities.

Quick tip

"Every action done in company ought to be with some sign of respect to those that are present."

George Washington

Knowledge of etiquette, then, is a key ingredient in human relations and in business and personal success. Such knowledge can help you feel comfortable because you know what to do and can do it with grace, style, and ease. Work situations that call for effective etiquette include relationships with coworkers, with managers above you, with people below you in the hierarchy, with customers and clients, and with the general public where you are seen as representing your organization. Away from work, you will enhance your chances for satisfactory relationships with people if your behavior says that you respect them.

An important point needs to be made about etiquette: what is appropriate will depend to a certain extent on where, when, and with whom the interaction occurs. Behavior considered appropriate with one group or individual might be considered offensive with someone else. Think, for example, about the different perceptions of the handshake around the world. For instance, in Italy, handshakes are common for both sexes, and may include grasping the arm with the other hand. You may even receive a kiss on both cheeks if you have developed really good working rapport. Often, etiquette will come down to learning a person's preferences, then respecting them.

Because etiquette depends on timing and setting, you must develop good judgment and sensitivity to people around you. This awareness will give you the best chance of success in your relationships, in business situations such as negotiations and sales, in leadership positions, and in any situation requiring cooperation and teamwork.

The remainder of this chapter will discuss etiquette as a typical worker might use it on a normal workday. Etiquette starts with dressing for work in the morning and carries through work activities such as writing and using the telephone and other forms of communication technology. It also applies to meeting people, introducing people, having lunch, networking, mentoring, and participating in office politics. As you read the following section, imagine yourself in the example situations and apply the suggestions to your own life and work situation.

*Fast*Chat

1. What other reasons for good etiquette can you imagine?

2. Which one of these reasons do you think is most important and why?

3. How can proper etiquette be used to demonstrate respect? Give examples of effective etiquette and etiquette blunders you have witnessed in the workplace.

Experts point out that we form our impressions of people in the first few seconds we see them and that initial impressions can be difficult to change. These initial impressions can be formed from a person's appearance, manners, and greeting. Because of this, we need to be aware of what impression our own appearance makes.

APPEARANCE

Consider what you wore to work or class today and your overall appearance, which includes hygiene. When dressing this morning, did you consider whether the statement your clothes would make would be the one you want to make? Did you ask yourself whether your appearance would indicate that you fit in with the environment in which you function? Did you consider how your appearance made you feel about yourself?

If etiquette pertains to appropriate behaviors, certainly it must be extended to include appropriate dress, hygiene, and grooming. Inappropriate dress suggests a lack of respect for the situation and the people involved. People who take their careers seriously know that image is important. You will be a poor representative for your company if your appearance is making a statement that does not agree with the image of the company.

Quick tip ....

"While being judged by what you wear may not be fair, it's one of the few tangible qualities that the interviewer can use to assess a candidate."

Mary Anderson, Human Resources Manager

Additionally, our clothing and accessories can help us feel better about ourselves, which can in turn make us feel more comfortable interacting with others. If we can forget about our appearance because we are satisfied with it, we are free to concentrate on the other person. The most important rule of dress for work: dress appropriately for your organization. Some organizations are conservative in nature and expect their employees to dress accordingly. Organizations that stress creativity expect that their

Would you send out a resume without proofreading it first? No! Then proofread yourself before you send yourself to an interview. Follow these basic guidelines and you'll be proofed to go:

- Conservative two-piece business suit—solid dark blue or grey
- Clean, long-sleeved white shirt/blouse. Pastel colors are okay.
- Clean, well-groomed hair, styled neatly.
- Clean, trimmed fingernails.
- Minimal, preferably no, cologne or perfume.
- No gum, candy, or cigarettes.
- Small briefcase or portfolio and pen.
- Most importantly, clean, polished, conservative shoes.

employees will reflect that creativity to a certain extent and will tolerate less conservative dress, although good taste is still expected.

The moment people look at us, they begin to form an opinion about our education and economic level, our social position, and our success level. Sexy clothes in most kinds of jobs are never considered to be in good taste. Neither are strong colognes, flashy jewelry, dirty or messy hair, unnatural hairdos and makeup, or extreme tattoos and piercings. Clothes and shoes do not have to be expensive, but they should fit well and be clean. Casual, dress-down Fridays do not mean sloppy weekend wear. Many experts still suggest following the adage "Dress for the position to which you aspire." Also important is consistency in dress. People will not be viewed as stable employees who know where they are going if they dress professionally one day and inappropriately the next.

Quick tip

Many organizations today have a *business casual* dress policy, but what does this mean for employees? Business casual means dressing in a professional yet relaxed manner. For men, this usually means khakis or dress trousers and a button-down or polo-style shirt. For women, it usually means conservative wool or twill pants with a sweater or blouse. Be sure to become familiar with the office attire policies outlined in your organization's employee handbook. Observe what your coworkers wear, and dress in a manner that makes you feel confident and will make others take you seriously.

TABLE MANNERS

Practically everyone shares meals with others at some time as a part of the workday. Whether you are eating in the company cafeteria with coworkers or attending a business luncheon outside the company, you can make these times more relaxed and enjoyable by understanding certain basic rules of etiquette. In general, the following rules should be used in any setting.

If you think good table manners are outmoded or, worse yet, overrated, think again. Etiquette is not outdated or something your parents used to do. It is still around and very much in use. Elena Brouwer, founder of the International Etiquette Center, had a client who blundered by not knowing how to order from a menu appropriately in a restaurant and lost a major financing account. Does this seem unimportant? Obviously not to the lender. Roberto Bianco, a career development counselor at the Massachusetts Institute of Technology, has developed a workshop to prepare students for careers in corporate America. They participate in role-playing exercises and mock job interviews and attend formal dinner parties to test their international protocol skills and table manners. Many of these students will work for cross-cultural corporations where these skills may make or break their careers.[7]

CASE STUDIES IN THE NEWS

"I was mortified!" This was the comment made by Bill Mahoney after observing one of his junior employees display horrific manners at a business dinner. She was speaking with a mouthful of food, waving her knife in the air while describing some sporting event, then literally sopped her bread in the gravy and downed it all with a slug of white wine held not by the stem. Mahoney runs a consulting firm in Fort Lauderdale and was hosting the dinner party in honor of one of his clients, the CEO of a billion-dollar company. Said Mahoney, "I noticed my client watching her, and the look on his face gave me the clue to call in an etiquette professional to train my key staff."

Judgments are often made about your competence, professionalism, and your character based on that critical first impression. Etiquette classes appear to be experiencing a renaissance, teaching manners to workers who grew up with TV trays and video games. Mahoney felt his money was well worth the investment at a cost of $2,500 per session, when he saw demonstrated improvements—and picked up a few pointers for himself.[8]

Why are proper manners and social etiquette especially important at business dinners?

Basic Table Manners

1. To keep people from bumping into each other, sit down from the left side of the chair when possible.

2. In general, wait until all people at the table are seated and have their food before beginning to eat. The company cafeteria, where people are on different schedules, may be an exception. Another exception may be when you are served a dish that will lose its flavor if cooled or warmed.

3. Place your napkin in your lap as soon as you are seated, and sit with both feet on the floor.

4. Avoid playing with your silverware or food.

5. Keep the hand not holding the fork in your lap (unless you need to use a knife). Do not place your elbows on the table while eating or lean on the table to eat. Remember to sit straight but not rigid throughout the meal.

6. Never reach for food or condiments across the table. Pass both salt and pepper together. Ask the person nearest the item you want to "please pass the..." Bowls are passed to the right.

7. Do not smack or slurp while eating or talk with your mouth full.

8. Do not groom at the table. If women need to add lipstick or men or women need to smooth wind-blown hair, they should go elsewhere to do so.

9. Excuse yourself to people on each side if you should leave the table.

10. Place your napkin in your chair if you have to leave the table during the meal.

11. When finished eating, lay your silver in your plate placed in a 5:20 position and your napkin on the table to the left of the plate. Do not shove your plate away from you or comment about how full you are.

12. Cocktails before or after dinner may be appropriate in a social setting, but alcohol is best avoided at work-related meals.

Correct table manners make business luncheons more comfortable and enjoyable.

©Getty Images/PhotoDisc

Human Relations

INTRODUCTIONS

We are constantly meeting new people in our jobs and at times must introduce people to each other. The latter situation is more likely to create anxiety. You can reduce your anxiety, be more comfortable, and create a gracious atmosphere if you remember the overriding goals of putting people at ease and showing them proper respect.

Introductions should put people at ease and show them respect.

General Rules for Making Introductions

1. Introduce younger people or people lower on the organizational hierarchy to older people (those appearing to be 15 years older) and superiors. Address the older person or person higher on the hierarchy first: "Dr. Rutherford, I would like you to meet Rhonda Elliott, the new associate in our office."

2. Introduce a man to a woman if they are about the same age and on the same level of the hierarchy. Address the woman first: "Ms. Salinas, I would like you to meet Mr. Freedman. He handles the new product line in the San Antonio office."

3. If you forget the name of someone you are introducing, as we all do occasionally, be honest and ask people to introduce themselves to each other, as follows, "My mind is not giving me names today. Will you please introduce yourselves?"

If you are the one being introduced and your name is mispronounced, you may give the correct pronunciation when acknowledging the person to whom you are introduced. For example, if your name is Dalton and you are introduced as Dawson, you may correct this mistake simply by saying, "Sam Dalton. I'm glad to meet you."

If no one introduces you in a group, you may handle the situation politely by smiling and saying something like, "I'm Danielle Muster from Accounting." Be gracious and friendly in order to put the group at ease.

The handshake, a common part of introductions, should be firm but not hand-breaking. It may include one or two gentle pumps and should be accompanied with a smile, eye contact, slight forward lean, and a short phrase such as, "I am happy to meet you." When you shake hands with someone, make it brief by releasing the hand after the pumps.

These days, your global village may consist of three clients in Canada, four in Japan, two in Mexico, and a new account in China. How are your cross-cultural "hobnobbing skills"? Okay with handshakes? What about proper introductions and titles? You can never do enough homework about the countries you will be visiting or with whom you will be doing business. A well-executed handshake is often the first step in developing a successful, long-term relationship. As our world gets smaller and smaller through globalization, we must become aware and respectful of the cultures and customs of others. Whether a hearty hand pump, a gentle grasp, or a respectful bow, the acknowledgment of others sets the tone for success.[9]

1. *In new business social settings, are you comfortable that you will make the right choice when introducing guests? What is the proper protocol—titles and order?*

2. *What type of handshake do you believe is most acceptable in a business situation? Why?*

Although in some social situations people routinely kiss or hug when meeting each other, such behavior is totally out of place in a U.S. business setting. You should not put an arm around coworkers of either sex, place a hand on his or her shoulder, or touch a coworker in any way. However, if you are involved in international business circles, following the norm for that culture is appropriate.

*Fast*Chat

1. Does your place of business have a dress code? Why do you think appearance is so important to success?

2. Have you ever had a bad first impression of someone? What was it about the person that created the bad impression? Did the impression last?

3. How many of these etiquette rules have you missed on occasion? Which one was news to you?

4. What types of greetings have you observed that are different than what you use?

As international, multinational, transnational, multidomestic and global businesses continue to shrink our world, people are "coming closer" and recognizing the need to learn how to work effectively both abroad and at home with other cultures. Cross-cultural communication and etiquette have become critical elements required for all international and global business executives, managers, and employees. Short courses on cross-cultural work relationships and workshops on international business etiquette are springing up all over. Ann Marie Sabath, author of *Business Etiquette: 101 Ways to Conduct Business With Charm and Savvy*, suggests that if you anticipate a foreign assignment, taking a vacation there for exposure would be a smart move.[10]

Some common stereotypes concern Japanese business practices. For example, many people have heard that American managers in Japanese firms have no real power, the Japanese punish initiative, the Japanese insist that management be by consensus or else, and the Japanese do not respect female employees. Americans experienced in working with the Japanese suggest that these stereotypes are not valid. Numerous authorities point out that experience with other cultures, even if only through travel, is helpful in working with foreign business people. Such experience is likely to give a person greater tolerance—even admiration—for ways unlike those at home.

> Tolerance and acceptance is necessary when working with people of other cultures.

uick tip ....

"It is the mark of a cultured man that he is aware of the fact that equality is an ethical and not a biological principle."

Ashley Montagu,
Anthropologist

International business assignments have their pitfalls. Experts who have worked abroad for many years warn to keep a sharp eye for cultural variances and learn to be tolerant of different standards of behavior. What is considered sexual harassment in the United States, for instance, may not raise an eyebrow in other cultures. Also, pantsuits, no matter how dressy, are not acceptable business attire in Japan, especially not in serious negotiation settings. The many cultural sensitivities required in today's business arena make fertile ground for business etiquette and protocol schooling.

Bobbi Marten, a professional etiquette consultant, says Americans are profoundly unprepared when it comes to international etiquette. Unfortunately, this has painted a negative image of U.S. workers abroad. Americans are generally perceived as pushy, brash, and rude. "The real problem is that most U.S. business people don't take the time to do their homework and learn the culture." She believes that the United States is the most culturally diverse country in the world but the most culturally inept. We cannot expect to do business the same all over the world, and we certainly cannot expect others to do it the way we do.[11]

If you are called upon to work with people from another country, as you probably will be, certain guidelines may help you.

International Work Guidelines

1. Learn as much as you can about the nonverbal communication and customs of the other culture. Numerous organizations offer such classes. Books and articles are available, and people familiar with the culture can be helpful. This aspect of communication is a ripe area for misunderstandings. For example, the Japanese almost always bow when exchanging their business cards. In Arab nations, a man will hold another man's hand a long time when they meet. Additionally, business transactions almost always take longer outside the United States. Knowing these cultural differences, you will not be caught off guard.

2. Learn some of the other language. Even a little knowledge will demonstrate that you are trying to meet people of other countries half way rather than insisting that everyone know your native language. Several language schools offer "crash courses" for the business traveler emphasizing frequently used terms and phrases that will get you through a day. By using a beginning like this, you are communicating that you do not necessarily expect others to know English. Also, it can help you get around when you're overseas. (Your business contact may speak English, but does the taxi driver?)

3. Talk to someone knowledgeable about the culture before offering gifts, inquiring about family members, or beginning business discussions. Norms for these behaviors vary from culture to culture, and the pace at which discussions flow from personal to business differs. The Japanese, for example, frequently give gifts, whereas Western European businesspeople generally do not.

4. Being courteous and sincere can help you over the rough spots.

As our world continues to shrink and international borders become more blurred, special attention must be given to our cultural IQs. The self-quiz on page 395 will introduce you to multicultural issues and terms dealing with gestures. Test your cultural IQ.

Keep Your Hands to Yourself

1. The two A-OK gestures (a circle of the index finger and thumb, or a thumbs-up) that are so popular in the United States are extremely rude in many parts of the world. Pick the country where one or both of these well-meaning A-OK gestures are obscene.

   A. Brazil   B. Australia   C. Spain   D. Middle Eastern countries   E. All of these

2. True or false: Asians may show disagreement by squinting and sucking air through their teeth.

3. Never demonstrate how big—or small—anything is in Latin America by measuring the space between your two extended index fingers. The correct way to illustrate length in Latin American countries is:

   A. Hold one hand at the appropriate height from the floor.

   B. Extend your right arm, and measure from your fingertips to the correct distance up your arm with your left hand.

   C. Use a measuring tape or slide rule.

4. True or false: In Chile, slapping your right fist into your left palm is obscene, and an open palm with the fingers separated means stupid.

5. U.S. executives are generally comfortable standing with about two feet of space between them. True or false: The normal speaking distance in much of Latin America is less than one foot.

6. You are late for your appointment with your new German boss; then you call him by his first name and move your chair closer to his desk. Which of the following might placate him?

   A. Ask him about his family.   B. Slouch.   C. Stick your hands in your pockets

   D. Apologize for being late and get right down to business.

7. True or false: In Japan, tapping one's finger repeatedly on the table signifies agreement and support of a speaker's statement.

8. People from different cultures point with various parts of their bodies—their chins, thumbs, or palms. True or false: A person from England will generally indicate something with his or her head.

9. A British professor was a guest lecturer at a university in an Islamic country. During his address, he unthinkingly insulted the audience by displaying a part of his body. What did he show the audience that was so offensive?

   A. His teeth   B. His left hand   C. The sole of his foot

Answers can be found on p. 414.

By Terri Morrison and Wayne A. Conaway. Copyright © 2004 Getting Through Customs. All Rights Reserved. Used by permission.

*Fast*Chat

1. How many different cultures do you encounter in a normal day? How do they influence your life?

2. What would you do to prepare for an international assignment?

How employees treat customers and clients is a crucial factor in the success of a business. Poor service or bad treatment will lose a company customers. And it loses more than just the customer who was treated badly because while customers will seldom tell the company about the treatment, they do tell their friends and others. Effective customer relations, then, is an important part of an organization's marketing strategy.

The best rule for customer relations is the new Golden Rule.

If you come in contact with customers in person, by mail, or over the telephone, the most important guideline that you can remember is, "Do unto others as they would have you do unto them." The ways that employees should treat customers seem so obvious that mistreatment seems almost unthinkable, yet it occurs every day and drives customers away by the dozens. One rude employee can do untold damage to a business, whereas one helpful employee is worth thousands in marketing dollars.

The three situations shown on page 397 could have been improved if the employees had remembered these basic guidelines pertaining to customer relations. In reviewing these incidents, think how you would have felt had you been the customer. If you are like most people, you would have been somewhat hurt or angered by the treatment and, more than likely, you would have been reluctant to return.

MANNERS IN CORRESPONDENCE AND ON THE TELEPHONE

Manners are as important in correspondence and on the phone as in person.

As an employee of a company, you portray the image of that company each time you write someone or use the telephone for a business purpose. Effective human relations is just as important in correspondence and on the telephone as in person.

In writing, the tone of a message is important. Polite requests, such as "Please return both copies" sound much more pleasant than "Return both copies." Including a person's name on all correspondence rather than just a company or department name can help to make the receivers feel that they are dealing with real people, not just an impersonal organization.

Additionally, because everyone's time is at a premium, unnecessarily long messages are a form of waste and poor manners.

When you answer the phone, you represent the company. Therefore, your voice and manner should present a friendly and professional image. Right and wrong ways to handle telephone communications exist—ways that are courteous and efficient and ways that are abrupt and rude.

Examples of Customer Treatment

Poor Treatment	Correct Treatment
Incident 1. About five minutes before Arnold was to leave for the day to start a two-week vacation, a customer, Helen Williams, came in wanting to submit an application for credit. When Arnold was told that the customer was in the outer office, his loud response was, "Well, she had better hurry. I have things to do." When the supervisor said, "Shhhh," with a finger to her lips, Arnold replied, again loudly, "Oh, she didn't hear me."	*Incident 1.* Arnold should have either handled the application or have politely asked someone else to help her. No comments about his leaving should have been made in front of the customer.
Incident 2. Wanda has been taken off the telephone to free her for handling customers. However, when all of the other clerks are on the telephone or busy, the calls roll over to her station. This chore displeases her so much that when she answers the phone, she is abrupt with her "Hello" and snaps out answers to the callers' questions.	*Incident 2.* Because callers do not know what a situation is in an office and have every right to expect the person answering to be ready to deal with their business, Wanda should treat each call with patience, respect, and consideration.
Incident 3. Ronald is busy waiting on a customer in the eyeglass shop when Angie walks in. He continues to help the customer with whom he was working, assuming that Angie can look around while she is waiting. After about five minutes of standing nearby and waiting for his attention without even getting a glance from the salesclerk, Angie leaves the shop.	*Incident 3.* Ronald should have acknowledged Angie as soon as she walked into the store. This he could have done with a friendly, "Hello. I'll be with you shortly. Would you like to look around in the meantime?"

The following guidelines for good customer relations will be helpful in your day-to-day interactions. The suggestions on page 399 are from Southwestern Bell Telephone's publication *Telephone Manners.* These telephone tips can help you present the best possible impression for your company and do an efficient job at the same time.[12]

Good Customer Relations Guidelines

1. Never say anything *about* a customer that you would not say *to* the customer.

2. When serving a customer by phone or in person, give that person your full attention. Do not shuffle papers or try to do other work at the same time.

3. Every customer who walks into your place of business should be acknowledged immediately. Your manner should be pleasant and helpful. The customer should not be left unattended long.

4. Consider the role you play in your company's marketing strategy by dressing appropriately each day. Remember to exercise good hygiene by having clean clothes, hair, and teeth. Do not chew gum or eat in front of customers. Your demeanor should be professional. A ready smile, eye contact, correct posture, and smooth voice are helpful in client relations.

5. Remember to use "please," "thank you," "thank you for your interest in our company," and "please come again." Calling people by name is an easy way to make them feel important.

6. Never conduct personal telephone calls or carry on personal conversations in front of clients or customers.

7. If you must answer a phone while working with a customer who is with you, ask that person, "Will you excuse me please while I catch this call?" Remember to take care of the first customer first by asking the second whether he or she can hold or would like you to call back. Use the telephone guidelines presented in the next section.

You represent the company each time you answer the telephone at work. Your voice and attitude should present a friendly and professional image.

©Thinkstock

Tips on Telephone Manners

1.	*Answer promptly*	Answer calls on the first ring, if possible, in a friendly, enthusiastic way.
2.	*Answer correctly*	Speaking clearly and enthusiastically, say, "Good morning (or good afternoon)," and on an outside line, give your company name. On an inside line, use your first and last names in answering instead of the company name. Adding "May I help you?" is a courteous way of letting the caller know that you are immediately available and interested.
3.	*If you are answering for someone else*	First, identify the department, office, or area, and then identify yourself as a substitute for the expected person and add "May I help you?"
4.	*Transfer calls only when necessary*	People may become irritated if their calls are switched from one person to another. Instead, put the caller on hold, get the information, and return to the line. If you cannot get the information, explain to the caller who can help, giving the name and number of that individual, then ask if you may transfer them to that number. Always ask first. Then indicate that you are transferring by saying, "I'll transfer your call now. One moment, please."
5.	*When the caller asks for someone you do not know*	Use a courteous, gracious manner and a tactful reply, such as, "May I have that name again, please?" or "I'm sorry. I don't find that name on our list. Could you tell me in which department she works?"
6.	*Calls on hold*	If you are going to be delayed in continuing a call, tell callers that you are going to put them on hold for a moment and then, before placing the instrument down, put it on hold.
7.	*If you are delayed*	Do not leave callers on hold more than 30 seconds without returning to say that you have not forgotten them. If you must leave the telephone for more than a minute, offer to call back and state the approximate time when you will do so.
8.	*If the requested party is busy*	Explain in a courteous manner that the person is unavailable and offer the caller the option of waiting on the line or being called back.
9.	*If the party is out*	Project your company's image by stating that "Ms. McWright is out of the office until..." Ask callers whether someone else can help or whether they would like to leave their names and numbers.
10.	*Taking messages*	Keep a message pad and pencil by your telephone. Request the information courteously, using a phrase such as, "May I have your name, please?" Correct spelling of names is important. Ask if you are unsure. Repeat the number to the caller to make sure that you have it right.
11.	*Saying good-bye*	Continue your professional demeanor by thanking the party for calling and saying good-bye.

Another suggestion offered by Southwestern Bell is to cultivate a good telephone personality. Be alert, keep a smile in your voice, speak clearly and distinctly, and greet the caller pleasantly. Other ways to project a good telephone personality include using the caller's name, treating every call as important, being tactful, apologizing for errors or delays, taking time to be helpful, and saying "please," "thank you," and "you're welcome."[13]

RULES FOR OTHER COMMUNICATION TECHNOLOGIES

We are drowning in a sea of communication. Office workers are feeling overwhelmed by the flood of faxes, phone calls, e-mails, and other interruptions. Technology has made information readily available and communication easier across boundaries of time and space.

Employees are being sent to netiquette school to learn the proper ways to handle e-mail and are provided process improvement techniques. This cyber-world approach to improving communication and information overload is only the beginning of things to come.

In 1922, Emily Post called Americans to action with her first book on etiquette, stating, "A knowledge of etiquette is essential to decent behavior." Nearly 80 years later, her great-granddaughter, Peggy Post, helped co-author the 75th anniversary edition of *Emily Post's Etiquette*.[14]

TECHNOLOGY CONNECTION

The tide is turning on rude cell phone users. Restaurant-goers are rebelling and asking for "no cell phone zones," much like no smoking sections. With sensitivity to their needs, The Brooklyn Café in Atlanta recently installed a red antique telephone booth, brought from the streets of London, as a conversation haven for cell phone users. Owner Greg Pyne actually guides patrons toward the booth when they are using their phones. Another booth has popped up at the Main Street Bistro in Sarasota, Florida, where the club owner says he gives his patrons a napkin, why not a phone booth so they can still demonstrate their manners?[15]

1. *What do you think about this new trend? Would you be willing to use an enclosed phone booth to make your personal calls?*

2. *Why do you think this situation has become such an issue? In what other ways could the problem be solved?*

The impact of the current explosion of electronic communications is reflected in the fact that Post's new edition provides such useful tips as how to use wireless phones in business and social settings without incurring the wrath of family, friends, and colleagues, and how to "behave" on the Internet and with other telecommunications forms. The netiquette tips on page 402 may be helpful when you have questions about proper use of the Internet for business.

An area of major concern for companies is how e-mail documents are showing up in courtrooms offered as legal documents. E-mail messaging may be a popular form of communication, but it is not a very private one and messages can be intercepted or in some way compromised. A good rule of thumb is if you don't want your message to wind up in someone else's hands, don't send it by e-mail.

The increased use of many other communication technologies has brought a whole new set of etiquette problems. Employees act inappropriately when they send personal messages over the company fax (no love notes or carry-out orders, please!), leave one caller hanging to talk with the second one, spend excessive time on personal telephone calls, or violate confidentiality of information they receive through computer usage. The guidelines offered on page 403 can help you use this multitude of communication forms in ways that are less likely to cause problems—for you as well as for others.

TECHNOLOGY CONNECTION

With more than 147 million cell phones in use as of 2001 and predictions that cell phones will be in the hands of 70 percent of Americans soon, Jacqueline Whitmore became the cell phone etiquette spokesperson for Sprint. She declared July as National Cell Phone Courtesy Month to encourage an awareness of the rampant misuse of this technology and help find a cure—one that will make everyone happy. At the request of commuters, Amtrak added a "Quiet Car" to each of its trains in the northeast corridor. These cars are free and clear of cellular and any other electronic sounds.[16]

1. *Do you have a wireless phone? Were you aware that how and where you use it can be offensive to others?*

2. *Are you sensitive to the feelings of others when using your cell phone? Discuss your thoughts on this subject.*

Netiquette Tips

1. Do not send formal thank you notes via e-mail.

2. Refrain from using "emoticons," those little facial-expression symbols. Most people find them annoying and unprofessional.

3. When applying for jobs via e-mail, don't provide a return e-mail address that starts with a funny nickname. Prospective employers are unlikely to be amused.

4. Do not write anything in all capital letters. This is the on-screen equivalent of yelling and is inconsiderate to the reader.

5. Avoid using slang, abbreviations, or acronyms that may be confusing to other people, especially in other countries.

6. Do not leave the "Subject:" field blank. Always provide a concise description of the content of an e-mail.

7. Avoid using heavy formatting, colored text, and images in e-mail. Readers may not be able to open the e-mails or see the formatting.

8. Do not forward jokes, chain letters, and other non-critical e-mails to others without their permission.

9. Understand that technology and netiquette rules are constantly changing. Make a concerted effort to stay on top of these changes, and be understanding of others.

10. Know your company's policies on e-mail transmissions.

CASE STUDIES IN THE NEWS

In her recent update to *Netiquette*, author Virginia Shea explains the most basic 10 rules, or the "Core Rules of Netiquette." The first is simply to apply the Golden Rule and respect the person. Second is to follow the same standards of behavior online as you do in your real life. Be ethical. Rule 3 reminds you to know where you are in cyberspace and to follow the lead of others in your chat domain. The fourth rule is to respect other people's time and limit the size of your messages, and the fifth is to make yourself look good online by using good communication skills, etc. Rule 6 is to share your knowledge; it's a tradition. Rule 7: Help keep flame wars under control—enough said. The eighth rule is to respect other people's privacy. Rule 9 is don't abuse your power. And the final rule is to be forgiving of other people's mistakes. Following these simple rules will make you very proper and appreciated by fellow Net users.[17]

1. *Which of these netiquette manners would be more difficult to follow? Why?*

2. *Why do you think these guidelines have had to be established?*

3. *Which one do you think is the most important and why?*

Etiquette for Telecommunication Methods

1. **Fax etiquette.** Be careful, be considerate, and be brief. Fax machines, while convenient, can be the cause of endless irritation. Know your fax recipient. To prevent problems, call ahead to check for any ground rules and to notify your recipient that a fax is on its way. Sending unwanted or long correspondence can tie up the machine unnecessarily. Be certain you have the correct fax number. Don't walk away from the fax machine—wait (or check back often), especially if you are using redial or multiple recipient features. (If you entered a home number, the machine won't hear the voice that answers, it will just keep calling back, which is a nuisance.)

2. **Call waiting etiquette.** The call waiting feature on telephones signals us while we are on the line that another call is coming in. Except in emergencies, the first caller should receive our complete attention. Many etiquette writers consider call waiting to be a rude interruption and suggest that the accounting method of first in, first out be used. That is, do not ask the person with whom you are speaking to wait while you handle a second caller. Instead, once you have determined that no emergency exists, politely ask the second caller to call back or offer to return the call yourself, stating when you will be free.

3. **Answering machine etiquette.** Messages on answering machines should be clear and precise. Jokes and blaring music are distasteful in any setting and totally inappropriate on office telephones.

4. **Voice mail etiquette.** Some people feel this may be the most infuriating of the electronic devices because callers receive instructions from a computer. However, it is generally a very reliable way to leave and receive messages. The best advice on using voice mail is to leave a straightforward message about your reason for calling and the information you desire.

5. **Pager and cell phone etiquette.** Remember to treat beepers and phones in public like babies: when they make a noise, remove them immediately to another room. Noisy users of beepers and cell phones can be politely asked to be quiet. Most theaters now require that devices be turned off before performances. If it is vital that you stay in touch, get a silent, vibrating pager or phone.

*Fast*Chat

1. What are some other forms of technology that you think will further advance our means of communicating?

2. How do you handle the overload of messaging occurring in your life?

3. What suggestions can you make that might be helpful to others?

With the 21ST century came a burst of new technologies advancing communication capabilities globally. At home, you may be enjoying the benefits of sending digital camera pictures to relatives halfway around the globe. Or, you may be sending your latest architectural drawings to the chief engineer on a jobsite in Bangladesh. Maybe you are text messaging your friend in the registrar's office about lunch.

We keep our hand-held computers close by, have our cell phone headset hanging loosely, and are poised for a camera phone snapshot at a moment's notice. Wireless Internet connections will further enhance our capabilities. These are but a few of the many forms of technologies we enjoy and use with comfortable ease.

In the workplace, many technologies have helped form the virtual office. According to Wainhouse Research, virtual meetings now outnumber in-person meetings with a 75 percent more productive ratio reported when using these services. Teleconferencing is the most familiar of these services and is still growing at a rate of about 60 percent a year. Web conferencing is the most popular because of the flexibility it offers. Some companies report a 100 percent growth in usage because they can point employees to a web address, lead them through a presentation, have them make any real-time changes to the shared documents during the meeting from their own desktops, solicit any further feedback, then wrap it up and call it a day. However, web conferencing calls for a unique set of etiquette guidelines, as does a videoconference, which requires its users to remain sharp and clear during transmittal time and has a few unique rules as well.[18]

While virtual meetings may save money and time, they create whole new areas of conferencing etiquette to remember. Just as shaking hands begins most face-to-face meetings, virtual meetings also have appropriate beginning and etiquette guidelines, whether you are teleconferencing, web conferencing, or videoconferencing.

According to the Emily Post Institute, virtual meeting basic etiquette ground rules include speaking clearly and distinctly, making eye contact with the camera and other participants, and turning off all cell phones, beepers, PDAs, and watch alarms. Don't speak over people and don't leave the room unless absolutely necessary. Following these simple courtesies may make you a star performer.[19]

Workplace surveillance, although not new, has taken on new methods and meaning that warrants some discussion. Gadgets and sensors are being used that track workers, while cameras in tiny places may be

Virtual Meeting Etiquette Guidelines

Teleconferencing

- Begin by introducing each participant by name, title, and location. Before speaking during the call, state your name.

- Speakerphones typically cut off when background noise is detected. Limit motion and sounds as much as possible.

- Interrupting is rude, whether face-to-face or on a conference call. Be considerate of others.

- Consider your location. Before dialing in, what is your background noise and could it seriously hinder the meeting's effectiveness? A baby crying, crowd noise, or static from a poor location could interrupt the clarity of the meeting transmission.

Web Conferencing

- Write clearly. When annotating a slide or changing a document, use a large font, with brief and clear language that is easily readable. Always proofread your message before sending it.

- Listen carefully. Pay attention to your meeting. The leader may ask for a poll of opinions or request input on the topic. Don't read and respond to other e-mails or work on other documents during the conference.

- Limit graphics. Keep presentation materials to a manageable size for those with slower Web connections. Unless all users have high-speed connections, limit graphic traffic also.

- Limit chatter and note passing. Resist the temptation to visit with others. Mind your manners.

Videoconferencing

- Dress appropriately. This is the same as an in-person meeting. Avoid wearing white or black, plaids, stripes, or busy prints because they confuse the monitor's transmission capability.

- Break for lunch. This is no place to eat your lunch while the meeting is going on. The noises can be very disruptive and the motion very annoying. And it is just plain rude.

- Follow basic good etiquette ground rules. Apply common courtesy and consideration.

---

looking when you least expect it. Employee abuse of Internet access has prompted employers to begin using software packages that can read, track, and archive all company e-mail records. Advances in global positioning systems (GPS) tracking help some companies track their company vehicles' movements—and the driver—in very close detail.

A recent study done by the American Management Association found that over half of employers monitor e-mail, and an earlier study revealed that 82 percent of the major U.S. corporations monitor employees through some type of videotaping or reviewing voice mails. Frederick Lane, a Vermont attorney, has written a new book, *The Naked Employee*, in which he describes his concerns about possible trouble in the future. Technological advances enable employers to collect unprecedented amounts of information about their employees. Lane advises employees that if they don't want companies to know something, they should not use the companies' systems.[20]

Bradley Alge, a Purdue University human resources expert, says that most employees sign a statement at the time of employment agreeing to surveillance policies without really noticing it. Dean Harold Krent of Chicago-Kent College of Law, who is a personal privacy expert, believes that few employees really know how far their rights go and where companies draw the line. As time and technologies advance, employees should become more familiar with surveillance policies.[21]

As technology advances, be sure you understand your employer's privacy policies.

"Last Thursday you whispered to yourself that our employee privacy policy stinks. Just what did you mean by that?"

©2001 Ted Goff www.tedgoff.com

*Fast*Chat

1. Which real-time communication method would you prefer using for your meetings? Why?

2. How do you feel about workplace surveillance? What problems do you see for the future, if any? What suggestions can you make to avoid problems in the future?

Having "a friend in the business" can be helpful when you face a problem or need advice. **Networking** is a process whereby you can get moral support, career guidance, and important information in areas outside your expertise by developing contacts with people in your place of employment and in professional organizations. Members can use networks to exchange information, ideas, and occasional favors.

Networking contacts should not be abused.

To be effective, you must use your networks appropriately. Members of a network will come to resent anyone who abuses the process, for example, by trying to solicit free advice from professionals such as doctors, lawyers, and accountants. You must also assist others in the network in turn. Needless to say, confidentiality is important, as it is in any relationship.

A **mentor** is an experienced person who will give you objective career advice. Such a person can give you pointers, offer advice concerning sensitive situations, and help you avoid mistakes. A mentor can be someone inside or outside your organization but in your profession. Your choice of a mentor should be someone you respect. Therefore, you should act in such a way that your mentor will admire both the way you behave and the way you handle your job. Do not abuse your mentor's time or position.

Respect your mentor's time and position.

Office politics are impossible to avoid but can be extremely sensitive. Discretion and courtesy should be your guidelines in participating in office politics. Participating in or even listening to gossip is not only ill mannered, but it can also kill your career. When confronted with gossip, avoid the discussion by simply saying, "Oh, I never pay attention to things like that."

Should conflict develop between you and a coworker, kindness and graciousness may restore your relationship. If you did something that offended the other person, you need to apologize. If you do not know why the person is upset, ask in a concerned manner. Refrain from making critical comments. Your goal is a win-win resolution of the conflict.

Etiquette can help coworkers resolve conflicts.

*Fast*Chat

1. What kinds of networking opportunities are available to you?
2. How can good manners help prevent conflict as well as resolve it?

How well you put etiquette into practice depends on your usual behavior. Three basic behaviors can be found in the workplace: passive, aggressive, and assertive. Understanding the different behaviors can assist you in becoming more effective on the job. Edward Charlesworth and Ronald Nathan, in *Stress Management*, define these behaviors.[22]

PASSIVE BEHAVIOR

Individuals who consistently engage in **passive behavior** value themselves below others, do not appear self-confident when they speak, want to be liked and try to please others, and avoid unpleasant situations and confrontation. Their passivity shows, in part, through their nonverbal communication. Passive people may look down or to the side in order to avoid eye contact. They will also mumble and hesitate when speaking. Slumped shoulders and poor posture may round out this person's passive demeanor.

Failure to communicate wants and needs is also part of passive behavior. Others may become angry, especially when they sincerely want to know the passive person's desires or preferences. A common example is the group questioning passive individuals about their choice of restaurants. Frequently, even after repeated questioning, the only response from the passive person is, "I don't care. You decide."

Others often become irritated at passive individuals' manner and begin to view them as "pushovers," "nerds," or "wimps." This loss of respect may lead some people to attempt to take advantage of passive individuals by burdening them with excessive work or responsibilities. Passive individuals will say nothing, but inside them anger is building and eventually that anger must be confronted.

AGGRESSIVE BEHAVIOR

People who consistently engage in **aggressive behavior** value themselves above others and say what they feel or think at the expense of others in an attempt to get anger off their chests. They may attempt to dominate or humiliate, use threats and accusations, or try to show up others. They also frequently choose for others and speak with an air of superiority and in a voice that is demanding or rude. Their aggressive behavior includes nonverbal communication intended to intimidate or put down other people. It consists of glaring at others with an angry facial expression or using a voice that is sharp and curt, demanding, and rude. An aggressive individual's stance makes him or her appear to be ready to fight, and fists may be clenched.

This type of behavior offends others, of course. They may feel angry, defensive, or humiliated and may possibly want to strike back at the aggressor. Often aggressors get what they want, but by offending others have trouble working with coworkers later.

Both of these behaviors—passive and aggressive—can damage your career. For instance, suppose that you are working on an important project for your supervisor and discover that your supervisor has made a huge mistake that will cost the company thousands of dollars unless corrected. If you are a passive person, you will not want to tell your supervisor about the mistake. You will be afraid of causing offense. What do you think will happen later, when your supervisor learns that you did not report the error? Is this the kind of person supervisors like to have on their teams?

If you are aggressive, you will not fare much better. You will tell your supervisor but will probably say something like, "Well, you really blew it this time." Such behavior will immediately make your supervisor defensive and unwilling to listen, even though you are right. The supervisor may look for something for which to reprimand you as a form of revenge.

ASSERTIVE BEHAVIOR

The situations above are better handled with **assertive behavior**. Assertive individuals are comfortable in using correct etiquette, feel that they are equal to others, and make their own choices. They also use "I" phrases and other effective communication techniques, appear calm and confident, and want to communicate and be respected. They have self-esteem and are respected by others.

Assertiveness requires that you speak clearly, calmly, and firmly. Maintain eye contact without staring. Have a relaxed facial expression with no evidence of tension in your body. Keep your shoulders back and your posture erect. This type of nonverbal communication is not intimidating but shows that you have confidence.

Assertive individuals are respected and valued by others and, therefore, often obtain what they want. Others do not feel offended or violated, and everyone's rights are respected. Even in situations that are not ideal or are potentially annoying, the assertive person remains calm, pleasant, and in control. For example, if the assertive person needed to repeat a message because another person did not pay attention the first time, he or she would repeat the message with firmness and respect.

Assertive individuals are comfortable using correct etiquette and making their own choices.

Learning to behave assertively takes patience and practice. The following steps can help you build assertive behavior skills.

Developing Assertive Behavior

1. Monitor your own behavior. Pay particular attention to your own responses—eye contact, gestures, body posture, facial expression, and voice tone and volume. Decide which behavior you usually exhibit.

2. Imagine situations at work and at home. What would have been the outcome if you had behaved differently? Practice how you would handle the situations assertively by saying the appropriate words aloud when you are alone. Practice nonverbal communication in front of a mirror.

3. Begin communication with "I" phrases. Opening a conversation with "I think" or "I feel" is particularly effective. Practice this phrasing and other communication techniques to become familiar and comfortable with them.

4. Enlist a friend to help you practice assertive behavior. Role-playing assertiveness with someone whose advice you trust and respect can be effective.

5. After you have practiced and are confident, try the new behavior on those around you.

6. If you need more help, consider enrolling in a short assertiveness training course. Your local community college and other groups probably offer one. Many people have benefited from such instruction.

7. If your lack of assertiveness results from negative feelings about yourself, professional counseling may help. Your school counselor is a good starting point in seeking assistance.

Remember that it will take some time for everyone (including you) to become comfortable with your behavior. If you are a passive person, those around you may be uncomfortable when you become assertive. Also, you may go overboard and become aggressive while trying to become comfortable with your new behavior. However, continued practice will help you become skilled and confident in dealing with other people.

*Fast*Chat

1. Among your acquaintances, can you think of individuals who fall into each of these behavior categories? How could you identify their behavior types?

2. Which of the tips in this section do you think will be most helpful to you?

CHAPTER SUMMARY

Etiquette, acting appropriately in social and business situations, is becoming ever more important in business. Etiquette involves following rules, using courtesy, and showing good taste. What is appropriate will depend to a certain extent on where, when, and with whom the interaction occurs.

Appearance is an important form of etiquette because it communicates respect for the situation and the people involved. Following basic rules of table etiquette can make these times more relaxed and enjoyable and can also potentially improve your business opportunities. Etiquette is used when making introductions to put people at ease and to show them proper respect.

Today's businessperson must be able to work effectively with people of other cultures. Studying the nonverbal communication of the other culture, knowing a little of the language, being sensitive to the norms of that culture, and using courtesy with sincerity will help.

Effective customer relations can make or break a business. Remember that to customers you *are* the company.

Many technologies have helped make our lives easier yet more complex. The virtual office has become an important part of conducting business and is expected to grow and become even more sophisticated as technologies advance. Regardless of the sophistication of the technology, there remains the most important part of consideration—the need for effective human relation skills. Workplace surveillance has taken on new methods and meaning in this millennium and remains an open subject for the present. The increased use of communication technology has brought with it a whole new set of etiquette problems. Exercise common sense in using faxes, cell phones, call waiting, voice mail, and pagers.

Networking and mentoring can help your professional development if you use your network appropriately and treat your mentor with respect. Discretion and courtesy should be your guidelines in participating in office politics. Passive, aggressive, and assertive are three types

Key Terms

etiquette

protocol

networking

mentor

passive behavior

aggressive behavior

assertive behavior

of behavior found in the workplace. Assertive behavior will bring you the best results.

REVIEW QUESTIONS

1. Define etiquette and protocol. What is the relationship between the two?

2. Why do many business experts believe that knowledge of etiquette is more important than ever today?

3. List three basic guidelines for table manners.

4. Name two points to be remembered in making introductions.

5. List at least one etiquette guideline for correct use of each communication technology discussed in this chapter.

6. How can you use networking, mentoring, and office politics to help, not hurt, your career?

7. Differentiate among aggressive, passive, and assertive behaviors and explain which is appropriate.

DISCUSSION QUESTIONS

1. Think of times when someone showed poor manners. What part of etiquette was violated? How did the violation make you feel? How did you respond to it?

2. Name some examples of protocol in your daily life or work.

3. Name some instances of workplace surveillance of which you are aware through experience, the media, or friends and a related potential problem. How do you feel about this potential problem, and how would you solve it?

4. You've just learned that your new job is in India. How will you prepare for your assignment? Discuss the logic of your course of action.

5. Are you a member of a professional network? If so, describe it. How do you use it? How do you contribute to it?

CHAPTER PROJECTS

1. As a group, discuss the resources available to you for inviting a guest speaker to class for a discussion of expertise or general information on topics from the chapter. This person may be a representative from the local phone company to speak on telecommunications etiquette. Perhaps a classmate knows someone who works for a multinational corporation who is willing to share some valuable work experiences with the class. Alternatively, invite a member of an ethnic group in to share the customs of his or her culture. In pairs, properly introduce one another to the speaker. Prepare written thank-you notes to the speaker indicating your grasp of sound business etiquette.

2. As a group, hold a mock "networking" meeting as a practice for your protocol and etiquette skills. Your may want to designate certain individuals as "titled" or "dignitaries" or as different levels of management in your company. You may want to have some class participants represent various cultures and demonstrate the uniqueness of their business protocols in their countries. Participants should dress appropriately. A sit-down meal is optional but would add an excellent dimension if appropriate. Perhaps a short test of those skills would be appropriate.

APPLICATIONS

In small groups, analyze the following situations:

Hot Times in Hamburger Heaven

"Yeah, what do you want?" Gary gruffly asked the lady on the other side of the counter at Hamburger Heaven.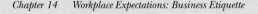

"Well, I'm not sure yet," Mrs. Chang said, as she looked at her two small children, who were trying to make up their minds.

Gary rolled his eyes and frowned. He stamped around in a circle and said, "You ready now?" When Mrs. Chang shook her head, Gary slammed down the tray and went to check the French fries.

"What's wrong with him?" Mrs. Chang's son asked. "Did I do something wrong?"

"No, son," she said. "I'll tell you one thing. I don't like his attitude. You can bet our next meal will be down the street at Bea's Burgers. He has just spoiled my appetite."

1. Was Gary displaying passive, aggressive, or assertive behavior?

2. How should Gary have behaved?

3. What has Gary cost his company?

Telephone Tales

Tom had just had a wonderful date, and he was busy telling his buddy, Carlos, about it on the phone. Things were slow in the plant, and Tom was bored with his bookkeeping job. As Tom was telling the story, the other line blinked. He picked up the phone and mumbled quickly, "Ashton Enterprises. May I help you?"

The caller on the other end of the line did not speak at first, and Tom said, "Hello, hello?" in an irritated fashion.

Mr. Zanigo said, "Oh, is this Ashton Enterprises?"

"Yeah, what do you need?" Tom said impatiently.

"Is Ms. Tate in?" asked Mr. Zanigo.

"Yeah, hang on," Tom replied. Tom then switched back to his friend. "Sorry about that, Carlos. I had to catch the other line. Let me tell you what a great dancer she is . . . ." When he went back to the caller's line 10 minutes later, it was dead.

About two hours afterward, Claudia Ashton, the president of Ashton Enterprises, called Tom into her office. "Tom," she said, "I'm going to have to let you go. My best client was trying to reach Ms. Tate and finally gave up in frustration. If we lose that contract, our business is ruined."

1. What telephone etiquette rules did Tom violate?

2. How should Tom have handled the telephone call?

3. What might Tom's behavior have cost the business?

ADDITIONAL READINGS AND RESOURCES

Lane, Frederik. *The Naked Employee: How Technology is Compromising Workplace Privacy.* New York: AMACOM, 2003.

Lewena, Bayer, and Karen Mallett. *Power Suit, Power Lunch, Power Failure.* Great Plains: Winnipeg, MB, 2000.

Lewena, Bayer, and Karen Mallet. *Pass the Promotion Please.* Great Plains: Winnipeg, MB, 2001.

Mohn, Tonya. "The Social Graces as a Business Tool." *The New York Times,* November 10, 2002.

Post, Peggy. *Emily Post's Etiquette—75th Anniversary Edition.* New York: Harper Collins, 1999.

Sabath, Ann Marie. *Business Etiquette: 101 Ways to Conduct Business with Charm and Savvy.* Franklin Lakes, NJ: Career Press, 2002.

Shea, Virginia. *Netiquette.* San Francisco: Albion Books, 2004.

For additional resources, refer to the web site for this text: school.cengage.com/career/dalton

---

Answers to "Keep Your Hands to Yourself" Quiz

1. E. We should all have a nickel for how many times a U.S. president or vice-president has inadvertently insulted foreign dignitaries by cheerily waving from Air Force One, and then giving a hearty A-OK or thumbs-up sign. 2. True. Many Asians find it difficult to say no, and instead more comfortably indicate their displeasure or disagreement with this gesture. 3. B 4. True. 5. True. In Brazil, many executives will stand approximately six inches away from each other when speaking. 6. D. If you are thoroughly prepared and sit ramrod straight in your chair without moving until he dismisses you, you may leave with your job intact. 7. True. This type of "mini-applause" was reportedly started in one of the courts of a Japanese emperor. 8. True. A proper Brit would never point at anything with a digit. 9. C. The professor's failure to respect Muslim decorum resulted in a student protest and newspaper headlines denouncing British arrogance.

Ethics at Work:
Your Attitude and Responsibilities

focus

Business Week proclaimed that the year 2002 would be remembered as the *annus horribilis* of business. Companies that had once been praised and trusted were tarnished with tales of corporate crime and greed. Outside auditors and members of the boards of directors pleaded ignorance as the stories unfolded. Among the accusations? Bernie Ebbers borrowed $408 million from WorldCom, a company that broke records with the size of its bankruptcy. The Rigas family was accused of defrauding Adelphia Communications of some $1 billion, while Sam Waksal urged his daughter and father to sell their ImClone Systems Inc. stock based on inside information. Enron reached new lows in corporate ethics, with the ex-chief financial officer, Andrew Fastow, facing 78 felony charges of hiding Enron's debt and manipulating its earnings. And Dennis Kozlowski, who had been named by *Business Week* as one of the best managers of 2001 for his ability to lead Tyco International, was charged with looting $600 million from his company to fund his own lavish lifestyle.[1]

Enraged, Congress enacted the Sarbanes-Oxley Act of 2002, which President George W. Bush signed into law. This law is primarily designed to end the "book-cooking" epidemic in public companies and in those planning to go public.[2]

What factors do you believe may have played a part in this eruption of corporate crime and greed? What effect does unethical behavior have on companies? Employees? Shareholders? The public?

After studying this chapter, you should be able to:

15.1 *Understand the differences among ethics, integrity, values, and social responsibility.*

15.2 *Describe methods of determining ethical standards and resolving ethical dilemmas.*

15.3 *Discuss how today's companies are addressing business ethics.*

15.4 *Understand your responsibility regarding ethical behavior at work.*

in this chapter

Integrity is strict adherence to a code of behavior.

We are faced with decisions every day that require drawing on our sense of what is right or wrong, good or bad, ethical or unethical. We make the ultimate choice from a set of values instilled early in life. The process of choosing can be complicated by many factors, so that we often find ourselves facing difficult situations with questions not easily answered.

Ethics, as defined by *The American Heritage Dictionary*, is "the study of the general nature of morals and of the specific moral choices to be made by a person; the rules or standards governing the conduct of a person or the members of a profession."[3] More simply stated, ethics is the study of what is good and right for people. Ethics involves not only telling right from wrong and good from evil, but doing what is right, good, and proper.

One term frequently linked with ethics is **integrity**, which is the strict adherence to a code of behavior. The lack of integrity has become a critical issue in individual and business behaviors today, causing some of the incidents discussed later in this chapter. Another term closely related to ethics is values. **Values** are principles, standards, or qualities you consider worthwhile or desirable. More specifically, your values are your beliefs about what is right or wrong, good or bad, and acceptable or unacceptable. These beliefs develop during your formative years and are heavily influenced by your family, friends, religion, schools, and the media. Values determine how we will behave in certain situations.

Values vary widely in our diverse society. In 1992, the Josephson Institute set out to determine whether a diverse group could agree on common core values. The 30 leaders they brought together agreed upon "Six Pillars of Character" that make up the ground rules for decision making: trustworthiness, respect, responsibility, fairness, caring, and citizenship. Along with these common values, each of us will have individual values such as family, specific beliefs, honor, duty, etc. We demonstrate our values by how we interact with others and make decisions in our daily lives. Ethics brings our value systems into play.[4]

UNDERSTANDING ETHICAL ISSUES

Ethics is not only an individual issue but also an organizational issue. We cannot avoid ethical issues in business any more than we can in other areas of our lives. Corporate culture influences decisions that affect an organization's employees, its customers, and the public in general.

In the 1980s, a *Wall Street Journal* article called business ethics "an oxymoron, a contradiction in terms like jumbo shrimp." Many felt it was the bottom line that counted and nothing more. As long as businesses obeyed the law, their obligations were fulfilled.[5]

But Ford Motor Company learned the hard way that just obeying the law is not enough. In 1978, three Indiana teenagers were killed when the Pinto they were driving was struck from the rear and the gas tank burst into flames. Ford was indicted and tried on charges of reckless homicide, marking the first time an American corporation was prosecuted on criminal charges. Prosecutors alleged that Ford knew Pinto gas tanks could catch fire during rear-end collisions but failed to warn the public or fix the problem out of concern for profits. Ford attorneys argued that the Pinto was in compliance with federal standards. Ford was acquitted but was forced to pay millions of dollars in dozens of civil suits. Inquiries found that design changes to make the gas tanks safer would have cost only $11 per car, but Ford's own cost analysis studies had determined that it would be less costly to pay for deaths and injuries.[6] This lack of safety concern seriously damaged Ford's reputation and ultimately led to stricter industry safety standards. Balancing the bottom line with ethics is now seen as a smart business move.

Balancing the bottom line with ethics becomes even more important as companies try to gain a competitive advantage by empowering employees

CASE STUDIES IN THE NEWS

A biology high school teacher resigned in protest when the school board ordered her to give her students partial credit for a school project. The teacher stated that 28 high school sophomores plagiarized their projects, which amounted to 50 percent of their grade. She had warned students that if they plagiarized their projects, they would receive no credit. This order by the school board enabled many of the students to pass the class.

The district superintendent and the principal sided with the teacher. However, the district superintendent pointed out that he takes orders like everyone else and that the board is given the authority to make final decisions within the school district.[7]

1. *Have you ever been in a position where your values differed from those of an employer? What did you do?*
2. *Would you leave your job if you felt your employer was behaving unethically even if the behavior was legal? Why, or why not?*
3. *What kind of message do you believe the action by the school board sent to students? To parents? To the community?*

and pushing crucial decisions down to individuals at lower levels of the organization. Companies must be able to trust that their employees are making ethical decisions. In 1995, a 28-year-old trader who made unethical decisions and took unjustifiable risks with other people's money single-handedly toppled Barings PLC, England's oldest investment firm, which was founded in 1762.[8]

Both individuals and corporations must deal with ethical issues on a day-to-day basis. James Stoner and R. Edward Freeman in their book *Management* describe four levels of ethical issues:[9]

Levels of Ethical Issues

1. **Societal issues**   At the societal level, questions deal with the basic institutions in a society. For example, are Chinese Communists ethically correct when they suppress, imprison, or kill those who challenge their power? Is it ethical for the U.S. government to extend Permanent Normal Trade Relations to China when human rights violations are common there?

2. **Stakeholders' issues**   Stakeholders' issues pertain to appropriate treatment of and relationships with employees, suppliers, customers, shareholders, bondholders, and others. They deal with business policy, such as how much obligation a company has to notify its customers about the potential dangers of its products.

3. **Internal policy issues**   Questions of internal policy pertain to the relationship between a company and its employees at all levels. Examples are policies dealing with employee rights, due process, free speech, employee participation, and others.

4. **Personal issues**   Personal issues are the day-to-day questions that occur in every organization. They revolve around two basic questions: Do we have the right to treat other people as means to our ends? Can we avoid doing so?

At work, ethics concerns the ground rules on all four of these levels. Because most of our personal ground rules are already in place, making ethical decisions requires us to be critical of our own ground rules and to improve them. Occasionally, situations in business result in applying a set of ground rules different from those used in personal life. For instance, an organization may set ground rules that prohibit accepting gifts from vendors while you may feel that accepting the gift would not violate your personal standards.

What other common situations involve making the distinction between ethical and unethical actions? The following box describes some possible unethical behavior in personal and business settings.

Human Relations

Some Unethical Behaviors

Personal	Business
• Cheating on exams/tests	• Copying software programs
• Accepting credit for favors not performed	• Accepting gifts from subordinates and vendors
• Cheating on income tax reports	• Falsifying time/expense reports
• Betraying personal confidences	• Keeping unauthorized materials/monies
• Plagiarizing papers and projects; borrowing content from other sources (including web sites) without permission or citation	• Doing personal business on company time
• Violating minor traffic rules	• Taking company materials and supplies for personal use
• Downloading music files without paying for them	• Using company phone service and Internet access for personal use
• Making unauthorized copies of CDs and DVDs.	• Polluting the environment with toxic waste

Unethical behaviors may lead people to financial gain or other benefits, but the consequences may range from a guilty conscience to a fine or prison term. Corporations may gain sizable market shares and higher profits but, if exposed, may be faced with large fines and serious penalties as well as decreased sales and a loss of confidence from customers and the general public. Ethics is a concern for both individuals and organizations.

Does It CLICK?

When faced with a tough decision, see if it "CLICKS."

Consequences: What are the consequences if I do this? Who will benefit? Who will suffer?

Legal: Is it legal?

Image: Would I like to see this on the front page of the newspaper? Would I like to tell this to my kids?

Culture: Does this decision support or damage our organization's culture or values?

Knot: Does it cause a knot in my stomach?

Developed for Florida Power Corporation by Lee Gardenswartz, Ph.D., and Anita Rowe, Ph.D., of Gardenswartz & Rowe, Los Angeles, CA and Patricia Digh of Realwork, Washington, D.C. and reprinted by permission from Society for Human Resource Management Mosaics Diversity Newsletter.[10]

SOCIAL RESPONSIBILITY

Social responsibility plays a key role in decisions about pollution, discrimination, welfare, and the well-being of society.

Social responsibility is the obligation we have to make choices or decisions that are beneficial to the whole of society. These types of decisions most commonly involve issues such as environmental pollution, welfare, inflation, discrimination, and homeless and hungry people. Corporate social responsibility may be viewed from one of three perspectives: classical, accountability, and public.

Three different perspectives may affect our views on social responsibility.

The **classical perspective** holds that businesses need not feel responsible for social issues and should concentrate on being profitable, as an economy based on strong businesses best serves society overall. This view suggests that ethics should have little influence on decisions and that profit is the bottom line. We need only consider the effects this approach could have on our environment if no concern were shown for air quality or water pollution.

The **accountability perspective** holds businesses accountable for their actions, with a responsibility to be fair and considerate in their business practices. This view requires sensitivity to environmental and social issues and prevents unethical decisions in such matters as toxic waste disposal and discrimination against minorities, women, aged, or workers with disabilities.

Social responsibility is the obligation to make choices or decisions that are mutually beneficial to the whole of society.

©Getty Images/PhotoDisc

The **public perspective** links businesses with the government and other groups to solve social and environmental problems actively. This view requires involvement by all parties in improving the general quality of life. Decisions are made with the goal of profit for the business but also with consideration of impact on pollution or unemployment.

Recent events suggest a need for more ethical decision making.

From any of these perspectives, ethics plays a critical role in the decisions to be made. Should a company pollute the air or water because control devices are expensive to install and would reduce profits? Should the company install expensive pollution devices that may have a negative impact on the budget and cause employee layoffs, affecting local unemployment problems? Considering these questions makes more obvious the relationships of values, integrity, and ethics. All three must be exercised in situations involving social responsibility.

With the enormous escalation in numbers of unethical practices in recent years, we are left wondering whether we are living in a mindless, valueless society on a path of destruction or whether we are overexposed to excessive media coverage of unethical behavior and corporate greed. In either case, individuals and organizations now have a greater obligation to improve current ethical practices.

CASE STUDIES IN THE NEWS

Unethical practices cut across all occupations.

 Unethical behavior has been with us throughout history. From all appearances, however, the United States is currently suffering a crisis in ethics. Television news broadcasts and newspapers (beginning in the 1960s and mushrooming through the 2000s) have been filled with reports of unethical business practices and unethical personal behaviors. Few professions or occupations are left unscathed. Corporate CEOs, bankers, doctors, lawyers, government officials, defense contractors, investment counselors, food and medicine manufacturers, and military employees are being indicted in unprecedented numbers for a variety of unethical activities.

1. *Were these kinds of events happening in previous years but unnoticed because the ethical culture of those times was different? Do you believe that Americans have become less ethical?*

2. *To what do you attribute the current trends in ethics?*

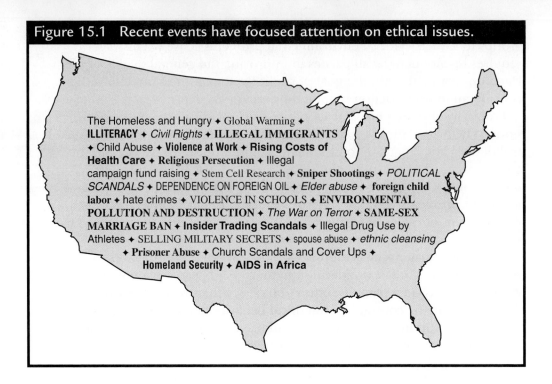

Figure 15.1   Recent events have focused attention on ethical issues.

The Homeless and Hungry ✦ Global Warming ✦ **ILLITERACY** ✦ *Civil Rights* ✦ **ILLEGAL IMMIGRANTS** ✦ Child Abuse ✦ **Violence at Work** ✦ **Rising Costs of Health Care** ✦ **Religious Persecution** ✦ Illegal campaign fund raising ✦ Stem Cell Research ✦ **Sniper Shootings** ✦ *POLITICAL SCANDALS* ✦ DEPENDENCE ON FOREIGN OIL ✦ *Elder abuse* ✦ **foreign child labor** ✦ hate crimes ✦ VIOLENCE IN SCHOOLS ✦ **ENVIRONMENTAL POLLUTION AND DESTRUCTION** ✦ *The War on Terror* ✦ **SAME-SEX MARRIAGE BAN** ✦ **Insider Trading Scandals** ✦ Illegal Drug Use by Athletes ✦ SELLING MILITARY SECRETS ✦ spouse abuse ✦ *ethnic cleansing* ✦ **Prisoner Abuse** ✦ Church Scandals and Cover Ups ✦ **Homeland Security** ✦ **AIDS in Africa**

Aside from the media keeping the subject in the forefront, the public seems to have reached the full span of the pendulum swing. Public opinion now reflects the sentiment, "We are fed up. Let's all play by the rules."

At the base of all these activities are human beings placed in positions of making ethical decisions. All bring their own set of standards, traditions, rules, and values, and all must struggle with deciding what is ethical.

*Fast*Chat

We hear reports of unethical behavior daily.

1. Name recent sports, business, religious, or political leaders whose ethical conduct has been exposed. What were the consequences?

2. Joseph de Maistre wrote in 1821, "Every nation has the government it deserves." That is, leaders reflect something about the people who vote for them and put them in power. In light of this statement, what American attitudes and values have been reflected by the ways in which the war on terror has been handled?

Experts in business ethics have identified many methods to assist workers in evaluating whether decisions are ethical. Five of these methods are described below.[11]

Methods for Evaluating Ethical Decisions

1. **Legality**	Is your decision within the legal limits? Laws governing situations usually correct some previous misjudgment or define the boundaries of an activity. Some people believe that if a decision complies with current laws, it will by definition be ethically sound. Other people suggest that the demonstration of ethics begins where the law ends.
2. **Personal morality**	Personal commitment to uphold human rights and dignity will almost always ensure ethical choices. This method reflects personal integrity and moral sensitivity.
3. **Enlightened self-interest**	Some people argue that organizations should promote socially responsible behavior because it is good business. This idea, termed **enlightened self-interest**, suggests that organizations' and people's best interests are served by being genuinely concerned for others. The internal payoff for being socially responsible may be self-esteem. External payoffs may be higher profits and other measurable consequences.
4. **Corporate or professional codes of ethics**	Many organizations attempt to institutionalize ethical policies and decision making in a number of ways, such as ethics committees and training in ethics. One popular approach is adoption of a **code of ethics** that requires and prohibits specific practices. Although few companies actually display their codes, most will dismiss, demote, or reprimand employees who intentionally violate the codes. Codes may not actually change people's behaviors, but proponents argue that they do communicate to employees that the company is committed to its standards and is asking employees to adopt them. Codes of ethics are sometimes categorized in two ways: corporate, if they are for business organizations, and professional, if they are for a specific professional group. The National Management Association's Code of Ethics appears on the next page. Following these types of standards when making your decisions will influence your choices in a positive manner.
5. **Common practices**	The means of ethical decision making known as common practices relies on the belief that "everyone else does it this way." This method is least likely to ensure ethical choices. If others accept gifts from contract bidders, following their example does not make you right.

The National Management Association's Code of Ethics[12]

- I will recognize that all individuals inherently desire to practice their occupations to the best of their ability.
- I will assume that all individuals want to do their best.
- I will maintain a broad and balanced outlook and will recognize value in the ideas and opinions of others.
- I will be guided in all my activities by truth, accuracy, fair dealing, and good taste.
- I will keep informed on the latest developments in techniques, equipment, and processes. I will recommend or initiate methods to increase productivity and efficiency.
- I will support efforts to strengthen the management profession through training and education.
- I will help my associates reach personal and professional fulfillment.
- I will earn and carefully guard my reputation for good moral character and good citizenship.
- I will promote the principles of our American Enterprise System to others by highlighting its accomplishments and displaying confidence in its future.
- I will recognize that leadership is a call to service.

The National Management Association
Reprinted by permission of the National Management Association

CONFLICTS IN ETHICAL DECISION MAKING

Legality, personal morality, enlightened self-interest, codes of ethics, and common practices may help you make ethical decisions.

Relying on our value system to guide us in our decision making will most often result in ethically sound judgments. We may, however, experience conflicts with this method when we operate in an environment that does not share similar values. Operating in certain other ethnic cultures, for example, may create difficulties. What may be considered unethical in our culture may be perfectly acceptable in another. In some cultures, for example, expectations are that government officials will be given "gratuities" for services rendered. In the United States, this is considered not only unethical but also illegal.

Ethical dilemmas challenge us to make the right choices.

The Foreign Corrupt Policy Act of 1977 was passed to guard against such conflicts. This law requires U.S. companies to operate ethically in their worldwide business dealings, and the U.S. Justice Department polices activities of U.S. companies overseas to prevent unethical actions. Specifically, the act makes it illegal for a U.S. person and certain foreign issuers of securities to make a corrupt payment to a foreign official for the purpose of obtaining or retaining business for or with, or directing business to, any person. Since 1998, the provisions also apply to foreign firms and persons who take any act in furtherance of a corrupt payment while in the United States.[13]

SOLVING ETHICAL DILEMMAS

Ethical dilemmas, or conflicts in values, arise when our sense of values or social responsibility is questioned internally or challenged externally. "Examples of Personal and Business Ethical Dilemmas," on the next page, provides examples of situations that may be considered ethical dilemmas. These dilemmas are separated into personal situations and business situations. Do any of these dilemmas seem familiar? Think about how you handled them or what ethical decision you might make.

The heart of ethical dilemmas is not whether you know what is right or wrong, but whether you will choose the right behavior. Individuals must decide whether they are willing to risk making a decision that challenges wrongdoing even though that decision may result in losing or not obtaining something desired. An example would be filling out your time sheet showing a few extra hours that you did not work because you want money to buy a new outfit. You feel that without the new clothes, you will not be able to impress your friends, which is very important to you. Obviously, the ethical choice would be to report your time correctly and find some other way to save or earn the money for the outfit.

GLOBAL CONNECTION

In 2000, Gap, Inc. was contacted by a TV journalist stating that a Gap supplier in Cambodia was using child labor and had in its employ a 12-year-old. At that time, Gap, Inc. allowed its Cambodian factories to verify employee ages by using a "family book" because through the decades of genocide and war these are often the only records of birth. The factory claimed the child was old enough to work legally. The journalist said he had verified the age of the child.

The garment industry in Cambodia accounts for about a third of that country's gross domestic product. The industry provides jobs for many, especially women and young people, who have very few income options. This steady income is essential for educating siblings and stabilizing families that struggle to exist on subsistence farming.[14]

1. *If you were in charge of a business in the garment industry, would you fire all the children who appeared to be under 15 (the legal age to work in Cambodia)? Why, or why not?*

2. *If you did not terminate the children and the American public learned you employed underage children, how would you handle it?*

Examples of Personal and Business Ethical Dilemmas

Personal	Business
Should I pay at the checkout counter for the grapes I tasted in the produce aisle?	Should I accept these basketball tickets from my contractors?
Should I tell the salesclerk that the item I am purchasing is mismarked with a lower price?	Should I pad my trip expense report to pick up a few extra dollars?
Should I turn in to lost and found the billfold I found in the ladies' lounge?	Should I copy this new computer software to load onto my PC at home?
Should I count cash payments as income on my taxes?	Should I use the office copier to run copies of the recipe for the cake Jane brought in this morning?
Should I tell the bank they have credited my account with extra amounts of money?	Should I type my term paper on the company's PC during duty hours?
Should I accept exam answers from another student?	Should I select my old basketball team member for the job opening or the most technically qualified applicant?
Should I take this book from the library without properly checking it out with the desk clerk?	Should I pressure my new employee for a date this weekend?
Should I completely stop at the stop sign even though there is no one around for miles?	Should I pay my quarter for the coffee or just enjoy a free cup?
Should I take credit for a school project even though I borrowed content from a web site?	Should I authorize the dumping of this waste material into a remote landfill site without proper hazardous waste handling and labeling?
Should I download music without paying for it?	
Should I buy/sell stocks based on insider information?	Should I modify reports to show a better financial picture to managers and stockholders?

Responses to value conflicts are different for each individual. Some people may respond physically with ulcers, alcoholism, or mental disturbance. Others will show no symptoms and easily adjust their value to the new accepted norm.

If your boss asked you to bend the rules, how would you react? An article in *Working Woman* by Pat Amend suggests the following steps:[15]

1. *Validate the conflict.* It may not be real. You may not have all the facts. Ask straightforward questions in a nonthreatening way: "Are we allowed to do that in our work agreement?"

2. *Assess the risks involved.* How much are you personally willing to risk? Amend quotes Barbara Ley Toffler, author of *Tough Choices: Managers Talk Ethics,* as saying, "Everyone has to decide where the line is. You have to pick your cause." Doing a cost-benefit analysis to assess the possible harm versus the probable benefits of your choice may clearly guide your decision.

3. *Act on your decision.* Decide, and then proceed with tact. If you are willing to take the risk, you might mention that you are uncomfortable with what you have been asked to do. Rather than making accusations, give your boss a chance to save face or reverse the request.

4. *Get help in a troubled situation.* If the talk with your boss does not resolve the situation, seek help from a slightly senior-level manager you know and trust. Reporting decisions, policies, or practices within the organization that we consider to be detrimental or illegal is known as **whistleblowing**. It also can include publicizing such behavior to people outside the organization, which is a sensitive matter. Correcting detrimental or illegal situations may involve replanning, redesigning, and reworking, hence, much time and money. For this reason, many managers choose to ignore these situations. If you go to someone above you, you should be subtle and not name names or point fingers. Approach this advisor with a general question, such as "Does the company usually do this?"

5. *Consider a change in jobs.* If your boss's ethics are in conflict with yours, you may choose to transfer or leave the company. The majority of business executives in the United States agree that in order to be ethical in business, you need the support of an ethical boss. Although individuals can behave ethically on their own, they may be "frozen out" by the boss. You may, therefore, adjust your ethics in order to survive professionally in this particular organization. Self-esteem begins to erode, and by age 50, you may not like yourself any more, but you may be reluctant to leave because you are locked into a high salary and comfortable benefits. You have become the organization.

> These steps may be useful in ethical decision making.

*Q*uick tip ....

Various federal and state laws protect whistleblowers from retaliation by their employers for reporting illegal activities. Despite these laws, those who blow the whistle often, if they are not fired, are isolated at work and made to feel irrelevant. Many suffer from depression or alcoholism. Cynthia Cooper, who revealed that WorldCom had covered up $3.8 billion in losses and was named by *Time Magazine* as a person of the year in 2002, said, "There have been times I could not stop crying."[16]

Before you blow the whistle, consider the following:[17]

- Is what you're about to tell everyone so bad that it is worth taking the risk?
- Would others agree with what you are about to say?
- Can what you say be proved?
- Will what you say make a difference?

Authors Kenneth Blanchard and Norman Vincent Peale provide a simple three-step approach to resolving ethical dilemmas. In their book, *The Power of Ethical Management,* they offer the following questions to be used in an ethics check of behavior:[18]

1. Is it legal? Will you be violating any laws or company policies?

2. Is it balanced? Will your decision be fair to all parties concerned, and will it promote a win-win situation?

3. How will my decision make me feel about myself? Will I be proud of my choice? Will I feel good when my family reads about my decision in the local newspaper?

Blanchard and Peale think that ethical behavior is strongly related to self-esteem and that people who feel good about themselves are more able to make ethical decisions and withstand the pressures against those choices.

One other approach to ethical decision making, suggested by Stoner and Freeman, is a questioning process using common morality. Common morality is a set of ground rules covering ordinary ethical problems. These questions may help you when faced with ethical dilemmas:[19]

Questions that May Help When You Are Faced with Ethical Dilemmas	
Promise keeping	Am I keeping promises that I have made?
Nonmalevolence	Am I refraining from harming other people?
Mutual aid	Am I helping someone else if the cost is not too great for me to bear?
Respect for persons	Am I treating people as ends in themselves, rather than as mere means to my own ends? Am I taking them seriously, accepting their interests as legitimate, and regarding their desires as important?
Respect for property	Do I have the consent of others before using their property?

*Fast*Chat

1. Review the "Methods for Evaluating Ethical Decisions" at the beginning of this section. Think of recent stories in the news where problems resulted from unethical decisions. Applying which methods might have avoided these problems?

2. Review the questions above that may help you when you are faced with ethical dilemmas. Which have you dealt with lately? Using situations you feel comfortable revealing, discuss how you handled these questions.

Companies are addressing business ethics by publishing written standards. According to a 2003 Business Ethics Survey conducted by the Society for Human Resource Management's Ethics Resource Center, 79 percent of respondents said that their organizations had written standards.[20] However, critics point to the fact that recent scandals have occurred at companies with big, well funded ethics programs such as Halliburton's Engineering and Construction Group and Boeing.[21] Even Arthur Andersen, the accounting firm that imploded after having signed off on Enron's books, had a strong ethics program.[22]

> Companies are working to improve their tarnished ethics.

To put more teeth into their written standards, many companies are doing such things as adding sanctions, requiring employees to sign off on policies, developing a confidential system for reporting wrongdoings, and increasing training. SAP, the German software giant, has added a sanctions section to their ethics code that warns that unethical behavior could lead to consequences affecting employment and to possible external investigations, civil law proceedings, or criminal charges.[23]

ETHICS CONNECTION

A workplace ethics survey released in 2004 by Watson Wyatt Worldwide of over 1,200 U.S. employees revealed that nearly 60 percent of workers believe that upper-level managers in their organization are lacking in integrity and honesty. Three-fourths of this same group, however, believed that their immediate boss was trustworthy. Hypocrisy and favoritism were the top reasons business leaders acted unethically according to those surveyed. Only 8 percent said dishonest financial dealings were at the root of unethical behavior.

When asked whether they were pressured to act unethically, fewer than 10 percent said they were often pressured, 22 percent said they were sometimes pressured, and 70 percent said they were infrequently or never pressured.[24]

1. *Have you ever felt you were being pressured to violate company policies in order to achieve business objectives? If so, what did you do?*

2. *What do you think employees should do when they observe their coworkers lying to supervisors, lying on reports, stealing, engaging in sexual harassment, abusing drugs, or engaging in conflicts of interest?*

Commitment, communication, mutual trust, and enforcement by top management are the keys to a successful ethics program.

Tyco International, which was embarrassed by the lavish spending and parties of its CEO L. Dennis Kozlowski, now requires employees to take an annual six-hour online training course that introduces concepts ranging from what you should do if you believe unethical behavior has occurred to sexual harassment. A hotline for employees to report violations has also been established.[25]

Even the most detailed, well constructed ethics program will not be successful without commitment, communication, and mutual trust, with the tone set by top management. The keys are the CEO, a board with independent members, a system of checks and balances on management in place throughout the company, and a mechanism to allow complaints to surface. A strong code of ethics, written rules, and corporate procedures are important, but without strong commitment and enforcement from senior management, they are merely words on paper. Communicating expectations through continuous training programs may serve to build the mutual trust required in an effective ethics program.

Additionally, publicly traded companies must comply with new federal regulations. In 2002, Congress enacted an important business reform act. The **Sarbanes-Oxley Act** of 2002 (named for the senator and congressman who drafted the bill) is a set of complex regulations that protects investors and enforces corporate accountability and responsibility by requiring

TECHNOLOGY CONNECTION

Technology brings with it the potential for a whole new range of unethical behavior. It is now possible to alter photographs and videos or to create viruses that will ruin thousands of computers. It is also easy to spread information widely via the Internet—and not necessarily accurate information. E-mail in-boxes fill up with unwanted advertisements, "urban legends," scams, and other e-mails of dubious origin.

1. *How can you discover what information is real and what has been distorted?*

2. *Is it wise to take things we read or see on the Internet without questioning the source or the validity? Why, or why not?*

3. *Do individuals who disseminate information over the Internet have an obligation to be truthful?*

4. *What steps can you take to protect yourself and others from untruthful, altered, or otherwise unethical material, both on the Internet and elsewhere (TV, bookstore, gossip, etc.)?*

accuracy and reliability of corporate accounting and disclosures. Also known as the Corporate and Criminal Fraud Accountability Act of 2002, the bill was passed quickly as a response to increased corporate fraud, accounting scandals, and record-breaking bankruptcies. The act grants the Securities and Exchange Commission increased regulatory control and imposes greater criminal and compensatory punishment on executives and com-panies that do not comply. It also establishes procedures for handling whistleblower complaints.[26]

©Getty Images/PhotoDisc

Companies today must be committed to preventing unethical and illegal behavior.

uick wit ....

"Anyone who proposes to do good must not expect people to roll stones out of his way, but must accept his lot calmly if they even roll a few more upon it."

Dr. Albert Schweitzer,
Humanitarian and Medical Missionary

*Fast*Chat

1. In what areas do you think companies can offer ethical guidance?

2. Sometimes people suggest that the government should establish more guidelines for behavior for individuals, both on the job and off. For what issues might government guidelines be helpful? What are the dangers of too much government intervention?

You are ultimately responsible for your own behavior.

Behaving ethically and responsibly enhances your life, makes human interactions less stressful and more rewarding, and boosts self-esteem. Additionally, understanding ethics and behaving appropriately can make or break your career. Anyone working today needs to take the following measures:

1. *Know your own value system.* Explore with yourself your own value systems and beliefs. Understand the events in your childhood that shaped your values. If you feel that some areas are not fully developed, pursue ethical teachings to help you fill any gaps.

2. *Learn about and respect the value systems of others.* Remember that others grew up in different circumstances and may have developed a different set of values. Learn to respect those values.

3. *Learn about the ethics and the norms of your place of business.* If your business has a written ethics policy or guidelines, be sure you are familiar with them. If there is no written code, then ask questions to determine how management views certain behavior. For instance, before giving a gift to a supervisor, inquire of others around you if this is an accepted practice.

4. *When confronted with something that feels uncomfortable, take time to think.* Use some of the techniques suggested in this chapter in order to sort out how you wish to handle the situation. Make a list of your options and the pros and cons before you decide what to do.

5. *The decision must be your own.* Remember, in the end, you must live with whatever decision you make. You will reap the benefits or pay the consequences.

*Fast*Chat

Individual values start developing in childhood.

1. Which values are you most likely to learn at home? How might a home situation affect your values?

2. What values should be taught in school?

3. When do you believe training in business ethics should begin—high school? College? Why?

4. Do you feel that it would be better to change your value system or to leave a job where your values differ from those of the company or your supervisors? Explain.

CHAPTER SUMMARY

Ethics is the application in decision making of values learned in early years. Our environment influences these values heavily. Personal ethics involves decisions outside work, whereas business ethics applies to work-related decisions. Beginning in the 1960s, unethical practices began to escalate, resulting in today's ethics crisis. Unethical practices have penetrated political, environmental, religious, military, business, and sports fields, affecting all of us. The topic of ethics is now receiving attention in hopes of reversing this trend.

The five most common methods for determining appropriate ethical standards are following common practices, checking the legality of the action, considering enlightened self-interest, abiding by codes of ethics, and relying on personal morality.

Each person is faced with ethical dilemmas in everyday life situations. These dilemmas involve making decisions on issues that question our value system. Several steps guide ethical decision making: validate the conflict, assess risk, decide, get help, and, if necessary, change jobs.

To improve business practices at publicly traded companies, the U.S. government passed the Sarbanes-Oxley Act in 2002. Companies also issue codes of ethics and ethical standards handbooks. Training programs are used to reinforce company positions on ethical issues. Top management participates in these programs to emphasize their importance. In order to deal more effectively with ethical issues, you need to know yourself and your values, know and respect the values of others, make an effort to learn your company's values, explore situations before acting, and then make the best decision you can.

Key Terms

ethics

integrity

values

social responsibility

classical perspective

accountability perspective

public perspective

enlightened self-interest

code of ethics

Foreign Corrupt Policy Act

ethical dilemmas

whistleblowing

Sarbanes-Oxley Act

REVIEW QUESTIONS

1. Explain the differences among ethics, values, integrity, and social responsibility.

2. Identify two recent events that have fostered the current emphasis on ethics.

3. What are some of the methods used in determining ethical standards?

4. What is meant by ethical dilemmas?

5. What methods can you use in dealing with ethical dilemmas?

6. What steps are companies and the federal government taking to improve the standards of ethics within companies?

DISCUSSION QUESTIONS

1. From the illustration at the top of page 422, select the three events that you think have had the most profound effect on ethics in business. Why did you pick those three events?

2. Review the figure "Examples of Personal and Business Ethical Dilemmas" on page 426. Which of the dilemmas in the chart have you faced? Are some of them ones that you have not faced but have seen others deal with?

3. Does the company for which you work have a code of ethics or some other form of ethics program? Discuss that program and its effectiveness.

4. Name an ethical issue with which you are faced or expect to be faced. Make a list of the pros and cons each decision will bring.

CHAPTER PROJECTS

TEAMWORK

WRITING

WEB

With your class divided into two groups, discuss the different sides of the following ethical dilemmas. Choose one of the dilemmas and write a position paper in which you defend your opinion and explain how you came to your decision.

1. The XYZ Company wants to build a new, modern facility on the outskirts of your town, which has been suffering economic difficulty for a long time with high unemployment and low wages for the jobs that do exist. However, an environmental survey discovered that a rare bird that lives only in the area has its main nesting ground where the company

Human Relations

wants to build the factory. If the factory is built there, the bird will most likely become extinct. The company has tax incentives from other cities that want the factory, but it prefers your site.

2. You are a high-level manager in the Last Chance Corporation. You have been in talks with the management of your company and know that a large layoff is about to take place. You are aware that one of your employees is about to close on the purchase of a new house. Shortly after the close, he will be laid off. You have been told that everything is strictly confidential and you are not to tell anyone about the layoff.

3. You and your best friend work at a fast food restaurant. Your friend has been giving free meals to his girlfriend who comes into the restaurant. Your friend feels that he doesn't get paid enough for what he does, and, since the company is so big, the meals will never be missed. You are behind the counter and the girlfriend comes in. She expects you to give her a free meal. What are your options? What should you do?

As an alternative project, locate an example of inaccurate, distorted, or damaging information spread via the Web or e-mail. Explain why you suspected the information was false or dubious. Find at least two sources that provide conflicting information on the subject and write a summary of your findings.

APPLICATIONS

In small groups, analyze the following situations:

All Money Is Green

Guy Walters is the chief executive officer of a major engineering firm. He has been appointed committee chair for the High Speed Transportation System (HSTS). This group is expected to develop a viable method of transporting mass quantities of products safely and quickly to major distribution points around the world. Funding for this project has come from many companies interested in rapidly moving their products into global marketplaces. Guy feels strongly about making a success of this project and believes that it will greatly benefit the transportation industry, his company, and his personal career.

In a meeting with Shalonda Hall, his chief financial officer, Guy discovers that his budget is too limited to complete the project. Shalonda explains that they are confined by the company's policies to using the HSTS funds and that getting approval for additional funding will be difficult.

"We'll just have to bring the matter before the executive board and request additional funds before we can go on," explained Shalonda.

Guy responded to the news with, "I don't want to do that! You know how they feel about budget overruns. Why can't we just divert some of the leftover funds from other study programs to wrap up this thing? What's the big deal anyway? All money is green! We are all working toward the same end—profits for the company. We're so near completion on this job that I don't want to slow the progress by begging for dollars. Go do some of that 'creative financing' for which you budget people are famous. They'll never know the difference!"

1. What is the ethical issue in this situation?

2. What does Guy mean by "all money is green"? Is he correct?

3. How should Shalonda respond to Guy's instructions?

4. How would you resolve the ethical dilemma Shalonda faces?

The Bootlegged Booty

TEAMWORK

John was to report to the office on Monday as the new supervisor. Alan was eager to make a good impression on his new boss and had heard John was fond of using his PC. As a special treat, Alan decided to load John's new laptop with all the bootlegged software that he had acquired over the last few years. He knew John would need some of the applications as soon as he hit the door. Getting software orders through the regular channels took as much as several weeks and then only if you knew someone to pull strings for you. He felt that John would appreciate his outfitting the laptop and he could make some points.

When John arrived on Monday and discovered that his PC was loaded with software that was not authorized, he immediately called his staff together for a meeting. He told them that he felt very strongly about the ethical issues in question in copying software and that he had asked the software specialists to unload the bootlegged copies from his machine. "I have also asked them to remove all illegal copies from your machines. We should be able to order whatever we need. That may take a while, but at least we'll be legal."

1. Why did Alan think that John would appreciate the added software?

2. Could Alan have handled this situation so that John would have felt more comfortable? How?

3. Do you think that John acted responsibly by ordering that all machines be legal, even though it might temporarily limit the working capability of his staff?

4. How would you have handled this dilemma?

ADDITIONAL READINGS AND RESOURCES

Alford, Fred C. *Whistleblowers: Broken Lives and Organizational Power.* Ithaca, NY: Cornell University Press, 2002.

Corey, Gerald. *Issues and Ethics in the Helping Professions (with InfoTrac).* Belmont, CA: Wadsworth Publishing, 2002.

Fritzsche, David J. *Business Ethics: A Global and Managerial Perspective,* 2nd ed. Columbus, OH: McGraw-Hill/Irwin, 2004.

His Holiness the Dalai Lama. *Ethics for the New Millennium.* New York: Penguin/Riverhead Books, 2001.

Maxwell, John C. *Making Decisions.* New York: Time Warner, 2003.

Meese, Edwin, and P. J. Ortmeier. *Leadership, Ethics and Policing: Challenges for the 21st Century.* Upper Saddle River, NJ: Pearson Education, 2003.

Miethe, Terance D. *Whistleblowing at Work: Tough Choices in Exposing Fraud, Waste, and Abuse on the Job (Crime & Society).* Scranton, PA: Westview Press, 1999.

Mitchell, Charles. *A Short Course in International Business Ethics: Combining Ethics and Profits in Global Business* The Short Course in International Trade Series. Novato, CA: World Trade Press, 2003.

Weber, Max, Talcott Parsons, and Anthony Giddens Routledge. *The Protestant Ethic and the Spirit of Capitalism,* 2nd ed. New York: Routledge, 2001.

For additional resources, refer to the web site for this text: school.cengage.com/career/dalton

Employee Rights:
Working Toward Mutual Respect

focus

Today's workers' rights are protected by federal and state regulations, and companies that do not comply are subject to severe penalties:

- The Wage and Hour Division of the U.S. Department of Labor secured over 80,000 workers in low-wage industries $39,000,000 in back wages in fiscal year 2003. Groups targeted included garment manufacturing, agriculture, day care, restaurants, janitorial services, and temporary help.[1]

- When charged with unfair labor practices by the National Labor Relations Board, the owners of South Coast Refuse Corporation agreed to make an $850,000 compliance settlement, pay $40,250 in fines, and recognize and bargain with the union.[2]

- The Occupational Safety and Health Administration issued citations alleging willful and serious safety violations and proposed monetary penalties to Triram Corporation after a worker died in the explosion of an asphalt tank. According to OSHA, the worker was directed to do welding work on top of the 10,000 gallon tank without being informed of the dangers of the tank's hazardous materials.[3]

Should federal and state governments do more to protect workers? Are you willing to pay extra taxes to increase compliance efforts? Why, or why not?

in this chapter

Local, state, and federal laws regulate various aspects of employment. These regulations cover employment discrimination, family and medical leave, fair labor standards, the right to bargain collectively, employee safety and health, employee benefits, and miscellaneous employee rights. Both individuals and organizations need to understand and abide by these regulations.

Individuals should understand what their rights are and how to take appropriate action when those rights are violated. Sometimes employees assume they have rights on the job that they, in fact, do not have. Problems may arise when employees act on these assumptions. The consequences can range from lost promotions or raises to disciplinary action or termination.

Organizations also need to be aware of, and respect, employee rights. Violating employee rights can lead to costly investigations by federal and/or state agencies. These investigations require the submission of paperwork and can disrupt the workplace by removing employees from the job to provide witness statements. In addition, employees may spend time discussing or worrying about the impending investigations rather than working. Violations may require payment of fines or back pay and reinstatement of employees. Payment for damages may be required as a result of a lawsuit. More important, employees whose rights are abused will be unhappy and less productive. Ideally, organizations will treat employees well and fairly not only because it is a smart business tactic, but also because it is the right thing to do.

Because laws in the area of employee rights change rapidly, both employees and organizations must keep track of changes. *Consult a lawyer for recent changes in legislation discussed in this chapter and for an explanation of state and local laws.*

> QUICK WIT
>
> "[Our mission is] to protect the workers in their inalienable rights to a higher and better life; to protect them, not only as equals before the law, but also in their health, their homes, their firesides, their liberties as men, as workers, as citizens; to overcome and conquer prejudices and antagonism."
>
> Samuel Gompers, American labor leader

EMPLOYMENT DISCRIMINATION

Abraham Lincoln abolished slavery on January 1, 1863, by signing the Emancipation Proclamation. However, in the late 19TH and early 20TH centuries, the freed slaves and their descendants continued to be deprived of their liberty and blocked in their pursuit of happiness through **discrimination**, or a difference in treatment based on a factor other than individual merit. A grassroots civil rights movement began in the 1950s, demanding that these inequities be corrected. As a result, several acts were passed to protect blacks and other groups against discrimination in the workplace.

Title VII of the Civil Rights Act of 1964, the Pregnancy Discrimination Act, the Equal Pay Act, the Age Discrimination in Employment Act, and the Americans with Disabilities Act were enacted to stop discrimination in the workplace. The **Equal Employment Opportunity Commission** (EEOC) is the federal agency responsible for enforcing these laws. These acts are briefly summarized below.

Title VII of the Civil Rights Act (1964) **Title VII of the Civil Rights Act of 1964** prohibits discrimination by companies that have 15 or more employees. Discrimination based on race, color, religion, sex, or national origin is forbidden. All terms, conditions, and privileges are covered—hiring, placement, training, promotions, transfers, layoffs, compensation, and terminations. This act also prohibits sexual harassment.[4]

Anyone Can Discriminate!

BIAS + INSTITUTIONAL POWER = DISCRIMINATION

Federal law requires equal treatment of workers, regardless of color, religion, sex, race, age, national origin, or disability.

In the past, some employers attempted to get around Title VII by setting specific qualifications for a position. For instance, some police departments set height and weight requirements that effectively eliminated females from the position of officer. Requiring a bona fide occupational qualification (BFOQ) curbed these practices. The employer must show a legitimate business necessity for eliminating certain groups of individuals from a job. Requiring proof that restrictions are bona fide has limited the use of discriminatory occupational qualifications by employers. However, some restrictions have been found to be valid. For instance, a producer may hire only women for a female role in a movie. Legitimate age limitations may be placed on some occupations, such as airline pilot. The courts have ruled, however, that preferences, such as females for airline attendants, are not BFOQs.

Quick tip

When determining whether you are being subjected to discrimination, remember the following:

• The law covers differences in treatment based on specific characteristics (such as race or gender). Adverse treatment because your boss "doesn't like you" or because you smoke is not covered by federal law.

- Civil Rights laws do not promise good treatment or even fair treatment, only equal treatment. You can be treated badly yet still equally.

- A disability or pregnancy does not give you permission to be less productive than other individuals in the workplace.

- Whether you have been sexually harassed depends on whether the behavior was "unwelcome." For example, you cannot laugh at off-color jokes or join in telling them and then complain that you have been harassed.

· ·

Pregnancy Discrimination Act (1978) The **Pregnancy Discrimination Act** is an amendment to the Civil Rights Act of 1964. An employer cannot refuse to hire a woman because of pregnancy as long as the woman is able to perform the job.[5]

A pregnant woman may work as long as she is able to perform the job and may not be required to stay out a certain length of time after the baby is born. Federal law does not require that special considerations, such as light duty, be made for pregnant women. It does, however, require that pregnant women be treated the same as other employees who are temporarily disabled. If nonpregnant individuals are given light duty, pregnant individuals must be allowed the same privilege.

A company is required to hold a job open for a woman on maternity leave the same length of time that jobs are held open for other employees who are on sick leave or disability leave but are not pregnant. This law does not guarantee a position upon return from maternity leave. If the company routinely fills positions of individuals who are sick for other reasons, it may legally fill positions of women who are on maternity leave. Some states, such as California, require that a position be held open for a certain length of time after the start of maternity leave.

Equal Pay Act (1963) **The Equal Pay Act** requires that men and women be paid the same for equivalent work. For instance, a male and female teacher with similar backgrounds and experience are to be paid equal salaries.[6]

Age Discrimination in Employment Act (1967) The **Age Discrimination in Employment Act** prohibits employers with 20 or more employees from discriminating based on age. The law covers individuals 40 years of age and older. As long as employees are able to perform their jobs, they cannot be forced to retire. However, an exception for highly paid corporate executives does exist.[7]

QUICK WIT

"We hold these truths to be self-evident, that all men and women are created equal."

Elizabeth Cady Stanton, American reformer and leader of the Women's Suffrage Movement

Employees must make clear that sexual harassment is unwelcome and report it immediately.

Sexual Harassment The Civil Rights Act of 1964 prohibits sexual harassment in the workplace. **Sexual harassment** includes any *unwelcomed* sexual advances, requests for sexual favors, or verbal or physical conduct of a sexual nature. Examples are telling sexually oriented jokes, standing too close, touching and making physical contact, displaying sexually oriented material, or making sexual comments about a person's body if these actions are unwelcome.[8b]

Either sex can commit sexual harassment. Men can harass women, and women can harass men. Additionally, men can harass men, and women can harass women. Harassment can be from a coworker, supervisor, an agent of the employer, or a nonemployee such as a repair person who comes on the company premises to perform work. Organizations are responsible for stopping the harassment from a coworker, nonemployee, or agent of an employer as soon as a management official becomes aware of the harassment. Furthermore, they are responsible for the harassment from a supervisor whether other management officials are aware of the harassment or not.

The law requires that employers provide an atmosphere free of sexual harassment. However, employees must make it clear that the harassment is unwanted. The individual being harassed should tell the harasser in no uncertain terms that the comments or actions are not appreciated and to stop. If the harassment continues, the victim should report the harassment to a management official or the human resources department.

The EEOC and Electrolux Home Products announced a voluntary resolution to allow more than 150 Somali Muslims a break to offer daily prayers at work at the Electrolux plant in St. Cloud, Minnesota. This break was already offered to other line employees. Allegations had been made that Muslim Somali employees were treated differently than similarly situated Somali employees with regards to the terms and conditions of their employment. Besides allowing employees to observe their sunset prayer, the agreement specifies that a Somali translator will be available on certain occasions, and policies and procedures will be available in Somali. Corporate managers, line leaders, and supervisors will undergo diversity training.[9]

In the past decade, religious discrimination charge filings with the EEOC have increased 85 percent. Why do you believe this has happened?

The Americans With Disabilities Act The **Americans with Disabilities Act** (ADA) prohibits discrimination against individuals who are disabled. Disabled individuals are those whose impairment (physical or mental) is severe enough to affect a major life activity. The individual with the disability must be able to perform the essential functions of the job, with or without reasonable accommodation. **Reasonable accommodation** is any

President Johnson signing the Civil Rights Act of 1964 into law.

©CORBIS

action that assists the disabled employee without imposing undue hardship on the company. It may include making existing facilities accessible to individuals with disabilities; job restructuring; part-time or modified work schedules; reassignment to a vacant position; acquisition or modification of equipment or devices; appropriate adjustment or modifications of examinations, training materials, or policies; the provision of qualified readers or interpreters; or similar accommodations for individuals with disabilities.[10]

RESPONDING TO DISCRIMINATION

If you think you have been the victim of discrimination, you should attempt to settle difficulties within your organization before resorting to outside sources. If your company has a grievance or complaint procedure, use this process. If such a procedure is unavailable, approach your supervisor or a responsible individual in the human resources department. Explain your concerns and difficulties in a calm, clear manner, using the communication skills from Chapter 4. Listen carefully to the explanations of the company officials. External circumstances of which you are not aware may exist. Work with your organization in good faith, giving the company a chance to correct the problem. Such action on your part demonstrates a belief that a person, not the company, is the problem.

QUICK WIT
"Injustice anywhere is a threat to justice everywhere."
Martin Luther King, Jr., American clergyman and Civil Rights leader

If the company will not take action, you should file a charge of discrimination with the Equal Employment Opportunity Commission or your state commission on equal employment. Employers, by law, cannot retaliate against individuals who have filed a charge of discrimination with the EEOC. However, companies can continue disciplinary action that is reasonable and expected and is administered to other employees not filing charges.[11]

Trends in Employment Opportunity **Affirmative Action**, a practice originally designed to correct past discriminatory practices against minorities and women in the workplace by setting goals for hiring and upward mobility, has become increasingly controversial. Companies who do business with the federal government as well as many who do business with state and local entities are still required to develop and implement an affirmative action program. Currently, the Supreme Court has ruled that these types of programs are constitutional only if they are "narrowly tailored" to remedy the lingering effects of past discrimination. However, the justices have not clearly defined how serious the effects must be to warrant favoring women and minorities in employment and contracting decisions. Increased dialogue on this topic can be expected. Lastly, current federal laws do not prohibit discrimination against gays and lesbians. Calls to

Human Relations

prohibit this type of discrimination can be expected to increase in the future.[12]

FAIR LABOR STANDARDS

As discussed in Chapter 1, the Industrial Revolution saw a major shift in the workforce from farms to factories. Unfortunately, this rush to fill the rapidly multiplying factories with workers often meant that children and women were exploited. Young children worked the same hours as adults, sometimes 12 to 14 hours a day or all night, and often worked in unsafe conditions. They were paid less than adults, which tended to lower the adult wage. Women also were subjected to low wages and long hours of work. Public concern mounted, and states began to pass laws restricting child labor and providing a minimum livable wage.

The mass unemployment during the Great Depression of the 1930s brought a public outcry to regulate hours of work in order to allow more individuals to be employed. The result was the first national legislation to regulate working hours, wages, and child labor, which is known as the Fair Labor Standards Act.

The **Fair Labor Standards Act** of 1938, as amended, sets the minimum wage, equal-pay, overtime, and child-labor standards for several types of employers and employees. These include employers engaged in interstate commerce or the production of goods for commerce and employees who are employed in enterprises engaged in commerce or the production of goods for commerce. Employers in retail and services whose sales volumes exceed a certain amount and agricultural workers are also covered. The minimum wage has slowly increased over the years and has been $5.15 an hour since September 1, 1997. A subminimum training wage allows employers to pay individuals under the age of 20 a training wage of $4.25 an hour for the first 90 days.[13]

Overtime provisions require payment of time and one-half of the employee's regular rate for all hours worked in excess of 40 hours per week except for those employees exempted from overtime (see box on next page). This base rate must include incentive pay or bonuses received in that week. A workweek is considered to be seven consecutive days and may begin on any day of the week. State and local governments are allowed to pay compensatory time in lieu of overtime.

Individuals under 18 years of age are not allowed to work in hazardous occupations. Individuals 14 and 15 years old are allowed to work in a limited number of industries and occupations, but work hours are restricted and duties cannot conflict with school. Exceptions to the age limitations are for actors and actresses, newspaper carriers, and those who work in the family business.

If you feel your rights to fair wages and hours have been violated, attempt to work it out with your employer first. If this attempt fails, contact the Wage and Hour Division of the U.S. Department of Labor.

Fair Labor Standards Act Exemptions from Overtime[14]

The following employees are exempt from the requirement that overtime be paid:

- White-collar workers—executives, administrators, professionals, computer professionals, and outside sales personnel;

- Workers in specific industries—transportation, bulk oil distributors, hospitals, seasonal business, communications, and agriculture;

- Workers performing specific types of work—commissioned retail salespeople, family members, fishermen, taxicab drivers, newspaper delivery people; and

- Employees working under special certificates—full-time students, learners, student-learners, apprentices, employees with disabilities, and messengers.

If you are uncertain whether or not someone is exempt, you can contact the Department of Labor regarding the application of current regulations.

Future Trends in Wage and Hour Issues Issues concerning payment of overtime are developing as companies are forced to become more competitive in the workplace and to respond to new federal legislation. Additionally, because of technology, work is becoming "virtual," enabling many employees to put in work hours away from the job.

Many organizations are finding that even with requirements to pay overtime, working skilled employees more than 40 hours a week is less expensive than hiring and training new workers. Also, employers, always eager to reduce costs, want to be able to offer compensatory time (time off for hours worked in lieu of pay) as state and local governments are allowed to do.

Furthermore, some professionals who are exempt from overtime are routinely putting in 70 to 80 hours a week. Many feel individuals working excessive hours are being exploited. Suggestions have been made to limit hours of work for everyone or to raise overtime pay to double pay.

Lastly, the idea of a livable minimum wage will continue to be an issue. Stories surface regularly of the working poor, who work 40 hours a week but earn so little that they are unable to afford decent housing or other basic necessities of life. Periods of inflation will further fuel this debate, as we search for a balance between the need for employers to remain competitive in the global economy and the need of the worker to survive.

CASE STUDIES IN THE NEWS

Since 1994, approximately 117 cities have enacted living wage ordinances requiring employers who work on public contracts or who receive government economic development subsidies to pay their employees enough to lift them out of poverty. This trend has occurred because the federal minimum wage has not risen since 1997 and many local governments have taken decently paid municipal jobs and put them in the hands of private contractors.

Two localities have expanded their regulations to cover all employers in their jurisdiction. In an effort to curb this trend, business groups are pressing state legislators to bar these types of laws.[15]

1. *Do you think that the minimum wage provides a viable living in a large metropolitan area? Why, or why not?*

2. *Do you think that jobs traditionally offered to minimum wage earners (mainly students or those with few skills) will disappear? Move to other locations? Why, or why not?*

3. *If companies were forced to pay more, what would be the effect on products you buy every day?*

4. *If wages are not increased, will charities and government aid programs be forced to provide increased assistance to employees and their families?*

"Who wants permission to stay late all next month?"

© 2001 Ted Goff www.tedgoff.com

Issues of overtime payment are a concern for companies as they try to stay competitive and comply with new federal legislation.

FAMILY MEDICAL LEAVE

As the workforce in the United States expanded with women, single mothers, and dual income families during the 1960s through 1980s, the need to balance work, health, and family responsibilities became more pressing. Many states began to pass laws designed to provide some sort of job-protected family or medical leave. Then, in 1993, the federal government addressed this need by passing the **Family Medical Leave Act (FMLA)**. The FMLA provides that eligible employees be allowed up to 12 workweeks of unpaid, job-protected leave within a 12-month period for:

- The birth or adoption of a child
- The placement for foster care of a child under 18 if not disabled, or over 18 if child is incapable of self-care
- The care of a child, spouse, or parent with a serious health condition
- An employee's own serious health condition.[16]

The leave can be taken consecutively or on an intermittent basis. Upon returning from leave, the employee, unless deemed to be a key employee, is entitled to return to the same position held before the leave or to a position that is equivalent in pay, benefits, privileges, and other terms and conditions of employment.

Eligibility Requirements for FMLA[17]

To be eligible for a job-protected leave under FMLA, you must:

- Be an employee who has been employed for a total of at least 12 months by the employer on the date on which any FMLA leave is to commence
- Have been employed, on the date on which any FMLA leave is to commence, for at least 1,250 hours with the employer granting the leave during the previous 12-month period
- Be employed in any U.S. state, the District of Columbia, or any U.S. territory or possession
- Be an employee who is employed at a work site at which the employer employs more than 50 employees, within a 75 mile radius, measured by the shortest route using surface transportation

---

*Fast*Chat

The federal government has passed legislation that restricts whom employers can hire and how much time off they must give employees.

1. Should the government intrude on the decisions businesses make? Why, or why not?

2. Are discrimination regulations still needed? Why, or why not?

Prior to the 1930s, working conditions for many of America's workers ranged from unpleasant to truly awful. Early in the Industrial Era, factories were little more than sweatshops, exploiting the worker with long hours, unsafe work conditions, and low wages—and even using child labor—as factories sprang up and the demand for goods exploded. Management emphasis was placed on the scientific approach popularized by Frederick W. Taylor (as discussed in Chapter 1). However, while Taylor's ideal was to make work efficient for the benefit of both management and labor, many adopted only the concept of maximizing productivity output, and workers' needs were ignored. Employers showed little concern for human relations, and workers had no voice in influencing their work environment.[18]

In an attempt to protect themselves, employees began to form associations to bargain collectively with employers over wages, hours, and working conditions and to protect themselves from unfair or arbitrary treatment. These organizations became known as **unions**.

These attempts by workers to unionize were resisted by management and routinely brought before the courts, which customarily ruled against labor union activities. Companies habitually used injunctions to halt strikes and boycotts to inhibit union activity. Other antiunion techniques used by management included firing labor agitators, blacklisting, yellow-dog contracts, and lockouts.[19]

> Early attempts to unionize were marred by conflict and controversy.

Management Anti-Union Tactics

Labor Agitators	Influential persons capable of rallying workers toward unionizing.
Blacklists	Names of labor agitators and other persons known to be sympathetic to unionizing efforts.
Yellow-Dog Contract	Condition of employment that required would-be employees to sign a statement that they would not start or join a union.
Lockouts	Company management locked the factory doors and shut down operations.

Labor agitators, once identified by company management, were immediately fired and their names placed on a blacklist. Company managers would pass these lists of potential troublemakers around to assure that union organizers were denied employment. The threat of unemployment had the desired result of discouraging active support for the labor movement.

When workers made demands for improved conditions or threatened early forms of strikes, company management could simply impose a lockout. Because companies could economically outlast the now unemployed worker, it was another effective means of discouraging union activities. The yellow-dog contract was also used until the **Norris-LaGuardia Act** of 1932 outlawed it, as a softening of antiunion attitudes began in the early 1930s. Occasionally, management of some shops even resorted to brutal and blatantly illegal methods to stop pro-union activities of employees.[20]

However, mounting public and congressional disfavor of these activities gave rise to the trend toward legalizing unions. Several key pieces of congressional legislation laid the framework for the labor movement and the unionization rights of workers. The Wagner Act of 1935, the Taft-Hartley Act of 1947, and the Landrum-Griffin Act of 1959 are of primary interest.

THE WAGNER ACT

The Wagner Act legitimized labor unions.

The National Labor Relation Act, passed in 1935, established the right of employees to form unions and bargain collectively with management on employment issues. More popularly known as the **Wagner Act**, this legislation ordered management to stop interfering with union organizing efforts and defined what constituted an unfair labor practice by management.[21]

Practices that Developed from the Wagner Act[22]

1. Management cannot fire or refuse to hire because individuals are union members.

2. Management cannot discriminate against a union member who files an unfair labor practice complaint or testifies before the National Labor Relations Board.

3. Management must bargain in good faith with a union and, once a union is elected, cannot recognize any other union.

4. Management can talk about the disadvantages of a union but cannot threaten, interrogate, or spy on individuals concerning union activities.

5. Management must allow union members to meet on their own personal time (such as lunch or breaks) to discuss union business but not on company time.

6. If employees strike for wages or working conditions, employers may hire replacements and are not obliged to rehire strikers unless so stated in the contract.

7. If employees strike over unfair labor practices (activities that violate the act), the employer must fire the replacements and take the strikers back when the strike ends.

The Wagner Act established the **National Labor Relations Board (NLRB)** as well. The NLRB is a government agency responsible for enforcing the provisions of the Wagner Act. Regional offices throughout the United States are often called upon to help resolve disputes and to police strike activities for violations of federal legislation.

Because the Wagner Act was so sweepingly pro-union, unions gained enormous power and frequently called strikes to force desired improvements in work conditions. In 1946, 113 million workdays were lost in union strikes, causing a major shift in public opinion about unions. Many industries were paralyzed, which affected the general public and set the stage for more restrictive labor legislation.[23]

The NLRB remains active in policing labor-management activities.

THE TAFT-HARTLEY ACT

The Taft-Hartley Act, also known as the Labor Management Act of 1947, was a series of amendments to the Wagner Act. It imposed certain controls on union organizing activities, internal union activities, and methods used by unions in collective bargaining attempts.

CASE STUDIES IN THE NEWS

In recent years, union membership has dwindled from a high of 36 percent of the workforce in the early 1950s to approximately 13.2 percent in 2002. In order to revitalize itself, the AFL-CIO (the federation of America's unions) launched Working America in 2003 to target U.S. workers who are not union members but who want to have their voices heard regarding important national, state, and local issues such as jobs, health care, and education. Dues will not be required, but a voluntary contribution of $5 is suggested.[24]

Working America will concentrate on concerns such as the gutting of overtime protections, privatizing Medicare and Social Security, and cutting back on education, health care, and homeland security programs for first responders. It will not be employment based, nor will it deal with employers for the purposes of collective bargaining, grievance handling, or any type of job-related representation.[25]

1. *Do you believe American workers still need traditional union protection? Why, or why not?*

2. *Would you join Working America? Why, or why not?*

1. Enables states to pass right-to-work laws (known as Section 14b).
2. Forbids discriminatory or excessive dues charging by unions of prospective employees.
3. Forbids make-work practices that force employers to pay for services not rendered.
4. Invokes the "cooling-off period," which allows the president to request an 80-day freeze on any strike that threatens national health or safety.
5. Requires unions to bargain in good faith with management.
6. Requires 60-day notices to be given of any impending contract termination.
7. Forbids unions to use coercive means for recruiting members.
8. Allows employees to settle grievances informally with management.

> Closed, union, and agency shops protected the union's rights to membership dues.

In a union shop, the worker need not be a union member at the time of hiring but is required to join the union within 60 to 90 days after employment. An agency shop requires workers to pay union membership dues whether or not they actually choose to join the union. This rule serves to protect the union from would-be free riders. Free riders are employees who received the same benefits as union members without paying dues. The group represented by the union, those for whom the union negotiates, is called a **bargaining unit**, and it is in the union's interest to have as many paying members as possible.[27] The Taft-Hartley

ETHICS CONNECTION

In a 2003 article in *Healthcare Financial Management,* Bernard Liebowitz states that most individuals agree practices such as allowing unsafe working conditions, exploiting foreign workers, or lying, cheating, and stealing are unethical for a business to utilize in order to make a profit. However, he raises concerns about what he calls "borderline ethical" practices such as cutting prices to destroy a competitor or keeping employee compensation low by cutting insurance benefits or paying minimum wage.

Other behaviors that can be considered "borderline ethical" are forcing suppliers to give steep discounts, delaying the payment of invoices for several months, and cutting corners wherever possible on workmanship or services.[28]

1. *Are these practices ethical? Why, or why not?*
2. *Should a publicly held company do everything humanly possible to keep expenses low and profits high to satisfy stockholders?*
3. *Are there any downsides to these practices?*
4. *Should the government force businesses to pay higher minimum wages and to provide health insurance at no cost?*

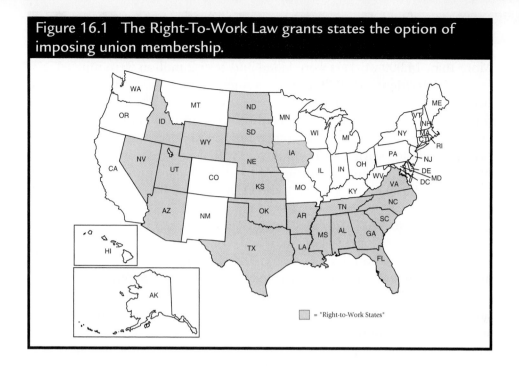

Figure 16.1 The Right-To-Work Law grants states the option of imposing union membership.

= "Right-to-Work States"

Act also contains a provision that individual states may pass right-to-work laws. The **Right-To-Work Law** allows states to give the worker the choice of union membership without compromise.[29]

Driven by reports of alleged corruption by union officials, Congress held extensive investigations that resulted in the passage of the Labor Management Reporting and Disclosure Act in 1959, also known as the **Landrum-Griffin Act**. This act requires unions to disclose the sources and disbursements of their funds, hold regularly scheduled elections of union officials by secret ballot, and restrict union officials from using union funds for personal means.[30]

> Corruption and misuse of funds by some union officials led to the Landrum-Griffin Act.

*Fast*Chat

1. What were the employment conditions in 1930s industrial America? Do any of these conditions still exist today in the United States? In other countries?

2. How do lifestyles, employment levels, and cost of living in some of these other countries differ from those in the United States?

3. Discuss two advantages of the Wagner Act and explain what the NLRB does.

4. What is the most important provision of the Taft-Hartley Act?

5. Why is the Landrum-Griffin Act important?

More than 14,000 workers were killed and over 2 million were injured in industrial accidents in 1970. Estimates suggested that 300,000 new cases of occupational disease were being discovered annually. These work-related injuries had steadily increased since the 1960s, and no end to this trend could be seen. Although many companies were concerned with safety and taking action to provide their employees with a safe environment, these individual actions were not considered sufficient. The public demanded action, which came in the form of the Occupational Safety and Health Act.[31]

Federal law requires employers to provide a safe work environment.

The **Occupational Safety and Health Act** was passed in 1970 to "assure so far as possible every working man and woman in the nation safe and healthful working conditions and to preserve our human resources." The act sets health and safety standards for U.S. businesses. **Safety** standards address hazards that can result in a direct injury, such as broken bones and cuts. **Health** standards address the role of the work environment in the development of diseases and illnesses, such as asbestosis and black lung. (Black lung, or pneumoconiosis, is a disease coal miners acquire from breathing air filled with coal dust.) These types of diseases are known as occupational diseases.[32]

The **Occupational Safety and Health Administration** (OSHA) was established as a federal agency to ensure that each employer provides a place of employment free of recognized hazards causing or likely to cause death or serious harm to employees. Almost all businesses that affect commerce (except government) are covered. However, only businesses with 10 or more employees, or those in certain retail, service, finance, real estate, or insurance industries, are required to keep records concerning occupational illnesses or injury.

OSHA establishes standards for safety and health in the workplace. These standards cover many facets of the work environment, such as training and safety procedures for operating hazardous machinery and equipment, instructions for handling dangerous chemicals, permitted noise levels, designation of protective equipment and clothing, and sanitation regulations.

In order to enforce the act, OSHA makes inspections of company sites. These visits may be unscheduled. Unscheduled visits may be in response to complaints of imminent danger or to deaths or catastrophes. Other visits are scheduled in advance. These visits can be prompted by a high injury rate or a specific type of injury reported. Sometimes OSHA chooses a certain industry to monitor.

Companies are responsible for providing a safe work environment.

©Getty Images/PhotoDisc

If violations are found during the visit, citations are issued. These citations must be posted in a public location in the workplace. In the case of gross violations, OSHA can secure a court order to close the facility. Failure to correct the infractions immediately can result in fines or jail sentences.

OSHA further requires that companies give employees access to certain information about the physical and health hazards of chemical substances produced, imported, or used in the workplace. This right-to-know regulation is known as Hazard Communication Standard (HCS).

Hazard Communication Standard (HCS) Requirements[33]

- Establish a written hazard communication program to inform employees of the potential dangers of hazardous substances used or encountered in the workplace.

- Train employees to handle hazardous chemicals as well as emergency and first aid procedures.

- Provide Material Safety Data Sheets (MSDS), which describe the chemical and the proper first aid treatment, and keep them where all employees have immediate access in an emergency.

- Place warning labels on all containers of potentially dangerous materials.

WORKING SAFELY

Every employee has a responsibility to follow OSHA and company rules concerning safety. If you work in an environment that requires goggles or a hard hat, your compliance with these regulations is extremely important. These measures may prevent your losing an eye or suffering a concussion. Even though workers' compensation helps support an employee who has been injured, payment in any amount can never make up for a lost hand or a damaged back. Specific tips for on-the-job safety are listed in Tips for Working Safely.

Tips for Working Safely

1. Observe all safety rules.

2. Wear personal protective equipment correctly.

3. Know how to operate all equipment properly. If you do not know, ask.

4. Check equipment before using to be sure it is in proper working condition.

5. Be alert for unsafe conditions.

6. Report any hazardous conditions or malfunctioning equipment immediately to your supervisor.

7. Do not participate in or condone horseplay while working in hazardous areas or while using equipment.

Accidents can be caused by incorrect lifting of equipment or supplies; careless operation of saws, lathes, or machinery with gears, pulleys, and belts; inattention while using hand tools; negligence while working with electricity; or falls on stairs, ladders, and scaffolds.

Office workers also need to be alert to safety. Time has been lost from injuries that occurred when file cabinets tipped over because too many drawers were opened at once. Falls on floors made slick by spilled coffee are another source of injury.

Those in the health care industry and those who deal with individuals in a variety of public settings need to follow guidelines on handling blood and other potentially infectious materials in order to minimize exposure risks to blood-borne pathogens such as hepatitis or human immunodeficiency virus (HIV).

OSHA also gives employees rights under the law. An employee may request an inspection and have a representative, such as a union member, accompany the inspector. Employees may talk to the inspector privately.

In addition, regulations must be posted regarding employee rights under the act, and employees can have locations monitored for exposure to toxic or radioactive materials, have access to those records, and have a record of their own exposure.

Employees may have company medical examinations or other tests to determine whether their health is being affected by an exposure and have the results furnished to their personal doctors. Furthermore, employers may not retaliate against employees for exercising their rights under the Occupational Safety and Health Act.

If you ever feel unsafe on the job, you should discuss the problem immediately with your supervisor or the safety committee if your facility has an active one. Should you feel that the danger is life threatening, you have the right, by law, to refuse to work. If the problem cannot be resolved by working within the company, you should, of course, contact OSHA.

FUTURE HEALTH AND SAFETY ISSUES

Health and safety will continue to be areas of concern for both employers and employees. Employers, faced with spiraling insurance and worker compensation premiums, will be searching for ways to reduce employment-related injuries and diseases, usually through the use of protective equipment and/or training in safe work habits. Furthermore, fit employees are more productive employees, adding incentives for organizations to provide a healthy work environment.

Because workplace violence and motor vehicle accidents are two of the top three causes of death in the workplace and account for 45 percent of occupational fatalities, health and safety experts will begin to focus on this area, which has not traditionally been addressed by OSHA. Less obvious hazards such as injuries caused by ergonomic factors and exposure to dangerous substances will remain a concern.

*Fast*Chat

Some employees still work in unsafe environments.

1. Why do some employers fail to provide a safe working environment?

2. Why do some employees fail to work safely?

3. What is your responsibility when you see someone working unsafely or notice an unsafe working condition?

Traditionally, care of those too infirm or too old to work was left to charitable organizations or to families. This method of caring for those unable to help themselves worked fairly well in an agrarian society where an extra mouth could be supported by planting another row of crops or raising extra livestock. However, urbanization and industrialization began to put a strain on the ability of individuals to care for extended families. Some organizations initiated benefit programs for their employees, but the majority of employees were left without assistance.

The Great Depression intensified the crisis, leaving a great many individuals without work and unable to provide the basics for themselves, much less for their dependents. As a result, legislation was enacted that required organizations to provide retirement benefits, benefits to those who became unemployed, and compensation to those injured on the job.

FEDERALLY MANDATED BENEFITS

Most employers must provide Social Security, unemployment compensation, and workers' compensation.

> Most employers must provide Social Security, unemployment compensation, and workers' compensation.

Social Security The **Social Security Act** was passed in 1935 and has been amended many times since. Social Security benefits include retirement insurance, survivor's insurance, disability insurance, and Medicare. These benefits are mandatory for approximately 95 percent of all U.S. workers. The benefits are summarized in the figure on the next page. Social Security was created to replace a portion of earnings lost as a result of old age, disability, or death—not all lost wages.

Social Security is funded through payroll taxes. Employees contribute 7.65 percent of their salary up to a maximum of $87,900 as of 2004. The company matches this contribution. Regardless of the number of companies for whom an employee works, benefits will accumulate in the employee's account. Anyone who is self-employed must pay both the employee's portion and the company match for this tax.[34]

The Social Security Administration manages the Social Security program. You may contact the administration to review your earnings statement to be sure that your earnings have been correctly recorded and to inquire about details of benefit programs.

Job Loss Compensation **Unemployment compensation** was created by the Social Security Act of 1935 to assist those who became unemployed until they find another job.

The federal government set up minimum standards for unemployment compensation, and the states developed their own standards around the minimums. For this reason, the state agency governing unemployment compensation should be contacted concerning specific benefits and qualifications.[36]

In most instances, employees who quit voluntarily are unable to receive unemployment compensation. Employees also are denied benefits in most states if they have been discharged for misconduct.

Individuals receiving unemployment compensation must be actively seeking employment and must accept suitable employment when offered. States may interpret these terms differently; therefore, you should consult your local unemployment agency when you have specific questions.

ETHICS CONNECTION

During fiscal year 2003, the Fraud and Abuse Division of the Kansas Division of Workers Compensation received the following complaints of fraud, abuse, or failure to comply with workers' compensation regulations allegedly committed by claimants, employers, insurance entities, and self-insured employers, as well as by health care givers and attorneys. During that year, the division collected $152,237.78 in restitution and civil penalties, the largest sum ever collected.[37]

Kansas Division of Workers Compensation, Fraud and Abuse Division Type of Fraud, Abuse & Compliance Referrals FY 2003	Total
Obtaining or denying benefits by making false statements	71
Failure to confirm benefits to anyone providing treatment to a claimant	12
Failure to initiate or reinstate compensation when due	5
Refusing to pay compensation when due	5
Refusing to pay any order awarding compensation	9
Failing to file accident reports in a timely manner	6
Receiving temporary or permanent total disability benefits while working	15
Failure to maintain workers' compensation insurance when required	130
All other Fraud and Abuse Practices	37

1. *Workers' compensation benefits do not come close to replacing the salary of an injured individual. Is working while receiving benefits justified?*

2. *If competition is tough, is it justified for businesses to cut corners by not filing timely accident reports or failing to maintain workers' compensation insurance?*

The unemployment compensation system is funded through employer taxes. The amount of tax depends on the total wages and the number of former employees drawing unemployment compensation. For this reason, employers have an incentive to keep undeserving former employees from drawing unemployment benefits.

Compensation for Injury on the Job **Workers' compensation** is a system that compensates individuals who have been physically or mentally injured on their jobs or who have developed an occupational disease. The compensation can include cash payments, reimbursement for medical costs, and, in some cases, the costs of rehabilitation for the employee or compensation for survivors of an employee killed on the job.

Employers are required either to purchase insurance to cover workers' compensation or to become self-insured, and state regulations vary on how they can acquire coverage. Employers do, however, have an incentive to reduce injuries, because injuries mean not only lost time from the job but higher premiums.

Each state has its own compensation laws. The Federal Employees' Compensation Act covers Federal employees, and federal coverage is extended to maritime workers on navigable waters of the United States. As with unemployment insurance, the state agency should be contacted for specific details.[38]

BENEFITS EMPLOYERS VOLUNTARILY OFFER

Employers typically offer a number of benefits voluntarily. They have found that attractive benefit packages help draw and keep qualified employees, allowing them to remain competitive in the workplace. The variety of benefits that may be offered by employers is listed in the figure on the next page. The employer may pay in part or in full for these benefits. An employer may give employees a choice of benefits so that they can design their own benefit packages. All benefits together, mandatory and optional, can average as much as 42.3 percent of salaries.[39]

> Voluntary plus mandatory benefits can average as much as 42.3 percent of salaries.

In 1974, the federal government enacted the Employee Retirement Income Security Act (ERISA). This act regulates benefit plans for health insurance, group life insurance, sick pay, long-term disability income, pension plans, profit sharing plans, thrift plans, and stock bonus plans. It sets legal standards around which employee benefit plans must be established and administered. In addition, ERISA requires that employees be given a summary plan description and have access to plan financial information. Plan termination insurance, which guarantees benefits if certain types of retirement plans terminate, is another provision of ERISA.[40]

If you have questions concerning your benefits or options, consult your supervisor or the human resources department. The company will have literature or other information that will explain the benefits available in detail.

The Future of Benefits Employee benefits will be a controversial topic in the 21ST century. An aging workforce will bring with it the need to revise Social Security regulations that specify how much work an employee is allowed to perform and still draw benefits. Funding can be expected to continue to be an issue because of the large number of individuals who will be drawing benefits. As of 2003, the Social Security fund is solvent until the year 2042 if no tampering with the funds is allowed.[41]

Voluntary Company Benefits

Financial Plans
Pension plans
Profit sharing
Thrift plans
Employee stock ownership plans
Individual retirement accounts

Insurance
Health—hospital, medical, dental, vision,
  prescription drug
Life insurance
Disability insurance

Payment for Time Not Worked
Vacation
Holidays
Sick leave

Other Benefits or Services
Housing or moving assistance
In-house health services
Flexible work hours
Parental leave
Child care programs
Social or recreational services
Educational assistance
Employee assistance plans
Legal services
Financial planning
Assistance or discounts on purchasing
  food or other goods
Credit unions
Medical savings accounts
Transportation services
Wellness programs
Concierge and personal benefits services

A crisis has erupted concerning medical benefits offered by employers. Many are hiring only part-time workers in an effort to avoid paying medical insurance premiums. Others are shifting the burden of rising premiums to employees or even dropping coverage altogether. In a further effort to reduce medical costs, some insurance carriers are dropping the amount of coverage allowed on some claims, which leaves the employee paying an increasing share of medical bills. On the positive side, employers are offering more wellness programs as a way to reduce medical costs, which is better for both employees and the health care system.

*Fast*Chat

Most companies offer more benefits than are legally mandated.

1. Why do companies offer extra benefits?

2. Would you work for a company that did not offer paid vacation time? Why, or why not?

In general, our rights as employees differ from those we have away from the workplace. Understanding our rights as employees is crucial to functioning in the work world. Using sound communication and human relations skills is important as we attempt to work out problems on the job.

The rights of employees of governmental bodies and union members are usually better defined than those of other employees. The rights discussed in the following sections are controversial at this time. Many areas are gray and subject to change. Changes in rights evolve from court and arbitration decisions. At times, court cases can be inconsistent, with one court deciding for an issue while another court rules against it.

As an employee, you should be aware that standing on principle over some of the issues discussed below might result in termination. A court case may be needed and years may pass before the case comes to trial.

State and local law varies in the areas discussed below. *Consult a local legal expert for additional details in these areas of the law.*

Employment at Will **Employment at will** means that an employee serves at the discretion of an employer and can be terminated at any time for any reason even if the employee is performing well. The employee also has the right to quit at any point. Presently, the legality of this practice is in question, and the law is rapidly changing in this area. In general, most states support the concept of employment at will. However, employees who have contracts or implied contracts should consult an attorney, since recent decisions have favored employees in cases where "at will" statements in employee handbooks or on contracts have been unclear.

> The principle of employment at will is eroding in the United States.

The exceptions to employment at will are individuals who assert their rights under certain federal legislation, such as the equal employment laws, Occupational Safety and Health Act, Fair Labor Standards Act, Vietnam Era Veterans Reemployment Act, Clean Air Act, and Federal Juror's Protection Law. These people cannot be terminated for exercising those rights.

Courts have also ruled that employees cannot be terminated for filing for workers' compensation benefits, obeying a subpoena, leaving for jury duty, refusing to participate in an employer's lobbying efforts, or reporting an employer's illegal acts.

Proof of Eligibility to Work The Immigration Reform and Control Act (IRCA) of 1986 bans employment of unauthorized aliens and requires employers to document the identity and authorization to work for all new employees. Employers are required, within three days of hire, to complete an employment eligibility verification form called an **I-9** on all new employees. The documents that may be used for identification are listed in the figure below.[42]

All individuals seeking employment should be sure that they have the correct documentation to provide proof of authorization to work in the United States. If you have any questions concerning your documentation, consult the Immigration and Naturalization Service.

Establishing Authorization to Work in the United States[43]

List A Documents that Establish Identity and Employment Eligibility	List B Documents that Establish Identity		List C Documents that Establish Employment Eligibility
1. U.S. Passport (unexpired or expired)	1. Driver's license or ID card issued by a state or outlying possession of the United States provided it contains a photograph or information such as name, date of birth, sex, height, eye color, and address	**and**	1. U.S. social security card issued by the Social Security Administration *(other than a card stating it is not valid for employment)*
2. Certificate of U.S. Citizenship *(INS Form N-560 or N-561)*			2. Certification of Birth Abroad issued by the Department of State *(Form FS-545 or Form DS-1350)*
3. Certificate of Naturalization *(INS Form N-550 or N-570)*	2. ID card issued by federal, state, or local government agencies or entities provided it contains a photograph or information such as name, date of birth, sex, height, eye color, and address		3. Original or certified copy of a birth certificate issued by a state, county, municipal authority or outlying possession of the United States bearing an official seal
4. Unexpired foreign passport, with *I-551 stamp or* attached *INS Form I-94* indicating unexpired employment authorization			
5. Alien Registration Receipt Card with photograph *(INS Form I-151 or I-551)*	3. School ID card with a photograph		
	4. Voter's registration card		
	5. U.S. Military card or draft record		

Employees must provide either one document from List A OR one document from List B and C.

This is an abbreviated list. Consult the U.S. Citizenship and Immigration Service or search its web site for a list of alternative documents.

WEB

Freedom of Speech Public employees, in general, cannot be terminated for speaking on matters of public concern. This right, however, can be limited if the speech interferes with the efficient operation of the government. They can be terminated for speaking on matters of personal interest. Public employees are not allowed to campaign for people who will become their bosses. The Hatch Act was passed in 1940, limiting the political activity of federal civil servants. Many states and large cities have passed their own Hatch acts.[44] Some states offer broad protection, whereas others offer little or none. In general, individuals in high positions in a company have fewer rights than individuals at lower levels. The potential impact of statements coming from individuals in higher positions of authority or prestige is greater.

Employment and Military Service The dependence on the Reserve/National Guard to assist in military actions has increased in recent years. In 1994, Congress passed the Uniformed Services Employment and Reemployment Rights Act. The act protects members of the uniformed services from discrimination and provides for reemployment rights as well as for protection of certain benefit rights.[45]

Defamation of Character Defamation is the open publication of a false statement tending to harm the reputation of a person. If the statement is oral, it is called *slander*. If it is in writing, it is called *libel*. If you feel that your character has been defamed, consult an attorney to determine your rights. Truth is considered a defense in defamation charges. Most courts consider a statement protected if it is made in good faith in the discharge of a public or private duty to someone else who has a corresponding interest, right, or duty. For instance, if a security guard reported to the managers that an employee had attempted to steal property, the courts would most likely not consider this defamation of character.

Smokers' Rights Courts are tending to side with the rights of nonsmokers. At present, an employer may totally forbid smoking on the job and, in some states, discriminate against smokers by not hiring them. Some companies that do not totally ban smoking may identify smoking and nonsmoking areas. Often, this is prompted by local ordinances that require the designation of nonsmoking and smoking areas in the workplace.

Medical Benefits The Health Insurance Portability and Accountability Act (HIPAA) was passed in 1996 to provide increased privacy for employee health information and greater portability of employee health care coverage, allowing employees leaving an employer health plan to have access to the new employer health plan without waiting periods or limitations because of preexisting conditions or health status.

In addition, the Consolidated Omnibus Budget Reconciliation Act (COBRA) requires employers with 20 or more employees to extend health care coverage to employees and dependents for 18 to 36 months in situations in which they would no longer be eligible for coverage. The individual must pay 102 percent of the premium, at a minimum.[46]

Personnel Files   Employers are compelled to protect themselves from charges of discrimination and unjust punishment or termination. Many rely on documentation in the personnel file to protect themselves in this area.

> Employee files store documentation on performance and behavior on the job.

Employees can expect to find reprimands, warnings, or write-ups concerning performance or behavior in their files. Most states allow access to personnel records by employees at reasonable times. Some states allow employees to correct documents or remove erroneous materials or insert explanations of disputed materials. Employees should consult their employee handbook and state laws to determine whether access to their personnel files is allowed.

Drugs on Personal Time   Currently, the courts do not give employees in private enterprise many rights in this area. Terminations of employees

GLOBAL CONNECTION

Companies around the world have vastly different views of employee rights. Some countries, for instance, do not support employment at will. The European Union has enacted strict employee privacy regulations that prohibit employers from using personal information without permission or tracking computer usage through software. In addition to limiting the freedom of the employer to fire employees, the freedom of employees to change jobs is also often limited. Many countries mandate that companies offer long vacations. In some countries, political power is tied up in issues of employee rights. Countries worldwide will have to weigh the pros and cons of maintaining local traditions versus competing globally. Although many will choose the higher profits offered by global opportunities, some will choose to protect their cultures.[47]

1. *What problems can different employment rights cause for companies operating globally?*

2. *Should employment practices be standardized worldwide? Why, or why not?*

Human Relations

who test positive for drugs whether used on or off the job are upheld. Governmental employees have more rights concerning drug testing than those in private industry. Even though some drugs can stay in the system up to 72 hours after use, the courts have made no allowances for use of drugs on personal time.

Search of Work Areas In general, employers have the right to search employee packages, files, desks, and cars in order to prevent theft and to control operations. Court restrictions on search and seizure are limited, particularly if the employer has warned employees that they are subject to search.

Polygraphs The Employee Polygraph Protection Act of 1988 prohibits most private employers from using lie detector tests to screen applicants. The tests cannot be the sole reason for discharge and can only be used if a reasonable suspicion of guilt exists. Because polygraph use is limited, some employers have turned to the use of pencil and paper tests concerning honesty and substance abuse in order to screen job applicants.[48]

Companies are concerned with employee honesty for several reasons. First, employers lose billions of dollars annually through employee theft. Then, substance abusers cost companies billions of dollars more in higher benefit costs, lower productivity, and absenteeism. Second, because of the "negligent hiring theory," employers can be held liable for crimes that an employee commits on the job if they fail to screen the employee for past misdeeds or personality quirks.

Currently, these tests are legal, and employers can use them to make decisions concerning hiring and firing. However, many see the tests as intrusive, subjective, and unreliable. Employers who administer these types of tests may offend potential applicants and send a message to future employees that they are not trusted.

Plant Closings The Worker Adjustment and Retraining Notification Act of 1988 requires that plants with 100 or more workers give 60 days advance notice of a shutdown affecting at least 50 workers. Layoffs of more than one-third of the work site employees for more than six months must also be announced in advance.[49]

Dress Codes Dress codes that are reasonably related to the business needs of the company and that are clear, consistently enforced, and communicated have generally been upheld by courts and arbitrators. Some reasonable accommodation, however, must be made if the employee asks to deviate from the dress code for religious reasons.

Technology allows employers to monitor employees' locations in the workplace—or on the road, if the employee is, for example, driving a delivery truck—at all times. In addition, today's technology allows monitoring of telephone conversations, keystrokes on the computer, and Internet access.

1. *Should employers have a right to monitor the activities of workers? Why, or why not?*

2. *Why do you think an employer might feel the need to monitor employees?*

3. *Would you work for an employer that required you to wear a badge to track your location on the work site? Why, or why not?*

Blowing the Whistle on Illegal Activities   The Sarbanes-Oxley Act protects officers, employees, contractors, subcontractors, or agents of publicly traded companies from adverse employment-related actions. If they report conduct they reasonably believe involves a violation of federal securities laws, the rules or regulations of the Securities and Exchange Commission, or "any provision of federal law relating to fraud against shareholders," they are covered by this act. Additionally, the law generally affords protection to federal and state employees. These employees cannot be terminated for reporting illegal activities within their organization.[50]

Electronic Surveillance of Employees   Currently, employers may legally survey employees electronically, particularly if they have advised the employees that surveillance may occur without the employees' knowledge and that refusal to permit it may be grounds for discipline. Some companies have employees sign waivers; others post copies of search policies. Some companies perform electronic surveillance to prevent theft and reduce unproductive time of employees not closely supervised.

Employers may eavesdrop with hidden microphones and transmitters attached to lockers or telephones that pick up office conversations or spy with pinhole lenses in walls and ceilings. Some companies record the length of telephone calls, when the calls were made, and where the calls were placed. They may also monitor the content of the telephone calls.

Employers may legally survey employees electronically to prevent theft and reduce unproductive time.

©Getty Images/PhotoDisc

E-mail Privacy   Currently, e-mail communications are not private and can be subject to subpoena. Even e-mails that have been erased can be retrieved.

Future Rights   The future will most likely bring extensive changes in the area of miscellaneous employee rights. As technology becomes more sophisticated and inexpensive, enabling companies to perform even more thorough surveillance on employees, a push to curb this "big brother" type of activity will most likely occur. Additionally, the courts are expected to continue to move away from the employment at will doctrine, granting employees even more rights.

*Fast*Chat

1. Have you benefited from any of the rights listed in this section? In what ways did you benefit?

2. How can strong human relations skills help you avoid having problems with any of the elements covered by these rights, either as an employee or as an employer?

Key Terms

discrimination

Equal Employment Opportunity
  Commission

Title VII of the Civil Rights Act of
  1964

Pregnancy Discrimination Act

Equal Pay Act

Age Discrimination in Employment
  Act

sexual harassment

Americans with Disabilities Act

reasonable accommodations

Affirmative Action

Fair Labor Standards Act

Family Medical Leave Act

union

Norris-LaGuardia Act

Wagner Act

National Labor Relations Board
  (NLRB)

Taft-Hartley Act

bargaining unit

Right-To-Work Law

Landrum-Griffin Act

Occupational Safety and Health Act

safety

health

Occupational Safety and Health
  Administration (OSHA)

Social Security Act

unemployment compensation

workers' compensation

employment at will

I-9

CHAPTER SUMMARY

Various federal, state, and local laws regulate the workplace. Federal laws protect employees from discrimination based on race, religion, sex, color, age, national origin, and disability. Employees may legally form unions in order to bargain collectively with employers over wages, hours, and working conditions. Health and safety of workers is regulated through the Occupational Safety and Health Act. Federal laws also mandate fair labor standards, family and medical leave, retirement, disability, survivor's benefits, and unemployment compensation through the Social Security Act. State laws control compensation for employees injured or killed on the job.

Many employers offer additional benefits, such as health insurance, retirement, savings plans, or child care, in addition to federally mandated benefits. These benefits, along with required benefits, can average up to 42.3 percent of an employee's salary.

In general, miscellaneous employee rights at work differ from those enjoyed away from the job. Public employees tend to have better-defined rights than private employees. Employees should learn what they can and cannot do in their locale.

REVIEW QUESTIONS

1. Which federal laws regulate discrimination in the workplace? What types of discrimination do they prohibit?

2. Which major laws regulate fair labor standards? Explain them.

3. What is a union? What is a union allowed and not allowed to do?

4. What is OSHA? How does it protect employees' safety and health?

5. Identify three benefits that are required by law and five that may be offered voluntarily to employees.

6. What miscellaneous rights do employees have at work?

DISCUSSION QUESTIONS

1. Review the employee rights discussed in the last section of the chapter. Do you think employees should have more rights or fewer rights?

2. Have you ever been confronted by an unsafe working condition on the job? What did you do about it?

3. Should an employer have the right to search your work area?

4. Social Security was not intended to support fully individuals who have lost income through death, disability, or retirement. Explain what other benefits companies provide to help fill the gap. Have you begun to plan for your retirement? Why, or why not? If so, how?

5. Do you agree with the teenage training wage? Why, or why not?

6. Does your school or place of work have designated smoking areas? Should smoking be banned altogether? Why, or why not?

7. Should employers be able to tell you what to wear to work? Why might an employer care about what you wear?

8. What are your feelings about electronic surveillance in the workplace? Should employers have the right to monitor employees to see that they are working during business hours and to assess the quality of their work?

TEAMWORK

CHAPTER PROJECT

Divide into two groups. Debate the following statements, one side supporting the statement and the other side opposing it. Support your arguments with information from the chapter and from information you find on U.S. Department of Labor and government web sites.

WEB

1. Unions are no longer needed. Employers treat employees fairly.

2. An employee has no obligation to report discrimination.

3. Employees should have the right to say anything they wish at work.

APPLICATIONS

It's Your Thing: Do What You Want To Do?

Dora had been employed at Seymour's Shop for five years. She and her supervisor, Herbert, had been at odds for months. Dora thought that he was obnoxious and disliked his ordering her around and making demands.

Dora began to complain about Herbert to others in her group. She criticized his decisions to Manuel and made fun of his clothes when talking to Chen Lee. Other workers began to pick up on this behavior and made fun of Herbert behind his back.

One evening, Dora noticed Herbert in the café across the street from the office. A young woman was with him. The next day she reported this scene to the group, and they began to speculate concerning the woman's identity and why she and Herbert were together. Dora and the group were standing in front of the water fountain, laughing and talking, when Herbert walked up.

"Dora, I want to see you in my office right now," he said abruptly. Dora followed him in and Herbert shut the door. "Dora, I'm going to have to let you go because you are a troublemaker. Every time I turn around, you are in someone else's office gossiping and interrupting work. You are causing too much trouble."

1. What employer right did Herbert exercise?

2. Should Dora have been allowed freedom of speech? Was the issue really about freedom of speech? How would you have felt if you were Dora? How would you have advised Dora to behave?

3. How would you have felt if you were Herbert? What might happen to a company if employees were allowed to disrupt business and undermine authority? What are some other things Herbert might have done, even if he still ended up having to fire Dora?

4. How do you think the other members of the group will react?

Equal and Fair Are Two Different Things

"I've had it," Carmelita said as she sat down next to Emilio. "That Elvin is a real monster. He yells at me, returns my work, and makes me do it over. He's always telling me that I'm stupid when I make mistakes. He makes me so nervous that I can't think straight. I'm tempted to go to the EEOC and file charges on him. I don't think he likes Hispanics."

"I know what you mean," Emilio said. "He chewed me out in front of the whole office. I was so embarrassed that I felt like hiding."

Just then Jan walked up and joined the conversation.

"You can try EEOC if you want," Jan said. "But he treats everyone that way. I was in Alice's office yesterday when Elvin told her what a simpleton she was because she had incorrectly added some figures. He threw the report on her desk, yelled 'Do it right or else!' and stormed out. Alice is white and she gets that treatment. I guess he treats everybody equally!"

1. What discriminatory treatment do federal laws prohibit? Would they be applicable to Carmelita and Emilio?

2. Does being treated equally mean that you will be treated fairly or as you would like to be treated?

3. How do you think Carmelita and Emilio might handle the situation?

4. Do any governmental regulations dictate the type of treatment to be received by employees?

ADDITIONAL READINGS AND RESOURCES

Arnesen, Eric, and Charles. W. Calhoun, editors. *The Human Tradition in American Labor History.* Wilmington, DE: Scholarly Resources, 2003.

Lake, Silver, editor. *Health Insurance Made E-Z.* Chicago: Socrates Media/Made E-Z Products, 2001.

Selby, Paul. *The Nearly-Complete Guide to Social Security, Adult Disability Benefits, & Work Incentives.* Greenwood, IN: Magic Wand Solutions, 2000.

The following helpful resources are available on the Internet and from the U.S. Equal Employment Opportunity Commission Clearinghouse, 2070 Chain Bridge Road, Suite 450, Vienna, VA 22182.

Fact Sheet: National Origin Discrimination
Fact Sheet: Pregnancy Discrimination
Fact Sheet: Religious Discrimination
Fact Sheet: Sexual Harassment
Fact Sheet: Age Discrimination
Fact Sheet: Race/Color Discrimination
Fact Sheet: ADA Discrimination

For additional resources, refer to the web site for this text: school.cengage.com/career/dalton

Maintaining Balance:
Work and Life

After studying this chapter, you should be able to:

17.1 *Define work-life balance and describe the benefits to both employer and employee.*

17.2 *Identify some of the physical and mental effects of stress and learn ways to minimize these effects.*

17.3 *Understand the effects of substance abuse on job performance and how companies try to minimize these effects.*

17.4 *Describe several methods of effective time management.*

17.5 *Discuss the importance of maintaining proper health practices.*

focus

Fistfights, shouting matches, throwing things, and damaging equipment are all symptoms of "desk rage." According to a 2000 study by Integra Realty Resources, Inc., this problem is not uncommon. A random telephone survey of 1,305 working adults revealed that 10 percent surveyed had been in an atmosphere where physical violence had occurred because of stress while 42 percent said yelling and verbal abuse occur in their workplace. Of those surveyed, 2 percent admitted to striking a coworker and 29 percent admitted to yelling at coworkers because of stress.

Causes of stress that pushed workers to desk rage included overcrowded physical conditions, unreasonable deadlines, excessive personal workload, rudeness of coworkers or clients, too much caffeine, and an excessive amount of e-mail.

How else did those in the survey react to the stress? They couldn't sleep, drank alcohol excessively, smoked excessively, and ate chocolate. Crying, calling in sick, or quitting were cited as coping mechanisms. Complaints of physical symptoms such as neck pain, stressed eyes, and hurting hands, as well as aching rear ends, were numerous.[1]

Should companies try to do something about employee stress? Is the problem of job stress getting better or worse?

in this chapter

Work-life benefits are benefits that employers offer to help employees gain some measure of balance between work and home. A 2003 survey by the Mellon Financial Corporation stated that over the past two years, almost 50 percent of employers increased the number of work-life programs they offer while only 5 percent decreased the number of programs. The top three reasons for offering these types of programs are to raise morale, enhance recruitment efforts, and remain competitive or increase image in their industry.[2]

Organizations have been offering work-life benefits in some form since the 1930s but, because of demographic changes, the increasing use of technology, and the changing relevance of work, work-life benefits have become more important than ever.

> Work-life balance programs help organizations raise morale, enhance recruitment efforts, and remain competitive in their industries.

DEMOGRAPHICS

The dominance of the traditional American family with a stay-at-home mother and working father is gone from today's workforce. Because of the large number of working parents—couples, single parents (fathers and mothers), and grandparents caring for children—maintaining a balance between work and home has become even more important than ever. Working parents have been demanding assistance, and employers have been responding with accommodations.

As reflected in the 2000 census, the number of Americans living alone has surpassed the number of married couples with children. Older workers are expected to shift to a working retirement. While working parents are interested in benefits that revolve around children, single and older employees are more interested in benefits such as gym subsidies, wellness programs, and training and development and educational assistance. Additionally, they expect benefits that are on a par to those offered to working parents.

TECHNOLOGY

Technology has enabled many employees to perform their work in places other than the office. Employers can now be more flexible in terms of the places and times work is performed without worrying about a decrease in productivity. However, this breakthrough is causing many workers to find themselves working 24/7 and blurring the lines between work and home.

Access to exercise facilities is a popular work-life balance benefit.

©Getty Images/PhotoDisc

THE MEANING OF WORK

Since 9/11, many people have been reevaluating their lives and the importance of work. Economist Charles Handy says that work is a fundamental part of life. However, he divides work into several areas, the first being paid work.

Besides paid work, he says there is home work (caring for home and family), gift work (volunteering), and study work (keeping abreast of developments in your area of expertise and upgrading skills). Some workers, he says, are trading security for independence to perform all types of work, interspersed with leisure time. Organizations, in order to entice the next generation of talent, will need to allow employees an opportunity to perform all types of work.[3]

CASE STUDIES IN THE NEWS

ABC News Commentator John Stossel, in a 2004 segment of *20/20*, said it is a myth that we have less free time than we used to, despite all the stories that Americans are more stressed and working more. He quotes sociologist John Robinson of the University of Maryland as saying that since 1965 we've gained almost an hour more of free time every day. Additionally, when individuals Stossel interviewed kept diaries on how they spent their time, they found they actually had more free time than they had estimated.

Experts say we have more free time because we're working less, marrying later, having fewer children, and retiring earlier.[4]

1. *Watching TV is the number one free time activity in America, according to Stossel. How much television do you watch? Does it affect your perception of how much free time you have?*

2. *If we have so much free time, why are we so stressed?*

Despite changing attitudes, the surest way to climb the corporate ladder is to work long hours and sacrifice personal and family time. Increasing workforce diversity and technology continue to put stress on employees while global competition puts pressure on employers to do more with less. U.S. workers have now surpassed Japanese workers in the number of hours worked per week, which is expected to further complicate the quest for work-life balance.

Examples of Work-Life Benefits

- Dependent care flexible spending account
- Vaccinations on-site (e.g., flu shots)
- Flextime
- Wellness program, resources and information
- Health screening programs (high blood pressure, cholesterol, etc.)
- Gym subsidy
- Family leave above required FMLA leave
- Compressed workweeks
- Casual dress days (every day)
- Bring child to work in emergency
- Weight loss program

- On-site fitness center
- Club memberships
- Career counseling
- Food services/subsidized cafeteria
- Elder care referral service
- Adoption assistance
- On-site child care center
- Company supported elder care center
- Career counseling
- Travel planning services
- Massage therapy at work
- Self-defense training
- Concierge services

---

*Fast*Chat

Employers want employees who are willing to devote themselves body and soul to the company, according to Jeffrey Pfeffer, Professor of Organizational Behavior at Stanford Graduate School of Business.[5]

1. Why do you think this attitude exists today despite the demand for balance between home and work?

2. What barriers do organizations face in initiating work-life benefits?

3. Do you think those who work part time or fail to put in extra hours deserve the same career advancement as those who do?

Excess stress may result in physical or mental disorders.

Stress is a physical response to environmental pressures. Basically any challenge, physical or psychological, triggers a stress reaction. The body reacts the same to both physical and psychological challenges—the mind actually prepares the body for some activity in response to the external stimuli. Stress is an unavoidable effect of living. Indeed, we could not live without stress. However, if stress is too powerful, or our defenses are inadequate, physical or mental disorders may result. Generally, the problem today is that, with the rapid pace of daily life and the pressures that seem to be ever present, we are almost constantly under stress and have no time to reenergize.

ORIGINS OF STRESS

Stress is not a new phenomenon, although the term "stress" was applied relatively recently to humans. The reaction now called stress was first recognized on the battlefield in the Civil War. Nervous and anxious reactions in the form of heart palpitations were so common among fearful soldiers that they became known as "soldier's heart." Stress was called "shell shock" during World War I and "battle fatigue" during World War II.

These reactions, in fact, existed in prehistoric times. When faced with possible danger, the autonomic nervous system responded by preparing early humans to face the situation with additional strength, energy, and endurance. Stored sugar and fat poured into the bloodstream to provide fuel for quick energy, breathing speeded up to provide more oxygen, and blood-clotting mechanisms were activated to protect against injury. Muscles tensed for action, digestion slowed to allow blood to be directed to the muscles and brain, pupils dilated to allow more light to enter the eye, and hormone production increased to prepare them either to fight or to run for safety. This response to anxiety is commonly known as the "fight or flight response."[6]

Physiological reactions occur in stressful situations.

Modern humans respond similarly to the pressures and demands of daily events. For example, you may worry or feel anxious about juggling family and job responsibilities, the local school board election, a career-limiting mistake you made at work, or a wreck you nearly had on the freeway. In each of these instances, your body reacts in much the same way that early humans reacted to a wild animal or attacking enemy. A series of biochemical changes occurs, and the body's system is thrown out of balance.

In today's fast-paced society, we are almost constantly under stress.

In today's society you can seldom fight or flee in these situations. The physiological responses get turned on without being used for the intended purpose. The body is unable to release its stored energy because aggressive behavior would not be appropriate in most social situations. Repeated or chronic preparation for action without the action following can lead to stress-related diseases and disorders.

STRESS OVERLOAD

Stress can be caused by either good or bad events. Holidays, weddings, births, and moving into a new house are examples of pleasant events for most people that are usually very stressful as well. The death of a loved one, divorce, being fired from work, or just experiencing trouble on the job are negative events that cause stress.

TECHNOLOGY CONNECTION

E-mail is the communication workhorse of the 21ST century, allowing instant communication around the world. Junk e-mail and unnecessary messages have become a problem, swamping workers and wasting precious time. Address lists that copy everyone on every message quickly clog electronic mailboxes. With so many other things to do, e-mail ceases to look like a convenience and starts to be an additional source of stress.

1. *What can individuals do to control the volume of junk e-mail?*

2. *Should companies regulate e-mail? Why, or why not?*

Since stress is, by definition, a challenge, then challenges such as exams, sports contests, or anything that includes competition can induce a stress response. Even simple daily stressors have an effect on your body. Fights with the kids, a missed bus, a flat tire, traffic, and a rush job at work—all these small stressors add up. And those are just the emotional stressors. Physical stressors, which can range from poor nutrition to allergies to illness, add to the load. Chemical stressors—such as too much caffeine, cigarette smoke, or any other substances that affect the body's response systems—can also contribute to becoming "stressed out."

Are You Suffering from Symptoms of Job Stress?[7]

If you are suffering from these symptoms, you may be suffering from job stress that could pose a threat to your health.

- Increased absenteeism
- Reduced civility
- Physical ailments
- Sleep dysfunction
- Reduced human interaction

 **uick tip** ....

The Rotarian magazine suggests the following lighthearted tips for relieving stress:[8]

- Pop some popcorn without putting the lid on the pan.
- Make a list of things to do that you have already done.
- Fill out your tax form using Roman numerals.
- Drive to work in reverse.
- Read the dictionary upside down and look for secret messages.
- Write a short story using alphabet soup.

Some experiences are obviously more stressful than others. Often, the same type of experience will be more stressful to one person than to another. Regardless of the varying intensities of the experience, each person has a limit, or a stress threshold, to the amount of stress that can be handled physically and psychologically.

As stress builds up, people will experience an overload, which results in negative symptoms or behaviors. Overeating, loss of appetite, overindulging in alcohol, ulcers, temper tantrums, headaches, hypertension, and heart disease are common results of stress overloads. Additionally, a decrease in the ability to concentrate, memory problems, insomnia, anxiety, depression, and other personality changes may accompany stress overloads. In fact, estimates are that as many as 75 percent of all medical complaints are stress-related illnesses.[9a]

Stress overload may cause various physical symptoms.

Learning to deal with stress, then, can literally be a matter of life or death. A healthy lifestyle can help you deal with stress and other health-related matters. It should include not abusing substances, effective time management, proper diet, exercise, relaxation, other leisure activities, and no smoking. It also involves changing stressful thoughts, attitudes, and behaviors.

CASE STUDIES IN THE NEWS

In 2003, Forbes.com reported that job stress is estimated to cost American industry $300 billion a year from factors like absenteeism and job turnover. This statistic has made some employers start looking for alternative ways to reduce stress in their workplaces.

One Buffalo law firm begins Monday meetings with meditation. A pharmaceutical company in Delaware offers Quigong sessions (Chinese exercise and mediation). Two hospitals in Cleveland offer breaks to nurses for aromatherapy, music therapy, and energy-stimulating massage. Skeptics are dubious, but proponents of stress reduction continue to praise the effectiveness of techniques like meditation, yoga, and other relaxation methods.[9b]

1. *How would relaxation techniques like mediation, yoga, and massage be received in your workplace?*

2. *Do you think they would reduce stress? Why, or why not?*

*Fast*Chat

Stress seems to be a way of life in today's society.

1. Do you believe modern technology has increased stress on the job? Why, or why not?

2. Do you expect stress at work to continue to increase or to begin to decrease?

3. Can companies lower stress and still be competitive?

Substance abuse is the misuse of alcohol, illegal drugs, or prescription drugs. It has become a great concern for organizations because of the millions of dollars lost each year through decreased productivity, absenteeism, theft, industrial accidents, and excessive benefits use. Estimates are that employee alcohol and drug abuse costs U.S. businesses $81 billion or more annually. Alcohol consumption is estimated to make up 86 percent of this cost.[10]

COMMONLY ABUSED SUBSTANCES

The U.S. Department of Labor Substance Abuse Information Database identifies the following substances, side effects, and signs of abuse.[11]

Alcohol is the most commonly abused drug in the United States.

Alcohol is the most abused drug in the United States. A depressant, it slows down the activity of the brain and spinal cord and knocks out the control centers one by one. Although it may produce feelings of well-being, it can lead to sedation, intoxication, blackouts, unconsciousness, and death.

Heavy consumption of alcohol may cause immediate physical problems, such as inefficiency, low energy, weight loss, lethargy, sleeplessness, accidents, and memory loss. Emotionally, it can cause a person to feel jealous, sexually aroused, impotent, moody, easily angered, guilty, depressed, worthless, despondent, and even suicidal.

Over a period of years, the effects of heavy drinking include malnutrition, brain damage, cancer, heart disease, liver damage, ulcers, gastritis, and birth defects in children whose mothers abused alcohol during pregnancy.

Cocaine is a stimulant derived from the coca leaf. It has been used in the United States for years and, prior to 1900, was an active ingredient in many soft drinks and patent medicines. Common feelings experienced by the person who has taken cocaine are hyperalertness, euphoria, and power. These feelings are short lived, typically not lasting more than 30 minutes. For these reasons, cocaine is highly psychologically addictive, and individuals begin to want more and more the sensations they receive from cocaine.

Heavy use of cocaine can lead to weight loss, insomnia, and anxiety reactions. Paranoid thinking may also develop, as well as severe anxiety and depression when the effects of the drug wear off. Long-term use causes serious physical damage and can result in death. Because of its temporary effects, cocaine has become popular among professionals who are achievement-oriented and feel an obligation to be "up" constantly. Crack, the street name for a powerful form of cocaine, is smoked rather than sniffed through the nose or injected. Crack creates the same side effects as cocaine but is even more addictive.[12]

The second most commonly abused substance in the United States is believed to be **marijuana**. Researchers are discovering that marijuana, the dried leaves and flowering tops of the distillate hemp plant, is a much more dangerous drug than was originally thought. Marijuana produces relaxation, spontaneity (because of loss of inhibition), disorientation of spatial relationships, heightened (although not always accurate) sensory awareness, and hunger. It also causes immediate memory loss, impairment in thinking, and a loss of motivation. These effects can be particularly disruptive in the workplace. The heavy smoker is detached, cannot judge or concentrate, and is not motivated. Psychologically, heavy usage can cause "flashbacks" (viewing scenes from the past) and acute adverse reactions.

The physical effects of heavy marijuana usage are cause for concern. Regular marijuana use appears to cause lung and other types of cancer and respiratory diseases more rapidly than does cigarette smoking. In addition, it has an adverse effect on both the male and female hormonal balance and reproductive functions. THC, the active ingredient in marijuana, also possibly suppresses the immune system, leading to lower resistance to disease.[13]

Sedatives (barbiturates) and **tranquilizers** include Seconal, Tuinal, Nembutal, Phenobarbital, Quaaludes, Glutethimide, Doriden, and Valium.

GLOBAL CONNECTION

Employees on overseas assignments need to be aware that the penalties for substance abuse in foreign countries can be vastly different—and usually far more severe—than those in the United States. Failure to respect the differences can result in jail time or worse.

1. *Should Americans working overseas be protected from foreign laws? Why, or why not?*
2. *Where can you get information concerning views about alcohol and illegal drugs in other countries?*

Street names may be downers, ludes, barbs, yellow jackets, red devils, or blue devils. Methaqualone is also known as quaaludes, ludes, or sopers. Some of them are legal drugs that can be obtained with a prescription.

Sedatives and tranquilizers are depressants and can cause drowsiness, agitation, intellectual confusion, and physical impairment. Abusers may have slurred or emotional speech as well as poor body coordination. Overdoses can be characterized by difficulties in walking and speaking, constant uncontrolled eye movements, lethargy, and coma.[14]

Amphetamines are synthetic nervous system stimulants. They have a number of street names, such as speed, ice, bennies, crank, uppers, meth, crystal, and pep pills. They are used to lose weight, stay awake, increase energy, and "get high." The physical effects are dilated pupils, rapid heartbeat, loss of appetite, anxiety, irritability, rapid speech, tremors, and destructive mood elevation.[15]

Club drugs are frequently used at dance parties such as "raves" or "trances" or at nightclubs. Ecstasy, commonly known as Adam, E, X, XTC, or Go, temporarily makes people feel more alive and sensitive to people around them. However, research shows that these drugs destroy cells in the brain that produce dopamine, a vital nerve transmitter. GHB, rohypnol, and ketamine are depressants known as soap, scoop, R-2, Mexican Valium, jet, or super acid. They are sometimes called "date rape" drugs because they are often colorless, tasteless, and odorless and can easily be added to beverages and ingested unknowingly.[16]

Inhalants are another category of abused substances. The practice of sniffing hydrocarbons contained in substances such as glue, gasoline, cleaning fluid, and aerosols is prevalent among children 11 to 15 years old. Symptoms include restlessness, excitement, lack of coordination, confusion, and coma. Long-term use of inhalants can cause damage to the brain, nerves, liver, and kidneys. Fatalities have occurred from suffocation caused when the abuser used a plastic bag to inhale the substance and lost consciousness.[17]

Hallucinogens produce chemically induced hallucinations. The list of hallucinogens includes LSD (acid), mescaline, MDA, and PCP (or angel dust). The fact that these hallucinogens can create immediate emotional disturbances or cause flashbacks years later makes them particularly dangerous in the workplace. Symptoms include euphoria, loss of inhibition, agitation, confusion, stupor, and paranoia. Violent or bizarre reactions are not uncommon, and extreme doses can lead to convulsions, coma, or death. In addition, these drugs can reduce or eliminate inhibitions, potentially leading to dangerous, illegal, or lethal behaviors.[18]

Narcotics include heroin, opium, morphine, dilaudid, and codeine. All are derivatives of the opium poppy. They can cause euphoria, sedation, nausea, vomiting, insensitivity to pain, watery eyes, and skin problems and infections. These drugs are physically addictive, and withdrawal causes painful physical symptoms. Death from overdoses is not uncommon.[19]

Anabolic steroids are legal, man-made drugs that are designed to build muscles. Athletes and others sometimes abuse steroids to enhance performance and improve physical appearance. However, abuse can cause serious side effects such as liver tumors, cancer, jaundice, fluid retention, and high blood pressure. Aggression and other psychiatric side effects such as extreme mood swings may also result from abuse of anabolic steroids.[20]

Other legal drugs that can be abused include prescription and over-the-counter medications, such as cold remedies. Even using them as prescribed can cause drowsiness, impairing an employee's ability to drive or operate machinery on the job. Employees operating equipment and taking medication should consult their supervisors.[21]

Don't let substance abuse jeopardize safety in your workplace.

© 1998 Ted Goff www.tedgoff.com

FIGHTING SUBSTANCE ABUSE IN ORGANIZATIONS

Organizations are using a variety of techniques, such as drug testing, employee assistance programs, and employee education, in an effort to curtail substance abuse at work. Testing can be performed on potential employees as well as current employees.[22]

Pre-employment drug testing requires job applicants to be tested for drugs in their system prior to employment. Applicants who do not pass or refuse to take the examination are not hired.

A growing number of organizations are also testing current employees for substance abuse. A variety of testing schedules is used, depending on the preference of the organization. One type of schedule is known as **expected interval testing**. Under this method, employees are informed ahead of time when testing will occur. It is then performed at the same time on a continuous basis. For example, the test may be scheduled for the first workday after each payday.

CASE STUDIES IN THE NEWS

The National Institute of Drug Abuse states that workers who smoke marijuana are more likely than nonsmoking coworkers to have problems on the job. Marijuana smoking has been associated with increased absences, tardiness, accidents, workers' compensation claims, and job turnovers.

Research has shown that marijuana's adverse impact on memory and learning can last for days or weeks after the acute effects of the drug wear off. Heavy marijuana users in a study of college students had more trouble sustaining and shifting their attention and in registering, organizing, and using information than did participants who had used marijuana no more than 3 of the previous 30 days.[23]

1. *How could marijuana use off the job affect your career in the long term?*

2. *Should companies be able to regulate use of marijuana off the job? Why, or why not?*

Organizations are testing employees for substance abuse.

Random interval testing involves giving tests at random to a particular group of employees. For instance, all employees in the accounting department may be informed that they are to report immediately for a drug test. This testing is most often used for job categories involving public safety or security.

A third type of testing schedule is called **"for cause" testing**. With this method, individual employees may be tested when they appear to exhibit signs of substance abuse, such as slurred speech or dilated pupils. Testing is sometimes done after industrial accidents or for reasonable cause.

Employees may also be expected to submit to **treatment follow-up testing**. This type of testing is used to monitor an employee's success in remaining drug free after being allowed to complete a substance abuse treatment program rather than be terminated.

Other organizations test only employees who are transferred or promoted or employees who are in critical positions. Examples of employees in critical positions are factory employees who work with dangerous equipment and airline pilots.

Company policies and procedures vary on what happens to an employee who fails or refuses to submit to a substance abuse test. Many companies require termination on the spot. Others may require mandatory enrollment in a substance abuse program. Generally, the policy will be more lenient for legal substances than illegal. Employees should be familiar with their company policy on this matter.

Companies take action against employees who abuse substances.

Quick tip ....

Just Say No.

Partnership for a Drug-Free America

Most companies reserve the right to search all areas and property over which the company maintains control without consent of the employee. On occasion, organizations have been known to call local law enforcement agencies or use dogs trained to locate illegal substances in an effort to curtail substance abuse.

Besides utilizing drug detection programs, many firms have established employee assistance plans to provide short-term counseling to employees and assist them in obtaining appropriate treatment for substance abuse. Employee education programs are also used to alert employees to the dangers of substance abuse and to encourage those who are abusing to seek treatment.[24]

COMING TO TERMS WITH SUBSTANCE ABUSE

If you are abusing substances, you need to take action before their use interferes with your current job, prevents you from obtaining a job, disrupts other major areas of your life, destroys your health, or kills you.

Check the telephone book for treatment and counseling centers. If you are employed and your company has an employee assistance program (EAP), use it. The program is designed to help employees with substance abuse and other personal problems. It is confidential and usually free.

Substance abusers need to seek help.

Many individuals are reluctant to use an employee assistance program for fear that their employer will learn they have a problem. Most plans ensure confidentiality and do not reveal to the employer which employees have used the services. Employers will eventually find out about untreated substance abuse problems when performance declines.

Seeking help is the first step in controlling a substance abuse problem.

©Getty Images/PhotoDisc

If you drink socially, take steps to ensure that your alcohol intake is under control and to keep it within responsible boundaries:[26]

- Limit drinking to under one ounce of ethanol, the intoxicating ingredient in alcoholic beverages, on any day that you drink. (One-half ounce of ethanol equates to 12 ounces of beer, 5 ounces of wine, or 1 ounce of hard liquor.) Measure your alcohol when making your own drinks.

- Abstain completely from alcoholic beverages for at least two consecutive days each week.

- Drink slowly and intersperse alcoholic drinks with nonalcoholic drinks while at parties.

- Don't drink on an empty stomach.

- Don't medicate yourself with alcohol. It will only make you feel more depressed.

- Avoid social patterns that revolve around alcohol, and associate with responsible drinkers or nondrinkers.

While some individuals are able to drink socially in moderation, others should not drink at all. Abstinence is usually the only way that recovering alcoholics and individuals from alcoholic families are able to prevent abusing substances. More information can be obtained from the National Council on Alcoholism, Alcoholics Anonymous, or other organizations that deal with alcohol abuse.

If you do not take action to correct your substance abuse problem, quite likely your supervisor will. Most organizations that operate drug-testing programs have trained their supervisors to recognize behavior that signals substance abuse.

Many substance abusers deny having a problem and fail to realize that the problem is interfering with their work. Because of employee denial, organizations usually instruct their supervisors to do the following about suspected instances of substance abuse:

- Judge on performance only and do not accuse the employee of having a substance abuse problem.

- Do not accept excuses for ongoing poor performance or absenteeism.

- Document all poor performance.

- Assist employees in obtaining treatment if asked.

- Do not preach or moralize.
- Begin action up to and including discharge if the employee does not satisfactorily perform the job.

Employees with substance abuse problems should recognize that supervisors have support from higher management in taking these actions. Abusers should address their problem if they wish to remain employed.

Two federal laws can assist substance abusers in getting treatment and keeping their jobs. One is the Americans with Disabilities Act (ADA) and the other is the Family Medical Leave Act (FMLA). The Americans with Disabilities Act requires that employers with 15 or more employees give a reasonable accommodation to individuals with disabilities. Under the act, alcoholism is treated as a disability. However, employees who abuse alcohol may be disciplined and discharged when their alcohol use adversely affects job performance. Users of illegal drugs are not protected and can be discharged for drug use. Former drug addicts, however, are covered.

Individuals who voluntarily check themselves into a drug treatment center prior to being identified by the company as a substance abuser will most likely be protected by the act and be allowed a reasonable amount of time to pursue treatment.

The Family Medical Leave Act requires employers with 50 or more employees within a 75-mile radius to provide employees who have worked for the company at least 1,250 hours in the past 12 months to provide 12 weeks of unpaid leave during a 12-month period for a serious health condition. Absence for treatment of substance abuse does qualify for FMLA leave.[28]

As these laws and their interpretations rapidly change, anyone wanting protection for treatment under these laws or any state laws should check with the company's human resource department or obtain legal counsel.

DEALING WITH ABUSERS AT WORK

Becoming aware that a coworker or supervisor is abusing drugs or alcohol presents a dilemma. If you allow such people to operate machinery or perform any activity that might injure them or others or destroy equipment or property and something actually happens, living with yourself will be difficult. If you report the individual to management, resentment will most likely result, causing future difficulties in working with this individual. Others in your work group may feel uncomfortable around you, thinking that you will report their activities to management.

Covering up for coworkers or supervisors by doing their work or making excuses for their tardiness or absence is called **enabling**. This behavior allows substance abusers to continue this conduct and to avoid confronting the problem. Enabling will keep peace in your work group. However, you will continue to perform extra work while the abuser carries on the pattern of missed hours and substandard performance. Resentment on your part will soon build.

Additionally, you may wish to assist the individual in trouble. You may give advice, preach, or moralize. This action generally does not help because substance abusers typically deny that they have a problem. The more you attempt to help, the more resentful the substance abuser will become, frustrating both of you.

Take action when a coworker abuses substances.

Dealing with substance-abusing coworkers and supervisors, then, requires human relations skills. Use tact and diplomacy, involving only those who need to know. Tell abusers that their behavior is making your working with them difficult. Point out a specific behavior, such as absence, that is causing you difficulty. Offer support by showing concern that they do not appear to be their old selves and asking what you can do to help. Be supportive if they decide to enter treatment.

Light and moderate drinkers cause 60 percent of tardiness, absenteeism, and poor quality work as a result of alcohol consumption while heavy drinkers and alcoholics cause the remaining 40 percent.

A study of over 6,000 people reported that the more frequently employees become high or drunk, the more likely they are to report work performance problems. Employees who abstained from alcohol reported an average of 4.2 work-performance problems in the past year; those who were high or drunk on 13 or more days in the past month reported an average of 7.5 problems.[29]

1. *While almost everyone recognizes the toll alcoholics and drug addicts take on productivity, almost no one notices the loss of productivity caused by light to moderate substance abuse. Do you agree? Why, or why not?*
2. *Are you being fair to your employer if you tie one on after work regularly? To yourself?*
3. *Should organizations be allowed to dictate substance avoidance during nonwork hours? Why, or why not?*

Not allowing impaired employees to operate equipment, refusing to "enable" by covering for them, and not preaching or moralizing are the best ways to help yourself and your fellow employees. Both of you benefit: the abuser is forced into treatment quicker, and you won't be worried about potential disaster or feel that you're being used or taken advantage of.

*Fast*Chat

1. K.R. Collins of Collins and Associates states that most employees do not seek EAP assistance on their own but get help only when forced to do so by their employer. Why do you think this is?[30]
2. Do you believe EAPs keep information confidential? Why do you feel this way?
3. What other methods of treatment are available in your community?
4. Why is denial a problem when dealing with substance abuse? Review the definition of "enable" in this chapter and the defense mechanism "denial" in Chapter 2.
5. Name some specific actions that are enabling.

Time is a precious commodity. Every individual has the same amount of time each day to be wasted or spent well. How we choose to use our time makes the difference in whether or not we achieve our goals. Effective **time management** is simply maximizing the time that we have to our greatest advantage. When we are in control of our time, we perform better, feel better about ourselves, and suffer fewer stress-related illnesses. We can develop better time management by assessing how we use time, identifying how we waste it, and planning to use it better.

ASSESSING HOW YOU SPEND YOUR TIME

The first step in assessing whether you are managing your time wisely is to determine if you are suffering any of the negative symptoms of poor time management. These negative symptoms are:

Symptoms of Poor Time Management

1. *Indecision.* You have so much to do that you cannot decide what to do first. You end up doing nothing and getting nowhere.

2. *White rabbit habit.* "I'm late, I'm late, for a very important date" accurately describes your life. Like the rabbit in Lewis Carroll's *Alice's Adventures in Wonderland*, you are always in a hurry, running late, and missing appointments and deadlines.

3. *Stress illnesses.* Responses to the pressures of poor time management include headaches, backaches, insomnia, and hives.

4. *Irritability and anger.* You stay angry and upset and have a tendency to take your frustration out on others.

Negative symptoms may make you look "out of control" and keep you from getting results. Good time management tends to be reflected in a confident and controlled approach to activities.

Another valuable step in assessing your time usage is to keep a time log, as illustrated in the Sample Time Log on page 495. Use a log for at least a one-week period. Logging your daily activities for this length of time will allow you to identify your major time-wasters. You may be surprised at the amount of time you spend on innocent activities that rob you of using your precious commodity more productively.

> Assess the effects of poor time management and then correct it.

Constant lateness is a symptom of poor time management.

©Getty Images/PhotoDisc

IDENTIFYING TIME-WASTERS

Lack of planning, drop-in visitors, telephone games, procrastination, meetings, overcommitment, fighting brushfires, personal disorganization, the inability to say "no," television, and Internet surfing are among the most frequent time-wasters. You may recognize some of them as being at the top of your list. Methods of handling some of the biggest time-wasters are described below.

Lack of Planning An old adage appropriate to this situation states, "If you fail to plan, you plan to fail." Planning a course of action is crucial in accomplishing your goals. One of the easiest methods of planning is to make a list of tasks to be accomplished. Ideally, you will have a daily list of 5 to 10 major actions in order of importance. Limiting your list to 5 to 10 items enables you to add unexpected or forgotten items while keeping the list manageable. The important point is to stick to your list and not overcommit. Carry over any unfinished tasks to the next day and integrate them into that day's priority list. An effective way of handling your priority list is to keep it on a calendar throughout the year. This practice also provides you with an excellent record of your activities.

Another useful method of planning is to use your "peak times" for tough tasks. You may be a morning person or a night person. Our body clocks, or biological rhythms, do tick strongest at different times of the

Human Relations

Figure 17.1   Sample Time Log

Time	Planned Work	Telephone	Interruption	Meeting	Unplanned/New	Reports	Other	Subject	Originator (Person)	Priority A	B	C	Other	Comments
7:30														
7:45														
8:00														
8:15														
8:30														
8:45														
9:00														
9:15														
9:30														
9:45														
10:00														
10:15														
10:30														
10:45														
11:00														
11:15														
11:30														
11:45														
12:00														
12:15														
12:30														
12:45														
1:00														
1:15														
1:30														
1:45														
2:00														
2:15														
2:30														
2:45														
3:00														
3:15														
3:30														
3:45														
4:00														
4:15														
4:30														
4:45														
5:00														

Priority Definitions:

A-Very important; high priority item

B-Important; have more time to complete

C-Less important; could be delegated or rescheduled for later time

Other-Could "not do;" wasted time

Figure 17.2 Assess Your Time Management Skills

DIAGNOSTIC TEST: YOU AND TIME

	OFTEN	SOME-TIMES	RARELY
1. Do you handle each piece of paperwork only once?	❏	❏	❏
2. Do you begin and finish projects on time?	❏	❏	❏
3. Do people know the best time to reach you?	❏	❏	❏
4. Do you do something every day that moves you closer to your long-range goals?	❏	❏	❏
5. When you are interrupted, can you return to work without losing momentum?	❏	❏	❏
6. Do you deal effectively with long-winded callers?	❏	❏	❏
7. Do you focus on preventing problems before they arise rather than solving them after they happen?	❏	❏	❏
8. Do you meet deadlines with time to spare?	❏	❏	❏
9. Are you on time to work, to meetings, and to events?	❏	❏	❏
10. Do you delegate well?	❏	❏	❏
11. Do you write daily to-do lists?	❏	❏	❏
12. Do you finish all the items on your to-do lists?	❏	❏	❏
13. Do you update in writing your professional and personal goals?	❏	❏	❏
14. Is your desk clean and organized?	❏	❏	❏
15. Can you easily find items in your files?	❏	❏	❏
Subtotal	———	———	———
	$\times 4$	$\times 2$	$\times 0$
Total	═══	═══	═══

What the Test Says About You

Give yourself 4 points for every *often* you checked. Give yourself 2 points for every *sometimes*. Give yourself 0 points for every *rarely*.

Add your points together and place yourself in the proper group.

- 49–60   You manage your time well. You are in control of most days and most situations.
- 37–48   You manage your time well some of the time. However, you need to be more consistent with timesaving strategies. Adding new techniques is allowed!
- 25–36   You are all too often a victim of time. Don't let each day manage you. Apply the techniques you learn here right away.
- 13–24   You are close to losing control and probably too disorganized to enjoy quality time. A new priority-powered time plan is needed now!
- 0–12   You are overwhelmed, scattered, frustrated, and probably under a lot of stress. Put the techniques in this book into practice. Star chapters—for special study—that treat your problem areas.

day for each person. Recognizing your peak performance time may assist you in planning your more difficult tasks for that time to maximize your effectiveness. For instance, if you are a morning person, you will want to complete a difficult report early in the morning rather than waiting until late afternoon when you are not as alert.

Another timesaving tip is to plan certain activities for their nonpeak times. For example, banking on Friday afternoons will most certainly cost you more time than a midweek visit. Attempting postal business during your lunch break will find you in long lines with other individuals who had the same idea. A midmorning or afternoon visit to the post office will probably save you time.

Drop-in or Casual Visitors Friends and colleagues may unwittingly rob you of precious time needed to meet personal or professional commitments. That drop-in visit from the coworker down the hall to discuss the Monday night football game may disrupt your concentration on an important report due by noon to your boss or throw your daily schedule completely off track. To control such intrusions, close your office door if you have one. If this signal is not successful, use your body language to show that you are busy or stand up and start toward the door. Additionally, the following phrases can be useful in controlling the length of visits:

"I appreciate your stopping by, but…"

"I have a tight schedule; could we talk about this on…" (and set a time and date)

"I have about 10 minutes before I have to go…" "How can I help you?"

GLOBAL CONNECTION

Americans perceive time as linear, with a past, present, and future. Because of this, Americans are future oriented and prepare for it by saving, wasting, making up, or spending time. On the other hand, many cultures treat time as a limitless pool in which certain things happen and then pass. Things come and go, as do the seasons.

1. *How can these differing views of time cause time management problems in the global workplace?*

2. *Have you ever been exposed to a different culture's concept of time? If so, what happened?*

Procrastination   One of the most difficult time-wasters to control is your own procrastination. **Procrastination** is defined as putting off or intentionally delaying activities that need to be done. Once you understand the problem, you can develop methods of overcoming it. Chapter 10 and the box entitled Major Causes of Procrastination present some of the reasons we procrastinate and describe when delaying is appropriate or inappropriate.

We often have hidden meanings in what we say.

We occasionally find ourselves saying and meaning two different things:

Saying:		Meaning:	
	I really should…		I don't really want to…
	I can't do…		I won't do…
	I might…		I won't…
	I'll try to…		I won't…
	Could we discuss this some other time?		I really don't *ever* want to talk about it.

Major Causes of Procrastination

Inappropriate Causes	**Appropriate Causes**
• *Perfectionism*: You put off tasks until you can do them exactly right, the very best you can. You fear they won't be right or good enough.	• *Stressed/exhausted*: You are too tired to think through the problem effectively. You might make a poor or wrong decision. You tend to use bad judgment and may wind up doing it over again.
• *Abdication*: You wait for things to "happen" rather than *make* them happen; you make panic decisions; you let someone else make the decision; you do nothing at all.	• *Impulsive/emotional*: You might make snap judgments or might do things in a fit of anger and regret them.
• *Overwhelmed*: Job/task appears too big to handle. It seems threatening.	• *Lack of information*: You need more facts to make a good decision.
• *Uncertainty*: You are unsure how to do the task.	• *Feel cautious/concerned*: You heed a subconscious message that you should not do that activity.

 **Quick tip** ....

Try tackling procrastination by using the following suggestions:

   1. Tackle tough problems at your body's peak performance times.
   2. Break large tasks into smaller segments so they will not seem overwhelming.

Human Relations

3. Use daily "to do" lists and set specific goals.

4. Fight perfectionism.

5. Seek help if needed.

6. Let go of low priority tasks in order to focus and concentrate on high priority ones.

7. Schedule appropriate blocks of times to do specific tasks.

8. Establish a reward system for positive reinforcement.

••

Telephone Games   You may have been involved in a game of "telephone tag" or applied evasive tactics with "Gabby Gerty." The game of telephone tag—two people calling numerous times, leaving messages but never reaching each other—can take hours of unproductive time. This "game" can be avoided in several ways. Leave a message specifying what you want or leave instructions concerning required actions. If someone you need does not return your call, you might try leaving a message such as, "Unless I hear from you by close of business today, I plan…" This warning will normally prompt action by the other party. If all else fails, try to get your information elsewhere.

An encounter with "Gabby Gerty" involves receiving a call from someone who wants to discuss everything but the important purpose of the call. The following phrases may help control the length of time you spend on these calls:

"I appreciate your call, but. . ."

"I'm working on a term paper due this week. Can we visit later when I am not so pressed for time?"

"Could you call back when we might have more time?"

MANAGING YOUR TIME AT MEETINGS

Endless, nonproductive meetings are some of the biggest time-wasters in the workplace. Practicing a few important meeting strategies can help all attendees manage their time and get the most out of the meeting.

A **planned agenda** is an outline or list of what is to be discussed or accomplished during the meeting. The agenda is a valuable tool for controlling your meeting. Ideally, an agenda should be distributed several days prior to the meeting time. People will be able to schedule their time to support the meeting and prepare information that may be needed.

Quick tip ....

Try these guidelines for running an effective meeting:

1. Provide advance agendas reflecting timed subjects.
2. Invite only those people who are needed.
3. Start on time.
4. Set clear goals/purposes for the meeting.
5. Set time limits on the meeting and discussion topics.
6. Strictly adhere to your agenda.
7. Record and assign action items during the meeting.
8. Distribute meeting minutes within 48 hours.
9. Schedule an action-item follow-up.

....

Hidden agendas can waste your meeting time.

The agenda will serve as your guideline for a smooth transition from topic to topic and prevent the introduction of hidden agendas. A **hidden agenda** consists of topics that attendees wish to discuss that have no relevance to the purpose of your meeting. A hidden agenda can be disruptive.

As the meeting leader, you have the responsibility for adhering to the planned agenda. A successful meeting should move quickly, sufficiently cover all scheduled topics in the shortest possible time, and accomplish the planned meeting objectives. To manage time outside of meetings, you may want to develop some definite action plans. The Sample Time Management Action Plan below provides you with a format and brief example of an action plan.

Sample Time Management Action Plan
....

Desired Result: *Quit watching excessive TV*
Change Required: *Be more productive; read more, watch less*
Target Date: *Within a week*
Actions Required: *Unplug TV*
Key People Involved: *Family—they won't like it*
Evaluate/modify: *Did I achieve desired results? If not, try another approach*

---

*Fast*Chat

1. Often, we spend time "efficiently" but are not "effective." What is the difference between *efficient* and *effective*?
2. Do you take time to determine what really matters and concentrate on that activity? Why, or why not?

Sound health practices are vital to a successful career. You can take responsibility for your own health by eating a balanced diet, maintaining an appropriate weight, limiting alcohol consumption, not smoking, and developing a mind-set that allows you to relax and enjoy leisure time while limiting stressful thoughts, attitudes, and behaviors.

A BALANCED DIET AND WEIGHT MANAGEMENT

The United States Department of Agriculture (USDA) recommends that we eat a balanced variety of foods to get the nutrients we need and at the same time the right amount of calories to maintain healthy weight. Their suggestions can be found in The Food Guide Pyramid below. Note that servings vary based on your age and other factors.[31]

Your eating patterns affect your mental and physical condition.

Being overweight or obese has been associated with increased risk of developing such conditions as high blood pressure, Type 2 diabetes, and coronary artery disease. To determine whether you are at risk because of your weight, determine your Body Mass Index (BMI) by using the chart below. Then, using your BMI and waist size, determine your health risk relative to normal weight.[32]

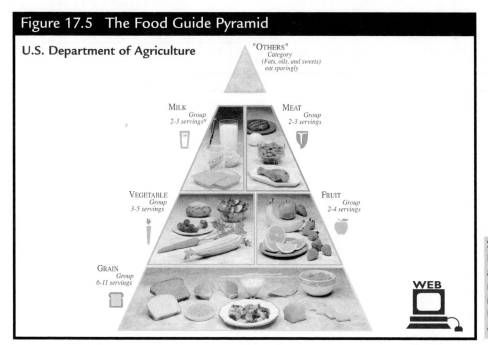

Figure 17.5   The Food Guide Pyramid

U.S. Department of Agriculture

"OTHERS" Category (Fats, oils, and sweets) eat sparingly

MILK Group 2-3 servings*

MEAT Group 2-3 servings

VEGETABLE Group 3-5 servings

FRUIT Group 2-4 servings

GRAIN Group 6-11 servings

WEB

Search online for BMI calculators and other nutrition resources at the U.S. Department of Agriculture.

Determining your Body Mass Index (BMI)

Find your height in the left-hand column. Move across that row to your weight. The number at the top of the column is the BMI for that height and weight.

BMI (kg/m^2)	19	20	21	22	23	24	25	26	27	28	29	30	35	40
Height (in.)	Weight (lb.)													
58	91	96	100	105	110	115	119	124	129	134	138	143	167	191
59	94	99	104	109	114	119	124	128	133	138	143	148	173	198
60	97	102	107	112	118	123	128	133	138	143	148	153	179	204
61	100	106	111	118	122	127	132	137	143	148	153	158	185	211
62	104	109	115	120	126	131	136	142	147	153	158	164	191	218
63	107	113	118	124	130	135	141	146	152	158	163	169	197	225
64	110	116	122	128	134	140	145	151	157	163	169	174	204	232
65	114	120	126	132	138	144	150	158	162	168	174	180	210	240
66	118	124	130	136	142	148	155	161	167	173	179	186	216	247
67	121	127	134	140	146	153	159	166	172	178	185	191	223	255
68	125	131	138	144	151	158	164	171	177	184	190	197	230	262
69	128	135	142	149	155	162	169	176	182	189	196	203	236	270
70	132	139	146	153	160	167	174	181	188	195	202	207	243	278
71	136	143	150	157	165	172	179	186	193	200	208	215	250	286
72	140	147	154	162	169	177	184	191	199	206	213	221	258	294
73	144	151	159	166	174	182	189	197	204	212	219	227	265	302
74	148	155	163	171	179	186	194	202	210	218	225	233	272	311
75	152	160	168	176	184	192	200	208	216	224	232	240	279	319
76	158	164	172	180	189	197	205	213	221	230	238	246	287	328

Risk of Associated Disease According to BMI and Waist Size

BMI		Waist less than or equal to 40 in. (men) or 35 in. (women)	Waist greater than 40 in. (men) or 35 in. (women)
18.5 or less	Underweight		N/A
18.5–24.9	Normal		N/A
25.0–29.9	Overweight	Increased	High
30.0–34.9	Obese	High	Very high
35.0–39.9	Obese	Very High	Very High
40 or greater	Extremely Obese	Extremely High	Extremely High

MAKING HEALTHY CHOICES

Cutting back on harmful substances and learning to practice stress management techniques can contribute greatly to overall health.

Limiting the consumption of caffeine   Regular consumption of caffeine (over 350 mg/day) through coffee or caffeinated soft drinks may not only cause dependency but chronic insomnia, persistent anxiety, restlessness, heart palpitations, upset stomach, and depression. Eliminating caffeine intake after 2:00 PM will allow deep, rather than restless, sleep, which is necessary for the body to produce high energy.[33]

Smoking   Cigarette smoking is the single most important preventable cause of death in our society. Cancers of the lung, larynx, oral cavity, esophagus, pancreas, and bladder; heart and blood vessel disease; chronic bronchitis; and emphysema have all been linked to smoking. Additionally, involuntary or passive inhalation of cigarette smoke can cause or worsen symptoms of asthma, cardiovascular and respiratory diseases, pneumonia, and bronchitis. Smoking during pregnancy has been associated with premature births, small or underweight babies, and respiratory and cardiovascular problems in infants. Besides these physical implications, smoking is a major contributor to death and injury from fires and other accidents.

In an effort to curb smoking-related problems, most states have passed legislation limiting or forbidding smoking in enclosed public places. Smoking has been banned on domestic and many international air flights, and more nonsmokers today are demanding and obtaining smoke-free environments at work and in public areas. Asking someone not to smoke around you should be done tactfully, however.

Giving up the smoking habit takes determination. Smoking often serves as an outlet for nervousness. The habit of smoking can become psychologically addictive. Nicotine, a key ingredient in cigarette smoke, is physiologically addictive, making it even more difficult to stop. Many programs designed to help people stop smoking are available, and some are covered by medical insurance.

Exercise   Exercise is one of the most effective methods known for reducing stress. Although it is not a cure-all, exercise releases the stored energies of the "fight or flight" response. Moderate running, swimming, biking, racquetball, and basketball are all good forms of exercise for reducing stress. Regardless of which exercise form you choose, fitness experts recommend a minimum of 20 minutes of continuous exercise, three or four times a week.

However, lighter forms of exercise can be equally effective stress reducers. Working in the garden, mowing the yard, playing ping pong or

QUICK WIT
"Put a pot of chili on the stove to simmer. Let it simmer. Meanwhile, broil a good steak. Eat the steak. Let the chili simmer. Ignore it."
Recipe for chili from Allan Shivers, former governor of Texas

Exercise can play a key role in relieving stress and controlling weight.

pool, or taking a brisk walk can disengage you from the sources of stress. These exercises provide a "mental break."

Exercise need not be dull or seem like a chore. Its benefits, such as relieving tension, helping control weight, and lowering cholesterol, can be obtained through small changes in your personal routine. You do not have to be an accomplished athlete or a physical fitness expert to achieve desired results through exercise. In addition to establishing a regular exercise program at home or at a gym, you might consider changing simple daily habits. The following small changes in your lifestyle can increase your physical activity: [34]

1. Use the stairs rather than the elevator.

2. Park your car at the back of the parking lot and walk to the store.

3. Put more vigor into everyday activities.

4. Take a walk each day at lunchtime or after work, and keep walking shoes in your car for these occasions.

5. Go dancing or join a square-dance club.

6. Use the restroom on a different floor at work and take the stairs.

Before starting any exercise program, however, you should consult a physician to determine what is appropriate for your age and physical condition.

Relaxation Learning the art of relaxation is crucial to controlling stress. Headaches, backaches, and nervousness can be reduced or eliminated by using progressive relaxation techniques. Nervousness wastes energy, making us more fatigued and less alert.

To relax, spend 20 to 30 minutes twice a day applying some of the various relaxation techniques. All that is necessary is a quiet place where you will not be disturbed. Mini-relaxation breaks of five minutes each throughout the day can also be invaluable in reducing stress. Only a comfortable chair or sofa is necessary. One of these techniques is described below:[35]

Loosen any tight clothing. Close your eyes and concentrate on breathing slowly and deeply into the lower part of your chest. As you exhale, imagine the tenseness leaving you. Begin to concentrate on your toes and feet, telling yourself that they are relaxing. Think slowly and deliberately. Concentrate on relaxing and breathing until your toes and feet feel thoroughly relaxed. Gradually progress to other parts of your body until you are completely relaxed.

After you are fully relaxed, you may wish to practice visual imagery, seeing yourself relaxing on a beach or gently swinging in a hammock. Your local library or bookstore can provide you with further exercises on relaxation. Additionally, audio and visual relaxation tapes and recordings of peaceful sounds are available. And simply looking at beautiful pictures of forests, meadows, or other peaceful, green settings has been shown to elicit the relaxation response quickly and refreshingly.

Spend time during the day mentally scanning your body. Are your muscles tense? Is your stomach in knots? Do you have a tension headache or a case of indigestion? If so, you may choose to spend a few minutes breathing deeply, concentrating on relaxation, and applying some of the stress and tension-relieving exercises. With practice, you can quickly bring yourself into a peaceful state.

Leisure Leisure time is important. It allows us a chance to relax and get away from daily stresses, permitting us to return refreshed and ready to work. Unfortunately, obtaining that time seems to be difficult at times. Although we live in what is often called the "short-cut society," we still have less time to enjoy stress-free activities. With the advent of fast foods, virtual offices, fax machines, cell phones, pagers and similar electronics, laptop computers, microwaves, satellites, and robotics designed to make our lives easier, the pace of life has simply increased, and we are part of the frenzy.

This inability to make time for leisure activity is part of the pattern of workaholism. **Workaholics** are individuals who are consumed by their jobs and derive little pleasure from other activities. These people are likely candidates for heart attacks, depression, hypertension, insomnia, and other physical ailments. They often view their lives as one long, continuous workday reaching well into the night and are rarely able to enjoy even the thought of leisure time. They are known to carry a briefcase full of work along anywhere they go and phone into the office frequently for messages that often add pressures. For workaholics, even vacations are seldom restful because they take thoughts and worries of their jobs with them, compounding the stress.

Personality traits can also contribute to stress conditions. Two well-known personality types have been identified by extensive psychological research on behavior patterns. **Type A personalities** tend to be highly competitive, aggressive, achievement-oriented, and impatient. They typically appear pressured, rushed or hurried, and volatile and dislike waiting in lines or for traffic lights to turn green. **Type B personalities** exhibit an opposite behavior pattern. They appear more relaxed, easy-going, and even-paced in their approach to life in general. The Type B individual seldom overcommits, can say no without feeling guilty, and takes time to smell the roses along the way.

Type A individuals are more likely to experience high stress levels and exhibit stress symptoms than Type B individuals. Type A personalities are twice as prone to cardiovascular diseases, such as heart attacks and

QUICK WIT
"If you look at what you have in life, you'll always have more. If you look at what you don't have in life, you'll never have enough."
Oprah Winfrey

Enjoying leisure time is an essential part of reducing stress.

clogged arteries, as Type B personalities. An important step in developing a healthy lifestyle may be to identify these patterns in your personality and strive to reduce negative Type A tendencies you may have.

Tips for Leaving Stress at the Office

1. Try to end the day as smoothly as possible. Start unwinding about one-half hour before you leave. Save easier jobs for last to assist you in unwinding.

2. To cut down worry about unfinished items, make a list of what needs to be done, imagine successfully completing these items, and leave them until the next morning.

3. Maintain a perspective. Remember that today's disasters are not the end of the world and will be of little importance in the future.

4. Use your commute to unwind. Listen to soothing music, read a good book, or enjoy a picturesque magazine if you are not driving.

5. Arrange with your family to be allowed a small bit of quiet time. This will help ease the transition between work and home.

6. Do not make dinner an ordeal with fancy meals. Turn off the television and limit interruptions. Limit work-related conversations at mealtime.

7. Do not overschedule your leisure hours. Do not bring work home on a routine basis, and discourage colleagues from calling in the evenings with work-related questions.

In addition to making the most of our leisure time, we should choose activities carefully. For highly competitive individuals, sports, such as softball and tennis, can be as stressful as work.

Reducing stressful thoughts, attitudes, and behaviors Setting realistic goals, learning to take risks, raising self-esteem, practicing positive self-talk, using communication skills, understanding the grieving process, and developing assertive behavior are discussed in other chapters. All of these skills can assist you in changing stressful thoughts, attitudes, and behaviors.

Another important skill that reduces stress is the ability to be self-focused. Harriet Goldhor Lerner, in her book, *The Dance of Intimacy*, states that individuals who are not self-focused see others as the problem and believe the solution is for the other person to change. These individuals are unable to achieve intimacy with those around them, which increases stress. The best idea is to focus on our own problems and work on resolving them rather than trying to change the behavior of others.[36]

Lerner also suggests avoiding what she calls "triangles." A triangle occurs when one person brings you into a problem that he or she is having with a third person. Refusing to be drawn into a problem between others is a healthy behavior to learn.[37]

> Changing stressful thoughts, attitudes, and behaviors takes time and practice.

You can cultivate other healthy attitudes and behaviors in these ways:

1. Do not try to change others; accept them as they are.

2. Do not expect actions from others. Thoughts such as "they should" and "they must" can cause anger and frustration.

3. Clarify what you want and firmly state your wants in an assertive manner.

4. Recognize situations in which you have no control. A traffic jam will unclog at the same time whether you remain angry at the inconvenience or attempt to relax and spend the time productively.

5. View situations realistically. What will failure in this situation mean next month, next year, in 10 years?

6. Recognize that you do have options and control of many situations. Review Chapter 3 on how to seek alternative ways of meeting wants and needs.

7. Develop a support system of friends and relatives with whom you can discuss stressful events and situations.

8. When choosing a relationship, ask whether it will be good for you or whether it will increase your stress.

9. Take coffee and lunch breaks away from the office.

10. Schedule some quiet time to be alone, during which you may dream, relax, or think.

Accepting and applying some of these attitudes and behaviors will ease feelings of stress that complicate your daily routine.

*Fast*Chat

Many individuals consciously participate in activities that are potentially harmful to their health.

1. Should companies have the right to refuse to hire individuals who smoke, even if they do not smoke at work? If not, what alternatives might companies have to keep insurance rates lower for others?

2. Should companies have the right to refuse to hire those who are over-weight or who participate in dangerous activities such as skydiving and mountain climbing?

Key Terms

work-life benefits

stress

substance abuse

alcohol

cocaine

marijuana

sedatives

tranquilizers

amphetamines

club drugs

inhalants

hallucinogens

narcotics

anabolic steroids

pre-employment drug testing

expected interval testing

random interval testing

"for cause" testing

treatment follow-up testing

enabling

time management

procrastination

planned agenda

hidden agenda

workaholics

Type A personalities

Type B personalities

CHAPTER SUMMARY

Work-life programs allow employees to gain some measure of balance between work and home. Organizations show interest in these programs because they raise morale, enhance recruitment efforts, and allow them to remain competitive or increase their image in their industry.

Stress is the physical state of the body in response to environmental pressures that produce emotional discomfort. Stress can result from good or bad causes. When the body reaches its stress threshold, certain physical and mental reactions occur. Overindulging, hypertension, insomnia, anxiety, depression, heart attacks, and mental disorders are only a few of the symptoms of stress illnesses.

Organizations are concerned about substance abuse because abusers cost them money in the form of lost productivity, industrial accidents, and excessive use of benefits. Individuals who are abusing substances need to take action to control their problem. If they do not, their supervisors may take action.

Lastly, a healthy lifestyle can help manage stress and prevent disease. Hallmarks of a healthy lifestyle include the ability to manage time effectively, a healthy diet, not smoking, and changing stressful thoughts, attitudes, and behaviors. Relaxation and leisure activities also contribute to a well rounded way of life.

REVIEW QUESTIONS

1. What are work-life benefits? Why are they good for both employer and employee?

2. What are companies doing to promote work-life balance?

3. What are the physical and mental results of stress overload?

4. What are companies doing to combat substance abuse?

5. What substances are commonly abused? What are the effects of these substances?

6. What actions can an abuser of substances expect from a supervisor who has been trained to deal with substance abusers?

7. What are the most effective methods of time management?

8. What is the importance of proper diet in minimizing stress effects?

9. How do exercise and relaxation help you stay healthy?

10. How can you change stressful thoughts, attitudes, and behaviors?

DISCUSSION QUESTIONS

1. Does your organization provide work-life benefits for employees? If so, what are the obvious benefits of these programs?

2. What symptoms of stress do you feel? What do you believe are the major causes? What do you do to reduce the stress?

3. Should employers have the right to administer drug tests to employees? Why, or why not?

4. What difficulty would you have in handling a coworker and good friend who is abusing substances? What might happen to the coworker if you became an enabler, allowing him or her to continue in the abuse? What might happen to you? To others? To the company?

5. What method of time management do you use? What benefits do you realize from your method? How might you improve your method?

6. Do you procrastinate? Why? How might you overcome your procrastination?

7. Do you have a problem finding leisure time in your daily schedule? Do you exhibit symptoms of being a workaholic? How might you better plan for leisure time?

8. Which of your thoughts, beliefs, or behaviors contribute to your feelings of stress? How might you reduce these sources of stress?

WEB

WRITING

CHAPTER PROJECT

On the Internet or at your local library, find an article about health. Write, prepare, and deliver a five-minute oral presentation to your class members on a health or wellness subject discussed in this chapter.

APPLICATIONS

In small groups, analyze the following:

TEAMWORK

Alice in Wonderful Land

Alice had just been awarded a contract to provide a training seminar on supervisory skills to a group of new first-line supervisors at a major oil company in Dallas. This opportunity could establish her as a leader in the training field, and with the right exposure she could receive more contracts with other companies. She already had a comfortable amount of business that pushed her busy schedule, but this job could really boost her practice into high gear. Alice smiled with satisfaction at the prospects.

The only problem was the amount of time and effort required in putting a new seminar together. "How can I crowd all this new preparation into my schedule?" she wondered out loud. "I already work 14, 16, … sometimes even 20 hours a day just keeping up with my current contract load." The day did not seem to have enough hours to do all that needed to be done. She was also teaching a class two nights a week at the local college and had just agreed to collaborate on a project for her community that was a full year's commitment of time and effort. Her work with the youth group at the church might have to be cut back if this wonderful opportunity really got off the ground.

"With a little luck, I'll be able to pull this off and get over the hump this time. If only I don't get those awful headaches I had last week. They certainly put a damper on my productivity."

1. What symptoms of stress is Alice exhibiting?

2. Do you believe that Alice is an effective time manager? How might she solve her problem?

3. Should Alice accept the new contract? Why, or why not?

Watch Out from Behind!

TEAMWORK

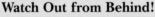

Carey had planned for weeks in advance to make this meeting successful. He had carefully selected the attendees, reserved the conference room well in advance, and prepared his briefing materials in plenty of time to go over them and make the necessary changes for clarity. He had even sent a well organized agenda a week ago to all attendees so that they could be prepared to discuss the topics outlined. Everything would go smoothly, and they would be finished before noon.

Carey started the meeting promptly at 10:00 AM and moved swiftly through the first several items with good decisions made and all action items appropriately assigned. The next topic generated a great deal of conversation.

Almost everyone was commenting on the plans he had outlined in his briefing. Suddenly, Frank from the engineering division put a new proposal on the table for discussion. Everyone was surprised that Frank had thought out this approach so thoroughly, but they were clearly interested. Some people began adding their ideas to Frank's, and before Carey knew it, they were completely off the primary subjects of his meeting. Somehow he had lost control of his meeting and wasn't sure how he would meet the noon deadline for getting the decisions and results he needed from this fiasco.

1. What caused Carey's meeting to get off track?

2. How might Carey have prevented this problem?

3. How would you have handled Frank's action?

ADDITIONAL READINGS AND RESOURCES

Allen, David. *Getting Things Done: The Art of Stress-Free Productivity.* New York: Penguin USA, 2003.

Dodes, Lance M. *The Heart of Addiction: A New Approach to Understanding and Managing Alcoholism and Other Addictive Behaviors.* New York: HarperCollins, 2002.

Emmett, Rita. *The Procrastinator's Handbook: Mastering the Art of Doing It Now.* New York: Walker and Company, 2000.

Harris, Clare. *Minimize Stress, Maximize Success.* London: Duncan Baird Publishers, 2003.

Kaye, Beverly, and Sharon Jordan-Evans. *Love It Don't Leave It—26 Ways to Get What You Want at Work.* San Francisco: Barret-Koehlar Publishers, Inc., 2003.

Kirshenbaum, Mira. *The Emotional Energy Factor.* New York: Delacorte Press/Random House, 2003.

For additional resources, refer to the web site for this text: school.cengage.com/career/dalton

CHAPTER 18

OBJECTIVES

Career Management:
Securing Your Future

After studying this chapter, you should be able to:

18.1 *Understand the forces shaping our economy and how they affect the types of jobs available.*

18.2 *Explain the skills needed to manage your career.*

18.3 *Explain how to learn about occupations, organizations, and job openings.*

18.4 *Write a solid resume.*

18.5 *Use appropriate behavior and communication during a job interview.*

18.6 *Identify ways to handle job search stress and respond to job offers.*

18.7 *Explain strategies for starting and ending jobs.*

focus

Tom Peters, management guru and author of numerous business books, gives his view of employment in the 21st century in his 2003 book, *Re-imagine!*[1]

1. Lifetime employment is over.

2. Stable employment at large corporations is gone.

3. The average career will likely encompass two or three "occupations" and a half-dozen or more employers.

4. Most of us will spend sustained periods of our career in some form of self-employment.

5. Bottom line: we're on our own, folks.

6. It's not theory. It's happening...NOW.

What is your plan for managing your future? Are you prepared for these employment trends?

in this chapter

The RAND Corporation's 2004 report, "The 21ST Century at Work: Forces Shaping the Future Workforce and Workplace in the United States," was prepared for the U.S. Department of Labor and cites changing demographics, technology, and globalization as driving forces of our economy.[2] Understanding these driving forces can help you plan your future.

DEMOGRAPHICS

Demographics are statistics showing population characteristics about a region or group, such as education, income, age, marital status, ethnic makeup, and other factors. Through the use of demographics, experts have determined that the composition of the U.S. population is changing, which will in turn affect the composition of the labor supply. By 2050, the Census Bureau expects that minority groups will make up 49.9 percent of the population and 21 percent of residents will be age 65 or older.[3] Women will continue to be an important factor in the workforce. These demographic changes are discussed in more detail in Chapter 9.

Declining birth rates and the tendency for men to retire at earlier ages has reduced the growth rate of the workforce. This growth rate is expected to decline even further in the future, forcing organizations to offer more flexible scheduling, part-time work, and telecommuting in order to attract parents, the disabled, and older workers into the workplace.

Three forces are shaping our economy.

Advances in technology, global communication, and lifelong learning will be the frontier of the 21ST century.

Figure 18.1 Bureau of Labor Statistics Releases 2002–2012 Employment Projections 2004[4]

The 10 Fastest Growing Occupations, 2002-2012 (Numbers in thousands of jobs)

Occupation	Employment		Change		Most significant source of post-secondary education or training
	2002	2012	Number	Percent	
Medical assistants	365	579	215	59	Moderate-term on-the-job training
Network systems and data communications analysts	186	292	106	57	Bachelor's degree
Physician assistants	63	94	31	49	Bachelor's degree
Social and human service assistants	305	454	149	49	Moderate-term on-the-job training
Home health aides	580	859	279	48	Short-term on-the-job training
Medical records and health information technicians	147	216	69	47	Associate degree
Physical therapist aides	37	54	17	46	Short-term on-the-job training
Computer software engineers, applications	394	573	179	46	Bachelor's degree
Computer software engineers, systems software	281	409	128	45	Bachelor's degree
Physical therapist assistants	50	73	22	45	Associate degree

Other changes will result from demographic changes, such as the aging population. Older people have different needs and are expected to spur the demand for health-care-related products and services. As family members who are responsible for caring for children or elderly parents enter or remain in the workforce, they are expected to "outsource" many routine household chores. Because of these needs, the lower-skill-level jobs in sectors such as retail trade, eating establishments, health care, child care, and other personal services are expected to be strong.

TECHNOLOGY

Ray Kurzweil, futurist, predicts there will be one thousand times the technological change in the 21ST century than there was in the 20TH century. The RAND Corporation says that the converging and interdependent trends in information technology, biotechnology, nanotechnology, and other technology areas have led experts to conclude that the pace of technological change will accelerate in the next 10 to 15 years.[5]

At the turn of the 20TH century, technology in the auto industry took away blue-collar jobs from skilled craftsmen who hand fitted components and allowed less skilled workers to assemble standardized parts on an assembly line. Now, in the 21ST century, robots are performing those assembly jobs. White-collar jobs are beginning to suffer the same fate, as routine, defined tasks such as those performed by bank tellers and telephone operators are being automated.[6]

CASE STUDIES IN THE NEWS

Cemex, Mexico's biggest cement company, has teamed up with FedEx, an American logistics management company, to cut wasted cement. Normally, about 50 percent of cement loads are dumped because construction sites are not ready for them. In a number of metropolitan areas, Cemex and FedEx have installed computers in the cement trucks. If the truck arrives at a site and the site is not ready for the cement, the driver launches a mini eBay-like auction and sells the cement to the highest bidder within the perishability radius. This has helped Cemex make considerable inroads into the U.S. market and reduce its lost truck share from 50 percent to 15 percent.[7]

What new skills did the cement truck drivers need in order to continue doing their jobs?

Quick tip ....

"For all workers, the premium on education, flexibility, and vision
has never been as important as in the years to come."

Ken Blanchard,
Management Consultant and Author

••

Routine tasks, both manual and cognitive, are the most easily computerized jobs. Those jobs involving nonroutine skills such as flexibility, creativity, problem solving, and complex communications are not as readily computerized.

This means that cognitive skills are growing in importance. In the manufacturing sector, production line employees now program and repair complex machines, and in the service sector workers are responsible for managing, interpreting, validating, transforming, communicating, and acting on information generated by new technologies.

Cognitive skills are growing in importance.

Technological advances increase the demand for highly skilled workers who stay current on the latest technologies. Businesses, in order to respond to market needs and utilize the latest technologies, will need to become more decentralized. This may result in more workers being independent contractors and performing project work. The cyber society will put a high premium on such entrepreneurship. Imaginative and energetic self-starters who can recognize emerging needs and create ways to fill them will be in high demand.

CASE STUDIES IN THE NEWS

Georgia Institute of Technology is building a 160,000-square-foot nanotechnology research facility with 30,000 square feet of its space dedicated to "clean" rooms. Clean rooms are specially designed to reduce the number of dust particles in the air. It will be the most advanced nanotechnology research facility in the southeast and among the most sophisticated in the country.

Nanotechnology allows scientists to manipulate individual atoms and molecules. Utilizing this technology makes it possible to build machines on the scale of human cells or build structures or materials that assume dramatically different properties by virtue of their size.[8]

What skills will employees need to do research at this new facility? To maintain the equipment? To produce reports of findings? To clean the building?

GLOBALIZATION

Globalization is a crucial piece of the change we face in the 21st century. Container ships, jets, satellite communications, and the Internet have created an international market. Manufacturing is relocating overseas, and workers now move around the world with increasing ease. The cost of transporting goods and communicating globally has dropped so dramatically that distance is no longer an issue. Buyers in Dallas are able to transact daily business needs with sellers in South Africa, for example.

This trend toward making goods and services worldwide in scope, with no national boundaries or trade barriers on where they are produced or sold, is called **globalization**.

Globalization is making goods and services available worldwide with no trade barriers or boundaries.

The globalization of manufacturing means that a metal bolt produced in Malaysia must precisely fit a nut made in Thailand and hold together parts made in Brazil and Chile. Electronic components may be bought from Japan, assembled in Mexico, and sold in the United States. Gone will be the days of "Made in Japan" or "Made in America" as true identifiers of product origins. Globalization of services means that the individual who takes your telephone call at a help desk may be located in India or Ireland.

GLOBAL CONNECTION

Ken Gaebler owns a Chicago marketing firm that produces nearly $1 million in sales with only three full-time traditional employees. When he needs assistance, he turns to independent contractors to complete projects rather than hiring traditional employees. He recently hired a man from the Ukraine to design a computer system to monitor sales results and paid him $118, much less than the $1,000 he would have paid someone in the United States.[9]

1. *Do you think more companies will resort to independent contractors for project work? Why, or why not?*

2. *While someone in the United States lost out on $1,000 worth of work, Mr. Gaebler has $882 to spend for other goods and services. Do you believe globalization is good for the economy? Why, or why not? How will you be impacted by globalization?*

While globalization has resulted in jobs being outsourced, it has also caused jobs to be insourced, with 6.4 million Americans working for foreign companies as of 2001. The number of new American workers employed by foreign companies more than doubled during the 15 years that ended in 2001.[10]

Globalization expands markets for U.S. goods and services as well as makes available a wider variety of goods and services to those living in the United States. According to the RAND Corporation, research suggests that more jobs are created than are lost through globalization. However, what this means is that employees who are in the manufacturing or service sectors whose jobs are lost because of globalization will be forced to develop other skills and move into sectors of the economy that have not been affected. This might require employees to move to other regions of the country in search of these jobs.[11]

The global market will continue to affect our nations in many ways and require a constant adjustment to changing environments.

©John Dakers; Eye Ubiquitous/CORBIS

The globalization of many industries has reduced barriers to offering goods in international markets.

*Fast*Chat

1. What technologies have been developed in your lifetime? How have they changed your life?

2. Can you name at least five products that were in demand in some part of the 20TH century that are no longer produced in any quantities?

3. What must the United States do to ensure that the workforce has the skills necessary to perform jobs of the future?

4. Review the chart on page 513 of the fastest growing occupations. What education is required for these jobs? Which of these jobs is higher paying?

Education and learning how to learn are keys to future career success.

If you want to thrive in this new work world, you will need a personal strategy to navigate the exciting and turbulent times ahead. Education—and learning how to learn—will be vital. Communication and human relations skills need to be honed. The jobs of the future will involve nonroutine skills such as flexibility, creativity, problem solving, and complex communications. Recognizing job trends and preparing for transitions into these jobs will be important to your success in the workplace. You will need to adjust to the new work environments and remain flexible in adapting to changes. Lastly, you will need the skills to find a job, which are perhaps the most challenging workplace skills to learn. You will have challenges, but you will have even more opportunities, and if you're prepared, your options will be almost unlimited.

PURSUE SKILLS AND KNOWLEDGE

Employees who can work with computers and who can also filter the incoming information, discern, make decisions, and address problems will be in great demand.

Education has become *more* important than ever as technology provides more information because machines cannot tell bad data from good, valuable information from useless, accurate information from inaccurate. Employees who can work with computers and who can also filter the incoming information, discern, make decisions, and address problems will be in great demand.

Do not wait for your employer to train you. Realize that you must take control of your own career and personal development and take advantage of courses at your community college. Get a degree or certificate. Learn a foreign language. Sign up for any optional training offered by your employer and volunteer for assignments that allow you to gain new knowledge. Associate with super-charged experts or stimulating conversationalists so you can learn from one another. Learn a new software application. Read about the cultures of countries where your company does business.

Read voraciously. Read books, magazines, newsletters, newspapers, and online articles in areas of interest. Watch meaningful TV features. Research interesting topics on science, technology, and professional interests. The more you understand about how business operates and what is going on in the world, the more effective you will be as an employee. Include information that will not become obsolete—topics that deal with life and human nature or that sharpen your problem-solving skills (many CEOs love reading mysteries, for example)—as well as keeping up with business topics and changing trends.

Acquire and practice effective communication skills (discussed in Chapter 4). As the workplace becomes more complex and fast-paced, these skills will become even more important. Good communication and human relation skills can make you more valuable as an employee and can help reduce stress, both yours and that of those around you.

One last reminder: the key to surviving in a knowledge-based economy is learning. Maintain a hunger for learning. Continue your education at any level to keep the momentum. Lifelong learning will be a way of life for anyone who wishes to succeed, in business or in life, in the 21ST century.

> The key to surviving in a knowledge-based economy is learning.

CASE STUDIES IN THE NEWS

In 2003, *Ladies Home Journal* profiled several mothers and their efforts to return to work. One woman, Vicki Locricchio, had been out of the workforce for two years when her husband's employment agency was hit hard in 1999 from the economic downturn. Fearing they would be unable to pay their mortgage, Locricchio began looking for work. Despite 17 years of human resource experience, she found her job search stalling because she had only an associate's degree. Employers wanted a bachelor's degree. Also, she found her Internet skills had slipped, as she did not know how to do Internet searches or e-mail her resume to others. She finally found a job but was back on the job market one year afterward when the company closed. Six months later, she found another human resource position but at $10,000 less than she had earned before she quit to stay home with her children.[12]

1. *Do you believe lifetime employment is a thing of the past? Why, or why not?*
2. *Why is it more important than ever to keep your skills current?*
3. *Is a bachelor's degree enough today? Why, or why not?*

RECOGNIZE JOB TRENDS

Recognizing job trends can help you plan your career. Job openings occur from both employment growth and replacement needs. Many new jobs are surfacing as our technologies advance and the shift to services continues to influence the workplace. Replacement needs arise as workers leave occupations, retire, return to school, or quit to assume household responsibilities, and replacement needs are expected to account for 60 percent of the approximately 56 million job openings that the U.S. Bureau of Labor Statistics projects between 2002 and 2012.[13] Understanding trends in employment by industry and occupation can help you plan your future education and career choices.

The Bureau of Labor Statistics expects professional and related occupations to grow faster and add more jobs than any other major occupational group, with 6.5 million new jobs expected by 2012. Three-fourths of the job growth in this area is expected among computer and mathematical occupations, health care practitioners and technical occupations, and education, training, and library occupations.

Service occupations are projected to have the largest number of total job openings, 13 million, with high replacement needs. Generally, those jobs with relatively low pay or limited training requirements such as food preparation and other service occupations have the highest replacement needs.[14]

Occupations Expected to Decline
. . . .

According to a 2004 U.S. Department of Labor report in *XX1* Magazine, the following occupations are losing the most jobs:[15]

- farmers
- ranchers
- word processors
- typists
- tellers
- loan interviewers and clerks
- secretaries (*except* legal, medical, and executive)
- switchboard operators (including answering services) and other office and administrative support occupations
- dishwashers
- railroad brake, signal, and switch operators
- utility meter readers

ADJUST TO NEW WORK ENVIRONMENTS

Recognizing trends and being flexible are crucial to your career.

The RAND Corporation study points out that the forces of technology and globalization are changing the nature of business organizations. Recognizing these trends and being flexible are more crucial than ever to career management. Business organizational forms are expected to move in three ways: 1) from vertically integrated to less vertically integrated, specialized firms, 2) from command-and-control leadership styles to decentralized management and employee empowerment across all levels of the organization, and 3) an increasing emphasis on knowledge as the key source of comparative advantage.[16]

The shift from vertically integrated to less vertically integrated means that many businesses are outsourcing functions that are not central to their business, such as security and cleaning, industrial design, manufacturing processes, business-processing tasks, human resources, information technology, and other business tasks companies used to perform internally. Additionally, outsourcing is now available on a global scale.

The result is that almost one in four workers is currently in an employment arrangement that is **not** permanent, full-time, year-round, and paid by the employer as a regular employee. These workers are independent contractors, on-call workers, temporary-help agency workers, self-employed individuals, workers employed by contract firms, and those working part-time. The trend is expected to continue.

Technologies that allow work products, data, and information to be transmitted quickly and inexpensively plus the need for firms to respond rapidly to changing technological and market forces will increasingly result in decentralized businesses. More and more, organizations are providing frontline employees with greater authority and decision making. Instead of serving as a command and control function, corporations of the future may exist to provide rules, standards, and cultures that define how more autonomous employees operate.

Knowledge will be valued to a greater extent. This also includes understanding technology, markets, customers, suppliers, business processes, and best practices. These changes mean that just doing your job will not be enough—you will need to intimately understand the forces impacting your position.

QUICK WIT

"The world is progressing rapidly and resources are abundant. I'd rather go into a grocery store today than to a king's banquet a hundred years ago."

Bill Gates,
Chairman and Chief
Software Architect,
Microsoft

DEVELOP JOB-SEEKING SKILLS

Job-seeking skills are skills that assist you in finding employment. They include the ability to determine the type of position that will satisfy your needs, to locate available positions, to obtain interviews for those positions, and to land the job.

Some people lose jobs because of layoffs, terminations, or downsizing, while others simply want to find positions that are more suitable, with working conditions, location, wages, or job duties that more nearly match their needs or interests. The Bureau of Labor Statistics states that the median number of years that wage and salary workers had been with their current employer was 3.7 years in January 2002.[18] The odds are that you will be looking for a job more than once in your life.

Strong job-seeking skills are necessary because finding a job can be one of the most difficult tasks you will ever face. It can be full of frustration and rejection. Although there are sources of help and guidance, most aspects of a job search are actions you must do on your own and for yourself. A carefully organized, well-executed job search is vital if you are to obtain the best possible job in the shortest amount of time. To begin, develop a profile of the type of position you would like to have.

IDENTIFY YOUR SKILLS AND VALUES

Analyzing your skills shows the types of jobs you would like and the skills you can market.

The first step in determining the perfect job for you is to review your previous activities—paid work, volunteer work, professional organizations joined, and educational courses taken. What things did you do well? What courses did you enjoy? Which activities did you like best? Richard Bolles, in the 2004 edition of his book *What Color Is Your Parachute?*, identifies three primary areas of skill: people, data, and things. Identifying where your greatest abilities lie can help you determine what kind of work would most suit you. Bolles suggests that you ask yourself the following questions to help analyze into which areas your skills fall.[19]

Identifying Skills

• **People** Do you communicate effectively orally and in writing, and do you get along with others? Do you know how to handle, motivate, organize, direct, persuade, and coach others? Are these activities enjoyable to you?

• **Data** Are you able to gather, compile, interpret, analyze, and problem solve around data (mathematical or other)? Do you enjoy these types of activities?

• **Things** Do you competently operate machines or tools? Do you like these activities?

After identifying your skills, determine how you might use them on the job. This process will assist you in identifying the type of job for which you are best suited as well as recognizing what skills you can market to your prospective employers.

The Transferable Skills Worksheet below will help you determine how the skills you have identified might transfer into a work situation.

Values are another important area to explore. What is important to you? Respect? Helping others? Having freedom of expression? Caring for the environment? Someone who values helping others, for instance, may be happier as a social worker or teacher than as an accountant.

Transferable Skills Worksheet Sample

Skills I Have	How and Where I Used These Skills	How I Can Use These Skills on the Job
People	Organized a 10K race open to all runners in the city for a charitable organization	Can organize, coordinate, and direct—can delegate responsibility. Follow up to see that everything is in order
Data	Prepared weekly sales report when I worked for XYZ Corporation	Collect, analyze, and prepare data in usable format
Things	Responsible for maintenance on photocopy machine— adding paper, clearing paper jams, replacing toner— for the church	Understand office equipment and can perform routine maintenance duties

Enter Your Own Information Here

People		
Data		
Things		

Visit CareerOneStop, the Department of Labor-sponsored web site, and use the Skills Profiler to help identify your skills, explore what jobs need your skills, and analyze any gaps in your skills.

Environmental preference is another factor to consider. Would you rather work inside or outside? Alone or with others? In a structured or unstructured environment? In a large or small organization? In another part of the country or the world? Pay requirements are an additional consideration. How much do you actually need to earn? Also, do you have any physical or mental disabilities that would prevent you from performing certain jobs?

Answering these questions will help determine the types of jobs for which you will be most suited. This activity is particularly helpful for the individual beginning a first career or seeking a career change. Complete your self-analysis by becoming aware of your personal strengths and potential obstacles to overcome.

IDENTIFY YOUR STRENGTHS AND OBSTACLES

Analyzing your strengths and potential obstacles helps identify your realistic prospects.

Become aware of the strengths you do have. Intelligence, punctuality, trustworthiness, sense of humor, patience, and loyalty are but a few of the personal characteristics that are valued by a company. The Personal Strengths and Potential Obstacles Analysis below shows you a way to chart both these strengths and potential obstacles to employment.

Ask friends and family members to help you identify strengths (you may have some you don't even realize you have). Discuss work experience that others have had to help you identify how strengths fit into various situations. If you want more help identifying your strengths, especially as they apply to business, numerous books and assessment tools have been developed. Visit Internet sites such as CareerOneStop or ask business associates, school counselors, or a librarian for suggestions on titles that might help.

Personal Strengths and Potential Obstacles Analysis

Personal strengths
Word process 65 words/minute; completed computer courses; know Word and Excel

Potential obstacles
Have been out of job market for six years, caring for three young children

How these strengths can be valuable to an employer
I can use my skills and knowledge to turn out work quickly with a minimum of training time for the company.

How potential obstacles can be turned into an asset
I'm mature, know what I want, and performed volunteer work while being out of the job market. I am a responsible adult.

What are your own strengths and obstacles?

Human Relations

According to a McKinsey & Company report, the most important corporate resource over the next 20 years will be talent: smart, sophisticated business people who are technologically literate, globally astute, and operationally agile. The caliber of a company's talent is becoming more important than ever in determining a company's success in the marketplace.[20]

Many applicants have obstacles to overcome. However, with careful thought and preparation, liabilities can be turned into assets. Review the following list and determine whether you have any of these concerns.

Obstacles to Overcome

- You have been convicted of a crime.
- You are older.
- You are unable to relocate.
- You have been away from the job market for a long time.
- You are young and have no work experience.
- You were fired from your previous job.
- You were not born in the United States.

- You have too much education.
- You have too little education.
- You have a physical disability.
- You have a mental disability.
- You are a minority.
- You are a woman.
- You have no experience in the industry for which you have applied.
- You have changed jobs frequently.

Being older, for instance, can be turned into an asset. You have maturity and poise and understand the nature of work. Develop a positive attitude and work on presenting your obstacles to employers in a positive light. Of course, you can work to remove some obstacles: gain more education, improve your skills, or gain experience, even if it is through volunteer work.

Once you have honestly evaluated yourself, you are ready to identify occupations that interest you. However, be realistic and do not set yourself up for disappointment by setting inappropriate goals (applying for a job that requires travel, for example, if you are unable to travel). Most obstacles can be overcome or turned to advantage if you are honest and open and have strengths and skills that you can offer to an employer.

*Fast*Chat

1. What skills do you need to be able to be a freelance or contract worker? Would that option appeal to you? Why, or why not?

2. Why is it important to consider your values when looking for a job? What happens if your values are not in alignment with those of your position?

3. What obstacles do you have? How are you going to present them as assets?

18.3 How Can You Learn About Careers and Job Openings?

Information on careers can be obtained through the Internet, library, or interviews.

The Internet, local library, and your school career-counseling center are the best places to start learning about careers and organizations. Many books, magazines, and journals concerning careers describe what different occupations entail. The librarian or career counselor can direct you to this information.

CAREERS

A good place to start researching careers is the CareerOneStop web site supported by the U.S. Department of Labor.

A good place to start is with the CareerOneStop web site supported by the U.S. Department of Labor. The site contains the O*Net Online, a database containing skills needed for different occupations. It additionally houses America's Career Infonet, an electronic storehouse of national, state, and labor market data with employment trends, wages, and more.

Several references, in particular, are extremely helpful. The *Occupational Outlook Handbook, Occupational Outlook Handbook for College Graduates, Occupational Outlook Quarterly,* and the *Occupational Outlook Handbook and Career Guide To Industries* are good starting places for your search. The *Occupational Outlook Handbook,* for instance, lists major occupations and explains what the future of those careers looks like, the nature of the work, earnings, working conditions, and usual training required.

If you are still unsure, try an informational interview. Start with your instructors. If you know they are familiar with a profession that interests you, ask to discuss it with them. They may know people in this profession who would be willing to talk with you about their jobs.

CASE STUDIES IN THE NEWS

In 2004, *Small Business Notes* reported that two-thirds of new employer firms survive at least two years, and about half survive at least four years. Despite these business failure rates, small businesses created three-quarters of the U.S. net new jobs (2.5 million of the 3.4 million total) in 1999-2000. Moreover, start-ups in their first two years of operation accounted for the majority of the net new jobs in the economy.[21]

1. *What might be some of the advantages of working for a smaller company rather than a large corporation? Disadvantages?*
2. *What kinds of small businesses do you see starting up in your community?*

ORGANIZATIONS

Before deciding which organizations will be the focus of your job search, you must make some decisions concerning the locations in which you are willing to work. In what area of the country do you want to work? Are you willing to relocate? How far are you willing to drive to a job? What areas of town are inaccessible to you?

Identify potential organizations online and research them carefully before interviewing.

Organizations in your area can be identified through the Internet and library resources. Some of the available resources are:

- Local business directories, such as the Chamber of Commerce directory

- Company reports, such as annual reports and *10K* reports (order reports over the Internet from the Public Register's Annual Report Service)

- *Business.com*

- *Hoover's Online*

- *Corporateinformation.com*

- *Encyclopedia of Associations*

- *Standard and Poor's Register of Corporations*

- *Dun and Bradstreet Directories*

- *Thomas Register of American Manufacturers*

- *Value Line*

- *Forbes 500 Largest Private Companies*

Local libraries contain information specific to your community. Ask the librarian for assistance in locating this information. These resources can tell you where organizations are located and other information about them. This information will be useful during the interviewing phase. At this point, a realistic look at the job market is in order.

Friends and neighbors are another source of informational interviews. Ask if they know someone who does the type of work in which you are interested. Also, you can call a company and ask for an informational interview. Ask the receptionist for the name of an individual who holds a position in the area in which you are interested. For instance, if you are curious about jobs in accounting, you may ask the name and correct title of the accounting manager. Then, armed with that information, either call or write that individual and ask for an appointment.

When calling, explain that you are interested in learning more about the individual's occupation and ask for an appointment at a time that would be convenient. If someone else referred you, mention that individual's name as your referral source.

Be prepared with some questions to ask, such as what tasks are performed, what entry-level positions lead to the individual's position, and what salary you could expect. Do not stay too long. Be sure to thank the individual speaking with you.

JOB OPENINGS

An effective job search includes several approaches to finding open positions.

You must take a number of approaches to find an open position. Networking, the direct approach, the Internet, newspaper want ads, hot lines, private employment agencies, public employment agencies, temporary agencies, job fairs, summer jobs, internships, and school placement centers are all ways in which individuals find jobs. After assessing the types of positions available, you will be able to determine realistically what type of job you will be able to obtain.

Networking is one of the most effective methods of looking for a job opening.

Networking **Networking** is one of the most effective methods of looking for a job opening. It involves telling people you know that you are looking for a job and asking them to contact you if they hear of any openings. These people include teachers, former employers, friends, parents of friends, former coworkers, and contacts in professional organizations. Ask these acquaintances to inquire on your behalf. Having a friend within the organization you are targeting deliver your resume and recommend you for a position will dramatically increase your odds of receiving an interview.

The informational interview mentioned previously can also be used in networking. Ask individuals with whom you speak to refer you to others who may know about jobs and to call you if they have any openings.

Last, networking should not stop after you get a job. Many career services professionals will tell you that the ability to build and keep working relationships is the number one job skill of the 21ST century.

uick tip ....

> Business consultant Susan Solovic offers this tip for building a network: focus first on what you can do for others before you ask for assistance or favors. She also suggests staying in contact with others by taking the time to write personal notes.[22]

Direct Approach The direct approach to a company is another extremely effective method of locating an opening. Many large organizations have human resources departments that post all job openings and accept applications for employment on a regular basis.

Before going to the company, call human resources to determine when the company takes applications and where jobs are posted. Going to a company unannounced is not recommended.

Another approach is to call the company, asking for the name of the individual who supervises the department in which you wish to work. For instance, you can call and ask for the name of the accounting manager and the correct company address, explaining that you are developing a mailing list. Then, call or send a target letter to that individual, giving your qualifications and asking for an interview. A sample of a target letter is illustrated on the next page. This letter should be modified to fit the qualities you have that may interest this particular employer. Follow up by telephone if you have mailed a target letter and ask for an interview. If you are told that the company has no openings, ask if you can call back later or if the official knows of any other job openings. Express thanks, and always be polite and professional.

The Internet The Internet is a popular way to search. You can check web sites for individual companies to learn about job openings with an employer in which you might be interested. You can also visit some of the many web sites that maintain lists of job openings.

Quick tip ....

According to Richard Bolles's 2004 *What Color is Your Parachute?*, success rates of certain methods of finding employment are as follows:[23]

Internet	4%
Mailing out resumes at random	7%
Answering ads in professional trade journals	7%
Answering local newspaper ads	5–24%
Using private employment agencies/search firms	5–28%
Networking	33%
Knocking on doors of employers	47%
Locating businesses in Yellow Pages and calling to see if they are hiring	69%

Newspaper Want Ads The want ads of the newspaper contain many positions. However, the newspaper is one of the least effective ways to find a job. Never depend totally on the newspaper to identify positions because the competition is fierce for the positions advertised. Scan the ads and answer only those advertisements for which you are qualified.

489 Longren Circle
Rancho Palos Verde, CA 90274
714-555-2645
lcolton@internet.com

August 28, 2004

Ms. Darnelle Johnson, Data Processing Manager
Springboard Products, Inc.
836 Spring Oaks Avenue
Los Angeles, CA 90047

Dear Ms. Johnson:

I recently obtained an Associate of Science Degree in CyberSecurity Technology. My willingness to work hard and my ability to collaborate with others, along with this degree, will make me a valuable member of your data processing staff. To further highlight my accomplishments, I have attached a copy of my resume.

I would appreciate an opportunity to discuss my skills and abilities with you. I will call in a few days to schedule a mutually convenient time for us to meet.

Sincerely,

Lucinda Colton

Lucinda Colton

Hot Lines Many large employers, such as hospitals, universities, corporations, and governmental entities, have 24-hour telephone hot lines that run a recording of open positions. These lines can be checked at your convenience. Develop a list of these numbers and check them weekly. Also, if you belong to any professional organizations, see if they have job hot lines or Internet sites.

Private Employment Agencies Private employment agencies have jobs for those with skills and a proven track record. However, carefully check to see what your financial obligations to the agency may be. Some require you to pay a fee for the job you obtain through them. Other jobs are fee paid. This term means that the employer, rather than the employee, will pay the fee.

Public Employment Agencies Public employment agencies operate in each state. Visit your state employment/workforce commission and find out how its services operate and what positions are available. Many organizations with government contracts are required to place job openings with the state employment commission, and federal and other government openings can be obtained through these agencies as well.

Temporary Agencies Individuals working with temporary agencies frequently find permanent employment through a long-term temporary job assignment. Finding a job in this manner can be beneficial because you have a chance to learn about the company and the people in it prior to accepting permanent employment. If you do not wish to stay there, you simply ask for a new assignment.

Job Fairs In some regions, job fairs are held to introduce companies to potential employees. Local firms will often offer on-site interviews or will at the very least accept resumes from interested searchers. These fairs can give you an opportunity to meet human resources representatives from several companies at the same time. Dress well and take lots of copies of your resume, plus a calendar, so you can write down any interviews you schedule.

Summer Jobs and Internships Summer jobs and internships are an excellent way to find a full-time position. After seeing the part-timer's skills and capabilities, companies will often offer full-time employment.

School Placement Office Do not overlook your school placement office. Assistance in interviewing, job leads, and moral support can be obtained through the center. Recruiters frequently come to campus and interview students through the office. The most efficient way to obtain a job interview is to take advantage of as many job search methods as possible. This will allow you to locate more positions and generate more interviews quickly. These interviews must happen before hiring occurs.

EVALUATING PROSPECTS

After reviewing what you would like in a job, what skills you have, and what types of companies and openings exist, you can realistically evaluate what type of job you will be able to obtain.

Using an assessment tool, like the Job Parameters chart on the next page, can help you evaluate your prospects.

Take into consideration your local economy. If the unemployment rate is high and layoffs are occurring, you may have to accept a position that is not quite what you want in terms of job duties and pay. (But don't worry—statistics show that, no matter where you are in your career, you will probably change jobs again at some point. So make the best of whatever jobs there are, and do whatever you can—on-the-job training, education, extra responsibilities—to prepare for your next job, which may be closer to your ideal.) With these realities in mind, applying for jobs can actually begin.

Quick tip

The Americans with Disabilities Act requires that employers make "modifications or adjustments to a job application process that enable a qualified applicant with a disability to be considered for the position such qualified applicant desires."

An employer may have to provide a number of possible reasonable accommodations in connection with the application process. These may include:

- making existing facilities accessible,
- changing tests or hiring practices
- providing qualified readers or interpreters

Also, be aware that employers must provide reasonable accommodations to employees with disabilities. Be prepared to ask about the following accommodations in an interview, if needed:

- restructuring jobs or tasks
- allowing modified work schedules
- changing the work environment

If you are a qualified individual with a disability and find you need an accommodation during the application process, you should immediately advise the organization's representative. You can find out more about reasonable accommodation by searching the Equal Employment Opportunity Commission's web site.[24]

WEB

Job Parameters		
	Ideal	**Realistic**
Salary	$37,000 a year	$32,000 a year
Location	Los Angeles	LA, Sacramento, San Francisco
Hours	9–5	7AM–7PM any time between these hours
People (Groups) Younger, Older, Individual	work by self	work with groups near my age
Outdoors/Indoors	outdoors	in and out
Size of Company	below 50 employees	any size
Dress Code/Supervision	no dress code minimal supervision	willing to conform to moderate dress code and closer supervision

*Fast*Chat

1. Determine a job that interests you. How would you obtain an informational interview? What questions would you ask?

2. Search the CareerOneStop web site and review the job skills requirements given for an occupation that interests you. How do your current skills fit? What can you do to develop these skills further?

3. What factors restrict us from obtaining our "perfect" job? What can we do to improve the chances of landing our ideal job?

A resume's sole function is to get you a job interview.

A **resume** is a sales tool designed to assist you in obtaining an interview. It provides a prospective employer with a brief summary of your skills, education, and job experience. The resume does not get you a job. However, a poorly written resume that does not identify your skills and abilities, contains typographical errors, and is unattractive will not get you an interview.

Here are some tips and guidelines to keep in mind while you're developing your resume:

Resume Writing Tips

1. Limit the resume to one page unless you have extensive work experience.

2. Target your resume to specific employers. With word processing software, you can easily customize objectives and emphasize skills that fit the job or company for which you are applying.

3. Do not enclose a photograph or list your marital status, number of children, height, weight, race, or other personal information. This information may disqualify you from the interview. Religion, too, should not be listed, unless it's specifically related to or required for the job.

4. List extracurricular activities or hobbies if they are relevant to the position for which you are applying, or highlight skills that could be useful in that position.

5. Be specific about your accomplishments. Use action verbs such as earned, planned, wrote, achieved, completed, increased, and improved when describing your accomplishments and achievements.

6. Avoid the use of "I."

7. Expect to complete several rough drafts. Ask someone else to read your draft critically, reviewing for clarity, spelling errors, and format. Some employers will refuse to consider a candidate with errors in a resume, so be sure your resume is error-free.

8. Be sure that your resume is pleasing to the eye. A well laid out resume with white space and one-inch margins will be easier to read.

9. A resume that has been printed on a laser printer and then cleanly photocopied on a higher-grade paper of at least 20 pounds is a relatively inexpensive alternative to a professional resume.

10. Use white or off-white 8 ½-by-11-inch paper when printing your resume.

TECHNOLOGY CONNECTION

Resumes are often separated from a job candidate's e-mail message, so it is imperative that contact information be easily accessible for recruiters. The Resume Doctor web site offers the following suggestions for e-mailing resumes:[25]

1. Include a professional e-mail address that you check regularly. Do not use inappropriate or funny e-mail addresses such as borntobewild@yahoo.com.
2. Transmit your resume as a Word file attachment and do not "zip" the file.
3. Name your file so it can be easily identified such as *Doe, Jane resume.doc* rather than *resume.doc*.
4. Turn off "Track Changes" in your word processing program so hiring managers cannot see your edits.

As more companies use scanners and accept resume files over the Internet, formatting your resume in such a way that it can be easily read is extremely important. Your resume must be clean and free of stray marks that a scanner might pick up. The Quick Tip below lists the most important considerations for making your document compatible with this technology.

uick tip ....

Dr. Randall Hansen, publisher of Web-based *Quintessential Careers,* recommends the following guidelines for making your resume text based and/or scannable ready:[26]

- Use words in your resume on which companies will perform key searches. Study current job listings for popular key words, especially ones appropriate to the field in which you're interested.
- Include these key words in your summary, which should be coherent and well worded.
- Print the resume in letter (highest) quality mode.
- Avoid bolding, italicizing, underlining, bullets, lines, tables, templates, headers or footers, shading, or graphics.
- Use Arial or Times Roman in an 11- or 12-point font size.
- Avoid folding or creasing a resume and do not staple the pages.
- Use only white or off-white 8 1/2- by 11-inch size paper.

FORMATS

Numerous formats exist for resumes. The two basic forms are chronological and functional. The **chronological resume**, which is illustrated on page 537, is the most common resume style. It lists experience in reverse chronological order, identifying the most recent employment first. This format is good when an individual has a continuous work history with progressively more responsible positions. However, it may not be helpful for those who have gaps in their employment or are attempting to return to the job market after a prolonged absence such as caring for a family.

The **functional resume** emphasizes special skills that can be transferred to other areas, making it useful for individuals reentering the job market or changing careers. Also, those with little work experience, extensive volunteer experience, or frequent job changes can benefit from this format. An example of a functional resume is shown on page 538.

Resumes can also be developed that incorporate both chronological and functional forms. These are called **hybrid** or **combination resumes**. This style of resume is illustrated on page 539.

ETHICS CONNECTION

Embellishing accomplishments or even lying about qualifications on resumes does unfortunately occur. ADP Screening and Selection Services, in a 2003 study, found false information on more than 50 percent of the people on whom it conducted employment and education checks. These falsehoods are not mere misrepresentations of facts. Some candidates are resorting to buying phony academic degrees over the Internet that include a toll-free number so that employers can "verify" the phony degree. Others are even paying hackers to plug their names into a class list database of a university they falsely claim to have attended.[27]

1. *How could these practices damage an individual's career?*

2. *How might they hurt companies?*

3. *How would you feel if you lost a job for which you were qualified to someone who lied?*

4. *How would you feel if you hired someone and found out that person had lied? What might you do?*

JANET D. HERNANDEZ
114 West 23rd Street, Nashville, TN 46302
615-555-1708   hernandezjd@provider.net

OBJECTIVE

Administrative Assistant position for MegaMall Property Management Company

EDUCATION

Associate of Applied Science, 2004, Nashville College, Nashville, TN
• Major: Administrative Office Technology, GPA 3.7

Related Courses and Skills
• Advanced Word Processing (Word, WordPerfect)
• Keyboarding at 75 words per minute
• Spreadsheet (Excel, Quattro Pro) and Database Management (Access)
• Records Management
• Bookkeeping I and Computerized Bookkeeping (QuickBooks Pro)
• Ten-key at 250 strokes per minute
• Presentation Software (PowerPoint, Presentations)
• Office Management
• Internet Software (Internet Explorer, Netscape)

EXPERIENCE

Community Volunteer, Nashville, TN   **December 2000-2004**
• **Humane Society:** Developed and customized spreadsheet report to track results of three fund-raising activities, reducing reporting time by 50 percent. Used Excel.
• **Secretary-Treasurer, Valley Elementary School Parent-Teacher Organization:** Published electronic newsletters, answered e-mail, maintained correspondence, maintained books for two years, and satisfied yearly CPA audits. Used Word and QuickBooks Pro.

Katz Department Store, Nashville, TN   **March 1998-December 2000**
• **Sales Supervisor, Part-time:** Supervised four sales clerks; trained new sales employees. Computed daily cash receipts, balanced two registers, attained highest part-time sales volume, and had fewest sales returned.

Value Variety, Nashville, TN   **Summers 1996, 1997**
• **Sales Clerk, Floater:** Provided complete customer service in sales and returns; coordinated weekly inventory deliveries.

Adapted from Your Career: How to Make It Happen, *5th ed., by Julie Griffin Levitt © 2004 Thomson Business and Professional Publishing.*

JANET D. HERNANDEZ

114 West 23rd Street, Nashville, TN 46302   615-555-1708   hernandezjd@provider.net

---

OBJECTIVE

Administrative Assistant position for MegaMall Property Management Company

EDUCATION

Associate of Applied Science, 2004, Nashville College, Nashville, TN
• Major: Administrative Office Technology, GPA 3.7

PROFESSIONAL SKILLS

Document and Report Preparation: Expert using Word, WordPerfect, PowerPoint, and Presentations. Enter text at 75 words per minute. Integrate tabular data and graphics into documents using Access, Excel, and Quattro Pro. Write, format, and proofread printed and electronic business correspondence, reports, and newsletters. Research topics on the Internet (Internet Explorer, Netscape).

• Published electronic newsletters and maintained correspondence for Valley Elementary School Parent-Teacher Organization (PTO) for two years.
• Developed spreadsheet to track results of three fund-raising activities for the Humane Society that reduced reporting time by 50 percent.

Bookkeeping: Perform manual (ten-key at 250 strokes per minute) or computerized (QuickBooks Pro) bookkeeping functions from journal entry to end-of-period reports.

• Maintained books for Valley Elementary PTO for two years and satisfied yearly CPA audits.
• Computed daily cash receipts and balanced two registers as part-time sales supervisor of a department store.

Human Relations: Successfully cooperate with store managers, representatives of delivery companies and community organizations, and the general public:

• Held positions of responsibility in two community organizations over the last three years.
• Worked in two department stores: promoted to supervisor, trained new sales clerks, coordinated weekly inventory deliveries, provided customer service in sales and returns, attained highest part-time sales volume, and had fewest sales returned.

EXPERIENCE

Community Volunteer, Nashville, TN	December 2000-2004
Katz Department Store, Nashville, TN	March 1998-December 2000
Value Variety, Nashville, TN	Summers 1996, 1997

Adapted from Your Career: How to Make It Happen, *5th ed., by Julie Griffin Levitt © 2004 Thomson Business and Professional Publishing.*

JANET D. HERNANDEZ
114 West 23rd Street, Nashville, TN 46302
615-555-1708   hernandezjd@provider.net

OBJECTIVE
Administrative Assistant position for MegaMall Property Management Company

RELATED QUALIFICATIONS
- Word Processing in Word and WordPerfect
- Spreadsheet generation with Excel and Quattro Pro
- Database design and maintenance using Access
- Keyboarding at 75 words per minute
- Write and proofread printed and electronic business correspondence, reports, newsletters
- Presentation preparation using PowerPoint and Presentations software
- Internet research using Internet Explorer or Netscape; e-mail correspondence using Outlook
- Bookkeeping using QuickBooks Pro and ten-key at 250 strokes per minute
- Proven ability to work successfully with store manager, delivery companies, community organizations, and the general public

EDUCATION
Associate of Applied Science, 2004, Nashville College, Nashville, TN
- Major: Administrative Office Technology, GPA 3.7

EXPERIENCE
Community Volunteer, Nashville, TN   **December 2000–2004**
- **Humane Society:** Developed and customized spreadsheet report to track results of three fund-raising activities, reducing reporting time by 50 percent. Used Excel.
- **Secretary-Treasurer, Valley Elementary School Parent-Teacher Organization:** Published electronic newsletters, answered e-mail, maintained correspondence, maintained books for two years, and satisfied yearly CPA audits. Used Word and QuickBooks Pro.

Katz Department Store, Nashville, TN   **March 1998-December 2000**
- **Sales Supervisor, Part-time:** Supervised four sales clerks; trained new sales employees. Computed daily cash receipts, balanced two registers, attained highest part-time sales volume, and had fewest sales returned.

Value Variety, Nashville, TN   **Summers 1996, 1997**
- **Sales Clerk, Floater:** Provided complete customer service in sales and returns; coordinated weekly inventory deliveries.

Adapted from Your Career: How to Make It Happen, *5th ed., by Julie Griffin Levitt © 2004 Thomson Business and Professional Publishing.*

REFERENCES

References are individuals who can vouch for your work abilities and personal qualities. They include former bosses, coworkers, teachers, and fellow professionals or sometimes acquaintances who know you socially. Employers expect applicants to have references but differ in their preferences regarding when and how they want to see a reference list. Experts recommend omitting references from your resume. Instead, do research to learn whether your target employer wants you to submit a list of references. Prepare a reference sheet that includes names, titles, addresses, and contact information for each reference and be ready to provide it to an employer that may request it.

Family members are not considered good references, as most employers do not view them as unbiased. Offer references such as former employers and teachers who can attest to your performance first. Only if you are asked for character references should you provide the names of others. Never use individuals' names for a reference without obtaining permission. Tell them about your job search plans and the type of work you are seeking. Be sure that you have their complete mailing addresses, daytime telephone numbers, and the correct spelling of their names. Between three and five references is the usual number. Be sure to express appreciation to references for being willing to assist you in your job search. Call them after an interview to let them know that they can expect a telephone call from your prospective employer.

Tips for Filling Out a Job Application Form

In addition to having an up-to-date resume, be prepared to fill out job application forms:

- Follow all directions carefully and answer all questions.
- Write neatly in black ink, type, or word process an application. Make sure each answer is correct and well phrased.
- Make sure your application is free from typing, spelling, grammar, and punctuation errors.
- Use complete and accurate addresses in the references section.
- Be sure the completed form is attractive, neat, and clean, and sign and date the application.

---

*Fast*Chat

1. Which of the resume formats do you think would work best for you? Why?

2. What sorts of questions do you think employers would ask your references?

An **interview** is a process by which the prospective employer learns more about you and evaluates whether you are the best-qualified candidate for the position. As the interviewee, you have the responsibility to sell yourself, allowing the interviewer to see exactly what you are capable of doing for the company. In addition, the interview is a time when you can evaluate the company and learn more about the position that is available.

CASE STUDIES IN THE NEWS

 Workforce, a magazine for human resource professionals, cites the following job interview incidents reported by readers:[28]

1. A candidate said she was no longer living at the address on her resume because her home had been taken over by aliens.
2. One applicant brought his lunch to an interview because it was scheduled during his lunch time.
3. Although an offer was never made, a candidate for a receptionist opening showed up and sat at the receptionist desk.
4. A job candidate searched through the interviewer's desk when the interviewer briefly stepped out of the room.
5. An applicant for a management position was so inebriated when he arrived for his interview that he could not stand up straight.
6. An applicant came for an interview wearing an ear on a chain around his neck.
7. A CEO went to the candidates' homes to conduct his interviews. He would ask the spouse why he should hire the applicant.

1. *If you were the recruiter, would you recommend these individuals for a position?*
2. *How would you feel if an interviewer came to your home?*

PREPARING YOURSELF

A number of steps can be taken to prepare for the interview. The first is to be prepared to answer questions that the interviewer might pose. Examples of the types of questions an interviewer might ask you are shown on page 542. Extensive time should be spent in developing honest, thoughtful answers.

The interview that obtains the job requires practice and planning.

Prepare a two-minute summary of yourself in response to the "tell me about yourself" question. Study potential weaknesses and learn how to present them in a positive light. For instance, if you are younger and have little work experience, present yourself as eager, energetic, and willing to work hard. Remember, interviewers will not believe that individuals have no weaknesses and appreciate frank answers to their questions. In addition, study the "Possible Questions to Ask the Interviewer" on page 543. These are samples of the kinds of questions you will want answered about the company and the position.

Questions an Interviewer Might Ask

- Tell me about yourself.
- What are your strengths?
- What are your weaknesses?
- Why should I hire you?
- Describe a time when you were faced with a challenging situation and how you handled it.
- What are you looking for in a job?
- Why did you leave (or why do you want to leave) your current job?
- Why do you want to work for this company?
- What are your long-term career objectives?
- What are your short-term career objectives?
- How long would you stay with us?

- What motivates you? How do you motivate others?
- What do you know about this organization?
- What do you find most appealing in a job? Least appealing?
- How would you describe your personality?
- What interests you most about this job? Least?
- What don't you do well?
- What did you think of your last boss?
- What would be an ideal job and/or boss for you?
- What are your salary requirements?
- Are you willing to relocate?

When an offer to interview is extended, be sure that you verify the correct time, date, location, and the name of the person with whom you will be speaking. Then, research as much information about the company as possible. You might go to the library or Internet, call a friend who is employed there, or read the annual report or *10K* report. Be sure that you know how to find the location; if necessary, make a trial run on the day before the interview.

> ### Possible Questions to Ask the Interviewer
>
> - What are the job duties of the position?
> - What types of skills are you looking for?
> - What type of training program do you have?
> - What will be expected of me within three months, six months, and a year?
> - If I perform well, what are the opportunities for promotion?
> - What hours would I be working?
> - What is the salary range for this position?
> - What benefits are available/provided?

Be prepared for the interview to take one of several forms—directed, nondirected, group interview, board interview, or stress interview. A directed interview has specific predetermined questions, whereas a nondirected interview is less structured, involving more frank and open discussion. At a group interview, several candidates are interviewed at one time by one or more interviewers. At a board interview, one individual interviews more than one candidate at the same time.

The stress interview may take place in any of these formats. This type of interview is designed to test an individual's reactions to uncomfortable situations. (Don't worry—this is only likely to happen if you are applying for a job where grace under pressure is vital.) The candidate may be subjected to verbal attacks, silence, or rapid questioning. Not allowing yourself to become flustered and remaining calm will earn you passing marks in this type of interview.

Sometimes you can expect a series of interviews. A representative from the human resources department may perform a screening interview to be sure that you meet the general job qualifications and then refer you to the department with the opening. The supervisor will then interview you. Sometimes you may interview with several individuals in management with whom you would be working.

SALARY QUESTIONS

Know ahead of time the least amount of money you require. This amount will most likely be quite different from what you would like. Knowing what the local market generally pays for that position is also important. This information can be found through library or Internet research or by asking individuals in similar positions or counselors at your school placement center.

Suggestions for Successful Interviews

1. Be on your best behavior from the time you drive onto company property. Many a job applicant has unknowingly run into the interviewer in the hallway, parking lot, or rest-room.

2. Arrive a few minutes early.

3. Dress appropriately for the position, as if you were working there. Clothes that are revealing are unacceptable. If you feel you can wear the outfit to a party or a picnic, it is unsatisfactory for the interview. Be sure that your clothing is clean and wrinkle free. Polish your shoes. Do not wear too much jewelry, perfume, or makeup. A watch, small to medium earrings for women only (men should not wear earrings), and one ring is considered appropriate. Do not wear large chains, ankle bracelets, or other heavy jewelry. Dressing conservatively is a good idea.

4. Be physically clean, with combed hair, clean nails, fresh breath, and deodorant.

5. Do not smoke or chew gum.

6. Smile and be pleasant. If offered a hand, make sure your handshake is firm.

7. Use eye contact but do not stare. Review the oral communication skills presented in Chapter 4 and make extensive use of them.

8. Remember that the first few minutes of the interview develop the all-important first impression. Small talk can be expected.

9. Explain how your qualifications make you the best candidate for the position. Use the knowledge you developed earlier about your skills to explain how you have used them in the past and how you will use them to the benefit of the company.

10. Never speak badly about a previous employer. Interviewers fear you will one day speak badly about their organization.

11. If you must, explain any negative work experiences in an unemotional manner, emphasizing how this experience makes you a better employee.

12. Remain enthusiastic even if you feel that this position may not be for you. Ask for the position. Ask the interviewer when the decision will be made and whether you may call to inquire about the decision.

13. Be prepared to take pre-employment tests, such as a word processing or proofreading test. Ask several questions about the job or the company.

With a bottom line in mind, you can decide whether a particular job is worth a lower salary because it offers a chance for rapid advancement or is in an industry that you are eager to enter.

Do not bring up salary first. If the interviewer asks what salary you had in mind, you may try something such as, "I'm fairly open. Do you have a salary range for this position?" Once you know the range, you can better handle negotiations.

Sometimes, if the salary is lower than you can comfortably handle and is on the low side for your skills, abilities, and the market, you may want to decline the position. Refusing is particularly important if you feel you would not be happy with yourself if you accepted the position.

INAPPROPRIATE QUESTIONS

At times, you may be interviewed by an inexperienced interviewer and asked questions that are inappropriate. Some of the inappropriate questions—and the ways in which the topics can be appropriately addressed or questioned—are shown in the box below.

Inappropriate Interview Questions

Topic	Inappropriate	Appropriate
Age	How old are you?	Are you at least 18?
Marital status	Are you married? Divorced? Single?	The job requires frequent overtime. Are you able to meet this requirement?
Children	Do you have children? If so, how many?	(Same as above)
Criminal record	Have you ever been arrested?	Have you ever been convicted?
National origin	Where were you born? Are you a citizen?	Not appropriate. New hires must provide proof of ability to work in the United States within three days of hire.
Religion	What religion are you?	Not appropriate.
Disability	What is your handicap?	Are you able to perform the essential functions of this job with or without a reasonable accommodation?

These types of questions usually indicate an inexperienced interviewer, but they may also indicate discrimination, which is why trained interviewers do not ask them. If these questions were used during an interview and you feel that they were the basis for the company's failing to hire you, contact your state fair employment commission or the Equal Employment Opportunity Commission.

Remember, however, that most interviewers are not professional interviewers; they are likely to be unaware of the law and probably do not intend to discriminate.

Being faced with one of these questions poses a dilemma. If you refuse to answer or if you tell the interviewer that the question is inappropriate, you may diminish your chances for employment because the interviewer may feel you have something to hide. Also, you may embarrass the interviewer or cause discomfort. On the other hand, answering it may decrease your chances for employment. An employer who learns that you are a single parent with four preschool children may not hire you for fear that you will be absent frequently.

Be prepared with an answer in the event you are asked any of these questions. For instance, a good response when faced with the question of how many children you have would be, "You need not worry about my family. I have made arrangements, and I do not let my personal obligations interfere with my work."

Cindia Cameron, organizing director of 9to5, National Association of Working Women, says that it is important to maintain a positive and professional tone. She says, "Don't refuse to answer questions, but work at drawing the conversation back to your skills and experience." Cameron advises to redirect the question with your response. For example, if you're asked about children or child-care arrangements, Cameron suggests you respond with, "I'm happy to discuss my qualifications and experience. Could you tell me how the issue of children, marital status, etc. relates to the job opening?" Or, "If you're concerned about my availability and attendance, I'm happy to provide references who can confirm I have an extremely high attendance record."[29]

FOLLOW UP

Immediately after the interview, write a thank-you letter to the individual with whom you interviewed. Express your appreciation for the interview, discuss your interest in the job, add any facts or points you may have omitted from the interview, and ask for the job. The sample thank-you letter on the next page shows how formal the letter should be, and how short it can be. This is another opportunity to make a good impression, so be sure the letter is neat and without errors.

Keeping progress charts will help you measure your job search progress. Keep track of the applications placed, resumes mailed, and follow-up telephone calls made each week. Also, develop an interview chart that will help you keep track of interviews and follow-ups. Samples of these charts are on page 548.

128 Daisy Trail Lane
Edmond, OK 73013
405-555-5432
mlottero@provider.net

September 20, 2004

Mr. Sam Hathaway, Accounting Manager
Von Rheen Enterprises
611 Cutler Lane
Edmond, OK 73018

Dear Mr. Hathaway:

Thank you for the opportunity to interview for the accounts payable position. My accounting coursework along with my proven attention to detail and ability to follow instructions will allow me to do an excellent job for you as accounts payable clerk. I look forward to hearing from you on September 26.

Sincerely,

Michael Ottero

Michael Ottero

At an interview, you learn about the company and the company learns about you.

©Getty Images/PhotoDisc

Sample Interview Chart

Company/ Official Name	Date Interviewed	Thank-You Note Sent	Follow-up Date	Analysis	Offer/ No Offer
1. *SPIDEX INC.* *Frank Turner* *President*	*3/26*	*Yes*	*4/4*	*good company; would like to work there*	*no offer*
2. *ART INC.* *Lois Frazier*	*4/8*	*Yes*	*4/10*	*salary not what I hoped*	*no offer*
3. *The Ray Company* *Lou Smith* *Vice President*	*4/4*	*Yes*	*4/12*	*good company, liked job and people*	*offer $27,000/yr*

Sample Progress Chart

	Applications	Resumes Mailed	Follow-ups/ Phone Calls	Interviews	Thank-You Notes
Week 1	*TᴴᴴᴴᴴΙ*	*///*	*////*	*//*	*//*
Week 2	*Tᴴᴴᴴᴴ ///*	*////*	*////*	*/*	*/*
Week 3					
Week 4					
Week 5					
Week 6					

*Fast*Chat

Review the list of inappropriate questions in this section.

1. Have you ever been asked one in an interview? How did you handle it?

2. What were the consequences of your answer?

3. Could you have handled it in another way?

How Do You Handle Job Search Stress and Repond to Job Offers?

18.6

Seeking employment can be one of the most stressful activities ever. Rejection abounds, and we hear "no" more than "yes." Picking up the telephone or writing a letter or going to fill out an application that may lead to rejection takes an unusual amount of self-confidence when we are feeling good about ourselves. Having lost a job or being unsure of our ability to do a first job plays on our self-doubt, making the task even more difficult.

To ease job-seeking anxiety, construct a less stressful environment.

HANDLING REJECTION

The rejection itself is not the only part of the job search that is stressful. Driving to new locations for interviews, meeting with unfamiliar people, waiting for telephone calls or letters, and worrying about finances all increase the tension. Learning how to cope with these strains is of the utmost importance for a smooth job search.

Arranging your environment is a first step in coping with job search stress. Statistics show that people who join a job search club or group find jobs more quickly than those who work alone. You can share your distress concerning rejection and receive support from others in the job search group. Ask your school counselor or inquire at your state employment commission concerning job groups. Or, start a group with a friend who is also searching for a job or search for a group on the Internet. Meet regularly for discussions and practice interviews.

Discuss job search problems with your family. Explain to them how rejection feels. Be sure family members understand how to answer the telephone and take accurate messages. If you do not have an answering machine, provide an alternate number of someone who has a machine or who is available to take messages.

Approach job seeking as a job. Work at least six hours a day on your job search—doing research, writing letters, making telephone calls, and completing applications. Spend some time each day exercising and doing pleasurable activities such as a hobby or volunteer work with others less fortunate. These types of activities will help you manage the stress.

The fear of rejection is the main reason job searches are unsuccessful. Keeping a positive attitude and concentrating on the adage "Nothing ventured, nothing gained" can counter this fear.

QUICK WIT

"A typical job hunt:
NO NO NO NO NO
NO NO NO NO NO
NO NO NO NO NO
NO NO NO NO NO
NO NO NO NO NO
NO NO NO NO NO
NO NO NO NO NO
NO NO NO NO NO
YES"

Tom Jackson,
Author, Guerrilla Tactics
in the Job Market

Keep a positive attitude: "Nothing ventured; nothing gained."

HANDLING JOB OFFERS

When you are offered a job, asking for 24–48 hours to decide is reasonable if needed.

Job offers can be made by telephone, letter, or in person. If the job, the organization, the location, and the salary are right, accept the job immediately. Be sure to inquire when you are to start, where and to whom you should report, and what time you should arrive.

Many times, however, you may want to think about a job offer. You may have another offer that you expect to materialize, or you may need to discuss the offer with your family or friends before accepting. Asking for 24 to 48 hours to allow for a decision is reasonable, with a maximum of 72 hours. Be sure that you have asked the company representative if a decision-making period is permissible and set a time when you will get back with the representative.

If you decide to reject a job offer, do so professionally.

If you decide to reject a job offer, do so professionally. Practice your reasons for refusing the job ahead of time. Avoid reasons such as a personality conflict with the new boss or an offer of more money from your old company. Acceptable excuses are:

"I want very much to work for the company but feel the position offered does not fit with my career objectives."

"At present, I am unable to relocate, but I expect to be able to do so in several years."

"Your offer is excellent, but the opportunity for promotion does not seem to be as great as I need to meet my career objectives."

After declining a job offer, you should write a thank-you letter. You may want, at a later date, to work for this company and should leave the door open for future employment.

*Fast*Chat

1. Why do you think individuals in job search groups find jobs faster?

2. What kind of support can you get from a group?

3. Imagine you have just received a job offer. What reasons might you have for wanting time to think about the job offer?

4. Why is it important to decline a job offer gracefully?

The first week on the job can be a frightening affair. Although we are excited to have the position, we have much to learn, everything from people's names to where the restroom is. These adjustments can be stressful even though we looked forward to beginning the new job. Be patient with yourself and with the job. Give yourself time to get adjusted before you make any judgments concerning your new position.

Your employer will want you to succeed and coworkers will help you get off to a good start. The following techniques will help you adjust to the organization and your job and help you succeed in your new position.

> The first week on a new job is both exciting and stress filled.

How To Keep a Job

In its *Job Search Handbook*, the Georgia Department of Labor recommends the following behaviors for starting and keeping a job.[30]

- Show a positive attitude and project a positive, competent image and appearance.
- Be on time for work and ask your supervisor for the proper method of notifying him/her if you are going to be unavoidably tardy or absent.
- Follow the rules and be dependable.
- Accept criticism as constructive and show appreciation for training, support, input, and feedback.
- Keep your emotions under control and your personal life and problems at home.
- Show initiative. Meet and exceed your employer's expectations.
- Try to solve problems before asking for help. Admit mistakes and learn from them.
- Be a team player and be willing to help.
- Be respectful and treat others the way you want to be treated.
- If you need help, try to find a mentor or role model.
- Treat everyone with courtesy and respect and avoid negative, critical, and gossiping people.
- Volunteer for projects and committees if your work is completed and your supervisor approves.
- Don't try to change things right away. For at least the first month on the job, focus on listening and learning.

Start off right in a new job by showing initiative and a positive attitude.

"I have a plan to make this company the greatest in the world, starting with the position you have open in the mail room."

© 1999 Ted Goff www.tedgoff.com

> Jobs do not last forever, and knowing when and how to leave is a must.

At the opposite end of the spectrum is leaving a position. Jobs are not forever. Individuals may become bored and find no opportunity for growth. Companies lay off workers because of economic conditions, mergers, or buyouts. Sometimes people are terminated because of ethical misconduct, poor work performance, or personal chemistry that is not right. Whatever the cause, almost everyone leaves a job for one reason or another. Warning signs of impending termination abound. Some of them are listed below:

Warning Signs

• You hate your job and spend more time thinking about what you will do after work than at work. You find getting out of bed in the morning difficult. These attitudes tend to show at work, and others on the job realize how you feel about your job.

• You lose your influence. Your ideas and opinions are not heard, and others around you pull back and quit communicating with you, perhaps because they realize your job is in danger. You see others being promoted around you as you stay in the same position.

• You begin to hear about layoffs because of a recession or a potential takeover.

• You're not personally productive, which appears in the form of missed objectives, poorly managed time, or confused priorities.

• You fail to change. You feel unwilling to adapt and learn new skills and ways of doing things.

If you see the handwriting on the wall and feel you will soon be terminated, or if you feel ready for a job change, decisions must be made. Just how bad is the job? Can you hang in there until you find another position? How will you support yourself if you resign? Can you draw unemployment if you resign? Will the company pay severance pay if you resign?

552

Human Relations

Quick wit

"When one door closes, another door opens; but we so often look so long and so regretfully upon the closed door, that we do not see the ones which open for us."

Alexander Graham Bell,
American Scientist and
Inventor of the Telephone

Finding another job is usually easier while you still have one. In fact, approximately one-third of all job seekers are looking for another position while employed. Never use company time to conduct your job search. Do research in the evenings or on weekends and schedule telephone calls on breaks and interviews during your lunch period. Many times, prospective employers will agree to see you late in the evening or even on Saturdays.

If you decide to resign, even if you have a new job, give two weeks' notice of your resignation. This length of notice is standard and proper. Your new employer usually will allow you time to give notice. Sometimes a company may ask you to leave immediately once your resignation is submitted, especially if you deal with trade or strategy secrets or if they feel that your immediate removal is in the best interests of the other employees.

No one is ever totally prepared for termination from a job. However, if you have been reading the warning signs and suspect it is a possibility, start preparing yourself. Expect to feel anger, shame, fear, sadness, and self-pity. Try to control these emotions during the termination interview and remain as professional as possible.

During the termination interview, find out what benefits, if any, the company may give you. Ask, if you think you will need it, for a reference that is positive or at least neutral. If you feel too out of control to discuss benefits, ask if you can return the next day to do so.

Be aware of the unemployment laws in your state. Some states will not pay unemployment if you resign but will if you are terminated. If you are asked to resign rather than be terminated, this may be important.

Never burn your bridges. Throwing a tantrum while being terminated, threatening to kill someone, destroying computer files, tearing up documents, or smashing furniture may make you feel better temporarily but will hurt you in the long run. You may need a reference or want to return to the company under different circumstances.

Checklist for Making a Successful Job and Career Change

- Keep yourself on the cutting edge of the workforce by continuing your education.
- Consider the pros and cons of staying in your current job before making a change. Avoid quitting until you've secured another job.
- Change to a new career if it's realistically available and meets your needs.
- Always resign professionally and courteously.
- In relocating, consider the impact on your loved ones, values and interests, costs involved, and impact on your career goals. Research a new community before moving, and build a new support network right away.

Do not be surprised if your supervisor or a member of security escorts you to your work area to remove articles. This procedure is standard practice in a number of companies because of terminated employees who have destroyed company property.

Many employees, after being terminated, react with disbelief. Some are relieved to be out of an uncomfortable situation; others turn to violence or drinking. Many experience a combination of reactions. Whatever your reaction, you can expect to grieve because of the loss of a job.

 **uick tip** ....

Remember the following dos and don'ts of termination:

- Do try to have a calm conversation with your supervisor to clarify the reason for your termination. Don't make things worse by verbally (or physically) attacking your supervisor or coworkers.
- Don't focus on how unfairly you were treated. Analyze objectively what you may have learned.
- Do reestablish your support system and contact network. Review your job search materials, update your resume, and develop new skills.
- Do use the term "laid off" rather than "fired" when asked about your past job experience. Remember that many people who have lost their jobs in the past have gone on to enjoy successful new jobs and careers.

CHAPTER SUMMARY

Changing demographics, technology, and globalization are altering not only the composition of the workforce of the future, but also the types of goods and services produced in our country. These changes will, in turn, transform the nature of work.

The new jobs of the 21st century will require new technological skills. Cognitive skills such as flexibility, creativity, problem solving, and complex communications are also growing in importance. To meet the challenges that the future holds, you must recognize trends in the job markets, adjust to the new work environment, remain flexible for the future, and make lifelong learning a permanent part of your life.

Job-seeking skills, which help us in finding employment, have become increasingly important as technology and globalization make some jobs obsolete while, at the same time, creating new types of jobs.

Finding employment can be one of the most difficult tasks we face and can be filled with frustration and rejection. Knowing how to prepare a resume, research occupational information, find job openings, and interview successfully is vital to success.

The job search can be stressful, and job seekers can expect many more rejections than offers. Discussing the situation with family members, joining others who are job seeking, getting regular exercise, and working at the job search at least six hours a day will help you stay focused and manage stress.

Once a job is obtained, new employees can expect a stressful first week. Give yourself time for transition to a new position. Leaving a job can be just as stressful. Learn to recognize the warning signs of impending termination and be prepared to leave a job gracefully, without burning bridges.

Key Terms

demographics

globalization

job-seeking skills

networking

resume

chronological resume

functional resume

hybrid/combination resume

reference

interview

REVIEW QUESTIONS

1. What are the major forces shaping our economy? Explain their effects.

2. What can you do to prepare yourself to enter the workforce of 2020?

3. How can you figure out an ideal job for your skills and abilities?

4. What are the obstacles to job-hunting, and how can you overcome them?

5. What resources for information on organizations and careers are available?

6. What goes into a solid resume?

7. Where can you locate job openings?

8. What behavior is appropriate for a job interview?

9. How can you handle the stress of the job search?

10. What are the early warning signs of impending termination?

11. How can you cope with the termination process?

DISCUSSION QUESTIONS

1. Imagine yourself in the year 2010. What job do you expect to be performing? From what age and ethnic groups do you expect your coworkers to be? What types of equipment do you expect to be using?

2. Are you fluent in another language? Why, or why not? What would be the advantages of learning another language?

3. Which of the major forces shaping the economy do you think is the most important? Why?

4. Have you ever looked for a job? Describe your job search and discuss the feelings associated with it.

5. Have you ever been terminated from a job? What happened? Could you have better handled the termination interview?

6. What is the economic situation in your community? Are jobs plentiful or scarce? What adjustments will you need to make in your search because of the economy?

CHAPTER PROJECT

Working in small groups, brainstorm a workplace of the future. You may choose any industry and bring outside source materials in for reference, check web sites for additional materials, or rely on the diverse ideas of the group members. Design an office setting of the future. You are encouraged to take pictures, draw graphic illustrations, or present items in real time. What kind of furniture will be there? What computer connectivity, if any, will be required? Present your design to the class with a verbal briefing on what is represented and why. Describe how it will work and who will be in it. Fully develop and present your ideal workplace of the future.

Develop a resume for a position at this workplace. Use the form of your choice. Share it with classmates for critiquing.

APPLICATIONS

In small groups, analyze the following situations.

R.I.P. Manufacturing

Ian, the production manager, wandered down the silent hall of the R.I.P. Manufacturing Company. He and Wilma, the human resources manager, were the last employees left. Everyone else had been laid off, and they would be leaving and locking the doors for the final time this afternoon. He stopped by Wilma's office one last time.

"I just don't understand what happened, Wilma," Ian said thoughtfully. "I thought those new precision machines would help us improve our quality. We just couldn't compete with the Germans, though. I could never get the product cost down as low as they could. And the quality just wasn't there. You know, I can't blame our customers for buying foreign-made products."

"I know, Ian," Wilma sighed. "I just couldn't find employees who care about quality. You know, some of those folks simply had no skills. Then, when we finally got them up to speed on the equipment, they would leave. That made keeping the plant running at peak capacity impossible."

1. To what forces did R.I.P. fall victim?

2. What changes would have been necessary to save the company? Is the company responsible? Society? Both?

3. Do you foresee this same fate for other U.S. businesses today? Why, or why not?

Nine O'clock Nightmare

TEAMWORK

Cindy breezed in for her 9:00 AM interview five minutes late. She always liked to attract attention and keep people waiting. As she told Darin, the office manager, that she was here for the data processing interview, she began to pull out her hairbrush and lipstick to freshen up a bit. Just as she was tucking everything away in her purse, Mr. Lightfoot walked out. He did a double take when he saw Cindy. She had on a low-cut dress that was bright red and yellow. She had applied heavy makeup and wore her favorite huge gold earrings.

Mr. Lightfoot escorted Cindy into his office. She plopped into her chair and exclaimed, "The traffic was awful! It really got my nerves jangled. I've just got to have a cigarette." She opened her purse and reached for her cigarettes, but Mr. Lightfoot explained that smoking was not allowed in the office.

Mr. Lightfoot proceeded to interview Cindy. She was well informed about the company, explained her extensive software and word processing experience, and emphasized how much she wanted to work for the company.

After the interview, Mr. Lightfoot walked Cindy to the door and, after she left, turned to Darin and asked, "Well, what do you think?"

"Seems like a real flake to me, Mr. Lightfoot. I wouldn't hire her if I were you. I see nothing but trouble."

"Darin, I think you're right. She has great technical skills and has mastered several software programs, but I don't think she would fit in here. Please call the woman I interviewed yesterday—Carlita—and offer her the job."

1. What interview rules did Cindy break?

2. What should Cindy have done during the interview?

3. Are skills always the most important factor?

4. What do you think would have happened if Cindy had been hired?

ADDITIONAL READINGS AND RESOURCES

Bolles, Richard. *What Color Is Your Parachute?* Berkeley, CA: Ten Speed Press, 2003.

Fox, Jeffrey J. *Don't Send a Resume: And Other Contrarian Rules to Help Land a Great Job.* New York: Hyperion Books, 2001.

Karoly, Lynn A., and Constantijn W. A. Panis. *The 21ST Century at Work: Forces Shaping the Future Workforce and Workplace in the United States.* Santa Monica, CA: The RAND Corporation, 2004.

Krannich, Ronald L. *America's Top 100 Jobs for People Without a Four-Year Degree: Great Jobs With a Promising Future.* Manassas Park, VA: Impact Publications, 2004.

Krannich, Ronald L., and Caryl Rae Krannich. *Job Interview Tips for People With Not-So-Hot Backgrounds: How to Put Red Flags Behind You.* Manassas Park, VA: Impact Publications, 2004.

Levitt, Julie Griffin. *Your Career: How to Make It Happen,* 5th ed. Mason, OH: Thomson Business and Professional Publishing, 2004.

Malone, Thomas W. *The Future of Work: How the New Order of Business Will Shape Your Organization, Your Management Style and Your Life.* Boston: Harvard Business School Press, 2004.

Peters, Tom. *Re-Imagine! Business Excellence in a Disruptive Age.* London: Dorling Kindersley, 2003.

Reich, Robert B. *The Future of Success: Working and Living in the New Economy.* New York: Vintage/Random House, 2002.

Rosenberg, Arthur D., and David V. Hizer. *The Resume Handbook: How to Write Outstanding Resumes & Cover Letters for Every Situation (Resume Handbook, 4th Ed).* Avon, MA: Adams Media, 2003.

U. S. Department of Labor. *21st Century Guide to Federal Job and Career Information – Labor Department Data on Future Jobs, Occupational Outlook Handbook, Government Jobs and Careers, Military Career Guides, Student Programs and Internships, Agency Career Information,* 1st ed. Washington: Progressive Management, 2003.

For additional resources, refer to the web site for this text: <u>school.cengage.com/career/dalton</u>

Notes

Chapter 1

1. Fiona Haley, "Fast Talk®: Smart Shops," *Fast Company*, December 2003. Retrieved March 15, 2004, from http://www.fastcompany.com/magazine/77/fasttalk.html.

2. Cited in Ralph D. Wray et al., *Fundamentals of Human Relations* (Mason, OH: Thomson/South-Western, 1996).

3. Robert J. Derocher, "Can Management Style at the CEO Level Predict a Company's Success?" *Insight*, February/March 2001.

4. Cited in Wray et al., *Fundamentals of Human Relations.*

5. Tracey Drury, "IT Industry Strategy Promotes 'Soft Skills,'" *Buffalo Business First*, February 2003.

6. Ted W. Hissey, "Enhanced Skills for Engineers," *Today's Engineer*, September 2002.

7. Cited in MECCA: Memphis Educational Computer Connectivity Alliance. "Now What? Relationships with Co-Workers." Retrieved March 15, 2004, from http://www.mecca.org/~tschieff/AVIATION/Online_CC/NowWhat.htm.

8. Frederick W. Taylor, *Principles of Management* (New York: Harper and Brothers, 1911).

9. Henri Fayol, *General and Industrial Management*, trans. Constance Storrf (London: Sir Isaac Pitman and Sons, Ltd., 1949).

10. Elton Mayo, *The Human Problems of an Industrial Civilization* (New York: Macmillan Publishing Company, 1934).

11. Gene Kranz, presentation at San Jacinto College, Pasadena, TX, November 16, 1998.

12. Thomas H. Davenport, *Process Innovation: Reengineering Work through Information Technology* (Boston: Harvard Business School Press, 1993).

13. James Martin, *Cybercorp* (New York: Amacom, 1996).

14. "Continental Airlines Implements New Airport Procedures, Offers Tips for Stress-Free Check-In," January 17, 2002. Retrieved March 22, 2004, from http://www.prnewswire.com/cgi-bin/micro_stories.pl?ACCT=204100&TICK=CAL&STORY=/www/story/01-17-2002/0001650190&EDATE=Jan+17%2C+2002.

15. "Culture and Globalization: Introduction," *Global Connections: A Student's Guide to Globalization* (Washington: Center for Strategic & International Studies, 2001). Retrieved June 3, 2004, from http://www.csis.org/schollchair/gc/culture/.

16. Bill Leonard, "Bank Mergers Lead to Job Loss and Insecurity," *HR Magazine*, April 2001.

17. Rick Dobbis, "Music Piracy Rises Worldwide," *BBC News Entertainment,* June 2002.

18. Thomas J. Peters and Robert H. Waterman, Jr., *In Search of Excellence* (New York: Warner Books, Inc., 1982).

19. Chip Bell, "Managers as Mentors," *Houston Chronicle,* December 13, 1996, p. 34.

20. Hissey, "Enhanced Skills for Engineers."

21. Jeffrey Hallett, *Worklife Visions* (Alexandria, VA: American Society for Personnel Administrators, 1987).

22. Thomas P. Murtha, *Managing New Industry Creations: Global Knowledge Formation & Entrepreneurship* (Palo Alto, CA: Stanford University Press, 2001).

23. David W. Moore, "Americans Say Internet Makes Their Lives Better," February 23, 2000. Retrieved June 3, 2004, from http://www.gallup.com/poll/content/login.aspx?ci=3202.

24. Robert Lemos, "Poll: Net Privacy Fears Increase," *ZDNet News,* February 23, 2000. Retrieved June 3, 2004, from http://news.zdnet.com/2100-9595_22-518749.html.

25. Douglas Dedo, "Mobile Devices in the Enterprise," Microsoft Corporation Mobility Group White Paper, October 2001. Retrieved June 3, 2004, from http://www.microsoft.com/windowsmobile/business/whitepapers/devicesinenterprise.mspx.

Chapter 2

1. CareerBuilder.com, "CareerBuilder.com Survey Finds Majority of Men and Women Satisfied with Jobs." Retrieved June 3, 2004, from http://www.creativepro.com/story/news/19429.html.

2. "Study Finds Women Denied High-Tech Jobs," *Houston Chronicle,* November 12, 2003.

3. Rita K. Baltus, *Personal Psychology for Life and Work* (New York: McGraw-Hill College, 1998).

4. ibid.

5. Joseph Luft, *The Johari Window: A Graphic Model of Awareness in Relations* (Palo Alto, CA: National Press Books, 1970).

6. ibid.

7. Joseph Luft, *Group Processes: An Introduction to Group Dynamics* (New York: McGraw-Hill College, 1984).

8. ibid.

9. ibid.

10. D'Arcy Lyness, "How Can I Improve My Self-Esteem?" *Teens Health,* 2001.

11. "Beyond Positive Thinking," *Success,* December 1988, pp. 31–38.

12. David D. Burns, *Feeling Good: The New Mood Therapy* (New York: Avon, 1999).

13. Stephen Strasser, *Working It Out—Sanity & Success in the Workplace* (Englewood Cliffs, NJ: Prentice-Hall, Inc., 1989).

14. Elwood N. Chapman, *Attitude: Your Most Priceless Possession* (Menlo Park, CA: Crisp Publications, Inc., 1995).

15. Career Solutions Training Group, *School-to-Work Series: Attitude* (Mason, OH: Thomson/South-Western, 1996).

16. Elizabeth Kubler Ross, *On Death and Dying* (New York: Touchstone Books, 1997).

17. Career Solutions Training Group, *School-to-Work Series: Attitude.*

18. Anna Freud, *The Ego and the Mechanisms of Defense,* cited in *Gale Encyclopedia of Psychology,* 2nd ed. (Farmington Hills, MI: Thomson/Gale Group, 2001).

19. ibid.

20. Walter D. St. John, "Successful Communications between Supervisors and Employees," *Personnel Journal,* January 1983, pp. 71–77.

21. "Managing Your Boss," *Government Executive,* April 1989, pp. 34–37.

Chapter 3

1. A. Overholt, "Des Moines: The Hippest City in the USA?" *Fast Company,* October 2003, pp. 96-98. Retrieved March 29, 2004, from http://www.fastcompany.com/magazine/75/desmoines.html.

2. L. W. Prencipe, "Mastering Motivation," *InfoWorld,* November 16, 2001. Retrieved March 29, 2004, from http://archive.infoworld.com/articles/pe/xml/01/11/19/ 011119pemotivate.xml.

3. Gary Applegate, *Happiness, It's Your Choice* (Sherman Oaks, CA: Berringer Publishing, 1985).

4. Abraham H. Maslow, *Motivation and Personality* (New York: Harper & Row, 1954).

5. "India's Call Centers Suffer High Quit Rate," *CNetAsia, News & Technology,* August 8, 2003. Retrieved March 29, 2004, from http://asia.cnet.com/newstech/industry/0,39001143,39145029,00.htm.

6. Frederick Herzberg, *Work and the Nature of Man* (New York: HarperCollins, 1966).

7. Frederick Herzberg, "One More Time: How Do You Motivate Employees?" *Harvard Business Review Classic,* September/October 1987, p. 112.

8. David C. McClelland, *Studies in Motivation* (New York: Appleton-Century Crofts, 1955).

9. David C. McClelland and David H. Burnham, "Power Is the Great Motivator," *Harvard Business Review,* January/February 1995, pp. 123–139.

10. Victor H. Vroom, *Work and Motivation* (New York: John Wiley & Sons, 1964).

11. Joseph L. Massie and John Douglas, *Managing—A Contemporary Introduction* (Englewood Cliffs, NJ: Prentice-Hall, Inc., 1992).

12. Peter Drucker, *Management: Tasks, Responsibilities, Practices* (New York: Harper & Row, 1993).

13. Claudia Coates, "Money Doesn't Buy Loyalty—Titles Do," *Associated Press,* July 19, 1998.

14. G. R. Emery, "Employees: Show Me the Recognition," *Washington Technology,* October 9, 2000. Retrieved March 29, 2004, from http://www.washingtontechnology.com/news/15_14/workplace/1871-1.html.

15. Albert J. Bernstein and Sydney Craft Rozen, "How to Re-Energize Your Staff," *Working Woman,* April 1989, pp. 45–46.

16. ibid.

17. Mary Beth Lamb, "Boosting Productivity through Recognition Requires Cultural Understanding," *Link&Learn Newsletter,* March 1, 2003. Retrieved March 29, 2004, from http://www.linkageinc.com/newsletter/archives/default.shtml.

18. Natalie Burke, "Gen X Entrepreneurs Embrace Self-Reliance," *Nevada Outpost,* June 1, 1997.

19. F. Warner, "Learning How to Speak to Gen Y," *Fast Company,* July 2003, p. 36. Retrieved March 29, 2004, from http://www.fastcompany.com/magazine/72/smartcompany.html.

20. ibid.

21. Bernstein and Rozen, "How to Re-Energize Your Staff."

22. Kenneth Blanchard and Spencer Johnson, *The One Minute Manager* (New York: William Morrow and Company, 1983).

23. "Bigger Carrot, Better Results," *Inc. Magazine,* September 1988. Retrieved March 29, 2004, from http://www.inc.com/magazine/19880901/5961.html.

Chapter 4

1. Phillip J. Harkins, *Powerful Conversations: How High Impact Leaders Communicate* (New York: McGraw-Hill, 1999).

2. Cynthia C. Froggatt, *Working Naked: Eight Essential Principles for Peak Performance in the Virtual Work Place* (San Francisco: Jossey-Bass Business and Management Series, 2001).

3. "Listening Factoids," International Listening Association, February 13, 2004. Retrieved April 12, 2004, from http://www.listen.org/pages/factoids.html.

4. ibid.

5. ibid.

6. "How Has Information Technology Changed Your Life?" *BBC News Online,* December 22, 2003. Retrieved April 12, 2004, from http://news.bbc.co.uk/1/hi/technology.

7. Alfred Hermida, "Nations Wrestle with the Internet Age," *BBC News Online*, December 15, 2003. Retrieved April 12, 2004, from http://news.bbc.co.uk/1/hi/technology/3318371.stm.

8. Ted Neilson, "Keep Your Essay Sentence Length Under Control." Retrieved April 12, 2004, from http://www.write-an-essay.com/.

9. Andrea C. Poe, "Hone Your E-Mail Messaging Skills to Improve Communications," *Managing Smart*, Winter 2002. Retrieved April 12, 2004, from http://www.shrm.org/managingsmart/.

10. A. Mehrabian and S. R. Ferris, "Inferences of Attitudes from Nonverbal Communication in Two Channels," *Nonverbal Communication*. (New York: Oxford University Press, 1974).

11. Geoff Ribbens and Richard Thompson, *Understanding Body Language: Barron's Business Success Series* (Hauppauge, New York: Barron's Educational Series, 2001).

12. "Evolutionary Etiquette and the Cellular Telephone," *Mannersmith Monthly*, no. 34, 2002. Retrieved April 12, 2004, from http://www.mannersmith.com/.

13. "Non-Verbal Communication: A Leader's Most Powerful, Revealing Tool— Q & A with Hal Movius," *Link&Learn Newsletter*, January 15, 2003. Retrieved April 12, 2004, from http://www.linkageinc.com/newsletter/archives/default.shtml.

14. "Instant Messaging," *Internet.com Small Business Channel*, February 20, 2004. Retrieved April 12, 2004, from http://www.internet.com/sections/sb.html.

15. "Top Text Tips: Useful Info for Trouble Free Texting," *Text.It: Text for Grown Ups*. Retrieved April 8, 2004, from http://www.text.it/grownups/default.asp?intPageID=200.

16. Frank Thorsberg, "Instant Messaging Etiquette," *PC World*, May 30, 2002. Retrieved April 8, 2004, from http://www.pcworld.com/howto/article/0,aid,99405,00.asp.

Chapter 5

1. Danielle Sacks, "The Gore-Tex of Guitar Strings," *Fast Company*, December 2003.

2. Mark Hunter, "Work, Work, Work," *Modern Maturity*, May–June 1999, p. 37.

3. "Computers Not the Real Reason for Rage on Job?" *Houston Chronicle*, March 26, 1999, 5G.

4. "New to Six Sigma: A Six Sigma Guide for Both Novice and Experienced Quality Practitioners," *iSixSigma*. Retrieved April 20, 2004, from http://www.isixsigma.com/library/content/six-sigma-newbie.asp.

5. Edward De Bono, *Six Thinking Hats* (Boston: Back Bay Books, 1999).

6. John F. Reh, "Pareto's Principle – The 80-20 Rule." Retrieved April 20, 2004, from http://management.about.com/cs/generalmanagement/a/Pareto081202.htm.

7. Lyle Sussman and Samuel D. Deep, *COMEX: The Communication Experience in Human Relations* (Mason, OH: Thomson/South-Western, 1997).

8. ibid.

9. Bill Schadewald, "There's a Buzzword Born Every Minute." *Houston Business Journal,* January 22–28, 1999, 24A.

10. Abraham H. Maslow, "The Scientific Study of Inventive Talent," in *A Source Book for Creative Thinking,* ed. Sidney J. Parnes (New York: Scribner, 1962).

11. "Creativity and Counseling. Highlights: An ERIC/CAPS Fact Sheet," *ERIC* Digest, 1984. Retrieved April 20, 2004, from http://www.ericfacility.net/ericdigests/ed260369.html.

12. Maslow, "The Scientific Study of Inventive Talent."

13. "Creativity and Counseling. Highlights: An ERIC/CAPS Fact Sheet."

14. Daniel A. Wren and Ronald G. Greenwood, *Management Innovators: The People and Ideas that Have Shaped Modern Business* (New York: Oxford University Press USA, 1998).

15. Gary Hamel and C. K. Prahalad, *Competing for the Future* (Concordville, PA: Soundview Executive Book Summaries, 1994), pp. 16–24.

16. Wren and Greenwood, *Management Innovators: The People and Ideas that Have Shaped Modern Business*

17. "How to Harness Creativity," *Personal Report for the Executive,* National Institute of Business Management, July 1, 1989.

18. ibid.

19. "Brainstorming: Generating Many Radical Ideas," *Mind Tools.* Retrieved April 20, 2004, from http://www.mindtools.com/pages/article/newCT_04.htm

20. Charles Warner, "How to Manage Creative People." Retrieved April 20, 2004, from http://www.charleswarner.us/mgtcreat.html.

21. Jim Barlow, "Nine Steps Toward a Great Workplace," *Houston Chronicle,* April 11, 1999.

22. Keith Hammonds, "Is Your Company Up to Speed?" *Fast Company,* June 2003.

23. Roger E. Axtell, *Do's and Taboos of Humor around the World* (Hoboken, NJ: John Wiley & Sons, 1998).

24. Ian Ayres and Barry J. Nalebuff, *Why Not? How to Use Everyday Ingenuity to Solve Problems Big and Small* (New York: Harvard Business School Press, 2003).

25. Axtell, *Do's and Taboos of Humor around the World.*

26. Jim Calano and Jeff Salzman, "Ten Ways to Fire Up Your Creativity," *Working Woman,* July 1989, pp. 94–95.

27. Eugene Raudsepp, "How Creative Are You?" *Nation's Business,* June 1985, pp. 25–26.

28. Bruce Tulgan and Carolyn A. Martin, "Managing Generation Y – Part 1," *Business Week,* September 28, 2001.

Chapter 6

1. Tom Peters, *Re-Imagine! Business Excellence in a Disruptive Age* (London: Dorling Kindersley, 2003).

2. Ron Ashkenas et al., *The Boundaryless Organization: Breaking the Chains of Organization Structures, Revised and Updated* (Hoboken, New Jersey: Jossey-Bass, 2002).

3. Thomas Claburn, "New Direction for the AP," *InformationWeek*, January 26, 2004.

4. Michael Warshaw, "Open Mouth, Close Career?" *Fast Company*, December 1998, p. 240.

5. "Straight Talk," *Boeing Frontiers*, February 2004, p.5.

6. Stanley M. Herman, *Rewiring Organizations for the Networked Economy: Organizing, Managing and Leading in the Information Age* (New Jersey: Pfeiffer Publishing Program, 2002).

7. Seth Godin, "There Is No Corporate Privacy, and That's a Good Thing," *Fast Company*, August 2003, p. 60.

8. Barry L. Reece and Rhonda Brandt, *Effective Human Relations in Organizations* (Boston: Houghton Mifflin, 2001).

9. Leslie Walker, "Mall's WiFi to Blur the Line between Work and Play," *Houston Chronicle*, February 29, 2004, 4D.

10. Warren Bennis, "News Analysis: It's the Culture," *Fast Company*, August 2003.

11. Steven Marlin, "The 24-Hour Supply Chain: 7-Eleven Depends on Store Managers," *InformationWeek*, January 26, 2004.

12. John A. Byrne, "How to Lead Now: Getting Extraordinary Performance When You Can't Pay For It," *Fast Company*, August 2003.

13. Joseph L. Massie and John Douglas, *Managing—A Contemporary Introduction* (Englewood Cliffs, NJ: Prentice-Hall, Inc., 1992).

14. "The Company of Friends Toolbook," produced by *Fast Company* for the 2000 Community@Work Leadership Summit. Retrieved April 20, 2004, from http://www.fastcompany.com/friends/toolbook.html.

15. Carleen Hawn, "The Global Razor's Edge," *Fast Company*, February 2004.

Chapter 7

1. F. J. Roethlisberger and W. J. Dickson, *Management and the Worker* (Cambridge: Harvard University Press, 1939).

2. H. Leavitt, "Suppose We Took Groups Seriously . . ." in *Man and Work in Society*, eds. E. L. Cass and F. G. Zimmer (New York: Van Nostrand Reinhold, 1975).

3. "Working Life at Shell." Retrieved July 22, 2004, from http://www.shell.com/home/Framework?siteId=careers-en&FC2=&FC3=/careers-en/html/iwgen/inside_shell/youask_weanswer_0912.html#1.

4. Marvin E. Shaw, *Group Dynamics: The Psychology of Small Group Behavior*, 5th ed. (New York: McGraw-Hill, 1996).

5. John Foley, "Blue Print for Change," *Information Week Magazine*, January 26, 2004, pp. 22-24.

6. Warren Bennis, *The Secrets of Great Groups* (San Francisco: The Drucker Foundation and Jossey-Bass Publishers, 1997), pp. 29–33.

7. Todd Leopold, "The Crowd is Smarter than You Think." Retrieved July 14, 2004, from http://www.cnn.com/2004/SHOWBIZ/books/07/14/wisdom.crowds/index.html.

8. Rensis Likert, "The Nature of Highly Effective Groups," in Rensis Likert, *New Patterns of Management* (New York: McGraw-Hill, 1961).

9. Adam Lucas, "Tar Heels of the Year Interview Outtakes," *NC Tar Heel Monthly*, June 24, 2004.

10. Likert, "The Nature of Highly Effective Groups."

11. ibid.

12. ibid.

13. Shaw, *Group Dynamics: The Psychology of Small Group Behavior*.

14. Irving Janis, *Victims of Groupthink* (Boston: Houghton Mifflin Company, 1992).

15. James Robertson, "Managing the Knowledge Worker." Retrieved July 15, 2004, from http://www.steptwo.com.au/km/km/index.html.

16. Tom Brinck, "Groupware: Introduction." Retrieved July 15, 2004, from http://www.usabilityfirst.com/groupware/intro.txl.

Chapter 8

1. Regina F. Maruca, "What Makes Team Work?" *Fast Company*, November 2000. Retrieved July 15, 2004, from http://www.fastcompany.com/magazine/40/one.html.

2. California Institute of Human Services, Sonoma State University, "Team Versus Group," *California High School Reform: Aiming High Toolkit*. Retrieved July 15, 2004, from http://www.bused.org/rsabe/rsabe10.pdf.

3. "Hopkins Surgeons Successfully Separate Nigerian Conjoined Twin Girls," Johns Hopkins Children's Center News Release, September 16, 2003. Retrieved July 15, 2004, from http://www.hopkinschildrens.org/pages/news/archivedetails.cfm?newsid=152.

4. Mark Samuel, *The Accountability Revolution: Achieve Breakthrough Results in Half the Time* (Tempe, AZ: Facts on Demand Press, 2001).

5. Donald Wallace, *One Great Game: Two Teams, Two Dreams, in the First-Ever National Championship High School Football Game* (New York: Atria Books, 2003).

6. Nancy Nelson, SPHR, "The HR Generalist's Guide to Teambuilding," Society of Human Resource Management White Papers, August 2002.

7. ibid.

8. ibid.

9. ibid.

10. Richard M. Hodgetts, *Modern Human Relations at Work* (Mason, OH: Thomson/South-Western, 2002).

11. Cornelius Grove, Willa Hallowell, and Kathy Molloy. "Protocols Make E-Mail More Effective...Fortunately!" Retrieved July 15, 2004, from http://www.grovewell.com/pub-email-solutions.html.

12. Sue Widemark, "Lessons from Geese: Who Is the Author and Is It Scientifically Sound?" Retrieved July 15, 2004, from http://www.suewidemark.com/lessonsgeese.htm.

13. B. Tuckman and B. & M. Jensen, "Stages of Small Group Development," *Group and Organizational Studies*, no. 2, 1977, pp. 419-427.

14. Hodgetts, *Modern Human Relations at Work*.

15. Jon L. Katzenbach and Douglas K. Smith, "The Discipline of Virtual Teams," *Leader to Leader*, no. 22, Fall 2001. Retrieved July 15, 2004, from http://leadertoleader.org/leaderbooks/L2L/fall2001/katzenbach.html.

16. Ann Rippin, *Teamworking* (Oxford, U.K: Capstone Publishing, 2002).

17. Ronald J. Burke and Cary L. Cooper, *Leading in Turbulent Times: Managing in the New World of Work* (Boston: Blackwell Publishers, 2003).

Chapter 9

1. Minority Corporate Counsel Association, "Employers of Choice: Spotlight on 2003 Award Winners." Retrieved March 1, 2004, from www.mcca.com.

2. Tex Texin, "Marketing Translation Mistakes," Internationalization, Localization, Standards, and Amusements. Retrieved July 13, 2004, from www.i18nguy.com.

3. Todd Campbell, "Diversity in Depth," Society for Human Resource Management Diversity, Hot Topics. Retrieved February 18, 2004, from www.shrm.org.

4a. United States Department of Labor Bureau of Labor Statistics, "BLS Releases 2002-12 Employment Projections," February 11, 2004. Retrieved July 13, 2004, from http://www.bls.gov/news.release/ecopro.nr0.htm.

4b. Michael Lewis, *Moneyball: The Art of Winning an Unfair Game* (New York: W.W. Norton & Company, 2003).

5. Society for Human Resource Management, "How Should My Organization Define Diversity?" Retrieved July 13, 2004, from http://shrm.org/diversity/definingdiversity.asp.

6. Karyn-Siobhan Robinson, "New Study Examines Changing Workforce," *Society for Human Resource Management HR News*, October 9, 2003.

7. ibid.

8. U.S. Census Bureau, "Table No. 577. Employment Status of Women by Marital Status and Presence and Age of Children: 1970 to 2002," *Labor Force, Employment, and Earnings, Statistical Abstract of the United States*, 2003. Retrieved July 13, 2004, from http://www.census.gov/prod/www/statistical-abstract-03.html.

9. United States Department of Labor Bureau of Labor Statistics, "BLS Releases 2002-12 Employment Projections."

10. AARP, "Staying Ahead of the Curve 2003: The AARP Working In Retirement Study," 2002 Retrieved July 13, 2004, from http://research.aarp.org/econ/multiwork_2003.html.

11. Judith Graham, "Oldest Worker In America Leads a Growing Trend," *Chicago Tribune*, November 12, 2003. Retrieved July 13, 2004, from http://www.centredaily.com/mld/centredaily/news/7242713.htm.

12. United States Department of Labor Bureau of Labor Statistics, "BLS Releases 2002-12 Employment Projections."

13. U.S. Newswire, "Foreign Born a Majority in Six U.S. Cities: Growth Fastest in South, Census Bureau Reports," December 17, 2003. Retrieved July 13, 2004, from http://releases.usnewswire.com/GetRelease.asp?id=24504.

14. Carol Hastings, "Tapping Into Your Foreign-Born, Spanish-Speaking Workforce," *Society for Human Resource Management: Mosaics* 8, no. 3, July/August 2002.

15. United States Department of Labor Bureau of Labor Statistics, "Table No. 5. Civilian Labor Force by Age, Sex, Race, and Hispanic Origin, 1982, 1992, 2002, and projected 2012," *Bureau of Labor Statistics Monthly Labor Review*, May 2002. Retrieved July 13, 2004, from http://stats.bls.gov/emp/emplab2002-05.pdf.

16. Society for Human Resource Management, "Where Will Employers Find Talent in the 21st Century?" *Diversity Hot Topics*, October 2003.

17. Catherine Donaldson-Evans, "Fortune 500 Companies See Money in Gay Families." May 26, 2004. Retrieved July 13, 2004, from http://www.foxnews.com/story/0,2933,120902,00.html.

18. Gary J. Gates and Jason Ots, "Why Study Gay and Lesbian Location Patterns?" *The Gay and Lesbian Atlas*. Retrieved July 13, 2004, from http://www.urban.org/pubs/gayatlas/chapter1.html.

19. Annie Murphy Paul, "Where Bias Begins: The Truth About Stereotypes," *Psychology Today*, May/June 1998.

20. Marilyn Loden and Judy B. Rosener, *Workforce America! Managing Employee Diversity as a Vital Resource* (New York: McGraw-Hill, 1990).

21. Janet Lockhart and Susan M. Shaw, "Rating Your Behavior Handout," *Writing for Change: Raising Awareness of Difference, Power, and Discrimination.* Retrieved July 13, 2004, from http://www.toleranceusa.net/teach/expand/wfc/pdf/section_1/1_03_rating_behavior.pdf.

22. "People Whose Ideas Influence Organisational Work: Geert Hofstede." Retrieved July 13, 2004, from www.onepine.info/phof.htm.

23. Devon Scheef and Diane Thielfoldt, "Engaging Multiple Generations among Your Workforce," *Link&Learn Newsletter*, November 15, 2003.

24. Deborah Tannen, *The Power of Talk: Who Gets Heard and Why* (Boston: Harvard Business School Press, 2002).

25. Joe Mullich, "The Language of Cooperation," *Workforce Management Magazine*, March 2004.

26. Jennifer E. Beer, "High and Low Context," *Culture at Work: Communicating Across Cultures*, 1997-2003. Retrieved July 13, 2004, from http://www.culture-at-work.com/highlow.html.

27. ibid.

28. Loden and Rosener, *Workforce America! Managing Employee Diversity as a Vital Resource.*

29. Deborah Tannen, *Talking from 9 to 5: How Women's and Men's Conversational Styles Affect Who Gets Heard, Who Gets Credit, and What Gets Done at Work* (New York: HarperCollins, 1994).

30. ibid.

31. HRZone, "The Pygmalion Effect: Belief in Potential Creates Potential," from Brian D. McNatt, "Ancient Pygmalion Joins Contemporary Management: A Meta-Analysis of the Result," *Journal of Applied Psychology*, 200 85, no. 2, pp. 314-322. Retrieved July 14, 2004, from http://www.hrzone.com/articles/pygmalion_effect.html.

32. Linda S. Wallace, "10 Practical Ways to Increase an Individual's Cultural IQ," *Houston Chronicle*, May 23, 2003.

33. William Sonnenschein, *The Diversity Toolkit* (Chicago, IL: Contemporary Books, 1999).

34. Caryl Stern-LaRosa and Ellen Hofmeire Bettmann, *Hate Hurts: How Children Learn and Unlearn Prejudice* (New York: Scholastic, Inc., 2000).

35. Stephan Dahl, "Hall's Classic Patterns," *An Overview of Intercultural Research.* Retrieved July 14, 2004, from http://stephan.dahl.at/intercultural/hall.html.

36. David Thibault, "Southwest Airlines Cleared in Race Discrimination Lawsuit," January 23, 2004. Retrieved July 14, 2004, from http://www.cnsnews.com/Culture/Archive/200401/CUL20040123b.html.

Chapter 10

1. Peter McWilliams, *Life 101.* Retrieved July 30, 2004, from http://www.mcwilliams.com/books/books/life1/.

2. Denis Waitley, *The Psychology of Winning: Qualities of a Total Winner* (Niles, IL: Nightingale-Conant, 1995).

3. Jim Loehr and Tony Schwartz, *Power of Full Engagement: Managing Energy, Not Time, Is the Key to High Performance & Person Renewal* (New York: Free Press, 2003).

4. Ramon J. Aldag and Timothy M. Stearns, *Management* (Mason, OH: Thomson/South-Western, 1987).

5. Peter Drucker, *Management: Tasks, Responsibilities, Practices* (New York: Harper & Row, 1993).

6. Brian Tracy, *Goals! How to Get Everything You Want – Faster Than You Ever Thought Possible* (San Francisco: Berrett-Koehler Publishers, Inc., 2003).

7. ibid.

8. Aldag and Stearns, *Management.*

9. Jack Canfield, Mark Victor Hansen, and Les Hewitt, *The Power of Focus: How to Hit Your Business, Personal and Financial Targets with Absolute Certainty* (Deerfield Beach, FL: Health Communications, Inc. 2000).

10. Robert Kriegel and Marilyn Harris Kriegel, "How to Reach Peak Performance — Naturally," *The Secretary,* March 1986, pp. 22–24.

11. Thomas E. Burdick and Charlene A. Mitchell, "Executives Face Freeze on Fast Track," *The Houston Post,* April 4, 1988, C1.

12. International Association of Administration Professionals, "Check Your 'Progress Pulse' to Measure Career Success," *The Secretary,* March 1986, p. 25.

13. "Management by Objectives," *George Odiorne Letter* 14, no. 20, October 19, 1984.

14. ibid.

15. Lester Bittel, *What Every Supervisor Should Know* (New York: McGraw-Hill, 1985).

16. Henry Mintzberg, "MBA Menace," *Fast Company,* June 2004. Retrieved September 30, 2004, from http://www.fastcompany.com/magazine/83/mbamenace.html.

Chapter 11

1. Ripley Hotch, "Letter from the Editor," *Success Magazine,* April 2001.

2. Warren Bennis, *On Becoming a Leader* (Reading, MA: Addison-Wesley Publishing Company, 1989).

3. ibid.

4. John Naisbitt and Patricia Aburdene, *Megatrends2000—Ten New Directions for the 1990s* (New York: William Morrow and Company, Inc., 1990).

5. Jennifer Reingold, "One Degree of Russell Simmons," *Fast Company*, November 2003, pp. 71-80.

6. Peter Drucker, *Effective Executive* (Burlington, MA: Elsevier/Butterworth-Heinemann, 1999).

7. Larraine Segil, James Belasco, and Marshall Goldsmith, *Partnering: The New Face of Leadership* (New York: American Management Association, 2002).

8. Joseph L. Massie and John Douglas, *Managing—A Contemporary Introduction* (Englewood Cliffs, NJ: Prentice-Hall, Inc., 1992).

9. ibid.

10. ibid.

11. Douglas McGregor, *The Human Side of Enterprise* (New York: McGraw-Hill, 1960).

12. ibid.

13. Robert Blake and Jane Srygley Mouton, *The Managerial Grid®—The Key to Leadership Excellence* (Houston, TX: Gulf Publishing Company, 1985).

14. Fred E. Fiedler, *A Theory of Leadership Effectiveness* (New York: McGraw-Hill, 1967).

15. Paul Hersey, *The Situational Leader* (New York: Warner Books, 1985), p. 63.

16. Paul Hersey and Kenneth H. Blanchard, *Management of Organizational Behavior: Utilizing Human Resources* (Englewood Cliffs, NJ: Prentice- Hall, 1982).

17. Hersey, *The Situational Leader*.

18. Deborrah Himsel, *Leadership Soprano's Style: How to Become a More Effective Boss* (Chicago: Dearborn Trade Publishing, 2003).

19. Gregory Smith, "Using Assessments to Develop Managers and Others for Professional and Personal Growth," *Link&Learn Newsletter*. Retrieved July 30, 2004, from http://www.linkageinc.com/newsletter/archives/pm/smith_using_assessment.shtml.

20. Brace E. Barber, *No Excuse Leadership: Lessons from the U.S. Army's Elite Rangers* (Hoboken, NJ: John Wiley & Sons, 2003).

21. Robert Rosen, "Ping An Insurance," *Training & Development*, May 2001.

22. John Naisbitt and Patricia Aburdene, *Re-Inventing the Corporation* (New York: Warner Books, Inc., 1986).

23. "What Is PHP?" Retrieved July 30, 2004, from http://www.php.co.jp/japaninface/phpguide.html.

24. Lester R. Bittel and John W. Newstrom, *What Every Supervisor Should Know* (New York: McGraw-Hill, Inc., 1992).

25. Segil, Belasco, and Goldsmith, *Partnering: The New Face of Leadership.*

26. Massie and Douglas, *Managing—A Contemporary Introduction.*

27. John P. Kotter, *The Leadership Factor* (New York: The Free Press, 1988).

28. Munir Kotadia, "Red Hat." Retrieved July 30, 2004, from www.zdnet.com.

29. Wess Roberts, *Leadership Secrets of Attila the Hun* (New York: Warner Books, 1987).

30. Warren Bennis, "How to Be the Leader They'll Follow," *Working Woman,* March 1990, pp. 75–78.

31. Bernard M. Bass, *Bass & Stogdill's Handbook of Leadership* (New York: The Free Press, 1990).

32. Bennis, *On Becoming a Leader.*

Chapter 12

1. Patricia Sellers, "The Business of Being Oprah," *Fortune,* April 2002.

2. ibid.

3. David Rynecki, "Golf and Power," *Fortune,* March 2003.

4. Patricia Sellers, "Most Powerful Women in Business," *Fortune,* April 2003. Retrieved July 30, 2004, from http://www.fortune.com/fortune/articles/0,15114,490359,00.html.

5. J. R. P. French and B. Raven, "The Bases of Social Power," in *Group Dynamics,* 3rd ed., eds. D. Cartwright and A. F. Zander (New York: Harper & Row, 1968).

6. James Stoner and R. Edward Freeman, *Management* (Upper Saddle River, NJ: Pearson Higher Education, 1991).

7. Robert Meier, "Power—Do You Lust for It?" *Success,* May 1984.

8. Sellers, "Most Powerful Women in Business."

9. Anthony Robbins, *Unlimited Power* (New York: The Free Press, 1997).

10. Andrew J. DuBrin, *Winning Office Politics* (Englewood Cliffs, NJ: Prentice-Hall, 1990).

11. ibid.

12. Wayne E. Hensley, "The Measurement of Height," *Adolescence,* Fall 1998. Retrieved July 30, 2004, from http://www.findarticles.com/p/articles/mi_m2248/is_131_33/ai_53368542.

13. Dress for Success, "What We Do." Retrieved July 30, 2004, from http://www.dressforsuccess.org.

14. Anne Fisher, "Ask Annie," *Fortune,* June 2003.

15. Michael Arndt, "Living Large in the Corner Office," *Business Week,* February 2004.

16. ibid.

17. Brent Schlender, "All You Need is Love, $50 Billion, and Killer Software Code-Named Longhorn," *Fortune,* June 2002.

18. Kenneth Blanchard, John P. Carlos, and Alan Randolph, *The 3 Keys to Empowerment: Release the Power within People for Astonishing Results* (San Francisco: Berrett-Koehler Publishers, Inc., 1999).

19. ibid.

20. Frances Hesselbein, *Working Smart* Newsletter, National Institute of Business Management. Retrieved July 30, 2004, from http://www.nibm.net/newsletter.asp?pub=PRE.

21. Warren Bennis, *On Becoming a Leader* (Reading, MA: Addison-Wesley Publishing Company, 1989).

22. R. W. Cuddy, "Executive Leadership Coaching." Retrieved July 30, 2004, from http://www.rwcuddy.com.

23. Patricia Sellers, "Power: Do Women Really Want It?" *Fortune,* September 2003.

Chapter 13

1. Marilyn Geewax, "Plan on Visiting India? Your Tax Returns Might," *Palm Beach Post,* March 28, 2004.

2. ABC News, "Fed OKs J.P. Morgan Chase-Bank One Merger," June 15, 2004. Retrieved July 30, 2004, from http://www.wjla.com/news/stories/0604/153309.html.

3. Joellen Perry, "Help Wanted," *U.S. News & World Report,* March 8, 2004.

4. Julekha Dash, "Employees Say Hunters Need Soft Skills," *ComputerWorld,* June 2001.

5. James Champy, "Create Jobs, Don't Protect Them," *Fast Company,* October 2003.

6. Champy, "Create Jobs, Don't Protect Them."

7. Simon Gompertz, "Working Lunch," *BBC News,* February 7, 2003. Retrieved July 30, 2004, from http://news.bbc.co.uk/1/hi/programmes/working_lunch/default.stm.

8. Michael Flaherty, "American Wood Furniture Manufacturers Losing Floor Space, Jobs," *Reuters News Service.* Retrieved July 30, 2004, from http://www.reuters.com/newsChannel.jhtml?type=businessNews.

9. ABI Rearch, "Hydrogen Infrastructure Deployment is Key Component to U.S. and Canada Having One Million Fuel Cell Vehicles by 2015," September 4, 2003. Retrieved August 10, 2004, from http://www.abiresearch.com/pdfs/HYD03pr.pdf.

10. Terry Costlow, "Fuel Cell Research Moving at Light Speed," *IEEE USA Today's Engineer,* April 2003. Retrieved August 10, 2004, from http://www.h2cars.biz/artman/publish/index.shtml.

11. Peter Drucker, *The New Realities* (New York: HarperCollins, 1990).

12. Kim Clark, "A Fondness for Gray Hair," *U.S. News & World Report*, March 8, 2004, pp. 56-58.

13. F. Becker and W. Sims, "Offices that Work," Cornell University International Workplace Studies Program, 2001. Retrieved August 10, 2004, from http://iwsp.human.cornell.edu/pubs/pdf/IWS_0002.PDF.

14. ibid.

15. Paul McDougall, "Offshore Outsourcing Projected to Grow," *Information Week*, January 29, 2004. Retrieved August 10, 2004, from http://www.informationweek.com/showArticle.jhtml?articleID= 17500699.

16. Jennifer Reingold, "Still Angry after all these Years," *Fast Company*, October 2003, p. 89.

17. The European Centre for Total Quality Management, *TQM Magazine*. Retrieved August 10, 2004, from http://www.brad.ac.uk/acad/ management/ectqm/MAGAZINE.HTML.

18. David A. Zatz, "Harnessing the Power of Cultural Change," *The OD Papers*, February 1994.

19. ibid.

20. ibid.

21. ibid.

22. Catherine D. Fyock, "Rocking the Boat without Falling Out," *HR Magazine*, January 2000.

23. James Champy, *X-Engineering the Corporation: Reinventing Your Business in the Digital Age* (New York: Warner Business Books, 2002).

24. David Sheff, "Levi's Changes Everything," *Fast Company*, June 1996. Retrieved August 10, 2004, from http://www.fastcompany.com/online/03/levi.html.

25. Fara Warner, "Inside Intel's Mentoring Movement," *Fast Company*, April 2002.

26. Leslie Haggin Geary, "Vanishing Jobs," *CNNMoney*, January 9, 2004. Retrieved August 10, 2004, from http://money.cnn.com/2003/12/17/pf/q_nomorework/index.htm.

27. "The Jobless Recovery," *CNNMoney*, April 1, 2004. Retrieved August 10, 2004, from https://www.timeinc.net/subs/secure/MO/mo_crtnb.html?url= http://premium.money.cnn.com/pr/subs/magazine_archive/2004/04/ DOB.html.

28. Warner, "Inside Intel's Mentoring Movement."

29. Jeffrey Zaslow, "Baby Boomer Managers Struggle with Mentoring." Retrieved August 10, 2004, from http://www.careerjournal.com.

30. NAMI, "Mental Illness in the News." Retrieved August 10, 2004, from http://www.nami.org.

31. William J. Rothwell, "Beyond Succession Management: New Directions and Fresh Approaches," *Link&Learn Newsletter,* September 2003. Retrieved August 10, 2004, from http://www.linkageinc.com.

32. Federal Occupational Health, "Documenting the Value of Employee Assistance Programs." Retrieved August 10, 2004, from http://www.foh.dhhs.gov/Public/publications/EAPROI_short.pdf.

Chapter 14

1. David Ho, "People Annoyed by Cell Phones Turn to Jammers." Cox News Service, February 15, 2004. Retrieved August 10, 2004, from http://www.coxnews.com/cox/news/Business/story/5408.

2. Maureen Rauscher, "The Global Etiquette Guidebook: Keys to Success in International Business." Retrieved August 10, 2004, from http://www.etiquetteexpert.com/global.htm.

3. Tonya Mohn, "The Social Graces as a Business Tool," *The New York Times,* November 10, 2002.

4. ibid.

5. Dorothea Johnson, "The Protocol School of Washington." Retrieved August 10, 2004, from http://www.psow.com/.

6. Phyllis D. Huguenin, "Mind Your Manners: Lady Protocol is Watching," April 3, 2003. Retrieved August 10, 2004, from http://www.etiquettecentre.com/MiamiPostArticle.htm.

7. Robyn Friedman, "Mind Your Manners: Proper Etiquette Can Make a Deal, Get You a Job," *The Sun Sentinel,* March 4, 2004. Retrieved August 10, 2004, from http://www.etiquetteexpert.com/news_article_march_04.htm.

8. ibid.

9. Carey Toane, "Shake Hands in 10 Different Languages," 2002. Retrieved August 10, 2004, from http://www.profitguide.com/magazine/article.jsp?content=692.

10. Ann Marie Sabath, *Business Etiquette: 101 Ways to Conduct Business with Charm and Savvy* (Franklin Lakes, NJ: Career Press, 2002).

11. Denise Kersten, "Mind Your Manners for a Good First Impression," *USA Today,* November 15, 2002. Retrieved August 10, 2004, from http://www.usatoday.com/money/jobcenter/workplace/successstrategies/2002-11-15-impression_x.htm.

12. *UPDATE: Telephone Manners—A Guide for Using the Telephone,* Southwestern Bell Telephone Company, n.d.

13. ibid.

14. Peggy Post, *Emily Post's Etiquette—75th Anniversary Edition* (New York: Harper Collins, 1999).

15. Amy Sims, "Businesses Encourage Mobile Manners," *Fox News,* July 23, 2003. Retrieved August 10, 2004, from http://www.foxnews.com/story/0%2C2933%2C92660%2C00.html.

16. Ben Charny, "Shhh! Cell Phone Carriers Call for Etiquette," CNET News.com, November 16, 2001. Retrieved August 10, 2004, from http://www.etiquetteexpert.com/shhh.htm.

17. Virginia Shea, *Netiquette* (San Francisco: Albion Books, 2004).

18. David R. Woolley, "Real-Time Conferencing: An Independent Guide to Software & Services Enabling Real-Time Communication." Retrieved August 13, 2004, from http://thinkofit.com/webconf/realtime.htm.

19. Emily Post Institute, "Technology Etiquette." Retrieved August 13, 2004, from http://www.emilypost.com/etiquette/technology/index.htm.

20. Frederik Lane, *The Naked Employee: How Technology is Compromising Workplace Privacy* (New York: AMACOM, 2003).

21. ibid.

22. Edward Charlesworth and Ronald Nathan, *Stress Management* (Tallahassee, FL: Anhinga Press, 1980).

Chapter 15

1. "The Best (& Worst) Managers of the Year," *Business Week,* January 12, 2003.

2. Jonathan A. Segal, "The 'Joy' of Uncooking," *HR Magazine,* November 2002.

3. "Ethics," *The American Heritage® Dictionary of the English Language,* 4th ed., 2000. Retrieved August 24, 2004, from http://dictionary.reference.com/search?q=ethics.

4. Michael Josephson, *Making Ethical Decisions* (Los Angeles: Josephson Institute of Ethics, 2002).

5. Roger Riclefs, "Ethics in America," *The Wall Street Journal,* October 31/November 3, 1988.

6. "Ford Pinto Reckless Homicide Trial." Retrieved August 24, 2004, from http://www.historychannel.com/speeches/archive/speech_465.html.

7. Diane Carrol, "Teacher Quits in Dispute with School Board over Student Plagiarism," *Kansas City Star,* February 8, 2002.

8. "Barings PLC," Retrieved July 28, 2004, from http://encyclopedia.thefreedictionary.com/Barings+PLC.

9. James A. F. Stoner and R. Edward Freeman, *Management* (Englewood Cliffs, NJ: Prentice-Hall, 1992).

10. Developed for Florida Power Corporation by Lee Gardenswartz, Ph.D., Anita Rowe, Ph.D., and Patricia Digh, "Does It Click?," Society for Human Resource Management *Mosaics* Diversity Newsletter, 1999.

11. Pat Amend, "The Right Way to Deal with Ethical Dilemmas," *Working Woman,* December 1988, p. 19.

12. National Management Association, "NMA Code of Ethics." Retrieved August 24, 2004, from http://www.nma1.org/aboutnma/ethics.htm.

13. "Deciphering the Foreign Corrupt Practices Act," *SHRM Global Forum.* Retrieved July 28, 2004, from http://www.shrm.org.

14. Gap, Inc., "2003 Social Responsibility Report." Retrieved July 18, 2004, from http://www.gapinc.com/social_resp/social_resp.htm.

15. Amend, "The Right Way to Deal with Ethical Dilemmas."

16. Richard Lacayo and Amanda Ripley, "Persons of the Year," *Time,* December 30, 2002.

17. "Workers' Whistleblower Protection Under Seven Federal Environmental Laws," *Factsheet of the "Protecting Workers Who Exercise Rights" Project of the National COSH Network,* July 28, 2004.

18. Kenneth Blanchard and Norman Vincent Peale, *The Power of Ethical Management* (New York: William Morrow and Company, Inc., 1988).

19. Stoner and Freeman, *Management.*

20. "Business Ethics Survey," *SHRM/Ethics Resource Center,* 2003. Retrieved July 28, 2004, from http://www.shrm.org.

21. Lisa Singhania, "Companies Embrace Ethics Guidelines," *Indianapolis Star,* July 25, 2004.

22. Amy Stone, "Putting Teeth in Corporate Ethics Codes," *Business Week,* February 19, 2004.

23. ibid.

24. Bill Leonard, "Workers Cite Hypocrisy, Favoritism as Top Ethical Concerns," *Society for Human Resource Management HR News,* January 15, 2004.

25. Singhania, "Companies Embrace Ethics Guidelines."

26. "Sarbanes-Oxley: Public Company Accounting Reform and Investor Protection Act." Retrieved August 24, 2004, from http://www.sarbanes-oxley.com/.

Chapter 16

1. U.S. Department of Labor Wage and Hour Division, "2003 Statistics Fact Sheet." Retrieved August 24, 2004, from http://www.dol.gov/esa/whd/statistics/200318.htm.

2. National Labor Relations Board, "Press Release: NLRB Settles Contempt Case against South Coast Refuse Corporation with Owners on Brink of Imprisonment," April 4, 2003. Retrieved August 24, 2004, from http://www.nlrb.gov/nlrb/press/releases/default.asp.

3. U.S. Department of Labor Occupational Safety and Health Administration, "Press Release: Fatal Explosion Brings Framingham Employer OSHA Citations," January 15, 2004. Retrieved August 24, 2004, from http://www.osha.gov/pls/oshaweb/owasrch.search_form?p_doc_type= NEWS_RELEASES &p_toc_level=0&p_keyvalue=.

4. Equal Employment Opportunity Commission, "Types of Discrimination: National Origin." Retrieved August 24, 2004, from http://www.eeoc.gov.

5. Equal Employment Opportunity Commission, "Types of Discrimination: Pregnancy." Retrieved August 24, 2004, from http://www.eeoc.gov.

6. Equal Employment Opportunity Commission, "Types of Discrimination: Equal Pay." Retrieved August 24, 2004, from http://www.eeoc.gov.

7. Equal Employment Opportunity Commission, "Types of Discrimination: Age." Retrieved August 24, 2004, from http://www.eeoc.gov.

8a. Juan Castillo, "A New Alliance in the Rights Struggle," *Austin American Statesman,* June 28, 2004, p. A1.

8b. Equal Employment Opportunity Commission, "Types of Discrimination: Sexual Harassment." Retrieved August 24, 2004, from http://www.eeoc.gov.

9. Karyn-Siobhan Robinson, "EEOC Reaches Voluntary Resolution in Religious Accommodation Case," *Society for Human Resource Management HR News,* October 1, 2003.

10. Equal Employment Opportunity Commission, "Types of Discrimination: Disability." Retrieved August 24, 2004, from http://www.eeoc.gov.

11. Equal Employment Opportunity Commission, "Filing a Charge of Discrimination." Retrieved August 24, 2004, from http://www.eeoc.gov.

12. Pamela J. Conrad and Robert B. Maddux, *Guide to Affirmative Action: A Primer for Supervisors and Managers* (Los Altos, CA: Crisp Publications, 1988).

13. U.S. Department of Labor, "General Information on the Fair Labor Standards Act." Retrieved August 29, 2004, from http://www.dol.gov/esa/regs/ compliance/whd/mwposter.htm.

14. U.S. Department of Labor, "DOL's FairPay Overtime Initiative." Retrieved August 29, 2004, from http://www.dol.gov/esa/regs/compliance/whd/ fairpay/main.htm.

15. Diane Cadrain, "States, Cities Squaring Off Over Living Wage Ordinances," *Society for Human Resource Management HR News,* January 15, 2004.

16. U.S. Department of Labor, "Compliance Assistance—Family Medical Leave Act." Retrieved August 29, 2004, from http://www.dol.gov/esa/whd/fmla/.

17. ibid.

18. Eileen Ahern et al., *Federal Policies and Worker Status since the Thirties* (Madison, WI: Industrial Relations Research Association, 1976.)

19. Wayne N. Dutton, Robert J. Rabin, and Lisa R. Lipman, *The Rights of Employees and Union Members* (Carbondale, IL: Southern Illinois University Press, 1994).

20. ibid.

21. National Labor Relations Board, "The First Sixty Years: The Story of the National Labor Relations Board 1935-1995." Retrieved August 29, 2004, from http://www.nlrb.gov/nlrb/shared_files/brochures/60yrs_entirepub.asp.

22. ibid.

23. ibid.

24. Karyn-Siobhan Robinson, "AFL-CIO Launches Membership Organization for Non-Union Workers," *Society for Human Resource Management HR News*, October 2, 2003.

25. AFL-CIO Executive Council Actions, "Working America," August 6, 2003. Retrieved August 29, 2004, from http://www.aflcio.org/aboutaflcio/ecouncil/ec08062003f.cfm.

26. National Labor Relations Board, "The First Sixty Years: The Story of the National Labor Relations Board 1935-1995."

27. ibid.

28. Bernard Liebowitz, "What's Wrong with Being 'Borderline Ethical'?" *Healthcare Financial Management*, September 2003.

29. National Labor Relations Board, "The First Sixty Years: The Story of the National Labor Relations Board 1935-1995."

30. ibid.

31. U.S. Department of Labor Occupational Safety and Health Administration, "About OSHA." Retrieved August 29, 2004, from http://www.osha.gov/about.html.

32. ibid.

33. U.S. Department of Labor Occupational Safety and Health Administration, "Hazard Communication." Retrieved August 29, 2004, from http://www.osha.gov/SLTC/hazardcommunications/index.html.

34. Social Security Administration, "The History of Social Security." Retrieved August 29, 2004, from http://www.ssa.gov/history/history.html.

35. ibid.

36. Social Security Administration, "Historical Development." Retrieved August 29, 2004, from http://www.ssa.gov/history/pdf/histdev.pdf.

37. Kansas Department of Labor, Fraud Abuse Unit of the Kansas Division of Workers' Compensation, "Annual Report FY 2003." Retrieved August 29, 2004, from http://www.dol.ks.gov/wc/html/wc_ALL.html.

38. U.S. Department of Labor, "Workers' Compensation." Retrieved August 29, 2004, from http://www.dol.gov/dol/topic/workcomp/index.htm.

39. Karyn-Siobhan Robinson, "Benefits Surpass 42 percent of Payroll Costs, U.S. Chamber Reports," *Society for Human Resource Management HR News*, January 23, 2004.

40. U.S. Department of Labor, "Health Plans & Benefits: Employee Retirement Income Security Act—ERISA." Retrieved August 29, 2004, from http://www.dol.gov/dol/topic/health-plans/erisa.htm.

41. Social Security Administration, "OASDI Trustees Report," 2003. Retrieved August 29, 2004, from http://www.socialsecurity.gov/OACT/TR/.

42. U.S. Citizenship and Immigration Services, "Immigration Laws, Regulations, and Guides." Retrieved August 26, 2004, from http://uscis.gov/graphics/index.htm.

43. ibid.

44. U.S. Office of Special Counsel, "Political Activity (Hatch Act)." Retrieved August 26, 2004, from http://www.osc.gov/hatchact.htm.

45. Kenneth H. Pritchard, "The Uniformed Services Employment and Reemployment Rights Act," *SHRM Whitepapers*, December 1995, reviewed June 2002.

46. U.S. Department of Health and Human Services, "Office for Civil Rights—HIPAA." Retrieved June 25, 2004, from http://www.os.dhhs.gov/ocr/hipaa/.

47. "Key European Employment Legislation," *Workplace Visions*, Society for Human Resource Management Workplace Trends Program, no. 1, 2002.

48. American Polygraph Association, "The Employee Polygraph Protection Act of 1988 (EPPA)." Retrieved August 29, 2004, from http://www.polygraph.org/eppa.htm.

49. U.S. Department of Labor, "Compliance Assistance—Worker Adjustment and Retraining Notification Act." Retrieved August 29, 2004, from http://www.dol.gov/dol/compliance/comp-warn.htm.

50. Paul Salvatore and Laurie S. Leonard, "The Sarbanes-Oxley Act of 2002: New Federal Protection for Whistleblowers," *SHRM Legal Report*, November/December 2002.

Chapter 17

1. "Is America Suffering from 'Desk Rage'?" *PR Newswire*, November 29, 2000.

2. Karyn-Siobhan Robinson, "Employers Increase Work/Life Programs, According to Mellon Survey," *Society for Human Resource Management HRNews*, January 16, 2004.

3. Cynthia G. Wagner, "The New Meaning of Work," *Futurist*, September 2002 36, no. 5, pp. 16, 2p, 3c.

4. John Stossel, "Commentary: Lies, Myths, and Downright Stupidity," *ABC News*, January 23, 2004.

5. Jeffrey Pfeffer, "The Real Keys to High Performance," *Leader to Leader*, no. 8. Spring 1998. Retrieved August 29, 2004, from http://www.pfdf.org/leaderbooks/L2L/spring98/pfeffer.html.

6. Michael E. Cavanagh, "What You Don't Know about Stress," *Personnel Journal*, July 1, 1988, pp. 53-59.

7. Stacy VanDerWall, "NIOSH Report: Job Stress a 'Threat' to Workers' Health," *Society for Human Resource Management HRNews*, January 15, 1999.

8. Philippine Rotary, quoted in *The Rotarian*, April 1999, p. 19.

9a. Andrew Golisek, *60 Second Stress Management* (Far Hill, NJ: New Horizon Press, 1992).

9b. Catherine Valenti, "Stress Busters," *Forbes.com*, September 16, 2003. Retrieved October 14, 2004 from http://www.forbes.com/execpicks/2003/09/16/cx_0916health.html.

10. U.S. Department of Labor, "Background Information: Workplace Substance Abuse." Retrieved August 29, 2004, from http://www.dol.gov/workingpartners/.

11. U.S. Department of Labor, "Working Partners Substance Abuse Information Database." Retrieved August 29, 2004, from http://www.dol.gov/asp/programs/drugs/said/SearchResult.asp.

12. Cynthia Kuhn et al., *Buzzed: The Straight Facts about the Most Used and Abused Drugs from Alcohol to Ecstasy* (New York: W.W. Norton and Company, 2003).

13. ibid.

14. ibid.

15. ibid.

16. ibid.

17. ibid.

18. ibid.

19. ibid.

20. OHS Health and Safety Services, Inc., "Steroids (Anabolic-Androgenic)." Retrieved August 29, 2004, from http://www.ohsinc.com/steroids.htm.

21. U.S. Department of Labor, "Working Partners Substance Abuse Information Database."

22. U.S. Department of Health and Human Services Substance Abuse and Mental Health Services Administration, "Drug Testing." Retrieved August 29, 2004, from http://www.drugfreeworkplace.gov/M_Level2.asp?Level1_ID=1.

23. National Institute of Drug Abuse, "NIDA Research Report—Marijuana Abuse," 2002. Retrieved August 29, 2004, from http://www.nida.nih.gov/ResearchReports/Marijuana/.

24. Shelly Prochaska, "Employee Assistance Programs: What does HR Need to Know?" Society for Human Resource Management White Paper, May 2003.

25. Robert B. Maddux and Lynda Voorhees, *Job Performance and Chemical Dependency* (Menlo Park, CA: Crisp Publications, 1986).

26. Robert W. Thompson, "Study Tallies Costs of Workers' Social and Problem Drinking," *Society for Human Resource Management HR News*, February 8, 1999.

27. About.com, "Alcoholism Screen Quiz." Retrieved August 29, 2004, from http://alcoholism.about.com/library/blalcoholquiz.htm.

28. U.S. Department of Labor, "Compliance Assistance—Family Medical Leave Act." Retrieved August 29, 2004, from http://www.dol.gov/esa/whd/fmla/.

29. National Drug-Free Workplace Alliance, "Drug Free Workplace Statistics." Retrieved August 29, 2004, from http://www.ndfwa.org/statistics.htm.

30. Prochaska, "Employee Assistance Programs: What does HR Need to Know?"

31. U.S. Department of Agriculture, "Food Guide Pyramid." Retrieved August 29, 2004, from http://www.health.gov/dietaryguidelines/dga2000/document/build.htm#pyramid.

32. U.S. Department of Agriculture, "Aim for a Healthy Weight." Retrieved August 29, 2004, from http://www.health.gov/dietaryguidelines/dga2000/document/ aim.htm#weight_top.

33. Jon Gestl, "Coffee, Caffeine, and Fitness," *Mama's Health*, 2004. Retrieved August 29, 2004, from http://www.mamashealth.com/exercise/caf.asp.

34. Ira Dreyfuss, "Wellness, Exercise Programs May Save Companies Some Money," *The Desert News* (Salt Lake City, UT), February 22, 1999.

35. Martha Davis et al., *Relaxation and Stress Reduction Workbook* (Oakland, CA: New Harbinger Publications, 1998).

36. Harriet Goldhor Lerner, *The Dance of Intimacy* (New York: Perennial/HarperCollins, 1990).

37. ibid.

Chapter 18

1. Tom Peters, *Re-Imagine! Business Excellence in a Disruptive Age* (London: Dorling Kindersley, 2003).

2. Lynn A. Karoly and Constantijn W. A. Panis, "The 21st Century at Work: Forces Shaping the Future Workforce and Workplace in the United States," The RAND Corporation, 2004. Retrieved August 29, 2004, from http://www.rand.org/pubs/monographs/2004/RAND_MG164.pdf.

3. Genaro C. Armas, "Stir Up the Melting Pot," *The Associated Press*, March 18, 2004.

4. U.S. Department of Labor Bureau of Labor Statistics, "Economic and Employment Projections: Table 3b. The 10 Fastest Growing Occupations, 2002-12." Retrieved August 29, 2004, from http://www.bls.gov/news.release/ecopro.t04.htm.

5. Karoly and Panis, "The 21st Century at Work: Forces Shaping the Future Workforce and Workplace in the United States."

6. ibid.

7. Peters, *Re-Imagine! Business Excellence in a Disruptive Age.*

8. Georgia Institute of Technology, "Governor Announces Major Nanotechnology Initiative for Georgia Tech," October 23, 2003. Retrieved August 29, 2004, from http://www.gatech.edu/news-room/release.php?id=201.

9. Nell Henderson and Kirstin Downey, "A New Kind of Workforce Emerges: Surge in Number of Contractors Helps Explain Why Recovery Adds Few Jobs," *The Washington Post,* January 27, 2004. p. E1.

10. Ken Belson, "Jobs: A 2-way Street: Some in U.S. Benefit from Insourcing," *International Herald Tribune,* April 12, 2004. Retrieved August 29, 2004, from http://www.iht.com/articles/514299.html.

11. Karoly and Panis, "The 21st Century at Work: Forces Shaping the Future Workforce and Workplace in the United States."

12. Janet Bailey, "Your Back-to-Work Success Guide," *Ladies Home Journal,* July 2003.

13. U.S. Department of Labor Bureau of Labor Statistics, "BLS Releases 2002-12 Employment Projections." Retrieved August 29, 2004, from http://www.bls.gov/news.release/archives/ecopro_02112004.pdf.

14. ibid.

15. U.S. Department of Labor, "Century XXI: It's Not Your Parents' Workforce." Retrieved August 29, 2004, from http://www.dol.gov/21cw/magazine/020314/parents.htm.

16. Karoly and Panis, "The 21st Century at Work: Forces Shaping the Future Workforce and Workplace in the United States."

17. Kim Clark, "Job Jitters," *U.S. News and World Report,* November 5, 2001, pp. 72-74.

18. U.S. Department of Labor Bureau of Labor Statistics, "BLS Releases 2002-12 Employment Projections."

19. Richard Bolles, *What Color Is Your Parachute?* (Berkeley, CA: Ten Speed Press, 2003).

20. "The War for Talent, Part 2," *The McKinsey Quarterly 2001,* no. 2. Retrieved August 29, 2004, from http://www.mckinseyquarterly.com/article_abstract.aspx?ar=1035&L2=18&L3=31.

21. "The Number of New Jobs Created by Small Firms," *Small Business Notes.* Retrieved August 29, 2004, from http://www.smallbusinessnotes.com/aboutsb/sbfacts/sbnewjobs.html.

22. Susan Wilson Solovic, "Why Networking Clubs Aren't Just for the Boys," CareerJournal.com. Retrieved August 29, 2004, from http://www.careerjournal.com/jobhunting/networking/20031104-solovic.html.

23. Bolles, *What Color Is Your Parachute?*

24. Equal Employment Opportunity Commission, "Types of Discrimination: Disability." Retrieved August 29, 2004, from http://www.eeoc.gov.

25. "Tips for an Internet Friendly Resume," *Resume Doctor.* Retrieved August 29, 2004, from http://www.resumedoctor.com/InternetFriendlyResume.htm.

26. Randall S. Hansen, "Scannable Resume Fundamentals: How to Write Text Resumes," *Quintessential Careers.* Retrieved August 29, 2004, from http://www.quintcareers.com/scannable_resumes.html.

27. "Resume Fraud Gets Slicker and Easier: Half of Job Seekers Submitted False Information in 2003, Survey Finds," *Reuters News Service,* March 9, 2004. Retrieved August 29, 2004, from http://www.msnbc.msn.com/id/4488908.

28. "The Interview Process," *Workforce Management Magazine.* Retrieved August 29, 2004, from http://www.workforce.com/section/06/.

29. Kiki Peppard, "Illegal or Just Inappropriate? Know Your Rights When It Comes to Interview Questions," Monster.com. Retrieved August 29, 2004, from http://interview.monster.com/articles/illegalqs/.

30. Georgia Department of Labor, "Chapter 12 Keeping Your Job: Your New Job," *Job Search Handbook.* Retrieved August 29, 2004, from http://www.dol.state.ga.us/pdf/replace/dol_4436.pdf.

Glossary

4 Cs of communication Reminders to improve writing; complete, concise, correct, and conversational/clear.

80-20 Rule Rule that says 20 percent of your problems will account for 80 percent of your losses or gains.

A

ABC analysis Concentration of decisions where the potential for payoff is greater.

Accountability perspective View that businesses are accountable for their actions, with a responsibility to individuals and the general public to be fair and considerate.

Active listening A conscious effort to listen to both the verbal and nonverbal components of what someone is saying, without prejudging.

Ad hoc committee A committee that has a limited life and serves only a one-time purpose.

Affirmative Action A practice originally designed to correct past discriminatory practices against minorities and women in the workplace by setting goals for hiring and upward mobility.

Age Discrimination in Employment Act Federal legislation that prohibits discrimination against individuals age 40 and over in the workplace.

Aggressive behavior Valuing ourselves above others and saying what we feel or think but at the expense of others; attempting to dominate or humiliate; using threats and accusations or trying to show up others; choosing for others; speaking with an air of superiority and in a voice that is demanding and rude.

Alcohol The most commonly abused drug in the country. Alcohol is a depressant that slows the activity of the brain and spinal cord.

Americans with Disabilities Act Federal legislation that prohibits discrimination against individuals who are disabled.

Amphetamines Synthetic nervous system stimulants.

Anabolic steroids Legal, man-made drugs that are designed to build muscles.

Assertive behavior Using correct etiquette; feeling equal to others; making our own choices; using "I" phrases and other effective communication techniques; appearing calm and confident; having positive self-esteem and being respected by others.

Autocratic leadership Leadership style that is task oriented and highly directive and involves close supervision and little delegation.

Avoidance Conflict resolution by totally refraining from confronting the conflict.

B

Baby boomers Those Americans born between 1946 and 1964, during the "baby boom" that followed World War II.

Bargaining unit The group represented by the union; those for whom the union negotiates.

BARS (Behaviorally Anchored Rating Scale) An appraisal system where the behavior an employee most often exhibits is measured against a scale developed for his or her position.

Behavioral school of management Study of management that focused on techniques to motivate workers.

Behavioral science approach Part of the behavioral school of management that began in the late 1950s and used controlled experiments and other scientific methods to view human behavior in the workplace.

Benchmarking A method of organizational change that involves comparing the company's practices, among internal divisions and/or against those of competitors, to determine which are best.

Bias An inclination or preference either for or against an individual or group that interferes with impartial judgment.

Brainstorming Group problem-solving technique that involves the spontaneous contribution of ideas from all members of the group.

C

Centralized management Distribution of power so that those high up in the organization make all major decisions.

Chain of command The direction in which authority is exercised and policies and other information are communicated to lower levels.

Change agent Person who diagnoses problems, provides feedback, assists in developing strategies, or recommends interventions to benefit the organization as a whole. Also known as an Organization Development practitioner or an OD consultant.

Checklist An appraisal instrument that offers a list of statements about performance and characteristics that supervisors can check off in order to rate an employee.

Chronological resume Resume that lists experience in reverse chronological order, listing the most recent employment first. This format is beneficial when an individual has a continuous work history with progressively responsible positions.

Classical organization theory Approach begun by Fayol that focuses on management of the organization as a whole. It is part of the classical school of management.

Classical perspective Belief that businesses need not feel responsible for social issues and should concentrate on being profitable.

Classical school of management Study of management that focused on the technical efficiency of work as a way to maximize production.

Club drugs Stimulant and depressant drugs frequently used at dance parties such as "raves" or "trances" or at nightclubs.

Coaching A method of employee development that closely resembles on-the-job training where a senior experienced and skilled employee helps develop or train a junior employee.

Cocaine Stimulant derived from the coca leaf or synthesized.

Code of ethics List that requires or prohibits specific practices by employees in a particular organization or by all members of a professional group.

Coercive power Power based on fear and punishment.

Cohesiveness Degree to which group members are of one mind and act as one body.

Committee Type of task group.

Communication Process by which we exchange information through a common system of symbols, signs, or behavior.

Communities of Practice (COPS) Highly synergistic peer groups working on projects or problems of shared interest; informal small groups working toward a common purpose.

Compensation A defense mechanism by which individuals attempt to relieve feelings of inadequacy or frustration by excelling in other areas.

Competition A healthy struggle toward goal accomplishment without interference, even when the goals are incompatible.

Compromising A method of conflict resolution that addresses the issue but seldom resolves it to the complete satisfaction of both parties.

Concentration Focusing intensely on a problem to the exclusion of other demands.

Conceptual skills Administrative or big picture skills; ability to think abstractly and to analyze problems.

Conflict Disagreement between individuals or groups about goal accomplishment.

Conflict resolution The active management of conflict through defining and solving issues between individuals, groups, or organizations.

Confrontation Conflict resolution by openly exchanging information and actively working through the differences to reach agreement.

Consensus A solution that all members of the group involved can support.

Context Conditions in which something occurs that can throw light on its meaning.

Continuous improvement teams Teams that focus on continuous process improvement. They are also known as quality circles or kaizen teams.

Conversational rituals Things we say without considering the literal meaning of our words.

Cooperative counseling A mutual problem-solving effort involving both parties in exploring and solving issues.

Cost-benefit analysis Examination of the pros and cons of each proposed solution.

Counseling A discussion technique used to assist employees with problems affecting performance on the job.

Counselor A person, usually a trained professional or a supervisor, capable of dealing with a wide variety of employee problems.

Creativity Thinking process that solves a problem or achieves a goal in an original and useful way; the ability to come up with new and unique solutions to problems.

Critical incident technique An appraisal technique in which supervisors record in writing actual incidents of behavior that they observe in employees.

Critical norms Norms considered essential to the survival and effectiveness of the group as a whole.

Critical Path Method (CPM) The critical path is the sequence of activities requiring the longest time for completion. It will show the minimum time to complete the project.

Cross-functional team A team composed of individuals from two or more different functional areas; commonly used to design and bring a new product to market and ensure its long-run success.

D

Decentralized management Distribution of power so that important decisions are made at a lower level.

Decision tree Graphic depiction of how alternative solutions lead to various possibilities.

Delegated method Giving employees the responsibility and authority to effect change.

Delegation Assigning tasks to subordinates and following up to ensure proper and timely completion.

Democratic leadership Leadership style, also described as participative, that is usually preferred by modern management and involves showing concern for followers, sharing authority with them, and involving them in decision making and organizational planning.

Demographics Statistics showing population characteristics about a region or group, such as education, income, age, marital status, or ethnic makeup.

Denial A defense mechanism by which a person refuses to believe something that creates anxiety or frustration.

Derivative power Power obtained from close association with a powerful person.

Deviance Not conforming to group norms.

Direct communication style Style of speaking that reflects a goal orientation and a desire to get down to business and get to the point.

Directive counseling A method of counseling that involves the counselor's listening to the employee's problem, allowing emotional release, determining an action plan, and advising the employee on what needs to be done.

Discrimination A difference in treatment based on a factor other than individual merit.

Displacement A defense mechanism by which an individual acts out anger toward a person who does not deserve it but who is a "safe" target.

Diversity Refers to differences. In people, it refers to differences such as race, religion, sex, age, disability, sexual orientation, national origin, educational levels, area in which you live, occupation, and job title.

Downward communication Communication that begins at higher levels of the organization and flows downward.

E

E-mail Communication medium that uses a computer, keyboard, and service provider to create messages and send them through electronic networks; also called electronic mail.

Emergent leader An informal leader who emerges without formal appointment and can exert as much or more power than the formal leader.

Empathy The action of understanding, being aware of, being sensitive to, and vicariously experiencing the feelings, thoughts, and experience of another.

Employee assistance program (EAP) A formal company program designed to aid employees with personal problems, such as substance abuse or psychological problems, that affect their job performance.

Employment at will A philosophy that states the employee serves at the discretion of an employer and can be terminated at any time and for any reason, even if the employee is performing well.

Empowerment Allowing others to make decisions and have influence on desired outcomes.

Enabling Covering up for or making excuses for the behavior and performance of individuals who are abusing substances, allowing them to continue their disruptive conduct.

Enlightened self-interest Belief that organizations' and people's best interests are served by being genuinely concerned for others.

Equal Employment Opportunity Commission (EEOC) Federal agency responsible for enforcing laws related to employment discrimination.

Equal Pay Act Federal law that requires men and women be paid the same salary provided they perform the same job and have the same experience and education.

Essay appraisal An appraisal instrument on which the supervisor writes a paragraph or more concerning employee performance.

Esteem needs Level of Maslow's hierarchy that includes the need for respect from self and others and that can be met by increased responsibility, recognition for work well done, and merit increases and awards.

Ethical dilemmas Conflicts of values that arise when our sense of values or social responsibility is questioned internally or challenged externally.

Ethics As defined by *The American Heritage Dictionary*, "the study of the general nature of morals and of the specific moral choices to be made by a person; the rules or standards governing the conduct of a person or the members of a profession"; the study of what is good, right, and proper for people.

Etiquette As defined by *Merriam-Webster's Collegiate Dictionary*, "the forms required by good breeding or prescribed by authority to be observed in social or official life"; i.e., acting appropriately in social and business situations.

Expected interval testing The process of giving drug tests at specific, preannounced times.

Expert power Power based on having specialized skills, knowledge, or expertise.

F

Fair Labor Standards Act Federal legislation that sets the minimum wage, equal pay, overtime, and child labor standards.

Family Medical Leave Act (FMLA) Federal legislation that provides eligible employees with up to 12 weeks of job-protected family or medical leave.

Feedback Information given back to a sender that evaluates a message and states what the receiver understood.

Follower readiness A worker's desire to achieve, willingness to accept responsibility, ability and experience with the tasks, and confidence.

"For cause" testing Drug testing of employees only when they are suspected of being under the influence of drugs or alcohol.

Force field analysis A technique used to analyze the complexities of a change and identify the forces that must be altered.

Forced distribution An approach to comparative appraisal where ratings of performances of employees are distributed over a bell-shaped curve.

Forcing Results when two persons or groups reach an impasse and allow an authoritative figure to choose one preference rather than work toward a mutually agreeable solution.

Foreign Corrupt Policy Act Law requiring companies to operate ethically in their worldwide dealings.

Formal communication Communication that flows up or down the formal organizational structure along the chain of command.

Formal group A group designated by the organization to fulfill specific tasks or accomplish certain organizational objectives.

Formal leader An individual who is officially given certain rights or authority over other group members and who has a degree of legitimacy granted by the formal group or organization.

Free-rein leadership Leadership style, also called laissez-faire or integrative, that allows followers to lead themselves, provides advice or information only when requested, and makes little or no effort to increase productivity or nurture or develop followers.

Functional authority Authority given to staff personnel to make decisions in their areas of expertise and to overrule line decisions.

Functional group Groups made up of managers and subordinates assigned to certain positions in the organizational hierarchy.

Functional resume Resume that emphasizes special skills that can be transferred to other areas. This resume is useful for individuals reentering the job market or wanting to change careers.

Functional work teams Employees from one particular function, such as accounting or human resources, who work together to serve various groups.

G

Globalization Making goods and services available worldwide with no national boundaries or trade barriers on where they are sold or where they are produced.

Goal Objective, target, or end result expected from the completion of tasks, activities, or programs.

Grapevine An informal person-to-person means of circulating information or gossip.

Graphic rating scale An appraisal instrument that outlines categories on which the employee is rated; the scale for each category can range from unacceptable to superior.

Great man theory A theory of leadership based on the belief that certain people are born to become leaders and will emerge in that role when their time comes.

Group Two or more persons who are aware of one another, interact with one another, and perceive themselves to be a group.

Group norms Shared values about the kinds of behaviors that are acceptable or unacceptable to the group.

Groupthink Process of deriving negative results from group decision-making efforts as a result of in-group pressures.

Groupware Computer software that has been developed to facilitate the use of groups and teams; technology that relies on modern computer networks, such as e-mail, newsgroups, video-phones, or chat to improve group interactions.

H

Hallucinogens Drugs that produce chemically induced hallucinations.

Halo effect A process by which an individual assumes that another's traits are all positive because one trait is positive.

Hawthorne effect The idea that the human element is more important to productivity than the technical or physical aspects of the job. The effect was identified through experiments conducted by Mayo.

Health The role of the working environment in the development of diseases such as cancer and black lung.

Hear To perceive sound with our ears.

Herzberg's two-factor theory A popular theory of motivation that says two sets of factors or conditions influence the behavior of individuals at work: one set to satisfy and the other to motivate.

Hidden agenda Topics that meeting attendees wish to discuss that have no relevance to the purpose of the current meeting.

High context group Group that values long-term relationships, communicates in a less verbally explicit fashion, and strongly defines who is accepted and who is considered an outsider.

Horizontal communication Communication that occurs between individuals at the same level in an organization.

Human relations Study of relationships among people.

Human relations approach Branch of the behavioral school during the mid-1920s and early 1930s that focused on how physical working conditions affect worker productivity.

Human relations skills Ability to deal effectively with people through communicating, listening, being empathetic, inspiring and motivating, being perceptive, and using fair judgment.

Hybrid/combination resume Resume that combines the format of functional and chronological resumes.

Hygiene factors Factors identified by Herzberg that are necessary to maintain a reasonable level of satisfaction, such as working conditions, job security, quality of supervision, and interpersonal relationships on the job.

I

I-9 Employment eligibility verification form all new employees are to complete within three days of hire.

Illumination The "Aha!" stage of the creative process; when solutions break through to conscious thought.

Incubation Stage of the creative process that is mysterious and below the surface and involves reviewing ideas and information.

Indirect communication style Style of speaking that reflects a focus on the relationship and is used to develop a rapport before getting down to business.

Influence Ability to change the attitude or behavior of an individual or group; the application of power through actions we take or examples we set that cause others to change their attitudes or behaviors.

Informal communication Communication that does not follow the chain of command.

Informal group A group created to satisfy the needs of individual members that are not satisfied by formal groups.

Informal leader A person within the group who is able to influence other group members because of age, knowledge, technical skills, social skills, personality, or physical strength.

Information Age The current economic era, characterized by increasingly large and complex organizations, advanced technology, and the computer.

Information overload An inability to continue processing and remembering information because of the great amount coming at us at one time.

Inhalants Hydrocarbon-containing substances that are inhaled for their intoxicating effects.

Innovation The end product of creative activity.

Instant messaging A method of sending and responding to written messages in real time over the Internet.

Integrity Strict adherence to a code of behavior.

Interview Process by which the prospective employer learns more about you and evaluates whether you are the best-qualified candidate for the position.

J

Job enlargement Increasing the complexity of a job by adding similar tasks to those already being performed.

Job enrichment Building greater responsibility and interest into task assignments.

Job redesign A method of bringing about change within the organization aimed directly at the tasks performed by individuals.

Job rotation Shifting employees from one job to another in hopes of reducing boredom and stimulating renewed interest in job performance.

Job-seeking skills Skills that assist us in finding employment.

Johari Window Model that helps us understand our relationships with others; panes represent parts of us known or unknown to others and ourselves.

L

Laissez-faire leadership Leadership style, also called free rein or integrative, that allows followers to lead themselves, provides advice or information only when requested, and makes little or no effort to increase productivity or nurture or develop followers.

Landrum-Griffin Act A federal law enacted in 1959 that requires unions to disclose the sources and disbursements of their funds, hold regularly scheduled elections by secret ballot, and restricts union officials from using union funds for personal means; intended as a means of control over possible corruption in union activities and misuse of union funds.

Leadership The process of influencing the activities of individuals or organized groups so that they follow and do willingly what the leader wants them to do.

Leadership style Pattern of behavior exhibited by a leader.

Legitimate power Power derived from formal rank or position within an organizational hierarchy.

Life cycles Stages of a business, consisting of start-up, expansion and growth, stability, decline, and phase-out or revitalization.

Linguistic styles characteristic speaking patterns, such as directness or indirectness, pacing and pausing, and word choice, and the use of elements such as jokes, figures of speech, stories, questions, and apologies.

Line and staff structure A complex organization structure in which the line (production employees) is given support by staff in such areas as law and safety.

Low context group Group that values the written or spoken word, is task oriented and results driven, and generally adopts a direct linguistic style.

M

Management Use of resources to accomplish a goal; may be nonbehavioral.

Management by Objectives (MBO) A method and philosophy of management that emphasizes self-determination and allows employees to participate in setting their own goals.

Management science school Branch of management that began after World War II and was used to solve complex management problems. The computer has played an important part in this school.

Managerial Grid® Leadership theory developed by Blake and Mouton that uses a grid to plot the degree to which leaders show concern for people and concern for production.

Marijuana Drug derived from the dried leaves and flowering tops of the distillate hemp plant.

Maslow's hierarchy of needs Motivation theory that recognizes five levels of needs. Individuals are motivated by the needs within each specific level. When these needs are met, individuals are no longer motivated by that level and move upward.

Matrix structure A complex organization structure that uses groups of people with expertise in their individual areas who are temporarily assigned full or part time to a project from other parts of the organization.

McClelland's acquired needs theory A motivational theory that states that through upbringing, individuals acquire a strong desire for one of three primary needs: achievement, affiliation, and power.

Medium The form in which a message is communicated.

Mentor An experienced person who will give you objective career advice. A senior-level manager or retired professional with political savvy and an interest in helping employees achieve both career goals and the objectives of the organization.

Mentoring A popular form of coaching on a personal level with the emphasis on helping employees develop to their fullest potential.

Message The content of the communication sent or received; may be verbal, nonverbal, or written.

Millennials Generation Y; members of the generation born between 1979 and 1995.

Monochronic work style Consists of doing one thing at a time and following plans closely.

Motivation Needs or drives within individuals that energize behaviors.

Motivational factors Factors identified by Herzberg that build high levels of motivation, such as achievement, advancement, recognition, responsibility, and the work itself.

Motivational source fields Forces that motivate; can be outside, inside, or early.

N

Narcotics Drugs that are derivatives of the opium poppy.

National Labor Relations Board (NLRB) A government agency responsible for enforcing the provisions of the Wagner Act, established in 1935.

Negotiation Discussion that leads to a decision acceptable to all involved.

Networking (1) Process whereby you give and receive moral support, career guidance, and important information by developing contacts with people in your place of employment and in professional organizations. (2) Method of finding employment that involves telling all individuals you know that you are seeking a job and asking them to contact you if they hear of any openings.

Nondirective counseling A method of counseling viewed as a mutual problem-solving effort involving both parties in exploring and solving issues.

Nonverbal communication Meaning conveyed through the body, the voice, or position.

Norris-LaGuardia Act A federal law enacted in 1932 to abolish the use of yellow-dog contracts by companies as an antiunion technique.

O

Occupational Safety and Health Act Federal legislation that sets safety and health standards and ensures that they are observed in the workplace.

Occupational Safety and Health Administration (OSHA) Federal agency that regulates safety and health in the workplace.

Official goals Formally stated, abstract goals that are developed by upper management.

Ongoing committee A committee that is relatively permanent, addressing organizational issues on a standing or continuous basis.

One-way communication Communication that takes place with no feedback from the receiver.

Operational goals Concrete and close-ended goals that are the responsibility of first-line supervisors and employees.

Operative goals Goals that are developed by middle management and are more specific than official goals.

Optimists People who always look on the positive side of situations.

Organizational culture A mix of the beliefs and values of society at large, the individuals who work in the organization, and the organization's leaders and founders.

Organizational development A holistic approach to organizational change involving the entire organization—its people, structures, culture, policies and procedures, and purpose.

Overachiever Individual who takes on unattainable goals, whose intent is usually to perform better or achieve more success than expected.

P

Participative method A method of implementing organizational change that uses employee groups in the problem-solving and decision-making processes preceding the actual change.

Passive behavior The valuing of ourselves below others; lack of self-confidence while speaking; wanting to be liked and trying to please others; and avoiding unpleasant situations and confrontation.

Passive power Power source that stems from a display of helplessness.

Perception (1) Way in which we interpret or give meaning to sensations or messages; (2) the first stage in the creative process requiring that we view objects or situations differently.

Perceptual defense mechanisms Mechanisms individuals use to handle anxiety.

Performance appraisal A measurement of how well an employee is doing on the job.

Peripheral norms Norms that, if violated, are not perceived as damaging to the group and its members.

PERT chart Graphic technique for planning projects in which a great number of tasks must be coordinated (Program Evaluation and Review Technique).

Pessimists People who always look on the negative side of situations.

Physiological needs A level of Marlow's hierarchy of needs that includes the desire for food, sleep, water, shelter, and other physiological drives.

Planned agenda An outline or list of what topics are to be discussed or what is to be accomplished during a meeting.

Planning An attempt to prepare for and predict the future; it involves goals, programs, policies, rules, and procedures.

PODSCORB An acronym for the functional abilities required of leaders—planning, organizing, directing, staffing, coordinating, reporting, and budgeting.

Polychronic work style Consists of doing many things at once, changing plans easily, and tolerating interruptions.

Power The ability to influence others to do what we want them to do even if we are not a formal leader.

Power-compulsive Power personality with a lust for power; seldom satisfied with the amount of power achieved.

Power politics Developing opportunities for success.

Power positioning Conscientious use of techniques designed to position an individual for maximum personal growth and gain in an effort to develop power.

Power-positive Power personality that genuinely enjoys responsibility and thrives on the use of power.

Power-shy Power personality that tends to avoid being placed in position that requires overt use of power.

Power symbols Physical traits, personality characteristics, and external physical factors that are associated with those who are perceived to be powerful.

Pregnancy Discrimination Act Federal law that prohibits discrimination against pregnant women in the workplace.

Pre-employment testing A test given to job applicants to determine whether they have drugs in their systems.

Applicants who do not pass the test or who refuse to take it are not hired.

Prejudice The act of prejudging or making a decision about a person or group of people without sufficient knowledge.

Preparation Acquiring skills, background information, and resources for sensing and defining a problem.

Primary group Group made up of family members and close friends.

Primary needs Basic needs required to sustain life, such as food, water, air, sleep, and shelter.

Proactive management Management that is characterized by looking ahead, anticipating problems, and determining solutions to potential problems before they develop.

Problem Disturbance or unsettled matter that requires a solution if the organization or person is to function effectively.

Process innovation A method of enhancing productivity that blends information technology and human resource management.

Procrastination The intentional putting off or delaying of activities that need to be done.

Production function The sector of an organization that actually produces goods or performs services.

Program Evaluation and Review Technique (PERT) A model used by managers to plan and control work.

Project teams Groups that come together to accomplish a specific project, frequently used in the engineering and construction industries to design and construct buildings or plants. Upon completion, the team disbands and team members are generally assigned to other teams.

Projection A defense mechanism whereby individuals attribute unacceptable thoughts or feelings about themselves to others.

Protocol Business, diplomatic, or military etiquette.

Public perspective View that links businesses with the government and other groups to solve social and environmental problems actively.

Pygmalion effect Psychological phenomenon whose premise is, "You get what you expect."

Pyramidal hierarchy Triangular shape of an organization with the single head of the organization at the top. Smaller pyramids appear within the larger.

Q

Quality circle Committee of 6 to 15 employees who meet regularly to examine and suggest solutions to common problems of quality.

R

Random interval testing The process of giving drug tests to employees at varying and unannounced times.

Ranking An approach to employee appraisal that involves comparing employees' performances, listing them from highest to lowest.

Rationalization A defense mechanism by which a person explains away a problem.

Reactive management Management characterized by being caught off guard and moving from one crisis to the next.

Realistic achiever Individual who sets challenging but attainable goals.

Reasonable accommodations Actions that assist people with disabilities to perform the essential function of their jobs without imposing an undue hardship on the company.

Receiver One to whom a message is transmitted; one who receives the message.

Reengineering The fundamental rethinking and redesign of business processes to achieve dramatic improvements in critical, contemporary measures of performance, such as cost, quality, service, and speed.

Reengineering processes Change processes designed to make an organization more competitive. They generally involve the fundamental rethinking and redesign of business processes to achieve dramatic improvements, such as eliminating unnecessary work, reducing cycle time, improving quality, and improving customer relations.

Reference Individual who can vouch for your performance and character.

Referent power Power based on respect or admiration.

Regression A defense mechanism whereby a person reverts to an earlier behavior pattern.

Relationship behavior Leader behavior with people; the extent to which the leader is supportive of followers and engages in two-way communication with them.

Repression A defense mechanism by which an individual cannot remember an unpleasant event.

Resume Sales tool designed to assist in obtaining an interview. It provides a prospective employer with a brief summary of a job seeker's skills, education, and work experience.

Reverse or tarnished halo effect A process by which an individual assumes that another's traits are all negative because one trait is negative.

Reward power Power based on the ability to give something of material or personal value to others.

Right-to-Work Law A provision of the Taft-Hartley Act that allows states to prohibit both the closed and the union shop contract agreements, thereby giving the worker the choice of union membership.

Role ambiguity Confusion that occurs when individuals are uncertain about what role they are to fill or what is expected of them.

Roles Differing parts that individuals play in their lives.

S

Safety Absence of or protection from hazards that could result in a direct injury.

Safety and security needs A level of Maslow's hierarchy of needs that reflects the desire for physical, economic, and emotional security, such as safe working conditions, job security, and periodic salary increases.

Sanctions Actions taken to force compliance with established norms.

Sarbanes-Oxley Act A set of complex regulations that protects investors and enforces corporate accountability and responsibility by requiring accuracy and reliability of accounting and disclosures in publicly traded corporations. The act grants the Securities and Exchange Commission increased regulatory control, imposes greater criminal and compensatory punishment on executives and companies that do not comply, and establishes procedures for handling whistleblower complaints.

Scapegoating A defense mechanism that relieves anxiety by blaming other persons or groups for problems.

Scientific management theory Approach begun by Taylor and enhanced by the Gilbreths that focuses on the work itself. It is part of the classical school of management.

Secondary group Group made up of fellow workers or social acquaintances.

Secondary needs Needs that include security, affiliation or love, respect, and autonomy; developed as a result of an individual's values and beliefs.

Sedatives Depressants that can cause drowsiness, agitation, intellectual confusion, and impairment.

Self-actualization needs A level of Maslow's hierarchy that includes the need for personal growth, freedom of creative expression, and using one's abilities to the fullest extent.

Self-directed work teams Teams that, to a certain extent, manage themselves; they may or may not have a leader. Often these teams are responsible for selecting and hiring their members, reviewing member performance, and making decisions regarding corrective action.

Self-disclosure Revealing information to others about yourself.

Self-esteem Feelings about yourself that can be high or low.

Self-talk Making positive statements to ourselves.

Semantics The study of the meanings and the changing meanings of words.

Sender Person who transmits, or sends, the message.

Sexual harassment Unwelcome sexual advances, requests for sexual favors, or verbal or physical conduct of a sexual nature found in the workplace.

Situational Leadership® Leadership theory developed by Hersey that says leadership style must be adapted to the situation and the readiness of subordinates.

Six Thinking Hats A method of lateral thinking designed by Edward de Bono that facilitates looking at issues in different ways at the same time; a form of group decision making that gives each person a role to play in wearing the six different "hats" of intelligence.

Six Sigma A sophisticated method of continuous process improvement that uses a structured statistical approach to improve bottom-line results; involves statistically measuring baseline performance to improve performance processes.

Smoothing Conflict resolution by playing down strong issues, concentrating on mutual interests, and seldom discussing negative issues.

Social needs A level of Maslow's hierarchy that centers on the desire for meaningful affiliation with others, such as love, affection, and acceptance.

Social responsibility Obligation we have to make choices or decisions that are beneficial to the whole of society; involves issues such as environmental pollution and welfare.

Social Security Act Federal legislation that mandates retirement, Medicare, disability, and survivors' benefits.

Span of control Number of people that an individual supervises.

Statistical models Mathematical models that assist managers with planning and controlling factors such as inventory, product mixes, and sales forecasts.

Stereotypes fixed or distorted generalizations made about members of a particular group.

Strategic planning The systematic setting of organizational goals, defining strategies and policies to achieve them, and developing detailed plans to ensure that the strategies are implemented.

Stress The physical state of the body in response to environmental pressures that produce emotional discomfort.

Sublimation A defense mechanism by which an individual directs unacceptable impulses into socially accepted channels.

Substance abuse The misuse of alcohol, illegal drugs, and prescription drugs.

Synergy Interaction of two or more independent parts, the effects of which are greater than they would attain separately.

T

Taft-Hartley Act A series of amendments to the Wagner Act that imposes controls on unions' organizing activities and methods used in collective bargaining attempts.

Task behavior The extent to which a leader directs and supervises a task.

Task group A group formed for a specific reason with members drawn from various parts of an organization to accomplish a specific purpose.

Team An identifiable group of people who work together toward a common goal and who are dependent upon each other to realize that goal.

Teambuilding A series of activities designed to help work groups solve problems, accomplish work goals, and function more effectively through teamwork.

Teamwork The work performed by the combined effort of several disciplines for maximum effectiveness in achieving common goals.

Technical skills Skills required to perform a particular task.

Telecommuters Term coined to describe people, frequently based at home, who use technology networks to send and receive work and information to and from different locations, locations (such as offices) to which they would once have needed to commute.

Text messaging Allows users of cellular telephones or other integrated voice and data devices to send text messages rather than voice messages.

Theory X and Theory Y Two sets of assumptions that leaders hold about followers, as outlined by Douglas McGregor; Theory X is a pessimistic view and Theory Y an optimistic view.

Time management Using the time available to the greatest advantage.

Title VII of the Civil Rights Act of 1964 Federal law that prohibits discrimination based on race, color, religion, sex, or national origin in the workplace. This law also prohibits sexual harassment.

Total person approach Human relations trend that takes into account needs and goals of the employee and acknowledges that a whole person, not just skills, is being hired.

Total quality management An organizational change method that focuses on involving employees in continuous process improvements to keep the organization on the cutting edge. TQM is rooted in the theories of American statistician Dr. W. Edward Deming.

Transactional leadership Leadership style in which leaders determine what followers need to achieve their own and organizational goals, classify those needs, and help followers gain confidence that they can reach their objectives.

Transformational leadership Leadership style that motivates followers to do more than they originally expected to do by raising the perceived value of the tasks, by getting them to transcend self-interest for the sake of the group goal, and by raising their need level to self-actualization.

Tranquilizers Depressants that can cause drowsiness, agitation, intellectual confusion, and physical impairment.

Treatment follow-up testing Drug testing used to monitor an employee's success in remaining drug free after being allowed to complete a substance abuse treatment program rather than be terminated.

Two-way communication Communication in which feedback is received.

Type A personalities Persons who tend to be highly competitive, aggressive, achievement oriented, and impatient and typically appear pressured, hurried, and volatile.

Type B personalities Persons who tend to be relaxed, easygoing, and even paced in their approach to life.

U

"Understanding strategy" Suggestion that once people know someone's preferences regarding business protocol, they will comply with them.

Underachiever Individual who sets goals that are lower than abilities in order to protect himself or herself from risk and anxiety.

Unemployment compensation Benefits paid to those who have become unemployed involuntarily.

Unilateral method A method of implementing organizational change that allows supervisors to dictate change with little or no input from the employees.

Union A group or association of workers who collectively bargain with employers for improved working conditions and protection from unfair or arbitrary treatment by management.

Upward communication Communication that begins in the lower levels of the organization and goes to higher levels.

Upward management Process by which individuals manage their bosses.

V

Value system A set of values that provides a road map for our behavior in a variety of situations.

Values Principles, standards, or qualities considered worthwhile or desirable; those things (as a principle or quality) intrinsically valuable or desirable.

Verbal communication Any message sent or received through the use of words, oral or written.

Verification Last stage of the creative process; testing, evaluating, revising, retesting, and reevaluating an idea.

Virtual office Computer and information networks that link people in different ("remote") locations, so that they can interact and share work as if they were located in one office building.

Virtual team A task- or project-focused team that meets without all members being present in the same location or at the same time.

Visualization A thought process by which you view yourself as being successful.

Voice mail System that extends a telephone's capabilities, receiving and storing incoming messages like an answering machine but with the added options of responding to messages or transmitting messages to the voice mails of others.

Vroom's expectancy theory A theory that views motivation as a process of choices and says people behave in certain ways based on their expectation of results.

W

Wagner Act A federal law enacted in 1935 that ordered management to stop interfering with union organizing efforts and defined what constituted unfair labor practices; established the right of employees to form unions and collectively bargain with management on employment issues; established the National Labor Relations Board.

Whistle-blowing Opposing decisions, policies, or practices within the organization if they are considered detrimental or illegal; can include publicizing such behavior outside the organization.

Win-win situation The result when negotiation is handled in such a way that both sides of an issue feel they have won.

Workaholics People who are consumed by their jobs and derive little pleasure from other activities.

Workers' compensation Compensation to those who have been physically or mentally injured on the job, or who have developed an occupational disease.

Work-life benefits Benefits employers offer to help employees gain some measure of balance between work and home.

Index

G

Gaddis, William, 319
Gaebler, Ken, 516
GameChanger, 178
Gap, Inc., 425
Gardenswartz, Lee, 419
Gates, Bill, 25, 307, 323, 337, 521
Gay Financial Network, 227
GE Capital, 62
Gender
  perception and, 30
  power and, 340
  women in workforce, 230–231
General Electric, 195, 363
General Foods, 213
General Motors, 78, 143, 168, 351, 363
Generations
  Baby Boomers, 75–76, 231, 238
  differing values in, 238
  Silent (Traditionalists), 238
  X, 75–77, 238, 351, 372
  Y, 75–77, 78, 144, 238, 351
Georgia Institute of Technology, 515
Gergen, David, 289
GHB, 484
Gilbreth, Frank, 8
Gilbreth, Lillian, 8
Girl Scouts of America, 15, 338
Global Connection
  child labor, 425
  communication, 159
  cross-cultural etiquette, 392
  cultural differences in planning, 262
  cultural perceptions, 44
  cultural values, 237
  decentralization, 167
  Economic and Monetary Union (EMU), 349

employee assistance programs (EAPs), 375
employee rights, 466
effects of globalization, 18
furniture manufacturing, 350
Generation Y and, 144
groups, 178
Internet usage, 97
Levi Strauss, 365
lifelong learning, 133
mentoring, 371
nonverbal communication, 107
offshoring, 170, 516
perception, 42
stress, 34
substance abuse, 483
teams, 218
time management, 497
Global positioning systems (GPS), 405
Global Workforce Diversity, 228
Globalization, 18, 516–517
Glutethimide, 483
Goals
  ambiguity in, 221
  changes in, 264–265
  characteristics of, 261
  definition of, 259–260
  official, 259
  operational, 260
  operative, 259
  prioritization of, 264–265
  setting of, 265–266
  successful attitudes, 267–269
  for teams, 212
Goals! How to Get Everything You Want (Tracy), 261
Goethe, Johann Wolfgang von, 139, 261
Goff, Ted (cartoons), 33, 35, 58, 121, 192, 216, 253, 257, 364, 383, 406, 447, 485, 552

Goldsmith, Joan, 289, 308
Goldsmith, Marshall, 290, 303, 311
Gompers, Samuel, 439
Good taste, 384
Gore-Tex Company, 117
Grapevine, 161–162
Graphic rating scales, 276–277, 278–279
Gray, Trevor, 288
Great Depression, 75, 445, 458
Great Groups, 184
Great man theory, 291
Grieving, 42–43
Group Processes: An Introduction to Group Dynamics (Luft), 36
Groups
  definition of, 176
  effectiveness of, 185–191
  formal, 180–182
  functional, 181
  future of, 195
  importance of, 177–179
  informal, 182–183
  leadership in, 184
  nature of the task, 191
  norms in, 187–189
  pitfalls in, 192–194
  primary, 180
  problem solving in, 128
  roles in, 193–194
  secondary, 180
  sizes of, 189–190
  status of members, 190–191
  task, 181
Groupthink, 126, 193
Groupware, 196, 214
Grove, Andrew, 355, 364
Grove, Cornelius, 208
Grovewell Global Leadership Solutions, 208

GTE Corp., 362
Guaranteed Overnight Delivery, 79
Guerrilla Tactics in the Job Market
    (Jackson), 549
Gulick, Luther, 305

H

Habitat for Humanity, 202
Hackett, Jim, 335
Hallett, Jeffrey, 21
Halliburton, 429
Hallucinogens, 484
Halo effect, 32–33
Hamel, Gary, 311
Hamlet (Shakespeare), 99
Handshakes, 391
Handy, Charles, 476
Hanks, Tom, 110
Hansen, Randall, 535
Happiness: It's Your Choice
    (Applegate), 59
Harassment, 188
Harkins, Phillip J., 86
Harvard Bureau of Vocational
    Guidance, 5
Harvard Business School, 9, 340
Hatch Act (1940), 465
Hate crimes, 34
Hawthorne effect, 9, 177
Hawthorne Plant, 177
Hayway, Justin, 65
Hazard Communication Standard
    (HCS), 455
Health, 501–507
Health Insurance Portability and
    Accountability Act (HIPAA),
    465
Health standards, 454–457
Healthcare Financial Management, 452
Heinz, 142
Hemingway, Ernest, 70
Hensley, Wayne, 333

Herman Miller, 163
Heroin, 485
Hersey, Paul, 294–296
Herzberg, Frederick, 63–64, 80
Hesselbein, Frances, 338
Hewlett-Packard, 121, 195, 307,
    327, 346
Hiatt, Arnold, 308
Hidden area, 37
Hierarchy of needs, 60–63, 65
High achievers, 256–268
High context groups, 240–241
Himsel, Deborrah, 298
Hispanic Association of Corporate
    Responsibility, 227
Hissey, Ted, 4
Hoftstede, Geert, 237
Holmes, Oliver Wendell, 355
Home Depot, 353
Hoover's Online, 527
Houston Business Journal, 129
Houston Chronicle, 163
*How to Win Friends and Influence
    People* (Carnegie), 3
HR Magazine, 203
Hudson, Eileen, 204
Hugs, 1
Human relations
    approach, 9
    defined, 2
    history of, 6–12
    importance of, 4–5
    in organizations, 13–19
    role of communication in, 87
    skills (*see* Human relations skills)
    technology and, 23–25
Human relations skills
    change and, 348, 370
    creativity and, 134–135
    in goal setting, 265
    key elements of, 2
    in leadership, 301, 310–311

in performance appraisals, 274
with substance abuse cases, 491
in teams, 213–214
Human Side of Enterprise, The
    (McGregor), 291–292
Humes, James, 108
Humor, 108, 141–142, 308
Hunt's, 142
Hygiene factors, 63

I

I-9, 464
Iacocca, Lee, 286
IBM, 137, 163, 170, 213, 228,
    307, 363
IFBI, 19
Illumination, 132
ImClone Systems Inc., 415
Immigration and Naturalization
    Service, 464
Immigration Reform and Control
    Act (IRCA), 463–464
Inc., 79
Inclusivity, 245
Incompatibility, 221
Incubation, 132
India, 62
Industrial Era, 6, 352, 449
Industrial Revolution, 346, 445
Influence, 288, 317
Information Age, 7, 352
Information overload, 93
Information technology, 347
Information Week, 167, 181
InfoWorld, 56
Ingham, Harry, 36–38
Inhalants, 484
Innovation, 131–132
Inside forces, 73
Insight Magazine, 3
Instant messaging, 111